Finally, we've lived to see a reliable and comprehensive work on the life and activities of Józef Retinger – a Polish politician with incredible connections and influence in the Western world, the Godfather of the European Union, founder of the Bilderberg Group, and author of many initiatives of international importance that shaped the political image of the world in the twentieth century. The author of this book made use of a broad base of sources, including sources not presented so far, which shed new light on the activities of this extremely interesting character. The work of Biskupski has high scientific value and the efficient narrative makes pleasant reading.

**Andrzej Pieczewski**, University of Łódź, Poland

The mystery of Europe's notorious éminence grise is finally unveiled in a fascinating deconstruction of the myth of Józef H. Retinger, international agent of Polish origin. Did Retinger really influence the results of both world wars, revolution in Mexico and the creation of the European Union? Was he a Jesuit, free-mason or Soviet spy? Biskupski's brilliant life's work provides the thoroughly documented answers.

**Władysław Bułhak**, specialist in the field of intelligence studies, Warsaw, Poland

Józef Retinger was a key figure in the Polish government-in-exile during the Second World War, often referred to as General Sikorski's *eminence grise*. His political career, before the war, in this government and as one of the founders of the movement for European integration has been the subject of much speculation and mystification. This well-researched and highly readable biography provides a definitive account of his political career and is essential reading for all interested in the history of World War II and of the post-war years.

**Antony Polonsky**, Emeritus Professor of Holocaust Studies, Brandeis University and Chief historian, POLIN Museum of the History of Polish Jews, Warsaw, Poland

# War and Diplomacy in East and West

*The New York Times* said of Józef Hieronim Retinger that he was on intimate terms with most leading statesmen of the Western world, including presidents of the United States. He has been repeatedly acknowledged as one of the principal architects of the movement for European unity after World War II, and one of the outstanding creative political influences of the postwar period. He has also been credited with being the dark master behind the so-called "Bilderberg Group," described variously as an organization of idealistic internationalists, and a malevolent global conspiracy.

Before that, Retinger involved himself in intelligence activities during World War II and, given the covert and semi-covert nature of many of his activities, it is little wonder that no biography has appeared about him. This book draws on a broad range of international archives to rectify that.

**M. B. B. Biskupski** holds the S. A. Blejwas Endowed Chair in Polish History at Central Connecticut State University, USA.

# Routledge Studies in Modern History

A full list of titles in this series is available at: www.routledge.com/Routledge-Studies-in-Modern-History/book-series/MODHIST
Recently published titles:

**15 Transnational Perspectives on Modern Irish History**
*Edited by Niall Whelehan*

**16 Ireland in the World**
Comparative, Transnational, and Personal Perspectives
*Edited by Angela McCarthy*

**17 The Global History of the Balfour Declaration**
Declared Nation
*Maryanne A. Rhett*

**18 Colonial Soldiers in Europe, 1914–1945**
"Aliens in Uniform" in Wartime Societies
*Edited by Eric Storm and Ali Al Tuma*

**19 Immigration Policy from 1970 to the Present**
*Rachel Stevens*

**20 Public Goods versus Economic Interests**
Global Perspectives on the History of Squatting
*Edited by Freia Anders and Alexander Sedlmaier*

**21 Histories of Productivity**
Genealogical Perspectives on the Body and Modern Economy
*Edited by Peter-Paul Bänziger and Mischa Suter*

**22 Landscapes and Voices of the Great War**
*Edited by Angela K. Smith and Krista Cowman*

**23 War, Peace and International Order?**
The Legacies of The Hague Conferences of 1899 and 1907
*Edited by Maartje Abbenhuis, Christopher Ernest Barber and Annalise R. Higgins*

**24 Black Cosmopolitanism and Anticolonialism**
Pivotal Moments
*Babacar M'Baye*

**25 Constructing Nationalism in Iran**
From the Qajars to the Islamic Republic
*Meir Litvak*

**26 War and Diplomacy in East and West**
A Biography of Józef Retinger
*M. B. B. Biskupski*

# War and Diplomacy in East and West

A Biography of Józef Retinger

M. B. B. Biskupski

LONDON AND NEW YORK

First published 2017
by Routledge
2 Park Square, Milton Park, Abingdon, Oxon OX14 4RN

and by Routledge
711 Third Avenue, New York, NY 10017

*Routledge is an imprint of the Taylor & Francis Group, an informa business*

© 2017 M. B. B. Biskupski

The right of M. B. B. Biskupski to be identified as author of this work has been asserted by him in accordance with sections 77 and 78 of the Copyright, Designs and Patents Act 1988.

All rights reserved. No part of this book may be reprinted or reproduced or utilised in any form or by any electronic, mechanical, or other means, now known or hereafter invented, including photocopying and recording, or in any information storage or retrieval system, without permission in writing from the publishers.

*Trademark notice*: Product or corporate names may be trademarks or registered trademarks, and are used only for identification and explanation without intent to infringe.

*British Library Cataloguing in Publication Data*
A catalogue record for this book is available from the British Library

*Library of Congress Cataloging in Publication Data*
A catalog record for this book has been requested.

ISBN: 978-1-138-21845-1 (hbk)
ISBN: 978-1-315-43765-1 (ebk)

Typeset in Sabon
by HWA Text and Data Management, London

Printed and bound by CPI Group (UK) Ltd, Croydon, CR0 4YY

Moim ukochanym dzieciom, Olesi, Jadzi, Mietkowi, Misi i Stasiowi, tę książkę poświęcam. Tata.

# Contents

| | |
|---|---|
| *Preface* | xi |
| Introduction | 1 |
| 1 The formative years, 1888–1914 | 6 |
| 2 World War I, 1914–1918 | 17 |
| 3 From Europe to Mexico | 60 |
| 4 "I got religion" | 93 |
| 5 The war begins | 114 |
| 6 First steps towards federation: the Czech frustration | 136 |
| 7 A wider federation | 150 |
| 8 Retinger and Polish–Soviet relations | 163 |
| 9 The collapse of Poland's international position | 181 |
| 10 Retinger's most controversial episode: the mission to Poland, 1944 | 190 |
| 11 "In twenty years Europe will be united, together with Poland": Retinger and the federal movement in European history | 220 |
| 12 Retinger and the building of a united Europe | 231 |

| | |
|---|---:|
| 13 The Congress of Europe, 1948 | 248 |
| 14 The Bilderbergs | 272 |
| 15 Conclusions | 291 |
| *Bibliography* | 295 |
| *Index* | 316 |

# Preface

Józef Hieronim Retinger, one of the most mysterious figures of the twentieth century, was a much misunderstood man.[1] Accused of everything, credited with prodigious accomplishments, cursed for supposed evil machinations, suspected of uncountable secret if not nefarious acts and missions, he was basically a man of large goals sought through complex methods. There is no part of his life which is free from controversy, and, at many points, his actions must either be inferred from scanty resources, or merely speculated upon. Nonetheless, when reconstructed in its whole, this is the career of a brilliant man: imaginative, influential, resourceful almost beyond belief, frequently disingenuous if not deceitful, but, withal, of singular motivation. But, we shall need to study the whole of his life to prove that final point. We should remember the observation of an English chronicler: "Every Pole has conspiracy in his blood."[2]

Relatively little has been written regarding Retinger. A version of his memoirs compiled by his secretary, Jan Pomian, is the usual source for virtually all writing on him. It has gaps, however. Despite this, it is an indispensable source containing excerpts from Retinger's letters and a shrewd commentary by Pomian, who was Retinger's secretary and friend. There are four different attempts at a full biography. Bogdan Podgórski's is most helpful and exploits a number of archival sources, but far from all. He is heavily indebted to Pomian.[3] The second is the "sketch" by Denis de Rougemont. The third is a Dutch-language biography by Taverne which is also heavily indebted to Pomian, and contains no reference indications, but includes a lengthy secondary-source bibliography.[4] All rely heavily on Pomian. A strange, anonymous, online minibiography is really quite good and contains many excellent quotations. It bears the odd title "Józef Retinger: Happy Birthday, Józef!"[5] A full-scale biography by Pająk is really an endless search for conspiracies with scant evidence in support.[6] In addition, there are a few books which discuss his post-World War II efforts at constructing a federal Europe, all of quite recent authorship, a good effort being Pieczewski's,[7] a shorter account by Witkowski, and the writings of Thierry Grosbois in exploiting Western European archives for Retinger's later career, but he does not know Polish. Hugh Wilford has integrated Retinger into his larger work on Cold War international politics. Two dissertations deal with Retinger's connections with the mysterious Bilderbergs.[8] Wapiński is the author of a fine, albeit very brief, biographical outline in the *Polish National Biography* series (Polski Słownik Biograficzny).[9]

Retinger makes brief appearances in many memoirs, letter collections, and studies of related themes: these are often tantalizing but not fully explanatory, leaving many blind allies. His materials, some quite skimpy, are scattered about in many archives. I have tried to exploit all of the major repositories in many languages, and as many of the minor ones as I could.

I would like to thank a number of colleagues who have been kind enough to tender me their advice over the years relating to Retinger and my depiction of him. These include Piotr Wróbel of the University of Toronto, Piotr S. Wandycz of Yale, Neal Pease of the University of Wisconsin, Milwaukee, the late Anna Cienciala of the University of Kansas, Grzegorz Witkowski of the University of Warsaw, Linda Biesele Hall of the University of New Mexico, Jean Szczypien of the Fashion Institute of Technology, Jürgen Buchenau of the University of North Carolina, Charlotte, Christopher N. Fritsch, and particularly Jan Pomian, Retinger's last secretary, with whom I kept in regular correspondence to discover his unmatched knowledge and insightful views concerning Retinger. I should also like to thank the late Feliks Gross, President of the Polish Institute of Arts and Sciences in America, Andrzej Pieczewski of the University of Łódź, and Richard J. Aldrich, of the University of Warwick. All of these scholars have helped me.

I am also grateful to Teresa A. Meade of Union College; Ann Hudak of the University of Maryland's Hornbake Library; Thierry Grosbois of the Catholic University of Louvain, Guido Koller, Eidgenössisches Departement des Innern EDI, Schweizerisches Bundesarchiv BAR, Dienst Historische Analysen; Mary Carr of the Historical Archives of the EU in Florence, Dobrosława Platt of the Polish Social and Cultural Association in London; Anna Stefanicka of the Polish Institute and Polish Institute and Sikorski Museum (PISM); Lucyna Janas, of the Archiwum Retingera at the Uniwersytet Ekonomiczny Krakowski, and Katarzyna Tarnawska of the same institution both for their extraordinary kindness in procuring vital documents.

There are those who deserve special attention for reading all or part of the manuscript and communicating their comments: Andrzej Pieczewski, Bułhak, and the late Michael Alfred Peszke deserve special thanks for this. Władysław Bułhak of the Instytut Pamięci Narodowej, also located and sent me invaluable documents on Retinger's World War II career, as did Pieczewski. My research assistants include Chris Abraham of the Dwight D. Eisenhower Library and Museum who carefully selected post-World War II Retinger documents; Hywel Masten, and Rosalie Spires for their tireless work at the National Archives in Kew, the Birmingham University Library, and at the Imperial War Museum. Wims Maas worked at the Dutch National Archives and Guido Perlini found much of value at the Historical Archives of the European Union in Florence. Martin McCarthy, now a practicing attorney in Rochester, New York, was long ago my research assistant assigned to ferret information from the press regarding the many suspicious characters that dot the text. I have later received additional research assistance from a number of people at Central Connecticut State University: I am especially indebted to Nick Pettinico of the university administration who supported my research efforts with intelligence and loyalty. My colleague, Renata Vickrey, always helped when I needed her, as did April C. Armstrong of the Seeley G. Mudd Library at Princeton. Of all, special thanks go to Magda Jacques, my secretary, who was unflagging in helping and dealing with my idiosyncrasies.

This book is dedicated to my beloved children who may wish to know about the most fascinating Pole of modern times.

Colchester, CT, 2016

## Notes

1 Robert Eringer, *The Global Manipulators: The Bilderberg Group, The Trilateral Commission: Covert Power Groups of the West*. Bristol: Pentacle Books, 1960, 16.
2 Ibid., 21.
3 Podgorski also wrote the much shorter "Józef Hieronim Retinger, 1888–1960," available online from Archiwum Retingera, Uniwersytet Ekonomyczny Krakowski.
4 W. Chr. Taverne, *Wat nemand schumt te weten: J. H. Retinger het striven naar enn verenigd Europe* (Hoogeveen: Horizont, 1987).
5 "Józef Retinger: Happy Birthday, Józef," http://bilderberg2013.co.uk/jozefretinger/. Accessed on May 9, 2013.
6 Henryk Pająk, *Retinger, mason i agent syjonizmu* (Lublin: Retro), 1996.
7 Andrzej Pieczewski, *Działalność Józefa Hieronima Retingera na rzecz intergracji europejskiej* (Łódź: Marszałek), 2008.
8 Ungeborg Philipsen, "Diplomacy with Ambiguity: The History of the Bilderberg Organisation, 1952–1977," København Universitet, 2009 and Thomas W. Gijswijt, "Uniting the West. The Bilderberg Group, the Cold War and European Integration, 1952–1966," Ph.D. diss., Ruprecht-Karls-Universitat Heidelberg, 2007.
9 Roman Wapiński, "Retinger, Józef," *Polski Słownik Biograficzny*, 1988, Vol. 128, 148–152.

# Introduction

He was the "Father of Europe."[1] At Józef Hieronim Retinger's funeral in 1960, Sir Edward Beddington-Behrens remarked that he had "complete entrée in every political circle." Prince Bernhard of the Netherlands reckoned him one of the few men to make an indelible mark on his time, albeit in virtual anonymity. The *New York Times* said of him: "Mr. Retinger... was on intimate terms with most leading statesmen of the Western World, including presidents of the United States."[2] He has been repeatedly acknowledged as one of the principal architects, indeed *spiritus movens*, of the movement for European unity after the Second World War, and "one of the outstanding creative political influences of the postwar period."[3] What Retinger was, or indeed, who he was, has baffled a generation of historians who have discovered his name or his influence in a myriad of places, seemingly unconnected, often implausible, sometimes incomprehensible.

Throughout his long and mysterious career on the international political scene, Retinger was described as an agent of British, American, French, German, Austrian, Mexican, or perhaps Japanese intelligence, and the chief architect of a Vatican-inspired plan to re-organize central Europe under the guidance of the Jesuit Order during World War I. He was also, simultaneously, a major link between, Polish socialists and the left-wing of British politics,[4] and, also, between London financial circles and the Warsaw government. A report to the Polish prime minister noted, almost with astonishment, that Retinger enjoyed the respect and friendship of the "highest English officials" who regarded him as a "politician of broad competence," whose views on European problems – not just Polish affairs – were accorded serious attention.[5] In the same decade, Retinger was the principal financial advisor to the revolutionary government of Mexico during the interwar era, and briefly the inmate of an American jail. Throughout much of the interwar era, Retinger inveigled himself in political plots and was deeply involved in the opposition to the increasingly authoritarian government in Warsaw, joining scattered, disgruntled émigrés like the erstwhile premier Ignacy Jan Paderewski, the populist leader Wincenty Witos, and the soldier and statesman General Władysław Sikorski among others. By the 1930s, however, he was back in Europe, again a link between Polish politics and the British political left; according to some he was a "fellow-traveler" at the very least if not an agent of the Comintern, perhaps even a link between the British Communist Party and the Kremlin.

By the outbreak of the Second World War, Retinger was rumored to be a major figure in "international Jewish masonry," and a high official of the British B'nai B'rith. Soon thereafter he was described – most ardently as a British agent, perhaps a Soviet asset, a patriotic Pole, and possibly all three. That he was the principal advisor to General Władysław Sikorski, Prime Minister of the Polish government-in-exile is beyond question. In April, 1944, though far from young, and in poor health, he was parachuted into German-occupied Poland. Though ostensibly on a mission from his own government, Retinger may also have then been acting for the British.[6] As late as 1966 Colonel Sir Colin Gubbins, chief of the ultimate secret agency, the Special Operations Executive (SOE), insisted that certain details of his remarks about Retinger's mission remain secret. Hugh Wilford has recently argued that Retinger acted as a SOE agent.[7] Certainly Retinger's World War II activities show very close relations with the British – often to the outrage of his own countrymen.

So secret was Retinger's 1944 mission that he entered the aircraft wearing a mask, and was clad in the uniform of a British army captain. Retinger's loyalties to Poland were so suspect that members of the Intelligence Division of the Polish General Staff decided to have Retinger assassinated in 1944. Retinger's activities during the war are still unclear and controversial. It is obvious, however, that he had direct access to the highest reaches of the British government

In the postwar era, Retinger was active in the movement for European unity, serving as co-founder of the European League for Economic Cooperation, and Secretary General – "his favorite function" – of the European Movement. In addition, he was dedicated to negotiating reconciliation between the Church of England and the Vatican, and even managed to have an audience with Cardinal Montini, the future Pope Paul VI, in this vain enterprise. Until the last months of his life, he was actively intriguing in Polish émigré politics; a figure of controversy to the end. Until his death and long after, an often repeated explanation for Retinger's actions was that he was, perhaps for many years, a secret agent of the British government acting under the direct orders of its highest officials. Finally, he has been credited with being the dark master behind the so-called "Bilderberg Group," described variously as an organization of idealistic internationalists, and a malevolent global conspiracy

Observers of Retinger's long career have repeatedly confronted severe difficulties. Many of the episodes in which he participated are impossible to reconstruct clearly. A sympathetic biography by his secretary, with frequent Retinger quotations, is indispensable yet incomplete.[8] Documentary evidence concerning his highly secretive "diplomatic" activities is exceedingly rare, fragmentary, and contradictory. Most of his contemporaries were suspicious of him, and all of them were bewildered by his mysterious travels, meetings, and activities. What or who guided his actions? Was he ultimately, a foreign agent, as has been repeatedly asserted by many Poles, or was he, as a contemporary historian has charitably deemed him, "a citizen of the world rather than a spy,"[9] perhaps, a global diplomat? Pieczewski describes him as "our greatest European," not a cosmopolitan, but rather, ultimately, simply – but not too simply, a Pole. Here we have a fascinating insight by a Czech writer who captures Retinger's grandiose schemes in a few words: a man obsessed with a goal and dedicated to launch great schemes to achieve it. As Vaclav Fiala rewrote:

> It is typical of the Polish nature that it conceives a great aim without being unduly concerned with the possibilities of attaining it, and without weighing the required strength on accurate scales. It prefers vain but grandiose efforts to moderate and repeated successes or to small settlements of current issues. In the Polish dictionary the word compromise is not an expression *comme il faut*.[10]

This volume has three goals. First, to reconstruct Retinger's activities to discern the motives and goals of his actions. He seemed to gambol about, always off to some adventure in a series of disconnected episodes. In reality, Retinger was guided by simple goals the fundamental one being how to serve Poland. Very early in his life he was painfully aware of the fact that Poland was not only lacking independence, but that its reconstruction seemed quite impossible, unless some outside powers could be involved. This led him to Austrophilism – a not uncommon disposition of Poles living under the Habsburgs. His efforts to help Austria leave the war – an effort, incidentally, which was repeated by other Poles – were not Austrian patriotism, but Polish. The failure of the Habsburgs to survive World War I was the end to his interest in Austria. Austria was a means not an end.

In the interwar period he tried to play a role in advancing the Polish cause both domestically and internationally. He thus was at work stimulating Polish-Mexican economic ties, and negotiating loans from England for Warsaw. The goal of his myriad but cloudy actions was to replace the Warsaw government with one more democratic with broader popular support. Poland's position in the world, never assured after 1918, declined during the 1930s, and Retinger's patriotism motivated his political activities.

In the midst of the interwar era, Retinger met with General Sikorski and they became both close friends as well as having many shared political beliefs. Central to this partnership was the belief that the geo-political arrangement of Europe did not secure Poland a position of security, possibly not even independence. The solution was an essential transformation of the continent along federalist lines which would protect members from the aggressive inclinations of powerful Germany and Russia. Poland, in an eastern bloc, could be defensible, and thus avoid both international threat and assure the basis of domestic political stability. Retinger's federalism was doubly rooted: an old Polish political tradition of strength through federal ties (beginning in the fourteenth century), and the ruminations of a long series of thinkers about uniting European civilization to avoid its disastrous in-fighting. If a free Poland could join a series of similar states, Europe would be transformed but, more important Poland would be safe and independent.

Retinger's fascination with European unity through federalism became especially evident during World War II when he became the chief political advisor of the Polish exile government under Sikorski. Retinger worked tirelessly to convince the other exile governments to create a postwar federated Europe – which would assure Polish independence. This effort eventually failed due to Czech intransigence, the lack of Western support, and Russia's overpowering role in the postwar world. During the war Retinger's dedication to European federation was inseparable from that of Sikorski. This was part of a larger Polish *Weltanschuung*. Federation required some reconciliation with Russia – a "realism" that they shared. Without this federation, Poland was doomed to Russian domination.

His actions were always rooted in Polish goals and connected with patriotic activities worldwide, thus he could be broadly defined as a Polish agent no matter which government he was working with. As his vision expanded to include the continent, then Atlanticism, and finally dabblings in global politics, Poland always was the center.

Two other questions remain. Chronologically the first is whether he was guided by a kind of political Catholicism. Was his vision of a united Europe both a solution for Poland as well as the advance of a – at least partially – unified Europe under Catholic influence? The episodes which reflect this are scattered about chronologically: his original Catholic roots; the early contacts with the Vatican and the Jesuits during World War I; his network of Catholic acquaintances both before and after World War II, and his repeated efforts to reconcile European Christians.

In the postwar world, he was in the pay of the CIA in his efforts to create the rudiments of an international consultative body, the Bilderbergs. Moreover, whereas the Bilderbergs have been repeatedly criticized for striving to be more than a loose body of important global figures, but an agency seeking a powerful world role, we must not forget that Retinger had long favored continental coordination to consider basic and pressing problems, a private, elite, international center of discussion of indeterminate consequence.

It is important to follow the bases of his actions: Poland, with horizons far beyond its truncated borders, what is deemed political Roman Catholicism (though his piety was dubious), and a blurry political leftism. He was always an elitist repulsed by mass politics. In his early life he was at least inferentially connected with rightist Polish organizations. Later his politics were clearly left, indeed, radically so. Finally, in the waning years, Retunger was seeking to create political influence by powerful people linked by common purpose and willing to impinge on national sovereignty.

The purpose of this study is an attempt to explain Retinger in his international context and in the Polish world into which he was born and really never left. It is my contention that amid the farrago of activities one can discern a design which remained constant throughout his long career.

## Notes

1 This is Thierry Grosbois' conclusion of how contemporary historians regard Retinger; see his "Activities," 13.
2 "Joseph Retinger, Polish Democrat," *New York Times*, June 24, 1960, 27.
3 David C. Riede, "Retinger, Joseph Hieronim," in Warren Kuehl, ed., *Biographical Dictionary of Internationalists* (Westport: Greenwood Press, 1983), 606.
4 Wincenty Witos, *Moja tułaczka* (Warsaw: Ludowa Spółdzielnia Wydawnicza, 1967), 460.
5 Adam Roniker to Grabski, March 12, 1924, in Zbigniew Landau and Jerzy Tomaszewski, *Kapitały obce w Polsce, 1918–1939* (Warsaw: Książka i Wiedza, 1964), 89.
6 Józef Garliński, *Poland in the Second World War*, New York: Hippocrene Books, 1985, 113.
7 Hugh Wilford, *The CIA, the British Left, and the Cold War*. (London: Frank Cass, 2003), 228.
8 Jan Pomian, Retinger's secretary and confidant during his last several years, published as *Joseph Retinger: Memoirs of an Eminence Grise* (Sussex: Sussex University Press, 1972). In 1990, a Polish-language edition, "corrected and enlarged," was published: *Józef Retinger: Życie i pamiętniki 'szarej eminencji'* (Warsaw: Pelikan, 1990). Yet another Polish edition appeared in 1994, *Józef Retinger: Życie i pamiętniki pioniera jedności europejskiej* (Warsaw: PAVO, 1994). The two Polish-language editions have identical texts, though they vary in format. All citations in this book are from the 1990 edition, hereafter cited as Pomian: *Pamiętniki*. A valuable critique of this work is Siemaszko, "Szara eminencja," 172–185. The fate of this version is unknown; see Spencer Curtis Brown to Retinger, March 24, 1953.
9 Roman Wapiński, "Retinger, Józef Hieronim," in *Polski Słownik Biograficzny*, 30/1 1988 (Wrocław: Ossolineum, 1988), 152.
10 This passage, translated from the French, is quoted in Piotr S. Wandycz, "Poland in International Politics," *Canadian Slavonic Papers*, Vol. 14, No. 3 (1972), 408.

# 1  The formative years, 1888–1914

Retinger was born in Kraków, which was under Austrian rule, in 1888. Despite his German name (his ancestors spelled it Röttinger), and original Bavarian ancestry, the family was completely polonized after their arrival in the late eighteenth century.[1] Retinger described his family as "ardent patriots and very ardent Catholics" with "a very strong anti-Russian and anti-German complex ... maybe reactionary ... and not without an anti-Jewish bias."[2] According to his grandson, the rumors that Retinger was of Jewish origin were created and circulated by his detractors and have no basis in fact, but is little more than an anti-Semitic invention.[3] However, Podgórski has uncovered documents which indicate that Retinger's great-grandfather was, indeed, Jewish but he and his family converted to Catholicism in 1827.[4] If this were a conversion to polonism it was rapid and profound: Retinger's grandfather was killed in the 1846 Galician jacquierie aimed at the Polish elite.[5]

Retinger's possible Jewish ancestry, despite his many denials, and the blunt rejection by his last secretary, Jan Pomian, has considerable support. In his papers, a French-language notation describes him as being "a good Jewish bourgeoisie family, Polish by façade."[6] Jan Hulewicz says virtually the same thing.[7] There are similar references sprinkled about, however the dispositive evidence was possibly provided by Retinger's own guardian Władysław Count Zamoyski, who referred to Retinger's father as a convert to Roman Catholicism from Judaism. Zamoyski, by way of explanation, noted that he had known Retinger for years and that Retinger's father was his attorney, until the former's death.[8]

Retinger's mother's family was not Jewish, and Retinger was raised a Catholic, hence the ultimate answer to the question whether Retinger was Jewish is: not by any reasonable standard. Zamoyski noted in what may serve as the final word on this subject: "On peut être absolument sûr de ses sentiments polonaises."[9] Retinger returned the compliment: Zamoyski was "a saint."[10]

Both Retinger's parents died when he was young, leaving five children.[11] From an early age, Retinger was intended for the priesthood. After initial preparations in Poland, he was sent to Rome at eighteen. Due to the influence of Cardinal Rampolla, he was admitted to the Academie dei nobili ecclesistici. Soon after he left: in his own words "to serve my faith and my country as part of the laity."[12]

Retinger's father was an intriguing personality. Born in Tarnów, and the descendant of successful merchants, the elder Józef was a devoted Polish patriot and fought in the Polish anti-Russian rising of 1863–1864 (the so-called January Insurrection). A lawyer by education, he was a prominent member of the Kraków urban patriciate and was decorated by the Habsburg government. He became a member of the city council and president of the advocates' society. He was a member of the literati: translator of German works, and a playwright as well, indeed man of many parts.[13] He was also a landowner – a category the significance of which is difficult to convey apart from its Polish context but it is more of symbolic than financial significance.[14] It denotes membership in the traditional elite of Polish society. He was closely connected to Kraków's famous Jagiellonian University, a relationship immensely strengthened when he married Marynia Czyrniańska, daughter of the rector of the university. The elder Czyrniański was a distinguished chemist and the co-founder of the Polish Academy of Sciences (Polska Akademia Umiejętności), there is a bust of him in Kraków's famous university church of St. Anne.[15]

The elder Retinger had a close relationship with Zamoyski which was of vital significance in his son's life. Retinger Sr. was the attorney for Zamoyski in the territorial dispute with Hungary over the territory of Morskie Oko.[16] Retinger won the complex legal battle and the territory has remained Polish ever since. The premature death of Retinger's father made young Józef the unofficial ward of the count, scion of one of the wealthiest families in Poland. Zamoyski supported Retinger generously, allowing him to complete his education at the Sorbonne, from which he received a doctorate in 1908, perhaps the youngest contemporary European to earn that distinction.[17] He later studied in Germany, Italy, and England, preparing his for his later continental career including the mastery of many languages. Zamoyski was also politically active in France in support of the Polish cause.[18]

Retinger later recalled the Zamoyski family as his "link to the legitimist tradition of European aristocracy from the era before Napoleon III ... the living example of the famous encyclical of Leo XIII, *Rerum Novarum*."[19] Beyond their profound intellectual imprint, the Zamoyskis allowed Retinger immediate access to the highest circles of European wealth and distinction; a world of influence that expanded rapidly over the next few years. In Paris, he became acquainted with the French cultural elite. Cousins of Retinger, the Godębski family (similarly French citizens of Polish origin) maintained a well-known Parisian salon to which he was at once admitted. Thus, in the years before World War I, Retinger established an extensive assortment of influential "contacts": Cardinal Alfred-Henri-Marie Baudrillart,[20] Marshal Hubert Lyautey, and the bizarre dandy, Marquis Boni de Castellane – of whom more later. This relationship was most fruitful, for de Castellane was on close terms with the then Prince of Wales, later King Edward VII, whereas

## 8  The formative years, 1888–1914

Boni's wife, the American Annie Gould, was reputed to be the wealthiest heiress in the world, the daughter of the financier Jay Gould.[21] De Castellane himself served briefly in the French parliament and had very powerful friends in both British and French political circles, especially on the left. In the world of the arts, Retinger became acquainted with André Gide,[22] Jean Moréas, François Mauriac, Arnold Bennett, Léon-Paul Frague, Valéry Larbaud, Paul Valéry, Maurice Ravel, Pierre Bonnard, François Poulenc, Léon-Paul Fargue, Claude Terrasse, Manuel de la Falla, Jean-Aubry (with whom Retinger wrote articles about Poland), Eric Satie, Edward Vuillard, and, from the political world: the aforementioned de Castellane, Prince Sixte de Bourbon-Parma (the exact date of their acquaintance is unclear), Charles-Louis Philippe, the press magnate Lord Northcliffe, and publisher Bernard Gasset, among innumerable others.[23] Retinger inherited 100,000 francs from his family but squandered it. Zamoyski described Retinger as having "too much self-assurance and too much imagination." He had powerful friends, but enemies as well.

After brief periods in London, Munich, and Italy, about which little is known, Retinger returned to Kraków, published a literary review which enjoyed a *success d'éstime*, and created thereby a network of friends among the Polish literary establishment.[24] The authors he published included such literary giants as Leśmian, Morstin, Staff, Strug and many others. It is probably during this brief stay (1911–1912) that Retinger's political career began.

Retinger had, apparently, been approached by the representatives of the National Council (Rada Narodowa, RN), a nationalistic organization of the Polish political right, headquartered in Galicia, (Austrian Poland) which was attempting to establish a network of filial organizations throughout Europe and North America.[25] The RN was militantly anti-German and emphasized that in any future war, Berlin would be the principal enemy of Polish independence. This meant that the geo-strategic disposition of the RN followed the line of the founder of modern Polish nationalism, Roman Dmowski.[26] This reflected Retinger's youthful rightist views which later moved dramatically to the left.[27]

Retinger was to establish an information office in London (1911) and, acting in the spirit of the RN's anti-German orientation, distribute propaganda in the English-speaking world in favor of the Polish cause.[28] Significantly, the anti-German position of the RN was coupled with a rather indulgent view of the Habsburgs; hence anti-Austrian propaganda was decidedly not one of Retinger's tasks.[29] His pamphlet – *The Poles and Prussia* – denouncing German policy towards Poland made him *persona odiosa* in Germany.[30] At the same time it endeared him to the Polish nationalist right.

The work argued to its British audience that the conclusion that the "Polish Question" was a closed chapter in European history was mistaken. The British did not realize that Prussia really had an incorporated Polish history and that the population there was "swallowed, but never digested."[31] To prove his point, Retinger essayed a highly emotional aperçu of Prussia's history. We may summarize this briefly to grasp the basis for Retinger's attitudes towards the Germans.

In Europe of the ninth and tenth centuries, the area northeast of an imaginary line drawn between Hamburg to Leipzig was populated by two equally uncivilized people: the "kindly and peaceable" Slavs and the "violent" "aggressively cohesive" Germans. The Germans used their penchant to "accept leadership" to conquer most of the land by "massacre and rapine." Then Poland emerged.[32]

Distractions to the east prevented Poland from "doing justice" to this problem in the north. The barbaric paganism of the "Borussians", that is, native Prussians, forced the Poles to seek to "repress the murderous raids," hence the appearance of the Order of Teutonic Knights and the long, complex and controversial epic of Polish relations with the Order.[33] Soon after moving to historic Prussia, the Knights became "monsters of greed and ambition."[34] The local population, suffering under their rule, rebelled and was virtually annihilated in response.

The Polish-Lithuanian union of 1385 brought powerful forces into the field against the Knights. The result was the crushing Polish victory at Grünwald (Tannenberg) of 1410, which Poland did not exploit because the "tolerant Pole" never takes "full advantage of his victories." Subsequently the Order became secularized, adopted Protestantism, and became the hereditary possession of the Hohenzollern family.[35]

The Prussians hated their former Polish overlords, and it was largely vengeance that motivated their participation in the Partitions of Poland at the close of the eighteenth century – perhaps "the greatest crime in history."[36] The ultimate result was the 1871 German Empire. Retinger is quick to remind his readers that Poles played an important role as unwilling soldiers of the Prussians and thus had an ironic part to play in the creation of the modern German Empire.[37] However, Berlin declared "war against" its Polish subjects which it declared historically or perhaps racially inferior (der minderwärtgen Nation)." In Prussian Poland the Poles offered resistance, but the Polish Jews were "always apt to side with those in power."[38] The Germans responded with a "monstrous" policy of repression – the Kulturkampf – which Retinger details.[39] A discussion of the later school-strikes and German mistreatment of children followed-a truly foul episode.[40]

Retinger concluded by urging the British not to ignore this Prussian chronicle of dastardly deeds which illustrate German behavior in the contemporary world: Prussian methods of empire building.[41] The purpose of this brief chronicle is obvious: the Poles are history's victims and the Germans seemingly-civilized barbarians. The British must familiarize themselves with the Prussian past to understand what they are facing in this Central European threat.

Retinger's prejudices are clearly indicated: Catholic loyalties, Polish patriotism, the conviction of the innate nobility and goodness of the Polish people, and the contrasting murderous traditions of the Germans. It is in this pamphlet, written on the eve of the war that we are given Retinger's conception of the Germans. Historical circumstances never allowed Retinger to essay a similar summary of Polish-Russian relations: it would have allowed an edifying comparison. Lacking that, we may conclude simply that he regarded the Germans as the historical enemies of the Poles and exceptionally foul ones at that. There is no evidence that this disposition changed. Indeed, twenty years later, Retinger wrote that Poland had been forgotten in the nineteenth century and had disappeared from the consciousness of the world; leaving the Poles beset by feelings of inferiority.[42]

At the end of 1911 (or perhaps in early 1912), Retinger moved to London, – "the center of world politics" – established a so-called Polish Bureau for the National Council, in a single pathetic room on Arundel Street,[43] attended classes at the London School of Economics, and avidly continued his practice of cultivating prominent and powerful Britons and others. He used his position at the Bureau to become involved with Polish relief agencies with distinguished patrons.[44] To the dramatist Arnold Bennet, whom he had net in Paris, he added Stafford Cripps, later a Labour politician.[45]

At the time he captured his political philosophy succinctly: "Russians were 'the enemies of my country'."[46] In his efforts on behalf of the RN, Retinger met and actively cultivated two of his countrymen, then in England, maestro Ignacy Jan Paderewski, and, more consequentially, novelist Joseph Conrad.[47] Indeed, Retinger rapidly became an intimate of Conrad who was a great admirer of the youthful Retinger, crediting him with almost limitless political and diplomatic talent.[48] Retinger, in turn, was able to use Conrad's fame as an entrée to influential circles in Great Britain. Indeed, so close was the Conrad-Retinger relationship that it has been noted by a contemporary Polish journalist, perhaps half-facetiously, that Conrad "recommended Retinger to British intelligence."[49]

Retinger arranged, through the family of his wife (the Zubrzyckis), Conrad's nostalgic visit to Poland in the summer of 1914 – the émigré's return after more than twenty years.[50] Podgórski has argued, persuasively, that Retinger may well have had political motives for arranging this trip: to win Conrad over to active support of the "Polish Question" in England. Conrad had not previously been open in his support of Polish issues.[51]

Unfortunately for Conrad, his arrival coincided with the mobilization antecedent to the First World War, bringing his visit to a dramatic close. However brief his stay, Conrad was most active regarding Polish affairs. He held a great many meetings with Polish political activists and produced a most intriguing memorandum. In this document, Conrad clearly enunciated what has come to be called the pro-Austrian or "Austrophile" position regarding Poland's possible rebirth. Conrad resolved to win British support for the Polish cause and London's sympathy for Austria. Russia, Conrad decided, would certainly be defeated. By contrast, the defeat of Germany was scarcely imaginable; hence England must support Austria against Germany at any future peace conference to lessen the danger of German domination. Ultimately, London should be encouraged to "support Austria's Polish policy" while opposing German and Russian goals.[52] The reconstruction of the Habsburgs Empire as a trialist state, with Poland, the third portion, was a first step to a federated Europe.[53]

For Retinger, also, the abbreviated visit had political significance. He later recalled that after seeing to the safety of the Conrad family he

> went to Lwów, knowing that the major Galician leaders [of Polish politics] were found there. I met with archbishop [Józef] Bilczewski,[54] with the Armenian-Catholic archbishop [Józef] Teodorowicz[55], and the representatives of the major political parties, [Tadeusz] Cieński[56] and [Jan] Dąbski,[57] and others. They asked me to go, as fast as possible to France and England on their behalf...I was to work on behalf of Polish independence with all the boldness and determination I could manage. They assured me that they would support all my actions in this regard.[58]

Retinger was given letters addressed to the French and British ministries of Foreign Affairs, a letter from the Polish episcopate to Archbishop Bourne of Westminster, and rather vague instructions. This was the beginning of Retinger's relationship with another Galician organization, the Central National Committee (Centralny Komitet Narodowy, CKN). The CKN was a short-lived political congeries of rightist parties which were moderately pro-Austrian as regards the war.[59] This new affiliation supplanted, though perhaps did not formally sever, his earlier linkage to the right-wing RN.[60]

Retinger's return voyage to London in the summer of 1914 was certainly "remarkable" as noted by Włodzimierz Suleja.[61] His journey from Kraków to Vienna was arranged by archbishop Bilczewski with considerable aid from the Austrian authorities. In Lwów a Pole, curiously named Rheinlander, arranged for him to meet the Austrian commander at Lwów. The Viennese Ministry of War provided him with an exit visa, initialed, notably, by the German ambassador in Vienna, Heinrich von Tschirsky, as well.[62] He met, serendipitously, an old man on the train who happened to be the chief of the railroad who facilitated Retinger's travels. Later Retinger would refer to this as "I had luck again."[63] Through the assistance of Retinger's Austrian contacts, and the efforts of the American ambassador in Vienna, Penfield, the Conrads were able to exit as well and return to England.

Arriving in Switzerland, Retinger received a visa from the French authorities – he also carried, *mirabile dictu*, a Russian passport. He made good use of his time there. He met with the French ambassador to Berne (Neau), and Grant Duff, the British ambassador. The latter did not trust him and even frisked him. He soon continued to Paris where, thanks again to Zamoyski,[64] he met with the highest officials in the Foreign Ministry, including Phillipe Berthelot, and Foreign Minister Stephane Pichon himself.[65]

His further journey to London was arranged by the French authorities who facilitated his travels. Berthelot, he claims, personally came to free him from the French jail where he was briefly held. This astonishing chain of immensely useful contacts propelled the twenty-six-year-old Retinger onto the international stage. He later claimed that his "amazing adventures" put him immediately good terms with Berthelot and was well regarded by both the British and the French who accepted him as "the unofficial representative of Polish interests."⁶⁶ His Galician origins and long residence in France had borne fruit.

During World War I, Retinger first became involved with Polish-Jewish relations. Although details are scanty, Retinger at this time befriended leaders of the international Zionist community, including Chaim Weizman, Wladimir Żabotyński, and especially Nahum Sokołow. Retinger criticized Roman Dmowski, the powerful leader of the Polish nationalist faction for his anti-Semitic views, which the latter dismissed.⁶⁷ Closely associated with Retinger's views regarding European unity, and a perennial problem for Poland, was the Jewish question. Retinger discussed the issue with Jews in 1915–1916 and had the notion that the Church in Poland should act as the "protector of the Jews." The details of this vision have not been recorded.⁶⁸ He also befriended Orthodox Jews from eastern Poland who, in Retinger's words, "had tender feelings for Poland." He also met a number of powerful American Jews: attorney Louis Marshall-who later played a prominent role at the Paris Peace Conference, Rabbi Stephen Wise, professor Magnus, and Judge Felix Frankfurter. This aspect of Retinger's activities seems largely to have convinced his enemies that Retinger was a Jew.⁶⁹ In any event, there is a bit of evidence to suggest that Retinger was later a member of the Polish section of B'nai B'rith.⁷⁰

## Notes

1 This is Aleksander Janta's argument as presented in his "Refleksye Retingerowskie: Czy był i czyim był agentem?" *Wiadomości*, No. 1325 (August 22, 1971), 2. Hereafter referred to as "Refleksye 1."
2 "Chapter I," Retinger Papers, drawer 4, Biblioteka Polska w Londynie (hereafter BPL).
3 This topic has evoked much contention. Retinger's non-Jewish origins are the rather fervent contention of his grandson; see Stanislaw W. Dobrowolski, *Memuary pacyfisty* (Kraków: Wydawnictwo Literackie, 1989), 10–11. When the author inquired of Jan Pomian, Retinger's last secretary, whether there was any truth to the rumors that Retinger was of Jewish origin, he dismissed them categorically (Pomian Interview). However, Stanisław Mackiewicz, a journalist au courant with twentieth-century Polish political gossip, regards Retinger as being of Jewish origin, stating that his father was a convert and a "great patriot." See his *Lata nadziei 17 wrzesnia 1939 – 5 lipca 1945* (Warsaw: Glos, 1945). It is significant that he was regarded as not always sufficiently sensitive to Jewish issues in this capacity, and Israeli historian David Engel suggests that Retinger was not well-disposed towards Jews (see his *In the Shadow of Auschwitz: The Polish Government-in-Exile and the Jews, 1939–1942* (Chapel Hill, NC: University of North Carolina Press, 1987), 53, 67–68, 85, 238 n. 79. Retinger claimed he was of German ancestry and never mentioned any Jewish origins; see Retinger to Gedda, July 17, 1949, Archiwum Narodowe w Krakowie (hereafter

ANK), s. 8064. Władysław Pobóg-Malinowski considers him a convert; see his *Z mojego okienka: Fakty i wrażenia z lat 1939–1945*. Vol. I (Łomnianki, 2013), 710.
4  Podgórski further argues that another branch of the family remained Jewish and retained the double 't' in the spelling of their name; see Bogdan Podgórski, *Józef Retinger: Prywatny politik* (Krakow: Universitas, 2013) 20.
5  Retinger to Gedda, July 17, 1949, ANK, s. 8064.
6  See the untitled French-language notes in Retinger Papers, Box 25a, BPL.
7  Z Papierow Hana Hulewicza, "Wspomnienia o J. H. Retingerze," ANK, s. 10371; cf. Władysław Pobóg-Malinowski, *Najnowsza historia polityczna Polski, 1864–1945. Tom III: Okres 1939–1945* (London: Gryf, 1981), 148n.
8  Zamoyski, 1853–1924, was scion of perhaps the most distinguished of all Polish families. Born in Paris, and a French citizen, he had also represented France abroad. Despite this, he was an ardent – and munificent – Polish patriot. Doubtless his profound French connections must have been an enormous aid to Retinger.
9  [Zamoyski] to NN, July 13, 1918, Retinger Papers, BPL, Box 17, BPL. Zamoyski's authorship is not certain, however.
10  Retinger, "Count Wladyslaw Zamoyski," Drawer 4, 1, BPL.
11  Grzegorz Witkowski, *Józef Retinger: Polski inicjator integracji europejskiej* (Warsaw: ZBLIŻENIE, 2000), 29; idem. *Ojcowie*, 36.
12  See the letter, marked "strictment personnelle et confidentielle," July 17, 1949 from Retinger to Luigi Gedda; Korespondencja Józefa Hieronima Retingera, s. 8064, ANK.
13  There is useful material about his in Dobrowolski, *Memuary*, 11ff.
14  See Longina Jakubowska, *Patrons of History: Nobility, Capital and Political Transitions in Poland* (Farnham: Ashgate, 2012).
15  Dobrowolski, *Memuary*, 17.
16  The literature on this episode is considerable; see, for example, Jerzy Roszkowski, "Rola hr. W. Zamoyskiego w spórze o Morskie Oko na tle dzieje kształowanie się granicy w Tatrach," http://www.zamoyski.pl; "Spór o Morskie Oko," http://www.scizga.pl both accessed on January 17, 2013.
17  There is some controversy over the year Retinger received his doctorate; see Wapiński, "Retinger," 148.
18  Podgórski, *Retinger*, 36.
19  Pomian, *Pamiętniki*, 16.
20  The Cardinal, something of a social butterfly, was close to the General Maurice Gamelin, of later ill-fame for his incompetence during the Second World War.
21  There is a brief biography "Anna Gould" in *Retratos de la Historia*," on-line at http://retratosdelahistoria.lacoctelera.net/post/2006/11/07/anna-gould, accessed on February 28, 2012.
22  Gide's memoirs indicate that he met Retinger – whom he described as "charming" – in May 0f 1907. Soon afterwards he referred to him as "le petit." Retinger was then nineteen. The meeting was via the neo-romantic artist Witold Wojtkiewicz; André Gide, *Journal, 1889–1939*. Paris: Bibliothèque de la Pléiade, 1951, 243, 477–478.
23  This list is a compendium of names drawn from Pomian, *Retinger* (22–23), as well as Pieczewski; see the latter's, *Działalność*, 67. Retinger referred to this period in his life as "Education in Paris," see his essay in 1, BPL.
24  Valuable comments about Retinger's brief publishing career and the cultural milieu in which he functioned can be found in the memoirs of his contemporary, Wacław Lednicki; see his *Pamiętniki, Tom II* (London: B. Świderski, 1967), 68–73, 98–105, 148; cf. Podgórski, *Retinger*, 31.
25  The RN was founded in Lwów in 1908 and was dominated by adherents of the right, despite its putatively all-Polish protestations. Its president was Tadeusz

Cieński (1856–1925). It established branches throughout Western Europe before 1914 and one in Chicago as well. See the correspondence between Retinger and Woźnicki of 1913–1914 about the establishment of Retinger's Polish Bureau under RN auspices in akc. 4386, Woźnicki Papers [34/I], Biblioteka Polska w Paryżu (hereafter BPP).

26 Grzegorz Witkowski, *Jozef Retinger: Polski inicjator integracji europejski* (Warsaw: Zbliżenie, 2000), 33. Witkowski here relies on the writings of Aleksander Janta.
27 Aleksander Janta, "Refleksye (3)," Janta says nothing about Retinger's putative Jewish origins.
28 Retinger was, at the time a proponent of the nationalist Roman Dmowski, Witkowski, *Ojcowie*, 41; cf. Podgórski, *Retinger*, 37.
29 He later noted that Poles were freer under the Habsburgs, which was certainly true; see his "My First Steps in Practical Politics," drawer 2, BPL.
30 Pieczewski, *Działalność*, 69. Podgórski argues that Zamoyski probably inspired and financed the book; Podgórski, *Retinger*, 38.
31 J. H. Retinger, *The Poles and Prussia*. No place of publication, nor publisher, nor date of publication is indicated. From other sources we know it was published in London in 1910 or shortly thereafter.
32 Ibid., 4–5.
33 Ibid., 5ff.
34 To the Germans they were – and remain – heroes.
35 Ibid., 6–7.
36 Ibid., 7.
37 Ibid., 7.
38 Ibid., 9.
39 Ibid., 9–13.
40 Retinger's emotional presentation and lurid details of the German brutality towards Polish parents and their children is an outrageous example of Berlin's mistreatment of its Polish minority; see John J. Kulczycki, *School Strikes in Prussian Poland, 1901–1907*. Boulder, CO: East European Monographs, 1981.
41 Retinger, *Prussia*, 15.
42 Józef M. Retinger, *Polacy w cywilizacjach świata*, (Gdańsk: np, 1991), 11–16.
43 For a characterization of the office, see Zdzisław Najder, *Joseph Conrad: A Chronicle* (New Brunswick: Rutgers University Press, 1983), 581 n. 3; cf. Pomian, *Retinger*, 28–29.
44 "Sprawozdanie Polskiego Katolickiego Towarzystwa Dobroczynności," [1914] in akc. 4430, Archiwum Kazimierza Woźnicki, BPP
45 Retinger, *Conrad and his Contemporaries* (Miami: The American Institute of Polish Culture, 1981), 55ff; Olgierd Terlecki, *Kuzynek diabła* (Kraków: Krajowa Agencja Wydawnicza, 1988), 11. There are multiple editions of Terlecki's brief yet important biography of Retinger. It was first published in 1971 in a four-part series in the Kraków periodical Życie Literackie (nos. 1015–1018) under the title "Wielka awantura." These parts were collected into a book bearing the same title and published by the Polska Fundacja Kulturalna in London in 1978. The identical text was re-issued as *Barwne życie szarej eminencji* by the Krajowa Agencja Wydawnicza (Kraków, 1981). Finally, an expanded edition, again *Kuzynek diabła* appeared in 1988. All references are in this work exclusively to the 1988 edition.
46 "My First Steps in Practical Politics," Retinger Papers, 2, BPL; Conrad regarded Russia as a "monster," Pomian, *Retinger*, 35.
47 Retinger was introduced to Conrad by Bennett; apparently in 1909; see Retinger, *Conrad and his Contemporaries*, 64; cf. Pomian, *Retinger*, 31.

48 The fullest account of the burgeoning Retinger-Conrad friendship is in the exhaustively documented work by Najder, *Conrad*, 381ff, cf. Retinger to Helena Żółtowska, December 15, 1948, folder S, Box 19, Retinger Papers, BPL.
49 Terlecki, *Kuzynek*, 11.
50 J. H. Stape "The Chronology of Conrad's 1914 Visit to Poland," *Polish Review*, 29 (1984), 65–71; John S. Lewis, "Conrad in 1914," *The Polish Review*, 20 (1975), 217–222. Retinger was married in 1912 to Otylia (or Otolyia) Zubrzycka, from a prominent family. Her family is discussed in an untitled biography with a number of errors in the archives of the Warsaw Instytut Pamięci Narodowej (hereafter IPN), file BU 01222/593/D.
51 Podgórski, *Retinger*, 314n.
52 This very important document was published as "Memorandum on the Polish Question," in Ludwik Krzyżanowski, "Joseph Conrad: Some Polish Documents," in Krzyżanowski, ed., *Joseph Conrad: Centennial Essays* (New York: Polish Institute of Arts and Sciences, 1960), 138–139. Regarding Conrad's geopolitical views concerning Poland see the essay by Eloise Knapp Hay, "Reconstructing "East" and "West" in Conrad's Eyes," in Keith Carabine, ed., *Contexts for Conrad* (New York: Columbia University Press, 1993), 21–40; cf. Conrad to Marian Biliński, November 9, 1914, Frederick R. Karl and Laurence Davies, eds. *The Collected Letters of Joseph Conrad: 1912–1916*, vol. 5 (Cambridge: Cambridge University Press, 1996), 258–259.
53 Dobrowolski, *Memuary Pacyfisty*, 37.
54 Józef Bilczewski (1860–1923) was Metropolitan of Lwów and also a professor at and later rector of the Jan Kazimierz University of Lwów. He was recently canonized.
55 Józef Teodorowicz (1864–1938), Archbishop of the Armenian Rite Catholic Church, Metropolitan of Lwów, member of the Austrian *Herrenhaus*, and after World War I, a member of the Polish parliament.
56 Cieński, earlier president of the RN, also became president of the CKN, established in Lwów in late July, 1914. Like the RN under Cieński it was pro-Austrian initially and only later became decidedly pro-Russian due to its antipathy to the Germans.
57 Jan Dąbski (1880–1931) was a populist leader in Galicia. His party was associated with the CKN.
58 This passage, ostensibly from Retinger's memoirs, is reprinted in Pomian, *Pamiętniki*, 40. In his essay "Trip to England, 1914," he also mentions meeting with Prince Czartoryski in Galicia in 1914; see drawer 3, BPL.
59 Regarding the CKN see Jerzy Holzer and Jan Molenda, *Polska w czasie wojnie światowej* (Warsaw: Wiedza Powszechna, 1973), 433. Cieński was the main figure in the CKN and Retinger met with him while in Poland in July 1914. Shortly afterwards the CKN was absorbed into the larger Supreme National Committee (Naczelny Komitet Narodowy, NKN) which was also a complex coalition of factions-across the political spectrum. The NKN worked closely with the Habsburg authorities and was, obviously, Austrophile.
60 Regardless of whether he maintained any formal connections with the RN, by the end of 1914 it was decided that Retinger was untrustworthy. Although evidence is scanty, the probable reason for its disenchantment with Retinger was the obvious connections he had already demonstrated with the CKN; see [Maciej] Loret to [Stanisław Osada], December 21, 1914, Papiery Wacława Gąsiorowskiego, s. 15226/II, Ossolineum, Wrocław.
61 See his "Szara eminencja" in Zbigniew Fras and Włodzimierz Suleja, *Poczet agentów polskich* (Wrocław: Ossolineum, 1995), 155–164.
62 Retinger's version of this episode strains credulity: He contends that he misled military authorities in Lwów into thinking that his voyage to the West was at

## 16  The formative years, 1888–1914

the behest of "very important personages," conveniently un-named. He used the same tactic in dealing with the Austrian General Staff in Vienna, and even with German ambassador Heinrich von Tschirsky, suggesting always that he had grave matters to attend in Western Europe, vouchsafed by the mighty; see Pomian *Retinger*, 40ff. Suleja judges Retinger's account "remarkable at the very least" (see his "Szara eminencja," 156.). Terlecki clearly regards Retinger's account of these extraordinary travels as implausible and concludes: "Ultimately we really know nothing about this episode" (see his *Kuzynek*, 18). Wapiński only notes laconically that Retinger moved about "without great difficulties;" see his "Retinger," 149.

63 Pomian, Retinger, 43.
64 Wapiński, Retinger," 149. Cf. Retinger, "Journeys Across Countries at War (August 1914)," drawer 2, BPL.
65 This account of Retinger's 1914 journey from Lwów to London is based largely on his memoirs as published in Pomian, *Pamiętniki*, 32–35. The detail concerning his possession of a Russian passport is from the files of the British Intelligence Service; see Ciechanowski, "Retinger w świetle raportów," 201. For the French Ministry of Foreign Affairs facilitating his international travels, see the untitled document attributed to French Intelligence in BPP, Woźnicki Papers; cf. Retinger, "Trip to England, 1914," sz. 3, BPL.
66 Undated, untitled document in Box 25a, folder "Życiorysy Józefa Retingera," 2., Retinger Papers, BPL. Podgórski presents this extraordinary voyage of Retinger matter-of-factly; it is not convincing; see, Podgórski, *Retinger*, 41.
67 Pomian, *Retinger*, 54.
68 "Jewish Problem," drawer 2, Retinger Papers, BPL, 12. There Retinger claimed he made representations to the Vatican in this regard.
69 Retinger "Jewish Problem," in J. H. Retinger Papers, BPL, drawer no. 2.
70 Pieczewski, *Działalność*, 70.

# 2  World War I, 1914–1918

In Paris, Retinger made the rounds of the Polish émigré leadership and implored them to undertake no action which would associate the Poles with support of France in the war, but rather to adopt an entirely neutral disposition. This impassioned effort made a particularly negative impression on those Poles who were already attempting to raise Polish volunteers to join the French war effort.[1] Retinger regarded his first mission in wartime London to get Polish internees released – Russian Poles were regarded as Russians and not interned. It was this task which brought him to the British Prime Minister.[2]

Soon after arriving in London, Retinger was able to meet Prime Minister Herbert Henry Asquith with whom he apparently established an instantly warm relationship.[3] This was an important step in what Retinger set as his goal: "penetrate into the inner circles of British politics."[4] Retinger was an enormously impressed by Asquith whom he regarded, even long afterwards, as a great statesman.[5] Retinger soon became a frequent guest at Asquith's home, and met a number of the British political elite including both Winston Churchill – whom he never trusted – and Lord Kitchener.[6] Retinger later provided a long list of his friends in key places in the British circles of power: Lady Maud Cunard – his link to Arthur James Balfour – Margot Asquith, Violet Asquith (later Lady Violet Bonham-Carter), the Duchess of Rutland, Lady Beresford, Lady Randolph Churchill, Lady Diana Manners – his link to Asquith: great ladies all, confirming the fact that for a man supposedly resembling a monkey, he had enormous appeal to females.[7]

Retinger's bizarre status in England is well captured by Pomian:

> Retinger's situation was delicate. Success-and even the possibility of acting – was due exclusively to the good will of people with whom he interacted. He was an Austrian subject, the citizen of an unfriendly state, beyond that, he tried to maintain contacts with a country controlled by the enemy from which also he received funds to undertake his activities. He was also an enemy of Russia, the ally of England. His letters of credence and his mandate could at any time placed in doubt both his countrymen, and his Western hosts. As it always is with émigrés in his sort of situation, he was taken and accepted as a Polish representative

only because, nobody better was around, and to the extent that it was decided to place faith in him. Were he to start to become weary, it would be easy to repudiate him as a pretentious sprig [młokos]. In this unclear situation, he had to act very carefully. He did not always do so which led him in the end to defeat.[8]

On August 31, 1914, Retinger called at the Foreign Office and presented a request, obviously from the Galician Poles (i.e. the CKN),[9] whom he had met in Lwów, that the British government undertake to guarantee, in some unstated way, the recent Russian approach to the Poles (the August 14, 1914 Proclamation of the Russian Commander-in-Chief, the Grand Duke Nikolai Nikolaievich) which promised unification of partitioned Poland in exchange for Polish support for the Russian war effort.[10]

The Austrian Poles were at pains to inform the British that whereas the large forces of international politics had ranged them with the Central Powers, they were, nonetheless, anti-German, though they maintained an affectionate loyalty regarding Austria. This was, in its infancy, the logic behind Retinger's later efforts to help Austria desert the Berlin alliance and come to a separate peace. Retinger was, throughout, anti-German.

George Clerk of the Foreign Office understandably rejected this request as "out of the question," but Retinger's *démarche* evidently elicited considerable reflection. Clerk wanted to maintain the contact with Retinger against future possibilities; Sir Arthur Nicolson (permanent Under Secretary) was decidedly opposed. He refused to meet Retinger, and referred to the whole issue as "foolish." The final determination was by Foreign Secretary Edward Grey who ordered that Retinger not be "snubbed," but rather furnished with a sympathetic yet anodyne written assurance that the British government was "in thorough sympathy" with the Russian declaration and that public opinion had "welcomed cordially" the Russian step. Retinger was even allowed to publish the letter containing these assurances.[11] Grey, Retinger concluded, knew nothing of Poland.[12]

Having completed his first "diplomatic mission," Retinger now apparently made himself useful to his new friends. Some high officials of the British government, and circumstantial evidence suggests Asquith himself, decided to send Retinger to the United States (or make use of his already decided intention of going there[13]) in order to ascertain whether the Poles of America were seriously contemplating raising volunteers from among their compatriots to serve the cause of Britain and her allies.[14] Retinger later claimed British initiative in the task a matter of controversy.[15] Retinger also attributes to Asquith a more fundamental goal: to urge the Poles in the United States to be pro-Allied.[16]

In October, the Polish community in America sent the British, via Retinger, an offer of 100,000 trained men. Later he referred to his initial actions in America as contributing to Polonia's efforts to raise an army.[17] The text is as follows:

The United Polish organizations of America, representing the whole of the three and one-half million Poles in the United States, have authorized me to offer to His British Majesty's Government and to the Government of France a body of armed Polish volunteers to serve, at their own risk and responsibility, with the Allies in the Western seat of war.

They are able immediately to supply 12,000 trained and fully equipped officers and men, and in the course of a very few weeks to increase this number to at least the strength of an army corps [!]. All these men have completed a course of military training in native organizations (one of which the 'Sokol,' numbered a few months ago no less than 30,000 drilled men).

In view of the active sympathy now manifested by the Poles in America with the common cause of the Allies are making on behalf of civilization, humanity, and the rights of oppressed nations, and in view of their own national aspirations, I am convinced that if the Governments of Great Britain and France are able to avail themselves of this offer, the Allies will have no more loyal and enthusiastic, enduring and courageous soldiers than the members of this potential Polish legion.[18]

The Foreign Office, after a plethora of minutes, decided to [probably the work of Arthur Nicolson] "give this very persistent gentleman a most civil refusal."[19]

Nonetheless, Retinger left for America. He arrived in the United States in November, 1914 letting it be known that he had access to the British government.[20] He journeyed from New York to Chicago, met with the major Polish leadership in the United States, and left them totally bewildered. His behavior oscillated between hauteur, with frequent claims of representing powerful forces, and virtual pan-handling as he asked his hosts to pay his hotel bills. In Chicago, Retinger explained that he had "received oral instruction from the English war ministry to come to the States in order personally to investigate the readiness of the local Poles to participate in the war."[21] Apparently the existence of a large Polish community in the United States was one of the arguments Retinger used to alert the British to the possible importance of the Poles, a people about which the British were "singularly unenlightened."[22] It was also useful that raising a Polonia legion was dear to the heart of Conrad.[23]

However, given American neutrality, the British were unable to accept any offers from the American Poles to volunteer. Hence, Retinger had nothing to say and there was a no purpose in his coming. The American Poles were stunned by Retinger's behavior, decided he was not to be trusted, and regarded the whole episode as incomprehensible.[24] An intriguing and characteristic sidelight of Retinger's brief mission was his devoted effort to meet as many "eminent Americans" as possible, to which end he carried letters of introduction.[25] The American Poles thought that Retinger intended to use these introductions to help create a pro-Polish lobby in the United

States; Retinger, however, seems to have been pursuing his traditional practice of ingratiating himself to anyone who might matter for his own purposes, since American Polonia gained no benefit from Retinger's efforts at self-promotion.[26]

When he arrived in New York, he told American immigration authorities that the purpose of his voyage was to visit his brother, Juliusz, who was a professor at the University of Chicago.[27] This verisimilitude served as a convenient pretext. Despite his brief stay, and apparently very limited funds, it is significant that Retinger went from New York to Washington to call at the British embassy before continuing to Chicago.[28]

Retinger's goals in his American mission are inexplicable. Was he really acting at the behest of the British government? What was he trying to accomplish in the United States? Was this, perhaps, another effort at personal ingratiation, albeit on a rather grand scale? But even if that were the only motive, why did Retinger trouble himself to come to the United States at all, especially just on the heels on an initial encouraging reception from Grey at the Foreign Office? Retinger sought two simultaneous and reciprocal goals: to convince the British that he had direct access to the leadership of the Polish community in the United States, and to impress the latter that he was had the confidence of the British government. He certainly conveyed the notion that he was acting on behalf of London, and others then, and later, drew the conclusion that he had become, in some measure, a British agent, the first step in the long legend.

The ultimate goal of Retinger's mission, as he later admitted, was to "get them on our side." Until he went to the United States, Retinger had a grand image of the American Polish community and regarded winning its support as a major coup. He was sorely disappointed.[29]

Retinger's own recounting of the episode deserves attention. He went, he said, to rally Polonia against Germany and Austria-not to investigate raising armies. The whole trip was "the greatest debacle for me and I can see now, entirely through my own fault." He was too "cocky"; "I was 'tactless'." I could have put the 'Polish problem on the map' for London but completely failed. 'I did everything wrong'." He had no preparation and left within a day of being notified of his mission. No one in America was informed of his coming except the British ambassador.[30]

Retinger's analysis of American Polonia was shrewd and insightful. They were "without Polish patriotism but had a sentimental remembrance of Poland." They were largely Americanized. They were poor and without any influence. They lived in "isolated ghettos." They had no understanding of how to use their electoral potential. Their leaders were not impressive. They "kow-towed" to any American politician who tried to woo them. They were rather pathetic.[31] In general, Retinger's impressions were negative: he was "deeply disappointed in Polonia," and as for the Americans he "disliked them intensely."[32] These views never changed.[33]

There is an important theme which should not be overlooked in considering Retinger's mysterious American "mission." Although he came, ostensibly, to investigate the question of Polonia, and volunteers for British service, he never said his purpose was to encourage such an effort. Indeed, his behavior in Chicago was exactly the opposite, and his visit did a great deal to smother the rising sentiment in American Polish ranks to organize volunteers.[34] Retinger was to claim shortly thereafter that he was opposed to the whole notion of raising a Polish volunteer force.[35] He later wrote that he did consider the "idea of a legion" for only two to three months, but concluded that it was impracticable.[36]

The explanation of this astounding offer, full of bombast and exaggeration, is a reflection of chronology. Despite his later refusal to stress his goal of recruiting a Polish army in the United States, at least at the outset, that is exactly what he was doing. He may well have been influenced by the baseless enthusiasm of American Polonia considering the numbers and ardor of their comrades, but nonetheless Retinger did make this proposal, with Polonia authorization. The only conclusion we can draw from this is as follows: Retinger was in touch with Polonia leaders in the early fall of 1914. They authorized him to act in their name and offer an army. Retinger, ignorant of the real state of affairs in Polonia, presented this project to the Foreign Office and they refused.[37] Shortly thereafter he went to the United States and found the situation not as Polonia's leaders had suggested. After several weeks of consideration, Retinger dropped the issue and rarely if ever referred to the army issue in his account of his trip.

There was even a rumor among the Poles of France that his American visit was financed by the Austrian Poles specifically to derail efforts at raising Polish volunteers in North America. There is even some evidence that, upon leaving the United States, Retinger traveled directly to Switzerland –where he is reputed to have moved in pro-Habsburg Polish circles – rather than to London.[38] Such actions would be consistent with Retinger's broader attitude towards the war which was pro-Austrian but anti-German.

Although Retinger may have managed to establish himself, however tentatively, as an *homme de confiance* to British authorities, "his alleged Austrophilism and some financial troubles" ended his work as the London representative of the Galician Poles.[39] Ninenteen-fifteen, is thus largely a gap in the record of Retinger's activities. His Polish Information Bureau closed – precisely when is unclear – and with it his official link to Galicia. As a result, when Retinger next appeared on the political scene, he would represent only himself.[40] Nonetheless, an important episode in 1915 allows us an insight into his political thinking.

Early in the year, Retinger had a noteworthy clash with the famous Polish pianist turned international lobbyist, Paderewski.[41] From the beginning of the war, Paderewski had been co-chairman (along with novelist Henryk Sienkiewicz) of a committee collecting aid for Polish victims of the war's ravages, the *Comité Général*, located in Vevey, Switzerland. Although the committee was strictly humanitarian in its activities, a close look at its membership and less public activities make it very clear that the Vevey committee was highly partisan regarding the war, ardently supporting England and France and, by necessity, their Russian ally. Moreover, Vevey was resolutely anti-German, and concomitantly anti-Austrian, although the later inclination lacked real passion. In early 1915, Paderewski decided to expand the eleemosynary activities of the Vevey committee by creating branches in Paris, London, and eventually the United States. He hoped to induce Conrad to join him in the British efforts. However, to Paderewski's consternation, Conrad reacted violently to the presence of Russian officials among the supporters of the proposed London branch and refused his cooperation. Paderewski discussed this matter with Retinger, who completely shared Conrad's sentiments, and probably inspired the novelist's response.[42] Paderewski was furious, and his relations with Retinger were irreparably damaged.[43]

The significance of this effort goes far beyond personalities, although Paderewski's ego was gargantuan while the young Retinger was both arrogant and often tactless. A real political division was reflected in the matter. Paderewski was committed to an allied victory in the war and supportive of Russia as an unavoidable concomitant. Retinger, like Conrad, could not support Paderewski's position which was functionally pro-Russian, and, perhaps worse, anti-Austrian. Retinger's falling-out with Paderewski in 1915 – which seems, incidentally, to have been his major political activity in that year – was part of the gradual formation of Retinger's conception of the war, and Poland's relationship which would only become clear in 1916.

## The 1916 mission to Poland

Retinger undertook another of his wartime missions in early, 1916. In February he suddenly arrived in the portion of Russian Poland just occupied by German and Austrian troops.[44] His appearance here was, prima facie, quite extraordinary. He came, ostensibly, to attend a meeting of the newly-formed National Central Committee (Centralny Komitet Narodowy, CKN).[45] One of this organization's founders, Karol Popiel, later disclosed this episode. According to Popiel, Retinger explained to the Poles that he was traveling at the behest of the British government, and that he had come (via Switzerland) to "acquaint himself with political conditions in the occupied Kingdom [of Poland]." The similarity to Retinger's 1914 appearance before the American Poles in Chicago is striking. Popiel observed that: "I did not need to make any inquiries to conclude that a man who, in time of war, can appear on the territory of a country occupied by the enemy, has definitely, and appropriately high, organizational or political connections."[46] The CKN, for its part, at least mused over the prospect of sending a representative to London.[47]

As was the case of his earlier visit to the Poles of America, this appearance followed a certain script. The hosts were not informed in advance of his arrival or the purposes of his mission. Retinger described himself as acting on behalf of the highest circles of the British government and claimed to be involved in political reconnaissance. Beyond these vagaries he said little or nothing and did not take the Poles into his confidence.

This early 1916 mission is again difficult to reconstruct due to lack of sources, and many questions remain unanswered.[48] However, certain features are clear and important to emphasize in order to bring into relief the political pattern that is gradually emerging from Retinger's melodramatic international "diplomacy." First, the meeting Retinger attended was comprised of representatives of what, in the complex world of wartime Polish politics, was regarded as the "left independence" or "activist" faction. This was a congeries of groups which, as regards the war, were decidedly anti-Russian and willing to work with (and hence the appellation "activist") the Central Powers for the purpose of reconstructing Polish independence. One of the hallmarks of their activities was the need for Polish armed units to fight against the tsar and hence, of necessity, on the side of Berlin, and more appealingly, of Vienna. It was, thus, functionally, Austrophile, as were Retinger and Conrad for that matter. The most prominent member of this grouping was Józef Piłsudski, the famed leader of the legions fighting against Russian under Austrian operational command since 1914. Thus the CKN, whose meeting Retinger had just attended, was the political antithesis of Paderewski and his rightist friends at Vevey who were forcedly pro-Russian. Significantly, Popiel recalled that the man who brought Retinger to the Warsaw meeting was Witold Jodko-Narkiewicz, then Piłsudski's most trusted lieutenant.

There are a few additional scraps of evidence to suggest that Retinger was attempting to establish contact with the Piłsudskiite camp early in the war, and this 1916 appearance in Warsaw can be seen as part of the project. Indeed, ever since February, 1915, Retinger had worked in London with August Zaleski who was favorably disposed towards Piłsudski and his legions in Austrian Galicia. There is little doubt that Zaleski encouraged Retinger in a pro-Piłsudski and pro-activist direction.[49] Retinger later acknowledged that from the very outset of the war he was fascinated with the legions and thought all Poles were.[50] He also met with a powerful legionnaire, Władysław Sikorski, though the circumstances of this have never been recorded.[51] It was the start of a long relationship.

Of course, how Retinger managed to cross several frontiers – both ways in 1916 – remains inexplicable, as does the validity of his claim that he was, in effect, a British agent assigned to canvass Polish issues. Perhaps an even more central question is not whether London sent Retinger, but who allowed him to cross into occupied territory? A convenient answer is that Vienna, or at least those with influence in Vienna, arranged for Retinger's visit, whether the British sent him or not. This would allow us to continue the assumption that Retinger had Austrian connections of some sort at least into 1916. The possibility of Retinger symbolizing, albeit in a small way, the notion of an Anglo-Austrian relationship is also intriguingly suggested.

## Austria, Retinger, and the separate peace

This mysterious trip to Warsaw was the immediate prelude to Retinger's most significant wartime "diplomatic" endeavor: the attempt to arrange a separate peace between the allies and Austria Hungary in 1916. In the same year, Retinger, often in conjunction with Conrad, inundated the Foreign Office with implausible proposals for the reconstruction of Poland. What historians have hitherto failed to realize, is that these were not separate enterprises by Retinger but part of the same project.[52] In 1916–1917, as would be the case later, he regarded Polish independence and more general schemes for European reorganization as inseparable and mutually supporting goals which could only be realized interdependently. Thus, although Retinger variously emphasized either the European – as against the more specifically Polish – aspects of his efforts, they were facets of the same project. Unfortunately some of the proposals were simply ridiculous: The novelist Arnold Bennett told Retinger that his "political ideas... [are] so extremely crude as to rob it [a memorandum] of all interest."[53]

In his memoirs, Retinger recalled that the initiative for his quixotic efforts to promote a separate peace came from the idiosyncratic French politician and social notable Boni de Castellane.[54] De Castellane was related by marriage to Polish noble families.[55] He had served in the French parliament for several terms, and his highly original and essentially Catholic view of international problems was well-known in Europe in the years before the war.[56] Retinger credits him with inspiring in him the idea of the "unity of Europe."[57] Retinger was overwhelmed by Boni:

> The most handsome, the most elegant, the flashiest, the most beloved dandy in France in the years before World War I. ... a man of the 18th century.[58]

By 1916, de Castellane had become convinced that Austria was the essential element to stabilize Central Europe under Catholic auspices and create a barrier to Russian penetration of the continent. Moreover, a rapprochement between Catholic France and Catholic Austria would serve both countries' national interests while simultaneously advancing the Vatican's cause.[59] Retinger introduced the Frenchman to Polish émigré politics and leaders, and won his sympathy for the Polish cause.[60] Retinger was a devotee of the aristocratic Catholic circles in which de Castellane moved, and was a man with connections among the Poles of Austria. Hence, de Castellane's notions about facilitating a separate peace for Austria were a most stimulating point of departure for the ambitious and resourceful Retinger. Retinger much later claimed that he learned many things from de Castellane; the two central one were the need for a "separate peace" with Austria, and the vision of an eventual "Unity of Europe."[61] De Castellane was a "cosmopolitan" not an internationalist, and a devoted patriot: Retinger could be describing himself.[62]

Here, a number of political trends and personal acquaintances came together. Retinger envisioned some amelioration of Poland's situation, perhaps the regaining of independence, through collaboration with Vienna. Austria would annex Russian Poland to the empire and create a much enlarged Poland, a solution which would induce the much bruited "trialism" for the Habsburg Poles and perhaps be a means to independence. This "Austro-Polish" solution to the Polish Question may have gained support even from Prime Minister Asquith.[63] Conrad, as we noted, shared this vision, and, like Retinger, wished to see a more active role for the Western allies in fostering the re-creation of Poland.[64] It was this position which dictated their unwillingness to cooperate with the seemingly pro-Russian activities of Paderewski; it was also evident in Retinger's missions to the United States in 1914 and occupied Poland in 1916. Saving Austria by arranging a separate peace thus had a particular Polish motivation.

But merely allowing Austria to avoid destruction was just the beginning. De Castellane introduced Retinger to a host of Catholic aristocrats with Austrian ties, notably Prince Sixte de Bourbon-Parma.[65] Charles, the new Austrian Emperor was married to Sixtes' sister, Princess Zita. These would provide the conduit for the approach to Vienna. This circle would also provide candidates for a simultaneous plan: to determine a future monarch for a restored Polish kingdom. Retinger apparently discussed this widely at the time. Conrad suggested a British candidate be found as a link to London's support for Polish aspirations. However, Retinger's Parisian friends suggested a Frenchman.[66] De Castellane, and thus Retinger, saw four elements in their solution to Europe's dilemma: the Pope, the Austrian Emperor, and the pretenders to the French throne (!). Prussia, Russia, and the United States were "extraneous bodies."[67]

De Castellane discussed a separate peace for Austria early in the war with the powerful political figure Joseph Caillaux. (Like Boni, Caillaux was pro-Austrian and anti-German, and also shared with the Pole a strong attachment to England.)[68] De Castellane cast his remarks in the context of close French cooperation with the Vatican in any effort in this regard which would, incidentally, also envision damaging Germany. Caillaux was, de Castellane concluded, impressed by his arguments.[69] Caillaux was known for his unorthodox political views and had been a controversial figure in French politics long before the war. By his own admission, Caillaux desired to arrange an early peace to save France, in contrast to the consuming dedication to victory associated with Premier Georges Clemenceau. Although regarded by many of his countrymen as a traitor, proponents of Caillaux have emphasized that his patriotism was incontrovertible, yet coupled with a broadly European orientation.[70] Caillaux was also a "prominent Catholic who shared the Holy Father's apprehensions ... about a peace which would not *desarticuler* Europe's internal and external structure."[71] The notion of a Paris-Vienna Catholic axis around which to reconstruct Europe – a revival of the Kaunitzian system – which would reduce the power of parvenu Germany[72] and keep Russia at bay, would appeal to de Castellane, Caillaux, and the Austrian Pole Retinger.[73]

Little is known concerning Caillaux's interest in Polish affairs during the war. However, late in 1916 he was one of the handful of French deputies urging a more vigorous Polish policy for his government.[74] This action by

Caillaux regarding Poland was especially significant when we couple it with Retinger's claim in his memoirs that it was Caillaux who "originated the idea of an eventual candidature of Prince Sixte de Bourbon-Parma to the Polish crown."[75] De Castellane knew Sixte well and kept in touch with him throughout the war. Sixte, in turn was a proponent of Austro-French cooperation, was militantly anti-German, and a devout Catholic. In addition, Sixte had been bruited as a possible candidate for the Albanian throne in 1912, and thus his availability for royal service was well-known in French circles.[76] Hence, we have a rather cloudy, yet nonetheless certain triangular relationship among Retinger, and the two powerful and controversial French politicians de Castellane and Caillaux.[77] There is speculation that Retinger acted as an intermediary between the Jesuits (especially the "Black Pope" the Polish Count Włodzimierz Ledóchowski), and Sixte.[78] A separate peace, Catholic politics, and Polish independence are all featured, though their interrelationship is quite unsure. The themes of international collaboration, monarchism, including preservation of the Habsburgs, and Vatican diplomacy are all elements of the intellectual context.

In the spring of 1916, Retinger began, at de Castellane's urging "a thoroughly unofficial investigation of the possibilities of concluding a separate peace with Austria."[79] Retinger was convinced that before any action he had to consult with the British. Hence, early in 1916 he met with Asquith who "had no objections."[80] Retinger later recollected, curiously, that he regarded the key to the whole enterprise was to "win over" the press magnate Lord Northcliffe: the reasons for this singularly odd determination he did not provide. In any event, using the intermediacy of Northcliffe's brother Lord Rothermere, another of Retinger's endless list of convenient acquaintances, he met the irascible Northcliffe and gained his support.[81] Northcliffe instructed his foreign correspondents, especially *The Times*' man in Paris, Henry Wickham-Steed, to facilitate Retinger's efforts. As a result, Retinger met with Clemenceau, and Berthelot of the Foreign Ministry.[82] These meetings were less than auspicious as Retinger acknowledged that his solicitude for Austria was prompted by the Dual Monarch's Catholicity, a feature of dubious merit to the atheist Clemenceau and the Protestant Berthelot. Despite this inauspicious inception, Retinger thence proceeded on his mission with what he regarded as Anglo-French blessing.[83] The only corroboration we have of his memoirs for these actions is a frustratingly vague letter from Conrad to Richard Curle of August 20, 1916:

> Retinger's activities go on at white heat – personal success immense, political what it can be and, indeed, better than one would have thought it possible in the hopeless state of the Polish question. He created for himself certain titles to a hearing by accomplishing a brilliant piece of work last month as an unofficial intermediary between the British and French Governments. In truth the position was delicate. But it's too long a story for this letter.[84]

Through de Castellane, Retinger met – though precisely when is unknown – with Prince Sixte and held a series of lengthy discussions with him.[85] The Countess of Montebello – royalist, pro-Austrian and a major influence on Boni – was also a link to the Habsburgs, but this relationship is elusive.[86] Retinger however had a double track approach to the Habsburgs. His guardian, Zamoyski, had arranged a meeting in Switzerland between Retinger and Ledóchowski. This linkage is significant because Ledóchowski was suspected by French intelligence of being the lynch-pin of the Vatican's efforts at pro-Central Powers diplomatic efforts.[87] A late 1915 report concerning Ledóchowski accused him of "animating a vast pacifist organization ... financed by Berlin and Vienna which ... disposes of many millions [of francs], [and] directs numerous Austrian, German, and Swiss agents."[88] The only prominent Poles we can associate with Retinger, other than Ledóchowski, are the historian Szymon Askenazy and the writer-scholar Władysław Tykociner, a putative German spy.[89]

Ledóchowski discouraged Retinger warning him that Vienna was so closely dependent on Germany that it was unable to act without Berlin's knowledge. For the next few months, Retinger shuttled back and forth between Paris, London, and Switzerland in pursuit of his diplomatic objectives. At some point, though the chronology is far from clear, he actually reached Vienna and held a number of meetings. His principal interlocutor was Count Mensdorff-Pouilly, the former Austrian ambassador in Paris and later himself an Austrian peace envoy. Retinger relates that he was asked, probably by the Austrian, to call the German Foreign Office and speak with Secretary Zimmermann, but refused. He did not explain why other than noting that he was too young to meet with such an esteemed personage; not a convincing argument from someone who had met with Asquith and Clemenceau.[90] He concluded that Berlin was refusing the Austrian *ballon d'essai*. In any event, Retinger feared that Berlin was monitoring his activities. He reported this, and dropped the effort. Clemenceau subsequently denied the episode.[91] Retinger later admitted that at the time of these frantic meetings he thought he was "playing a great role in international politics."[92]

German diplomats discovered that Retinger was meeting with Caillaux and traveling from France to Switzerland in April, June, September, and December of 1916, and in late March or early April of the next year. The Germans were highly suspicious and labeled Retinger an "English spy." However, the German consulate in Bern also reported that he was not trusted by the Poles in Switzerland, especially Roman Dmowski, and the pro-Entente Polish political right which he led.[93] The evidence should have immediately called into question the determination that Retinger was simply an "English spy." Indeed, British intelligence in late 1916 confirmed that Retinger was unpopular with the largely pro-Entente Poles of Switzerland and suspected that he has Austrian connections.[94] Conrad, who seems to have been kept reasonably abreast of Retinger's wanderings, was aware of the surreptitious and dangerous nature of his young friend's activities, referring to him as having "put his head in a noose for the Polish cause."[95] Unfortunately, Retinger's meetings with Caillaux – which would tie many ends together – remain very mysterious, although their authenticity was later confirmed by British intelligence as well.[96]

In the summer of 1916 Retinger again came calling on the British Foreign Office. These approaches were part of his larger effort to conclude a separate peace with Austria. A close friend was exasperated by Retinger's complex meanderings: "I do not know how you stand politically now, with the Poles or with anybody else."[97] This conclusion become clear if we examine closely what Retinger specifically presented to the British in 1916.

Retinger had induced Conrad to prepare a proposal for an "Anglo-French protectorate" over a "new Polish Commonwealth"; an effort to be undertaken "of course with the fullest concurrence of Russia." Poland was to be a "hereditary monarchy" and part of some rather vague Anglo-French alliance system. The future of this monarchy was a defined against a background of presumed Polish hostility to *both* Germany and Russia. The compatibility of this scheme for Polish restoration and the notions of an Anglo-French separate peace with Austria – arranged, notably, through essentially Polish channels – is striking. Unfortunately for Retinger, this grandiose project was virtually ignored by the Foreign Office which instantly recognized that an Anglo-French initiative regarding Poland would be utterly unacceptable to the Russians which held veto power over allied action regarding Poland.[98]

Retinger's frantic activities in 1916 had two ostensible motives: a separate peace for Austria, and the resurrection of Poland under Western auspices. It is intriguing to consider the possibility that Retinger's actions were inspired if not coordinated, with a rising initiative regarding Poland undertaken by the Poles in Austria. In early 1916, leading Poles from all three parts of the partitioned country met in Kraków to discuss a reunited Poland under Habsburg auspices, the so-called "Austrian solution" to the Polish Question. The reborn country would not press major territorial demands against Germany, though it had extensive desiderata as regarded Russia. To advance this goal, plans were made to establish propaganda bureaux throughout neutral countries.[99] Significantly, in early 1916 the most optimistic Polish proponents of a major Austrian move as regards the Polish issue were the leaders of the Kraków urban patriciate, Retinger's ancestral milieu.[100] Given Retinger's extensive connections in Austrian Poland, especially Kraków, it is difficult to believe that he was unaware of this development which so perfectly explains his otherwise separate 1916–1917 initiatives. We are again required to speculate based on suggestive, yet not definitive, evidence.

Retinger later admitted that he deluded himself into thinking he was playing a major role in international politics as a result of this complex, idiosyncratic and futile personal diplomacy of 1916–1917. Whereas it is impossible to discern any effect of Retinger's actions on the powers' actions at the time, the consequences of these melodramatic shenanigans for Retinger were considerable. His seemingly effortless travels across frontiers in wartime certainly suggested he was the servant of powerful forces. The frequent speculation that Retinger was an agent not only of the English, but perhaps a multiple agent, was certainly derived from this era. It is noteworthy that the accusations that Retinger was a British agent – which adhered to him for the rest of his life – probably had its source in Retinger himself: he used his implied close relations to facilitate his to-ing and fro-ing during the war. Thus the ultimate source of the charge that Retinger was a British agent was Retinger.

Late 1916 was something of a watershed in Retinger's activities. The available scraps of evidence suggest that he moved his activities from London to Paris. Retinger's relationship with the Foreign Office had been damaged earlier by accusations of Austrophilism. In 1916, Retinger was denounced by the pro-Entente Poles associated with Dmowski as "perhaps unwittingly being used for pro-Austrian purposes." MI5 was informed by the Foreign Office and Retinger was investigated. As a result, in December 1916, the Foreign Office decided to have no further dealings with him.[101]

The Polish Question advanced dramatically on November 5, 1916 when the Central Powers announced the reconstitution of Poland. Though obviously an insincere attempt to rally Polish support in occupied territory, and especially to gain recruits for its diminishing army, the German move obviously had repercussions. Retinger was concerned that the Germans might be able to raise significant numbers of volunteers and warned the Foreign Office: the idea of Germany emerging as the leader in solving the issue of Polish independence must have been horrifying to Retinger. He hatched a plan to forestall the German initiative: the Germans hoped to gain one million Polish troops by this action, but, if the British issued a statement of support for Polish aspirations and created a propaganda bureau in Switzerland the German effort would fail. The support of France and Russia was assured, he noted, the inclusion of Russia hardly comporting with the situation. The propaganda bureau should be under the direction of the Aga Khan! I cannot explain this bizarre touch, or what in the world the Khan to do with Poland.[102] Nonetheless by this time, the Foreign Office was no longer taking him seriously.[103] His innumerable lengthy memoranda on Poland and international politics were considered little more than an annoyance.

Retinger was interviewed by the War Office on November 8, 1916. He presented a complex, but insightful, analysis of the Polish situation which he explained in some detail. The text of the interview was later sent to the Foreign Office where Retinger was not in its good books. Nonetheless, his analysis of the Polish Question in light of the German proclamation is fascinating.

He judged the November 6 proclamation as "better than anything they [the Poles] had heard yet." He estimated that the Germans might be able to raise 50,000 volunteers, but conscript ten-times that many more. Moreover, the 700,000 Poles working in German industry could also be raised to a million and a half "if pro-German propaganda is successful." In Russian Poland the Poles were very anti-Russian, though they were pro-French and pro-British. This inclination was waning, however, due to their failure to take any steps "as to Poland's future": an accurate remark. The conscription of Poles to the allied colors would thus require that "some declaration should be made by the allies which would bear the distinct mark of Great Britain and France", that is, not Russia which had no Polish support. Hence, a declaration made by Russia alone would be worthless. By contrast, pro-British propaganda in Poland would fall on fertile ground, and it would reach Poles working "on munitions work in Germany."

Finally he played the Austrian card. "Approaching Austria with the idea of offering to accept her solution of Poland as a third member of the *Ausgleich*, and so induce her to make a separate peace with the Entente accepting this peace this solution as a recompense for losses in Transylvania, Croatia and Slavonia." He (Retinger) was "convinced that Austrian Foreign Minister Burián was favorably disposed towards this project."

The document, received by the War Office, was sent to Foreign Office on November 9, and to Lord Hardinge, Under Secretary of State of State for Foreign Affairs by the DMI. It anticipates Retinger's opposition to a pro-Russian policy by the Poles – such as raising an army to fight on the allied side, especially in conjunction with the Russians. It also purports to be an insight into Vienna's war policy in late 1916. Its meanderings through British governmental offices indicated that Retinger's views were still of interest to London.[104]

## Polish armies and Austrian initiatives

Retinger's subsequent actions during the war remain most obscure. Here, personal elements may have played the decisive role. Sometime in 1917 he endured a series of misfortunes: his first child was born with serious health problems. His marriage went into an irretrievable decline, ending in divorce and he began a lengthy affair with the singularly bizarre American adventuress Jane Anderson. His financial situation, always parlous, became so desperate that Conrad was required, surreptitiously, to subvent him.[105] His manifold flings into international diplomacy had accomplished nothing, and convinced many people that he was untrustworthy. His relationship with the British authorities had ended in failure, indeed, disaster.[106] His memoirs speak of being abandoned and shunned by those whom he had trusted. In despair, he attempted suicide.[107] Both the French and the British were highly suspicious and the British military authorities were watching him "very closely." They neither wanted him to return to Great Britain from France or go to the United States as he wished. The French regarded him as "a suspicious individual, mysterious, cunning and insinuating."[108] He was also infamous for not paying his bills – despite allied financial support – and of loose morals.[109] Retinger, too, despaired of his former patrons and later lamented that "Montenegro" mattered more to Paris than Poland.[110]

Retinger again made an attempt to play a role in the Polish aspects of international politics in late 1917. His actions have been previously dismissed as additional examples of political mischief, the product of mere idiosyncrasy, or simply left unexplained. However, they can be shown to be consistent with the motives attributed to him. Retinger admitted years later that his grandiose plan for European unity faded by 1917; he was "solely engaged in the fight for the independence of my country." This reflected "the personal, nationalistic, selfish point of view of a Pole."[111] Specifically, Retinger tried mightily to prevent the formation of a Polish volunteer army to fight on the side of the Entente.

This army project had long fascinated Poles of all political camps and many abortive efforts had been undertaken from the very beginning of the war to raise Polish units. We have seen Retinger's involvement in the Polonia efforts of 1914. However by 1917, other than a few minor and disappointing efforts, the only serious specifically Polish units to appear in the war were the legions associated with Austria and led by the charismatic Piłsudski, but the legions were in the process of dissolution by 1917. The Poles supporting the Entente were convinced that a Polish military force of substantial size, fighting alongside the Western allies would immeasurably increase the leverage of Polish émigré efforts to gain allied support for the cause of Polish independence. Finally, after endless efforts, in the summer of 1917, the French government agreed to sponsor such a force, with the close cooperation of the British and the Americans. The army was to be raised from the Polish population of the United States, officered largely by veterans of Polish nationality from the ranks of the fast collapsing Russian army, and raised largely with American financing. It would, after training in Canada, fight on the Western front. Political control would be by the Polish National Committee (Komitet Narodowy Polski, KNP), an émigré political body dominated by the political right under Dmowski in Europe, and Paderewski from his influential vantage point in the United States.

For Retinger, however, the creation of such an army was potentially disastrous. What he tried to do to stop it, and why he did this, are two fascinating questions which bring Retinger's whole World War I career into clear relief. News that a Polish army was being organized in France was similarly alarming to the leaders of the Austrophile camp in Galicia, who reacted by urging redoubled efforts to advance the goal of pushing Vienna to take steps regarding Poland.[112] Retinger's efforts in Switzerland logically complimented the notions of a separate peace and an associated reconstruction of Austria along trialist lines, including a restored Poland. Moreover, his opposition to the Polish army project would facilitate Austrophile efforts to win over the Poles and avoid a final break with Vienna.[113] The separate peace effort in 1917, coupled with the notion of an independent Poland, involved, as we see, many Austrian Poles.

Retinger was again in Switzerland in the first months of 1917, working assiduously to undermine the efforts of Dmowski and specifically trying to prevent the organization of Polish recruitment for the army in Russia. According to the German Swiss consulate and Berlin's operatives there, Retinger was well financed and even recruited "agents" to travel to Russia to further his plans. The Germans did not know what to make of these reports and concluded that Retinger was merely an "English spy." His contact with British military representatives in Switzerland seemed to confirm that.[114] London was, it would seem, not entirely through with Retinger.

In January, 1917 London reported the first highly tentative peace overtures from Vienna made via an Austrian industrialist in Copenhagen. Prime Minister David Lloyd George told the American ambassador that he was convinced that Vienna sincerely wished to leave the war as soon as possible.[115] Within Austria, Foreign Minister Count Ottokar Czernin told a Crown Council that Austria's desire to solve the Polish Question by establishing Poland as part of the Empire would require negotiations with the Entente.[116] In April, Count Mensdorff, contending that he was acting at the behest of Czernin, made more concrete overtures, and the British became first involved in the famous affair of Prince Sixte de Bourbon-Parma. Also in April, Retinger met with Caillaux and traveled to Switzerland; it was the latest in a series of visits since the preceding spring which had been monitored by German intelligence.[117]

Prince Sixte de Bourbon-Parma, who had met with Retinger in 1916 to discuss peace overtures to Austria, made his first efforts as an intermediary in January, 1917. Privately, Czernin assured the emperor that the time was perhaps propitious for some approach to Paris, as he anticipated the return to power there of Caillaux who would represent a "Peace Government."[118] The fact that Czernin linked the possibilities of peace with France and Caillaux is highly intriguing.[119]

When the French informed Lloyd George of this in April, "his commitment to a separate peace with Austria was total."[120] Thus the efforts that Retinger had vainly attempted in 1916 –approaches to Sixte, cooperation with London, a link to Austria via Switzerland, meetings with Caillaux – seemed to be materializing the next year. By spring 1917, the War Cabinet in London was told that the Austrian press was seething with reports about peace overtures, a break with Germany, and that the reconstruction of Poland was acceptable to Vienna.[121] Washington was considering the possibility of serving as a catalyst for secret negotiations between Vienna and the Western powers.[122] The Austrian diplomat, Adam Count Tarnowski, approached the Wilson administration about a separate peace with Austria which would include an independent Poland. Notably, Tarnowski was a Polish patriot.[123] Reports arrived in London of a direct peace offer from Vienna to be made in The Hague, or perhaps Stockholm. The Foreign Office showed a guarded interest, and interviewed Prince Sixte when he visited London at the end of spring.[124] It should be recalled that British involvement in these *pourpalers* was highly secretive: the Foreign Office was generally not apprised of the negotiations which Lloyd George pursued as a "behind-the-scenes intrigue with a shadowy outsider."[125]

In late summer, the British envoy to Switzerland noted that an Austrian diplomat – the Pole Władysław Count Skrzyński– was trying to urge the Polish émigré network in Switzerland to remain neutral in order to aid

Vienna's efforts at improving relations with the Western powers.[126] Efforts were reportedly underway to convince the Poles to assent to the notion of a Habsburg candidate for the Polish throne, the Archduke Charles Stephen.[127] Emperor Charles privately assured Polish politician in Vienna that he favored "trialism," that is the reconstruction of the Habsburg Empire with a third, Polish, state, equivalent to Austria and Hungary.[128] Charles Stephen, ostensibly a candidate for the throne of a restored Poland joined to Austria, lamented that Poles in the West were actively harming the Polish cause by efforts to create a volunteer military force, and specifically noted the malign influence of the pro-Entente Dmowski.[129]

By fall, however, the efforts of Prince Sixte de Bourbon-Parma had proved fruitless. New possibilities, however, arose in November when Skrzyński told the British in Bern that Czernin sought a high-level meeting. The result was a December interview between General Jan Christian Smuts of the Imperial General Staff and Count Mensdorff in Switzerland. Mensdorff was a noteworthy choice as he had been in Switzerland in March during the tentative Franco-Austrian negotiations of Sixte Bourbon-Parma. Mensdorff raised the Polish issue as central, to which Smuts responded that, should the Habsburgs really break with Berlin, the Austro-Polish solution would be favorably greeted in London.[130]

Over the next several weeks, London rapidly evolved a policy towards Austria which envisioned "extensive concessions" including specific support for the so-called Austrian solution to the Polish Question. Despite this, the second planned meeting between Smuts and Mensdorff never occurred, and by late spring, the prospect of a separate peace with Austria disappeared from the British diplomatic agenda as it had earlier from the French.[131] How serious was the possibility that these high-level secret negotiations would lead to peace remains doubtful.[132]

Ultimately, two possibilities were widely bruited: a separate peace for Austria, and a major initiative regarding Poland by Vienna. For those Poles who, like Retinger, saw the restoration of Polish independence in collaboration with Austria, this was perhaps the critical moment in the war. The imperial court was sending clear signals that it had positive plans for Poland but required some reciprocity, especially from the Polish émigrés in Western Europe, like Dmowski, who were actively pushing Polish opinion into an unfriendly direction. At the center was the prospective Polish army, especially one built in good part on the basis of officers recruited in Russia. In fact, although the army took form on the basis of a decree by the French government on June 4, 1917, it was clear that the instigation for it had involved Russian military representatives, and the project enjoyed the support of the Russian General Staff.[133] Thus the Polish army in the west had a clearly-and perhaps ironically – Russian origin. This alone would make it not only suspect, but also anathema to Austrophile Poles.

Given the many close relationships Retinger had with leading Polish political circles in Austria, it is certain that he must have been aware that a decisive moment had been reached; hence Retinger's efforts to block the Polish army. His efforts were protean if ineffective. In May, 1917 for example, Retinger sent the Foreign Office a rather fanciful proposal suggesting that London encourage the Americans to raise a large force of many divisions and send it across Siberia to join with a Polish nucleus winnowed from the collapsing Russian imperial forces. The result would be a reinvigorated Eastern front with an American-Polish nucleus. At first this seems a most peculiar proposal to come from Retinger as it would involve Poles in a direct military confrontation with the Central Powers, obviously anathema to an Austro-Polish orientation. However, if we look more closely at the proposal – which was given some attention by the Foreign Office before being rejected – it would have anchored the Poles of Russia there for a very considerable time (London estimated at least six months) awaiting a slowly forming American contingent. If the Poles in Russia were to await the Americans, they could not be available to aid the Polish army forming in France. Thus, this would have delayed Polish participation in a military force to be used against the Austrians, and gained Retinger and his cause a temporary delay.[134]

He campaigned tirelessly against the Polish army project in 1917, earning the disgust of Dmowski and the KNP.[135] Reports from KNP members indicate that Retinger was battling for influence in Paris against Dmowski and his entourage. However, since the French openly proclaimed their support of the Polish army in June, 1917, Retinger's efforts were foredoomed; indeed, they destroyed his position in both London and Paris.

### Retinger's Austrophilism in retrospect

Retinger's 1917 activities regarding the nascent Polish army in France were motivated by his desire to keep alive the prospect for a separate peace for Austria, a separate peace which would be linked to the re-establishment of Poland as a third element in a reconstituted Habsburg Empire. By 1917, however, Retinger's actions on behalf of Austrian interest – or perhaps on behalf of *Polish*-Austrian interests – had become very dangerous. This was the decisive year in the evolution of the international politics of the Polish Question, the year in which the Western powers, notably the United States in Wilson's "Peace without Victory" speech, had made the restoration of Poland a war aim, and they had recognized one faction in Polish politics, namely Dmowski's KNP, as the future country's exclusive representative. Retinger's position had been thereby rendered impossible, and his influence in London was replaced by another Pole, notably similar in background, who reflected this new Polish policy of the Western powers. Hence by late 1917, Jan Maria Horodyski, an Austrian Polish nobleman, corpulent and often ridiculous, with manifold international connections, had become an influential advisor to the British government regarding Polish matters. He also became a British spy.[136] Horodyski was closely associated with the Dmowski-Paderewski faction in Polish politics and thus was a sworn enemy of Retinger. Both Retinger and the British policy towards Austrian problems he represented had been supplanted by Horodyski.[137]

In a desperate move to replace the KNP, Retinger founded the "Pour la Pologne" organization in September. It was a clever idea. An international committee would be established "in favor of Poland." Marshal Joffre was to be offered the presidency, and the English branch would be led by Asquith, with (Wilson's confidant) Colonel Edward M. House in America. There were also to be branches in Italy and, oddly, Japan. The French branch, the organization's center would have a number of vice presidents. From politics this included Senator Pams, later a member of government, Aristide Briand, and Albert Thomas as well as religious, and other notables. The first meeting was followed the next day by a second, and a third the following day. The organization, however, soon disappeared – if it ever materialized beyond Retinger and two prominent Frenchmen. This is typical of Retinger: elite international cooperation, dependency of France, and the utilization of contacts assembled over the years.[138]

By October, 1917 Retinger was denied re-entry to England and thus marooned on the continent.[139] Furthermore, his agitation against the Polish army had resulted from his eviction from France.[140] He had been, according to the Foreign Office, "found out." Moreover, London knew that he had been well-supplied with money in 1917 – as the German consulate in Switzerland confirmed, but had not been able to ascertain the source. Arthur Nicolson of the Foreign Office suspected that Retinger's funds came from France, specifically Caillaux; he concluded that Retinger was simply "an international spy."[141]

## Conclusions

Integrating the reported Austrian peace initiative of 1917 (especially its Polish aspects) with Nicolson's comments allows some very interesting deductions. Obviously, Retinger was not on His Majesty's business in Switzerland in the summer of 1917, as the German consulate in Bern assumed. Just as obviously, London was not the source of his considerable funds. Moreover, his actions were hardly in concert with British policy at the time regarding a Polish army; they were directly contrary. Indeed, Eric Drummond of the Foreign Office had decided to break off contact with Retinger already in December, 1916, although he received various memoranda from him thereafter.[142]

However, Rothwell has underscored that the 1917 peace pourpalers between London and Vienna were very much a matter of Lloyd George's personal diplomacy. He always preferred confidential envoys and secret intrigue to normal diplomatic procedure whose practitioners he despised. It is possible that Retinger was acting as the Prime Minister's *personal* representative in his activities in Switzerland. Analogously, Retinger had claimed that he had been Asquith's agent when he came to the United States late in 1914. We know that the Foreign Office was later furious about its exclusion from the peace discussions in Switzerland, and that Lloyd George on one occasion during this period even took the extraordinary step of preventing minutes from being taken at the War Cabinet meeting.[144]

Retinger was probably not a British agent during World War I; though he may have served intermittently as one, and certainly often wished this conclusion to be drawn. He may well have undertaken certain actions at London's behest: the 1914 visit to the United States is the most likely example. But, insofar as Retinger worked for British interests, he was doing so ad hoc and probably as a personal emissary of Prime Minister Asquith not as an operative of the Foreign Office or MI6. Retinger's purposes in these activities were always to serve his own view of Polish interests, and not British policy regarding Poland. Whatever clandestine relations Retinger had with the British certainly came to an end by 1917, although this may well have recommenced later, perhaps as early as the 1920s.

Finally, some of the Austrians prominently associated with the peace bid were Retinger's fellow Poles, drawn from his social milieu. Hence, three possibilities arise. Hence we have three possibilities. The first is the unpersuasive notion that Retinger was a British agent. The second possible explanation is that Retinger was acting as an Austrian agent in 1917, or at least as an agent of pro-Austrian Poles who combined a vision of a restored Poland with loyalty to the Dual Monarchy. Here we should remember that some of the Austrians prominently associated with eh peace bid were Retinger's fellow Poles, drawn from his social milieu. This was essentially the position Conrad had assumed at the war's outbreak, and it was more or less what Retinger had espoused then and later.[143]

The third possibility begins with the assumption that both German sources in Switzerland and Nicolson's reconnaissance in Paris were correct in connecting Retinger with Caillaux. The latter, let it be remembered, was accused in 1917 of seeking to negotiate with the Central Powers to arrange early French exit from the war.[145] Collaboration between Caillaux and Retinger is not impossible – they had some dealings at least in 1916.[146]

Switzerland was the center of virtually all of the 1916–1917 peace overtures, from the Mensdorff mission to Retinger's meetings with Ledóchowski.[147] In Bern, the Pole Skrzyński was part of the Habsburg delegation to the Vatican. British and German intelligence both noted Retinger's frequent visits to Switzerland, and both connected him with Caillaux.[148] Ledóchowski, we know from French sources, was close to Skrzyński, and played a role in the tentative efforts of Sixte Bourbon-Parma. The Vatican Secretary of State's office also met with Caillaux or his representatives at this time regarding peace overtures.[149] Moreover, as noted earlier, Retinger's 1917 efforts to block the creation of a Polish army made him *persona odiosa* with the pro-Entente in Switzerland, especially the powerful Dmowski, yet they coincided perfectly with Vienna's efforts, epitomized by Skrzyński, to win over the Polish émigrés of Western Europe.[150] Retinger was concerned that his Polish contacts would become public knowledge and urged the utmost discretion.[151]

What was the source of Retinger's lavish funds in Switzerland – funds of which the British and Germans were equally unaware and concerning which were equally surprised? These funds, it must be noted, vanished suddenly in late 1917, leaving Retinger destitute. At this same time, he became *persona non grata* with the French. This collapse of his fortunes, literally and figuratively, coincides precisely with the arrest of Caillaux, on charges of treason. Over the next few weeks, a vast network of agents and activities was unearthed, all financially linked to Caillaux.[152] Retinger's name was never mentioned in the press reports or the several trials of Caillaux's putative confederates. Despite this, British sources reported that in Paris Retinger "was reputed to be an agent of Caillaux."[153] Hence, we may offer the tentative hypothesis that Retinger was, indeed, connected with Caillaux, and that the latter's catastrophe in 1917 brought about Retinger's disaster. Thus, a connection with Caillaux would explain the sudden and dramatic end to Retinger's wartime career. In 1917, he was reported, by both British and German sources, to be very well financed. By 1918, however, he was literally destitute and living on charity, probably Conrad's. He was driven from France and refused entry into England. This would doubtless be the fate of someone who had been connected with Caillaux, "the most hated man in France," whose arrest and trial were pursued with a merciless vengeance by Clemenceau, driving the pro-Caillaux forces into disgrace,[154] and creating "an atmosphere supercharged with fear, suspicion, and animosity."[155] Clemenceau's victory and Caillaux's fall coincided with the final consolidation of Polish émigré politics.

Dmowski, by late, 1917, had gained recognition for his KNP as a virtual provisional government in exile, a "government which enjoyed the recognition of most of the organized Polish community worldwide, especially in the United States," where Paderewski dominated Polish affairs. Austria was in thrall to Berlin, incapable of independent diplomatic initiative, and approaching dissolution.[156] Efforts by the Vatican to arrange a negotiated end to the war were bootless, as Woodrow Wilson was determined that "the role of mediator should go to only one nation and one leader – the United States and himself."[157] The structure of the world in which Retinger had launched his vain, quixotic, and shadowy efforts, had collapsed, and he had become a pariah in Western diplomatic circles. Nevertheless, the Germans regarded him as a British spy, while London seemed equally sure that he was spying for others, perhaps, *mirabile dictum*, the Japanese![158]

Even the putative Retinger-Caillaux connection may disclose only part of the complex picture. The great missing piece which may knot so many threads is Vatican diplomacy. Retinger, Skrzyński, Castellane, Zamoyski, Caillaux-to say nothing of Ledóchowski – all had clear links to the Vatican. The correspondence between the Pope and the devoutly religious Austrian imperial couple, Zita and Charles, regarding peace, and the future of Central Europe, is well-known.[159] Certainly ascribing a large role to the Vatican provides a triple context for Retinger's activities. First, it furnishes an intellectual matrix, a common framework, in which a disparate group of many nationalities could work together with certain fundamental shared values.[160] Second, the abundant but mysterious monies that seem to have been available would be conveniently attributable to Vatican sources. Finally, the diplomatic machinery of the Vatican immediately becomes the network which allows explanation for what are otherwise the strange movements of Retinger – among others – who often seemed to cross frontiers effortlessly.[161] This may be the first inkling of Retinger's "Catholic politics." Unfortunately, if the secret of Retinger's actions can be uncovered only by exposing the structure of the most intimate connections of Vatican diplomacy during the Great War, we shall have to wait long for an answer.

## Retrospection

Perhaps the most logical candidate for Retinger's clandestine employer was Vienna. He was born in Austrian Poland, and associated with Austrophile Poles in the early stages of his political career. He never acted against Austrian interests. His movements throughout would be far more explainable if we assume he could use Austria as a base of operations. The meeting in Warsaw in 1916 is a prime example.

Retinger was not emotionally *Kaisertreu*, but supported the Austrians for reasons of rational geopolitical analysis. In this, he clearly anticipated his later activities. In World War I he worked for some international settlement which would preserve order, avoid either Russian or German domination of Europe, and prevent the passions of the modern world from creating chaos. Notably, he posited the same goals during and after World War II. The preserved world would be all the better if it could include a restored Poland as an element of international equilibrium. In 1916–1917 Retinger propagated the idea of a Polish "buffer" against German expansion which would thus serve both Western and, perhaps surprisingly, Russian interests. Here Retinger's cosmopolitan Catholic background played a role in directing his thought: in the world of 1914–1918, the Vatican was the obvious international agency to aid in stabilizing the international system. And Europe's architecture required a functioning Austrian, perhaps tripartite, state with Poland as the third state equal to Austria and Hungary.[162]

Finally, Retinger was connected with Caillaux in 1916–1917. The latter was the likely source for Retinger's funds in that period. However, Caillaux's activities regarding international diplomacy – if which Retinger was a likely part – are still very little known, despite Jean-Claude Allain's Herculean efforts at reconstruction. Both British and German intelligence linked Retinger to Caillaux. Certainly a separate peace preserving Austria, safeguarding the interests of the Catholic nations of Europe, and weakening aggressive Germany – especially one that involved some possibility of a French candidate for a reconstructed Polish kingdom – would be a logical, and attractive cause to enlist Retinger. Caillaux always defended his actions on the grounds that he was a patriot who sought only "European conciliation," a goal which would later describe Retinger's own activities. The Caillaux-Retinger relationship was probably part of a network of connections involving, at the minimum, de Castellane, Prince Sixte de Bourbon-Parma, possibly the Duchess of Uzès, and perhaps Retinger's "godfather," Władysław Count Zamoyski. The degree to which Vatican diplomacy can be factored in remains unknown.

Retinger's "internationalism" is essential to understanding him. Its intellectual roots are Catholic and Jesuit, but also reflect his precocious cosmopolitan upbringing and education, and had secular results. As a schoolboy he dreamed of both "living beyond borders" and dedicating his efforts to the fatherland: "to serve my country by returning Poland to an international life."[163] In World War I, the vision of the rearrangement of Central Europe, including the Austro-Polish solution, and a Franco-Austrian rapprochement to end the war, embodied this. In late 1916, Caillaux argued that the Entente should have as its goal "maintenir une Europe," and he described himself as representing "une grande politique qui s'oppose au nationalism." The Frenchman was afraid of the "balkanization" of Central Europe and feared the consequence of Habsburg collapse and German expansion." Here he is at one with Retinger.[164]

Retinger was a patriotic Pole who worked for the reconstruction of his ancestral homeland and tried to interest the Western powers in championing the Polish cause, particularly England. Efforts to involve the British in Polish affairs run like a red thread through all of Retinger's actions. He convinced the British – at least some of them – that he was fanatically patriotic: "I'm sure if you died you would not forget to sing, in heaven, the Polish national anthem."[165] He was, a close friend concluded, "100 percent Polish." He told his wife on their wedding day: "Realize you will never be first – the first is Poland."[166]

Retinger consistently opposed the creation of a Polish army in the west. A Polish army, fighting alongside England and France, organized with Russian collaboration, would preclude any Austro-Polish solution. Moreover, because Polish units already existed in Austria (the Piłsudski legions), a Western Polish force would hopelessly split and embitter Polish ranks. Retinger was not loath to note that former soldiers from the German or Austrian army, serving in the Polish forces, would probably be regarded as traitors if captured. Perhaps worst of all, this Western Polish army would perforce be dominated by the political right who were antithetical to Retinger. Thus, his opposition to the army – in France in the summer of 1914, soon after in the United States, and later in Western Europe in 1917 – was a consistent and logical concomitant to his vision of the Polish Question during the war. His opposition to the army caused him no end of difficulties; it "ended my political career."[167]

Retinger had an essentially pre-modern geopolitical vision of the world. His intellectual world was alien to the modern passions of both nationalism and class warfare. His Polish and later French political connections were with elite conservative circles, an integrating political tradition in opposition to the nationalist right, which was hostile to both socialism and tradition. Retinger was conservative, not nationalist, a difference fundamental to Polish politics. Later, during his bizarre career in Mexican politics, he veered sharply to the left and was even referred to as a "Bolshevik."[168]

Situating Retinger in the Polish political landscape is problematical. Certainly, the wartime reports that he was a man of the right and even a pro-Russian, "Moscophile" are completely wrong. He wished to work closely with the Western powers in order to increase Polish abilities to resist Russian or German pressure. His attitude towards Austria, however, was very different from that associated with the Piłsudskiites because he seemed to have genuine sympathy for its preservation, while the Piłsudskiites had a much more instrumental, if not to say cynical view of Vienna, which was for them merely an ally of convenience. Of course, we could also argue that Retinger already viewed Polish problems in a larger European context than many of his Polish contemporaries, and that his support for the empire reflected this. At about this time Retinger described himself as representing the "Catholic and Democratic Parties."[169]

### Retinger's early vision of Poland in a federal Europe

Retinger's visions transcended the borders of a future Poland and foreshadow the later internationalism which was to characterize him. This Retinger tradition is captured in what we may call the "Capel" episode. He met the young, rich and hopelessly naïve Englishman Arthur Capel, who envisioned an Anglo-French union as a means to European peace. This was to be part of a continental-wide federation to ensure order. Capel was close to many prominent English political figures including General Sir Henry Wilson, as well as Frenchmen like Briand, Clemenceau, and Boni. Retinger apparently met him through his cousin Godębska. Capel's dream of a federal Europe was cut short by death, but not before he – assisted by Retinger – produced *The World on the Anvil*. Pomian argues that though initially skeptical it was Capel's vision that later influenced Retinger's federalist plans.[170] On his own motion. Retinger produced two Polish propaganda pamphlets: *La Pologne et l'équilibre européen* and *Considérations générals sur l'avenir* économique *de la Pologne*.

Retinger's 1916's *La Pologne* in 1916, and the next year's *Considérations* are both arguments for the restoration of a free Poland. He also issued an anonymous pamphlet "Petit Manuel de la politique anglaise" in an astounding 250,000 copies; a book with a preface by oft-Foreign Minister Stephan Pichon.[171] *La Pologne* begins with the lament that the Poles are not a people but now a geographical expression, whose past is forgotten, and present ignored.[172] It is a very brief work characterized by cliché, sweeping judgments, and efforts to associate Poland with France as linked, indeed similar actors on the European scene. Poland was historically a major power which restrained Germans and held Russia at bay; it was the embodiment of civilization. In addition to its geo-strategic role, it was a moral example by its devotion to liberal and democratic internal politics during its golden centuries (the fifteenth to the seventeenth). All the while the parallels with France were striking and the contacts with Paris particularly close.[173]

Poland, Retinger argued deserved greater attention to and appreciation for what he calls its "vitality." He contends that the Poles were the fastest growing nation on earth.[174] Historic Poland, the pre-partition frontiers, contained a population which would give the country – with forty-eight millions – third place in Europe, ahead of France. He down-played minority issues as without great significance; emphasizing the Polish tradition of a multinational homeland: "conquest" is a practice foreign to the Polish tradition.[175] Jews are virtually ignored. The large size of the Polish emigration was noted.[176] He compared Lithuanian or Belarusian as languages playing a role not dissimilar to Basque in France, or Scottish Gaelic in Great Britain.[177] "Colonisation" by the partitioning powers faces an "insurmountable obstacle."[178] He reminded Frenchmen of the more than 1 million men serving in foreign forces and insisted that this number was actually small compared to what it could be.[179]

Retinger's comments on geopolitics presages, *en passant*, his later devotion to European federation. Two bases provide the future for Europe: rights for the population of each country, and the general good of the ensemble of states regarded collectively. These were of particular significant with the war raging. The partitions of Poland (1771–1795) moved the axis of European power to the east – diminishing, *pari passu*, French significance. The partitions were responsible for this, and damaged the architecture of European security and equilibrium. Writing in France during the war, Retinger was much retrained in his criticism of Russia. He quoted Talleyrand to the effect that the division of Germany between Austria and Brandenburg – and the reconstitution of Poland were the keys to European security. The Congress of Vienna (1815), dominated by Russia and Prussia, acted unscrupulously in failing to restore Poland, and in their selfish interest Retinger suggests.[180] The restitution of Poland was necessary for the equilibrium of Europe.

Retinger here demonstrated his profound devotion to the Polish cause and belief that a restored – i.e.–very large – Poland was necessary for the world. Poland had a mission and Europe was its beneficiary. As de Rougemont noted after Retinger's death: "his idea of an independent Poland foreshadowed his idea of a united Europe."[181]

During World War I, Józef Retinger was a recklessly ambitious and arrogant young man who threw himself into intrigue and surrounded himself with an air of theatrical mystery. He claimed powerful sponsors and mighty assignments and sometimes told the truth. For those who remain baffled by Retinger and see him either a mercenary spy or cynical adventurer, this chapter, indeed, this book, contents that early on he left a blurred but nonetheless discernible profile of what he would always be, a cosmopolitan European who envisioned a future continental federated unity based on the

Christian heritage of Rome, a unity in which his Polish homeland would occupy a free, untrammeled, and worthy place.

Indeed, Poland was central to his Weltanschauung: as an old man he listed the "freedom and well-being" of Poland as the first goal of his life, "better understanding among peoples", some sort of "general ideology," a vague and rather ominous goal, and lastly, the "unity of Europe." Moreover, Retinger left a specific style. Many years after the war he wrote that he worked "behind the scenes" by "persuading others to act." This reflected his policy "from which I have not deviated since I came to adult age."[182]

## Departing Europe; an explanation

Retinger was forced to leave France in the spring of 1918. He tried first to go to the United States but his passport was refused.[183] The Americans thought he was guilty of too many "intrigues: including with 'political women'." Pomian insists that the main culprit in his eviction was Dmowski and the other supporters of the Polish Army in the west, which he insists, created a "storm." American diplomatic sources insist that it was the fact that Retinger was associated with a Polish policy simply in contradiction to that of France was the deciding factor in his eviction. By 1917 Paris wanted a Polish army created; Retinger did not. The positions were irreconcilable.[184] For Retinger "the concern was that prisoners who during the war would fight on the opposite side would no longer be subject to the protection by the Geneva Convention. If they were caught, they could be shot. Retinger protested as he was able, by sending memoranda to all Western governments.[185]

Doubtless this added to his difficulties, but it was Retinger's unhappy involvement with Caillaux and the labyrinth of French politics which was the principal cause. Influential circles in London, including the Foreign Office had been won over to the Paderewski-Dmowski faction and came to view Retinger's idiosyncratic geopolitical advice as somewhere between annoying and dangerous.[186] There is a simultaneous rumor that Retinger had convinced Pams, then a French senator and, Clemenceau's "Colonel House," to have the Russian general Lukvitzky rally Russian troops to overthrow Lenin and Trotsky. Only Clemenceau's official blessing was required. Pams supposedly discussed the matter with Clemenceau and Georges Mandel was tasked with the project in which Retinger placed great faith. Mandel had worked closely together in opposition to the Ribot government. Mandel rejected the project and left Retinger without support in Paris, causing him to be expelled probably at Mandel's insistence. Retinger had insisted that he be sent to Russia where "through moral forces" he would oust the Bolshevist regime: as a Pole in opposition to the then Polish government dominated by strongman Piłsudski) exiled from France, deported from the United States he would *sauf que peut* by being permitted to enter Bolshevik Russia. It was nonsense.[187]

If we are to believe Pomian, closely constructing his account on Retinger's reminiscences, Mandel, Clemenceau's intimate, wanted Retinger out of the country at once and told de Castellane as much.[188] Derivatively, Retinger was called to the office of the Minister of the Interior, Pams, who told Retinger he must leave or be ejected: he had "too many enemies."[189] Apparently Mandel was the most influential of these. Paris told the Americans that Retinger was "engaged in intrigue" and a US passport was refused.[190] As French Intelligence later noted he was expelled from France "par arrêt ministériel."[191] Lord Northcliffe was among his enemies-probably over a woman, Jane Anderson.[192]

With his usual thoughtless panache, Retinger insisted on taking the next departing train, without arranging to take any money. (His haste might also be explained by the fact that he owed the Hotel Meurice 9, 000 francs which he never paid.[193]) There was, nonetheless, a letter from de Castellane to the powerful Spaniard the Duke of Alba,[194] which finally overcame Spanish reluctance, and he crossed the border after being bidden farewell by a galaxy of French notables – including de Castellane, and his fellow French aristocrat, Marquis Pierre de Dampière,[195] who had tried to block the order to deport Retinger.[196] His enemies, plus his openly associating himself with the political losing side overcame what seems to have been a powerful coterie of supporters in both England and France.[197] In addition to his French and British enemies, the KNP conspired against him.[198] Retinger left a France in which he had lived a world of dreams and adventures, illustrated by his relationship with Isadora Duncan who, for some inexplicable reason, wanted to go to America and "dance for Poland" but, Retinger wrote wistfully, "spy mania 'forced' her to leave France."[199] As Pomian perceptively noted years later, Retinger was "peddling" a cause which was of no interest to anybody and could only gain influence if he could be of use to them. It meant taking a keen interest in their problems and trying to gain their confidence.[200]

A rather more elaborate explanation for Retinger's expulsion comes from the pro-Dmowski Jan Zamorski. According to this rather fanciful account, Retinger knew Asquith well but still could not get back to England. This was due to two reasons. First, Pichon backed Dmowski and Retinger tried to secure a position in the *Mirabile dictum*, Italian army and was close to the the Spanish ambassador to France who was an Austrophile. Paris had further suspicions of Retinger of a political nature; he was, perhaps, a German spy. He was reportedly in close relations with one Gaston Flegenheimer, identified by the French Consul General in Geneva as a German spy. Retinger also had close ties to Count Skrzyński, a Pole in the Austrian diplomatic service who was Vienna's agent in Switzerland. These were, the French concluded, the reasons Retinger was expelled from French territory, not just the Polish army issue.[201] This made him very suspicious, though the details cannot be proven.[202]

According to Retinger, he had no destination in mind and found himself, sick, bewildered, and destitute in Spain where he stayed for some months, mostly at the obscure frontier village of Fuenterrabia. He had 7,000 francs and lived in absolute destitution. He got drunk for the first, but not last, time.²⁰³ He had left Jane Anderson at a Parisian hotel.²⁰⁴ It is apparent that Conrad provided, after some interval, a subvention and at the writer's plea, Hugh Walpole and others may well have aided Retinger. Conrad described Retinger as "deserted by God and humanity."²⁰⁵ Retinger wrote a pathetic letter to Harold Nicolson at the Foreign Office describing himself as "totalement ruiné." The Foreign Office advised him to stay in Spain and return to Poland when the war ended: they would not allow him to enter Great Britain. Retinger asked as a *faut le mieux* for a safe conduct to Mexico or Argentina. It was refused.²⁰⁶ The Americans decided, disingenuously, to admit him, and then immediately send him to "some detention camp."²⁰⁷

Harold Nicolson of the Foreign Office having disliked and distrusted Retinger since the autumn of 1914, had the final word on Retinger's exile from European politics and isolation in Spain. If he were to return to England, wrote Nicolson, "he would probably be interned on arrival." This because, "I am inclined to regard Dr. Retinger as an international spy. He has had many influential friends here, but I think he may be considered to have been 'found out' more than a year ago. We agreed not to allow him in England: 'the evidence against him as a definite spy is indubitably rather flimsy'. But, until the French ejected him, he was well financed in Paris: now he is penniless. I am sure that we should do nothing to assist him or give him any facilities for travel." Nicolson was authorized by the Foreign Office to reply in this vein.²⁰⁸ Retinger described the letter as "contemptible."²⁰⁹

Nicolson detested Retinger and personal malice may well have motivated the tone if not the content of this message. However, it makes an important point. Retinger had not worked for the British – if at all – for some time by 1917. Indeed, London suggested that he was a French agent. The Foreign Office disavowed him and followed Nicolson's advice about abandoning him under suspicion. Retinger was only a British agent until 1917 if he had ever been, or, his connections with the British bypassed the Foreign Office and were directly with the Prime Minister.²¹⁰

In a pleading letter to Pams, Retinger summarized his wartime service: it is a précis of what he regarded as his major contributions and thus bears summary. All his political efforts were aimed at the re-establishment of an independent Poland within its historic frontiers. This, in turn would require an allied victory so he embarked on dangerous work. "Carrying confidential documents, I traveled at the risk of grave danger to get to Switzerland across enemy territory" (this probably refers to the Conrad trip). "I went to France with letters of introduction. Without explanation I was twice arrested at the French border. I finally got to the Foreign Ministry and gave it the letters I was carrying from Polish notables." For the next two and a half years he worked "on my political program." which he did not explain. He went to America at British request. He supplied regular reports to London and Paris and made twenty trips between the cities, plus a few to Switzerland. All of these were to gain French and British support for Poland. Some of his work was quite important and had "profound" reactions in Poland. He had always been an independent actor, not an agent. He wanted to go back to this work, but on medical advice he had to desist from politics for some time.[211]

While in exile Retinger penned a hysterical letter to the president of France which described his conduct since 1914 in terms both revealing and absurd. It makes a number of points: namely, he worked for Poland from the beginning of the war in conjunction with Britain and France; he contributed to American Polonia's interest in a Polish army (!); his efforts were denied by the French Foreign Minister.[212] Therefore he decided to go to the United State to await the outcome of the war. His efforts were not appreciated and, indeed, he was the target of a campaign of "mensonges and calumnies indignes" which resulted in his expulsion from France. This was – he noted queerly – an insult to the Poles (i.e. American Polonia) who sent him (back to Europe) and would have "graves consequences."[213] Obviously, the abrupt end to Retinger's surreptitious career had consequences for his mental stability.

## Notes

1 Wacław Gąsiorowski, *1910–1915: Historja armji polskiej we Francji* (Warsaw: Dom Książki Polskiej, 1931), 218–219.
2 Retinger with his usual modesty notes that "after a talk with me" Asquith had the Poles released and they were never again harassed; see his "Back in London during World War I," drawer 4, 1, BPL. He also credits Lord Kitchener's intervention for this solution; see "London 1914," drawer 2, BPL.
3 Retinger claims Asquith invited him to lunch; *why* is not explained; see "London 1914," drawer 2, Retinger Papers, BPL. Retinger boasts that he quickly made or already enjoyed acquaintances with high figures in the British government and convinced Asquith to free Poles interned in the Crystal Palace; this cannot be verified. Pieczewski notes that Retinger wrote Asquith a particularly moving note on behalf of the prime minister's son's death that it ingratiated Retinger to him; see Pieczewski, *Działalność*, 69. Retinger claimed he had "free access" to Asquith; Retinger, "London, 1914," drawer. 2, BPL. Pomian claims a "journalist" arranged Retinger's meeting with Asquith, but provides no details; see his. *Retinger*, 44.
4 "World War I," Retinger Papers, drawer 3, BPL. Retinger attributed his access to Asquith as due to "his secretary" and his friendship with Sir Maurice Bonham Carter," World War I," Retinger Papers, shelf 3, BPL.
5 The specifics of Retinger's meeting with Asquith are, like so many aspects of his life, very vague, ibid. Pomian's account is most unsatisfactory as it provides no specific date, mentions that a "journalist friend" arranged Retinger's invitation to lunch with the Prime Minister, and even refers to Asquith as "Arthur"; see *Retinger*, 35. Note also Siemaszko, "Szara eminencja," 173. Terlecki avoids the whole episode by the elliptical reference to the fact that Retinger "already knew" Asquith by 1915; see his *Kuzynek*, 20.
6 For the Churchill meeting, which took place at the same time he met Asquith see "W. Churchill" in drawer 1, BPL, referring to early October, 1914.
7 "World War I," Retinger papers, BPL. Pomian also refers to Retinger as looking like an "aged monkey," Pomian, *Retinger*, 9; the SOE thought so too: see Major R. Hazell to Roberts, January 25, 1944, file 233, FO371/39421, National Archives (hereafter NA).

8 Ibid., 46.
9 Maciej Loret, the RN's representative in Rome, referred to the documents Retinger received in Galicia in 1914 as "really opening the door for him [Retinger] to the most significant personages" in London: a summary of this observation is in "Wyciąg ze Sprawozdania sekretarza Polskiego Centralnego Komitetu Ratunkowego w Ameryce," undated, in Papiery Rozwadowskich: Jana Rozwadowskiego działalność publiczna, s. 8005/II, 3, Ossolineum.
10 This episode is noted in Kenneth J. Calder, *Britain and the Origins of the New Europe, 1914–1918* (London: Cambridge University Press, 1976), 23–24, but the details concerning its Polish aspects are inaccurate. See also Paul C. Latawski, "Great Britain and the Rebirth of Poland, 1914–1918: Official and Unofficial Influences on British Policy" (Ph.D. diss, Indiana University, 1985), 73f.
11 "Wyciąg ze Sprawozdania," 3–4.
12 Retinger, "London 1914," drawer 2.BPL. A similar ignorance Retinger noted in Undersecretary Tennant.
13 There is circumstantial evidence-rather flimsy – that Retinger literally escaped to America due to having fallen into awkward relations with Polish groups in France because of his connections with the Russian police. Bizarre to be sure, but it would explain the ill-prepared and haphazard quality of his trip; see Ryszard Świętek, *Ludowa ściana: Sekrety polityka Józefa Piłsudskiego, 1904–1918*. Kraków: Platan, 1998, 658, n. 244.
14 See Retinger's "London, 1914," drawer 2, Retinger Papers, BPL. Elsewhere he contends that the army issue was not part of his mission; see "The United States, 1914," Retinger Papers, drawer 3, BPL; cf. "America and the Americans," Retinger Papers, shelf 5, BPL; cf. "The United States," drawer 3, BPL.
15 See Retinger, "My First Steps in Practical Politics," drawer 2, BPL.
16 "London 1914," drawer. 2, BPL; M. B. B. Biskupski, "Pierwszy występ 'szarej eminencji? Józef Retinger, Polonia amerykańska I sprawa wojska polskiego na obczyźnie, 1914r," *Niepodległość*, 20 (1987), 181–187. Retinger did possess a letter from Asquith which purportedly thanked him for acquiring information about the Poles – this is from American diplomatic sources, Memorandum, Wiley to Winslow, November 13, 1919 contained in Joseph Grew to Gibson, February 12, 1926, 812.202./11/10, USNA, RG 59.
17 Retinger to NN, December 20, 1915, "Korrespondencje," Box 17, Retinger Papers, BPL.
18 Retinger to Under Secretary of State for Foreign Affairs, October 6, 1914, FO 371/2201/56795, NA.
19 See the minutes on the aforementioned document especially the concluding one initialed "AN" and dated October 21, 1914. For the army issue and American Polonia see M. B. B. Biskupski, *The United States and the Rebirth of Poland, 1914–1918* (Dordrecht: Republic of Letters, 2012).
20 He left England on November 17; little more is known of the chronology of his movements.
21 "Wyciąg ze Sprawozdania," 2, this corresponds to Retinger's own later remarks; see "America and the Americans," drawer 5, BPL.
22 Denis de Rougement, "A Biographical Sketch," in Centre Européen de la Culture. *Tribute to a Great European, J. H. Retinger*. np, nd, 28.
23 Pomian, *Retinger*, 49.
24 The Polish political right tried to warn its Polish American allies not to trust Retinger (Loret to [Osada], December 16, 1914, Papiery Gąsiorowskiego, s. 15226/II, Ossolineum.
25 For the issue of Retinger's letters, his efforts at cultivating influential Americans, and the reaction of Polish American leaders, see Biskupski, "Pierwszy występ," 183–185.

26 As early as late 1914, Retinger was criticized for claiming he had some nebulous charge from both the British and French governments in his activities; see Loret to [Osada], December 21, 1914, Papiery Gąsiorowskiego, s. 15226/II, Ossolineum. Cf. Osada to Sienkiewicz, March 9, 1915, Papiery Gąsiorowskiego, 15227/II, Ossolineum.
27 Regarding Retinger's movements and contacts with American immigration authorities, see the report of Emil A. Solana, March 9, 1921, in Record Group (hereafter RG) 65: Records of the Federal Bureau of Investigation, file BS 202600-966, microfilm reel 935, USNA.
28 About all we have is a report from the St. Louis jail where Retinger was held in 1925; see ibid.
29 "America and the Americans," drawer 5, Retinger Papers, BPL.
30 "London, 1914," shelf 2, Retinger Papers, BPL; "The United States, 1914," Retinger Papers, drawer 3, BPL.
31 "The United States, 1914," Retinger Papers, drawer 3, BPL; "America and the Americans," drawer 5, Retinger Papers, BPL. Cf. "World War I," Retinger Papers, drawer 3, BPL.
32 "America and the Americans," shelf 5, Retinger Papers, BPL. These remarks were written about 1955. In 1947 Retinger's daughter wrote him that she remembered "you telling me you didn't like the Americans," Marya to Retinger, February 16, 1947, ME 328, HAEU.
33 Retinger later wrote that the Polish Jew (later a Roman Catholic) art historian Bernard Berenson, "explained" America to him; cf. ibid.
34 Gąsiorowski, *1910–1915*, 220–221.
35 Henryk Sienkiewicz to Stanislaw Osada, February 12, 1915, in "Sienkiewicz o legionach, NKN i akcie 5 listopada 1916 r," in *Komunikaty towarzystwa im. Romana Dmowskiego*, Vol. 1 (1970–1971). London, 1970), 289; cf. *Czyn zbrojny*, 141.
36 "The United States, 1914," Retinger Papers, drawer, 3, BPL.
37 This explanation is supported by an off-handed reference Retinger made in 1916; see untitled memorandum by Retinger to [Foreign Office], ca. May, 1916 in FO 371/2747/98112, NA.
38 Gąsiorowski, *1910–1915*, 220.
39 The Polish political right contended that Retinger was secretly promoting the interests of the pro-Austrian Poles from the start of the war; see the memoirs of Marjan Seyda, *Polska na przełomie dziejowa* (Poznań: Księgarnia św. Wojciecha, 1927), 294; cf. Wiktor Sukiennicki, *East Central Europe during World War I: From Foreign Domination to National Independence*, two volumes (Boulder, CO: East European Monographs, 1984), 1:205; hereafter *ECE*.
40 By late 1915 "Retinger did not belong to any political organization or group, but he consistently upheld the idea of Polish sovereignty vis-à-vis all three partitioning powers," in Najder, *Conrad*, 407.
41 Paderewski doubtless anticipated difficulty with Retinger. As early as December, 1914, he stated his mistrust of Retinger – for political reasons apparently – and had been warning his supporters regarding him; see Loret to Osada, December 21, 1914, Papiery Gąsiorowskiego, s. 15266/II Ossolineum.
42 This is the contention of Najder, whose knowledge of Conrad is unmatched; see his *Conrad*, 406; cf. Retinger, "Back in London during World War I," 12, BPL, drawer. 4.
43 The contretemps between Paderewski and Retinger is mentioned in Terlecki, *Kuzynek*, 21–23; this section, incidentally, does not appear in the earlier versions of Terlecki's account of Retinger. Retinger notes an argument with Paderewski over the maestro's pro-Russian statements at a social event in London early in the war; see "World War I," Retinger Papers, BPL; cf. Retinger, "America and

the Americans," 12–16, drawer 5, BPL. Retinger later recalled that his loathing for Russia caused him constant problems with Petrograd's ambassadors in both Paris and London; see Retinger to Jens Christian Hauge, September 18, 1957, Retinger Papers, box 25a, BPL. The influential Erazm Piltz tried to convince Paderewski to work with Retinger, but to no avail: see Piltz to Comité Général de Secours à Lausanne, Woźnicki Papers, BPP, folder 4384.

44 This episode, like so many in Retinger's career, remains murky. For example, Wapiński's otherwise well-researched biography of Retinger reports only that "in 1916 he arrived in the Congress Kingdom (i.e. Russian ruled Poland) and established contact with the activist National Central Committee," see his "Retinger," 149. Suleja omits the episode entirely. One source insists that the appearance was really in December 1915; see Janta, "Refleksye, 1," 2.

45 The CKN was founded on December 18, 1915. It was a congeries of the activist Left; it is not to be confused with the organization of the same name of which Tadeusz Cieński was president and with which Retinger was associated before the war. The latter was politically Right.

46 Popiel's recollections are presented in Terlecki, *Kuzynek*, 26–27; cf. Witkowski, *Retinger*, 35–36. There is a brief mention in Aleksander Janta, "Refleksye Retingerowskie: Czy był i czyim był agentem?" *Wiadomości*, No. 1325 (August 22, 1971), 2.

47 Jerzy Z. Pająk, *O Rząd i armię: Centralny Komitet Narodowy (1915–1917)*. Kielce: Akademia świętokrzyska, 2003), 114.

48 There is an intriguing remark in the unreliable and tendentious work by Jędrzej Giertych, *Rola dziejowa Dmowskiego: Tom I: Rok 1914* (Chicago: Towarzystwo imienia Romana Dmowskiego, 1968) which reads: "I learned from the lips of a Polish officer who during the war had Retinger's personal file in his hands that, during the First World War, Retinger traveled from London to Kraków as an emissary (łącznik) to establish contact with the legionnaire camp (i.e. the Piłsudskiites). Retinger's relationship with the Piłsudski camp, then and later, is most intriguing, but very little evidence is available (Dmowskiego, 1: 53n). For example, in May, 1926, when Piłsudski took power via coup d'état in Poland. Retinger made efforts to convince the British that Piłsudski represented a pro-British orientation and thus betokened improved relations between London and Warsaw; Tadeusz Piszczkowski, *Anglia a Polska, 1914–1939: w świetle dokumentów brytyjskich* (London: Ofycyna Poetów i Malarzy, 1975), 293–296. Soon thereafter, however, he became a devoted opponent of Piłsudski

49 Regarding Retinger and Zaleski, see Sukiennicki, *ECE*, 1:205; 2:984 n. 15. For Zaleski's London activities see Piotr Wandycz, *August Zaleski* (Paris: Instytut Literacki, 1980), 9ff.

50 "World War I," Retinger Papers, drawer 3, BPL; Conrad to Retinger, August 21, 1916, *Conrad's Letters*, 260–261.

51 Witkowski, *Retinger*, 37. For the relationship of Piłsudski and Sikorski at the time see Włodzimierz Suleja, "Spór o kształt akytywizmu: Piłsudski I Sikorski w latach I wojny światowej," in Henryk Zieliński, ed. *W kręgu twórce myśli politycznej*," Wroclaw: Ossolineum, 1983, 141–199.

52 A friend reminded Retinger that all he was doing was not for the good of Austria, but for "une question Européenne" for which they were acting "comme Polonais". Retinger was urged to remind Britain and France of that fact; see NN to Retinger, August 5, 1916, ANK, s. 8061. See also the letter by Conrad which praised Retinger's "diplomatic genius" and urged him to be in touch with press magnate Lord Northcliffe; see Conrad to Retinger, April 2, 1916, ANK, s. 8062.

53 Arnold Bennett to Retinger, May 15, 1916, Retinger Papers, folder K, box 18, BPL. Retinger later retaliated with a brief biographical sketch of Bennett which made him look a fool; see Retinger, *Conrad*, 52–64.

54 Pomian, *Pamiętniki*, 39; Retinger, "Separate Peace with Austria," drawer 3, BPL.
55 De Castellane's aunt, Elisabeth, married a Radziwiłł in 1857. As a result, Boni was related to several Potockis and Branickis as well. Through unexplained family connections, he was related to Ksawery Count Orłowski and the German diplomat of Polish nationality, Hugo Prince Radolin. See Emmanuel de Waresquiel ed., *Mémoirs de Boni de Castellane, 1867–1932* (Paris: Librarie Academique Perrin, 1986), 27, 49–50, 117, 155–156, 263, 278, 292.
56 Heinrich Seeholzer, *Die Politik des Grafen Boni de Castellane* (Zürich: Leemann & Co., 1913).
57 Pomian, *Retinger,* 20.
58 Ibid., 18.
59 "The Vatican had long considered the Austro-Hungarian Empire its strongest ally in Europe," in David Alvarez, "A Secret Agent at the Vatican: The Gerlach Affair," *Intelligence and National Security*, 2 (1996), 345; see also Francis Latour, "De la specificité de la diplomatie vaticane durant la grande guerre," *Revue d'histoire modern et contemporaine*, 43 (1996), 360; cf. Derby to Balfour, May 21, 1918, Balfour Papers, file 49743, British Library (hereafter BL).
60 *Mémoires de Boni*, 362. De Castellane's recollections of Retinger are very brief. However, he also notes his being a habitué during the war, of the home of the Edwards family, where "je voyais beaucoup d'hommes politiques." Misia Edwards, née Godębska, married to Alfred Edwards, co-founder of *Le Matin* was Retinger's cousin and part of the family which had facilitated his introduction to Western Europe in his Sorbonne days (*Memoirs de Boni,* 340). The much-married Godębska is a character as fascinating as Retinger. She was variously a model for Renoir, Vuillard, and Bonnard, and Coco Chanel's mentor. Her salon was attended by the most influential people in France. Retinger claimed that he met "all the leading intellectuals" in pre-World War I France there; see the draft entitled "Domestic and External Politics" in drawer 1, Retinger Papers, BPL.
61 Retinger, "Boni de Castellane," Retinger Papers, drawer 1, BPL.
62 Ibid. The list of international notables Retinger met via de Castellane is long indeed.
63 Podgórski attributes this to Pomian, see the former's *Retinge*r, 44.
64 See Retinger's remarks about Conrad – which are virtually about himself – in his *Conrad*, 171.
65 Pomian, *Pamiętniki*, 49. Boni had maintained ties with Austrian aristocrats in Switzerland during the war.
66 Retinger, *Conrad*, 172.
67 See the draft of Retinger's chapter on de Castellane in Retinger Papers, drawer 1, BPL, 7–8.
68 *Mémoires de Boni*, 11, 49, 151, 339, 370.
69 Ibid., 350–351.
70 For example, see Maurice Barrès, *En regardant au fond des crevasses* (Paris: Émile-Paul Frères, 1917), 13ff. For Caillaux's own explanation of his wartime vision, see his *Devant l'histoire: mes prisons* (Paris: Éditions de la Sirene, 3rd ed., 1920), 128, 337–350, and *Mes Mémoirs*, III, 224–225. John M. Sherwood's argument that Caillaux was, in effect, a "created" traitor used by Clemenceau for partisan political purposes should be noted in this context; see his *Georges Mandel and the Third Republic* (Stanford, CA: Stanford University Press, 1970), 23ff.
71 Arno J. Mayer, *Wilson vs. Lenin: Political Origins of the New Diplomacy, 1917–1918* (Cleveland, OH: World Publishing Co., 1964), 281. Regarding Caillaux's religious views, see the lengthy and subtle presentation in Jean-Claude Allain, *Joseph Caillaux*, 3 vols. (Paris: Imprimière Nationale, 1978–1981), 1: 94ff.

72 Caillaux specifically endorsed the notion of strengthening Austria, and weakening Germany as a positive goal; see *Mes Mémoires*, 3: 192. Retinger admits that his studies at Munich University resulted in "a strong anti-German bias"; see "Studies in Germany, Italy, and England," BPL, drawer 3.
73 Circumstantial evidence suggests the possibility of a yet more complex series of personal and political linkages at work. De Castellane was very close to the Asquiths dating from the prewar era. Indeed, it was possible that he was the source of Retinger's seemingly instant acceptance by the Prime Minister. Further, Asquith had a very high opinion of Caillaux, which he vouchsafed to de Castellane; see *Mémoirs de Boni*, 326.
74 Janusz Pajewski, *Wokół sprawy polskiej: Paryż – Lozanna – Londyn, 1914–1918* (Poznań: Wydawnictwo Poznańskie, 1970), 52–53. It is not without significance that Caillaux was very close to Phillipe Berthelot of the Foreign Ministry whom Retinger had met with upon his return from Austria in the summer of 1914; see Henry Wickham-Steed, *Through Thirty Years, 1892–1932: A Personal Narrative*, 2 vols (Garden City: Doubleday and Co., 1924) 2:157 Bertie to Hardinge, June 11, 1917, Bertie Papers, MS 63035, BL. Caillaux was very suspicious of Russia and indeed it had foul designs for Poland; see "Affaire Caillaux," in 605 AP, Fonds Théodore Lescové: 3 Affaire Caillaux, Archives Nationals, Paris (Hereafter AN).
75 Retinger, *Conrad*, 172–173.
76 It should be noted that Sixte's principal motivation in 1916–1917 was to lessen Austria's dependence on Berlin and encourage Franco-Austrian cooperation, goals which were congruent with those of Austrophile Poles; see Philippe Amiguet, *La vie du Prince Sixte de Bourbon* (Paris: Les Éditions de France, 1924), 57ff., 93, 102ff.
77 Comparisons between Retinger and Caillaux are fascinating. Caillaux was regarded by many Frenchman, especially those of the right, as being a traitor. His defenders regard him as combining French patriotism with a larger, European view of affairs. He was a man of the left who nonetheless regarded the Roman Catholic Church with admiration, moved in powerful circles, had financial and political influence in South America, and was known for his sangfroid and sharp tongue. Retinger enjoyed a virtually identical position among Poles including, soon after the war, a Latin American position of influence. For an important intellectual aperçu of Caillaux see Emile Roche, *Avec Joseph Caillaux: mémoires, souvenirs et documents* (Paris: Publications de la Sorbonne, 1980), especially the essay therein by Jacques Chastenet, "Joseph Caillaux: un home d'état aux vues prophetiques," 33–40; cf. Jean-Claude Allain, "Joseph Caillaux et la seconde crise morocaine" (Ph.D. thesis, Université de Paris, 1974), 1, 13. Both men had close connections with the Spanish diplomatic corps in Western Europe and murky but significant Vatican ties; see Caillaux, *Devant l'histoire*, 210ff. Finally, and most bizarre, both had, or were reputed to have mysterious and highly significant connections to freemasonry. As regards Caillaux, see Charles Johnston, "Caillaux's Secret Power through French Masonry," *New York Times*, February 24, 1918, section 7, 11. Caillaux, according to Wolfgang Steglich, had some contacts with German intelligence via members of the Grand Orient Lodge (Steglich, *Der Friedensappel Papst Benedikts XV, Vol. I, August 1917 und die Mittelmächte* Wiesbaden: Fritz Steiner Verlag, 1979), 439–440, 482, a claim which appears less farfetched if it is remembered that Caillaux himself once claimed that the only forces that really mattered in France were the church and freemasonry (*Mémoires de Boni*, 351).
78 So concludes Podgórski, but he provides no documentation; cf. his *Retinger*, 44 Ledóchowski had certain features which would attract Retinger to him: he was an ardent Polish patriot; he had an intelligence gathering operation: and, in his

eyes, "the cause of Poland was identical with that of Catholicism"; see Wickham Steed, *Through Thirty Years*, II, 113–114.
79 Pomian, *Pamiętniki*, 39. We know that de Castellane was eager to see Retinger in April arguing that they had much to talk about; see Boni to Retinger, April 2, 1916 folder C, Box 18, Retinger Papers, BPL.
80 Pomian quoting Retinger in ibid., 39. Asquith insisted that Retinger act "privately," see Retinger, "Separate Peace with Austria," drawer 3, BPL.
81 Conveniently, Northcliffe was close to Joseph Conrad and Retinger was able to trade on the impressive network of his acquaintances; see Conrad to Richard Curle, August 20, 1916 in G. Jean-Aubry, *Joseph Conrad: Life and Letters* (New York: Doubleday, Page & Co., 1927), II:1 73. Confirmation of Retinger's approach to Northcliffe is the letter the latter wrote which was "intercepted by the War Office and sent to the FO;" see Wilfried Fest, *Peace or Partition: The Habsburg Monarchy and British Policy, 1914–1918* (New York: St. Martin's Press, 1978), 99; Pomian, *Retinger*, 50–51.
82 Berthelot was part of the salon of Retinger's cousin Misia Godębska (Pomian, *Retinger*, 35); cf. Retinger, "Separate Peace with Austria."
83 De Rougemont argues that Asquith and Clemenceau orally authorized Retinger's mission, but did not commit it to paper and, moreover that Clemenceau later mendaciously denied knowledge of the issue later before the Chamber of Deputies; see de Rougemont, "A Biographical Sketch," 29.
84 Quoted in Jean-Aubry, *Life and Letters*, 2:174.
85 This account of Retinger's diplomatic démarche is based on his subsequent rather sketchy presentation as presented in Pomian, *Pamiętniki*, 40–41.
86 Retinger, "Separate Peace with Austria;" see also Retinger, "In the Rear of the Great War," drawer 3, BPL.
87 Concerning Ledóchowski church connections see Taverne, *Wat Niemand*, 5–6; it is not much.
88 Quoted in Anne Lacroix-Riz, "Le Vatican et les buts de guerre germaniques de 1914 a 1918: le rève d'une Europe allemande," *Revue d'historie modern et contemporaine*, 42 (1995), 530. Ironically, the Kaiser regarded Ledóchowski rather differently: the center of a Catholic, Austrian, and possibly Polish plot to ruin Germany. In early 1918, he wrote: "The whole unsavory Parma-Rome-Habsburg campaign of agitation is represented, inspired, and directed by the *Jesuit General Count Ledóchowski*" (emphasis in original); quoted in Fritz Fischer, *Germany's Aims in the First World War* (New York: W. W. Norton, & Co., 1967, 434. Ledóchowski was able to arrange secret meetings at Zizers in 1917 involving prominent Germans; whether there were earlier meetings is unknown; Podgórski, *Retinger*, 43–44. Retinger was apparently present at one or more of the meetings.
89 French intelligence labeled "Tajne" (secret) it had neither day nor author in AKC, 4386 34/I, "Retinger," Archiwum Kazimierza Woźnickiego, BPP. Tykociner was suspected of being a German spy and close to the Pole Aleksander Count Skrzyński who was in Switzerland at the behest of Count Gyula Andrássy, the Habsburg Foreign Minister.
90 Retinger was not the only one to attempt the same network of relationships to arrange a separate peace. Bourbon pretenders, the "Black Pope," Habsburg court circles, and much clandestine to-ing and fro-ing in Switzerland was also the modus operandi of the Duchess d'Uzès at the behest of Aristide Briand of the French government (see C. A. Court Repington, *The First World War, 1914–1918: Personal Experiences* (Boston, MA: Houghton Mifflin Co., 1920), 2: 210–211. Briand's dealings with the duchess, which lasted approximately from January through March, 1917, are confirmed by his correspondence; see Georges Suarez, *Briand: Sa vie-son oeuvre-avec son journal et de nombreux*

*documents inedits. IV: Le Pilote dans la Tourments, 1916–1918* (Paris: Librarie Plon, 1940), 136–137, 143, 145–146. The activities of Anne de Rochechouart-Mortemart, Duchesse d'Uzès are particularly significant because she was closely involved with Polish affairs in Paris; see Gąsiorowski, *1910–1915*, 258. The duchess was also close to Boni, Retinger's friend who Retinger contended, first proposed to him the "peace mission"; see de Castellane. *Memoires*, 143, and Pomian, *Retinger*, 39. She was, like Retinger, simultaneously associated with aristocratic and monarchist circles as well as the political left, whence her sobriquet "la duchesse rouge." Hence the possibility of her connections with Retinger – again via the intermediacy of de Castellane – are obvious though I cannot establish a direct link. She was, incidentally, of distant Polish origins; see Bertie to Balfour, Bertie Papers, MS 63048, British Library (hereafter BL).

91 Retinger, "Separate Peace with Austria," BPL, drawer 3.
92 Retinger quoted in Pomian, *Retinger*, 53.
93 Romberg to Bethmann Hollweg, April 2, 1917, as repeated to the Polizeipräsident in Posen via the Minister des Innern, April 20, 1917, in Polizeipräsidium, s. 2721, Archiwum Państwowe w Poznaniu (hereafter APP).
94 Latawski, "Britain and the Rebirth," 141ff.
95 Quoted in an August, 1916 letter from Conrad to NN in Retinger, *Conrad*, 177.
96 See Harold Nicolson's minute of September 20, 1918, FO 371-3282, document no. 158193, NA.
97 J. E. Slocombe to Retinger, June 1, 1916, ANK, s. 8060. Retinger owed Slocombe £29.
98 Sukiennicki, *ECE*, 1:216–217; cf. Najder, *Conrad: A Chronicle*, 416–417. It is notable that this 1916 effort is analogous to Retinger's 1914 attempt to convince London, somehow, to "guarantee" the promises made to the Poles by the Russian commander-in-chief the Grand Duke Nikolai. The memorandum expressing these views was titled "A Note on the Polish Problem" and was ostensibly the work of Joseph Conrad, although Retinger's inspiration, and perhaps far more, is widely acknowledged; see Najder, *Conrad: A Chronicle*, 416, 586 n. 67. The arguments of this memorandum – including a prophetic endorsement of a Polish-German border along the Odra (Oder) – were adumbrated in 1915 in a pamphlet Retinger published in Paris titled *La Pologne et l'equilibre européenne*; see Bogusław Leśnodorski, "Conrad a sprawa niepodległości," 354–355.
99 There is a useful though now dated account in J. Lewin, "Die polnische Frage in Russland während des Weltkrieges," *Osteuropa*, Vol. 3 (1927–1928), 421–422. Lewin reports a specific January, 1916 meeting at which these plans were formulated. Lewin bases his conclusions on Russian intelligence reports which, he contends, highly agitated Petrograd in the first half of 1916; However, exhaustively researched work by Włodzimierz Suleja makes it clear that various forms of the "Austrian solution" were under discussion for many months, though they reached a particularly intensive level in early 1916; see his *Orientacja austro-polska w latach I wojny światowej [do aktu 5 listopada 1916 roku]* (Wrocław: Wydawnictwo Uniwersytetu Wrocławskiego, 1992), 204ff.
100 I have in mind people like Władysław Leopold Jaworski, leader of the Kraków conservatives; see Suleja, *Orientacja*, 265; cf. Andrzej Pańkowicz, "Działalność ugrupowań prawicowych w Galicji 1914–1918," in Michał Pułaski, ed., *W 70-lecie odzyskania niepodległości przez Polskę, 1918–1988* (Warsaw: Państwowe Wydawnictwo Naukowe), 145–156.
101 Calder, *Britain and the Origins*, 89–90; Latawski, "Great Britain and the Rebirth," 129.
102 Harold Nicolson to NN, November 6, 1916, FO 371/2747/225639, NA; Drummond to Rumbold, December 7, 1916 Rumbold to Drummond, December 16, 1916, Sir Horace Rumbold Papers, Oxford-Bodleian, deposit 17 (hereafter

OB). Retinger once mentions the Aga Khan-that he met him in 1914: nothing else is recorded; see Retinger, folder marked "Sikorski," in drawer 3, BPL.
103 Arthur Nicolson minute on Retinger to [Foreign Office], ca. May, 1916, FO 371/2747/98112; Grant Duff to FO, June 21, 1916, FO 371/2747/119621 NA.
104 "Summary of an Interview with Mr. Retinger," November 8, 1916, WO 106-963, NA.
105 Conrad apparently had an affair with Anderson in 1916; his colleagues in this endeavor were his son Borys and Retinger; see John C. Edwards, "Atlanta's Prodigal Daughter: The Turbulent Life of Jane Anderson as Expatriate and Nazi Propagandist," *Atlanta Historical Journal*, (summer, 1984), 26ff. Anderson's life was described as "worthy of a TV series"; see Jim Peglolotti to Nancy Howe Webster, April 17, 2000; in the possession of the author. Among her many oddities is her claim to be Buffalo Bill's daughter; see "Memorandum," August 8, 1941 in FBI Records, Federal Bureau of Investigation Archives.
106 Drummond to Rumbold, December 23, 1916, Rumbold Papers, OB deposit 17.
107 There is also a report that he suffered a heart attack in this period (Terlecki, *Kuzynek*, 30-35; Pomian, *Retinger*, 44). Retinger attempted suicide at least one further time, in 1923 (Drohojowski, *Wspomnienia dyplomatyczne*, 50-51).
108 See the French intelligence clipping of August 17, 1941, in Woźnicki Papers, AKC, 4386, BPP.
109 Ibid.
110 Józef H. Retinger, "Historja i polityka: O obiektywny komentarz," *Wiadomości Literackie*, November 13, 1938.
111 "My Past in the Movement for the Unity of Europe," Retinger Papers, drawer 2, BPL.
112 In July 1917 Władysław Sikorski prepared a memorandum urging renewed efforts by the Poles of Galicia in light of the reports of the Polish army in France; see the untitled document in Materiały Michała Bobrzyńskiego do dziejowa I wojny światowej. Formowanie się państwa polskiego, 1917-1919, s. 8121 III, BUJ: MSS.
113 For Retinger's precocious austrophilism see his "First Political Activities," Drawer 2, Retinger Papers, BPL.
114 Romberg (Gesandtschaft in Bern) to von Bethmann Hollweg, April 2, 1917, Polizeipräsidium, s. 2723 APP.
115 Walter Hines Page to Secretary of State, February 11, 1917, 763.72119/488, Record Group (hereafter RG), 59, Microfilm 367: Records of the Department of State Relating to World War I and its Termination, roll 374, USNA.
116 "Protokoll des zu Baden am 12 Jänner 1917 abgehaltenen Ministerrates für gemeinsame Angelegenheiten unter dem Allehöchsten Vorsitze Seiner Majestät des Kaisers and Königs," on PAI K 1092a: Nachlass Czernin, Haus- Hof und Staatsarchiv (hereafter HHSA), Vienna.
117 Romberg to Bethmann Hollweg, April 2, 1917, APP, 2721.
118 Czernin to Empress Zita, February 17, 1917, in Gottfried Zarnow, *Verbundet-Verraten!: Habsburgs Weg von Berlin nach Paris* (Bern: Buchverlags-Aktien-Gesellschaft, 1936), 3rd ed., 55; Wolfgang Steglich, *Die Friedenspolitik der Mittelmächte, 1917-1918* (Wiesbaden: Franz Steiner Verlag, 1964), 423 n. 7.
119 Czernin only informed Zita that his information about Caillaux came from "good sources" (aus gutter Quelle); Zarnow, *Verbundet*, 55.
120 V. H. Rothwell, *British War Aims and Peace Diplomacy, 1914-1918* (London: Oxford University Press, 1971), 83-85.
121 "Draft Memorandum," July 7, 1917, FO 371, 2864, 2;, NA cf. Egan [Copenhagen] to Secretary of State, April 1, 1917, 763.72119/532, RG 59, roll 374, USNA.

122 Robert Lansing to Woodrow Wilson, March 17, 1917, 763.72119/544a, RG59, roll 374, USNA.
123 See Biskupski, *The United States and the Rebirth*, 277–278.Tarnowski was the designated ambassador to Washington, but the Americans never accredited him. Nonetheless he spent some time in the United States in 1917 and worked closely with Polonia; see M. B. B. Biskupski, "Polonia's Ambassador to the United States: The Mystery of Jerzy Jan Sosnowski, 1917–1918," *Polish American Studies*, Vol. 73, No. 1 (Spring, 2016), 83–95.
124 Sir W Townley to the Foreign Office, August 22, 1917; Townley to FO August 23, 1917; FO 371/2864, 35, 37–38, NA see also the attached minutes on p. 36. Cf. Stanisław Koźmian, "Podczas czteroletni wojny," s. 8533, entry for August 11, 1917, 155, Biblioteka Uniwesytetu Jagiellońskiego: Dział Rekopisów (hereafter BUJ: DR). Note the comments in Rothwell, *British War Aims*, 11.
125 Quoted in ibid., 116.
126 Rumbold to FO, August 11, 1917, FO 371/2864, NA, 23. Skrzyński even held a highly secret meeting with Dmowski in August, 1917 to try to sway him regarding Austria but failed and concluded that Dmowski and his faction were inveterately opposed to the monarchy; see Pajewski, *Wokół sprawy polskiej*, 146–148.
127 E. Howard to FO, August 13, 1917; a message circulated to the king and the War Cabinet, FO 371/2864, NA, 417.
128 Koźmian, "Podczas czteroletni," s. 8532, 114–139; entry for May 26, 1917, 585, Biblioteka Uniwersytetu Jagiellońskiego (hereafter BUJ): MSS.
129 The remarks were part of a long conversation the archduke had with Stanisław Koźmian, a leading conservative Pole; see Koźmian's diary entry in "Podczas czteroletni," s. 8533, 140–165, entry for May 26, 1917, 585, BUJ:MSS.
130 Mensdorff to Czernin, December 19, 1917, PAI K 1092a: Nachlass Czernin, HHSA. Regarding the Polish aspects of these negotiations, see the discussion in Pajewski, *Wokół sprawy polskiej*, 153ff. As early as May the British were already reluctant to help Retinger with his endless commuting; see Clerk to Retinger, May 28, 1917, Retinger Papers, Box 18, folder C, BPL.
131 In March, 1918 Phillip Henry Kerr (later Lord Lothian) met with Skrzyński in Switzerland, but the talks were fruitless; Pajewski, *Wokół sprawy polskiej*, 161ff.; Rothwell, *British War Aims*, 160–171.
132 The key work in this regard is still probably Robert A. Kann, *Die Sixtusaffäre und die geheimen Friedensverhandlungen* Österreich-Ungarns *im ersten Weltkrieg* (Munich: Oldenbourg Verlag, 1966), 75ff. Kann does not mention Retinger or Caillaux.
133 Very important in this regard is "Protokół z posiedzenia pełnego Wydziału Narodowego PCKR w Ameryce," Nr. 55, December 11, 1917, Papiery Gąsiorowski, s. 15226/II, Ossolineum. Cf. Mirosław Frančić, "Entre la France et les États-Unis: le cas de Wacław Gąsiorowski pendant la première guerre mondiale," and Marian Zgórniak, "L'Armée polonaise en France, 1917–1919," in Marian Zgórniak, ed., *Studia Gallo-Polonica* (Warsaw: Państwowe Wydawnictwo Naukowe, 1988), Vol. 1, 93–94, 99.
134 Retinger to FO, May 7, 1917, and minutes of May 8, 1917; FO to Director, Military Intelligence, May 26, 1917, FO 371-3003-97976-98066, NA.
135 Terlecki, *Kuzynek*, 31; cf. Jan Zamoyski, "Pamiętniki," s. 9075 III, BUJ:MSS, entry for October, 1917, Vol. 23, 7. Retinger claimed that he was neutral in the war as far as Polish politics go, probably true, but the *endecja* hated him, undeniably true; see Retinger to NN, August 30, 1930, Retinger Collection, 68/11, Polish Institute and Sikorski Museum, London (hereafter PISM).
136 Paul Latawski, "Count Horodyski's Plan to 'Set Europe Ablaze, June, 1918," *Slavonic and East European Review*, 65 (July, 1987), 391ff. Horodyski was

as ardent an opponent of a separate peace with Vienna as Retinger was its proponent; see Norman Davies, "The Poles in Great Britain, 1914–1919," *Slavonic and East European Review,* 50 (January, 1972), 79.
137 Latawski, "Britain and the Rebirth," 131ff. Horodyski and Retinger were simultaneously clamoring for an audience at the Foreign Office from early in the war; see Mirosław Frančić, "Ignacy Jan Paderewski widziany oczyma historyków," *Przegląd Polonijny,* Vol. 9, No. 1 (1983), 95.
138 "Pour la Pologne," see the memoranda for the meetings of September 21, 22, and 23 in Korespondencja Jozefa Hieronima Retingera, s. 8067, ANK.
139 Zamorski, "Pamiętniki," 157.
140 Suleja, "Szara eminencja," 157.
141 Nicolson minute of September 20, 1918; FO 371-3282, doc no. 158193, NA. The putative Caillaux connection is fundamental here. As David French noted, the Foreign Office hated and feared Caillaux since long before the war. Any connection with Caillaux would make Retinger anathema (David French, *British Strategy & War Aims, 1914–1916* (London: Allen and Unwin, 1986), 9–10, 62, 110, 142, 166–167, 183. Retinger's Polish political rivals were surprised by his sudden fall from grace in London and could not understand how Asquith, with whom Retinger was known to be very close, could not protect him. That he was suspected of collusion with Vienna was their only conclusion; see Zamorski, "Pamiętniki," s. 9075 III, 7; Retinger, "London 1914," drawer 2, Retinger Papers., BPL.
142 Calder, *Britain and the Origins,* 89–90.
143 Giertych suggested the Retinger-as-Austrian-agent hypothesis some time ago; see Siemaszko, "Szara eminencja," 181.
144 Rothwell, *British War Aims,* 164.
145 Caillaux's secret wartime diplomacy, including known contacts with representatives of the Central Powers in Switzerland, is still largely unknown, see the frustrated remarks by Guy Pedrocini, *Les négociacions secretes pendant al grande guerre* (Paris: Flammarion, 1969), 53ff.
146 Caillaux does not mention Retinger in his lengthy apologia (Caillaux, *Devant l'histoire,* nor in his memoirs, written long afterward, *Mes mémoirs. III: clairvoyance et force d'âme dans les épreuves, 1912–1930* (Paris: Librarie Plon, 1947).
147 It is impossible to date the Retinger-Ledóchowski meetings. I have found a single document, from the Count expressing his willingness to receive Retinger; see Ledóchowski to Retinger, March 27, 1917, Retinger Papers, Box 19, folder L, BPL.
148 Caillaux apparently met with Mihály Count Károlyi, the Hungarian statesman, in Switzerland in August, 1917 to discuss a separate peace, "Reports Károlyi in Peace Plot," *New York Times,* October 12, 1917, 3.
149 Regarding both the Ledóchowski-Skrzyński connection, and the contacts between Caillaux and the Vatican's Secretary of State, see Lacroix-Riz, "Le Vatican," 530ff.
150 For Skrzyński's role in these affairs, see the documents assembled by Janusz Pajewski, "Politycy polscy w relacjach dyplomatycznych francuskich, *Dzieje Najnowsze,* 6 (1974), 209–213.
151 Retinger to Berbecki, nd, Box 18, folder b, Retinger Papers, BPL.
152 Regarding Caillaux's supposed network, see the useful, though intemperately partisan contemporary account "The Caillaux Case," in *The New York Times: Magazine Section,"* January 20, 1918; the vitriolic L. Marcellin, *Politique et politiciens pendant la guerre* (Paris: La Renaissance du livre, n.d. [1924]), Vol. 2, 29, 37, 39–40, 167ff., 193, 262–315; Roger de Fleurieu, *Joseph Caillaux au cours d'un demi-siècle de notre histoire* (Paris: Raymond Clavreuil, [1951],

216–217; and the highly detailed work by Georges Suarez, *Briand: sa vie – son oeuvre – avec son journal et de nombreux documents inédits. III: Le Pilot dans la Tourmante, 1914–1916* (Paris: Librarie Plon, 1939), 392ff. As regards the elaborate Italian aspect of Caillaux's actions, see the apologia by Filippo Cavallini, *Il processo Cavallini: storia di un delitto giudizario* (Milan: Modernissima: Casa Editrice Italiana, 1921). Notably, none of these accounts mentions Retinger.
153 Nicolson minute, September 18, 1918, FO 371, 3282, NA.
154 Retinger recollected that late in 1917 Georges Mandel, Clemenceau's "right hand," personally denounced the Pole to the "Tiger." See Pomian. *Retinger*, 46. By the end of the year, the American press reported regularly concerning the hatred in France for Caillaux – for example *New York Times*, December 17, 1917, 3.
155 Sherwood, Mandel, 22; Cf. Malcolm Anderson, *Conservative Politics in France* (London: George Allen & Unwin, 1974), 47, 67.
156 Gary W. Shanafelt, *The Secret Enemy: Austria-Hungary and the German Alliance, 1914–1918* (Boulder, CO: EEM, 1985), 183.
157 Constantine Peter Soustos, "Vatican Peace Diplomacy during World War I," (M.A. thesis, University of Virginia, 1992), 115.
158 Jan Ciechanowski, "Józef Retinger (1888 - 1957) w świetle raportów brytyjskiego wywiadu z lat 1913 do 1941," Zeszyty Historyczne, Vol. 59 (1982), 201; cf. FO Minute, September 20, 1918, NA, FO 371.3282, NA.
159 See Giorgio Rumi, "Correspondenza fra Benedetto XV e Carlo I D'Asburgo," in Giorgio Rumi, ed., *Benedetto XV e la pace – 1918* (Brescia: Editrice Morcelliana, 1990), 19ff.
160 This also applies to matters of internal Polish politics. Whereas Retinger's pro-Austrian sympathies would give him a common perspective with the Vatican, the anti-Central Powers orientation of the Dmowski camp made their approaches to the Vatican difficult until the Habsburgs were clearly *in articulo mortis*; see the useful essay by Stanisław Sierpowski, "Benedetto XV e la questione polacca negli anni della 'Grande Guerra'," in Rumi, *Benedetto XV*, 213–232. Also important are Dmowski's observations in his *Polityka polska i odbudowanie państwa* (Warsaw: no publisher, 1928), 208f.
161 Retinger, like Horodyski later, made Switzerland the center of his activities and worked closely with Ledóchowski. The importance of Switzerland and Ledóchowski for the Vatican's pro-Austrian efforts vis-à-vis the Poles is indicated by Lacroix-Riz, "Le Vatican et les buts de guerre germaniques," 517–555, esp. 539.
162 Retinger noted that Roman Catholicism was "a very profound factor in my life" and signaled out March Sangnier, the liberal theologian, as an important influence; see "Christian Politics and Religious Problems," a draft chapter in drawer 1, Retinger Papers, BPL. In "Introduction: European Perspectives on Unity and Diversity," Johann P. Arnason and Natalie J. Doyle argue a vision of the Habsburg empire as a "new order that would do justice to national aspirations while avoiding a destructive break-up of the imperial polity." See their edited volume *Domains and Divisions of European History* (Liverpool: Liverpool University Press, 2010), 11. Curiously, the Polish secret agent "Oskar" concluded his 1957 report on Retinger that he had a "materialist worldview," see Oskar,"Notatka służbowa," IPN BU 01136/69/D. INSTYTUT PAMIĘCI NARODOWEJ, [hereafter IPN].
163 Pomian, *Retinger*, 15.
164 M. B. B. Biskupski, "Polish Conceptions of Unity and Division in Europe: Speculation and Policy," Aranson and Doyle, *Domains and Divisions*, 105.
165 W. Athelstan Johnson (British Ambassador to Paris) to Retinger, November 9, 1917; Box 18, folder H, Retinger Papers, BPL. Retinger was despised by some

British officials-like Nicolson and the press's Northcliffe, but held in high esteem by others, like Gregory and Asquith.
166 Cited in Podgórski, *Retinger*, 319.
167 Retinger to Jens Christian Hauge, September 18, 1957, Box 25A, Retinger Papers, BPL. Retinger tried to get French and British help to get to Italy in November, 1917. Many of the Poles held prisoner by the Italians-captured from the Habsburg forces – wanted to join the Polish Army in exile. It was this issue which probably attracted Retinger to Italy; but this is only speculation. He also wanted to go to the United States where the army was forming. See the undated report by French Intelligence; in AKC, 4386 34/I, "Retinger," Archiwum Kazimierza Woźnickiego, PPL.
168 Typescript "Joseph Retinger Profile," *The Observer*, nd, Retinger Papers, box 25a, Retinger Papers, BPL.
169 Wiley to Winslow Memorandum; cf. Retinger, "Christian Politics and Religious Problems." To emphasize this he mentions his loyalty to Boni whose Catholicism was well-known.
170 Pomian, *Retinger*, 42. Retinger later claimed that he wrote the book; see "Notes," Retinger Papers, box 25a, BPL; "Unity of Europe," Retinger Papers, shelf 5, BPL. Cf. Taverne, *Was niemand*, 9–10. Retinger boasted of the link between the book and the later League of Nations; see Witkowski, *Ojcowie*, 55; cf. the untitled memorandum by Retinger in teczka (folder) 79, Retinger Papers, PISM; the British Journal, *The Contemporary* rejected Capel's article on federalism arguing that they had already published on that theme; see the journal's editor to Retinger. May 13, 1916, ANK, 8060. For Capel see the brief "Capt. Arthur Edward 'Boy' Capel." http://www.findgrave.com/cgi-bin/fg.cgi?page=gr&GRid=68789001, accessed on July 9, 2015.
171 De Rougemont, "A Biographical sketch." 29. De Rougemont claims Clemenceau "devoted an article to it" cf. Stanisław Lam, Materiały do słownika biograficznego polaków w świece litera "R"; Sygn 1263, BPP.
172 J. H. Retinger, *La Pologne et l'equilibre européen* (Paris: H. Floury, 1916), v–vi.
173 Retinger, *La Pologne*, 2–12.
174 Ibid., 13–16.
175 Ibid., 25.
176 Ibid., 30.
177 Ibid., 21.
178 Ibid., 20.
179 Ibid., 27–28.
180 Ibid., 66–69.
181 De Rougemont, "A Biographical Sketch," 48.
182 "Introduction," Retinger Papers, drawer 4, BPL.
183 "Retinger, Joseph, MID, F101101,"nd. Report from the French Embassy in Washington; RG165: War Department General and Specific Staffs: Military Intelligence Division, [hereafter MID] USNA.
184 Wiley to Winslow Memorandum; Retinger regarded his opposition to the army as having ended his World War I career; see "Confidential," September 18, 1957, Box 25a, Retinger Papers, BPL.
185 Pomian, *Retinger*, 56.
186 Paderewski refused to work with Retinger; see Erazm Piltz to Lausanne Committee (CAP); Archiwum Woźnickiego, 4384, BPP.
187 Wiley-Winslow Memorandum.
188 In AKC, 4386 34/I, "Retinger," Archiwum Kazimierza Woźnickiego, PPL.
189 Pams was pro-Polish; he had edited one of Retinger's pamphlet, but not known for his courage; see Retinger quoted in Pomian, *Retinger*, 59.

190 File "Retinger, Joseph," August 16, 1918; #10471NA, RG 165, micro. 1194, USNA. The Military Intelligence Division described him as having "intimate relations with political women" (?) and that, "many of his friends are suspects. His opposition to Dmowski's Polish army in France was dismissed as "intrigue." He was a "German Jew." See July 20, 1918m MID files, USNA, RG 165.
191 French intelligence clipping, dated August 17, 1941, Woźnicki Papers, akc. 4386, BPP.
192 Pomian quoting Retinger in his *Retinger*, 59.
193 Ibid.
194 Don Jacobo Fitz-James Stuart y Falcó, seventeenth Duke of Alba de Tormes, Grandee of Spain. The British and French apparently did not allow Retinger to withdraw funds from his accounts; see Podgórski, *Retinger*, 52.
195 De Dampière had spent some time in Switzerland during the war. He was in touch with the Poles fighting alongside Austria through (then) Colonel Władysław Sikorski. He traveled about Europe with Retinger on his several mysterious missions but details are not known other than the fact that the Frenchman noted that the trips were "en faveur de votre chère patrie"; see Dampière to Retinger, September 5, 1930, ANK, s. 8060; see also Wiesław Śladkowski, *Opinia publiczna we Francji wobec sprawy polskiej w latach 1914–1918* (Wrocław: Ossolineum, 1976), 208–209.
196 There is evidence that Paris was pressuring Madrid to refuse Retinger a passport; this was the work of Pierre de Margerie, a Foreign Ministry official who had experience with Polish affairs, "who hates him." See Wiley-Winslow Memorandum.
197 A partial list is in "Biographical Note: Jozef H. Retinger," Retinger Papers, box 25a, BPL. Retinger listed the army issue as decisive in ending "his political career"; see Retinger to Jens Christian Hauge, September 18, 1957, Retinger Papers, Box25a, BPL. It did not help that the press Lord Northcliffe detested Retinger; Retinger Papers, "Exile in Spain," drawer 1, BPL. Retinger's devoted friend Dampière insisted that the expulsion was exclusively due to Great Britain. He spent the next several years trying to get Retinger exonerated-perhaps he did; see Dampière to Retinger, September 5, 1920, ANK, 8006.
198 Retinger to "Panie Hrabio," September 27, 1917, Retinger Papers, box 17, BPL.
199 Folder marked "America and the Americans", written probably in 1955, in drawer 5, 14, BPL. Her devotion to Poland was short-lived: she was a Communist by 1920, if not earlier, and became a Soviet citizen. An odd biography for a lover of Poland. Duncan and Retinger were still in correspondence in 1948; see the plastic bag on shelf 6 labeled nr. 3; Retinger Papers, BPL.
200 Jan Pomian to author, nd (ca. February, 2000), author's collection.
201 French intelligence clipping, dated August 17, 1941, Woźnicki Papers, AKC, 4386, BPP.
202 See Jan Zamorski, "Pamiętniki," BUJ: DR, S. 9075 III, 7. Diary entry from October 7, 1917.
203 "Exile in Spain," drawer 1, Retinger papers, BPL.
204 French intelligence clipping, dated August 17, 1941, Woźnicki Papers, akc. 4386, BPP.
205 Conrad to Hugh Walpole, August 21, 1918, quoted in Pomian, *Retinger,* 63.
206 Retinger to Nicolson, September 9, 1918, FO 371-3282, doc. 158193, NA; Nicolson to Retinger, September 26, 1918, FO371/3282, NA.
207 Attorney General, August 15, 1918; no addressee given. RG 165, USNA.
208 Nicolson minute to Retinger to Nicolson, September 9, 1918, FO 371-3282, doc. 158193, NA, with minute "OK so reply." In Pomian's version of Retinger's memoirs Retinger notes that his position was "shaky in 1918"; actually he originally wrote 1917 – this comports with Nicolson's remarks; see draft chapter

"Exile in Spain," drawer 1, Retinger Papers, BPL. It should be noted that the Caillaux group had "extraordinary financial backing," Lord Derby to Balfour, June 17, 1918, Balfour Papers, folder 49743, BL.
209 "Exile in Spain," Retinger Papers, drawer 1, BPL.
210 One source claims that Retinger called at Downing Street virtually monthly during Asquith's premiership. Once Asquith "impetulously promised him support for a free Poland after the war. This would be the first such promise made by any Western statesman in the First World War." Retinger, discreetly, only published this statement much later, after Asquith's death. Perhaps it is true. See the typescript entitled "Joseph Retinger Profile" and signed "The Observer," nd. Box 25A, folder "Życiorysy J. Retingera," Retinger Papers, BPL. Indeed, Asquith did make such a statement, but it was in 1916; as for 1914, perhaps; see Asquith to Retinger, August 28, 1916, Retinger Papers, box 17, BPL.
211 Retinger to Pams, April 10, 1918, ANK, Korespondencja Józef H. Retingera, ANK, s. 8065, 15–18.
212 The French, his nephew remarked, neither heeded nor trusted him, despite his long residence there and many connections. See Dobrowolski, *Memuary Pacyfisty*, 35.
213 Retinger to President of France, May 10, 1918, box 17, Retinger Papers, BPL.

# 3  From Europe to Mexico

Nobody wanted Retinger. He had to leave Europe. His world had collapsed. Political dreams were dashed in the formation, and his personal life disintegrated. He claimed he had suffered a heart-attack, perhaps more than one.[1] Understandably, his general health deteriorated alarmingly. Even his personal life was in ruins. A year before he had begun an affair with the bizarre Jane Anderson an American journalist and adventuress. Anderson had, rumor suggests, at least a virtual affair with Conrad at about the same time. This resulted in damage to Conrad's own less than blissful marriage and an obvious strain on the Conrad-Retinger friendship. In the midst of this romantic farrago, Retinger's wife had a baby; the marriage ended not long thereafter.

There is an amusing story of Retinger's first meeting with Anderson's father. Before the meeting he was alerted by a friend that the father would kill him. Anderson was dressed "like the laughing cavalier." He was wearing a huge hat and brandishing a revolver. "I'm going to kill you, for what you did to my daughter." Despite this melodramatic beginning, the whole episode ended peacefully.[2]

Retinger was alone.[3] He went first, briefly, to Spain, next to Cuba, and, finally, then to Mexico, a country with which Retinger had a single link: a dreadful play he wrote, but never finished, with Conrad. But there was more, Retinger relates: there was a girl he loved, probably Jane Anderson, in the United States.[4]

Spain proved a brief interlude. Retinger's own recollections are both pathetic and humorous and culminate in his decision to abandon Spain for Cuba. His doctor had advised a long sea-voyage and no allied country would admit him so, seemingly, by chance he chose Havana. It was April, 1918. He was so emaciated that he fainted from hunger at the steamship company and received the ticket on credit.[5] A possible explanation was that Retinger really wanted to go to the United States, but his brother, Juliusz in Chicago, had only enough money to get Retinger to Havana and would send him the remainder later.[6] His trip was preposterous, in the hands of an incompetent captain and a drunken crew.[7]

On board ship to Mexico for thirty-one days, seasick and eating, quite literally, crow, Retinger met the Mexican politician Luis Negrete Morones, whom Retinger called "one of my best friends." In Havana he found some incomprehensible job as a lecturer in Spanish, a language he did not know, in a cigar factory. It seems obvious that he wanted to go to Mexico to exploit his relationship with Morones.[8] He also admitted an early interest in protecting Mexico from the exploitation of the United States, though this sounds like a retrospective justification.[9] As plausible as this appears, there is yet another variation on this explanation. According to this, Retinger was sent to Mexico by "parties in New York" under the guarantee that he would not return to the United States. The central figure in this episode was Gilbert Seldes, the anti-Communist writer and critic, but Jane Anderson, Retinger's once and perhaps continuing paramour, was also involved.[10] Conveniently Seldes had had an affair with Anderson during the war.[11] For Retinger the whole imbroglio was something of a lark: he went to Mexico "merely to make the trip."[12] Pomian argues more simply: Retinger was "besotted with" Anderson and wanted to be in Mexico to be as close to her as possible.[13]

The Mexican phase of Retinger's life from 1919–1936 is impossible to reconstruct clearly due to a dearth of materials.[14] He later wrote that these years were a period of "private socialism," International Socialism," and "London–Mexico–Poland."[15] Circumstances can be made comprehensible, but the motives and consequences of deeds are lost. All we know is that Retinger was involved in Mexican politics at the apogee, undertook crucial – preliminary – negotiations (or at least furnished advice to the highest levels of the Mexican government), and traveled about constantly on obscure missions or just as a series of adventures. What follows is a reconstruction from a very modest archival base which tries to separate fact from fiction and expose what is left.

## Retinger and Mexican politics

The corrupt Luis Morones was deeply involved in Mexican politics which were in convulsion for decades after 1910. There was a growing and occasionally violent labor movement, and widespread peasant unrest which also erupted into land seizure and murder. Names like Pancho Villa – who, from a base in northern Mexico, engaged in robbery, and seized and redistributed land – and Emilio Zapata, in the south, became famous for their escapades in rural Mexico leading a restive peasantry in violent revolt. Retinger's first job for Morones was as a translator for $150.00; hardly a prestigious appointment. According to American sources this was the humble beginning of his "service to the Mexican government."[16]

Morones was a supporter of General José Álvaro Obregón, who became president in 1920 and began widespread program of land reform and a banking system free from American control. Morones was the most prominent labor leader in contemporary Mexico, head of the Confederación Regional de Obreros Mexicanos (Regional Confederation of Mexican Workers, or CROM).[17] He was a survivor in the bewildering world of violent Mexican politics.[18] Morones signed a "secret pact" with Obregón in 1919 which enormously increased the political power of CROM: Morones "emerged as one of Mexico's most influential politicians."[19] Obregón also supplied Morones with money.[20] Morones soon introduced Retinger to the key people who would create the Mexican Labor union movement.[21] Obregón was the object of Retinger's great admiration.[22]

Nick Buford, Morones biographer, has described Retinger's patron this way:

> Reminiscent of a Chicago gangster par excellence during the prohibition era, this well-groomed, pistol-toting [man] ... had opposition congressmen kidnapped or gunned down in the streets. ... His name became synonymous with crime, violence, venality, and corruption.[23]

Morones worked closely with Samuel Gompers of the AFL-CIO to create a Mexican equivalent of the American organization: British intelligence even described Morones as one of Gompers' "lieutenants."[24] As early as 1918, CROM and the AFL had held joint meetings. Gompers was at the international meeting in Laredo, and became close to Morones.[25] When the Pan-American Federation of Labor" – presided over by Gompers – was founded; Morones was vice-president. Retinger reminds us that Communists were suspicious of Morones after this because of his association with a moderate rather than a revolutionary labor movement.[26] The Federation held regular meetings including Mexico City in 1921, El Paso-Ciudad Juárez in 1924, and Washington in 1925. Morones also traveled to Europe to make contacts with the Labor movement there.[27] Morones' delegate to the Amsterdam European Labor League was Retinger. He was assigned by Morones to "establish contacts" with European Labor circles.[28] By 1924, Retinger spent months in England trying to bring the Mexican labor movement and the British left into coordination. This led, Retinger claims, to the British sending "fraternal delegates" to the joint AFL-Mexican meeting in December 1924[29] Obregón and his successor, the repulsive Plutarco Elías Calles (president in 1924–1928), consulted Retinger a number of times, though Retinger never disclosed the details to Pomian. Working with Morones, Retinger had helped convince Calles to let a trade union movement develop in Mexico and link it to European and American counterparts, but not to the Communists.[30] Retinger even urged Calles to deport all Communists from Mexico. Retinger's introduction to the Labor Left in Europe came thus by way of Mexico.

Retinger recalls that "in 1921, when I knew something about the country and its people, I was asked for political advice." He concluded that the "basic question" was liberating Mexico from the threat of intervention by foreign powers – especially the United States, but also, though to a lesser degree, Great Britain.[31] The latter renewed diplomatic relations with Mexico and sent what Retinger regarded as an "outstanding" ambassador, Sir Esmond Ovey. By contrast, the American chargé, George Summerlin was, a mediocrity who disliked the Mexicans, and, in Retinger's words, followed the "big stick" philosophy.[32] Retinger apparently told him that he was "attached" to the Polish Mission in Washington and knew other "distinguished persons." Summerlin, nonetheless, had "violent antipathy" towards Retinger.[33]

In Morones' trips to New York and Washington to meet with American labor and political leaders, Retinger may well have accompanied him. At least we know that he was in New York City shortly after arriving in Mexico. Retinger, an outside observer noted, had a significant influence on Morones.[34] In fact, Katherine Ann Porter attributes Retinger's success in modulating some of Morones' more radical views.[35] By comparison to the Mexican, Retinger was, Porter thought, a "reactionary:" though later she called him a "fascist" and devotee of Mussolini."[36] Besides, Retinger "stinks."[37] Whereas we may reject the cogency of this political analysis, we are left with a useful observation. Retinger, Porter later said, "taught Morones his politics."[38] Retinger was, unquestionably, Morones' chief advisor in international matters.[39]

The Mexican government offered Retinger the assignment of helping it extricate itself from dependency on British – and especially American – economic manipulation. Retinger dealt easily with the British ambassador, Ovey, but did not like the American representative James Sheffield.[40] Retinger had considered the chargé, Summerlin, as suspicious of him and a "spoke in his wheels"[41] Sheffield was of limited intelligence and inclined to bully. Retinger's memoirs indicate that he found the British a far safer partner than the "imperialist" United States.

To Retinger, Morones was a giant. This, in turn, reflected his enormous devotion to Mexico and concomitant criticism of the United States as dismissing the Mexicans as racially – and otherwise – inferior.[42] In his unpleasantly hagiographic biography of 1926, Retinger refers to Morones, in just a few pages, as "more than any other ... responsible for the recent advance in the social life of Mexico." He is "the greatest moral leader of his country." More, he is "the object of hero worship. He is "the most important leader of labour in Latin America, indeed, one of the most important on the American continent," and so on.[43] Morones is, in fact, the symbol of the oppressed workers of Mexico, with whom Retinger had boundless sympathy. An American diplomat described the book as "highly eulogistic."[44] It is noteworthy that Sheffield loathed Morones and regarded him as very radical, as well as being the chief influence on President Calles (1924–1928).[45] This criticism was despite the fact that, in his racial profiling of the Mexican government, Sheffield commented that Morones had "more white blood but [was] not the better for it."[46] Incompetent and abrasive, Sheffield alienated many in Mexico.[47] He was was genuinely repulsed by the Mexican government and regarded Calles as "insane." Morones, in turn, would be, in Sheffield's view, the most important influence on Calles. Hence we have a Retinger-Morones-Calles linkage.[48] It is thus not surprising that Retinger had difficulties working with the Americans.[49]

Morones was a key member of the Obregón government and ran both the labor movement and the government' ministry of industry and trade. He was regarded widely as one of the two or three most powerful men in Mexico.[50] In Janta's words, Retinger served Mexico with his "skills, political, negotiation and intermediary abilities."[51] Over the several years he lived in Mexico, he never spent more than nine months in at any time. Otherwise he was gadding about Europe.

## General José Álvaro Obregón

Obregón is a significant actor in Mexican-American relations. In 1917 the Mexicans adopted a Constitution, whose Article 27 the Americans regarded as not protecting their property rights in Mexico.[52] After recognition by the Americans (relations had been severed in 1920), the optimistic Charles B. Warren was briefly ambassador, and then he was replaced by Sheffield. Petroleum interests in the United States feared the 1917 Constitution would nationalize sub-soil rights and wished Washington's support in asserting their claims. Washington made it clear that certain provisions of the 1917 Constitution would have to be excised before recognition would come. By comparison, American manufacturers, burdened with wartime overproduction, saw in Mexico an ideal market and supported recognition. Over time the American attitude, which had virtually regarded Obregón as a Communist, softened and his status grew in Washington which came to regard him a reformer not revolutionary. The complex affair ended with the return of an ambassador in 1923.[53] Shortly thereafter, in the so-called Bucareli Accords, Obregón promised Washington he would not enforce the Constitution against oil fields and mines already worked by foreigners.[54] The United States now supported Obregón, and decided he was a vigorous reformer rather than a dangerous revolutionary.[55] The way was now paved for an eventual agreement (of 1928) between the Mexicans and petroleum producers.

## Retinger's first mission

Retinger's first mission, or perhaps unprompted adventure, was in the summer of 1919 when he left Mexico for the United States traveling on a "French safe conduct card" issued in Barcelona by the French consul there.[56] In his memoirs, Retinger describes an episode which, though not impossible, has bizarre elements to it that deserve highlighting. A few months after his arrival in Mexico, he wanted to go to the United States and thence to Poland because of the Polish-Soviet war then raging. What use would Retinger have been in the war? He had no connections with the Piłsudski regime then in power, though he may have had, as noted, some previous contacts. In addition Retinger had no military credentials whatever. The only role Retinger might have served is as a link to the British but his odor in London in 1920 was probably foul.

He continued that, whereas Cuba, where he had spent time, and Mexico where he now resided, did not require passports, the United States did, and thus going through America would require an act of "self-smuggling." It is most likely that he went to the United States to visit his paramour, Jane Anderson,[57] hence, his peculiar route through the United States. The FBI later described Retinger at this time as, "an intelligence agent ...of some European Government."[58] Of course, at the same time, he was rumored to be having an affair with writer Mary Louise Doherty.[59]

Morones decided to help his friend.[60] He acquired the service of two smugglers (przemytniki) – whom Retinger was horrified to meet as they looked like "scoundrels" and "bandits" (probably named Esperan and Torres) – who would take advantage of the long and porous border with Texas. Both were wanted men on both sides of the frontier, and Morones threatened them with arrest if they did not accomplish their mission. After wandering in the scorching desert they came to the Rio Bravo, low in the summer. His guides demanded $3000.00 to cross the border which Retinger somehow paid, probably with money furnished by Morones.[61] They then refused to take him to San Antonio, fearing arrest. He wandered in the desert, was almost arrested for smuggling by a policeman he encountered by chance. He told him he was en route to visit his Mexican uncle.[62] He crossed the border, after first undressing – for reasons not clear – and covered himself with plants; soon he was wandering the desert in rags. He finally got to Laredo whence he took a train to San Antonio. He found nobody waiting for him and was lost. In San Antonio he did not find Morones who was supposed to be there. Why, of course, he did not accompany Morones in the first place is never explained. Morones soon showed up and bought him clothes ending Retinger's preposterous attire.[63]

From Texas, Retinger made his way to Washington. We do not know what he did there or with whom he met; save a brief and corroborated meeting with Justice Felix Frankfurter whom he describes as "my friend," and had cultivated during the war. Frankfurter was dubious about Retinger's recounting of his adventures, but nevertheless he apparently helped Retinger obtain a Polish passport, and later possibly helped get Retinger released from prison.[64] Earlier, Retinger had befriended Prince Kazimierz Lubomirski, the Polish Minister in Washington, probably a useful relationship now. He lived briefly in New York, with Jane Anderson.[65]

After a few months in the United States and some time in Mexico, Retinger went to Poland at the request of Obregón for "political reasons."[66] He left for Poland on the basis of documents issued by the Polish consulate in New York. While in Poland he supposedly was hired by something called the "Administrative Department of Volynia and Podolia," eastern Polish regions, to "assess the possibility of timber sales" to the United States. The University of Poznań also contracted him to obtaining American medical supplies. Despite these connections, Retinger was known to be an opponent of the regime of Marshal Józef Piłsudski which dominated Poland from

1918–1922.⁶⁷ Retinger claimed, however, that in 1921 the Polish Foreign Ministry offered him a diplomatic position in Moscow!⁶⁸

Leaving Poland in June of 1920 he returned to the United States, lived in New York and Washington, and concentrated on timber and the export of medical instruments as he had been asked – though working without remuneration. At the end of 1920 he returned to Mexico supposedly to "regain his health." Another explanation is that president Obregón asked him to return.⁶⁹

He decided to return to Mexico because the Obregón presidency offered him a political role; the details of which are unclear. The twin opponents of the regime were the influence of the United States and the Roman Catholic Church. The latter was under sever persecution from the Mexican regime. Retinger maintained this obscure governmental role – apparently without title – into the Calles administration which followed in 1924. Indeed, with interruption for visits to Poland, Retinger continued his role as a senior advisor to the highest reaches of the Mexican government until 1936.

Retinger explained his geopolitical orientation at the time: to guard Mexico against American – and to a lesser extent – British interference in Mexican internal affairs. However, Retinger reckoned that the two powers owned 97% percent of Mexican oil production.⁷⁰ This resulted in his conclusion that European and American "capitalists" had done a "fatal penetration" of Mexico over the last several years.⁷¹ To Mexico, Retinger argued, "the capitalist is always a foreigner."⁷²

Retinger was busy on many fronts, the economic promotion of Mexico, the labor movement, exploiting myriad European contacts to Mexico's benefit, service to Poland, journalism and propaganda, acting as Morones' publicity agent, and more besides.⁷³ Retinger was instrumental in creating contacts between Mexican leftist circles and the Labourites in Great Britain.⁷⁴ He was particularly interested in promoting Polish-Mexican economic relations.⁷⁵ One of these escapades seems especially lucrative. Retinger, staying at Warsaw's elegant Hotel Bristol, was commissioned by a Polish company to go to Mexico for three months. He would be paid lavishly for expenses; receive $3000.00 with an additional $2000.00 later, and $5000.00 more for any business he established between the Polish firm and Mexico, a total of $10,000.⁷⁶

## The failed coup: a complex plot

Details of Retinger's involvement in the abortive Mexican political crisis of 1920 are very sketchy, and the source is one of Retinger's lovers the American journalist and later novelist Katherine Anne Porter.⁷⁷ Porter worked in some mysterious capacity for Morones, as did Retinger, and the two soon had a torrid love affair.⁷⁸ She referred to herself as Retinger's "mistress."⁷⁹ He was even a character in one of her stories.⁸⁰ Porter was impressed with Retinger in early years; later she grew to loathe him.

The extraordinary tale begins in late 1920 when Porter, working as a journalist in Mexico met the elderly and idiosyncratic mineralogist and archeologist William Niven near Pococatépetl.[81] Niven had powerful friends in Mexican politics, but this network cannot be reconstructed beyond a few asides. Porter noted that Niven had a pile of letters which he let her read. They were politically explosive: "There was enough political dynamite in these casually written letters to have blown sky-high any number of important diplomatic and financial negotiations then pending between powerful governments" in her words.[82] Although Porter copied portions of them, they have never surfaced. One, according to Robert S. Wicks and Roland H. Harrison, was a description of a plot by American businessman Harry S. Bryan to overthrow the Obregón regime, just installed. In late December, Bryan wrote from Washington in a vague yet threatening manner about getting rid of Obregón, despite his efforts to ingratiate himself to the Americans. A central figure in this was the powerful and ambitious Senator Albert Fall – later jailed for his role in the Teapot Dome scandal – who had chosen two men to be "secretary and assistant secretary of war" in the incoming Harding administration who will "give me what I want."[83]

The chief of the plot was a Mexican general, Pablo González and his confederate and fellow officer Sidrónio Méndez.[84] American sources were supposedly funding them.[85] The latter went to Washington with Bryan to meet Fall. Fall had repeatedly accused Mexico of being the source of Bolshevik propaganda in the United States.[86] González promised an end to the Mexican government's war against the Church and to dispose of Article 27.[87] Fall had considerable investments in Mexico, and he was no friend of the Mexican government.[88] Moreover, Fall had recommended American intervention as recently as 1919 to overthrow the regime.[89] American intelligence predicted a revolution in Mexico worked by the radicals in the Obregón government.[90] This notion was complimented by Obregón's open intention of establishing diplomatic relations with Soviet Russia.[91] Bryan then went to Mexico to meet with Méndez to explain that the plot had been hatched. He was perhaps the key middleman. In the meantime Méndez had assembled troops should Obregón prove recalcitrant, and González was prepared to "move arms across the border."[92] The plot now took on a clear form:

> Bryan and González had visited him [Randolph Robertson, US Consul in Nuevo Laredo] on their way to Washington, where they would promise elimination of Article Twenty-seven along with the overthrow of Obregón. Fall apparently had guaranteed recognition by the United States if all factions unfriendly to Obregón should unite and cross the border.[93]

On May 7, 1920 González's troops entered Mexico City. The coup, large and violent, was short-lived. González was, however, released from prison soon after.

Porter showed the letters she obtained from Niven to Retinger who immediately decided to inform Obregón of the plot. Retinger then left Mexico for the United States ostensibly to buy saddles, but really to interfere in the Fall-González negotiations. He was sent as an agent of Morones.[94] Morones himself went to Washington at this time – as an unofficial envoy – to meet with President Wilson, Secretary of State Bainbridge Colby, and Gompers who acted as intermediary with the politicians.[95]

A yet more bizarre episode concerns archives. An American at the legation had sold, surreptitiously, a huge number of documents from the files of correspondence with the State Department.[96] In Retinger's words, they consisted of "five thousand documents including correspondence between the American government and their embassy in Mexico as well as a large number of documents from the State Department." A certain "high official of the American embassy and one of the most important members of the State Department had been selling these secrets to the Mexicans for over a year." Calles referred to it as his "secret weapon."[97] They disclosed a most unsavory aspect of American policy and oil interests. Retinger spent the Christmas holidays of 1925 going over the documents and decided the evidence was sufficient to blackmail the Americans. A planned invasion of Mexico was supposedly unearthed.[98] He suggested he go to Washington to meet with Secretary of Commerce Herbert Hoover, "one of the most honest American politicians."[99]

Before traveling to meet Hoover, Retinger had lengthy consultations with President Calles.[100] Since he was denied a visa at Nuevo Laredo on the 28th, Consul Robertson's work, he continued to travel on his Polish passport.[101] Retinger met the journalist Paul Hanna in St. Antonio en route to Washington on March 3, here the chronology appears logical. It was probably then that Retinger disclosed the contents of the Niven letters (or perhaps the stolen embassy letters) to Hanna. But Robertson, either in hot pursuit, or by the oddest coincidence, intercepted Retinger on the train in St. Louis on March 5 and had Retinger arrested on the incomprehensible charge, "that I was not Józef Retinger,"[102] and held him incognito for seven days. There was some speculation that Retinger was a victim of Morones' feuds with American officials. Porter was sent to Laredo to try and get Retinger released."[103] In a political version of *ménage a trois*, Jane Anderson was also importuning Polish authorities in Warsaw to intervene.[104]

From St. Louis he was sent to Houston, and then to Laredo where a judge freed him. He was immediately arrested again, in the same building in Laredo "on the charge of being a burden on the American Administration" and confined for another thirty days.[105] Retinger's transfer from decent circumstances in St. Louis to "wretched" jails in Houston and Laredo lasted a tortuous four months. Porter describes Retinger's place of confinement as "Very hot ... full of cockroaches, and the food abominable."[106]

Immigration officials refused him bail despite his raising the original sum from Mexican sources. Retinger's relationship with Morones was a doubtless cause of the ever increasing bail, because the labor leader was thought by many in America to be a virtual Communist.[107] This almost certainly refers to the Fall-González conspiracy. In other words, Retinger was Calles' agent to diffuse a coup. Porter provides the crucial evidence when she writes of Retinger's "Preparation for a secret diplomatic journey of investigation to Washington. (His pretext, was the aforementioned buying saddles for Morones, who was head of munitions army supplies in general.)"[108] Eventually, he tried to leave for Poland, but was deported to Mexico instead.[109]

Holding Retinger incommunicado, hardly a normal procedure for a mere border violation, is more comprehensible were we to assume international politics were in the making. With Retinger helpless in a St. Louis and then Laredo jail, the plot continued. Retinger gave a ridiculous account of his activities to the American jailers on March 7. Consul Robertson was part of a plot to unhorse the Obregón-Morones establishment of which Retinger was an important member.[110] Retinger argued that the long delay in releasing him was politically motivated: "The only possible explanation for all of this was that my enemies (whom he does not specify) wanted me to be taken out of circulation until their plans were realized." [111]

Hanna, a friend of Porter, published a quite detailed-though carefully censored–version of the coup in *The Nation* which corroborated Porter's revelations via Retinger. Hanna referred directly to the existence of the letters.[112] The plot unraveled in June: it was thwarted by the Calles' government and the top conspirators were killed.

Equally bizarre is Retinger's report that Washington was pressuring the Mexican government to expel him – their why is not explained by Retinger – and he went to see the Briton Ovey. Ovey presented Retinger with a number of documents of American "spying" and "crime" which were explosive but, nonetheless negotiable. This change Retinger apparently attributes to Sheffield's dismissal and replacement by Dwight Morrow with whom, Retinger claims, he immediately struck up a close friendship. Morrow "asked my advice" on the Mexican situation and Ovey acted as an intermediary. Morrow wanted the United States to do the right thing in Mexico, Retinger noted: the United States "changed its policies." But Sheffield's removal was, according to Retinger, part of a much larger intrigue. Retinger

> Informed [ambassador Ovey] about the documents collected over the last two years by the Mexicans which demonstrated, among other things, that Frank Kellogg, the Secretary of State, as well as Sheffield, the ambassador of the United States in Mexico, tried to find some pretext for armed intervention. It would show a scheme of intrigue and corruption of [American] officials, and in the States, where still fresh was the memory of the "Teapot Dome" scandal, a new scandal which certainly would be fatal for the administration. ... some London journalists already scented something, and the Mexican government was weighing the possibilities of allowing them access to information.[113]

Retinger's report to Ovey was conveyed to the American embassy and the storm quickly passed. President Calvin Coolidge, who was kept informed, Retinger argued, recalled Sheffield and replaced him with Morrow.[114] This is an amazing episode for the oft-noted change in Washington's policy toward Mexico, associated with the arrival of Morrow and suggests, if Retinger is to be believed, was due to very large and sordid motives.

## Red Mexico

Morones' politics were very radical. He was considered to be a Communist by both Katherine Anne Porter as well as the American government. He spoke of his desire to destroy capitalism, and was referred to as a "good Bolshevik."[115] Retinger moved in very Left Mexican circles indeed.[116] Though, to be fair, everyone who favored reform in Mexico was labeled a "Bolshevik."[117] In his book *Tierra Mexicana* Retinger lamented that "the landowners were not dispossessed of their properties" unlike, say, Soviet Russia, leaving the agricultural problem unsolved.[118] Retinger praised Morones for "studying" the AFL, the European version, the Federation of Trade Unions of Amsterdam, and "the Communistic organization with its centre in Moscow."[119] Retinger was very sympathetic to the cordial relations between Mexico and Soviet Russia which he regarded as quite natural. Stories abounded of connections between Mexican officials and Russian agents and government members. Retinger himself wrote: "Mexican Labour ... appreciates that the Union of Soviet Socialist Republics is the only workers' Republic outside of Mexico and for this reason it has always insisted that, no matter what are the social, political and theoretical differences between the two, some direct contact must be maintained." Mexico soon had the first Russian legation in the Western hemisphere.[120]

Ultimately, Retinger never admitted to being a Communist – which is convincing – but he was a political radical. The devoted Pomian even describes him as a "fervent socialist" in the 1920s–1930s.[121] He had many radical connections throughout the world many of which proved long lasting. In Mexico Retinger was a socialist, friendly towards the Soviet Union, anti-capitalist, and anti-American. These attributes would later haunt him.

The State Department had been suspicious of developments in Mexican politics in the post-World War I years, after suspecting Mexico of pro-German sympathies during the war.[122] Mexico as a scene for the repetition of the Bolshevik Revolution was bruited about. American investors were chary of Mexican radicalism.[123] A peasant revolt of massive dimension and radical coloration was feared in the United States. However, such observers as Holland Dempsey Watkins dismissed this as a fantasy give the abysmal level of Mexican poverty and ignorance, and even Retinger labeled the idea of a rural revolution as "ridiculous."[124]

Criticism of the United States was interpreted in Washington as a prelude to revolution and the establishment of a Communist regime. Indeed, Mexico was suspected as the possible source of Communist propaganda entering the United States.[125] In many ways the focal point of these fears was Morones. According to American diplomats in Mexico City, Morones had regular contacts with Soviet officials and even went to Moscow in 1923 and subsequently maintained relations with Soviet agents.[126] Despite pressure from American business circles, Washington recognized the Obregón regime in 1923.

Relations initially improved, but soon soured again and in 1925 Secretary of State Frank B. Kellogg issued an open threat to the Mexicans over mistreatment of Americans, and there was even talk of war.[127] Reflecting this instability, the import of Mexican oil to the United States fell disastrously.[128] This doubtless reflects the abrupt downturn in Mexican oil production: begun in 1901, it grew, with some interruptions to 193 million barrels by 1921, only to bottom out in 1932 at 33 million.[129]

A new crisis with the Americans erupted, and Pomian insists a letter from them included a demand that Retinger be fired.[130] In any event, the threat was aborted, and with the arrival of Ambassador Dwight Morrow in 1927, the situation quickly improved and Morrow established good working relations with the Mexicans.[131] Morrow was highly regarded in Washington, as someone "who can get us a fair deal."[132] In 1928 the virtual war with foreign, largely American oil companies, in suspense for a decade, was settled.[133] A foreign diplomat in Mexico accounted for this by noting that Charles Lindbergh flew from capital to capital in 1927. At Morrow's request, Will Rogers toured the country, and Morrow arrived: a blessed American "trinity" indeed.[134] Retinger described Morrow as his "great friend" though nothing in the Morrow papers reflects this.[135] This continues the tradition of Sheffield's tenure. Sheffield had never mentioned Retinger.[136]

Retinger wrote a biography of Morones, apparently with Porter's assistance.[137] The editor of the volume insisted that, at least at the time, Retinger was a "British Marxist" with close ties to the British Communist Party. He was also supposedly linked to the Comintern.[138] Retinger's book is a passionate defense of labor and pleads its case. His real target is "imperialism" by which we should understand American influence – and not the overthrow of capitalism by socialism.[139] Janis P. Stout is correct in labeling Retinger's proscriptions "gradualist."[140] Stout refers to Retinger as a "Polish intriguer" and a "mysterious foreigner."[141] Retinger's rival in labor politics was one Robert Haberman, an American citizen from Romania with radical views. Retinger looked upon Haberman with disdain; Haberman happily denounced Retinger to American intelligence operatives.[142] Both moved in the same circles and were obviously seeking to outdo each other as men of mystery.[143] By 1923 they worked together to influence Morones not to go to Russia and demonstrate the accusations that he had Communist sympathies.[144]

Retinger's denunciation of American policy towards Mexico took in broad geopolitical dimensions in a work he wrote entitled "Memorandum on the North-American Mexican Controversy." In this, Retinger argues that the ultimate American goal was to control all the area up to the Panama Canal thus dominating world trade. Washington needed Mexico's petroleum and ore. And there was a possibility that pressured by "threats and blackmail, Mexico might accept American demands. After all the Americans "have been imperialistic since the Cleveland administration, especially so in the case of Wilson." Under Harding this imperialistic pressure had become enormous. He here gives a list of large oil companies and banks involved in the rape of Mexico and cites Secretary of State Kellogg's speech of June 13, 1925 which had as its theme the "complete economic and financial control" leaving Mexico independent only "in name." "The Americans will coerce Mexico to accept, using the exportation of American food to Mexico as a lever."[145]

Retinger was a great backer of Calles and speaks of him warmly in solving agricultural problems. After all, the Government of Calles was convinced that Marx "was right in many of his theories." Hence regarding agriculture "the Mexican government is Marxist."[146] Americans and other outsiders had systematically exploited the Mexicans and used their governments to shield them.[147] Of course, Calles was also the man who said to Retinger "the most beautiful day of his life was when he hanged thirteen generals."[148]

## Retinger and the Mexicans

Retinger traveled about Mexico, trying to avoid the patronizing attitude of the tourist. He likened Mexico to Europe of 500 years earlier and described what were often dismissed and violent and corrupt as romantic figures trying to build a country from deep poverty. He presented his time in Mexico as having three goals: he wanted to understand Latin American politics and psychology and he thought this could best be done from Mexico; he wanted to "help" the Mexicans. The latter was, in his eyes prompted by his conclusion that after 1919 Mexico's relationship to the United States was similar to Poland's with Russia in 1750–1900: Mexico would have to protect itself from the Americans. Third, he "sought adventure," whatever that means.[149] He had "a built-in instinct for intrigue.[150]

The disturbingly ugly Morones was, in Retinger's eyes, enormously gifted. Surrounding him was a group of absolute devotees, all young and ambitious, like Retinger, who regarded them as "exceptionally dear" (wyjątkowo mili). They supported Retinger and paid for his excursions throughout the country though they themselves were poor. Retinger was passionate about learning as much as he could about Mexico, and was an ardent advocate of Mexico's position. There is no record, for example, of his criticism of the Mexican government's ruthless persecution of the Church which Retinger claimed to hold in such loyalty.[151]

He wrote a considerable amount about Mexico; all favorable; for example a pamphlet in 1925 about the "social movement" in Mexico, that is, the revolution continuing since 1910. In the same year appeared his aforementioned biography of Morones. The next year, 1927, he wrote a large volume on Mexican agriculture, *Tierra Mexicana*, which had been so convulsed of late. Retinger praised Mexico for tackling its rural problems, beginning in 1917, with such audacity and suggested it did, or at least could, serve as a model for other countries.[152] Retinger combined his passion for agricultural reform with an equal interest in the workers' movement, through Morones.

## The chaos of Mexican politics

Calles, described by Jim Tuck as a "fanatic" in his anti-clericalism, had been elected in 1924 to follow Obregón and started a convulsive persecution of the Church, a model of bigotry and persecution.[153] The war against Roman Catholics resulted in tens of thousands of deaths, the "Cristero" Rebellion. Although out of office by 1928, Calles would still rule Mexico indirectly. Calles apparently ended his career as a fascist reading *Mein Kampf*. Religious toleration was only later introduced by president Ávila Camacho, a declared Roman Catholic.[154] Retinger, Jesuit trained and a professed believer, found himself in odd circumstances. How he resolved his service to the Mexican government with its crusade against the Church is problematical. Years later he explained that the laicization of Mexico, and the simultaneous destruction of the latifundia, was the means by which the last vestige of Spanish imperialism could be removed and hence was an act of patriotism on the part of the government. This was not a convincing argument given the brutality of the undertaking.[155] He also argued that the "Religious War in Mexico" was due to a Roman Catholic plot to overthrow the Mexican government with the aid of American business interests."[156] Nonetheless, Retinger seems to have played no part in the convulsive religious war.[157]

Retinger's memories of his adventures became more complex and colorful with the passage of time: that details of smugglers, and wandering in rags were either later accretions or matters he did not think important until many years later. On the other hand Retinger liked to diminish his role and dangle misleading details, many probably false, in his recounting of his adventures. In his major political activities Retinger always worked in secret; in his memoirs he always beclouded issues with colorful distraction. Porter became disillusioned with Retinger whom she described as living in a "fog in the midst of which he moves fevered with visions."[158]

## Oil politics

Retinger was appalled at the huge American role in the Mexican petroleum industry. Bribery and corruption were rampant. They even had private armies and virtually ran Vera Cruz and Tamalpias. "Los petroleros," the American oil barons, were described as a "seething whirlpool of ambition and greed," characterized by "deceit, corruption, chicanery, theft, kidnapping, murder, and assassination."[159] Given this, it is perhaps not surprising that Retinger wrote: "I ... advised the Mexican government to take the only measure which could suppress the influence of the foreign oil interests, namely, to nationalize oil." He, however, "had no voice in the tactics, which were, he thought, "bungled." Direct American interference was thus feared.[160] Retinger even recalls speaking with an American Senator who had tried to bribe Calles with 13 million dollars. Retinger claimed he saw, though he did not explain, cables from President Harding, urging pressure to be put on the Mexican government.[161]

In 1925 the Mexicans took the first steps towards petroleum nationalization. Retinger recalled later what the American reaction was:

> The foreign oil concerns reacted immediately. The American businessmen began an offensive under the leadership of Bill Green, the director of the firm "Huastec" having in Washington the support of [Senator] Fall, the Minister of Internal Affairs [sic], and also even President Harding himself. Fall ... exerted enormous pressure He was the owner of a quarter of a million hectares of land in Chihuahua, as well as other possessions. He had long been active in Mexico, and his wealth in the country was enormous.[162]

By the late 1920s, the Mexicans feared American seizure of oil lands. The Mexican government reached an impasse with England and the Americans over the petroleum question.[163] The Americans were willing to spend millions on the negotiations including, according to Terlecki, considerable amounts for bribery.[164] Retinger represented Mexico in talks with ambassador Ovey, and prepared the Mexican case for dealing with the Americans. Retinger addressed "Mexican oil situation to Secretary of Commerce Herbert Hoover; apparently without result."[165] The Mexicans, Terlecki suggests, feared an American invasion and seizure of territory.

## The oil negotiations

This period is the most controversial in Retinger's Mexican sojourn. He was supposedly sent to the Geneva Conference to make a speech denouncing American "imperialism," a standard canard from the Mexican left. According to the State Department, Retinger had, by this time, "the entire confidence of the Mexican government" and was in effect Morones' personal agent. The American consul reported to the State Department that Retinger was an "intimate friend" of both Morones and President Calles who called upon Retinger to "give advice." Retinger had been preparing for this appearance by writing articles for the "Mexican White Book" regarding foreign involvement in the Mexican economy.[166] He carried documents which described him as "chief of section, specialist of the department of commerce."[167] Pomian, insists that Retinger was involved in a broad variety of undertakings designed to modernize Mexico from the educational system to building roads.[168]

The American Minister in Mexico insisted that Retinger would proceed from Geneva to Moscow to interview Soviet officials regarding a disarmament conference; A few weeks later one Antonio Reichis made a speech in Moscow which American observers regarded as "fomenting trouble in the US." Reichis was supposedly really Retinger and he was one of about six agents traveling about doing Mexican work of some kind.[169] The American legation in Mexico had already assumed that Retinger was an operative of the Third International.[170] However, Retinger's appearance in Moscow never, it seems, happened.[171] He was certainly an *homme de confiance* in Mexico but never its agent in Moscow, sporting a *nom de plume*.[172] That the Americans were willing to entertain the notion that Reichis was Retinger shows the suspicion in which he was held in Washington. He was also known to be in correspondence with Stanislav Pestkovsky of the Soviet Consulate in Mexico.[173] This doubtless helped the American view of Mexico's close relations with Bolshevik Russia. British Intelligence suspected him of Communist ties and close cooperation with the Profintern.[174] These machinations are the more important because the US ambassador in Mexico City warned Washington that CROM, that is, Morones, was about to take over Mexico by coup.[175] CROM, the American embassy concluded, "enjoyed almost absolute power."[176] Washington pressured Calles to fire Retinger.[177]

Retinger quickly found himself in oil issues. Mexico was a major producer, and the British and American owned 70 percent of the exploitation, making "fantastic" profits. They retained private armies and interfered in Mexican internal affairs. The country was in chaos. Retinger advised the Mexican government to nationalize the oil industry as early as 1924.[178] Morones led the fight to limit the degree of foreign exploitation of Mexican petroleum; in fact he escalated it.[179] The chaos which followed Retinger blamed the inexperience of the Mexicans: "I admit that I had partial responsibility for nationalization, but only for the idea."[180] He qualified that somewhat in his memoirs when he noted that he had nothing to do with the way in which it was carried out, which was often "brutal."[181] His motives were to aid their "struggle with the American penetration: which reminded him of Russia's role in Poland in the eighteenth century. This put the Mexicans in a difficult position with their erstwhile partners.[182] Their very independence was under threat from the petroleum industry. Retinger later claimed that, working with the newly arrived American ambassador Morrow, he could claim, a role in the "good neighbor policy" which emerged in the late 1920s.[183] Retinger noted that he had been in Mexican affairs since the early 1920s and told the American representative that Mexican politics vis-à-vis the United States was simply adolescent nationalism: if allowed ten years of "non-interference," the situation would change fundamentally.[184] Retinger shared with Obregón the desire to lessen American influence in Mexico; one of the reasons for Obregón's interest in Soviet Russia.[185]

The problem with the notion that Retinger worked with the Americans regarding the petroleum issue is complicated by the complete absence of any mention of him in the papers of Ambassador Dwight Morrow. There is a massive amount of memoranda and correspondence about this issue but Retinger's name cannot be found. We are left to conclude that Retinger's role was as a confidential advisor to the Mexican government, not as a quasi-agent to the Americans. He claimed to have had "no voice in the tactics" – which would explain his absence from the documents.[186]

## The last Mexican involvement: Retinger's oil company?

If Retinger's very superficially explained role in the nationalization of Mexican oil is anywhere near accurate, it is probably the most important political role he ever played. He obviously had dealings on behalf of the Mexicans with foreign embassies though he later claimed he never worked for any government till 1939.[187] In 1926 Retinger received 240 shares of "the Mexican Syndicate" which suggests his personal involvement with the oil industry.[188] In 1927 he was described as "Secretario de Industria" in a letter which describes a "great Mexican future" by a Detroit industrialist.[189]

Nineteen twenty-eight was the pinnacle of Retinger's involvement in Mexican business and politics. He was attempting to establish a Mexican news agency in Europe and other forms of promotion.[190] He carried on business, representing Mexico.[191] This involvement with economic promotion was complimented with journalism about Mexico, and here we have interesting texts, probably by Retinger, denouncing American "imperialism" in Mexico[192], and constant correspondence with British labor and business circles. Indeed, Retinger became caught up in the horrors of American interests in Mexico. The latter needed certain basic changes he noted, but all of these depended on the country being able to "overcome foreign capitalistic interests, sponsored as they are by the American government always."[193]

While in Europe he kept in close touch with the British legation in Mexico.[194] Of course, one must not be too sure: shortly before he dabbled in the pottery business.[195] He wandered about Europe in the 1920s, wheeling and dealing principally, according to one cynical source, because he did not like to work.[196]

Retinger had assembled a bizarre three-some of agents to promote the sale of Mexican oil assets and develop multi-faceted trade, including his beloved Poland. It consisted of very mysterious figures: de Dampière, the French aristocrat Retinger had known during the war years, the shadowy F. A. Boyer (also in Paris, but better known for his efforts in Washington), and Retinger.[197] Boyer, even by Retinger's standards, was very odd, and Retinger's willingness to be involved with him in fairly large business efforts, is an indication of the kind of people with whom Retinger was willing to surround himself.[198]

According to Retinger, Boyer was a "gangster." He claimed descent from both Indian and Puritan ancestors. But at other times he admitted he did not know who his father was. He inherited vast amounts of money, wasted it, on "grandiose fantasties." He was a pioneer in the American oil industry.

He traveled in Mexico with cars full of girls whom he paid. He fought in the Resistance in France in 1940 and died there in poverty. Lurking on the fringes was the indefatigable Ukrainian lobbyist Longin Cegelsky, and the colorful, and erstwhile lover of Retinger, Jane Anderson.[199] This was Retinger's business team.[200]

This group negotiated with the Mexicans as an intermediary between them and the "concessionaires." Following their success, probably with the foreign oil companies, they would then seek the approval of the Mexican government. In a "Memorandum" sent to Retinger in 1928, regarding the state of negotiations regarding concessions "on all federal lands" it speaks of a fifty-fifty split between the concessionaires and the Mexican government."[201] Retinger was openly credited with using his influence with the Mexican government to arrange foreign companies to become involved in Mexican oil.[202] Frustratingly, Retinger's name does not appear in the list of those involved in the oil compromise.[203]

Retinger's bewildering business adventures had two characteristics: first they included England, but not France, as much as possible, and second they were all designed to aid Poland, with foreign money. A list is quite enlightening. Boyer and Dampière's role in Mexican oil took up a great deal of time in 1928–1930, all of it confusing.[204] In 1929, Retinger was involved in complex correspondence with a Pole named Julian Brygiewicz regarding Mexico's exports to Poland and the attendant re-organization of the Mexican consulate in Warsaw.[205] Brygiewicz was also keen on constructing a new water supply for Łódź. He also wanted Retinger to join him in apartment construction in Warsaw.[206] Retinger, with or without Brygiewicz, had a series of construction projects in Poland from which he was paid handsomely.[207] Here Boyer again surfaced.[208] One of the more fascinating of his "deals" was to be involved in the building of the port of Gdynia, which would later prove a major Polish accomplishment of the interwar years.

Brygiewicz prepared a résumé which was quite exceptional: he controlled international firms for water and electricity, large mines in Polish Upper Silesia (Friedenshütte and Bismarckshütte); he ran an exporting business and was consumed by the prospect of Polish trade with Latin America, especially Mexico.[209] He became, after 1927 Mexico's honorary consul in Poland and sent representatives to both countries.[210] Brygiewicz wanted to entice Retinger to come back to Mexico from Europe in 1927 and offered him $5000.00.[211] It was probably Brygiewicz who provided Retinger a detailed memorandum in mid-1930 whereby petroleum rights would be shared equally 50 percent–50 percent after intermediaries were paid off.[212] Brygiewicz, along with Dampière, Boyer, and a Polish engineer named Kazimierz Jan Jaskulski had ambitious, and variegated, plans for Polish projects but could not find financial backers due to difficult economic conditions in Europe in 1931.[213] Retinger did not give up; as late as July 1939 he was involved in some business transactions in Lwów.[214]

A memorandum addressed to Retinger in 1930 spoke of creating a "syndicate" and later an "operating company." Retinger's "Mexican lawyer," and a certain Lt. Col. W. H. Mitford would be given "suitable commissions." Retinger would be a major beneficiary of the company; one vague reference speaks of 33 percent, but it is not completely clear whether this was to be Retinger's share or not. Retinger would provide, it seems, and here the proposal is blurry, certain "rights" and his partner would put up the financing. Retinger would transfer to some syndicate Mexican oil properties for £5,000 and the aforementioned 33 percent in return the syndicate would possess the oil. The creation of refineries was discussed and Retinger was the intermediary between British commercial interests and the Mexicans. Retinger's main interest was, it seems, to get the British involved.[215] It is all quite complex and shadowy. Regardless, this was a large undertaking. One of his jobs was to ensure that the Mexican government maintained enough control of the venture that none of the major petroleum companies could intervene. How much, if anything, Retinger profited from this cloudy episode cannot be found.[216]

By 1930, Retinger's involvement with international oil politics was well known. British sources credit him with being "of considerable service" to the Mexican government and as a result the latter had "entrusted him with the preliminary negotiations in connection with the exploitation of the Government's extensive oil lands."[217] Retinger proposed that a British oil company be formed on a 50 percent–50 percent profit basis with the Mexicans. The company would need 2 to 3 million British pounds, but money could come from French and German sources as well.[218] Circumstantial evidence suggests that Retinger's oil politics were motivated in part to promote British, as against American interests. Retinger was also working with Polish firms to stimulate trade with Mexico; though whether petroleum was involved is unclear. His travels throughout Europe in search of Mexican business relationships was paid for by the Mexican government.[219]

By 1930, Retinger ended his active role in Mexican oil negotiations and moved to other things.[220] Some documents suggest that his oil consortium was not an entirely ethical or legal undertaking.[221] There are possibilities that he found his activities lucrative, despite later references to his leaving Mexico as poor as when he arrived. He contented himself that he "contributed greatly towards the modernization of Mexico."[222]

For all his service to the Mexican oil politics, he was very critical of their management of their assets: he observed that "it never occurred to the Mexicans that none of them, even to a small degree, understood the petroleum business, its technology, and organization" and that "nationalization without indemnification …was of course disadvantageous to the Mexican government."[223]

## The Vatican episode

Although he claimed to have taken no part, he did play a role in the nasty politics of the Mexican government towards the Catholic Church which Retinger claimed to deplore. He was sent by President Calles, a colorful drunk and Retinger's "friend", to the Vatican where he had a series of meetings with Msgr. Borgoncini di Duca to settle the Catholic embroilment with the Mexican government.[224] In an effort at reconciliation, Retinger urged the Mexican Catholic Church to avoid involvement in politics. For this he was criticized for being anti-clerical and a mason, both of which attributions Retinger later denied.[225] Indeed, Retinger was so aggrieved by rumors, throughout his life, that he was not a Roman Catholic that he wrote this singular declaration which has been uncovered by Thierry Grosbois:

> I solemnly declare that I never participated in any way in a struggle against the principles of the Catholic Church and that I never consented, even passively, to make the slightest criticism of the dogmas of Catholic doctrine or even the general tactics of the Church
> 
> I defy anyone to find in my twenty books and some hundred articles a single word that could be interpreted as distrust of the precepts of the Church. To be sure I have committed a number of sins in my private life, but I have never stopped calling myself a Catholic and during important crises in my life I always submitted to the rules of the Church and accepted the duties imposed on Catholics.[226]

The exact date of Retinger's intervention between the Vatican and Mexican politics is hard to date. Obviously Calles was president which would locate the incident to after 1924. Calles was known for his opposition to the Church; it "hated him."[227] Evidence suggests that Retinger himself was under increased hostility from Rome. Vatican sources suspected him of being part of a group wishing to promote a national church in Mexico.[228] The biographer of Morrow credits the ambassador with working an end to the church-state feud in 1929 and does not mention any role for Retinger.[229]

## Conclusions

The Retinger of the Mexican years was not the man of 1914–1918. In the earlier period he was the ally of the Vatican, and the Austrian monarchy, the confidant of the conservative, and aristocratic, French right. In Mexico he associated himself with a radical regime, frequently used words like "imperialism," practiced labor politics, and spoke of the masses and the downtrodden; terms far from his wartime vocabulary which was notably elitist. We should remember that Retinger was associated with an openly socialist regime (Obregón and Calles) and therefore distrusted by the capitalist West but attractive to Europe's left. In a sense Retinger represented the political culture of Mexico. The Jesuit educated and devout Roman Catholic was an advisor to a government which massacred Catholics. Certainly Retinger had turned to the Left.

Retinger was a Polish patriot with large dreams of international cooperation willing to explore different avenues for an unchanging goal.

Retinger's interest in international comity and cooperation was not only motivated by the values inherent in those goals, but by something more. Late in life he noted that by the end of World War I, "I began to realize that Poland's fate depended on international affairs and I decided for this reason to start getting involved in international affairs."[230] Years later, Retinger's presence in Mexico was controversial for the anti-Catholic events of the era.[231] His earlier connections with the Jesuits and the Vatican make this a most intriguing episode.

The difficulty in discussing Retinger's actions in Mexico is the dearth of sources, many irreconcilable contradictions, and the absence of his name from what accounts we do have. There are two explanations for this. First, and this would correspond to his life-long preference for surreptitious activity and restricting himself to acting as a mysterious behind-the-scenes operative, is that Retinger was an intimate advisor and not a public negotiator. The second explanation is that Retinger was really a much less influential figure than he himself, and others, have claimed for him.

## The Mexican links to Europe

Retinger's travels in Europe as a representative of the Mexican labor movement brought international labor leaders to Mexico, including the socialist Zygmunt Żuławski from Poland. Calles and Morones, in turn, visited Germany and France. Retinger interested the *Daily Herald* in his claim that Mexico was very important "from the Labour point of view."[232] While in England Retinger met with parliamentarian E. D. Morel and bruited the idea of a secret international workers' movement; "a clandestine organization working for the unity of Europe." Retinger recollected that "big problems were dealt with by a kind of Mafia and an open conspiracy of people in different countries."[233] Soon he was part of this "open conspiracy of people in different cities."[234] The "Mafia" would, a generation later, appear as the Bilderbergs.

He credits the British Member of Parliament, E. D. Morel, for his first steps. Retinger envisioned an: "economic solution to the European problems." He referred to it as a "scientific approach." In this he had much help from Labour Party activists. Retinger married Morel's daughter, Dr. Marion (Stella) Phillips[235] (so much for Jane Anderson). Stella, Ben Spoor (an anti-imperialist Labour delegate who died prematurely of alcoholism), Richard Wallhead (another Labour MP), Graham Poole, and Clement Attlee among others became his closest confederates.[236] Though Morel's death brought an end to this strange plot, to a certain degree, Morel was replaced by Labour parliamentarian Sir Stafford Cripps, a relationship later important for Retinger.[237] Cripps' profound religiosity appealed to him.[238] These whirlwind efforts may explain Retinger's involvement on behalf of British firms investing in Mexico, oil politics, and a myriad of other things we may generally call "economic." But Ernest Bevin, then General Secretary of the Transportation Workers' Union was uninterested in Retinger's projects and the whole thing collapsed.[239] Bevin was, Retinger lamented, too "provincial"; "the whole thing was beyond him,"[240] though Cripps finally proved a lasting ally.[241]

Retinger was already working in England to drum up support for the idea of European unity but made no appreciable gains.[242] He later lamented that European unity was not an idea popular among either politicians or the general public in the era.[243] Retinger's leftist connections are demonstrated by letters he received addressed to "Comrade" and his lecturing and traveling about in labor circles.[244] Retinger's first foray into international politics, the only kind that mattered, had gotten nowhere. In despair he began writing for the British press to sustain himself.[245]

Bored, disillusioned, melancholic, and in poor health Retinger was appalled by the impression Western labor leaders made on him. He wrote, not very graciously, to a former lover:

> I have seen most of the prominent leaders of the world of any kind of race, creed, and party, during the last few months in Europe again, while doing some important work, did I meet many more, especially labor leaders, I did not meet yet a single one who was entirely square, who would not sell for someside [sic] outside his ideals, his convictions, and his followers.[246]

Retinger retrospectively regarded this early 1920s dabbling in international politics of a leftist coloration, his first steps into the movement for European unity, and he labeled a second effort, a few years later, to produce, along with MP Seymour Cox, an encyclopedia aimed at the masses (also an abortive effort) his second episode in the unity movement.[247] Doubtless a companion to this effort was the notion of an international socialist periodical which would combine some of his British leftist colleagues with Morones, and Żuławski in a kind of Polish-Mexican-Labour journal which made sense if Retinger was added as *spiritus movens*.[248] In his writings, he wished to emphasize socialism in Polish history and its contributions to *Russian* socialism.[249]

It was only with the Second World War that Retinger acknowledges his third effort. This, curiously, omits his activities during World War I. On the face of it this seems a simple omission, but perhaps there is nothing other than a mere oversight, Perhaps Retinger was telling us that restoring Poland, protecting the Habsburgs, and ending the war without German hegemony, lofty goals to be sure, did not, of themselves, constitute work for European unity. Perhaps they were too modest, a goal too easily espied. Retinger repeatedly dated his efforts at international leftist cooperation to the end of his World War I career and exile in Mexico. His omission of the war years and the pro-Habsburg separate peace efforts do not seem to belong to the same world he is telling us about. Perhaps, but if we include the centrality of the Polish issue, we see his efforts more clearly than he did. Whatever the combination, Retinger was gradually involving himself in European politics, as some sort of elitist socialist, and perhaps as a pacifist. Retrospectively a sympathetic and thoughtful observer commented on Retinger's years in the Mexican oil business as "irrelevant."[250] In the outline he provided of his own life, near its end, he devotes little attention to Mexico.[251]

## The Moroccan adventure

An episode, difficult to integrate into Retinger's life, is his supposed gun-running to Muhammed Ibn 'Abd el-Krim el-Khettabi (Abd el-Krim) in Spanish and French Morocco between 1921 and 1926 when he was also involved in Mexican and European affairs. After World War II, Polish Communist intelligence placed him in interwar Morocco but provided no other information.[252] Stanislaw Mackiewicz, the colorful Polish journalist, claims that in his efforts, Retinger acted as a British agent, but offered no proof.[253] Another explanation is that Retinger was acting as an agent of the European Left which supported the rebellion against Spanish and French imperialism. Lacking further details, we may more easily conclude that, if he was involved at all, it was to make money.[254] Witkowski is correct in exasperatedly concluding that this episode cannot be reconstructed.[255]

## Notes

1 Pomian claims, based on Retinger, that it was Conrad's son Borys who at one point nursed Retinger back to health; *Retinger*, 49.
2 Retinger quoted in Pomian, *Retinger*, 57–58.
3 To arrange his divorce, Retinger and his wife had to become temporary Calvinist. When he rejoined the church and by which formalities cannot be reconstructed; see Dobrowolski, *Memuary*, 41. Retinger's episodic though nonetheless torrid love affair with Anderson drove him, at least once to an attempted suicide, probably in New York in the early 1920s; see John Carver Edwards, *Berlin Calling: American Broadcasters in Service to the Third Reich* (Westport, CT: Praeger, 1991), 48.
4 See "Exile in Spain," drawer 1, BPL.
5 Wiley to Winslow Memorandum.
6 Terlecki makes this claim in *Kuzynek*, 38; it is supported in Bernard Grasset to Retinger, April 30, 1918, ANK, s. 8060.
7 Pomian, *Retinger*, 65.
8 Ibid. 52; Roman Wapiński, "Retinger, Józef," *Polski Słownik Biograficzny*, Vol. 31, No. 128, 150.
9 Retinger Papers, drawer 1, "Arrival in Mexico," BPL, 16.
10 Janis P. Stout, *Katherine Anne Porter: A Sense of the Times* (Charlottesville, VA: University Press of Virginia, 1995), 49.
11 Edwards, "Anderson," 29.
12 Wiley to Winslow Memorandum.
13 Pomian Interview; cf. "The real reason I wanted to go to Mexico was because the girl I loved was in the United States, and I hoped to be able to smuggle into the United States from Mexico"; Retinger, "Exile in Spain," drawer 1, BPL; cf. Pomian, *Retinger*, 64.

14 Tadeusz Łepkowski has virtually nothing to say about Retinger in Mexico save that he was "active for several years with CROM," see his *Polska-Meksyk, 1918-1939* (Wrocław: Ossolineum, 291m. The post-war Polish Intelligence service admitted it had no specific information on this period; see Sienkiewicz, "Notatka służbowa," November 6, 1957, IPN BU 01136/69/D.
15 "Życiorys H. Retingera," by Retinger. nd, Retinger Papers, box 25a, BPL.
16 Ibid. 75.
17 The best study of CROM, though too sketchy on the earliest era is Fabio Barbosa Cano, *La CROM: de Luis Morones a Antonio Hernández* (Puebla: Universidad Autonoma de Puebla, 1980); see the remarks in Buchenau, Calles, 98–99.
18 Michael J. Gonzales, *The Mexican Revolution, 1910-1940* (Albuquerque, NM: University of New Mexico Press, 2002), 178–181.
19 Ibid. 186.
20 Donald Hodges and Ross Gandy, *Mexico 1910-1976: Reform or Revolution?* (London: Zed Press, 1979), 27, 52–53.
21 Demonized: "Luis Napolean Mornoes and the Mexican Anarchist Movement, 1913-1920," *Secolas Annols* 37 (2005), 17.
22 Retinger quoted in Pomian, *Retinger*, 69.
23 Mick Buford, "A Biography of Luis N. Morones, Mexican Labor and Political Leader," Ph.D. diss, Louisiana State University, 1971, x.
24 "A Monthly Review of Revolutionary Movements in British Dominions Overseas and Foreign Countries," April, 1920, NA, CAB 24/04, 46.
25 Retimger, *Morones*, 39–40.
26 Retinger, *Morones*, 37–38. The labor movement in Mexico was, Retinger averred, "much misunderstood," ibid., vii.
27 Ibid., 42–4.
28 Retinger, *Morones*, 44.
29 Ibid. 46.
30 Walsh, *Porter*, 142.
31 Pomian, *Retinger*, 75.
32 Ibid., 75.
33 Walsh, *Illusion of Eden*, 25.
34 Walsh, *Porter*, 26.
35 Ibid., 48. Morones flirted with the IWW; see "Monthly Review," 46. To both American petroleum interests and the American ambassador, Morones was "a Bolshevik"; see Meyer, *Mexico y Estados Unidos*, 160; Walsh, *Illusion of Eden*, 26.
36 Walsh, *Porter*, 26, 197.
37 Ibid., 197.
38 Walsh, *Porter*, 197: Retinger played the same role for Porter; see Unrue, *Porter*, 81.
39 Reiner Tosstorff, *Profintern: Die rote Gewerkschaftsinternationale 1920–1937* (Paderborn: Schöningh, 2004), 472; Janta, "Refleksye Retingerowskie (2)," *Wiadomości*, September 12, 1971, No. 1328, 3.
40 Retinger claimed that Ovey was suspicious of American intentions in Mexico; see "Oil Intrigues in Mexico." Regarding Sheffield see "America and the Americans," 26. Both in BPL. In turn the Americans had a low opinion of Ovey; see Frederick S. Hibbard to Sheffield, July 27, 1927, Sheffield Papers, Box 6, folder 55.
41 "America and the Americans," shelf 5, 25, BPL. To Morones, Sheffield was an "unyielding enemy of our country." Quoted in Melzer, "Dwight Morrow," 1:162.
42 Retinger, *Morones*, xiff.
43 J. H. Retinger, *Morones of Mexico: A History of the Labour Movement in that Country* (London: The Labour Publishing Company Limited, 1926), xv–xvi.

44 Schonfeld to Secretary of State, July 25, 1927, RG 59, 812.504/870, USNA.
45 Taft to Sheffield, nd, James Rockville Sheffield Papers, Yale: Sterling Memorial Library, Box 5, f. 53. Pomian describes Retinger as "playing an essential role" in the Mexican government, but provides no details; see Pomian's "Słowo o autorze." In Józef H. Retinger, *Polacy w cywilizacjach świata*.
46 Sheffield to N. M. Butler, nd, 3, Sheffield Papers, Box 5, f. 48.
47 Buford, *Morones*, 117. For an analysis of Sheffield's relations with the Calles government see Melzer, "Dwight Morrow," 1:159ff. For a contrast between the naïve Warren who foresaw good relations and the acerbic Sheffield, see Sister M. Elizabeth Ann Rice, "The Diplomatic Relations between the United States and Mexico, as affected by the Struggle for Religious Liberty in Mexico, 1925–1929," (Ph.D. diss., Catholic University of America, 1959), 32ff.
48 Sheffield to Taft, April 22, 1927, Sheffield Papers, Box 5, f. 53. See the discussion of Sheffield and the Mexicans in the memoirs of Gil, *Autobiografia*, 391ff.
49 See the following: Sheffield to N. M. Butler, nd, 3; William Howard Taft to Sheffield, nd; Sheffield to Taft, April 22, 1927; Sheffield to Taft, May 12, 1927 all in Sheffield Papers, Box 5, folders 48 and 53.
50 Cf. Emilio Portes Gil, *Autobiografía de la revolución Mexicana: un tratado de interpretación histórica* (Mexico: Instituto Mexicano de Cultura, 1964), 631.
51 Aleksander Janta quoted in Terlecki, *Wielka awantura*, 38.
52 The Mexicans were very sensitive about this clause; see Calles letter of September 1, 1927 which in tone and substance is quite harsh. Morrow Papers, Box 1, folder 84. Ambassador Sheffield was recalled in October 29, 1927. For a discussion see Buchenau, *Calles*, 85ff.
53 Though complicated, this is a well-known story, a handy summary is N. Stephen Kane, "American Businessmen and Foreign Policy: The Recognition of Mexico, 1920–1923," *Political Science Quarterly*, Vol. 80, No. 2 (summer, 1975), 297ff.
54 Linda B. Hall, *Oil, Banks, and Politics: The United States and Postrevolutionary Mexico, 1917–1924* (Austin, TX: University of Texas Press), 1995), 8–9.
55 See Donald C. Hodges and Ross Gandy, *Mexico, the End of the Revolution* (Westport, CT: Praeger, 2002), 42.
56 Wiley to Winslow Memorandum.
57 See the speculation in Siemaszko, "Retinger w Polsce," 59. One quite plausible source purports that Retinger and Anderson plotted Lenin's assassination in her New York apartment in the 1920s. Given Retinger's supposedly pro-Soviet sympathies, this is difficult to comprehend; see Edwards, *Berlin Calling*, 47–48.
58 FBI report, January 6, 1943, FBI, 2.
59 These letters also mention Porter to make understanding even more difficult; see Mary Louise Doherty to NN, 1923, Korespondencja Retingera ANK, pp.31–42. Doherty was the author of a series of affectionate and zany latters to Retinger in the early 1920s; see her correspondence to him of November 10, 1923, March 22, 1923 (?), and December 7, 1924 in ANK, s.8060.
60 "Oil Intrigues in Mexico," drawer 2, Retinger Papers, BPL.
61 FBI report, January 6, 1943, 3, FBI. Morones did not tell Retinger that they were wanted men; Pomian, *Retinger*, 72.
62 Ibid. 73.
63 Retinger, "Oils Intrigues in Mexico," Retinger Col., drawer 2, BPL. Mesquite apparently ripped his clothing apart.
64 See the untitled and un-dated document in Box 25A, Retinger Papers, BPL; cf. Siemaszko, "Retinger w Polsce," 59; Pomian, *Retinger*, 74.
65 FBI report, January 6, 1943, Jane Anderson Papers. FBI, Federal Bureau of Investigative Archives, FBI, 3.
66 Pomian, *Retinger*, 74.

67 Ibid. This Polish episode cannot be reconstructed; see Siemaszko, "Retinger w Polsce," 59.
68 Ibid.
69 This is Pomian's thesis repeated by Podgórski in his *Retinger*, 55.
70 Pomian, *Retinger*, 75ff.
71 Retinger, *Morones*, xv.
72 Ibid., 32.
73 See the cache of correspondence in Retinger Papers, box 15 BPL including the memorandum "Comisión de Informes y Propaganda." The memorandum "Conference on Relations between Mexico and the United States. Some of his correspondents refer to him as "Secretario de Industria."
74 Retinger kept in close touch with the British left; see the several letters in ANK, s. 8061.
75 See NN to Retinger, [1929], "Bracia Brygiewicz" and Józef Werner to Retinger, April 13, 1929, MS 1280 in Retinger Papers, box 16, BPL.
76 Ibid. The company was controlled by a Polish merchant named Juljana Brygiewicz who was Mexico's honorary consul in Warsaw and had relations with German firms as well; see "Notatka o działalność Juljan Brygiewicza," April 20, 1929, folder 1929–1930, Retinger Papers, box 16, BPL.
77 Porter at least suspected that Retinger was involved in secret activities. On October 20, 1922, she wrote to him: "I hope your errand [of which I know nothing] is successful"; Retinger Papers, box 15, BPL. By the mid-1920s they were carrying on a considerable, if wistful, romantic correspondence; see folder K, box 18, Retinger Papers, BPL.
78 Stout, *Porter*, 47, 49. In 1922 it was apparently Retinger who used his influence with Morones to get Porter a lucrative contract to stage a Mexican art exhibition in Washington Unrue, *Porter*, 92; Stout, *Porter*, 51–54. She was penniless at the time; see Porter to Retinger, Retinger Papers, box 18, BPL. Regarding the exhibit see Porter's letters to Retinger in ANK, s. 8061; Porter to Retinger, nd, Retinger Papers, Box 15, BPL.
79 Walsh, *Porter*, 26.
80 Stout, *Porter* 50. Retinger was deemed "the Austrian" in "The Dove of Chapacalco," Walsh, *Porter*, 54. Porter apparently introduced Retinger to Diego Rivera who painted a rather grotesque portrait of him, ibid.47. In a later work he is Tadeusz Mey-sort-of a Polish name; see Walsh, *Porter*, 67.
81 This account, except where otherwise notes, follows closely the presentation of Thomas F. Walsh, *Katherine Anne Porter and Mexico: The Illusion of Eden* (Austin, TX: University of Texas Press) and the much abbreviated Robert S. Wicks, and Roland H. Harrison, *Buried Cities, Forgotten Gods: William Niven's Life of Discovery and Revolution in Mexico and the American Southwest* (Lubbock, TX: Texas Tech University Press, 1999), 185–193.
82 Walsh, *Porter*, 23.
83 Ibid. 35. Fall was in favor of American intervention in Mexico and the erection of a compatible government by force; see Spenser, *Impossible Triangle*, 17; Buchenau, Calles, 85ff.
84 González was described as "the most reactionary general" in the Mexican army known for his brutalities; see Hodges and Gandy, *Mexico*, 31.
85 Porter as quoted in Walsh, *Porter*, 23.
86 Hall, *Oil, Banks, and Politics*, 48.
87 Ibid. 36. Fall was deeply involved with the plot including both American and Mexican confederates one of which was William F. Buckley, Sr., father of the famous conservative journalist.
88 "Oil Intrigues in Mexico, Retinger Papers, drawer 2, BPL.

89  Walsh, *Porter*, 36; Lorenzo Meyer, *Mexico y Estados Unidos en el conflicto petrolero (1917–1942)*. Mexico City: El Colegio de México, 1968, 100ff.
90  Spenser, *Impossible Triangle*, 29.
91  Hernández, *La CROM*, 28–29.
92  Wicks and Harrison, *Buried Cities*, 190. There is a slightly different and more plausible account in Walsh, *Porter*, 36–37.
93  Darlene Harbour Unrue, *Katherine Anne Porter: The Life of an Artist* (Jackson, MS: University of Mississippi Press). 2005, 82.
94  Ibid. 82. Journalist Paul Hanna was involved with Morones in sending Retinger to America; but the evidence for this is very poor; see unsigned note of March 3, 1921, USNA, RG 165, micro 1194; Walsh, *Porter*, 37–38.
95  Buford, *Morones*, 39–40.
96  For this colorful tale see Melzer, "Dwight Morrow," I: 99 which dates Mexican acquisition of the American documents to post-1925. Curiously, it was Retinger's friend Morones who played a central role here.
97  Pomian, *Retinger*, 80.
98  The whole episode of the planned invasion, "Plan Green" and the diplomacy of blackmail remains very murky; see Buford, *Morones*, 126–130. Retinger's role, if any, typically, cannot be reconstructed. Melzer dismisses the so-called plan; see his "Dwight Morrow, 1:89; cf. "Oil Intrigues in Mexico."
99  Pomian, *Retinger*, 81.
100  Retinger, "Jail Experiences in U.S.," sz. 2, BPL.
101  Somehow, Hanna got the letters-from Porter or Retinger. The source is unclear and even Walsh who has a firm grasp of the details, cannot answer this question.
102  Ibid.
103  Stout, *Porter*, 49.
104  Grew to Gibson, February 12, 1926, 812.202/11/10, USNA.
105  Ibid.
106  This account follows Walsh very closely; see *Porter*, 39.
107  "Jail Experiences," drawer 2, BPL, 9.
108  Walsh, *Porter*, 38. Walsh dismisses the notion of a secret Washington mission for Retinger as "fictional"; in reality it appears to be a simple and truthful summary; cf. Grew to Hugh Gibson, February 12, 1926, USNA, RG 59, 812.20211/18. Grew refers to Retinger as a "special agent for Obregon."
109  Gibson to Secretary of State, February 12, 1926, 812.202/11/10, USNA; Terlecki, *Wielka awantura*, 42–44; Pomian, *Retinger*, 84. Porter raised bail money for Retinger with the help of, mirabile dictum, Summerlin! See Walsh, *Porter*, 39.
110  Duncan Sandys contends that Retinger's arrest made him a life-long "anti-Yankee" see Dobrowolski, *Memuary*, 40.
111  As quoted in Pomian, *Retinger*, 85.
112  Walsh, *Porter*, 36.
113  Pomian, *Retinger*, 86.
114  Ibid., 85–86.
115  Janis P. Stout, *Katherine Anne Porter: A Sense of the Times* (Charlottesville, VA: University Press of Virginia, 1995), 48.
116  Just to make Retinger's politics the more confusing, he was involved in a plot to kill Lenin about this time in league with his beloved Jane Anderson see Edwards, "Anderson," 30. It is probably this ridiculous rumor that resulted in Retinger being accused of being an American spy; see Pieczewski, *Działalność*, 93.
117  See the statement by president Calles quoted in Carl Henry Marcoux, "Plutarco Elías Calles and the Partido Nacional Revolucionario: Mexican National and Regional Politics in 1928 and 1929," Ph.D. diss, University of California, Riverside, 1994, 77–78.

118 J. H. Retinger, *Tierra Mexicana: The History of Land and Agriculture in Ancient and Modern Mexico* (London: Noel Douglas, 1928), 88.
119 Retinger, *Morones*, 35. As Łepkowski rather sarcastically notes, Retinger's books on Mexico had no influence in Poland: they were not written in Polish and not without misleading arguments; see his *Polska-Meksyk*, 14. 291n.
120 Retinger, *Morones*, 50.
121 Pomian, *Retingerx*, 98.
122 Hindman, "Obregon," 157ff.
123 Holland Dempsey Watkins, "Plutarco Elias Calles: el Jefe máximo de Mexico (Ph.D. diss, Texas Technological College, 1968), 157.
124 Watkins, "Calles," 53–54. Retinger seems to have been referring to the Indian population; Retinger, *Morones*, 97.
125 See, for example, John Page to US Embassy, Mexico City, January 23, 1926; 812.20211/2, USNA, RG 59, and the report from the legation in Mexico City of March 3, 1923, 812.20211.9. USNA; cf. Hall, *Oil, Banks, and Politics*, 48.
126 Clarence Dawson to Secretary of State, January 19, 1923, RG 59 812.20211/3, USNA George T. Summerlin to Secretary of State, March 17, 1923, 812.20211/9, USNA. Apparently Morones stay in Mexico was not a happy one: Horn dates his anti-Soviet inclination to his poor treatment in the Soviet capital; see James J. Horn., "Diplomacy by Ultimatum: Ambassador Sheffield and Mexican-American Relations, 1924–1927" (Ph.D. thesis, SUNY Buffalo, 1969), 128.
127 British Legation in Mexico City to FO, December 16, 1926; Ovey to FO, December 23, 1926; Ovey to Foreign Office, January 8, 1927; Ovey to Foreign Office-reporting a revolt in Mexico City – January 5, 1927; Ovey to Austen Chamberlain, January 13, 1927; Ovey to FO, January 15, 1927; Esmé Howard to FO, January 22, 1927; Esmé Howard to FO, March 19, 1927; NN to Esmé Howard, September 28, 1927; Esmé Howard to FO, October 31, 1927 all in FO371/1191-1999, and FO 371/12000.
128 Ibid., 175.
129 Jesus Silva Herzog, *Historia de la expropriación de las empresas petroleras* (México, DF: Instituto Mexicano de Investigaciones Económicas, 1964, 63–64).
130 Pomian, *Retinger*, 85.
131 See Richard Melzer, "Dwight Morrow's Role in the Mexican Revolution: Good Neighbor or Meddling Yankee," Ph.D. diss., University of New Mexico, two. vols. 1979. Melzer does not credit Morrow with the improvement in relations, but looks to larger factors; see iI70.
132 Grew to Morrow, October 6, 1927, Morrow Papers, Box 2, folder 92.
133 Ibid., 184. The stress of constant negotiations seems to have sapped Morrow's energies: by mid-1929 he described his work in Mexico as "discouraging"; see Morrow to Senator Borah, July 10, 1929, Dwight Morrow Papers, Amherst College, Box 1, folder 53. Melzer tends to deflate Morrow's accomplishments; see Melzer, "Morrow," 1:15. There is controversy over Morrow and the Mexicans; a balanced, though older account, is Ross, "Morrow and the Mexican Revolution," 510ff. 528.
134 Ibid., 180. Regarding Lindbergh, see Melzer, "Dwight Morrow," I:215–222.
135 Retinger. "Confidential," September 18, 1957, 4; Box 25a, BPL.
136 A thorough search of these materials in the Sheffield Papers produces no trace of Retinger.
137 There is a report that Porter had an affair with Morones; see Walsh, *Porter*, 28.
138 Stout, *Porter*, 50.
139 Retinger, *Morones of Mexico*, 32ff. See also the documents in "Four Presidential Elections," Retinger Papers, Box 15, BPL.
140 Stout, *Porter*, 51.

141 Ibid., 47. Retinger apparently acted as some sort of middleman between Obregón and Porter; see Darlene Harbour Unrue, "Antonieta Rivas Mercado: Katherine Porter's Horror and Inspiration," *Journal of the Southwest*, Vol. 47 (2005), 625 n. 16; cf. Porter to Retinger, September 22, 1925, box 15, BPL.
142 Walsh, *Porter*, 24–28. Apparently, so did Porter!
143 Retinger was obviously involved in Labor politics and close to Morones: both had leftist connections. He was supposedly collecting materials for a book on labor conditions in Mexico.
144 Walsh, *Porter*, 89.
145 Retinger, "Memorandum on the North-American Mexican Controversy," nd [probably 1927], box 15, Retinger Papers, BPL, esp. 4–5.
146 Retinger, *Tierra Mexicana*, 93–94.
147 Ibid., 100–101.
148 Retinger, "Arrival in Mexico," drawer 1, Retinger Papers, BPL. Pomian tells the same story but makes the figure 300 generals; see Pomian, *Retinger*, 70.
149 Retinger's views on Mexico are quoted in Pomian, *Retinge*r, 54ff.
150 C. D. Jackson quoted in Hatch, *H.R.H. Bernhard*, 213; cf. Pomian, *Retinger*, 70.
151 The aposotolic delegate to Mexico concluded that during his Mexican stay, Retinger was a communist; see Mikołajczyk to Sikorski, Retinger Collection, 68/28, PISM.
152 Terlecki, *Kuzynek*, 44–46.
153 A good biography of Calles is Jürgen Buchenau, *Plutarco Elias Calles and the Mexican Revolution* (Lanham, MD: Rowman and Littlefield, 2007). The meaning of the Church-government war in Mexico has generated much controversy. A good introduction is Donald J. Mabry, "Mexican Anticlerics, Bishops. Cristeros, and the Devout during the 1920s: A Scholarly Debate," *Journal of Church and State*, Vol. 20 (1978), 81–92.
154 There is a useful summary of these complex events by Jim Tuck in "Plutarco Elias Called: Crusader in reverse," at http://.mexconnect.com/articles/302-plutarco-elias-called-crusader. Accessed on February 21, 2012. Retinger was not known to condemn the Church; see Podgórski, *Retinger*, 63.
155 See his nephew's reminiscences in Dobrowolski, *Memuary Pacyfisty*, 40. The American ambassador, Morrow, had similar views; see Morrow to Frank Kellogg, July 16, 1928, Morrow Papers, Box 2, folder 171.
156 Retinger, "The Religious War in Mexico," box 15, Retinger Papers, BPL.
157 Podgórski, *Retinger*, 63–64; cf. Grosbois, "Activities,"14–15.
158 Quoted in Walsh, *Porter*, 39.
159 Horn, "Diplomacy by Ultimatum," 4.
160 When Retinger provided the Mexicans with this advice is unclear; Calles favored the move by 1924 if not earlier; see Sheffield, "Memoir," 14, Box 20, Sheffield Papers.
161 "Oil Intrigues in Mexico"; Pomian, *Retinger*, 79–80.
162 Pomian, *Retinger*, ibid.
163 The 1925 Retinger oil negotiations are based, except where noted, on Terlecki, *Kuzynek*.
164 Terlecki, *Kuzynek*, 42.
165 "Jail Experiences in the U.S.," Retinger Papers, drawer 2, BPL.
166 Grew to Gibson, February 12, 1926, 812.202/11/10; Schonfield to Secretary of State, September 18, 1925, 812.20111/40.RG 59, USNA.
167 Document dated January 19, 1927, in Spanish, folder 8066, KJHR, Archiwum Narodowe w Krakowie, 38; John Page to US Ambassador in Mexico City, January 23, 1926, RG 59, 812.20211/21, USNA. Page was a reporter; Department of State to Sheffield, January 26, 1926, RG 59, 812.20211/18, USNA. Retinger's supposed denucnciations of American imperialism caused him to be monitored

by the State Department in Europe; see Grew to Secretary of State, [February 13, 1926], USNA, RG 59, micro. 274; Grew to Secretary of State, 812.20211/18, February 13, 1926, RG 59, m. 274, USNA.
168 Pomian, *Retinger*, 88.
169 Report from Mexico to Secretary of State, April 26 and April 28, 1926; 812.20211/33 and /34. RG 59, USNA.
170 E. F. Arthur Schoenfeld to Secretary of State, September 18, 1925, 812.20011/40, RG 59, USNA.
171 Schoenfeld to Secretary of State, September 18, 1926, RG 59: Internal Affairs of Mexico, USNA, 812.20211/40. Schoenfeld was not an able representative and the Mexican despised him and found him impossible to work with.
172 Sheffield to Secretary of State, February 3, 1926, 812.20211/33, RG 59, USNA.
173 Stanislaw Pestkowski to Retinger, June 18, 1925, Retinger Papers, BPL, Box 15.
174 Ciechanowski, "Retinger," 201.
175 Sheffield to Secretary of State, June 23, 1926, 872.20211/18, RG 59: Central Decimal File, Box 7883, micro. 274, USNA.
176 See Stanley Robert Ross, "Dwight Morrow and the Mexican Revolution," *The Hispanic American Historical Review,* Vol. 38, No. 4 (November, 1958), 525.
177 Pomian, Retinger, x, 85.
178 Pomian, *Retinger*, 61. Buford's detailed biography of Morones does not mention a role for Retinger in this process; see his *Morones*, passim.
179 Buford, *Morones*, 113ff.
180 Pomian, Retinger, x, 78, 61.
181 Pomian, *Retinger,* x, 78–79.
182 Pomian, *Retinger*, 60.
183 Retinger to Luigi Gedda, July 7, 1949, marked "strictment personnelle et confidentielle," in file 8064 PAU-PAN , Korespondencja Józefa Hieronima Retingera (hereafter KJHR). Some have claimed that Retinger was the main advisor on oil politics to the Mexicans; see Siemaszko, "Szara eminencja," 177.
184 Schonfeld to Secretary of State, September 18, 1925, 812.20111/40, RG 59, USNA.
185 Daniela Spenser, *The Impossible Triangle: Mexico, Soviet Russia, and the United States in the 1920s* (Durham, NC: Duke University Press), 3.
186 "Oil Intrigues in Mexico," Retinger Papers, drawer 2, 1, BPL.
187 Terlecki, *Wielka awantura*, 41–42.
188 L. W. Kendall to Retinger, July 3, 1926, file 8060, KJHR, ANK, 120; Retinger to Phillip E. Hill, folder G, box 18, Retinger Papers, BPL. He was referred to at the time as enjoying influence "in the proper circles" in Mexico; see NN Mitford to "Sir Murdoch," folder M, box 19, Retinger Papers, BPL.
189 Milford Stern to Retinger, February 19, 1927, Retinger Papers, BPL, box 15.
190 NN to Retinger, September 24, 1927; Margaret M. Green to NN, August 4, 1927: folder "Meksyk 1922–1928: Artykuły," Retinger Papers, BPL, box 15. This effort met with at least evanescent success; see NN to Retinger, July 23, 1925, Retinger Papers, box 19, folder P, BPL.
191 This is ironic – and probably explains why Retinger never was wealthy – he knew, Pomian insisted, "next to nothing about business or law," Pomian Interview.
192 See the document, signed "Salamander" – i.e. Retinger – entitled "Four Presidential Elections" which denounces American "imperialism," Retinger Papers, BPL, box 15.
193 Retinger to Lord Oliver, May 13, 1927, BPL, Box 15, BPL.
194 See for example, NN to Retinger, August 20, 1927, Retinger Papers, BPL, box 15.
195 Kendall to Retinger, October 6, 1923, file 8060, KJHR, ANK, 117.
196 Hulewicz Papers, "Wspomnienia o J. H. Retingerze," ANK.

197 See, for example, McLaughlin to Retinger, April 28 and May 9, 1926 in Folder M, Box 19, Retinger Papers, BPL; cf. Retinger to Boyer wherein he asks Boyer about what funding he has acquired; see ANK, s. 8064; "Memoir pour M. Retinger [1928]," Retinger Papers, box 15, BPL.
198 Boyer again became interested in Mexico, in conjunction with Retinger after the war; see Boyer to Retinger January 28, 1948; November 24, 1949; January 16, 1950 in Folder B, Box 18, Retinger Papers, BPL. See also his correspondence with Morones from 1944 in August–September, 1944 in Retinger Collection, PISM, folder 38.
199 Anderson had, reportedly, advocated for the Balkan states during the Paris Peace Conference, but this reference is mysterious even for her; see FBI report dated December 17, 1942, Jane Anderson Papers, FBI; she was also, shortly after World War I involved, it was rumored, "interested in promoting a movement to create a Polish Navy," see FBI report, May 3, 1943, 2, FBI. Due to the constantly reported affinity for the British by Retinger, it is perhaps noteworthy, that a witness described Anderson at this time as "British in her manner and very pro-British"; FBI report, July 19, 1945, 17, FBI.
200 "America and the Americans," Drawer 5, Retinger Papers, BPL.
201 "Memorandum pour M. Retinger," [1928], Retinger Papers, BPL box 15.
202 NN to Count de Rochefort, April 18, 1928, folder R, box 19, Retinger Papers, BPL.
203 Melzer, "Dwight Morrow," 1: 264–274. Obregón. The same is true of the British records; see FO 371/11998, NA.
204 Michel Marie Dampière to Retinger November 17, and December 18, 1928, September 5, 1930; Dampière to Retinger, June 27, 1931; see Dampière had to warn him he had enemies in both France and England; Noel Dorveille to Retinger, a large cache of letters from 1928–1930; Viggs Gandil to Retinger, April 30, 1930; Aleksander Lipiński to Retinger, July 9, 1929; s. 8060 KJHR, ANK, s. 8060.
205 Zygmunt Merdinger to Retinger, December 15, 1929, KJHR, ANK s. 8061.
206 Julian Brygiewicz to Retinger, September 11, 1929 and February 7, 1931; December 5, 1929; KJHR, ANK, s. 8060.
207 See the considerable correspondence from Jaskulski to Retinger in folder J, box 18, Retinger Papers, BPL. Again, in the Morrow Papers, which contain voluminous correspondence regarding the petroleum problem, Retinger's name does not appear.
208 Jaskulski to Retinger, January 24, and February 7, 1931; Maclenger (?) to Retinger, October 3, 1929, ibid., s. 8061.
209 "Notatki o działalności Juljana Brygiewicza," April 20, 1929 by Retinger, box 16, BPL.
210 [Retinger] to NN, 1922; Box 15, BPL.
211 Brygiewicz to NN, September 16, 1929; Brygiewicz to Retinger, April 13, 1929; in box 16, BPL.
212 There is a possibility this rather complex and incomplete note was provided by or for someone whose initials were VS, but that is only a possibility; see VS (?) to Retinger, June 18, 1930 with attached memorandum; box 16, BPL; a few hints are available in Dampière to Retinger, ND in ANK, 8060.
213 See Jaskulski's letters of February 7, 1931, April 27, 1931, June 24, 1931, July 4, 1931, July 24, 1931, August 1, 1931, August 3, 1931, August 12, 1931, August 27, 1931 in ANK, 8060. Jaskulski described financial conditions in Europe, in his increasingly pessimistic correspondence as "fatalne." For a similar report to Retinger from British sources see Maurice Bonham Carter to Retinger, January 31, 1929, ANK, s. 8061.
214 Marian Reich to Retinger, July 16, 1939, ANK, s. 8061.

215 Kazimierz Jaskulski to Retinger, January 29 and January 31, 1929, KJHR, ANK, s. 8060.
216 Francisco de A. Benavides to Retinger, August 13, September 5, September 10, and November 11, 1929; NN to Retinger, June 18, 1930; "Memorandum Relating to Mexican Government's Oil Properties"; all in Retinger Papers, BPL, folder 1929–1930, box 16.
217 Viggs Gandil to Clifford J. Cory, May 7, 1930. File 8065 KJHR, ANK.
218 Ibid.
219 Podgórski, *Retinger*, 88
220 There is a considerable correspondence in this regard which makes it very clear that by the end of 1930 the complex oil project involving Retinger had collapsed; see "folder D," box 18, Retinger Papers, BPL. For an overview of Retinger's frantic business activities see the letters from"Noel" to Retinger, folder box 19, Retinger Papers, BPL.
221 See Boris Woulbroun's correspondence with Retinger in folder R, box 19, Retinger Papers, BPL.
222 Untitled document, begins "I began my international life...," Retinger Papers, Box 25a, BPL.
223 This is Witkowski's quotation from Pomian, see the former's *Retinger*, 44.
224 Monsignore Bogoncini di Duca was the negotiator for the Vatican in the talks between Poland and Holy See, over a series of months in 1924–1925 that produced the concordat of the latter year. He is better known for having been appointed nuncio to Italy after conclusion of the Lateran Accords in 1929. He was made a cardinal in 1953. Neal Pease to author, July 3, 2012. After World War II, Retinger was involved in an effort to reconcile the Anglican Church with Rome. The details of this episode are virtually unknown see Siemaszko. "Szara eminencja," 174.
225 Retinger says virtually nothing about his approaches to the Vatican other than implying that they were ultimately successful; see his "Confidential," September 18, 1957, 4; Box 25a, BPL.
226 Quoted in Grosbois, "Activities," 15.
227 Hodges and Gandy, *Mexico 1910–1976*, 31.
228 Siemaszko, "Retinger w Polsce," 61.
229 Melzer, "Dwight Morrow," 439–449.
230 "Życiorysy J. Retingera," Retinger Papers, BPL, box 25a.
231 During World War II, Sikorski had to defend Retinger against charges of anti-Catholicism stemming from the Mexican years; see Retinger Collection, 68, teczka 79: "Materiały dotyczące biografii Józefa Retingera," PISM.
232 *Daily Herald* to Retinger, July 23, 1925, Retinger Papers, box 19, folder P. Interestingly, the *Herald* wrote to Retinger care of Morones.
233 Retinger, "My Part in the Movement for the Unity of Europe," shelf 2, ANK.
234 Ibid.
235 Study of Retinger leads to espying strange linkages: Morel was a supporter of Roger Casement; Conrad was close to Retinger; Retinger was close to Morel; Conrad supported Casement. For the Morel-Casement connection see Andre Tardieu's memorandum (June 1914), in 324 AP, André Tardieu: Guerre 1914–1918. Documents et Raports, Archives Nationales, Paris. Retinger claimed that in 1914 Asquith asked the young Pole his opinions on the Casement matter; see "London. 1914," drawer 2. BPL. Stella died in 1931 leaving Retinger with two young daughters
236 Siemaszko, *Szara eminencja*, 173; Pieczewski, *Działalność*, 73.
237 Siemaszko, "Retinger w Polsce," 59–61. Phillips was a prominent proponent of womens' issues.
238 Pomian, *Retinger*, 169.

239 Ibid., "Trade Unions," Retinger Papers, drawer 3, BPL. Retinger, "My Part in the Movement for the Unity of Europe," drawer 2, BPL.
240 Retinger, "My Part." Poles in general had no use for Bevin: in 1920 he helped organize a strike to prevent desperately needed supplies from reaching Poland during their war with the Russians; see Halik Kochanski, *The Eagle Unbowed: Poland and the Poles in the Second World War* (Cambridge, MA: Harvard University Press), 2012, 559.
241 "Trade Unions," Retinger Papers, drawer 3, BPL. Retinger paints a somewhat different picture and leaves out the notion that the labor movement would be secret in "Notes," Retinger Papers, box 25a, BPL.
242 Pomian, *Retinger*, 69–70. Benedetto Croce and Seymour Cocks were associated with this effort; see Witkowski, *Retinger*, 47.
243 See the untitled memorandum in Retinger Papers, PISM, folder 79.
244 George Hicks to Retinger, April 27, 1927; Reginald Stump to Retinger, May 24, 1927 Retinger Papers, Box 16, BPL.
245 See folder 4, Box 19, BPL, for this voluminous material.
246 Retinger to Mary Louis Doherty, April 5, 1923, Mary Louis Doherty Papers, Special Collections, University of Maryland Libraries, Hornbake Library.
247 See Retinger memorandum, file 79, PISM.
248 Retinger to Dürr [1927], box 15, BPL
249 Retinger, "Unity of Europe," Retinger Papers, drawer 5, BPL
250 See "Joseph Retinger Profile," Box 25A, Retinger Papers. BPL.
251 See "Introduction," drawer 4, Retinger Papers, BPL.
252 "Amnestia," probably reprinted from an article by Stanislaw Stroński in London's Wiadamości," IPN BU 0 1178/694 the article is dated October 25, 1950. Pobóg-Malinowski makes a passing reference to Retinger's activities in Morocco, but no more; see his *Z mego okienka*, 713.
253 Terlecki, *Wielka awantura*, 72.
254 See Stanisław Mackiewicz, *Zielone Oczy* (Warsaw: Pax, 1958), 101. For the role of the Left, see Podgórski, *Retinger*, 78. For Labourite sympathy for the Riff see the passage in Marion (Phillips?) to Retinger, nd, ANK, 8061.There is a brief letter to Retinger by his business partner Kazimierz Jaskulski, April 24, 1924, regarding getting into Riff country, and to General Lyautey but it tells us little; see KJHR, ANK s. 8060. In 1925 Lyautey was replaced in command of French forces facing the Riff by Pétain. An even more ambiguous letter regarding Riff activities was written to Retinger can be found in NN to Retinger, nd, ANK, s. 8061.
255 Witkowski, *Retinger*, 46. Pobóg-Malinowski even credits Retinger with playing "no small role" in the rebellion; see his *Najnowsza polityka*, III:148.

# 4 "I got religion"

Retinger's conversion to the cause of European unity and "world government" he ascribed to a period of "germination" from 1916–1924. He was only in Mexico from time to time, never more than several months, and managed to obtain a British visa in 1924 and the Home Office assured him that renewing it would be effortless. Thus, Retinger was free to travel about Europe again.[1] He arranged press credentials for the United States and Mexico for the "Weekly Westminster."[2] He was busy arranging commercial contacts between British firms and Mexico.[3] He embarked on what he later called his "first attempts to make the unity of Europe work."[4] He, in his words, "got religion."[5]

Disappointed with London, Retinger began commuting to Holland where he met with Edu Fimmen, a labor leader in the International Federation of Trade Unions. Retinger held him in high esteem for starting the Dutch trade unions.[6] Fimmen was concerned about rumors of a war between Poland and Soviet Russia and asked Retinger to go to Poland to discuss the matter bluntly with Prime Minister Władysław Sikorski, just ensconced in power after a tumultuous year in Polish politics.[7] Retinger's relationship with Sikorski would last until Sikorski's death in 1943 and was the most controversial, significant, and mysterious activity in Retinger's life leading to innumerable charges and endless speculation.

## Retinger and Sikorski: origins of a relationship

General Władysław Sikorski and Retinger knew each other for a long time. They probably met first in Poland in 1916. Sikorski was devotedly pursuing an effort to recruit volunteers for a Polish Legion fighting alongside Austria. This put him in conflict with the efforts of Piłsudski who was convinced that Vienna was insincere in its promises to the Poles and that more recruiting simply meant more Polish casualties without political gain. It led to a terrible contretemps.[8] It goes without saying that the Austrophile Retinger would support the Sikorski position. Retinger told Sikorski, on whose authorization is unstated, that he was representing the interests of the Poles of Britain and France.

Retinger met with Sikorski at Fimmen's urging. The conversation was wide ranging but concentrated on foreign affairs which the two found themselves in substantial agreement.[9] Sikorski supposedly told Retinger that there were some in Warsaw who favored hostilities with Russia. This disposition was, according to Sikorski, being supported by the Western powers. The general insisted that his position was different and he wanted to improve relations with Moscow. In 1925, probably as a result of these conversations, Retinger was able to arrange a meeting between the Soviet ambassador in London, Christian Rakovsky, and the Polish diplomat Aleksander Skrzyński.[10] Skrzyński supported Sikorski's pro-Russian notions although the general was no longer Prime Minister.[11] This moderation in Retinger's view of Russia stands in stark contrast to his earlier Russophobia.[12]

Retinger claimed for himself a large role in Sikorski's later wartime actions: "the main lines of many of the things he achieved and planned to do we had discussed as early as 1922, when I first became on intimate terms with him."[13] Later reports insist that Retinger introduced Sikorski to prominent Britons during the interwar period.[14] Seeking Polish reconciliation with Russia became a major reason for condemning Retinger during World War II.

## A shared conception of Europe

A willingness to work with Russia was a common thread joining Sikorski and Retinger, but this communality was complimented by many others. The Russian problem verged on the insoluble Sikorski mused: how to achieve some understanding with Moscow without risking the "Bolshevization of Europe?" It is rarely noted that, despite their conviction that Poland must find a way to work with Russia, both despised it. Retinger inherited Russophobia from his family and demonstrated during World War I, only jettisoning it when it proved disastrous for Poland's long-term security. Sikorski, for all his supposed accommodation with the Russians also despised them. He referred to them in conversations with Retinger as "oriental and barbaric" in contrast to the Poles who epitomized a "Roman western cult." Poland, not Russia was the country "on which turns the future of the world." Despite this, reconciliation was, sadly, required.[15]

Germany was Poland's chief enemy; indeed Sikorski's obsession.[16] France was a vital ally and must be courted and the countries' foreign policies work in tandem. Poland was too weak to face Germany alone. Great Britain was a country desperately important but was very reluctant to involve itself in continental affairs: more, it had a disinterest verging on dislike for Poland which was regarded as part of the barbaric east, and in the French orbit as well. This explains Sikorski's constant feelers to London, of which Retinger is the personification.[17] Both countries, however as Sikorski wrote in the 1930s were ill-prepared to face Germany militarily. In 1936 he emphasized the importance of a united Poland in a column for *Kurier Warszawski*. This stress on national unification as a preparation of foreign policy reflects the various émigré combinations which involved Sikorski, all aimed at replacing the so-called sanacja government, that is, the Piłsudskiite regime of 1926–1939, with one with a broader basis of support.

In a larger geopolitical vision, Retinger was able to convince Sikorski of the value for Poland of a European federation, something he had long advocated. The compelling reason for this vision was based on Polish necessity: caught between two much larger powers, Poland needed to be part of a continental security system.[18] Czechoslovakia received special attention, as it was the object of possible harmonious cooperation. This alone would be a revolutionary step in Polish foreign policy as Warsaw and Prague had oft been at loggerheads and the sanacja regime was known for its dislike of the Czechs.[19] Retinger speculated on the value of "smaller states" working together; a theme he later advocated during and after World War II.[20] For his part, Sikorski courted Czech leader Edvard Beneš.

## Sikorski: Retinger's hero

Sikorski had a complex path to political power. He was born near Kraków, in Austrian Poland, as was Retinger – in 1881; seven years before him. Part of the patriotic movement since early youth, he was active in the famous Polish legions during the First World War along with his rival, Piłsudski. In 1920 he played a major, indeed, decisive role in the Polish Russian War when his Fifth Army halted the Bolshevik drive north of Warsaw. He was a gifted soldier, a quality even Piłsudski acknowledged, an astute military thinker, and a man of great dignity which served Poland well. He was also vain and vengeful.

In 1921 he became the army's Chief-of-Staff. Piłsudski was by then Marshal of Poland and Head of State. The next year Sikorski moved into government as Prime Minister during the crisis following the assassination of President Gabriel Narutowicz. His term of office was short, just until 1923. By 1924 he was Minister of Military Affairs and retained this post until Piłsudski launched a successful *coup d'état* in 1926 which ended any further political career for Sikorski: again foiled by Piłsudski. Although he remained in the army until World War II, he was without assignment after 1928, the obvious sign of the Piłsudski administration's disfavor. Instead, he turned his attention to writing, much of it still worth reading, and political intrigue, little of it worth recounting.

The bond between Sikorski and Retinger established almost immediately in 1923, was reinforced according to some evidence by a strange ingredient, Freemasonry. This is certainly a controversial and mysterious topic, but shreds of evidence exist. According to one source, Retinger became a Freemason in 1918. There is evidence that he was involved with French Freemasonry in his youth.[21]

The Grand Orient of Poland lodge was ostensibly established by Retinger and a handful of others; its Grand Master was Sikorski. This in turn was a Polish affiliate of a French lodge.[22] The Grand Orient was conspicuous for its Sikorskiite nucleus.[23] In addition to Retinger this included Professor Stanisław Kot, a friend of Sikorski from Legion days.[24] This, as the argument continues, helps explain the strangely intimate bond between the two, even during World War II when Retinger was the object of ferocious criticism. Both supposedly also belonged to another secret organization, the White Eagle (Biały Orzeł), of which Sikorski was also the head, but this has left no trace.[25] Leon Mitkiewicz, friendly with Retinger and often in close contact with him, was the Chief of Polish Counter Intelligence during the war. As far as he was concerned, Retinger was a Mason *and* a member of British Intelligence.[26] Paradoxically, it was the senior Piłsudskiites who were conspicuous in their Masonic ties.[27] Thus, linking Retinger with the masons, to say nothing of the fanatical anti-Piłsudskiite Sikorski, is a difficult problem to solve. As a man of the Left, Retinger would more likely have been a Mason than a staunch rightist, but this would put him in secret league with the Piłsudskiite camp. Indeed, Retinger himself argued that it was freemasons who were responsible for spreading the theory that he was a Mason "in order to distance me from my friends."[28]

But is this all nonsense? Rather, does it have any significance? Certainly Freemasonry was a serious topic in pre-World War II Poland, and a number of prominent political and military figures were members. It should not be rejected *prima facie*.[29] Retinger, however, categorically denied the attribution or the suggestion that he belonged to *any* secret organization.[30] Perhaps the best explanation is the most obvious: Retinger told the truth; he was not a Mason. Indeed, the whole Masonic tale is probably nonsense, but it was widely believed about Retinger and another reason for his enemies to loathe him.

There is yet another bond that possibly existed between Retinger and Sikorski. An unconfirmed report argues that Retinger joined Polish counter intelligence in 1922 and British service the next year. In this context he was part of the so-called "Salamander Affair" which is unknown to subsequent researches. The other Sikorski link to Retinger outside normal channels was Retinger's supposed gun-running, first to the Berbers in the Rif revolt, as already noted, and then on a larger scale to *both* sides in the Spanish Civil War. Retinger apparently fell into serious difficulties over these escapades and only Sikorski's influence saved him. This is a fascinating link between them which has left very little evidence.[31]

## The collaboration begins

Almost immediately after their meeting, the two entered into a steady correspondence. Sikorski displayed trust and confidence in Retinger from the very beginning. For example, in summer, 1923, Sikorski requested Retinger to furnish him with a detailed report on the possibilities of Poland receiving a loan from the British.[32] In response Retinger provided Sikorski with very long memorandum which combined Polish problems with international labor issues. In February, 1924, for example, when Retinger was also deeply involved in Mexican politics and had just received a British visa, he wrote to Sikorski. At the outset he appealed to Sikorski's legendary vanity by telling him that the general's new position as War Minister made a very favorable impression in London–"especially in the Labour Party."[33] England, according to his sources in Labour had new interests in economic investment in Poland, possibly in conjunction with Russia. In his endless quest for sources, Retinger asked Sikorski to tell the Polish Military Attaché in London to be in touch with him. Intriguingly, he spoke of "their policy" regarding Russia as one of seeking cooperation.[34]

Retinger had played the key role in establishing a linkage between the British Labour Party and the PPS (Polska Partia Socjalistyczna), the Polish Socialist Party. As early as 1922, Mieczysław Niedziałkowski of the PPS asked Retinger to act as the party's representative to Labour, and abroad in general in 1930.[35] Nonetheless Retinger never joined the party; despite the fact that he was a member of its Executive Board, a curious situation. Soon at least intermittent contacts were established. Retinger wanted Sikorski to help him send PPS representatives to a major Labour meeting. Retinger attended the meetings of the Central Executive Committee of the PPS and was even a candidate for the Polish parliament, the *sejm*.[36] Retinger was in a whirlwind of activities in British Labour circles in 1924. He was, reportedly, overworked and exhausted.[37]

Retinger also established direct communication with the then Polish Prime Minister, the crafty and unscrupulous Wincenty Witos. Retinger quickly fell into a very awkward position because Sikorski had designated Retinger his representative to deal surreptitiously with British political circles, especially the Labour Party. However, Konstanty Count Skirmunt, ambassador in London, did not like Retinger's shenanigans and this led to Retinger's offer to Prime Minister Witos, to resign because he did not wish to be involved, *mirabile dictum*, in conspiratorial work![38] Skirmunt told Retinger he did not want any unofficial channels opened with British political factions and wished to keep all relations in his own hands. The whole matter was further complicated by the fact that the Prime Minister, Witos, was reportedly the object of intrigue by Sikorski from his residence in France.[39] Retinger, Sikorski's man in London, would therefore be logically mistrusted by Skirmunt, the representative of the Witos government.[40]

Thus Retinger became part of a larger chapter in Polish economics and, relatedly, politics. The Poles were seeking a major foreign loan and accompanying investment. The new Treasury Minister, Władysław Kucharski and his ridiculous companion, Ludwik M. Hammerling, were touring European capitals looking for money.[41] They did not coordinate their efforts with the Polish diplomatic representatives abroad, which understandably infuriated Skirmunt, who, by the way, did not like his superior Foreign Minister Aleksander Count Skrzyński. [42] Sikorski had nebulous "plans" of which Retinger was a part. These were surreptitious, and involved private contacts, largely with Labour, the perfect environment for Retinger. But

Labour was also involved as an active agent. Certain circles in Britain wanted to bypass official representatives, Skirmunt, and deal with unofficial channels, Retinger. However, Skrzyński left office in May, 1923, making his relationship to Retinger moot. Whether his successor, Marian Seyda, continued communication with him or not is unknown, evidence suggests not. Retinger was thus caught in an impossible situation and he blamed internal Polish politics for the problem which was probably true.

The Witos government (1923) was notoriously weak and brittle. A large loan would have been a favor in light of the barrage of criticism they were under from their critics. Retinger was briefly optimistic about the loan, but soon condemned Kucharski's ineptitude and fell into despair.[43] A scandal involving Hammerling added to the government's difficulties.[44] The Witos administration collapsed in ruins in late 1923 and Witos was out of office.

Ironically, the British Labour Party, which Retinger had been cultivating – gained a parliamentary plurality for the first time days afterwards in January 1924. Retinger was optimistic about Labour's victory, and thought it heralded much for Poland. He wanted to work, in combination with the French, to encourage Western investment in Poland and cultivate members of the new government: something Warsaw had neglected for five years.[45] Retinger arranged a busy schedule for a delegation from the PPS, Mieczysław Niedziałkowski and Zygmunt Żuławski, to meet members of the British government, MPs, and other prominent people.[46] He told them he wanted the "moral support" of Labour for the PPS.[47] The PPS representatives, met with Arthur Henderson, and Arthur Ponsonby as well as a number of prominent socialists like Sidney Webb. The Poles were assured that 50 million pounds would soon be invested in Poland.[48] Labour was already planning foreign policy before the election. The visit was a complete success and helped establish harmonious relations between the Left in both countries.[49] This, however, resulted in little subsequent help for the Poles.

Retinger also acted as an intermediary in London during Premier Władysław Grabski's soundings about a British loan. Grabski had supported, clandestinely, the Niedziałkowski-Żuławski mission in which Retinger had played a major role. He recommended fervently to Grabski that Skrzyński be restored as Minister of Foreign Affairs; it was advice which mattered.[50] It is possible that Skrzyński had worked with Retinger in 1923 causing, as we have seem problems with ambassador Skirmunt. Retinger may have worked more closely with Skrzyński than can be proven. He is credited with being the real author of Skrzyński's *Poland and Peace* (1924), a book associated with Skrzyński's address at Williams College in 1924, a claim never proven but quite possible.[51] Authorship or not, Retinger played a major role in London in 1923–1924 in being an unofficial representative of the Foreign Affairs Ministry in seeking loans for the Polish government. His influence was considerable at the top of the Ministry.

The new Grabski government was on a mission to persuade London to have greater cooperation with Warsaw. In this effort, Retinger was used to place articles in the British press. The substance of the argument was, in Marek Baumgart's words: "Present Poland as a bridge connecting the Soviet Union with the Western powers, accenting in this way the significance for Great Britain-Polish-Soviet economic cooperation."[52]

Retinger also tried to arrange for Sikorski to visit London. It was a minor disaster. The British ambassador to Warsaw, Max Muller, called on Foreign Minister Skrzyński to describe the whole effort as a "fiasco" which he blamed on "intrigue" involving Retinger and warned the minister to avoid contacts with Retinger. Sikorski's standing in London had been damaged. Skrzyński's answer was probably a surprise to Muller. The Minister said Retinger had proved of value, was useful in maintaining relations with Labour, and sometimes it was necessary to employ such channels. Skrzyński denied any official role in Retinger's efforts to arrange the meeting and doubted whether Sikorski himself knew this. It was another attempt by Retinger to increase his importance. Muller was not pleased with Skrzyński's reaction.[53] Whereas nothing immediately arose as a result courting of Ramsey MacDonald's Labour government, which fell after only nine month in office), it was developments in Poland which shattered Retinger's dreams of close Anglo-Polish cooperation.

The new Treasury Minister, after the fall of the Witos government, was the highly competent Władysław Grabski (who, as we have noted, was simultaneously Prime Minister) who also wanted to arrange a large loan in London. In these efforts he used confidential agents, including Retinger.[54] Retinger offered advice and suggested candidates for the ambassadorship to London.[55] Most of all, he furnished Grabski with an elaborate plan to change fundamentally the British approach to Poland. A mission would be created in Britain of politicians and financiers. They would study the Polish economic situation, he hoped, with positive results. He went on to note that a British loan would have to be in the form of government credit for private investment in Poland, or many direct loans. The latter, he admitted, would take a long time to prepare.[56] Grabski was open to these suggestions and realized that a broad array of channels, especially with the British Left, must be created. He was not averse to using Retinger, and others, to establish them.[57] Retinger, who unceasingly tried to promote closer British-Polish economic and political cooperation, was perfect for the job. He had many contacts on the Left, and his business adventures in Mexico brought him in touch with British banking and business interests.[58] Unfortunately, there were no results.

## The Piłsudski coup and the Sanacja government

On May 6, 1926 Marshall Piłsudski staged a successful *coup d'état* and disposed of the government of Prime Minister Witos, and seized power. He dominated Polish politics in a semi-authoritarian manner until his death in 1935. When Piłsudski had come to power he announced a revolution in Polish politics and indeed society, called the *sanacja*, a sort of moral cleansing, an ethical transformation of sordid Polish politics, a word difficult to translate and harder to understand.

Following Piłsudski's death in 1935, his epigone ruled Poland, increasingly dictatorially, until the outbreak of the Second World War. Retinger opposed the Piłsudski regime, which he exaggeratedly referred to as "semi-totalitarian,"[59] and tried to create a web of connections within Polish politics in opposition. By the late 1920s he was close to a number of Christian Democrats, moderates in the complex world of Polish politics.[60] The relationship with the left wing of the PPS was even older and, via Witos he would ingratiate himself into the rightist Peasant Party (Stronnictwo Ludowe-Piast, SL-P). As Retinger acted to build a coalition of opposition, his once close ties with the PPS weakened; he was searching for a wider series of contacts.[61]

Sikorski was aghast at the 1926 coup and condemned the PPS for its support of Piłsudski[62] Retinger was convinced that the deteriorating interest of the British in Poland was entirely the fault of Piłsudski's action.[63] He redoubled his efforts as devoted member of the opposition to the sanacja and became, in Popiel's words, a "propaganda agent."[64] His relationship with Sikorski became palpably closer.[65]

## Disloyal opposition: the Front Morges

Something called the *Centrolew* arose in Poland in opposition to the sanacja. Six parties combined to resist the government from their combination of center and Left groups hence their name *Centrolew*.[66] Retinger was a central figure in the founding of the cobbled-together party in 1929. A sanacja observer reported that: "The mainspring of the gathering was Dr. Retinger. He pushed forward the most far reaching revolutionary ideas, anarchism against the state and against the government."[67] Retinger's nephew claims that he organized Centrolew meetings but provides no details.[68]

Relations grew rapidly worse between the coalition and the Piłsudskiites. The Centrolew adopted radical tactics and called for Piłsudski's removal in the sejm. Piłsudski responded by arresting eleven of them. The arrests increased with time and reached considerable numbers by October, 1930. Opposition leaders were incarcerated under harsh circumstances in the fortress of Brześć. During their trial, Retinger "tried to gain support for the Polish political prisoners in the English press and in the House of Commons. He frequently travelled between London and Warsaw."[69] In the next parliamentary election, however, the ramshackle Centrolew gained only 17 percent of the vote and was effectively destroyed. Other means of combating the sanacja had to be found.

This proved a major development in the relationship between the sanacja and its now outraged opponents.[70] Witos and Eugeniusz Kiernik of the SL-P, Herman Lieberman of the PPS and the Christian Democrat Wojciech Korfanty fled to Czechoslovakia rather than face trial after Brześć. The result was a series of evanescent combinations of exile political opposition which never lasted or congealed.[71] Opposition politics now had a domestic as well as in émigré center.[72] Retinger acted as a perpetually-in-motion go between among those in exile. This was an odd function for Retinger who despised internal politics, though he was often caught up in them.[73] Retinger's motives were quite simple: if the Polish regime could return to a fully-functioning democracy the "psychological" effect would be "enormous" as it would be the first country to restore the rule of law.[74]

According to Żuławski, Retinger was constantly in motion between Warsaw, London, Paris, Prague and Morawa-Ostrawa meeting with Niedziałkowski, Stanisław Kot, General Sikorski, Witos, and Korfanty and arranged their meetings with European politicians.[75]

In the 1930s, a number of prominent opponents of the Piłsudski regime congregated in an unwieldy agglutination called the Front Morges from the name of the Swiss village where it was founded. It was, from the start, composed of strange bedfellows: Sikorski and Witos, who did not like or trust one another, Korfanty a political moderate and leader of the Christian Democratic Party, the PPS's Herman Liebermann, General Józef Haller, a brave soldier and charismatic leader, but a political naïf associated with the political Right. Also, Karol Popiel, a prominent Christian Democrat was also a member. Witos was the central political actor.[76] The titular head however was Paderewski though Sikorski seemed to have been the initiator.[77] He sought Paderewski's benediction and his money. Paderewski eagerly joined the group, though adding that he would prefer not to resort to violence while ousting the sanacja.[78]

Paderewski, was a gifted pianist, a hero of Poland, but an abominable politician. In 1919 he was Prime Minister of Poland, while Piłsudski held the real power as head of state. Paderewski grew to loathe Piłsudski and never forgave him for his 1919 fall from power. We have to understand that Paderewski had dreamed of leading a reborn Poland, and that mantel shrouded Piłsudski's shoulders to the maestro's eternal resentment. After Paderewski left the premiership, he went into bitter exile in Switzerland.

Briefly, the political Right in Poland, the now quite radical National Democratic Party (or *endecja* after their Polish initials for *Narodowa Demokracja*) flirted with collaboration but this infatuation faded. For the followers of the rightist Dmowski, the endecja's leader, however, the Front was too liberal and probably under Jewish influence. For the socialist Left, it was too moderate.[79] It was as well Paderewski hated the endecja almost as much as he did Piłsudski.[80] Other than Witos, the populists were conspicuous by their absence. This put Paderewski in an incomprehensible place in Polish politics: a moderate rightist, who loathed the Right and opposed the Piłsudskiites who had traditionally represented the Left but were moving right! The Front Morges was thus a confederation of the moderate Right; even the socialist Liebermann was on the Right in the PPS.[81] It was best thought of as a largely Christian Democratic coalition of big names, and little real power.[82]

The origins of the Front are unsavory. Some who would soon become members contemplated a march of Warsaw and a military coup.[83] Witos proposed an émigré opposition meeting with Paderewski, but the effort proved abortive.[84] Piłsudski's death in 1935, however, and the resultant trepidation in sanacja ranks motivated Sikorski and others to greater efforts.[85] There followed a long and complex history of minor – and some not so minor – plots and notions in opposition ranks.[86]

Sikorski met Witos in Prague on January 1, 1936. He conversation was utterly unrestrained: President Ignacy Mościcki was "a common thief"; Foreign Minister Józef Beck was a "paid German agent," as so forth. Sikorski had already met with Generals Haller and Marian Januszajtis and considered the possibility of causing a "violent upheaval" in Poland. Witos, who loathed the sanacja, was fascinated.[87] Since, in Sikorski's view, all the Polish parties were worthless or corrupt, it would be necessary to gather together a group of prominent individual actors. Sikorski, the rather slow-witted Haller, and Witos would lead the organization. Witos was apparently stunned when Sikorski argued that the coup would be in the spring if not earlier. Moreover Sikorski told Witos that he had a subvention of 10,000 zlotych a month – the source was not divulged – and was going to ask for more from Paderewski. The preamble to this was to have Witos visit the maestro.[88]

Sikorski, whose visions were always grand, even involved foreign figures. Czechoslovakia's President Edvard Beneš promised a cordial reception to the putative new government. Sikorski visited France where he supposedly convinced powerful French figures to support his plans, including World War II's ill-fated General Maurice Gamelin.[89] Sikorski had long friendly relations with the French and was a passionate Francophile.[90]

Finally Haller and Witos were on a pilgrimage to Riond Bosson, Paderewski's home in Switzerland, to seek the benediction of the maestro. After meeting for three days in February, Paderewski released a press communiqué expressing the "complete unanimity" of the participants regarding the situation in Poland. The full program of Front Morges was released in April, omitting the possible coup.[91] It emphasized national unity in threatening times. On foreign policy it was anti-German and pro-French, also mentioning favorably French clients Czechoslovakia and Romania. There was to be a new democratic government replacing the praetorians of the sanacja, whose program since 1926 was to be, at least in part, dismantled. Finally it included a series of points to stimulate the sluggish Polish economy.[92]

Informally, the Front envisioned a new government for Poland with Witos as Prime Minister as he had unmatched experience in creating and leading cabinets, and the fast aging Paderewski as president, a wholly ceremonial position, but it added great panache to the Front. The target of the Front was the Piłsudskiite government in Poland. Piłsudski had died in 1935 and he was succeeded by various combinations of his devotees. The dominant figures were the soldier Edward Śmigły-Rydz, and the chemist and politically ambitious president Ignacy Mościcki. Although exercising power only in foreign affairs, a powerful figure was also Foreign Minister Colonel Beck. The sanacja of post-1926 Poland went through a rather rapid evolution. Piłsudski and his followers had their origins on the Left. Piłsudski had founded the PPS, but once restored to power by the coup, the Piłsudskiite regime became increasingly authoritarian and rightist, virtually co-opting the ethos of its eternal opponent the politically Right, and now quite radically so, endecja. The sanacja had many enemies: the Right, a traditional opponent despite increasing similarities and the Left, which regarded it as little more than a pack of fascists, the conservatives who were not the same as the Right in the galaxy of Polish politics, the traditionally minded who felt that the morality of the sanacja was lax as some were even divorced! The Communists, of course, hated them-and all the other factions as well. Among the Front's leaders was a perfect list of anti-Piłsudskiites: Paderewski who never forgave Piłsudski, Sikorski who hated him perhaps more, Witos, whom Piłsudski had removed from power in 1926. Witos, for example would not even recognize Independence Day (November 11) because it was too closely associated with Piłsudski.[93] Of course, this large, vague, and incompetent conspiracy would have to include Retinger.

Pomian insists that Retinger played the key (istotna) role in the initial negotiations to draw the founders of the Front together. However, he admits that Retinger did not speak about this issue with him and left no relevant correspondence.[94] The first definite reference we have regarding Retinger is a note that he, in conjunction with Sikorski, had co-opted two prominent socialists into the ranks of Front supporters in January, 1937.[95] This suggests that Retinger was working closely with the Front and, as usual with Sikorski, but tells us little more. Moreover this was a year after the Front was established and long after the preliminary versions had been adumbrated. It seems that it is more realistic to date Retinger's serious role in the Front only to 1938.

By then the Front had built up a political following by co-opting prominent people from cities across Poland. This was part of the group's strategy of creating a group of worthies rather than a mass party. The inductees would be drawn from every political faction that accepted the Front's appropriate call for national unity. A formal political group, the Labor Party (Stronnictwo Pracy) was born by combining members of the moderate Right in October 1937. In Jerzy Holzer's words, the new party was born under the watchwords of Christianity, patriotism, social and political unity. The idols of the SP were Paderewski, Sikorski, Stanisław Grabski, Stroński, and Stanisław Wojciechowski, all known for their anti-Piłsudskiite disposition.[96] Holzer omits anti-sanacja passion, its driving force. Its brief electoral history was dismal.

In late February, 1938 Retinger came to meet with Witos. Witos had heard of him, he recalls, but suggests he had never met him before. He was a man used for "various unofficial missions, especially in the West." Retinger was optimistic that something could be done, though he had been inactive in the cause previously, and Witos was known for his cynicism. Poland's image, argued Retinger, had declined drastically in the West which now regarded the country as virtually uncivilized. Beck's foreign policy was leading to disaster. Within Poland the situation was also pitiable; the sanacja administration was corrupt and incompetent. Retinger had harsh words for much of the PPS leadership, "cretins" and "fools" being among them. He had various notions about combinations of the socialists and peasant parties and even criticized Sikorski for his inactivity. Retinger told Witos he was returning to London to meet with the former the British Chancellor of the Exchequer to explain to him the Polish internal situation. Witos, characteristically, said nothing: "it was none of my business," he concluded oddly.[97] Witos never liked Retinger though he availed himself of his services many times.[98]

Later in the year, the two were in dialogue about a possible farm strike, perhaps as a preamble or accompaniment to overthrowing the government. Retinger was attempting to find out how the army would react to a peasant strike and had been assured that only some of the border guards (KOP) would stand by the government, which, he noted was in a state of chaos. He put himself at Witos' disposal.[99]

Nineteen thirty-eight seems to have been a year of unusual activity for Retinger in conjunction with if not as a member of the Front. His main focus was reporting to them that London was very unhappy with Poland, especially its foreign policy under Beck. Retinger claimed that the British wanted to see the end of the sanacja regime and its replacement by something akin to the Front and attached huge importance to internal changes in Poland.[100] The British inclination to interfere in Polish politics long predated World War II.

Retinger, Witos concluded, was in close touch with members of the government, MPs, and especially Labour. Retinger was acting closely with Sikorski and the PPS's Stanisław Kot. Retinger told Witos of Sikorski's ceaseless activities to alert Europe to the pending war danger.[101] He later reported that England needed time to rearm, Hitler's seizure of Austria (the Anschluss of March, 1938) was alarming and Poland's aggressive policy towards Lithuania was considered as virtually blackmailing Europe.[102] Retinger wanted Witos to issue a statement of support to the Lithuanians, but Witos ignored it.[103] The Polish situation in Europe was grave and Retinger was pessimistic.

Nonetheless in August, 1938, two weeks after Retinger's hand-wringing, one of his friends, Mander, the MP, raised the issue in the House of Commons.[104] Retinger urged Lord Addison, a Labour peer and a specialist on agrarian affair, to come to Poland. Retinger, incidentally extended the invitation "in the name of the Peasant Party." This alone shows the power Retinger had obtained from peasant leader Witos. Addison was to "meet people" but go to Czechoslovakia first to confer with Witos and Korfanty. There would be "mass demonstrations" Retinger promised.[105]

Retinger's plan to use the British to overthrow the Polish government came to an end when the PPS's Niedziałkowski arrived in September, 1938. The PPS member assured the British that no strike was brewing in Poland and that prominent peasant leaders (i.e. Maciej Rataj) opposed one. If there was a strike, it would fail because it would be unwise under the present conditions and there was no socialist support. In fact it was only the émigré leaders who wanted one. Retinger was appalled and opportuned Witos to pressure Niedziałkowski to stop promoting these arguments.[106] By November, Retinger was in despair, admitted that Beck had support within Poland and urged Witos to do something, and stay close to the Polish border just in case.[107] The same day he made a similar proposition to Korfanty.[108]

Retinger was, in effect, asking the British to interfere in Poland's internal affairs. Thus a very dangerous relationship was begun by Retinger a year before the war commenced: Britain would be invited to solve Poland's internal political difficulties. Retinger arranged for a petition of twenty MPs to be sent to President Mościcki calling for Korfanty-Witos leadership.[109] To be sure, Poland was in a supplicant's position after the war commenced but this dependence on Britain was a very dangerous tradition.

Retinger arranged a meeting between Witos and Sikorski at Morawa-Ostrawa in Czechoslovakia in August, 1938 where a dramatic, indeed, fantastic plan was discussed, though Retinger's role in its formulation cannot be gauged. Witos was to issue a ringing declaration and then return to Poland from Czech exile. Sikorski would prepare the ground in Poland. Witos obviously, blamed Retinger for this whole plan which he rejected. Witos was warned by prominent Polish socialists that Retinger was unreliable and probably a rogue (łobuz).[110]

Despite this, Witos came to value Retinger, noting that his political predictions often proved accurate. As 1938 progressed, Retinger met repeatedly with Witos, and they exchanged frequent letters and phone-calls. Witos praised Retinger's' perspicacity, and awaited his reports with anticipation.[111] Witos, at least, regarded Retinger as an important, though probably ancillary figure in opposition politics. We may hazard the opinion that Retinger was closer to Witos in 1938 than he was to Sikorski.[112] The latter's nasty comment to Witos about Retinger's reliability is yet another demonstration of Sikorski's very sensitive *amour propre*.

Retinger was predicting the outlines of the approaching war. Poland had alienated Britain and could not expect help from that quarter. Beck wanted to return Danzig (Gdańsk) to Germany for the sake of good relations as a war would ensue between Germany and Russia with Poland on Germany's side. The situation was deplorable and the Poles had much to blame for not overthrowing the government in Warsaw.[113]

Retinger hatched a rather dramatic plan. He would arrange a secret conference with powerful English leaders. Korfanty said he would come if the conference could be organized. Socialist Niedziałkowski did as well. In a particularly bold move, Retinger promised to use his influence in England to insert clauses in the loan the Polish government was seeking in London to insist the money would be dependent on Britain insisting on a more representative government in Warsaw, having London, in effect, lead the Front's program. This was so audacious a plan that Retinger asked Witos's advice which, we have no record of. Retinger claimed the support of "several dozen" British politicians, and urged the Poles at least to "embarrass" the Warsaw government.[114]

Probably acting on his own, Retinger launched another, or perhaps, linked, bold initiative, a plan to grant favors to important circles in London, whose names were unknown, that they should assist Sikorski and Witos in seizing power in Poland. Retinger assured Sikorski that he was highly thought of in London. Sikorski's response to Retinger's was merely a tut-tutting about not acting rashly: not a denunciation of violent undertakings. This episode demonstrates that on the eve of the war Retinger was already acting as Sikorski's representative to powerful circles in London.[115]

Frantically, he had Cripps give him a letter of introduction to influential Anthony Eden – (Foreign Secretary until February, 1938),[116] and carried on "ceaseless conversations" with politicians and journalists. His conclusions were that British public opinion sided with Poland in a possible war with Germany, that the United States would enter soon, and that the Soviets had no hostile plans regarding Poland, and a government of national unity would engender Western support.[117]

Soon he insisted that the situation was even worse, if that were possible. The Poles were pro-Western and anti-German, a cliché. The Front opposition was important, dubious. A movement for national unity was coming probably the work of the Front, no. Britain should refuse any support unless a government of national unity was installed, virtually an act of treason by Retinger.[118] Shortly thereafter Retinger added a few additional observations: all British politicians wanted a change in Poland. Retinger claimed he heard Eden say this to Foreign Minister Viscount Halifax. But they shied away from actively helping the opposition to overthrow the Polish government.[119]

At the end of December 1938, Retinger had already sent a very pessimistic report saying that Poland's fate was pre-ordained. The West would do nothing and the Germans would do as they please. The only hope was getting rid of the sanacja. Danzig would return to Germany within a year. Retinger, by 1939, was trying to peddle a more aggressive version of the Front.[120] He wrote to Sikorski in mid-March:

> Would it not be time to put forward an initiative about the creation of a Committee of Defense and National Unity, concluding all the former premiers from pre-coup [i.e. pre-1926] and the chief Polish notables. Perhaps at this moment of crisis has matured enough to that four

opposition parties; acting with their collective force would be able to issue a kind of manifesto for national unity and discipline.[121]

Retinger would return to Poland to put himself at the disposal of Witos, Korfanty, and Sikorski. After all, in England all the talk was about the necessity of Sikorski's and Witos's return to power. This would prompt the greatest possible help from Britain.[122] He had prepared a lengthy, March, 1938, memorandum analyzing the current state of internal affairs in Poland. It was damning. The sanacja was "in a complete state of collapse," it had no policy, no ideology, nor did public opinion support it. Indeed 90 percent were opposed. All parties were in opposition.[123] However, if the sanacja were to go, and Sikorski and Witos were in power, a major loan could be expected from Britain because the current regime was disliked abroad.[124]

A few days later Retinger continued this bombardment of Sikorski. Retinger had told Lord Oliver of the Board of Trade that Beck was unpopular and if Britain were to help Poland, Beck would be replaced by government of a national unity. He outlined for Oliver the state of the opposition parties which he assured him were trying to establish a government of national unity under Witos and Sikorski. If Beck failed to act accordingly, London should make a public statement as regards its attitude towards him. If the British government must be publicly "polite," it could at least be "cold." Stanley promised to raise it in parliament.[125] Retinger tried to arrange, via Cripps, an invitation for Sikorski to visit London. He failed. Perhaps the British were less interested in overthrowing the Polish government than Retinger had imagined.[126]

Korfanty wrote to Retinger what could only be described as sympathetic letters.[127] And Sikorski with Retinger came to Paris and then to Prague (Witos).[128] On the eve of the war, Retinger was flitting about trying to overthrow his own government with foreign help.

## Notes

1 Home Office to Marion Phillips, March 7, 1924, folder P, box 19, Retinger Papers, BPL.
2 NN Fuller to Retinger, Retinger Papers, folder P, box 19, BPL.
3 See the correspondence in Retinger Papers, box 15, BPL.
4 Retinger Papers, "Introduction," drawer 4, BPL.
5 "My Part in the Movement for the Unity of Europe," drawer 2, Retinger Papers, BPL.
6 "Trade Unions," Retinger Papers, shelf 3, BPL. An anti-Retinger source claims that the Labour Party grew disenchanted with Retinger and he felt it necessary to move on; a possibility: he was always feuding with various factions. See, Hulewicz, "Wspomnienie o J. H. Retingerze," ANK.
7 Retinger, "Polish Relations with the USSR and the Polish-Russian agreement of 1941," Retinger Papers, BPL, drawer. 2.
8 For the general question see Suleja "Spór."
9 Pomian, *Retinger*, 71–72.

10 See Piotr Wandycz, *Aleksander Skrzyński: Minister Spraw Zagranicznych II Rzeczypospolitej* (Warsaw: Polski Instytut Spraw Międzynarodowych, 2006), 97.
11 "Polish Relations with the USSR," Retinger Papers, drawer 2, BPL.
12 By the 1920s, exactly when is unclear, Retinger genuinely feared a Polish-Russian war which he regarded as a "cataclysm" for Poland. Poland would probably win, but alienate the West in the process and acquire territories populated by minorities. Here Retinger disclosed that he was not a supporter of the restoration of a pre-partition Polish east in some sort of federal relationship with Poland, the quintessence of Piłsudskiite federalism. See Retinger's "The Guardians of Peace and their Victims: The Russo-Polish Incident," drawer 2, BPL. Retinger encouraged any pro-Russian inclination of Sikorski's before the war; see Retinger, "Political Relations with the USSR and the Polish-Russian agreement of 1941," Retinger Papers, drawer 2, BPL.
13 "Introduction," Retinger Papers, drawer 3, BPL.
14 "Notatka," June 15, 1966, IPN BU 0 1178/694.
15 Retinger, "Are the Poles Necessary," drawer 1, BPL.
16 Many of these appear in the important collection of Marek Jabłonowski and Zbigniew Anculewicz, eds., *Generał Władysław Sikorski. Publicystyka generała Władysława Sikorskiego w łamach "Kuriera Warszawskiego" w latach 1928–1939*," Warsaw: Oficyna Wydawnicza ASPRA, 1999, 90.
17 Pomian, *Retinger*, 74–75.
18 Grosbois ("L'action," 64) argues that the federal concept was Retinger's and he convinced Sikorski of its merits; cf. Antoni Marszałek, *Z historii europejskiej idei integracji międzynarodowej* (Łódź: Wydawnictwo Uniwersytetu Łódzkiego, 1996), 37. Pomian shares the view that Retinger expanded Sikorski's geo-political horizons and was the source of his thinking in federative terms; Pomian Interview. See also Retinger's "My Part in the Movement for the Unity of Europe," Box 20, Retinger Papers, BPL. Szerer, a Polish theorist of federation simultaneously stressed two points: Poland was too small to exist outside a federation, but perhaps the major powers did not wish to include Poland within their putative federations; see his *Federacje*, 10–11, 37.
19 Unless otherwise noted this constitutes a compendium of Sikorski's journalistic essays on foreign policy appearing in *Kurier Warszawski* in the late 1930s; see Sikorski Papers, Collection 1, f. 1a, PISM.
20 "Notes on Recent European Politics," July, 1938, s. 8067, KJHR, ANK, s. 8067.
21 Podgórski, "Retinger," 57–59, 342–353. Podgórski is convinced that Retinger was a Mason.
22 The existence of multiple competing lodges and the consequences for politics is absolutely bewildering; see Tadeusz Katelbach, "Loże," *Zeszyty Historyczne*, 3 (1963), 199–208.
23 Leon Chajn, *Polskie wolnomularstwo 1920–1938* (Warsaw: Czytelnik, 1984), 135.The émigré press named Retinger, Litauer, Kot and others as being Grand Orient members supportive of and supported by Sikorski. Putting aside the Masonic rubbish this does suggest close relations; see British Intelligence files NA "Stanislaw Kot," February 12, 1943, KV2/3429 Stanislaw Kot. At about the same time the British surveilled a Retinger-Litauer-Kot "faction"; see "Polish M. of T.," and "Extract," June 6, 1941, NA, KV2/3429.
24 Tadeusz Pawel Rutkowski, *Stanislaw Kot 1885–1975: Biografia polityczna* Warsaw: DiG, 2000, 112–113. To his credit, Rutkowski admits that these attributions are very amorphous and drawing conclusions is dangerous; cf. Stanislaw Kot, *Listy z Rosji do Gen. Sikorskiego* London: Jutro Polski, 1956, 548–549 Katelbach, "Loże," 205, 207.
25 "Notes,"Retinger Papers, box 25a, BPL. See also Rutkowski, *Kot*, 112.
26 Mitkiewicz, *Z Gen. Sikorskim*.

27 See Neal Pease, *Rome's Most Faithful Daughter: The Catholic Church and Independent Poland, 1914–1939* (Athens, OH: Ohio University Press, 2009), 80.
28 Thierry Grosbois, "The Activities of Józef Retinger in Support of the European Idea: 1940–1946," in Thomas Lane and Marian S. Wolański, eds., *Poland and European Unity: Ideas and Reality*. Wrocław: Wydawnictwo Uniwersytetu Wrocławskiego, 2007, 15.
29 Pease, *Rome's Most Faithful Daughter*, 80–81. In 1949 Retinger declared that the Masons were pursuing a "campaign against" him; see Retinger to Luigi Gedda, July 17, 1949, s. 8064, KJHR, ANK; Jędrzej Giertych regards Retinger as closely associated with the Masons without being a member: a reasonable theory; see "O Józefie Retingerze," *Komunikaty towarzystwo im. Romana Dmowskiego*, I (1970–1971), 373–374. Retinger was also accused of being a Jewish mason, a member of the B'nai B'rith – dubious.
30 Thierry Grosbois, "L'action de Józef Retinger en faveur de l'idee européenne 1940–1946," *European Review of History*, 6 (1999), 60. During the Second World War, some in American Polonia distrusted the Sikorski government for its reputation of Masonic penetration; see Pestkowska, *Za kulisami*, 119n.; Retinger wrote later: "I never had any contacts with the Freemasons' community," Retinger, "Domestic and External Politics," drawer. 1, BPL.
31 "Notes, shelf 25a, Retinger Papers, BPL. Supposedly in the Spanish affair he worked with Tadeusz Katelbach. Davies contends that Retinger was in Spain during the Civil War, but offers no evidence; see *Rising '44*, 53. Communist era intelligence on Retinger insists that Retinger was involved in large-scale arms smuggling to the Spanish Republicans which, by some means fell into Francoist hands. The whole issue including suggestions of a role to British Intelligence or Freemasonry is very mysterious, and lacks supporting evidence; see "Retinger," IPN, BU 01222/593/D.
32 Sikorski to Retinger, August 22, 1923, Retinger Collection, PISM, folder 1.
33 Retinger to Sikorski, February 25, 1924, Retinger Collection, 1, PISM.
34 Ibid., Pomian, Retinger, x, 135. Retinger mentioned the PPS members he wanted by name Żuławski and Niedzialkowski. They attended the conference and, at least according to Retinger, made a favorable impression and met a number of prominent Labourites. See Retinger to Sikorski, April 4, 1924, Retinger Collection, no. 4, PISM. Pomian insists that Retinger played a large role in Polish-British relations in the interwar era; see Pomian, *Retinger*, 74; Niedziałkowski to Retinger, February 13, 1924, Retinger Collection, 68/8.
35 For the original appointment in the 1920s see Niedziałkowski and Barlicki to Retinger, February 16, 1922(?), in Retinger Papers, Box 7, coll. 68, PISM. He took part in the PPS executive Committee's meetings from 1924–1928 and was even considered a candidate for election to the sejm; Pomian, *Retinger*, 96. See Retinger's credentials of June 5, 1930. His instructions on how to perform were given only orally by Niedziałkowski. See KJHR, folder. 8066, 38, ANK. Ironically, Retinger was never a member of the Party; see Andrzej Suchcitz, "Listy Wojciecha Korfantego do Józefa Retingera," *Zeszyty Historyczne*, 73 (1985), 222; Retinger Papers, "Domestic and External Politics," shelf 1, 8, BPL. Retinger was also purportedly close to Herman Lieberman and Kazimierz Pużak, and was regarded by them to have served the PPS well in Great Britain; see "Dr. Józef Retinger," October 29, 1952, IPN, BU 01222/593/D.
36 Pomian, *Retinger* 71.
37 See the scattered correspondence throughout Box 8 of the Retinger Collection, February 15, 1923 68, PISM.
38 Retinger to Sikorski and Skrzyński, ND, Retinger Collection, #4, PISM; Retinger to MSZ, May 5, 1923, Retinger Collection, #6; Retinger to Witos, May 5, 1923 Retinger Collection, #7, PISM.

39 This is the conclusion of Henryk Bułhak based on French sources; see his "Działalność Władysława Sikorskiego w dziedzinie polityka zagranicznej w latach 1922–1925," in Henryk Bułhak *et al.*, eds., *Z Dziejów polityka i dyplomacji polskiej* (Warsaw: Wydawnictwo Sejmowe, 1994), 258.
40 Roniker to Kauzik, February 14, 1923, Kauzik Papers, collection 10, reel 30949, AAN.
41 For the Kucharski-Hammerling peripatations see M. B. B. Biskupski, *The Most Dangerous German Agent in America: The Many Lives of Louis N. Hammerling* (DeKalb, IL: Northern Illinois University Press, 2015).
42 [Retinger] to Sikorski and Skrzyński, nd, Retinger Collection, #43; Retinger to "Prince," Retinger Collection, #8, PISM.
43 A. Woytkiewicz to Retinger, October 5, 1923; Retinger to Witos, August 24, 1923 [Retinger] to NN, Retinger Collection, # 19, # 14, #6; NN to NN, September 30, 1923; Retinger Coll, Box 10, PISM.
44 See Biskupski, *The Most Dangerous German Agent in America*. (DeKalb, IL: University of Northern Illinois, 2015).
45 NN to Witos, March 12, 1924, Retinger Collection, #19 Retinger to NN, May 5, 1924, Retinger Collection, #44, PISM.
46 Żuławski and Retinger had been friends for some time, and Retinger's efforts with Morones in labor politics had brought the two Poles closer; "Trade Unions," Retinger Papers, BPL, shelf 3. Both Poles stayed in touch with Labour circles at least until 1927 if not later; see Retinger to Zygmunt [Niedziałkowski], September 24, 1927, ANK, s. 8063.
47 Retinger to NN, February 15, 1923, Retinger Collection, #4, PISM. See the packet of documents in Retinger Collection, # 32; [Retinger] to NN, [ca. March 25, 1924], Retinger Collection, #66, both in PISM; Nowak-Kiełbikowa, *Polska-Wielka Brytania w dobie zabiegów o zbiorowe bepieczeństwo w Europie 1923–1937* (Warsaw: Państwowe Wydawnictwo Naukowe, 1989), 61.
48 [Retinger] to NN, February 15, 1923, Retinger Collection, PISM, 4.
49 The conservative Adam Roniker also went on a visit to London seeking funds. Retinger apparently was useful in his contacts as well; but the details are not known. See Wandycz, *Skrzyński*, 91.
50 Ibid. 90–91 [Marion Phillips] to Retinger, November 16, 1925, ANK, s. 8061.
51 Wandycz, *Skrzyński*, 41, 83; Pobóg-Malinowski, *Z mojego okienka*, 714.
52 Marek Baumgart, *Wielka Brytania a odrodzona Polska 1923–1933* (Szczecin: Uniwersytet szczececiński, 1990), 34, n. 52. I am grateful to Piotr S. Wandycz for bringing this material to my attention.
53 Max Muller to Gregory, November 3, 1924, FO 688-14/49, NA.
54 Maria Nowak-Kiełbikowa, *Polska-Wielka Brytania*), *W dobie zabiegów o zbiorowe bezpieczeństwo w Europie, 1923–1937* (Warsaw: PWN, 1989), 53.
55 Ibid., 55.
56 Ibid.
57 Ibid., 60–61, 155.
58 Retinger to Sikorski, February 25, 1924, Retinger Collection, 68/1, PISM.
59 "Introduction," Retinger Papers, drawer 4, BPL.
60 Bożena Krzyobłocka, *Chadecja 1918–1937* (Warsaw: Książka i Wiedza, 1974), 164.
61 Aleksander Janta, "Refleksye Retingerowskie (2)," *Wiadomości*, No. 1328 (September 12, 1971), 3.
62 Sikorski to Retinger, July 18 and July 26, 1928, Retinger Collection, PISM , 68/1. Curiously, Sikorski went out of his way not to criticize the Marshall directly. See Antony Polonsky, "Sikorski as Opposition Politician, 1928–1939," in Sword, *Sikorski*, 44–46. He once referred to Piłsudski as a "genius." See ibid., 58.

63 Retinger to Zygmunt [Żuławski?], November 4, 1927, Retinger Collection, # 9, PISM; Retinger to Zygmunt [?], September 24, 1927: The Left in England neither cared about nor understood Poland, Retinger lamented.
64 Terlecki, *Wielka awantura*, 53–54.
65 Janta, "Refleksye Retingerowskie," 3.
66 There are two standard histories of Centrolew; viz. Stanislaw Piotr Stęborowski, *Geneza Centrolewu, 1928–1929* (Warsaw: Książka i Wiedza, 1960), and the broader work by Stanisław Lato, *Ruch Ludowy a Centrolew* (Warsaw: Ludowa spółdzielnia wydawnicza, 1965. Both are tendentious and neither so much as mentions Retinger.
67 Witkowski, *Retinger*, 36 idem, *Ojcowie*, 44–45; Podgórski, *Retinger*, 80.
68 Dobrowolski, *Memuary*, 42. For Retinger's involvement in 1929 Polish politics see the brief remarks in Bożena Krzyobłocka, *Chadecja, 1918–1937* (Warsaw: Książka i Wiedza, 1974), 164.
69 Andrzej Suchcitz, "Listy Wojciecha Korfantego do Józefa Retingera," *Zeszyty Historyczne* 73 (1985)," 222.
70 See Henryk Przybylski, *Front Morges* (Toruń: Marszałek, 2007), 14. Przybylski published an earlier-and somewhat different version of his book in 1972. All references to his work will be based on the newer edition unless otherwise noted. For Centrolew see the succinct remarks in 172–175; R. F. Leslie, ed., *The History of Poland since 1863* (Cambridge: Cambridge University Press, 1980), 172–175.
71 Pomian insists that Retinger was a major figure in these various combinations. There is little evidence to support this. On the other hand these were highly secret meetings and left no records; Retinger was characteristically reticent to provide details of his political machinations. See Pomian, *Retinger*, 81–82. Żuławski, of the PPS, also gives Retinger credit for these arrangements; but admits his knowledge is slim; see a quotation from Żuławski in Pomian *Retinger* 82.
72 Retinger claims he pressured the British to aid those arrested; he provides no details; see Box 25a, folder "Życiorysy Józefa Retingera," 6, Retinger Papers, 6, BPL.
73 See his "Domestic and External Politics," drawer 1, BPL.
74 Retinger to Witos, March 9, 1938 in Kisielewski, "Z Archiwum," 92.
75 Żuławski quoted in Pomian, *Retinger*, 82; Retinger aided those driven out of Poland by the sanacja regime, see Pieczewski, *Działalność*, 73.
76 Antoni Czubiński, *Centrolew: Kształtowanie się i rozwój demokratycznej opozycji antysanacyjnej w Polsce w latach 1926–1930* (Poznań: Wydawnictwo Poznańskie, 1963), 265.
77 Waldemar Bujak, "Stronnictwo Pracy-Partia Generała Władysława Sikorskiego," *Przegląd Polonijny*, Vol.7, No. 2 (1981), 89–90.
78 The fullest account of these negotiations is H. Przybylski, *Front Morges* (Warsaw, 1982). There is a very good –and very brief– summary in Henryk Lisiak, Paderewski: *Od Kuryłowki po Arlington* (Warsaw: SAWW, 1992), 170ff.
79 For some intriguing remarks about the Front and Jewish issues see Karol Popiel, *Polityczne Wspomnienia*, (Warsaw: Ośrodek dokumentacji i Studia Spółecznych, 1983), 90–91.
80 Adam Zamoyski, *Paderewski* (New York: Atheneum), 1982, 14.
81 The leadership of the PPS did not follow Lieberman's position; Przybylski, *Paderewski*, 282.
82 The constituents of the Front are discussed in great detail in Przybylski, *Front Morges*.
83 Sword, *Sikorski*, 60.
84 Przybylski, *Front Morges*, 29–30.

85 Ibid., 30ff.
86 See Wincenty Witos, *Moja tułaczka* (Warsaw: Ludowa spółdzielnia wydawnicza, 1967), 54–56.
87 Ibid., 61; Polonsky, "Sikorski as opposition politician," 60–62.
88 Witos, *Moja tułaczka*," 62–63.
89 Ibid., 62–63.
90 Polonsky, "Sikorski as opposition Politician," passim.
91 For the initial actions of the Front, a valuable source is Witos, *Moja tułaczka*, 56ff.
92 Pomian insisted that Retinger was the *spiritis movens* for the Front; there is no evidence.
93 See M. B. B. Biskupski, *Independence Day: Myth, Legend, and the Creation of Modern Poland*. (London: Oxford University Press, 2012).
94 Pomian, *Retinger*, 104–105.
95 Przybylski, *Front Morges*, 120.
96 Jerzy Holzer, *Mozaika polityczna Drugiej Rzeczypospolitej*. Warsaw: Książka I Wiedza, 1974, 422ff.
97 Witos, *Moja tułaczka*, 460–461.
98 Dobrowolski, *Memuary*, 43.
99 Retinger to Witos, June 28, 1938, Retinger Collection, 68/14, 10, PISM.
100 Retinger at this time wrote a very odd piece in *Wiadomości* title "Imponderabilia and Tabu" (the Impoderable and the Taboo) in which he discussed a Polish foreign policy which was radically different from that then promoted by Sikorski, He saw the post-World War I ascendancy of France "artificial" and the inevitability of German recovery. Both Britain's Macdonald and Sikorski-Piłsudski (!) in Poland were right to try to come to terms with Germany and free Poland from the status of a "satellite of France." If we contextualized this to the pre-sanacja era it would be in accord with some of Sikorski's views, though the positive reference to Piłsudski, as well as the disparagement of France were odd positions in 1938; see the December, 1938 issue of the journal.
101 Retinger to Witos, June 28, 1938, in Kisielewski, "Z Archiwum," 94.
102 Ibid., 469, 563. The Polish-Lithuanian imbroglio of 1938 is rather complex: Poland insisted in 1938 that normal diplomatic relations be created with Poland by Kaunas. But the Lithuanians were given only forty-eight hours to reply and in the meantime Polish troops were mobilized. The very sensitive Wilno issue – a Polish city that had been the historic capital of Lithuania – was menacingly in the background. The Polish insistence on the establishment of diplomatic relations was part of Beck's plan to create a bloc of states running from south to north across central Europe which would be able to defend itself against either Germany or Russia. The Western powers neither supported or even understood this policy and saw the whole issue as Warsaw blackmailing a small state. This summary is based on Anna M. Cienciala, *Poland and the Western Powers, 1938–1939: A Study in the Interdependence of Eastern and Western Europe* (London: Routledge & Kegan Paul, 1968), 48ff.
103 Ibid.
104 Parliamentary Debates: House of Commons Official Report, Vol. 333, No. 152, Wednesday, July 20, 1938 (London: HMSO, 1938). Not satisfied with this, Retinger tried to coax other MPs to raise the question as well; see Retinger to "Miss Hill," July 25, 1938 Retinger to Witos, August 11, 1938; Hill to Retinger, September 1, 1938; Hill to Retinger, September 15, 1938; Retinger Collection, col. 68/26, 31, 35, PISM.
105 Retinger to Lord Addington, March 31, 1938, Retinger Collection, 68/22, PISM.
106 Retinger to Witos, September 10, 1938, Retinger Collection, 68/38, PISM.

107 Retinger to Witos, November 1, 1938, Retinger Collection, 68/44, PISM.
108 Retinger to Korfanty, Retinger Collection, 68/45, PISM. As this file shows, the triangular correspondence among Retinger, Witos, and Korfanty was very voluminous in this period.
109 Hill to Retinger, July 14, 1939, BPL, 6819, folder 16.
110 The two critics were Kot and Rataj; see *Moja tułaczka*, 566 584. Sikorski, *mirabile dictum*, made similar remarks to Witos; ibid., 581.
111 Retinger enlarged his radius of information gathering and influence extending to Hungary by mid-1938.
112 There is a report that Witos, Sikorski, and the PPS's Lieberman (also a member of Front Morges) paid Retinger for his services; see 'Z papierów Jana Hulewicza: Wspomnienia o J. H. Retingerze," ANK, s. 10371. Retinger once referred to Witos as a "legend"; see Retinger to Witos, November 11, 1938; Kiselewski, "Z Archiwum." 100. He wanted, more than anything, to have Witos return to power in Poland; see Retinger to Witos, December 20, 1938; Kisielewski, "Z archiwum," 101.
113 Retinger to Witos, December 20, and 27, 1938; Retinger to Korfanty, December 27, 1938 (twice), Retinger Collection, 68/56, 57, 58, 59, PISM.
114 Retinger to Witos, July 6, 1938; Retinger to Korfanty, March 9, 1938; Retinger to Witos, March 17, 1938; Retinger to March 20, 1938; Retinger to Witos, March 30, 1938; Retinger Collection, 68/16. 8, 13, 15, 21, PISM.
115 Dymarski, *Stosunki wewnętrzne*, 22, 70.
116 Hill to Retinger, July 22, 1939, Retinger Collection, 68/24, folder 16, PISM.
117 Retinger to NN, August 26, 1939, Retinger Collection, 68/27, folder 16, PISM.
118 "Memorandum on the Political Situation in Poland," March, 1939, Retinger Collection, 68/13, folder 16, PISM.
119 Untitled memorandum, April 13, 1939, Retinger Collection, 68/15, folder 16, PISM.
120 Witos, *Moja tułaczka*, 498 595.
121 Retinger to Sikorski, March 17, 1939, Retinger Collection, 68/1, PISM.
122 Ibid.
123 "Observations on the Present Political State of Poland," Retinger Collection, 68/23, PISM.
124 Retinger to Sikorski, March 14, and March 16, 1939, Retinger Collection, 68/1, PISM.
125 Retinger to Sikorski, March 22, 1939, kol. 68/1, nr. 39, Retinger Collection, PISM.
126 NN to Retinger, April 21, 1939, Retinger Collection, 68/2, PISM.
127 See "Listy Wojciecha Korfanty do Retingera," 68/3, Retinger Collection, PISM.
128 Sikorski to Retinger, March 23, 1939, Retinger Collection, 62/8, PISM.

# 5 The war begins

Retinger's diagnosis of the state of European affairs as the war commenced rested on the conviction that Europe had lost its original unity as a result of the following: colonial imperialism and the discovery of sources of wealth beyond the borders of the continent; the end of religious unity, and the development of nationalism. This led to faith in the state as the central social institution, and the growth of an individualistic point of view of state standing in opposition to humanitarianism.[1] These led to rivalry and war, which would ultimately be ruinous to European civilization. The solution was a United States of Europe which required a remaking of the European world.

The key to this problem, as Retinger adumbrated in Britain, was essentially economic rather than political.[2] The aggressive behavior of Nazi Germany and a fascist Italy resulted from economic differences among the powers: Great Britain, the United States and France, plus their satellites, on the one hand, and the autarky of Germany, Italy and Soviet Russia on the other. It was not a struggle between democracy and fascism that lay at the root of the current conflict; it was economics. The Western nations must admit Germany and Italy "to their monetary system."

The Germans attacked Poland early in the morning of September 1, 1939 and made rapid headway against Poland's overstretched, outnumbered, and weakly armored opposition. After days of fighting, withdrawal, with elements of chaos and demoralization, ensued. Soviet Russia invaded from the east on September 17. This repulsive "stab-in-the-back" was arranged by the Hitler-Stalin pact of late August which partitioned Poland by secret accord before the war commenced. The Poles were virtually defenseless from such an assault, and the Russians stormed across eastern Poland. The government in Warsaw rushed to the southeastern corner of the country. It shared there a common border with Romania and a prior agreement allowed the Poles *droit de passage* to escape across Romanian territory to the Black Sea coast where they would, ostensibly, board allied ships for evacuation. However the Romanians neither honored their prewar agreement to come to Poland's defense, nor the more important promise to allow the Poles an escape route. A large number of them were trapped in Poland, interned by the Romanians, or able to sneak out only after harrowing adventures.

Even before the invasion the restless and ambitious Sikorski convened a meeting of Front worthies to denounce the defensive plans of the government.[3] From the very outset Sikorski predicted a rapid defeat for Poland, but after September 3, when Britain and France belatedly declared war, he argued that the Western powers would eventually prevail over the Germans. As for himself, he noted that perhaps he should like to die on the battlefield.[4] Obviously, he was under considerable strain and was immediately rejected by his own government for service, and was long-enmeshed in an opposition movement of uncompromising hostility.

Sikorski, who was without an assigned command for years, was still technically a serving officer in the Polish army. He immediately placed himself at the disposal of the Chief of State, Śmigły-Rydz. Sikorski realized from early in the war that the situation was hopeless and tried to meet with his colleagues to discuss how the prewar opposition could continue its existence in the crumbing ruins. He met in Warsaw with a number of opposition loyalists and discussed how an alternative regime could be erected in Poland while the war still raged.[5] Sikorski nominated the respected peasant leader Maciej Rataj. He, in turn, suggested Sikorski, and Witos's name was also bandied about. On the night of September 6–7, Sikorski left Warsaw and tried again to obtain an assignment from Śmigły-Rydz. He failed, and made his way to Dęblin in central Poland with an odd assortment of devotees. Others in his entourage reached Brześć to meet with Śmigły-Rydz, all to no avail. He had a series of meetings in Dęblin, of which no records survive. The conversations were certainly focused on two subjects: establishing a government in exile, and creating an underground authority for the soon-to-be occupied Poland.[6]

On September 10, Sikorski went southeast to Lwów, where another center of political opposition had formed. This was still a week before the Russian invasion and the city was reasonably safe. Sikorski continued to pressure Śmigły-Rydz for a posting. In Lwów he met the leaders of the prewar opposition, a slightly reformed Front Morges: Kot, Haller, General Marian Kukiel, Karol Popiel and other lesser lights. Witos was not among them because he had been arrested by the Gestapo.[7] A number of propositions were considered: leave for France, or have General Lucjan Żeligowski, famous for occupying Wilno in 1920 a fine officer, but a bit unpredictable, announce a plan to seek help from the Russians.[8] Sikorski laid the groundwork for an underground government.[9] Soon after he was in communication with General Kazimierz Sosnkowski, an ardent Piłsudskiite, but one who had feuded with the sanacja and been exorcised. With his blessing, Sikorski began an anabasis through the sites of historic Polish lore: Beresteczko, Krzemieniec, Zbaraż, Tarnopol, Trembowla, Stansławów, and finally to Kut on the Romanian frontier. He had already planned to evacuate Poland. It was decided to reconvene as many of the members of the opposition as possible in France. They implored Paderewski's intervention.

Reports, indicate that the morose Sikorski anticipated a Russian invasion at any time.[10] There he made the following proposition. They would go to

Romania, from which Śmigły-Rydz would travel on to France. Sikorski's network of contacts in the high reaches of French military and political circles would allow Śmigły-Rydz to create the basis of assembling an army in exile.[11]

Accordingly, Śmigły-Rydz had already decided to seek passage through Romania and ordered Sikorski to report to him there. Both crossed the frontier the next day.[12] Sikorski met with high-ranking French representatives, and apparently he decided to travel on to Bucharest. Contact with Śmigły-Rydz was broken. Sikorski was informed there that the internment of Polish officials was inevitable. Frantic discussions ensued during which Leon Noël (ambassador to Poland), and General Louis Faury, the Military Attaché to Warsaw, proved the decisive influence on Sikorski. He was convinced of two things: it was unlikely the sanacja government would continue its activities in the West – Sikorski suggested they go to Algeria – and that he would have much support from French political circles. He sent an emotional, but insulting, letter to Śmigły-Rydz and Chief of Staff General Wacław Stachiewicz that he would no longer recognize them as his superiors.[13] He was already acting as commander-in-chief. One of Sikorski's allies, Popiel, was gently interned in Romania. He immediately wrote to Paderewski to intervene on his behalf. He also wrote to Retinger in London to do the same. It is noteworthy that the channel he would pick to beseech his ally was Retinger.[14] Pobóg-Malinowski argues persuasively that Retinger and Sikorski were in close contace in the period from the invasion of Poland until the French campaign of summer 1940.[15]

Sikorski gave Polish ambassador to Romania, Roger Count Raczyński, a complex task to perform in creating a new Polish authority in France. Mościcki, the president, now interned in Romania, would be superseded by Cardinal Primate August Hlond as a provisional head of state. Paderewski soon intervened and had Hlond replaced by Witos. In an ominous foretaste of Sikorski's political designs, Raczyński was to send to France only officers "useful in this action," that is, no Piłsudskiites. Guilt for the defeat was to be ascribed to the sanacja not Poland *tout court*. A host of Front notables and their close associates were to be sent to Paris: Haller, Kukiel, the violently anti-Piłsudski soldier Izydor Modelski, Major M. Malinowski, Aleksander Ładoś, Rataj, Niedziałkowski, Popiel, Jan Stańczyk, Kot, Franciszek Bujak, the politically vacillating Eugeniusz Romer, Jan Kwapiński, and all the reasonable endecja figures. This was a pantheon of Sikorski loyalists and no Piłsudskiite was included.

On September 22, Sikorski, together with French and American ambassadors, Noël and Anthony J. Drexel-Biddle, left for Paris, where Stroński was waiting for them to explain the political landscape He had just arrived after meeting with Paderewski en route. They were faced with two questions. Who should form a new government and who should command the Polish soldiers in France. The sanacja was unable to compete with the insurgents and Mościcki, exercised his constitutional authority by choosing the Polish ambassador in Rome, General Bolesław Wieniawa-Długoszowski to replace him as president. Wieniawa had a colorful history as a cabaret habitué and, though he had put his unbridled past behind him, many both mistrusted and disdained him. France intervened in Polish internal affairs, a taste of the future proclivity of the Western Powers, and said they would not recognize Wieniawa. Mościcki's choice was soon ignored and the titular president, despite Sikorski's initial objections, became the lukewarm Piłsudskiite and intellectually limited Edward Raczkiewicz. Sikorski and Stroński failed to arrange Paderewski gaining the role: he was too old and feeble. Raczkiewicz willingly agreed to consult Paderewski on important matters, a testimony to his weakness. Meanwhile Sikorski was busy preparing lists of those he would allow to go to France: many were purged and only Front allies were included. The selection among officers was especially scrupulous.[16]

A government of "National Unity" was created, a motto used continuously by the Front after 1936. It had a number of specifics: the presidency had no power; besides, Sikorski would succeed to that office should it become vacant. Stanisław Stroński, Sikorski's long-term ally, was tasked with forming a government. Sikorski would be prime minister. A few weeks later he would also become commander-in-chief. It was September 30, 1939 and Sikorski had thus taken over the government of Poland.[17] He had finally equaled Piłsudski in 1918: all real power was in his hands. Sikorski approached Retinger and asked him to join the government, but his status was never clarified. He was referred to as an "advisor" and his real function was to "retain contacts, propaganda, and other questions in the field of foreign affairs."[18]

Retinger, for the first, and last, time, received an official position with the Polish government now relocated to Paris. Stroński, an old colleague of Retinger in the Front, named him advisor to the "Presidium of the Council of Ministers and tasked him with conducting Polish propaganda on British territory." The disquiet of official Polish circles was great because Retinger was regarded by many Poles as someone with "radical-communist" background.[19] His policy towards Russia was also highly suspect and he was considered pro-Soviet by many Poles, especially the Piłsudskiites. Moreover, Retinger was, in the polite language of Mitkiewicz, a virtual spy for Sikorski on all the members of the government.[20] His exact duties were obscure but his work consisted of "propaganda, lobbying, and negotiations."[21]

Terlecki made an insightful commentary of Retinger's usefulness to Sikorski. This was not France were Sikorski was comfortable and well connected, but London where he was neither.

> Retinger had influence on all political decisions. He was essential from the first minute. He knew the situation through and through and enabled any sort of helpful contact. Labour activists helped him. They went into the ranks of the Churchill cabinet of national unity. Almost everybody was either his acquaintance, or even his friend... [Retinger and Sikorski] were closely attached to one another.[22]

This was all the more important because "Sikorski, like his country, were quite unknown to the British."[23] Retinger was not.[24] A less flattering portrayal of Retinger's usefulness to Sikorski is provided by Hugh Dalton: "He's similar to a sewer-rat; nonetheless he enjoys the complete trust of Sikorski. Beyond that he is very susceptible to flattery. It's necessary to deal with him as he is."[25] Despite this unappetizing appraisal, Retinger and the influential Dalton dined together frequently and apparently became close.

Dalton created the SOE (the Special Operations Executive, the ultimate intelligence service) in 1940, Churchill's" secret army." He was moved to a pro-Polish orientation by Retinger; a vital connection for the Poles.[26] Dalton even learned to speak Polish-badly.[27] The possibility of the Poles staging an uprising was a major concern for British intelligence. This supports the notion of Retinger's close cooperation with the SOE who sadly misled the Poles into thinking major British assistance would be available.[28]

Retinger faced immediate problems in London. The Polish military attaché mistrusted him, and the ambassador, Count Edward Raczyński, disdained him and insisted that Retinger undertake no action without his approval.[29] This was quite a change for Retinger. He had spent years plotting against the government and gaining support anywhere it could be found. Now to be instructed to obey government policy must have seemed revolutionary to him. He attributed it to rumors that he was a "Bolshevik agent." And now he had to be reined in. He asked for Sikorski's intervention.[30] Over the next several weeks Retinger's relationship with Raczyński improved, but was never cordial.[31] Raczyński was furious when he received a letter from Stroński, countersigned by Zaleski, and initialed by Sikorski. It said, in its crucial passage: "Dr. Retinger would personally carry out propaganda in political and official circles, whereas the controversial Stefan Litauer – of whom more later – would be responsible for relations with the press 'in accordance with the ambassador's instructions and in close cooperation with Dr. Retinger'." Raczyński was "incensed at this cavalier treatment of an ambassador."[32]

Despite these accusations, if we search Retinger's correspondence and memoranda in the fall of 1939, a different picture emerges of Retinger as a friend of the Soviet Union. He warned against Soviet pressure on Poland and evil designs and he worried over British dependence on the Russians. He spoke of the need for federal combinations in Europe to forestall both German and Russian imperialism. This was not the voice of a communist sympathizer. But it is indirect confirmation of the attaché's concerns that not long after meeting with Raczyński to establish harmony, Retinger met with Stefan Litauer of the Polish Press Agency (PAT), regarded by many Poles as a Soviet agent, to discuss fruitful collaboration.[33] Sikorski apparently trusted Litauer[34] whom he had known since 1914 and who idolized him.[35] In November Sikorski discussed with Litauer Polish cooperation with the Soviets.[36] He floated the idea of the sacrifice of Polish eastern territories for compensation at German expense and some form of federation with

Czechoslovakia. The Foreign Office found Sikorski "sensible" as a result.³⁷ As Tadeusz Katelbach lamented: "Retinger and Litauer, the first one, as is generally spoken, is a British agent, the second one, whom I know extremely well, is beginning to look to me much worse, like a Soviet one."³⁸

Retinger outlined a complex plan of pro-Polish propaganda in Britain for Stroński. Litauer and Reginald Leeper from the British Political Intelligence Department were both assets due to their press connections.³⁹ There were several goals to work on: confront anti-Polish propaganda; win the British Catholics; mollify the Jews; and establish working relations with the Czechs. This work was already undertaken by fall. Additional goals were to combat Ukrainian propaganda and create a "post-war [i.e. post 1939] political ideology based on Sikorski's views."⁴⁰ Retinger even compiled lists of pro-Russian Britons who needed to be worked on among the political and literary communities. It was to be internationalist in tone and not a direct attack on the Soviets, although Soviet outrages in occupied eastern Poland would be stressed.⁴¹

Retinger proposed a plan whereby Polish propaganda in the United States would be carried on as part of the British effort. Britain would have to pay for it. Retinger brought this up with London and they seemed well-inclined. Within a week Retinger met with Leeper and an agreement was concluded.⁴² Hessel Tiltman in New York told Retinger that he must hurry in these efforts because the American knew nothing about Poland or its efforts in the war: "you'd be horrified" and Tiltman reminded Retinger that the United States was very important for Poland in the last war and might well be again.⁴³ However, someone would have to be sent to America to study the situation first as no Pole in the United States could be trusted with such a responsibility. This is further testimony of Retinger's absolute contempt for the Poles of America. During his long career, he seemed never to have been involved with anyone from Polonia.⁴⁴

A few months later Retinger tried to get General Sosnkowski, a distinguished soldier, to go to the United States to improve the Polish image in the country. That seems to have not interested the general.⁴⁵ Retinger found the task of propaganda in favor of Poland in the United States daunting indeed: general ignorance and unconcern; inability to differentiate the exile government from the sanacja; the lack of a constant stream of attractive personalities to gain attention; insufficient funds, and so forth.⁴⁶

## Sikorski, Retinger, and the British

But Retinger was less interested in arranging means, and trips to America. In November he sent Sikorski a memorandum arguing the existence of British support for European federalism. He included a sketch of his plan for a postwar federated East Central Europe. It would be based on a Polish-Czech cooperation, and include Lithuania, Romania, Hungary and, in the future, an independent Ukraine. Economic cooperation would serve as the chief motivating element. It would be the only way to protect the region from absolute Russian domination. It would be part of a series of federations encompassing the entire continent.[47]

Less than two-weeks thereafter, Sikorski issued a declaration in the name of the Polish government with a similar, rather grander federal plan.[48] He was repeatedly to return to this theme.[49] Witkowski goes so far as to argue that it was Retinger's pressure which made federalism one of the main components of Polish foreign policy of the war era.[50] Retinger himself dates Sikorski's efforts to "develop" his federalist ideas as "our point of view" – from November, 1939.[51] He openly claims that Sikorski's federalism was due to him.[52]

Sir Colin Gubbins, replaced Dalton as head of the SOE and become immediately a liaison between London and the duo of Sikorski and Retinger. Gubbins and Retinger became life-long friends from the start. The three held a meeting in Paris in February of 1940. It signaled what was to be a characteristic feature of Retinger's relationship with the British. It was primarily via the intelligence services-especially Gubbins' SOE, and not with the Foreign Office nor Military Intelligence (MI6). Indeed, Foreign Minister Anthony Eden and Gubbins disliked each other.[53] Eden was no friend of the Poles, and was known for his efforts to "conciliate" the Soviets.[54] Harrison regards the Foreign Office as being characterized by "Polonophobia."[55] By contrast, Gubbins, a most impressive man, had been with the British military mission in Warsaw at the start of the war and he had high regard for them.[56] Sikorski's involvement in subsequent contacts with Gubbins is not known; it seemed to be Retinger's task.[57] Garliński, a Pole and a student of the SOE states that the organization "always defended our interests to the best of its ability."[58] Gubbins had, say his biographers, "a strong sense of obligation to the Poles."[59]

Unlike Gubbins, the Foreign Office was, from the outset, suspicious of Retinger. As early as June 9, 1940 it ordered a full-scale investigation and received very negative material: Retinger had no standing in Poland other than being an opponent of the interwar government. However, he was later close to Sikorski's exile government, except for the military which disliked and mistrusted him. He was not highly regarded by many Poles. He deserted his first wife and left her penniless. He treated his second so badly that the Labour Party, with which she was affiliated, despised him and his boasts about close connections with them were dubious.

The report went on that after 1919 for a few years the British refused him a visa because he was "suspected of Bolshevist leanings" by the relevant office. The Foreign Office investigator, however, dismissed this charge. In the interwar period he was very close to Skrzyński and acted as his link with the British which was quite true.[60] The Foreign Office felt his cozying up to Sikorski was a replay of the policy he pursued earlier. Retinger had feuded with Jan Ciechanowski, secretary general of the Polish Foreign service, and used his influence with Minister Skrzyński to have the former replaced. Retinger was said to have abandoned politics after 1936, which was untrue because of his known involvement with the Front Morges. A report mentions his close ties to Witos and Rataj two of the Front's key players along with Sikorski, of course.

His Mexican years are given some valuable attention. Although Morones' name is not mentioned, it was obvious that the Foreign Office was speaking of him when they discussed Retinger's close relations with the Mexican authorities. He made, they concluded, a considerable amount of money from this linkage. Morones "paid him well" and he was "pretty flush of cash" which seems possible from a close analysis of both Retinger's dabbling in oil politics and his close ties to the CROM leadership.[61] If this were true, this contradicts the widely repeated view that Retinger left Mexico in poverty.

On the basis of these pages of information, London concluded that Retinger should not be acting as Sikorski's unofficial agent behind Raczyński's back: his past was too dubious and his activities were alienating and he was a "busybody" and intriguer. He was a "bohème" untrusted by Minister Stroński who was a source for some of the Retinger gossip contained in these reports. In conclusion Retinger was not "suitable" for his role and Sikorski was "quite wrong" to be using a man under suspicion. We may thus conclude that the Foreign Office began the war distrusting Retinger and not understanding his relationship with Sikorski. There is little evidence to suppose that this changed.[62] If Retinger were a British agent, he was not in the employ of the Foreign Office.

## The Poles and the fall of France

Germany invaded France in mid-May 1940, after sweeping through the Low Countries. Sikorski was very optimistic about French defenses, indeed, delusional in Panecki's words.[63] In a few days the situation was clarified: Sikorski had few options and the Polish situation was dire. Their troops were scattered about and under French operational command. On June 11, Polish forces evacuated Paris for Angers and Sikorski and the makings of his staff went to Bourlemount. The northern French front was collapsing. The French army was in disorder. Polish forces fought almost in isolation. The decision was made to evacuate the army and government to England. By 16 May the French defense was in ruins, Marshal Pétain asked for an armistice the next day: Retinger was with Sikorski when Pétain told him, on June 17 at Bordeaux, "France ought to do its penitence."[64] Sikorski had now reestablished his headquarters at nearby Libourne. He met with British officers and apparently with Retinger, though this conversation has not survived, and by the 24th Franco-British forces were pinned at Dunkirk. Belgium surrendered on May 28, and the British fled by June 3. On June 14 undefended Paris fell, and the armistice was signed on the 22nd. It had been a matter of a few weeks. Hitler had conquered France, the Netherlands, Luxembourg, Belgium, and the bulk of the British army in little more than the time he had taken to overcome Poland fighting alone and also invaded by the Soviets.

## 122  The war begins

The stunning defeat brought with it a disaster for the Polish units serving with the French. Two Polish divisions were part of the defense. There was an armored brigade and several companies scattered throughout the French forces; Garliński put the total number at 40,000, but Panecki, counting training units and command staff put the total much higher–85,000.[65] The German attack meant that large French units retreated leaving Polish forces vulnerable, as at Lagarde. Other Polish units crossed into Switzerland and were interned. Polish forces were shattered in the West.[66] Sikorski appealed personally to Churchill to rescue his men on June 18.[67]

Sikorski was profoundly shaken. Just days before the surrender he and his intimates had denounced those predicting the French collapse as defeatists and cowards, in a panic and lacking resolve.[68] Now his excessive optimism had led to a disastrous situation with Poles trapped in France. He moved his government briefly to Angers as we have seen, and then moved about as the vagaries of war demanded. His faith in the French was so unreasonably elevated that he made no plans for the evacuation of his government which was scattered about. The French offered no help. Chaos ruled.

### Retinger and the rescue of Sikorski

And then, "like a *deus ex machina* Józef Retinger appeared in France."[69] This is the first great Retinger puzzle of World War II. We must consider "the then universal opinion that Retinger acted at the orders of Churchill who desired the fastest possible discussions with Sikorski."[70] Tebinka even concludes that the rescue plane was sent "personally" by Churchill.[71] Other sources also credit Churchill directly with the initiative.[72]

Pomian, ostensibly basing himself on Retinger's recollections, makes the following account: "The Chamberlain government fell and Churchill came to power. Retinger was immediately invited for a consultation, about which he leaves this brief remark in his notes." He then quoted Retinger:

> In May 1940 Churchill became the premier. The Polish government still found itself in Paris and I received a telegram requesting that I come, because the [Polish] government was considering the position which it should adopt.
>
> I met with general Sikorski and his immediate co-workers and suggested, to Churchill – a man in private life sensitive and loyal, a devoted husband and good father that it was necessary to act in the name of humanity. General Sikorski as well as other Poles should try to gain his personal friendship. Churchill, a great patriot, profoundly believing in his country, and even more in his genius and destiny, was also devoid of any party prejudices. Although it did not occur to me, that we would be able to rely on him politically, we could rely on his personal loyalty. Unfortunately! Time showed that I was too right. I have to admit that

General Sikorski complied with my advice and through my personal grace I was successful in winning the friendship of Churchill.[73]

Podgórski argues the opposite: it was Retinger who prevailed upon Churchill to evacuate Sikorski and Polish troops from France. Retinger, this thesis contends, importuned Churchill to rescue Sikorski, and in so doing gained Churchill's loyalty-at least on a personal level.[74] Kot paid Retinger a back-handed compliment when he said that Retinger arranged the flight because of his "relations with certain bureaus" in the British government.[75]

Retinger was understandably concerned about Sikorski's fate and that of the Polish army in France. It was vital that some means be found by which the Poles could be evacuated, with British help, from collapsing France. Virtually no news from France was reaching London and nothing directly from Sikorski. Retinger approached the British Air Ministry and requested a military plane to take him to Bordeaux, find Sikorski, and gain reliable information.[76] (Why the Ministry would pay any attention to Retinger is a question in itself.)[77] Colonel Leon Mitkiewicz who was with Retinger the last few days discussing Sikorski's plight, joined by Colonel Bohdan Kwieciński, the Polish Air Attaché, and a long Retinger acquaintance, in a hurried meeting. It was decided by the three that it would be Reinger who would seek out Sikorski.[78] At 5:00 pm on the 17th June, Kwiecieński, "went to the command of the British air force" and asked, at Retinger's request, for a plane for Retinger to Bordeaux.[79]

"The plane was given at my disposition," Retinger writes, and "the pilot was to take me anywhere in France in my search for Sikorski."[80] The orders, however, say nothing about the plane being at Retinger's "disposal" but refer to him vaguely as "a passenger" who was Sikorski's personal advisor."[81] Two hours before Retinger's departure, the War Cabinet meeting of June 18 discussed the question but attributed the motivation to the Poles, but was vague regarding the authorization. The Chief of the Air Staff (Marshal Sir Cyril L. N. Newall) said declared that:

> He had received reports from Polish sources that General Sikorski was somewhere in France, probably in the Nancy area. The Poles were very anxious that he should be brought over to this country. He [Newall] had accordingly arranged to send a machine to Bordeaux with General Sikorski's personal advisor on board, with instructions to find the General, if possible, and to bring him back to this country.[82]

The War Cabinet "took note." Churchill was not at the meeting which was presided over by Chamberlain. We do know that the Cabinet was concerned that the Soviets "would not make a common front against Germany" and were thus anxious to speak with Sikorski about luring Moscow to an anti-German coalition.[83] The impetus, to fetch Sikorski, however almost certainly came from the Poles and was readily accommodated by the English. Any action by Churchill is neither proven nor dismissed.

124  *The war begins*

The English were delighted, and that the seaplane with Retinger and an English officer was to fly out that morning.[84] Did this request to the Air Ministry require the prior approval of Churchill? This seems likely. Otherwise we have an odd-looking Polish civilian asking to borrow a British aircraft from out of the blue, and the request being immediately granted. Was this perhaps the moment when Retinger began his cooperation with the British?

But, perhaps, the solution is simpler and ends speculation. On June 15, two days before Retinger claimed to have approached the British, Polish Foreign Minister August Zaleski asked ambassador Kennard for help in getting Sikorski and his government to England. No response is recorded. Thus much hinges upon who the "Polish sources" discussed by the Cabinet were. Were they Retinger or Zaleski?[85] Thus it may not have been Retinger's private proposal but the earlier action of the Polish government which prompted the flight. The Poles wanted Sikorski out and the British agreed. The action of rescuing Sikorski was a British action prompted by the Polish government: Retinger's involvement seems to have been parallel rather than causative.

## France to London

Retinger flew to Bordeaux. There was chaos there. "Nobody knew anything." Retinger could not find ground transportation. By accident he met Colonel Iżycki. They hired a chauffeur, and were accompanied by Squadron Leader Biddle, the pilot. They reached the British embassy in Bordeaux. It was a terrible sight. He could not find any trace of Sikorski from the hundreds of panicked British. Retinger realized there must be a Polish consul in Bordeaux. He found out from someone there that Sikorski must be in Libourne nearby where the Polish base was situated. After an arduous journey, he found Sikorski, alone, in the town. The general was startled and asked why he had come: "To have lunch with you" Retinger answered. Sikorski said he would go with Retinger back to England only on the condition that he could meet Churchill at once. It is significant that Retinger told Sikorski that he was inviting him to London on the express wish of Prime Minister Churchill. This was a clear indication of contact between the two.[86]

The meeting must have been of lightning speed. General Kazimierz Sosnkowski recalled with pique that Retinger's mission took place without warning and with such speed that

> The hurry was so great that I barely had a chance to stuff in the General's hand the notes containing the essential information concerning the transport of the rest of the army from French ports to the British Isles in the lobby of the restaurant.[87]

They flew back on the same plane. Sikorski had two or three people with him but Retinger did not disclose who they were.[88] Once in London they went to the Dorchester Hotel where Sir Charles Peake and Major Victor

Cazalet, (who soon thereafter became the Military Attaché to the Polish government) were waiting for them.⁸⁹ Cazalet, who conveniently owned the Dorchester, worked closely with Sikorski.⁹⁰ Soon Sikorski was visited by Colonels Mitkiewicz and Kwieciński, who had been instrumental in his rescue. They came at the bidding of Retinger.⁹¹

Sikorski also met with Litauer.⁹² Litauer carried a copy of an English-language memorandum Sikorski had asked him to prepare for delivery to Churchill later that day.⁹³ Sikorski, minutes before the Churchill meeting, asked Raczyński to translate it for him. In Anna Cienciala's words, "Raczyński was horrified" and apparently Sikorski was similarly displeased with what Litauer had written.

Litauer, had had earlier meetings with Andrew Rothstein of TASS in London.⁹⁴ Rothstein apparently acted as the Soviet embassy's liaison with the Poles, probably Litauer, Retinger, and perhaps with the British.⁹⁵ He was the one to signal that the Soviets were prepared to hold discussions with the Poles.⁹⁶ Mitkiewicz, who was very close to Sikorski, records that Sikorski told him that the Litauer memorandum concerning the basis upon which Polish-Soviet talks could be held was unacceptable because Litauer's reported conditions were too unclear and far-reaching. ⁹⁷

The Litauer memorandum had promised postwar Polish friendship with Moscow, differentiating it from the sanacja's attitude and expressed the willingness to consider "territorial changes" in the east, and expect, in response, an improvement in Soviet treatment of Polish nationals in Russia, and raised the prospect of creating an army from Poles under Soviet control.⁹⁸ Zaleski, newly arrived from Paris, wanted the document destroyed because it was too accommodating to Moscow, as did President Raczkiewicz. This led to a confrontation between Sikorski and Raczkiewicz, who always regarded Sikorski as too sympathetic to the Russians.⁹⁹ The memorandum was ultimately not presented to the British. Raczyński persuaded Sikorski to present "a rather different version" to Churchill and rewrote it on the basis of "notes" which Sikorski gave him.¹⁰⁰

Litauer is a fascinating personality. He was in the Polish diplomatic service for many years and developed an affinity for the Soviet Union. In the 1930s he was an open Piłsudskiite and a proponent of Colonel Józef Beck's foreign policy, regarded by Sikorski and the Front Morges as disastrous. With the war, Litauer's relations with ambassador Raczyński cooled and he fell in with Retinger who arranged, as we have seen, meetings at Litauer's home. Stroński appointed Litauer to handle press propaganda for Poland and Retinger in charge overall of propaganda. He would keep his position with PAT but in effect be a Polish agent. Litauer is often noted as an indication that Retinger was moving in communist and pro-Soviet circles, but there is perhaps another explanation. A letter from Retinger exists in which he cautions about Litauer and describes him as a "political opportunist" who cannot always be trusted. Retinger was not beguiled by Litauer and the possibility arises that the shrewd Retinger was actually using him.¹⁰¹ This possibility is further enhanced when we find a memorandum from Retinger criticizing a potential story for the press too critical of the sanacja,[102] and especially another memorandum, from November 3, 1939, in which he warns of profound rusophilism in England; that the Soviet embassy is doing a successful job cultivating the press. Most of all Retinger warns that this is an ill-omen: close British-Russian cooperation after the war would be "catastrophic for Poland" and deprive it of any chance of regaining its eastern territories.[103] As for Litauer, in the late stages of the war, he became an open apologist for Soviet imperialism and later was a journalist for Communist Poland.[104]

For his part, Raczyński despised Retinger and his unorthodox methods, reminiscent of the friction between Retinger and Skirmunt in the 1920s. Retinger was either too unorthodox or too unreliable for the official of the Polish government. Pobóg-Malinowski quoted Sikorski's lament "I don't know for whom he is working," as an indictment of Sikorski's judgment. On the other hand Retinger's endless efforts to ingratiate himself to the general especially during the extremely taxing first several months of the war must have been of considerable solace to Sikorski's enormous ego.[105] They also occasionally redounded to his disadvantage. Members of the Polish government, particularly those on the political right, criticized Sikorski for receiving bad advice from his immediate advisors, which always implied Retinger.[106] He was regarded as leftist and pro-Russian and thus a bad influence on Sikorski. The Polish government was in crisis and Sikorski was hanging on to power by a thread. The British were pressuring the Poles to resolve the situation of their leadership.[107]

On July 18, Sikorski, Raczyński, Retinger, and possibly others – met with Lord Halifax and Secretary of State Malet. Halifax suggested that civil and military leadership be divided, something which had been discussed in Polish circles for some time. The British were well-informed about the most secret inner workings of the Polish government. Obviously they had been kept *au courant*: Retinger was a good candidate for their informer.[108] London backed Sikorski; his dismissal would have been in Szumowski's judgment "catastrophic."[109] London had saved Sikorski, and the Poles knew it.[110] Sikorski raised with the British, the possibility of forming a large army, perhaps 300,000, from Poles in Soviet occupied Poland. This project was only later revealed to the Polish government but it reflected Sikorski's desire to work closely with the Russians.[111]

Retinger had met with his usual left-wing colleagues and was aware that the Soviets had furnished London with an aide-memoir calling for an ethnographic Poland, politically dependent on Moscow. However, Retinger's role in the later Litauer memorandum cannot be verified.[112] We know that Litauer had hosted a gathering of what Raczyński called "malcontents" at his home in London and Retinger had convened the meeting.[113] As if Rothstein did not link closely enough with the Soviets, Retinger also befriended Soviet Ambassador Alexander Bogomolov and sang his praises to Sikorski.[114] However, there is another way of looking at Retinger's courting of the British Left. As Lerski argues, they were deeply penetrated by Soviet agents one of whose main tasks was to damage the Polish image in British eyes. Knowing what the Left was doing was a vital interest of the Sikorski government.[115] Perhaps this was Retinger's goal. As a sort of double agent, Retinger consorted with the Russians to dig out information for the Poles.

Sikorski returned to France for a day-and-a-half and then again to London to arrange evacuations. Retinger tried to talk him out of the idea but failed: he even appealed to the general's patriotism: "The General cannot and may not risk his life, he is necessary for Poland."[116] Retinger's relations with Sikorski, already very close before the war, became even closer as a result of his rescuing the general from France. From that moment on, Retinger became his most trusted colleague, advisor, and an inseparable friend.[117] Retinger had reached a very high position in the world of Polish politics, ruined as they were. He was aided by his utter selflessness.[118]

The British were desperate for Soviet support after the catastrophe in France, and thus wanted to promote Polish-Soviet reconciliation. Terry has argued persuasively that the "initiative came from the British side." Her conclusions are:

> Having dispatched Cripps to Moscow for the transparent purpose of weaning the Soviet Union away from Germany, by mid-June the British found themselves in the unhappy position either of withdrawing him ... or of offering Stalin 'greater inducements' to curtail Soviet-German cooperation. Among the 'greater inducements' suggested was one that 'the British government, with the consent of the Polish, should discuss...a new Soviet-Polish frontier...'[119]

This argument, most persuasive, would help explain Sikorski's dramatic flight from Bordeaux: either Churchill needed him immediately to discuss this demarche, or Sikorski, of his own motion, elected to leave at once upon learning of the British action.

He also wanted to make sure that the British were intimately involved. Sikorski was being drawn into a web of influences, all sympathetic to Soviet demands on Poland, which was quite apart from the normal workings of the Polish government. The Cabinet knew that the Polish government was growing hostile to Sikorski by July and was understandably concerned.[120] This is one of many episodes which leaves Retinger's biographer perplexed. It is perhaps some solace to read a letter he wrote to the Belgium politician Paul-Henri Spaak in 1953 when he referred to writing his memoirs: "where I shall pass with silence many facts which the two of us know well, and that deserve not to be mentioned."[121]

## Was Retinger acting as a British agent?

The British spy theory cannot be proven when applied to World War I, though we can argue that he might have been sent on one or more missions by Asquith, It would make more sense to link him with the Caillaux theme and make him thereby a French agent, though unofficial. As we have noted, Retinger seems to have used the supposed connection with the British to enlarge his own position. As we have seen, there were other explanations for his actions. He was, really a Polish spy in foreign pay.

The interwar years in Britain also do not suggest intelligence operations. This are years of network building; creating linkages to the international Left, and collecting names for the future. It is during World War II when Retinger acting as a spy begins to take on some plausibility. He was intimately involved in most of the major episodes in Polish wartime diplomacy, but always in the background. Evidence of Retinger's influence must often be inferred rather than demonstrated. Olgierd Terlecki is absolutely right when he concludes that "It is a terrible shame that the witness to such huge events [koronny] left so little."[122] Retinger "had decisive influence not only on Sikorski, but in general on the course of Polish wartime policy."[123]

The evidence from the Sikorski rescue episode does not demonstrate that Retinger was thenceforth a British agent. Churchill could use Retinger, and he could spare a plane to go and get Sikorski. Zaleski probably proposed the plan, though it might have been Retinger. If it had been the prime minister's, idea he probably would not have chosen an unhealthy man in his fifties to undertake it.

The bond between Retinger and Sikorski is also not surprising: they had been on close terms for almost twenty years and shared dangerous experiences. We do not need to factor in British influence here. Hence, my conclusion to this episode is that it does not prove that Retinger was a British agent although it does demonstrate his infuriating habit of omitting vital details. If he was a man of mystery, he did much of the manufacturing. The idea that Retinger was already a British agent seems needlessly dramatic and not supported by clear evidence.[124]

Retinger proved of inestimable value to Sikorski in monitoring and reporting to him regarding the highest reaches of British politics, to which he had been ingratiating himself for years.[125] Sikorski depended on Retinger for both contacts with the British political world and reports from that source. Sikorski was, in the words of Sir Peter Wilkonson

> Absolutely helpless, whose name was unknown in England at that time to anybody, outside the Foreign Office. I shouldn't think that anybody in the War Office had ever heard of him. He was really impotent because he knew no English and knew nobody at the Polish Embassy. ....He was also in a slight state of shock, frankly, as a result of the French collapse.[126]

The Foreign Office was fascinated, and impressed, by the closeness between Sikorski and Retinger. Raczyński, with obvious disgust, noted that Retinger referred to Sikorski as "my friend" from early in the war, a reference he might well have saved for him. The British made the following fascinating conclusion which, by the way, does not suggest any subterranean connection with Retinger:

> On personal points it is quite clear that Retinger has, for good or ill, enormous influence with the Prime Minister. The latter laughs at him, it is true, and calls him *'le cousin du diable'*, but he is clearly regarded, both by Sikorski and by his family, as a sort of household pet and everything of importance is discussed with him. It is no good, therefore, trying to circumvent Retinger. The only thing is to confide in him and hope for the best.[127]

It is vital to underscore what Retinger meant for Sikorski and his government. It was Retinger who arranged meetings with both government leaders and powerful politicians, accompanied Sikorski to all meetings, took notes, acted as translator. Sikorski spoke no English so he was dependent upon Retinger's rendering of events. Retinger prepared the summary of key meetings which would be used by Sikorski for future diplomacy. We can only imagine what discussions the two of them must have had after an important meeting.

Certainly, Retinger provided the British with detailed reports regarding the internal politics of the Polish exile government, its personalities and problems. Whether this was merely done to win over British confidence or as an act of service to a British pay-master is unclear.[128] Retinger was the major source for information about the Poles, but various Foreign Office minutes indicate that he was widely regarded as dubious. As for Gubbins and the SOE, that was a different story.

Finally there is the question of the state of Retinger's relationship with Rothstein and, to a lesser degree, with Litauer. The former was a Soviet agent and the latter must have been as well. It was not surprising that by mid-1940, Retinger was mistrusted and despised by Polish military and political circles. Stanisław Mikołajczyk, the peasant leader in the Polish government thought Retinger was a bad influence on Sikorski and wanted him removed as early as the summer of 1940.[129] Criticism of Retinger reached such a point that he tried to resign in the fall of 1942, but Sikorski did not take cognizance of it.[130]

## Notes

1 Pieczewski, *Działalność*, 77.
2 Ibid., 78.
3 Roman Wapiński, *Władysław Sikorski*, (Warsaw: Wiedza Powszechna, 1978), 222–223.
4 Ibid., 223.
5 Wapiński, *Sikorski*, regards the report that Sikorski sent Rataj to Lwów to create a government in early September as unlikely. He is persuasive. See ibid., 224.
6 Walentyna Korpalska, *Władysław Eugeniusz Sikorski: Biografia Polityczna* (Wrocław: Ossolineum, 1981), 189–190.

7 Miroslaw Dymarski, *Stosunki wewnętrzne wśród wychodżstwa politycznego i wojskowego we Francji i Wielkiej Brytanii, 1939–1945* (Wrocław: Wydawnictwo Uniwersyteta Wrocławskiego, 1999), 22.
8 Wapiński, *Sikorski*, 225.
9 Ibid.
10 Wapiński, *Sikorski*, 226.
11 Korpalska, *Sikorski* 201.
12 Wapiński, *Sikorski*, 226–227.
13 The letter is quoted extensively in Wapiński, *Sikorski*, 230.
14 Karol Popiel, *Wspomnienia polityczne* (Warsaw: Ośrodek dokumentacji i studio spółecznych, 1983), 114.
15 Pobóg-Malinowski, *Z mojego okienka*, 714.
16 Wapiński, *Sikorski*, 231–232.
17 Korpalska, *Sikorski*, 204.
18 Pomian, *Retinger*, 109.
19 Dymarski, *Stosunki wewnętrzne*, 106.
20 Leon Mitkiewicz, *Z Gen. Sikorskim na obczyźnie* (Paris: Instytut Literacki, 1968), 40.
21 Witkowski, *Ojcowie*, 46.
22 See Terlecki, *General ostatniej legendy*, 123; cf. Tendyra, "Władysław Sikorski," 27.
23 Bernadeta Tendyra, "Władysław Sikorski w oczach brytyjczyków," *Zeszyty Historyczne* 97 (1991), 26.
24 Ibid., 27.
25 Dalton quoted in Tendyra, "Sikorski," 27n.
26 Grosbois, "Activities," 28–29, 30.
27 Harrison, "Britain and the SOE," 1075. Dalton once said: "On the day of Victory Poland ...should ride in the van of the victory march," ibid., 1075.
28 Retinger to Dalton, November 15, 1947, Edward Hugh John Neale Dalton Papers, London School of Economics, (hereafter, LSE); folder 2/10/16; "Note on S. O. E.'s Work with the Poles, nd, HS4/136, NA." See also Eugenia Maresch, "SOE and Polish Aspirations," in Tessa Stirling, Daria Nalecz, and Tadeusz Dubicki eds., *Intelligence Co-operation between Poland and Great Britain during World War II. Vol. I* (London: Valentine Mitchell, 2005), 198–215.
29 Retinger to Stroński, October 13, 1939, Retinger Collection, 68/21/4, PISM.
30 Retinger to [Sikorski], October 31, 1939, Retinger Collection, col. 68, file 18, 1, PISM.
31 Retinger to Stroński, October 18, 1939, Retinger to Sikorski, October 25 and 28, 1939; Retinger Collection, 68/18/10, 11, PISM.
32 Count Edward Raczyński, (London: Weidenfeld and Nicolson, 1962), 45, cf. the memorandum entitled "Propaganda polska w Anglii," Retinger Collection, 98/2, PISM. Litauer was paid £10 per month by the embassy but £70 by Military Intelligence; Świderska, "Drobiazgi," 67.
33 Retinger to Stroński, October 10, 1939, Retinger Collection, 68/21/3, PISM. There are a few fascinating remarks about Litauer in Bułhak, The Foreign Office," 55n.
34 Tendyra, Wladyslaw Sikorski," 28; Tadeusz Katelbach, *Rok złych wróżb* (Paris: Instytut Literacki, 1959), 36; see the excerpts entitled "Lack of Understanding," September 15, 1944 in the British Intelligence file on Stanisław Kot in National Archives, KV2/3429 (Stanislaw Kot); hereafter (NA).
35 Świderska, "Drobiazgi," 67–68. Prażmowska calls Litauer Sikorski's "friend"; see Prażmowska, *Britain and Poland*, 64.
36 Ibid., 68.
37 Ibid., 68–70.

38 Tadeusz Katelbach, *Rok zlych wróżb* (Paris: Instytut Leteracki, 1959), 68. Litauer, Katelbach notes, used to be a great champion of Beck of the sanacja. He lionized him in the late 1930s. and accused him of being a Quisling during the war; Świderska, "Drobiazgi" 66.
  Katelbach was a former intelligence officer and journalist-hence his links to Litauer. He was a Piłsudskiite. Oddly, Retinger maintained his friendship with Litauer in the postwar era; see Oskar, "Notatka służbowa," July 2, 1957, Instytut Pamięci Narodowej, BU 01136/69/D (hereafter IPN).
39 Leeper had been chargé d'affaires in Warsaw in the 1920s.
40 Retinger to Stroński, nd, Retinger Collection, 68/21, PISM.
41 Ibid.
42 Leeper, it should be remembered, was very close to Litauer.
43 Hessel Tiltman to Retinger, March 2, and May 27, 1940; Retinger to Tiltman, June 11, 1940; Retinger Collection, 68/36 PISM. Tiltman was an old friend of Retinger's. His comments about Poles who could fill the job: "Stroński is impossible. I'm more afraid of him than of Hitler." Drohojowski doesn't know what he is doing. It had to be Retinger. See Tiltman to Retinger, April 15, 1940, Retinger Collection, 68/46, PISM; See Retinger draft letter of November 8, 1940, Retinger Collection, 68/28, PISM.
44 "Notatka w sprawie polskiej akcji propagandowo-politycznej w Ameryce," February 21, 1940, Retinger Collection, 68/25, PISM.
45 Retinger to Kot, Retinger Collection, June 6 and 11, 1940, 67/70–72, PISM.
46 Retinger to Stroński, November 20, 1939; Retinger to Sikorski, December 20, 1939; "Akcja polityczno-propagandowa w Londynie," January 31, 1940; Retinger Collection, 68/21, PISM.
47 Podgórski dates this document to September, 1939; see his *Retinger*, 97.
48 Sikorski broadcast to Poland, on December 18, 1939, the idea of a "Central-Eastern European Federation"; see Walter Lipgens to Polish Underground Movement Study Trust, May 25, 1964 in WL 295, Historical Archives of the European Union [HAEU].
49 Pieczewski, *Działalność*, 100–101. In 1942 Sikorski stated that he had continuously endorsed federalism as early as October, 1929. See Sikorski's undated latter to Sumner Welles; Pomian, *Retinger*, 124.
50 Witkowski, *Ojcowie*, 47. The underground press in Poland often discussed postwar European federalism; see H. Czarnocka to Walter Lipgens, January 15, 1965; [Lipgens] to Czarnocka, February 15, 1965, WL 295, Historical Archives of the European Union (hereafter HAEU).
51 See untitled memorandum by Retinger, teczka 79, PISM. Retinger also writes that Sikorski accepted "his idea completely" and became in time "a convinced federalist." See Retinger's "My Part in the Movement for the Unity of Europe," Retinger Papers, BPL.
52 Pomian, *Retinger*, 125.
53 Peter Wilkinson and Joan Bright Astley, *Gubbins and SOE* (South Yorkshire: Pen & Sword Books, 1993), un-numbered front pages; MP to CDS, March 17, 1944, NA, HS4, 144.
54 Polonsky, "Polish Failure," 578. It is not surprising that Eden's secretary, Oliver Harvey, was very critical of the Poles. Passages like "typical Polish folly"; and the Poles being "almost incurably foolish and short-sighted" dot his memoirs. He even suggests that the war was, somehow, ultimately, Poland's fault. See John Harvey ed., *The War Diary of Oliver Harvey, 1941–1945* (London: Collins, 1978; 113), et passim.
55 Harrison, "British SOE," 1076. It was Cripps at the Foreign Office and the SOE's Dalton and Gubbins who were Retinger's most pro-Polish British contacts. Grosbois, "L'action," 69. In an internal memorandum draft, the British

## 132  The war begins

claimed that "without the support given by the S.O.E. to the Polish Underground Movement, they could not have carried on." See HS4, 4/139, draft, nd, NA.

56 Cookridge, *Europe Ablaze*, 22–23; Peszke, *The Polish Underground Army*, 18–19; Wilkinson and Astley, *Gubbins*, 38–45. Gubbins became close to Col. Stanislaw Gano, head of Polish Military Intelligence, Wilkinson and Astley, *Gubbins*, 47. MP to CDS, March 17, 1944, NA, HS4, 144. Gubbins' diary indicates that he met Retinger several times over 1940–1945, usually at the Ritz at 7:30; often with "vodka" noted. There is no mention of Sikorski. See the Papers of Major General Sir Colin Gubbins, Diary, 1941–1945, Imperial War Museum.

57 See Stroński's Memoirs in Volume 1/2 of Stroński Papers, PISM, collection. 183. Gubbins' first SOE assignment was liaison with the Poles and Czechs; by 1942 he headed all SOE operations; see E. H. Cookridge, *Set Europe Ablaze* (New York: Crowell, 1967), 21 –22. The Poles had a special body, Section III, to liaise with the SOE; there was no direct linkage to the highest ranks of the British forces; see Peszke, *Polish Underground Army*, 56, 66.

58 Garliński, *Poland, SOE and the Allies*, 123.

59 Wilkonsin and Astley, *Gubbins*, 180.

60 Frank Savery, 371/24476 to R. Makins, May 16, 1940, FO, NA.

61 Ibid.

62 This description of the Foreign Office's analysis of Retinger is based on the following documents: a FO minute of May 9, 1940 written on a memorandum concerning Sikorski and Retinger which is untitled; R. M. Makins to Savery at Angers, May 9, 1940; Savery to Makins, May 16, 1940; illegible to Jebb, July 5, 1940 all in FO 371/24476, NA.

63 Tadeusz Panecki, *General Władysław Sikorski: Pierwszy premier rządu RP na obczyźnie i naczelny wódz polskich sił zbrojnych*, Stefan Zwoliński ed., *Naczelni wodzowie i wyżsi dowodcy polskich sil zbrojnych na zachodzie* (Warsaw: Wojskowy Instytut historyczny agencya wydawnicza 'Egros', 1995), 42.

64 "La France devait faire pénitence," in Marcel-Henri Jaspar, *Souvenirs sans retouche*, Paris: Libraire Arthéme Fayard, 1968, 468.

65 Panecki, "Sikorski," 41. Cazalet's biographer claims 66,000, probably not including air force personnel; see James, *Cazalet*, 234.

66 There is a concise description of the Polish role in the campaign in Józef Garliński, *Poland in the Second World War* (New York: Hippocrene Books, 1988), 54–57, 76–82.

67 Jacek Tebinka, "Wielka Brytania dotrzyma lojalnie swojego słowa: Winston S. Churchill a Polska (Warsaw: Neriton, 2013), 47.

68 Tadeusz Szumowski, "Wokół przesilenia lipcowego 1940 roku," *Kwartalnik Historyczny*, Vol. 87, No. 1 (1980), 86.

69 Dymarski, *Stosunki wewnętrzne*, 96.

70 Maria Pestkowska, *Za kulisami rządu polskiego na emigracji* (Warsaw: RYTM, 2000), 44.

71 Tebinka, *Churchill a Polska*, 47.

72 Olgierd Terlecki, *General ostatniej legendy: Rzecz o Gen. Władysławie Sikorskim* (Chicago, IL: Polonia, 1976), 114; Witkowski, *Ojcowie*, 46; Józef Garliński also speaks of Retinger being "sent" by Churchill; see his *Poland, SOE and the Allies*. London: George Allen and Unwin, Ltd., 1969, 35, 53; cf. Tebinka, "Wielka Brytania," 47.

73 Pomian, *Retinger*, 87.

74 See Ciechanowski, "Józef Retinger," 196.

75 Kot, *Listy*, 536; the feeling was apparently mutual; see Janta, "Refleksje (3), 3.

76 Retinger unreservedly takes credit for the idea of his going: "my initiative"; the "first idea was mine"; see Retinger, "Journey to Bordeaux," shelf 2. BPL. He also said he went to "fetch" Sikorski, but does not mention Churchill in a

letter about, appropriately, Sikorski and Churchill; see "General Sikorski and Mr. Churchill," *The Times*, December 18, 1944, 5.
77 The Foreign Office noted in 1944 that Retinger "as always...has the ear of the Air Ministry." See Frank Roberts's memorandum of December 6, 1944, NA, FO 371/39541.
78 Włodzimerz Onacewicz "Komentarze do książki Leona Mitkiewicz 'Z Generałem Sikorskim na obczyźnie'," *Zeszyty Historyczne*, 18 (1970), 169) argues that the choice of Retinger was predetermined, but does not say why. Kwieciński, as air attaché actually obtained the plane "which [effort} fell within his professional competence]."
79 "Materiały dotyczące biografii Józefa Retingera," Retinger Papers, teczka 79, (PISM), 2; Retinger, "Sikorski," shelf, 2, BPL.
80 Pomian, *Retinger*, 89.
81 Stanislaw Stroński, *Polityka Rządu Polskiego na uchodźstwie w latach 1939–1942*, 3 vols (Nowy Sącz: Goldruk, 2007), 1: 280.
82 War Cabinet 171 (40), June 18, 1940, CAB 65/7/66: Second World War conclusions, NA, 506.
83 Ibid., 509.
84 Mitkiewicz, *Z Gen. Sikorskim*, 49 Cienciala, "The Question of the Polish-Soviet Frontier," 301–302. Pomian referred to the acquisition of the plan as "'"Kwieciński's work"; Pomian Interview. Pomian however allowed that the British Air Minister, Hugh Sinclair, was a friend of Retinger's; ibid. However it was apparently Air Chief Marshall Newall, and not Secretary of State for Air, Sir Archibald Sinclair, who authorized the flight.
85 General Kazimierz Sosnkowski, highest ranking soldier in the Polish army, requested an appeal to Churchill on the 18th, the day Retinger departed for France. Thus, permission for Retinger to leave could not be a response to Sosnkowski's request, but Zaleski's earlier appeal might have been the impetus. The three-day gap between the two Polish initiatives is curious.
86 Nurek, *Polska w polityce*, 295. Dymarski doubts that this was a British intelligence operation, but it did correspond to Churchill's disposition at the time: saving Sikorski meant invaluable Polish soldiers; see his *Stosunki wewnętrzne*, 96–97.
87 Kazimierz Sosnkowski, *Materiały Historyczne* (London: Gryf Publications, 1966), 3. Sosnkowski implies that Sikorski left so hurriedly that he left the evacuation plans in chaos; see Sosnkowski quoted in Babiński, *Przyczyniki*, 568–569.
88 Almost certainly one of the two was Sikorski' adjutant Janusz Tyszkiewicz-Łącki. See his "Byłem adiutantem Generała Sikorskiego," *Zeszyty Historyczne*, 89 (1989), 71cf. Zygmunt Borkowski, "Wspomnienia z Drugiej wojny światowej-1939–1943," *Zeszyty Historyczne*, Vol. 29 (1974), 199 who confirms Tyszkiewicz as one of the passengers.
89 James, *Cazalet*, 229, 232. He assumed this position at Sikorski's request.
90 Terlecki sees the Retinger-Cazalet combination as both representing British interests; see his *Wielka awantura*, 68–69. Cazalet described Retinger as Sikorski's "confidential adviser and lifelong friend"; see Cazalet, *With Sikorski to Russia*, 1. Cazalet and Sikorski became friends indeed "the closest friend in his life" the first time they met in April, 1940; see Robert Rhodes James, *Victor Cazalet: A Portrait* (London: Hamish Hamilton, 1976), 226, 232. Leon J. Waszak, *Agreement in Principle: The Wartime Partnership of General Władysław Sikorski and Winston Churchill* (New York: Peter Lang, 1996), 32–33. Retinger and Cazalet were very close.
91 Mitkiewicz, *Z Gen. Sikorskim*, 52–53, 252–253.
92 Anna M. Cienciala, "The Question of the Polish-Soviet Frontier in British, Soviet, and Polish Policy in 1939–1940: The Litauer Memorandum and Sikorski's Proposal," *Polish Review*, 33 (1988), 296.

93 Retinger contends that Sikorski asked Raczyński and him to prepare the memorandum, but that the first, rejected draft was by Litauer; quoted in Pomian, *Retinger*, 136–137; cf. Prażmowska, *Britain and Poland*, 64.
94 John Coutouvidis, "Sikorski's thirty-day crisis, 19 June–19 July 1940," in Sword, *Sikorski*, 116. For Litauer's connections with Rothstein and the Soviets see Jerzy J. Lerski, "Socjaliści polscy do brytyjskich," *Zeszyty Historyczne*, 75 (1986), 124–125; Terlecki, *Generał*, 119–120. It was about this time when Retinger was involved with a convoluted effort to publish a pro-government newspaper; the details are sketchy; see Dymarski, *Stosunki wewnętrzne*, 192n, 308. For Rothstein see Świderska, "Drobiazgi," 65.
95 Litauer, it seems, may well have also been a British agent; see Władysław Bułhak, "Wokół misji," Józef H. Retingera do kraju, kwiecień – lipiec 1944r. "*Zeszyty Historyczne*, 168 (2009), 74–75. Świderska, "Drobiazgi," 70. Rothstein was, not surprisingly, a member of the Party, but from when is unclear; see Prażmowska, *Britain and Poland*, 60.
96 Terlecki, *General*, 140.
97 Mitkiewicz, *Z Gen. Sikorskim*, 65. In 1945 Litauer claimed that as early as November, 1939 Sikorski had given the English a memorandum, prepared by Litauer which was not dissimilar to the current document, both in Stanislaw Mackiewicz's eyes, "philorussian"; see his *Zielone Oczy* (Warsaw: Instytut Wydawniczy Pax, 1958), 101. Pobóg-Malinowski brackets Retinger with Litauer as "inspirers" of the memorandum; see his *Najnowsza Historja*, 3: 151.
98 Here we follow closely the evidence presented by Cienciala in ibid.; cf. Terry, *Poland's Place*, 53, for a similar synopsis.
99 Raczkiewicz was always critical of what he considered Sikorski's pro-Russian disposition; see Kochanski, *Eagle Unbowed*, 341.
100 Retinger claimed, rather vaguely, that he had a part in composing Raczyński's version; this seems implausible given the latter's disdain for Retinger; "Polish Relations with the USSR and the Polish-Russian Agreement of 1941," Retinger Papers, shelf 2, BPL.
101 Retinger to NN, October 28, 1939, 68/1/12, PISM. Retinger does, however, credit Litauer with being an "ardent patriot." Retinger Collection, PISM.
102 Retinger to Stroński, November 1, 1939, 68/9/12? Retinger Collection, PISM. He also, however, criticized stories too pro-sanacja; see Retinger to Stroński, November 1, 1939, Retinger Collection, 68/20., PISM.
103 "Polska polityka w Anglii," November 3, 1939, 12. Retinger Collection, PISM.
104 There is a good biographical sketch of Litauer in Hanna Świderska, "Drobiazgi jałtanskie," *Zeszyty Historyczne*, 106 (1993), 63–83. As late as fall 1944 British Intelligence was meeting with Litauer; see "Report on a conversation with Dr. Litauer on September, 24 [1944]," HS4/136, NA. The British regarded Litauer as unreliable; see Moscow Embassy to FO, December 22, 1944, FO371/39421.
105 Władysław Pobóg-Malinowski, *Najnowsza historia polityczna Polski, 1864–1945. Tom trzeci: Okres 1939–1945*, 2nd ed. (London: Gryf, 1981), 148, n. 118 Ciechanowski, "Retinger," 197.
106 A prime example of this is a July, 19, 1940 meeting of the government; see Eugeniusz Duraczyński and Romuald Turkowski, *O Polsce na uchodzstwie: Rada Narodowa Rzeczypospolitej Polskie, 1939–1945* (Warsaw: Wydawnictwo Sejmowe, 1997), 51.
107 Barbara Berska, *Kłopotliwy sojusznik: Wpływ dyplomacji brytyjskiej na stosunki polsko-sowieckie w latach 1939–1943* (Kraków: Księgarnia akademicka, 2005), 52.
108 Szumowski, "Wokół przesilenia," 93.
109 Ibid., 93.

110 This is the conclusion of Szumowski, but he admits the lack of confirming British archival evidence; see ibid., 93.
111 Babiński, *Przyczynki*, 50–51.
112 Wapiński argues that Retinger helped in the preparation of the Litauer memorandum; see Wapiński, "Retinger,"150. Litauer is not an attractive figure. He met with Soviet representatives before drafting the memorandum. Evidence suggests that he was a Soviet agent; cf. Stroński, *Polityka*, 1:523n; Terlecki, *Generał*, 119.
113 Raczyński, *In Allied London*, 45.
114 Bogomolov was Soviet ambassador to France; after that he was a rather nebulous representative to allied governments in London, including the Poles. For Retinger's relationship with him see the frustrating letter NN to NN, nd, BPL. When Sikorski died off Gibraltar in 1943, Bogomolov's complete commentary was "he was anti-Russian," see Ladislav Karel Feierabend, *Beneš mezi Washingtonem a Moskvou: vzpomínky z Londýnske vlády. Od jara 1943 do jara 1944* (Washington, DC: PRO, 1966), 46.
115 Lerski, "Socjaliści polscy," 124.
116 Mitkiewicz, *Z Gen. Sikorskim*, 56.
117 This long summary is from Pomian, *Retinger*, 88–91. There is a report that Retinger was to be decorated for his action; it is apparently untrue; see Z. S. Siemaszko, "Szara eminencja w miniaturze," *Zeszyty Historyczne* 23 (1973), 177.
118 Terlecki, *Wielka awantura*, 70.
119 Sarah Meiklejohn Terry, *Poland's Place in Europe: General Sikorski and the Origin of the Oder-Neisse Line, 1939–1943* (Princeton, NJ: Princeton University Press, 1983), 54n.
120 War Cabinet Meeting, July 19, 1940, CAB65/8/20, NA130.
121 Retinger to Jaspar, May 18, 1953, Box 20, Retinger Papers, BPL.
122 Terlecki, *Wielka awantura*, 72.
123 Pobóg-Malinowski, *Z mojego okienka*, 714.
124 Terlecki argues that Retinger was a British agent from the start of World War II if not earlier; see his *Wielka awantura*, 61ff. Mackiewicz writes that Retinger admitted being a British agent while in Mexico and Morocco; Mackiewicz, *Zielone oczy*, 105.
125 Ibid., 69.
126 Sir Peter Wilkinson, "Sikorski's journey to England, June 1940," in Keith Sword, ed., *Sikorski: Soldier and Statesman: A Collection of Essays*. London: Orbis Books, 1990, 159–160.
127 Quoted in Coutouvidis, "Thirty Day Crisis," 101.
128 See, for example, H.D. to Jebb, forwarded to FO; March 3, 1941, NA, HS4, 325.
129 Mikołajczyk to Sikorski, July 24, 1940. Retinger Collection, 68/28, PISM.
130 Retinger to Sikorski, October 13, 1942, Retinger Collection, #40, PISM.

# 6 First steps towards federation
## The Czech frustration

**Sikorski's first trip to America**

In March of 1941, Sikorski made his first trip to America. It was preceded by lengthy meetings with Churchill. Retinger accompanied him along with two officers, including Leon Mitkiewicz, the peasant leader Mikołajczyk, and Cazalet.[1] The motives of his mission were rather vague and consisted essentially of winning American goodwill and support for his large postwar plans for European federation,[2] and to put Poland on the list of those nations eligible for lendlease. There was a bit of a cloud hanging over the visit: the possibility that Polonia would duplicate the enthusiasm to serve Poland evidenced a generation earlier when tens of thousands of Poles in America joined a Polish volunteer army. Retinger, to his credit warned Sikorski about recruiting: Polonia would give money but not volunteers.[3] The Roosevelt administration told the general that Washington could not allow the creation of such an army, but it did suggest some arrangement with Canada might be possible.[4]

A second problem was who to appoint as ambassador to Washington. Sikorski apparently wanted either General Sosnkowski or Zaleski, but had to settle for Jan Ciechanowski, who had held the position earlier and had the burden, as far as Sikorski's government was concerned, of being a member of the sanacja administration. It was a compromise choice; whether a good one is hard to judge. Retinger thought poorly of him, as did Sikorski, and regarded him as having no respect from a Democratic administration given his earlier days under Republicans Coolidge and Hoover.[5] The embassy in Washington produced one odd feature hitherto unremarked. The assistant military attaché in Washington, Rotmistrz (Senior Captain) Stefan Zamoyski, would report developments directly to Retinger; sometimes for indirect communication to Sikorski. Retinger thus had his own top level sources in America.[6] He was running his own military intelligence.

Soon after arriving, Sikorski held a press conference which won him the support of the reporters in answer to a question as to why he had come he answered that "as a salesman" (komiwojażer) of the Polish Question, "I have to go wherever I can do business."[7] Retinger was the translator.[8] Sikorski grandly announced that he came "not only as a Pole but as a spokesman of the smaller European nations to find out how much they could count on American support."⁹

Sikorski met with Secretary of State Cordell Hull, Under-Secretary Sumner Welles, at least twice, and the assistant, Adolf Berle, as well as Secretary of War Henry L. Stimson, and Roosevelt as well. He used his time to describe Polish suffering. He asked that American aid for Poland be accelerated.[10] He brought up the Jewish question. Terlecki claims that he was the first European statesman to raise to the Americans the idea of postwar reconstruction along federal lines, emphasizing the centrality of a Polish-Czech confederation. These giant plans surprised Roosevelt who expressed his enthusiastic support for the notions.[11] Welles added that Sikorski insisted that "no peaceful and prosperous Europe can be built up without a political and economic federation between Poland, Czechoslovakia and Hungary – and perhaps Rumania."[12] Sikorski had met with Czechoslovak, Greek, and Yugoslav leaders in the United States and told Roosevelt theat they supported a "regional federated Europe."[13] The significance of this is problematical: Secretary Stimson suggested that Roosevelt did not take the discussion seriously which reflected a " happy-go-lucky" attitude towards European problems.[14]

Retinger's activities in Washington are hard to reconstruct. There is a faint suggestion that he met with Hull, but that is not certain. The American ambassador to the Sikorski government, Biddle, wrote to Hull about him at the time, referring to him as "Sikorski's confidential political advisor."[15]

Poland was also quietly added to the lendlease recipients; though initially Washington wanted the Poles to work through London.[16] Hence, Sikorski got all that he had come for except rousing Polonia which was a major failure but an historic inevitability. They had become too Americanized to maintain devotion to their Polish heritage. Raczyński publicly referred to the Sikorski mission as one of the "historic moments" of the government, not that the list was long. In the north it was otherwise. The meetings with Canadian Prime Minister Mackenzie King produced nothing of substance, nor were they anticipated of doing so.[17] Before he left, Sikorski met with the Canadian Defense Minister, James Ralston, who was so negative as to be rude. The King visit was anticipated as accomplishing little and did not disappoint.[18]

The fiasco of Polonia volunteers in 1939–1940 was a major disappointment to Sikorski. . He had attached great significance to North American Polish recruiting, which was begun by negotiations with the Canadians, as Washington had suggested. Sikorski placed his confidence in the experience of the First World War.[19] At one point Sikorski anticipated raising 4,000 men in the first eight months.[20] However, he failed to consider the effects of time and assimilation: Polonia's greatest generation was gone. By the time America entered the war, Sikorski had dropped the issue. The Polonia recruiting failure was a blow to Sikorski and his brief meeting with Polonia leaders did nothing to assuage that.[21]

Retinger's successes in England were based on years of cultivating the Labour Party, the intellectual left, and key politicians. He had no such base of operations in the United States. And, whereas he often complained about powerful pro-Soviet propaganda in England,[22] in America the real problem was a combination of indifference and increasing hostility from the Roosevelt administration which found Poland an obstacle to building cooperative relations with the Soviets.[23] Roosevelt was, after all, the man who said shortly thereafter, that Poland has been "a source of trouble for over five hundred years."[24]

Retinger continued his efforts to cooperate with the Jews, something he had attempted years before and dabbled with in the interwar era. He met with British Jewish leaders in 1940, and now, during his trip with Sikorski, he met with leaders of the World Jewish Congress and the prominent rabbi from New York, Stephen Wise. Despite this, Retinger's involvement in Jewish affairs is an oddly marginal aspect of his activities and is difficult to explain.

## The Polish–Czech confederation

Poland's relations with its southern neighbor, Czechoslovakia were foul from the end of World War I. There was no history of close cooperation between the two peoples, and during World War I the Poles thought of the Czechs as excessively obedient to the Habsburg Empire, good soldier Švejk writ large. When the war ended territorial issues at once poisoned relations. The new Czech state and Poland both wanted the territory of Cieszyn (Teschen), and despite a local agreement dividing the area along ethnic lines, in which Poland prevailed, the Czechs seized the territory in January 1919 in an attack on Polish forces. The Poles, then involved in a bitter war with the Ukrainians in western Galicia, were unable to respond and the bulk of the territory remained with the Czechs, to the outrage of the Poles. Poland regained the territory during the Munich crisis of fall 1938 when the Germans seized western Czechoslovakia. The Polish government thereafter refused to discuss this Teschen issue, regarding it as settled.[25]

The Czechs, especially President Beneš, had been ardent opponents of Piłsudski's plan to build a Polish-led federation in the east of Europe and subsequent efforts at regional cooperation, Beck's "Third Europe" scheme. This first modern attempt by the Poles at European federation prompted Czech resistance who resented the notion of restored Polish influence.

The Western Powers did not recognize President Edvard Beneš as the head of an exile government and hence, Czechoslovakia has effectively ceased to exist. Since Poland played a part in the dismemberment of the country in 1938–1939, the two decades of bad relations between the countries was much worsened by the start of World War II. This state of affairs was not improved by Beneš's fundamental animosity for the Poles and the almost national disdain the Poles harbored for the Czechs.[26] The Czechs, too, had a long history of Russophilia which was abhorrent to the Poles but which influenced Czech policy decisively during World War II; in sum if the Czechs had to choose between Warsaw and Moscow, it would not be the Poles.[27]

The Polish-Czech relationship did not develop in a vacuum. As Thierry Grosbois has pointed out many of the smaller states came to the conclusion after the French defeat that they were "incapable of insuring their own defense." An alliance system of some sort would be necessary in the face of German power.[28] Various forms of confederation were "quite fashionable" during World War II, both among politicians and scholars.[29]

In October and November, 1939 Sikorski met with Beneš and denounced the policy of the both Piłsudski and the later sanacja regime towards Prague, a relationship which had caused considerable bitterness regardless of the causes. This perhaps tasteless rebuking of prewar foreign policy gave Sikorski a convenient way of suggesting that a new Poland was ready to discuss traditional grievances.[30] Sikorski had been openly advocating Polish-Czech reconciliation, and more, for years.[31] He was also known for his more "flexible" policy towards the Russians, something likely to appeal to the Czechs.

The British reaction to Polish-Czech talks was positive.[32] On December 18, 1939 the Polish government released a statement to the effect that it was necessary for the united front against Germany to create a union (zespół) of "Slavic States" in pursuit of an "East Central Europe."[33] Poland obviously intended to play the leading role in this creation and this desire led to negotiations with the Czechs in London. To create such a bloc, as Piotr Wandycz has indicated, would require a rapprochement with the Czechs. This did not appear an easy goal as Beneš was adamant about Poland surrendering its eastern territories to Russia and agreeing to become an ethnographic state.[34]

After the fall of France the meetings resumed. The Czechs now were recognized as a legal entity and vague plans for a collaborate state were sketched.[35] More serious talks were begun in late July, 1940. Nonetheless Beneš's caution and pro-Soviet attitude disquieted the Poles.[36] Raczyński had more formal talks with Beneš in September. Raczyński was cautiously optimistic.[37] In November, 1940 Beneš submitted a proposition for the Poles which was unappetizing: it started with insisting on the need for a *modus vivendi* with Russia, Poland had to denounce its seizure of Czech territory in 1938, and Russia would keep the Polish territory it occupied in 1939. For the Poles, who looked for a confederation to help protect themselves from Russian imperialism, this was hardly an attractive offer.[38] Shortly before, Beneš had the gall to tell the Poles that he was not prepared to accept the principle that "both sides made mistakes" during the interwar period: all the transgressions were on the Polish side.[39] Beneš issued the first "official document" about the talks on November 1, 1940.[40] Shortly thereafter, Sikorski asked Beneš to support Polish claims for the restitution of Poland's eastern territories. It was a step, the Pole though, in collaboration. Beneš was hostile and informed the British.[41]

From the outset Sikorski and Retinger relied on the smaller powers to begin the process of European federation.[42] Poland and Czechoslovakia were to be the nucleus:

> The union between Poland and Czechoslovakia was meant to be a customs union. It was assumed that other countries of East-Central Europe would enter the union in due course. This assumption implied that the Polish-Czechoslovakian union was to become the core of a broader federation that would embrace Central European countries.[43]

Retinger tried to propagate the idea among the major powers, beginning with the notion of economic cooperation. His first step was the founding of a journal called *New Europe*, whose influence is impossible to gauge, but was probably small.[44] Retinger used his years on network building to spread the Polish plan.

It seems clear in retrospect that the efforts by the Sikorski government to convince London of the values of postwar federation were designed to convince the British to take the Poles seriously by imitating a discussion of war aims. In November, 1940 the Sikorski government proposed a "counterweight" to Germany in the form of a "Middle European Federation dominated by Poland and Czechoslovakia." The Foreign Office was not interested.[45]

Further proof of Retinger's important role in proffering the notion of federation is the first (there would be four) of the so-called Bevin memoranda, sent by Sikorski to the Labour leader. It discussed Polish-Czech relations which were contextualized in a larger framework of Central European federation. Retinger had known Bevin for perhaps twenty years and was a well-established figure in leftist British politics. Hence his utility as a link for Sikorski is obvious. Sikorski met with Bevin shortly before issuing the memorandum; the only other person present was Retinger.[46]

However, enemies of Retinger insisted that the idea of federation was entirely Sikorski's program of 1940–1942.[47] Kot particularly resented Retinger's claim to co-authorship of even the ideas behind federation. Kot was sure those familiar with the situation would have been shocked. This, like so much Kot had to say about Retinger, is not convincing: Retinger had spoken of federation as early as 1915 and his discussion with Sikorski on the subject goes back to the 1920s. To argue that Sikorski was the sole author of these ideas is not persuasive.[48]

Sikorski also met with Milan Hodža, president of the Slovak National Council in Paris.[49] Hodža did not acknowledge Beneš's pseudo government, and was more receptive to the Poles than was his rival. Hodža envisioned a tripartite state of Poland, Czechs, and Slovaks, close to the Sikorski position.[50] He was also a convinced and proselytizing federalist.[51] Beneš opposed the division between Czechs and Slovaks contained in this plan. Retinger later admitted that the Poles were too close to the Slovaks.[52] Unfortunately, but not unexpectedly, the Poles chose Beneš. Slovakia, a virtual satellite of the Germans carried quite a burden in dealing with the allies.[53] Retinger also met frequently with Czechs Hubert Ripka and Jan Masaryk, unofficially, to circumvent Beneš. The key to Polish wartime federal plans was some arrangement with Czechoslovakia. As long as Beneš were in power, it would foreclose any Polish-Czechoslovak federation. Beneš thus was a major obstacle to Polish plans.[54]

> He rejected Hodža's idea of a tripartite Czecho-Slovak-Polish union. He opposed any real limitations of national sovereignty. He occasionally invoked the Little Entente as a useful model of regional cooperation. In this respect also his policy in exile was a continuation of the past for which largely he had been responsible.[55]

Retinger had a significant role in the Polish-Czech talks, though details are hard to uncover.[56] As Pieczewski has noted, the Polish-Czech union was not to be an end but a means for the federal reconstruction of Europe; something Retinger had long embraced. Pieczewski goes so far as to describe Retinger as "guide and initiator." Poland was too small to be "utterly independent." During the war Retinger regarded his closest colleagues in the federalist plans to be, in addition to Sikorski, Stafford Cripps, Panayotis Pipinelis, the Greek ambassador, and Milovan Gavrilović the Yugoslav ambassador. Ripka and Masaryk, who also cooperated, have already been mentioned.[57]

In February 1940 Retinger received, by a circuitous route, a note on Polish-Czech federation which pleased him immensely. It was from Zygmunt Hladka who had been Polish Councilor of Embassy in Prague in the 1930s. It listed a number of points explaining the Czech view regarding negotiations with the Poles. It listed these as political indecisiveness: a tendency to let larger powers make decisions for them; the reluctance to use force; "lack of heroic ambition"; practical, and with a gift for organization; a "cult of democracy"; and a tendency to model their political system on that of France. Retinger was delighted with the document. He thought it conveyed am outline of the Czech political mentality that could be exploited.[58]

In November, London informed the Poles that they had been musing over Central European federation; notably among Poles, Czechs, Greeks, and Yugoslavs.[59] The Poles were delighted that their federative ideas did not stand in isolation. More concrete actions regarding Polish-Czechoslovak federation soon followed, of which the center piece was Beneš's letter to Sikorski of November 1. Though differences were apparent, the basis for cooperation was achieved. Beneš wished to dilute the term "federations" by speaking of "confederation." On November 11, 1940, coincidentally Polish Independence Day, an official declaration, "The Confederation of Poland and Czechoslovakia" was issued. It was vague and more a statement of future discussions than already accomplished agreements; notable for placing past differences behind.[60] Despite this, a tentative program was announced in

December, and a joint committee established which met through the first months of 1941. Sikorski was generally recognized as the *spiritus movens* behind this.[61] Beneš, on the other hand was dismissive of the document, at least that was what he claimed in 1944.[62] He also attributed it to British pressure.[63] Wandycz suggests the whole policy can be traced to Retinger.[64]. Indeed, Retinger never abandoned the Polish-Czech federation as central to his geopolitical conception.

But in summer, 1941 the Germans invaded Russia, and Beneš wanted no serious dealings with the Poles. By 1942 Retinger was convinced that Russia would defeat the Germans, and by 1943 he concluded that only a Polish-Czechoslovak confederation would allow them to escape Russian domination. Here we may profitably consider Retinger's Catholicism in his federative ideas as discussed at the outset. A Christian community of nations would be most agreeable to a man caught praying devoutly in 1944.[65]

The Foreign Office, in June 1942, concluded that of the various confederative plans for Eastern Europe, a Polish-Czech relationship was central: "none of these small areas can easily be envisaged as members of the Confederation, unless the Polish-Czech Confederation turns out to be closer than our present information gives us conclusive evidence to expect."[66] Sikorski had proposed to Eden some sort of "Polish Balkan bloc" earlier, as a barrier to Soviet Pan-Slavism. Eden did not react at once, but the Poles soon regarded him as supportive.[67] A few months later, Churchill made positive noises about federalism which raised hopes in some circles.[68]

Eden seems to have been converted to federal notions regarding the east of Europe. When he was preparing his trip to Moscow in late 1941 he explained that one of the main goals of his meetings was "encouragement of confederations among the weaker European states." The British wanted to "strengthen" these countries to be able to resist Germany. As a result of this, London backed Polish-Czech negotiations and hoped to see other states included.[69]

The Polish-Czech negotiations proved impossible. Beneš was preemptively concerned with maintaining close relations with Moscow, and working with the Poles was therefore virtually precluded.[70] Moscow's entry into the war was, for the Czechs, the real end to federative flirtations with the Poles. Polish-Czech relations, though decorated with various committees, were at an impasse, and a rather rancorous one at that.[71] Beneš generally regarded the Polish émigré government as "reactionary."[72] There were so many factors working against a rapprochement between Prague and Warsaw that Wandycz has concluded, citing Jaroslav Valenta, "even without Soviet vetoes the chances of creating a postwar alliance between Poland and Czechoslovakia were really scanty."[73]

The Poles were stymied by a host of secondary factors: Jan Masaryk and Hubert Ripka were the biggest proponents of working with the Poles, but in Retinger's words, Masaryk was "weak." Further the Czechs did not want any Polish meetings with the Slovaks. If this were not all, Sikorski and Beneš did not like each other, and many of Sikorski's advisors disliked the Czechs.[74] When the joint Polish-Czech negotiators produced a draft agreement in June 1942 it was so vague as to be meaningless.[75] It was the failed Polish-Czech negotiations which prompted Sikorski to charge Retinger with sounding out the smaller West European states as regards forming a European Union. As was Retinger's tradition, these pourparlers were to be informal. "I am a poor manager and a poor chairman" he once lamented.[76]

During Sikorski's second visit to Washington in March 1942, the Americans were decidedly hostile to his federal plans, quite a reversal from their attitude the previous April. The general even provided Welles a "secret memorandum" from Cripps noting that the ambassador had presented advocating a postwar federation to the Cabinet a few weeks before. It was of no effect. Sikorski mused over the possibility of two blocs in Eastern Europe, one the Balkans, the other with Poles and Czechs as the nucleus possibly with Hungary and Romania as well; perhaps even Austria but, he noted, Beneš was opposed to that. Sikorski expanded his conversation to somehow include Turkey, and Scandinavia which in toto, would become "one of the main pillars of European peace."[77] Welles agreed to "consider" the ideas; Berle, "Roosevelts right-hand" according to Retinger found it "worth exploring."[78]

Washington was openly supportive of Russian ambitions in Eastern Europe, and feared that Sikorski would offend the Russians. Berle told the Poles that Washington understood Russia's need for security, a dangerous sign for the Poles.[79] Indeed, Berle had no hope for the Poles: they were the victims of Russian "imperialism" and all the Americans could do was "trust in God." Thus the Roosevelt administration deemed Sikorski's federal plans, designed to prevent Soviet domination of Eastern Europe as "doomed to failure."

Sikorski was naively pleased by the results of his second American trip which, in reality, were a blow to Polish hopes and plans.[80] Secretary Hull makes no mention of ever meeting Sikorski in his extensive memoirs. The general's long and detailed discussion of European strategy with Secretary Stimson was without consequence.[81] Retinger at least, had a long private meeting with Berle. It was Retinger's job to convince him to provide aid to the underground in Poland. Retinger met the under-secretary for two hours and, among others, gave him a horrific portrait of Poles under Russian control. They were ill and starving, and being worked to death. Berle made no comment. To his credit, Berle promised to do all that he could and later promised $12,000,000.[82] This was the only success of the trip.

The Poles would have been less optimistic about any support from Washington if they had known of Jan Masaryk's conversations with the State Department shortly before. Masaryk told Berle that the exile governments were "stupid," to which Berle assented. Besides, the Czech continued, it was "too early" to discuss postwar changes in Europe; with which Berle also agreed.[83] Besides, although "the smaller countries cannot exist as isolated units," I see no reason why we should object to their being within the orbit of Russia."[84] This was the atmosphere in Washington when Sikorski visited.

Sikorski met with Eden in August 1942 and reported his conversation with Beneš. They agreed that the question of the "Polish-Czechoslovak frontier" would be "deferred" to "some later date." If this did not end negotiations, Sikorski's conviction concerning Beneš's "obsession" with Russia caused Sikorski to conclude that he could not completely "collaborate" with Beneš. Eden seemed disappointed but negotiations between the Poles and the Czechs had really ended.[85]

Despite British efforts to intervene to resuscitate Polish-Czech planning, it was over. London substantially mirrored the American inclinations. Even Masaryk, who was close to the Poles, and Retinger personally, told Raczyński in May, 1943 that the border issue was still important and that the Czechs would not become involved in Poland's problems with the Russians; it would observe "La neutralité la plus stricte."[86] Sikorski failed to see that the rationale of pursuing a federation with the Czechs was evaporating.[87] Sikorski's death in 1943 and the end of the war ended these wartime plans: "all our schemes came to nothing" said Retinger.

## A final consideration of a Polish-Czech federation

By 1943, the American ambassador in Moscow Averill Harriman was searching for a "Polish Beneš" who would be as cooperative regarding the Soviets as the Czech was. Poland would, he hoped, adopt the "Czech solution."[88] This essentially was to seek Moscow's "benevolent protection." In December 1943 Beneš signed, in Moscow a Czechoslovak-Soviet Treaty of Alliance." Beneš apparently hoped this would be a model for the Poles. Harriman monitored the Beneš talks and shared his pleasure at the Soviets' seeming interest in good relations with the Czechs, a hopeful model for the Poles. Harriman advocated Polish capitulation to Soviet demands as regards to territorial issues as well as the composition of their own government. He had, after all, made disparaging remarks about the Poles as "feudalistic" and reactionary."[89] As for Roosevelt, he was not "interested in Eastern European matters."[90]

Harriman supported the emergence of a pro-Soviet Polish government under Moscow's tutelage.[91] Retinger and Sikorski were naïve and misled as to the chances of cooperation with Beneš. It would be the Soviets and not some federation which would speak for Central Europe, an idea supported by the Americans. During Beneš's 1943 visit to Moscow, in addition to speaking critically and condescendingly about the Poles, he discussed a tripartite union which would link Poland and Czechoslovakia as junior partners with Russia, exactly what the Poles were attempting to avoid. Beneš's naiveté here is amazing.[92]

In 1944 Beneš had a revelatory discussion on his retrospective views of the federation with Molotov and Stalin in the Kremlin. First he admitted that he fell under considerable British pressure to enter the talks with the Poles.

Second, he was "from the start" opposed to any federation; the most would be a *sui generis* arrangement which would at best be a "confederation." Even this would require the Poles to make radical internal change; they were a "feudal" society which needed to settle the outstanding territorial issues with the Czechs, and be friendly with the Soviets. In reality the whole issue was moot because Beneš would sign nothing abroad, that is, it would have to await the end of the war.[93] In the spring of 1944, a Polish underground paper concluded angrily: "The battle between the Sikorski's and Beneš's conceptions of Eastern Europe has ended with Beneš holding the field, and he is to all intents and purposes a Soviet agent."[94]

## Notes

1 Stroński, *Polityka* 1:480. The Americans referred to him as Sikorski's "principal private secretary," Chief of Staff Reference Card, RG 165, file 1, microfilm 1194, USNA. The press did not report Sikorski's mention of federal planning; see "U.S. Aid Reported Promised to Poles," *New York Times*, April 16, 1941, 3. Retinger was, he claims, initially refused a visa due to his frictions with the American earlier in Mexico; see Retinger, "Journey to Washington," shelf 2, BPL.
2 Sikorski referred to Poland and Czechoslovakia as in the van of a "regenerated federal Europe as the surest basis of lasting security." Sikorski to Roosevelt, April 28, 1941 in FDR, Papers as President: The President's Personal File, 7543, Part 16, Franklin D. Roosevelt Library and Museum, Hyde Park, NY (hereafter FDR Library).
3 Mitkiewicz, *Z Gen. Sikorskim*, 106. There is a good account of this, stressing the Canadian aspects but noting Sikorski's little-known negotiations with Roosevelt in Szymon Szytniewski, "Teofil Starzyński's Activities to Recruit Polish Soldiers in Canada during the Second World War," *Polish American Studies*, 63 (2006), 59–77; from the point of view of the exile government see J. Smoliński, *Polonia obu Ameryki w wojskowo-mobilizacyjnych planach rządu na wychodźstwie, 1939–1945* (Warsaw: 1998). Retinger wanted Haller to come to France to organize a Polish force there, as had happened in World War I, incidentally a phenomenon which Retinger opposed. See Retinger to Karol Popiel, September 23, 1939, Retinger Collection, 68/17, PISM; cf., Andrzej Brożek, "Polonia w Stanach Zjednoczonych wobec inicjatyw Ignacego Jana Paderwskiego oraz Władysław Sikorskiego w I i II wojny światowej," in Bloch, *Sikorski-Paderewski*, 269–303.
4 Welles, "Memorandum of conversation," February 21, 1941. Welles to Orme Wilson, July 22, 1941. Welles told ambassador Ciechanowski that it was impossible; Welles Papers, container 165, FDR Library. Welles to Roosevelt, April 7, 1941, *Foreign Relations of the United States*, Volume 1 (hereafter FRUS) (Washington: Government Printing Office, 1958), 232–233.
5 Mitkiewicz, *Z Gen. Sikorskim*, 126, 130. Sikorski reported his distaste for Ciechanowski to the British; see Strang to NN, August 16, 1941. FO 371/26759, NA.
6 Duraczyński, *Rząd Polski*, 217, 226, 233. Władysław Bułhak, "The Foreign Office and the Special Operations Executive and the Expedition of Józef Hieronim Retinger to Poland, April–July 1944," *Polish Review*, Vol. 61, No. 3 (2016), 42–43.
7 Terlecki, *General*, 135.
8 Mitkiewicz, *Z Gen. Sikorskim*, 129.

9 Wandycz, "Recent Traditions," 49.
10 Sikorski to Welles, April 27, 1941, Welles Papers, container 73. FDR Library.
11 Terlecki, quoting Ambassador Jan Ciechanowski, *Generał*, 135–136; Wandycz, "Recent Traditions," 49.
12 Wandycz quoting Welles in "Recent Traditions," 49–50; cf. Welles to Roosevelt, April 7, 1941, *FRUS Volume I*, 232–233.
13 Sikorski to Roosevelt, April 28, 1941, Roosevelt Papers as President, file 7543, FDR Library.
14 Henry Lewis Stimson, Diary, entry for April 9, 1941, Stimson Papers, reel 8, (vol. 41), Sterling Library, Yale University.
15 Biddle to Hull, June 28, 1941, ibid., 238–239.
16 Welles to Roosevelt, April 7, 1941, FRUS, 1941, Volume I, 232–233; Hull to Biddle, June 19, 1941, ibid., 236.
17 King was very impressed by Sikorski and his military analysis; see Mackenzie King Diaries, item No. 23970, Public Archives of Canada, Ottawa. Online at http://www.collectionscanada.gc.ca/obj/001059/f4/50003V60.gif
18 Dymarski, *Stosunki wewnętrzne*, 137ff.
19 Czesław Bloch, "Starania Sikorskiego o pomoc Polonii amerykańskiej," in Bloch ed., *Sikorski-Paderewski*, 230; cf. M. B. B. Biskupski, "Canada and the Creation of a Polish Army, 1914–1918," *The Polish Review*, Vol. XLIV, No. 3 (1999), 337–378.
20 Bloch, "Starania," 240.
21 Terlecki, *Wielka awantura*, 73. General Józef Haller, who led the army recruited in the United States in World War I, was even sent to the United States to rally support; it was a failure; see Bloch, "Starania," 234–237; Brożek, "Polonia w Stanach Zjednoczonych", 46–48.
22 For example, Retinger to Sikorski, October 14 and 16, 1939, Retinger Collection, 685, PISM, and later "Count Raczyński's Report…, September 9, 1943, *DPSR*, II: 50, Retinger was even asked to prepare a report for Eden on Russian propaganda.
23 The American scene is discussed in detail in M. B. B. Biskupski, *Hollywood's War with Poland, 1939–1945* (Louisville, KY: University of Kentucky Press, 2010).
24 Quoted in Piotr Wandycz, "Western Images and Stereotypes of Central and Eastern Europe," in Andre Gerrits and Nanci Adler, eds., *Vampires Unstaked: National Images, Stereotypes ND Myths in East Central Europe*. (Amsterdam: No. Holland, 1995), 15.
25 See Milan Hauner's review of Andras D. Ban ed, *Pax Britannica: Wartime Foreign Office Documents Regarding Plans for a Postbellum East Central Europe*. H-Net Reviews, online at http://www2.h.net.msu.edu/reviews/showrev.cgi?path=10556883998229, accessed on April 11, 2001.
26 Useful here is the interview with Kazimierz Wierzbiański entitled"Benesz a Polska," *Zeszyty Historyczne* 76 (1986), 79–88.
27 Beneš later wrote how difficult the Poles were to deal with, painting them as bellicose and unreasonable; see his *Memoirs of Dr. Eduard Beneš: From Munich to New War and New Victory* (New York: Arno Press, 1972), 147–148; for a commentary of Beneš-Sikorski relations see Luboš Kohout, *Edvard Beneš-demokrat, vlastenec, politycký realista* (Prague: np, 1984), 38–39; a tendentious work which shows Beneš in a very positive light.
28 Grosbois, "L'action de Józef Retinger," 64–65.
29 See Andras D. Ban's introductory remarks to his edited collection, *Pax Britannica: Wartime Foreign Office Documents Regarding Plans for a Postbellum East Central Europe* (Boulder, CO East European Monographs, 1997), 9.
30 Wandycz, *Czechoslovak-Polish*, 36.

31 Polonsky, "Sikorski as Opposition Politician," 69.
32 Nurek, *Polska w polityce*, 287; Wandycz, *Czechoslovak-Polish*, 37.
33 Mieczyslaw Nurek, *Polska w polityce Wielkiej Brytani w latach 1936–1941* (Warsaw: PWN, 1983), 287.
34 Piotr Wandycz, "Dwie próby stworzenia związków regionalnych w Europie wschodniej," in his *Polska a zagranica* (Paris: Instytut Literacki: 1986), 109–111; Raczyński, *In Allied London*, 46. Wandycz sees Retinger's hand in the December exposé.
35 Pieczewski, *Działalność*; Benes's letter to Sikorski was probably the first tentative step in these pourparlers; Pieczewski, *Działalność*, 103.
36 Marszałek refers to the Czechs' attitude towards federation with the Poles "opportunistic," see his *Z historii*, 137.
37 Raczyński, *In Allied London*, 69.
38 Wandycz, "Dwie próby," 111–112.
39 Beneš to Sikorski, October 27, 1941, NA, FO 800/871; FO 371, Sir Robert Bruce-Lockhart Papers, file 18, NA.
40 Pieczewski, *Działalność*, 103.
41 R. H. Bruce Lockhart to Strang, "President Beneš's Conversation with General Sikorski on Polish-Czechoslovak Co-operation," January 31, 1941, FO 371/26755, NA.
42 Retinger Papers, shelf 6, no title, BPL.
43 Pieczewski's "Retinger's Conception," 584.
44 In 1945, and probably earlier , the journal was badly underfunded, and narrowly distributed. See "Proposed budget for *New Europe* for 1945," nd, Feliks Gross Papers, Polish Institute of Arts and Sciences in America (hereafter PIASA), f. 4.28.
45 Prażmowska, *Britain and Poland*, 67–68.
46 Terry, *Poland's Place*, 87.
47 The pamphlet, which we shall discuss later, was entitled "The European Continent?" The address was given on 9 May, 1946.
48 Kot, *Listy*, 538m. Kot worshiped Sikorski; see his remarks quoted in Dymarski, *Stosunki wewnętrzne*, 71.
49 Retinger might have been involved with the talks as well but Hodža's biographer Pavol Lukáč, does not mention him. He does add Zaleski however; see his "Stredoeurópanstvo Milana Hodžu," 28. Pomian dates the first Polish-Czech discussions to late in 1939; see his *Retinger*, 121.
50 Tadeusz Kisielewski, *Federacja środkowo-europejska: Pertraktacje polsko-czechosłowackie, 1939–1943*. (Warsaw: Ludowa Spółdzielnia Wydawnicza, 1991), 29; Ivan Stovicek and Jaroslav Valenta, eds. *Ceskoslovensko-polska jednani o konfederaci a spojenectvi, 1939–1944*. Prague: Karolinum vydavatelstvi univerzity karlovy a historicky ustav akademie ved Ceske Republiky, 1995, 1:11.
51 Ibid., 31. Lukac, "Strednoeurópanstwo," 33. Hodža considered the January 14, 1940 agreement between the Czechs and Slovaks a model for Polish-Czecho-Slovak confederation; see Milan Hodža, *Federácia v strednej Európe a iné štúdie* (Bratislava: Kalligram, 1997), 239
52 Pomian, *Retinger*, x, 125, 127.
53 The greater receptivity of the Slovaks see Mateusz Gniazdowski, "Kontakty Piłsudczyków ze Słowakami w latach 1939–1945," *Niepodległość* 55 (2005), 136–137. Hodža, during the interwar period, floated the idea of a central European federation. Beneš's opposition ended the effort; see Piotr Wandycz, "Tentatives et projets d'union regionale en Europe central (XVIII, XIX, XX siècles)," *Les Cahiers de Varsovie*, 1991, No. 22, 441–442.
54 "Polish Situation Report," March 17, 1943, NA, HS4, 144.
55 Wandycz, "Recent Traditions," 41.

56 Nurek, 287. Andrzej Pieczewski, "Joseph Retinger's Conception of and contribution to the early process of European Integration," *European Review of History*, 17 (2010), 584–586.
57 Retinger, "My Part in the Movement for the Unity of Europe," BPL, Box 20.
58 Kiesielewski, *Federacja*, 45–50.
59 Ibid., 63.
60 "Declaration of the Provisional Czechoslovak Government and the Polish Government," in Ivan Štoviček and Jaroslav Valenta eds., Československo-polská jednáná o konfederaci a spojenectví, 1939–1944, four vols., Prague: Karolinum vydavatelstvi, 84–85; Wandycz, "L'éurope central," 442–443.
61 Dymarski, *Stosunki wewnętrzne*, 137–138, "The Establishment of Cooperative Peace in Europe," nd, Box 17, folder 2, Retinger Papers, BPL. Beneš obviously detested Sikorski; Kohout, *Edvard Beneš*, 39.
62 Mieczysław Szerer notes that Beneš spoke of "confederation" not federation, a major difference Szerer concludes because the former does not imply the construction of a single state and the latter does. See his *Federacje a przyszłość Polski* (London: P. S. King & Staples, 1942), 28.
63 Stanisław Kirkor, "Rola Benesza w sprawie polskiej w 1944 roku," *Zeszyty Historyczne*, 26 (1973), 47.
64 Wandycz, "Recent Traditions," 42. This seems to have been Retinger's view as well; see Podgórski, *Retinger*, 100.
65 Ibid., 19.
66 "Confederations in Eastern Europe," in Bán, *Pax Brittanica*, 45.
67 Eden to Dormer, July 4, 1941, FO 371/26755, NA. Sikorski told Eden that the Poles favored "inter-State organization." see Memorandum of July 3, 1941, FO 371/26755, NA; Cripps to FO, August 1, 1941, FO 371/ 26757, NA. "Memorandum of Conversation," November 27, 1942, [Welles and Ciechanowski], Welles Papers, FDR Library.
68 Churchill had mused over federalism in the east of Europe since the beginning of the war; see Reinhold Schairer, "Proposals and Suggestions by the US Committee on Educational Reconstruction," wherein the author speaks of Churchill and others speaking favorably about federalism "in the last weeks." In Gross Papers, PIASA, f. 4.45.
69 "Memorandum," February 5, 1942, Berle Papers, container 212, FDR Library.
70 See Beneš's advice to Feierabend, in the latter's *Beneš mezi Washingtonem a Moskvou*, 79.
71 Raczyński, *In Allied London*, 86–87.
72 Piotr Wandycz, "O stosunkach polsko-czechosłowackich: garść refleksji," *Zeszyty Historyczne*," 119.
73 Piotr S. Wandycz "Konfederacja polsko-czechosłowacka: Dokumenty," *Zeszyty Historyczne*, 116 (1996), 189.
74 Retinger Papers, "My Part in the Movement for the Unity of Europe," shelf 2, 15–17, BPL; Witkowski, *Retinger*, 57. For support of a Polish-Czech relations among anti-Beneš forces both in exile and at home, see Mateusz Gniazdowski, "Kontakty piłsudczyków ze słowakami w latach 1939–1945," *Niepodległość*, Vol. 55 (2005), 133–143.
75 Bán, *Pax Brittanica*, 49–57; Wandycz, *Czechoslovak-Polish Confederation*, 79; cf. Piotr Wandycz, "O trójkatach, pentagonach I heksagonach. Z dziejów współpracy państw Europy środkowo-wschodniej," in his *O czasach dawniejszych I bliższych" Studia z dziejów Polski i Europy* Środkowo-Wschodniej (Poznań: Wydawnictwo poznańskie, 2009), where he regards the 1942 events as the "pinnacle" (punkt szczytowy) of the Polish-Czech federative effort, 310; cf. Piotr Wandycz, "Benešův rozhovor se Sikorským 3. února 1942," *Acta universitatis carolinae. Studia historica* 42 (1995), 345–353.

76 Retinger, "Introduction," shelf 4, BPL, 1.
77 "The Problem of Central and South-Eastern Europe," in Welles "Memorandum," of December 7, 1942, Welles Papers, container 165, FDR Library. The document stressed the centrality of economics.
78 "Memorandum of Conversation," December 4, 1942, Welles Papers, container 165, FDR Library. Sikorski gave Welles a memorandum which, note, included Lithuania in the federated Poland. It was a very long memorandum and spoke about the Polish-German border issue at length. See also "Memorandum," March 28, 1942, Berle Papers, container 213, FDR Library.
79 "Memorandum of a Conversation," [with Raczyński], February 24, 1942, Berle Papers, container 213, FDR Library.
80 Wandycz, "Recent Traditions," 57–58.
81 Stimson was impressed by Sikorski and had his assistant, John McCloy come to the meeting. See Stimson Diary, March 27, 1942, Stimson Papers, reel 7, (vol. 38), Yale: Sterling Memorial Library.
82 Hull cites the figure of $12.5. It was to be paid yearly. When Sikorski died, in July 1943, a credit advance was arranged; see *The Memoirs of Cordell Hull, Volume II*, New York: Macmillan, 1948, 1270.
83 "Memorandum of Conversation," February 10, 1942, container 213, Berle Papers, FDR Library.
84 "Memorandum," February 5, 1942, container 213, Berle Papers, FDR Library.
85 Eden to C. Dormer, August 20, 1942, FO/954/19B, NA; British Intelligence reported that the Poles were convinced that Beneš was acting under Soviet "directives"; "Comments on London Reports," December 16, 1942; cf. London Report Number SO/576, December 14, 1943, HS4/243, NA.
86 Masaryk to Raczy ski, May 14, 1943, Gross Papers, PIASA, f. 4.32. Berle of the American State Department, referred to Beneš as the "field agent for the Russians," cf. "Memorandum," December 7, 1942, Berle Papers, container 214, FDR Library.
87 Ibid., 58.
88 William Larsh, "W. Averill Harriman and the Polish Question, December 1943–August 1944," *East European Politics and Societies*, Vol. 7 (1993), 514.
89 Wandycz, "Western Images," 15.
90 Larsh, "Harriman," 544.
91 Ibid., 549–550.
92 See Wandycz, *Polish-Czech Confederation*, 91ff; Stanislaw Kirkor, "Rola Benesza w sprawie polskiej w 1944 roku," *Zeszyty Historyczne*, Vol. 26 (1973), 39–56.
93 Stanislaw Kirkor, "Rola Benesza w sprawie polskiej w 1944 roku." *Zeszyty Historycne*, 26 (1973), 46–47.
94 See the excerpt in Lipgens, "East European Plans," in Lipgens and Loth, *European Integration*, 1:648.

# 7  A wider federation

After Sikorski's death in July, 1943 Retinger recalled: "We spent 1939–1940 maturing our ideas," though they were clear before the war. However: "The first inkling" was Sikorski's speech of November, 1939 at the Foreign Press Association in London. Sikorski was the first significant European statesman to indicate publicly and clearly that the European states ought to relinquish part of their sovereignty for the common interest.[1] In the key part of his address Sikorski said:

> The convolutions which were shaking the old content led now to the emergence of the idea of European solidarity. This idea would sooner or later unite all nations in a community of free and independent States, to whom it would bring home a European consciousness of common citizenship.[2]

This conclusion was the result of "a turning point in history, when mankind must choose between two forms of collective existence which were contending for supremacy in the world." The first was represented by Britain, France, and the United States, and the second by the aggressors in the war.[3] In the original, much longer, Polish version he adds at this point:

> Poland, its people and its new government have made the choice. Today there is not a Pole who doesn't see that that a free Poland can exist only in a united and consolidated Europe. Certainly it is too early to visualize how this future Europe will look in detail. However we can say with certainty ... is not this view the natural outcome of the spiritual, moral, and material outcome of Greco-Roman, and Christian civilization?[4]

Sikorski later explained some of his references in a press interview. The plans for Central Europe would give rise to a Scandinavian and Iberian federation, which Sikorski already saw in the offing. Germany and Italy were, for the nonce, not trustworthy. And, finally "there must be a world government" with its own military force.[5]

It was probably at this time that Retinger prepared a memorandum making a series of significant points. He began by arguing that Polish "political ideology" should be based on the creation of a regional federation. Which would result in powerful economic units. Which, in turn, would create a barrier against "Russian or German imperialism."[6] A bloc of Poles, Czechs, Slovaks, Lithuanians, Romanians, Hungarians and later Ukrainians; with a joint army and tariff system; but otherwise separate, was the dream. The members would enjoy complete autonomy. Simultaneously a Balkan and Scandinavian federation should be sought. They would form a future European structure strong enough to oppose the "imperialism" of Russia, America, or Great Britain.

Regional blocs were nothing new to Europe; it was the notion of the federation of these blocs which made Sikorski's speech noteworthy. In the interwar period, Také Ionescu's notion of a bloc vertically from the Baltic to the Aegean, or the Central European Bloc of Colonel Józef Beck of Poland are well known. Earlier, the weak Little Entente, which linked non-adjacent states, the Balkan Entente, and the Baltic Entente, had achieved nothing.[7]

The winning over of public opinion was to be the next task, not so much as that of Central Europe, but of France, England and America. The wartime journal Retinger created "Free Europe" would be the means for this campaign in Europe and America. But more importantly, an organization must be created to promote these solutions, perhaps resembling the earlier "Friends of the League of Nations."[8]

Retinger had adumbrated a plan for a continent-wide federation of two levels. The first would consist of smaller countries of limited potential. They would form local units: Scandinavia, Central Europe, and the Balkans. Alongside them would be Germany, Italy, and France. The function of this second grouping was vague but implied that each would function as the equal of the smaller federations. This would provide them with security from the imperial powers: Russia, America, Britain, and Japan. Germany and Poland would have some sort of connection but it was not detailed. Nationalism and economic competition were the causes of wars in Europe. Poland must be prepared for a new organization. This memorandum was both bold and annoying due to its omissions and vaguery. Nonetheless, it demonstrated that Retinger, from the beginning of the war, was caught up by broad schemes of federation.[9] He sought "federated blocs and the construction of cooperative peace."[10]

In November 1940, Sikorski delivered a memorandum to the British government outlining a plan for the federal reconstruction of Europe. Grosbois credits Retinger with being the moving force behind this action. This would reflect the Retinger memorandum of the previous September. Here Retinger's prewar connections with the British Left began to pay dividends. In Churchill's cabinet such Labourites as Hugh Dalton and Ernest Bevin were available to Retinger to link him to the government.[11] Sikorski also entrusted Retinger with conducting informal negotiations with a number of foreign statesman in search of allies for a confederative response to Europe's dilemma. The Belgians proved the most tractable.[12]

Apparently, Europe was envisioned as consisting of five blocs: first, a Central European one consisting of Poland, Czechoslovakia, Lithuania, Hungary, Romania; second, a "Mediterranean-Latin" bloc of France, Italy, Spain, and Portugal; Germany and Austria would be the third, the German bloc; fourth, the "North Sea Coast Bloc" would comprise Belgium, Holland, Luxembourg, Denmark, Norway, Sweden, and finally Yugoslavia, Bulgaria, Greece, and Albania would form the "South-Balkan Bloc." This plan stimulated discussion and federation theories among some of the listed states, notably Yugoslavs and Greeks, and led to the formation of a number of intragovernmental bodies.[13]

Retinger was directly responsible for the meetings between the Prime Ministers of the governments in exile in London.[14] This idea had been bruited by Sikorski in February, 1941 at a meeting at the Dorchester Hotel which included Cazalet, hence the link to the British-and Belgian representatives. Cazalet expressed British support. He also accompanied Retinger to subsequent meetings between Retinger and the Belgians. The latter were favorable to what Grosbois deemed the "Polish proposition." [15] This Western European combination would be the example and part of a Europe which would include a Polish federation in the east of Europe, the main reason the Poles were so interested in the Belgian attitude. Close cooperation between Belgium and Holland might presage, at least by example, a Polish-Czech rapprochement.

The key next step, in 1942 was the actions of the Belgian statesman who was the bridge, along with Retinger, from Sikorski's speech to the first postwar organizational efforts for continental cooperation, the "The European League for Economic Cooperation" of which there will be more later. Paul Van Zeeland, according to Belgian scholar, Dumoulin, formulated, in the context of Sikorski's Plan, several important considerations concerning the regional economic organization of Europe.[16]

In Pieczewski's words: "Retinger strengthened his personal connection with leaders of European countries such as the Belgians Paul-Henri Spaak (Minister of Foreign Affairs), van Zeeland (former Prime Minister), Roger Motz (former member of parliament), Marcel-Henri Jaspar (another former Prime Minister) and the prominent Catholic Pieter Kerstens which enabled him to establish close cooperation with those politicians after the war."[17] Retinger acted as a proponent and go-between among the exiled Belgian and Dutch governmental figures and constantly promoted the idea of a federated Europe: "the European idea." Retinger was able to combine a group of like-minded people to the federation concept with Jaspar in the forefront. By late 1940, he had Cripps's support, and Sikorski and Retinger met with Eden, Lord Sinclair of the House of Lords and "especially" Bevin to discuss the matter (the date or dates are not known). In January, 1941 Sikorski was speaking of an "Inter-Allied governmental declaration," but its contents were also unknown.[18] It was obvious that the Poles wished to assume the leadership of the exile governments and increase their leverage with the major powers. It was, as Retinger noted: "the beginning of a new idea."[19]

## A wider federation 153

Sikorski hosted a luncheon at the Dorchester suggesting the combination of the eight exile governments in Europe in favor of a "communauté européenne" which would, temporarily have its headquarters in London. Spaak wanted an exchange of views on the proposal as long as the Netherlands and Norway served as intermediaries and that a hostile attitude towards Soviet Russian was avoided. The Czechs were reserved, having already signed agreements of friendship and cooperation with Moscow. The Greeks feared that Sikorski was "anti-Russian" and confided this to the British.[20]

Retinger met with the Foreign Office's Sir William Strang and explained, innocently, that the exile governments were "engaged in trying to draft an agreement by which they would declare their intention to maintain relations of friendship and solidarity after the war".[21] British cooperation was eagerly sought, and formally requested shortly thereafter. A draft about postwar cooperation was in the offing. It included calls for a Polish-Czech and a Greek-Yugoslav confederation. The British were very unhappy as it saw the Polish initiative being essentially anti-Russian. London also feared that calls for an international economy might trouble the Americans. Unfortunately for the Poles, most of the exile governments were also opposed; especially Beneš. London rejected participation. Eden was "not enthusiastic." Retinger tried to mollify the British, but to no avail. The Polish draft died aborning.[22]

Sikorski later had talks with the Dutch, Eelco Van Kleffens, who signed the Benelux treaty for Holland and Pieter Gerbrandy, Prime Minister of the Netherlands in exile, and Belgian leaders on February 7, 1941. This was a major meeting and something of a transition. A number of Belgians, notably, Spaak had become converted to the idea of a west European federation but, as Grosbois notes, this would by definition exclude Poland. Van Kleffens had even prepared a memorandum opposed to Poland and the rest of East Central Europe joining a federative system.[23]

Sikorski invited the Belgian Prime Minister Hubert Pierlot to the Dorchester for a luncheon meeting. Also present were Cazalet, a link to Churchill, former ambassador Józef Lipski, Poland's last envoy to Berlin, Jaspar, and Retinger. Spaak and Jaspar immediately seized upon the "Polish idea" of a federal bloc. Pierlot was reluctant and lamented the excessive ambition of the Poles.

Jaspar has left a vivid impression of the February 7 luncheon convened by Sikorski:

> The general told us, with a puerile pride, that he was the greatest ally of the British, because he had more than 30,000 men, 30,000 soldiers on the soil of Britain.

Sikorski spoke again:

> To explain to us that the allied governments resident in London, should meet in conference to examine their war goals and post-war problems. Cazalet approved of the proposition of the President [sic] of Poland.[24]

Sikorski had taken the initiative in this proposal and we have the work of Fernando van Langenhove to expand on its particulars.[25] He summarized the "Polish propositions" as having the following points. First, replace the separate "bases" of a European community with issuing a public declaration of the change to a functioning entity. Second, establish "modalities de realisation" of the various delegates of their governments. Third, convince the British that there is a cohesion of these governments. And, finally, declare no intention of desiring a separate peace. Among the Belgian critiques was the difference between the Western and Eastern powers, namely Poland. Poland would be given too much power, and the Czech opposition would cause the plan to be doomed at the outset.[26]

Despite these Belgian concerns, and Czech hostility, they established a "Continental Foreign Ministers" group. Raczyński and Retinger were both members. The group had thirty to forty meetings and sometimes Eden, or the Americans Harriman or Ambassador Biddle would attend. In January, the Belgians established the "Commission pour l'étude des problems d'après-guerre, CEPAG," under the leadership of the prominently Catholic van Zeeland.[27] The Belgians then decided to discover the opinions of the major powers on the subject of European union. They regarded a Polish-Czech reconciliation as a model for a Belgian-Dutch one.[28]

The federation marketed by the Poles and supported by the British became more urgent after the Soviets launched an obvious plan to resuscitate pan-Slavism.[29] There was even a "Pan-Slavic Congress" in Moscow which much discomfited him.[30] Retinger was horrified and feared for both Poland and Britain. Retinger worked closely with the exile Yugoslav and Greek ambassadors, both fearful of the Soviet initiative. By early 1942 a public agreement on Balkan union was issued under Retinger's influence.[31] In February 1942 Moscow dropped what Wandycz calls a "bombshell" denouncing a Polish-Czechoslovak confederation.[32] In any event, the meetings with the exile leaders ended with Sikorski's death in 1943. Retinger concluded, wistfully, that only a future federation could save Europe, and Poland. The British, however, would not support federation in the face of Soviet opposition.

Sikorski had tasked Retinger with acting as a mediator between the exile participants, and both were at the decisive meeting in late 1941.[33] Spaak, perhaps the largest figure to emerge from the negotiations said this about Retinger and the Polish efforts:

> The politicians who had spent the war years in Britain knew him well. ...An intelligent, active, and slightly mysterious individual, he would have luncheon every day with one British politician or another, or with a member of one of the governments in exile. He knew everybody and no door was closed to him. During those years he was one of the best informed politicians. He helped to initiate the discussions we Poles, Czechs, Dutch, Norwegians and Belgians held in order to establish new links between us.[34]

Soon thereafter Sikorski, at Retinger's prompting, proposed postwar cooperation to Belgium, the Netherlands, Norway, Luxembourg, Yugoslavia and Greece. The British were also involved, and the preliminary discussions with Eden were led by Retinger.[35] Sikorski discussed the federation issue with Eden as his main topic even though there were seemingly more pressing matters. In early 1942, a group of eight states were rounded up. Whether this was at the Poles' initiative or not is unknown but circumstantial evidence suggests that it was, to sign a common declaration.[36] At the same time Retinger was happily speaking of another federation, involving Poland, Lithuania, part of Latvia, which would constitute "East Central European Federation." It was, essentially, pre-partition Poland. Cripps was supposedly enthusiastic.[37] What was needed was Western support. The Russians rejected the whole idea as without significance and made it clear that they would be the decisive voice in Eastern Europe and all these declarations were so much nonsense.[38]

Sikorski had produced a draft "declaration of principles to serve as a basis for postwar collaboration."[39] Some initial meetings were held, an Inter-Allied Secretariat created, and the first full gathering took place in October, 1942.[40] Twenty meetings were held at the Polish embassy and the Poles were represented by Retinger and ambassador Raczyński, indicating the seriousness with which they viewed the process. However, the group eventually fell apart. Sikorski was rejected as anti-Soviet and the meeting as worthless. Even earlier, nonetheless, from these combinations Benelux emerged.[41]

Retinger later blamed the idea's failure on Sikorski's death in 1943, his own trip to Poland in 1944, and the allied invasion of the continent. The role of the Poles, Retinger insisted, was crucial, and their distraction removed the "premier promoters of these discussions."[42] Nevertheless, Retinger deemed this the conception of the later European Union.[43] Thomas Lane believed that these activities by Sikorski and Retinger "laid the groundwork for the unity of the whole of Europe after the war:"[44] They were the Polish godfathers of the European Union, with Retinger almost certainly the initial moving spirit.

In what may have been a rogue operation, Retinger conceived the idea of creating a joint "Minor Allied SOE." The British were none too keen on this and tried to discourage this notion of the exile governments operating their own intelligence system. Gladwyn Jebb of the Foreign Office met with Retinger about it and was not helpful. Retinger openly regarded the composite organization as a wartime step in the direction of postwar European unity. Sikorski, in Scotland at the time, might not have known of Retinger's notions, but the British were not sure.[45]

These postwar speculations took on a wider and more specific framework in the creation of the Central and East European Planning Board in New York created (officially) on January 7, 1942 and was maintained by the eminent Polish sociologist Feliks Gross which brought together representatives of Poland, Czechoslovakia, Greece, and Yugoslavia.[46] In addition to Gross, who performed the role of general secretary, Minister Jan Stańczyk who represented Poland, and Jan Masaryk (a very active participant)

Czechoslovakia, were both deputy chairmen, as was Aristides Dimitratos of Greece. The powerless chairman was Yugoslavia's Sava N. Kosanovich. Gross was convinced that the Board had both significance and prospects. In 1943 he wrote, retrospectively, "General Sikorski saw in the Planning Board the first sign, however weak it may be, of the coming close cooperation and perhaps confederation of the suffering peoples of Europe."[47]

By the second meeting in February 1942, the Polish role had become overwhelming with ambassadors Raczyński and Ciechanowski, Minister to the League of Nations Sylwin Strakacz, former Minister of Industry Alfred Falter, two members of the Ministry of Foreign affairs, and at least one other.[48] Retinger was the moving force behind the body and long wanted such an organization to be created in the United States.[49] Since the beginning of the war Retinger had sought an American agency supporting European federation. On November 4, 1941 an agreement of representatives of the four countries plus labor leaders signed an agreement in favor of influencing American public opinion as well as the government.[50] The next day, *The New York Times* labeled this undertaking the "United States of Central Europe."[51]

Gross averred that support for European federation was popular in the United States and the Planning Board had a positive role to play.[52] Soon the Board, whose heart and soul was Gross, was in close touch with Adolf Berle of the State Department.[53] Gross, however, complained to Retinger that there was a dearth of interest in Eastern Europe in the United States and that many governments failed to pay their dues. Poland was an exception. Each country was assessed $3,000.00 per annum. Poland doubled that amount voluntarily. The Czechs paid $250.00.[54] Gross hinted that certain American agencies were supportive, but this is vague.[55] By 1943 it was Poland's doubling its assessed payment that "in this way prevented the liquidation of the Board."[56]

Because Gross was very close to Retinger (indeed, the only Pole in America with whom he maintained a close friendship even after the war) the former's views on federation are important. The sociologist envisioned that first, Poland's security required a continent-wide solution. This, in turn, assumed the close cooperation of all "free European nations." The latter would create: a European Federal Reserve Bank, centralized federal control of all colonies, similar management of key industries and raw materials. Armed forces, "national militaries," were to be only "small territorial forces." The whole would function in a contingent based on regions which would send representatives to a "European executive." Russia might be a member, but Germany not. Poland would be part of a "Baltic-Danubian region," whose details were not specified but posited as being large enough to maintain security between Russia and Germany. Within Poland there would be "autonomous regions," evidently for the large ethnic minority population of prewar Poland. The whole would reflect the "transvaluation of meaning of state frontiers." Gross foresaw possible problems with this vision. An Anglo-American bloc would be too big and the British Empire alone could possibly enter or perhaps an independent British Commonwealth. The whole was to be informed by Montesquieu's "division of powers." It is noteworthy that Christian principles or some reference to a Roman Catholic moral basis were omitted: though we should regard Gross and Retinger as having similar visions for Europe. Gross was a Jew and Retinger a Catholic.[57]

After the war, and much changed circumstances, the Planning Board quickly ceased functioning. Czechoslovakia stopped cooperating and as Masaryk reportedly said ironically "there be no Czechoslovakia without Poland, and no Poland without Czechoslovakia." Gross and Strakacz, the only ones left, applied for American visas.[58] However, federalist Poles living in the United States were active for many years later.[59]

## The Jewish issue

Whilst dealing with the Czechs and the federative plans in general, Retinger orchestrated a series of meeting between the Polish exile government and British Jews. This was a particularly sensitive topic because Polish-Jewish relations, had become severely strained in the last years of the sanajca regime, and anti-Semitism had been growing alarmingly. The agent decided to discuss these issues was Stanisław Kot, a devotee of Sikorski, but poorly chosen because of his aggressive anti-Semitism. In his closing remarks, which must have left the representatives of the Board of Deputies of British Jews flabbergasted, Kot suggested that the Jews be relocated somewhere between the Baltic and the Black Sea, a new pale of settlement. The Jews understandably rejected the notion. The meeting had been arranged by Retinger who must have felt awkward at so stark a proposal.[60] He had, however, himself called for Jewish emigration from Poland before the war, and early in the hostilities.[61] As Hamerow has argued, Retinger was "no racist, no anti-Semite. He was a typical centrist." However, like so many of this description he regarded the huge Jewish population of Poland as seemingly reluctant to assimilate. "Emigration" was the only answer.[62] "Retinger's low opinion of Kot's diplomatic skills seemed justified.[63]

Whereas these meetings proved abortive, the Poles pursued relations with the Zionists whose plans they regarded as complimentary. By early 1940, Retinger was "an ongoing link" with Abraham Abrahams head of the Revisionist New Zionist Organization's Political Department in London.[64] Retinger continued these activities. He was having a series of meetings with Jewish leaders and trying to convince them that the anti-Semitism they had noticed among the Poles was disappearing. The populists (peasant parties) were never anti-Semitic, and even the endecja was getting better. Retinger tried to create a "Special Commission" for Polish-Jewish relations and had virtually endless meetings with Jewish leaders in 1940 to 1942.[65] The Jews, however, had mixed feelings about the exile government.[66]

Retinger was obviously frustrated in his dealing with the Jews. The British Jews wanted some sort of declaration by the émigré government regarding Jewish rights in Poland. The Poles were very resistant. Selig Brodetsky, president

## 158  A wider federation

of the Board of Deputies of Polish Jews had a long meeting with Retinger in March 1940. In response to the demand for a declaration,[67] Retinger responded that things had already been undertaken, and he pointed to the *liberalność* of Sikorski, Kot, and Zaleski. Brodetsky said, to the contrary, that Koc and Haller were anti-Semites. Retinger responded, which must have been offensive to Brodetsky, that the Jewish question was not the only important issue facing Poland. He was not in a position to determine government staffing and he would not tolerate "Jewish interference in fundamental questions" [ingerencja żydowska w sprawach zasadniczych]. There needed to be Polish-Jewish reconciliation, but the Jews must do the most and here he brought up the anti-Polish press campaign and the still very controversial issue of the behavior of the Jews in eastern territories when the Soviets invaded.[68]

In 1941 he had broadened his support in the government and, to quote Engel: "the Washington [Polish] embassy did play an important role in introducing Revisionist representatives to leading American journalists, clergymen, and political figures, and it appears that the Information Ministry did eventually subsidize the English-language Revisionist monthly, *Jewish Standard*."[69] Retinger's interest in the American Jewish community was apparent at least as early as 1939 when he wrote to Sikorski that a Polish mission to the United States should be preceded by a meeting to discuss Jewish issues due to the "enormous influence and significance of Jewry" in America.[70] Unfortunately, the problem was not resolved.

A most unpleasant chapter in these negotiations was a pamphlet by Retinger, of which the exact date of issue is unclear, which Engel described as disconcerting. Its authors were Retinger and Kazimierz Głuchowski, a Polonia journalist. In it the authors argued that the only a mass emigration of Jews from Poland would provide a permanent answer to the Polish-Jewish problems. The Polish government did not repudiate these views, which, of course were not made in their name. Relations with the Jews were strained.[71] Nonetheless, Polish representatives countered that this was the view of many Jews themselves and reflected Jewish support.

## Notes

1  Retinger Papers, shelf 6, no title, BPL. c.f. "Konferencja Generała Sikorskiego w Bejrucie, 23 kwietnia 1943: Ostatnia wypowiedź Sikorskiego," *Zeszyty Historyczne*, 74 (1985), 147. Taverne argues that Sikorski's statements on European unity were made "at the insistence" of Retinger; see his "*Wat niemand*," 17.
2  "The Spirit of Poland: General Sikorski's Confidence," *The Times*, November 17, 1940, 10.
3  Ibid.
4  "Z prezydium Rady Ministrów," *Monitor Polski*, November 28, 1939.
5  General Władysław Sikorski, "Poland Wants Peace, [as told to Alfred Toombs]," *Colliers*, April 3, 1943, 11, 61–62.
6  This document bears no date or title. It can be found in the Retinger Papers at PISM.

7  Piotr S. Wandycz, "Recent Traditions of the Quest for Unity: Attempted Polish-Czechoslovak and Yugoslav-Bulgarian Confederations, 1940–1948," *Cahiers de Bruges*, nd, 38.
8  Ibid.
9  Pieczewski, *Działalność*, 116–117.
10  "The Establishment of Cooperative Peace in Europe," Box 17, Retinger Papers, BPL.
11  This material appears in the study by Grosbois, "L'action de Józef Retinger," 68.
12  Thierry Grosbois, *L'idee Européenne en temps de guerre dans le Benelux (1940–1944)* (Louvain-la-Neuve: Academia, 1994), 101–102.
13  Pieczewski, "Joseph Retinger's Conception," 585-where this formulation is outlined.
14  "Souvenirs de Denis de Rougemont."
15  It is not without meaning that the Belgian group was all Catholic.
16  Douli "Les debus"1.
17  Jaspar later tried to get Retinger the Noble Prize; see May 6, 1953, Retinger Papers, Box 20 BPL. A Belgian source suggest that Retinger may have been informing Soviet agents, in collusion with Jaspar and Ripka the Czech about federative negotiations affair – this is mere speculation; see Ciechanowski, "Retinger," 202–203. Curiously, it was Jaspar who Retinger regarded as his first co-worker in the struggle for European unity; Retinger, "Unity of Europe, drawer 5, BPL, 1–3.
18  Biddle, "Memorandum," January 21, 1942, United States Holocaust Museum Archives, Record Group 1998A.0371. Poland: Government in Exile. Records, 1940–1945 [hereafter Exile Government], reel 14; cf. Retinger memorandum, undated, folder 79, PISM.
19  Ibid.
20  Polonsky, "Polish Failure," 579.
21  Ibid.
22  Ibid., 580–586.
23  See Van Kleffens "Memorandum" in Grosbois, *L'idée européenne*, 101–107.
24  Jaspar, *Souvenirs*, 474.
25  Fernand Van Langenhove, *La securité de la Belgique: Contribution à l'histoire de la période 1940–1950* (Brussels: Editions de l'Université de Bruxelles: 1971).
26  Van Langenhove, *La securité*, 73ff.
27  For this issue see Thierry Grosbois, *L'idée européenne en temps de guerre dans le Benelux 1940–1944* (Louvain-la-Neuve, 1994); cf. his "Activities," 35. Grosbois suggests that Retinger may have had some role in the creation of CEPAG; see "L'action" 59; cf. Witkowski, *Ojcowie*, 82–83.
28  Grosbois, *L'idée européenne*, 18. See the valuable untitled memorandum by Retinger in folder 78, col. 68, Retinger Col., PISM Belgian documents confirm Retinger's important role as mediator. See Podgórski, *Retinger*, 106.
29  Pieczewski, *Działalność*, 109.
30  Detlaf Brandes, *Grossbritannien und seine osteuropaischen Alliierten, 1939–1943*. (Munich: R. Oldenbourg Verlag, 1968), 161–162.
31  Witkowski, *Ojcowie*, 74–75. It is an intriguing possibility that Retinger was not fully informed regarding what the other exile leaders were doing surreptitiously. Prażmowska has unearthed evidence that suggests that the Greeks, for example, were keeping Eden informed about Polish efforts at constructing a coordinated group of exile governments. The three main arguments used by the Greeks was the fear of keeping the British in the dark; provoking the Russians, and acceding to Polish leadership. The British, apparently took these reports seriously. Whether Sikorski and Retinger were aware of this behind-the-scenes activity is not known. See Prażmowska, *Britain and Poland*, 140–141.

32 Wandycz "Traditions," 5.
33 Pieczewski, "Joseph Retinger's Conception," 585–586; idem, *Działalność*, 120.
34 Spaak, *Continuing Battle*, 202.
35 Biddle to Secretary of State, October 8, 1942, including a "Memorandum" dated September 30, 1942; Exile Government, reel 4.
36 Piotr Wandycz, "Rozmowa Beneša z Sikorskim 3 lutego 1942 roku," in Wandycz, "O czasach,"357–365.
37 Mitkiewicz, *Z Gen. Sikorskim*, 223. The author adds to this new federation idea "And so much for Dr. Retinger." Cf. Prażmowska, *Britain and Poland*, 70.
38 Berska, *Kłopotliwy*, 160–161.
39 Biddle "Memorandum," February 26, 1942, Exile Government.
40 This is almost certainly October 8, 1942. Eden attended one of the meetings whose initiative was accorded to Sikorski; see Biddle to Secretary of State, November 4, 1942, Exile Government, reel 4.
41 Polonsky, "Polish Failure," 588.
42 Retinger, memorandum, folder 79, Sikorski Instytut.
43 Witkowski is here quoting Pomian; see the latter's *Retinger*, 74; cf. Retinger memorandum, folder 79, Sikorski Instytut; the formative role of the Poles, and a characterization of other participants is to be found in Retinger's "Unity of Europe," shelf. 5, BPL, 7–15.
44 Thomas Lane, "East Central Europeans and European Union 1940–1970: Ideas, Pressure Groups and Disillusion," in Lane and Wolański, *Poland and European Unity*, 82.
45 Jebb to R. Makins, February 24, 1942, NA, HS4 325.
46 Other members of the Board were Sava N. Kosanovic of Yugoslavia, chairman; Jan Masaryk his assistant; Jaromir Necas also a Czech; Emmanuel Tsouderos, the Prime Minister of Greece, and Jan Stańczyk for the Poles. Cf. Wandycz, "Recent Traditions," 55. Wandycz's list does not represent the original membership; it is unclear what moment he refers to. For a statement of purpose see "The Central and Eastern Planning Board," January 14, 1942, and "Report of the Secretary General," April 15, 1942, both in Gross Papers, PIASA, f. 4.40 and 4.42.
47 Report of the General Secretary, July, 1943, Gross Papers, PIASA, f. 4.46. Masaryk, with his usual insouciance said he was constantly traveling around the United States "trying to make the Americans indebted to us"; see Gross Papers, PIASA, f. 4.42.
48 See "Protocol" of meeting of February 27, 1942 in Gross Papers, PIASA, folder 4.42.
49 Here we depend on Witkowski, *Retinger*, 64–65. Gross had only the fondest memories of "Recio" decades later. Conversation with the author in 1999.
50 See Gross's "Project for a European Planning Board [1941]; Gross Papers, PIASA, f. 35.9 Pieczewski, *Działalność*, 113–114. Close relations were established with the ILO in Montreal and dozens of agencies and organizations; though most of these appear to have been very superficial.
51 Anne O'Hare McCormick, "U.S. of Central Europe," *New York Times*, November 5, 1941.
52 Gross and Dziewanowski, "Plans by Exiles," in Walter Lipgens and Wilfred Loth, *Documents on the History of European Integration*, 4 vols. Berlin: Walter de Gruyter, 1985–1911, 2: 355–362; Federalism, Gross averred, has always been popular in the United States; see "Quarterly Report of the Secretary General," April 18, 1944, PIASA, f. 4.47; cf. Gross's memorandum simply titled "Central and East European Planning Board," nd, f. 4.41, Gross Papers, PIASA.
53 "Notatka w sprawie Polskiej Grupy Studiów na terenie Stanów Zjednoczonych," nd, Gross Papers, PIASA, f. 4.39.

54 "Protocol" of first meeting, January 8, 1942, Gross Papers, PIASA, f. 4.40. Gross took only $100.00 monthly for himself; the Board's Associate Editor was paid $250.00; see "Expenses for January 1945," Gross papers, PIASA, f. 4.28. See also Gross to Necas, February 17, 1942, Gross Papers, PIASA, f. 4.32.
55 See Gross to Retinger, January 9, 1943; Gross to Sikorski, April 20, 1943; Gross's "Report" of January 1942–April 15, 1943"; Gross memorandum of June 3, 1943; Gross to Retinger, June 3, 1943; "Report' [by Gross], April 16–June 30, 1943; Report of CEEPB Educational Commission, June 14, 1943 all in Retinger col. 68. folder 45, PISM. The Board was always in search of funds see Gross to NN, nd, Gross Papers, PIASA, f. 4.41.
56 "Report of the Secretary General," April, 1943, Gross Papers, PIASA, f. 4.45; see also "Protocol" of eighth meeting November 19, 1942; Gross Papers, PIASA, f. 4.43.
57 Gross, "Poland and the European Settlement" a draft representing "personal views," Gross Papers, PIASA, f. 4.40. Gross later endorsed the idea of European countries having to "sacrifice a substantial share of their sovereignty to a supranational organization" with a common parliament, judiciary, and currency. See his "The Future of Mid-European Union," *Journal of Central European Affairs*, Vol. 16, No. 4 (January, 1957), 356.
58 Gross to M. A. de Capriles, August 3, 1945; cf. "Sprawozdanie z działalności CEEPB," both in Gross Papers, PIASA, f. 4.47 and f. 4.48 respectively.
59 Sławomir Łukasiewicz, "Dzieje Związku Polskich Federalistów w Stanach Zjednoczonych," 143 (2003), 57–84. Retinger's connections with these efforts is unknown.
60 Dymarski, *Stosunki wewnętrzne*, 160.
61 David Engel, *In the Shadow of Auschwitz: The Polish Government-in-Exile and the Jews, 1939–1942* (Chapel Hill, NC: University of North Carolina Press, 1987), 53; 233 n. 46; 85.
62 Theodore S. Hamerow, *Why we Watched: Europe, America, and the Holocaust* (New York: W. W. Norton & Co., 2008), 58–60; 300. David Engel, *Facing a Holocaust: The Polish Government in Exile and the Jews, 1943–1945* (Chapel Hill, NC: University of North Carolina Press, 1993), 25, 47, 218. Retinger had toyed with the idea that Jews may wish to go to Canada as farmers just before the war in correspondence with Marian Reich. See "Memorandum on the settlement in Canada of Polish Jewish agriculturalists," in ANK, s. 8067. See also Zygmunt Birnbaum to Reich, August 5, 1939 in *Guide to the Zygmunt William Birnbaum Papers. 1920–2000* [with appended documents] online at http://nwda.orbiscascade.org/ark:/80444/xv09585. Accessed on July 7, 2014.
63 Retinger to NN, July 11, 1940, Retinger Collection, 68/28., PISM. In a paroxysm of emotion, of which he was noted, Kot said about Retinger's mission to Moscow: "You are the first ray of hope," when he arrived; see Retinger, "Sikorski," Retinger col, BPL, drawer 3.
64 Ibid., 66. Regarding Sikorski's pro-Zionist views, see Kochanski, *Eagle Unbowed*, 197.
65 Retinger to Kot, April 19, 1940; I. Schwartzbart to Sikorski, November 19, 1942 and many additional documents in the same vein about Retinger's meetings with Jews; especially Selig Brodetsky, Leonard Stein, Abraham Abrahams, Lionel Cohen, and Ignacy Schwartzbart; see Retinger Collection; 68/29, PISM. Sikorski had told Roosevelt in the spring of 1941 that the Jews of America gave "loyal support to Poland," a bit sanguine; see Sikorski to Roosevelt, April 28, 1941, Roosevelt Papers as President, file 7543, FDR Library.
66 Engle, *Auschwitz*, 54.
67 Ibid., 58.
68 Retinger to Raczyński, March 19, 1940, 68/50, Retinger Collection, PISM.

69 Ibid., 111.
70 Retinger to Sikorski, October 16, 1939, Retinger Collection, folder 68/2, PISM.
71 Engel suggests this pamphlet appeared in spring, 1941 under the auspices of the Polish Information Center in New York; see his *Auschwitz*, 85. The whole episode suggests further investigation of Retinger's views of the Jewish question about which, unfortunately, virtually nothing exists. We do know that Retinger shared the view, common among Poles, that many Jews in the eastern Poland welcomed the Soviet invaders warmly, still a controversial question. See Engel, *Auschwitz*, 238n.

# 8 Retinger and Polish–Soviet relations

Just before the German-Soviet war, Ambassador Cripps came home from Moscow. He met with, among others, Sikorski and Soviet Ambassador Ivan Maisky. On the 18th Retinger and Sikorski, held a rather long meeting with Cripps. Sikorski and Cripps agreed that the attack on Russia by Germany was imminent; Cripps told the general that Retinger had been reporting to him about Sikorski opposition activities in the post-1926 era. Cripps announced his "greatest admiration." Retinger obviously had been distancing Sikorski from the sanacja regime to his old acquaintance Cripps. Retinger "did not disguise his belonging [przynależność] to British intelligence, but here he appeared as a Pole."[1] Retinger's close association with Cripps raises questions. The ambassador had, in late 1940, virtually offered the Soviets the portions of Eastern Europe they occupied, including all of eastern Poland. In doing so he went far beyond what the Foreign Office had authorized him to do: he was very sensitive to Russian desiderata.[2]

In addition to the war, the two spoke of the need to evacuate Polish soldiers from the Soviet Union. Sikorski put the number at 300,000. Cripps's response regarding this was not optimistic.[3] He spoke of getting the fifty most important Poles out of the Soviet Union, hardly what Retinger and Sikorski had in mind.[4] Immediately after the meeting, Retinger prepared an aide-mémoire. Sikorski told Cripps that Polish sources reported an imminent attack on Russia and a possible campaign against the British by winter. Cripps's information confirmed this. The issue of postwar Soviet territorial demand in Eastern Europe was also discussed; without conclusion. By then, doubtless many had been murdered at Katyń. Retinger apparently played no role in the conversation which was not recorded.[5] Nonetheless, Retinger was charged with conveying the conversation to President Raczkiewicz.[6]

## The Sikorski-Maisky Pact

On June 22, 1941 the Germans invaded the Soviet Union in Operation Barbarossa.[7] Their progress was extraordinary, and Soviet defensive efforts were incompetent. The forward air units were destroyed on the ground, and hundreds of thousands surrendered. The Germans reached Moscow and Leningrad by the end of the year. Behind schedule, despite their great victories, Operation Typhoon, designed to take the Russian capital failed, and by December the Germans were thrown on the defensive under the severest winter conditions. Having lost the initial goal of the war, it could be argued that the Germans, poorly prepared for defensive operations had just been defeated on the Eastern Front, though it would take overwhelming manpower, stupendous amounts of equipment, and almost four years to conquer them.

In the first weeks of the war, with the Germans making a lightening advance, Eden asked Sikorski and Retinger to come see him. Eden was in despair over the military situation and handed the Poles a note from Soviet Ambassador Maisky proposing immediate negotiation regarding the Poles in the Soviet Union. There was no mention of the sensitive border issue.[8] As a matter of fact, Retinger has already been in contact with Maisky who told him that the Russian favored some agreement with the Poles. Initially Sikorski rejected the Maisky proposals. But it was this document, Retinger later argued, that induced Sikorski to negotiate.[9] Eden, acting as intermediary, "never bullied," Retinger insisted.[10] Retinger later claimed he had supported accommodation with the Russians from 1941.[11]

July 4, 1941 was the first meeting with Eden. Sikorski was accompanied only by Retinger. Babiński comments:

> From this moment in the conversations concerning Poland and Russia, the Premier used almost exclusively the help of Retinger, and often with Litauer too, withdrawing himself ever more from cooperation with the Ministry of Foreign Affairs.
>
> Retinger was regarded by almost universally established opinion as an English agent and the close connection with Litauer and his with the Soviet embassy suggesting worse presumptions.[12]

Sikorski at once realized that the war had come to a turning point. He referred to the situation as "very favorable to Poland."[13] Negotiations between the Poles and the Soviets, the British acting as intermediaries, began almost at once. Eden alerted the Poles and said he had spoken with the Soviet ambassador who supported an agreement with them. Eden and Sikorski came to a gentleman's agreement: Sikorski agreed to negotiate and Eden promised to exert no pressure. He did the opposite.[14] The Poles had a brief agenda: the incarcerated Poles were to be freed; Moscow would recognize the Polish exile government; the 1939 Molotov-Ribbentrop Pact, which had given much of Poland to the Russians, would be ignored; and, the Polish army, which the Russians claimed was only 25,000 and the Poles estimated as much higher, was to be evacuated.[15]

Two weeks before the Sikorski-Maisky treaty there was a meeting at Maisky's residence to which he invited Sikorski, along with Retinger and Raczyński, Foreign Minister Vyacheslav Molotov, then in London, was present, as was Ambassador Bogomolov. The British were represented by Eden and Deputy Foreign Minister Alexander Cadogan. A three-hour discussion ensued which focused on the British-Soviet agreement. It was in many ways a preamble to the Polish-Soviet Pact of a month later. Sikorski gave an optimistic report of the discussions to his government and emphasized that the powers agreed not to interfere in each other's internal affairs. Border issues do not seem to have been discussed.

Whereas the British press hailed the Polish support for the July 12, 1941 British-Soviet Pact, Nagórski commented that it really indicated the already much weakened position of Poland; it was already in desperate straits.[16] It was dramatic proof of how the British viewed the Polish viewpoint, "brutal" in one opinion.[17] Essentially the British saw the Sikorski-Maisky negotiations as another means of cultivating the Soviets. It is indicative of the way Eden saw the negotiations that the ambassador to the Polish exile government told President Raczkiewicz that the "Poles could afford to yield a little ground more easily than the Russians."[18]

At the negotiations the British acted as intermediaries, and more. Sikorski and Zaleski were the Polish representatives; the British provided Cadogan, later replaced by Eden. This left only Retinger and the suspicious Litauer to see to the details of the negotiations. Retinger never left Sikorski's side.[19] Only Retinger was Sikorski's advisor.[20] It was he who orally translated the document to Sikorski.[21] The fact that Retinger often represented Sikorski at meetings with high-ranking British diplomats doubtless raised the suspicions of those who had come to mistrust Retinger. Moreover, it certainly helped to convince Sikorski's critics to be more critical of the general. Retinger's cooperation with Sikorski did not just concern diplomacy but extended far.[22] Indeed, British intelligence concluded that Retinger and Kot hoped that, on the basis of their "contacts" they could gain support for the idea of Sikorski remaining in power "beyond the end of the war."[23] Retinger and Kot, the report continued, were very close to Sikorski and "intensely ambitious." [24]

Sikorski, astoundingly, not only conferred with Retinger about his conversations with Eden, but amazingly met with Litauer as well, despite the fact that his function as a Soviet agent was already widely known.[25] Litauer was regarded by many Poles as Rothstein's spokesman.[26] Ironically, and perhaps more shrewdly, some London Poles regarded Litauer, as well as Retinger, as an "agent" of Sikorski.[27] Retinger was everywhere: he met frequently with Strang (counselor at the Foreign Office), Eden and others. On at least one occasion (July 20) Retinger insisted on changes in the draft proposal. Retinger informed Eden of dissensions within the Polish cabinet. [28]

Immediately they reached an impasse. The Poles wished to use as the point of departure the 1921 border set by the Treaty of Riga which the Soviets had violated in their attack on Poland on September 17, 1939. The Soviets demanded that Poland surrender its eastern territories and be transformed into an ethnographic state. There were many other differences but this was the fundamental one.[29]

This impasse, and the Russian dishonesty that accompanied it, caused direct talks to fail quickly and the British stepped in as intermediaries. Contrary to Eden's promise, "the pressure brought to bear on us from Downing Street was tremendous," Retinger recalled.[30] "The Foreign Office was also aggressive."[31] Cienciala concludes that Eden "took charge of the negotiations...and steered them to the end." The pro-Soviet Cripps played a large role in the concluding phase.[32] Eden also sent Cripps to see Stalin, three times, and discovered that the dictator was eager for an accord.[33] Eden later claimed that he viewed the weak Polish position with "anxiety," and credited Sikorski with the success of the negotiations.[34]

There were essentially two contradictory Polish positions regarding the putative settlement. Members of Sikorski's cabinet argued that the Soviets were losing the war to Germany. This was the time to press for concessions and use hard bargaining which was essentially the General Sosnkowski position. Sikorski, on the other hand, was convinced, under British pressure, that Polish failure to accept what amounted to Soviet demands would lose Poland the support of the British, and leave it isolated and helpless. It was evident that the British blamed the Poles for their intractability regarding their eastern borders and Sikorski was having trouble bringing the Polish government round to his policy of concessions. He had, in British eyes, "gone some way to meet the Soviet demands."[35] Retinger was in full support.[36] Retinger also argued later that German victory would mean more of Poland would be occupied.

Sikorski and Retinger both thought that the treaty represented "a final, historical settlement with the Russians."[37] The principal reason for Retinger's advocating a rapid conclusion of a pact with the Soviets was to free the huge number of Poles under Russian control.[38] If not already Retinger soon concluded that Russia, not the West, would free Poland and the price would be the eastern territories.[39] Retinger conferred with the British and hoped Sikorski's internal difficulties with Polish critics would be quieted by information that the British supported the accord.[40]

British policy was doubtless aided by Retinger's services: he kept them informed of the inner politics of the Polish government. He told Strang that three ministers of the Polish government opposed the treaty.[41] He asked the Foreign Office to help him silence a number of Polish officers and politicians who were critical of the proposed treaty. Retinger was "disappointed" when the British told him that there was nothing they could do.[42] He even forecast the likelihood that President Raczkiewicz would not sign, but that it was of little significance. Retinger informed Eden directly of this. [43] The American State Department listed Retinger, laconically, as a "British Government employee."[44]

In the end President Raczkiewicz refused to sign and Sikorski, in an unorthodox if not an illegal move, signed what became known as the Sikorski-Maisky Pact of July 30, 1941: the Poles had just willingly surrendered eastern Poland.[45] Whether they could have maintained their claim to it is dubious at best. Marian Seyda, Zaleski, and Sosnkowski all resigned and the Polish government was plunged into disorder. Jan Stańczyk, the PPS leader in Great Britain and a minister in the Polish government was also opposed. Retinger, making use of his pre-war connections, went to Hugh Dalton a Labour Cabinet minister who had long relations with the PPS. Retinger requested Dalton to bring Stańczyk on board, and in Retinger's presence, Dalton made a call to Stańczyk which was shocking in its abusiveness.[46] It was also successful; and repulsive. Added pressure on the Poles was the fact Maisky had signed a protocol with the Czechs two weeks earlier.[47] Retinger was convinced of the necessity of the pact. All opponents were "utopians" and "anti-Russians." The fact that Retinger would castigate opponents of Russia is significant and helps explain the hatred they had for him.[48]

Retinger here played a typically back room deal at this point. Sikorski was afraid his signature on the treaty would be meaningless without his government's support. Retinger met with the Foreign Office's Strang, who convinced Retinger that such an action by Sikorski would still be valid. Retinger, it seems, convinced Sikorski in turn.[49]

Most scholars agree that circumstances prevented Sikorski from refusing to sign the pact. He was under severe British, and perhaps American, pressure to sign.[50] Public opinion in Great Britain was pro-Russian, and Poland's military position was weak. The Western allies wanted Russia in the war as a wholly committed participant and if that meant sacrificing Poland, it was of no concern.[51] Even British Intelligence admitted that Sikorski was "forced" to sign, and that the Soviet success "will undoubtedly be the cause of trouble in the future."[52] Days after the pact, Eden let the Poles know that they should "pipe down" regarding the "frontier issue in broadcasts to Poland" because Moscow was getting "irritated." Retinger agreed.[53]

The only good news for Sikorski was that the Polish government in the occupied country endorsed the pact. For the British it was the overcoming of the first major obstacle to workable British-Soviet relations. Richard C. Lukas's comment probably sums up Sikorski's reasoning:

> Whatever Sikorski's true feelings were at the time of the signing of the Polish-Soviet Treaty, he later developed a realistic, if not fatalistic; sense that it would be difficult, probably impossible, for Poland to restore the Riga Line with the Soviet Union. Had he given expression to these sentiments, Sikorski probably would have been thrown out of office.[54]

In reality, Sikorski's decision was foreordained: Poland had very little to offer the British, but the Russians a great deal. Without a major ally, the British would lose the war: Poland could never be a major ally. Sikorski knew this. His countrymen could not accept it, even if they realized it. Poland was forced to make another dreadful decision which characterized its history in the war.

A military mission was sent by Sikorski to Moscow in early August headed by General Zygmunt Bohusz-Szyzko, but almost immediately thereafter

Retinger arrived. His mission was hurried due to British pressure. It is an eloquent indication of the degree to which Sikorski allowed Retinger to make policy when, before his departure to Moscow, the general told Retinger "I do not wish to give you too many instructions as we have discussed matters in general outline."[55] The task of the interim Polish diplomatic representative consisted in making administrative arrangements to the effect of the formation of the Polish army and securing consular protection for all deportees." Sikorski was convinced that Retinger knew the situation as well as he did.[56]

As he has underlined, there is another version of the story, courtesy of Kot. According to this Retinger came to Kot after the military mission left and asked to be sent to Moscow as a courier because "there was room on a British plane."[57] He would return with vital information about the situation to aid Kot in his ambassadorship.[58] According to Kot, since he knew of Retinger's connections with suspect people in London like Litauer and Rothstein, "he was strengthened" in his conviction to send Retinger who would have a convenient entrée to Soviet officialdom.

A perhaps more plausible account is provided by Retinger himself: Eden called him and asked him to go to Moscow to represent Polish interests. Retinger repeats this story in his memoirs, adding that Eden noted that Retinger was "the most important participant in the negotiations after Sikorski." The Foreign Office was pressuring Retinger to go.[59] The fact that London was selecting Polish representatives in vital areas is striking. If Retinger faithfully recalled Eden's words, it would mean that London regarded Retinger as more important in determining Polish policy than any Polish diplomat. This involvement with Eden has probably prompted Józef Garliński to conclude that Retinger was "almost certainly a British political agent," who was "more concerned with interests other than those of Poland."[60]

But, Retinger told Kot that Sikorski had denied him the mission. Kot, at Retinger's urging, called Sikorski to change his mind and let Retinger go.[61] According to Kot, Sikorski rained abuse on Retinger and mentioned specifically his flitting about. He ended by saying he had no idea who Retinger would be working for. Kot eventually talked Sikorski into the idea which Sikorski unenthusiastically allowed.[62] Retinger would, "open diplomatic channels between Poland and Soviet Russia."[63] Ironically, Kot bitterly remarked later that Retinger supplied him with nothing.[64]

Sikorski stressed that his main job was to have released as many Polish prisoners from Russian captivity as possible and create an army in Russia to be led either by General Stanisław Haller (not to be confused with his relative, general Józef Haller) or his fellow general Władysław Anders.[65] Haller died, leaving only Anders who was originally designated to be Haller's assistant. In Retinger's view his other two goals were to free the Poles languishing in concentration camps, and, most controversial and difficult, convince Moscow to disregard the Molotov-Ribbentrop Pact.[66] Anders quickly learned to respect and appreciate Retinger.[67] In turn, Retinger intervened with Sikorski to hurry Anders' promotion which would give him greater prestige with Moscow.[68]

## Retinger in Moscow

Arriving in Moscow (August 13th), Retinger was greeted by the Polish military delegation, Cripps, and a large number of Soviet dignitaries. *They* greeted him as chargé, and the Poles later assented.[69] The British were convinced that without this title, Retinger would not be able to obtain amnesty for the Poles.[70] The Ministry was horrified at the idea, as was Sikorski. Retinger filled the position until September when Kot arrived as the first post-1939 Polish ambassador.[71]

Retinger, immediately met with Molotov, and, true to his usual behavior, quickly got to know the chief Soviet officials.[72] He was able to progress on the amnesty quite rapidly.[73] However, it seems clear that Retinger's path to obtaining amnesty for the Poles was cleared before he arrived by Cripps who had met with Stalin and Molotov on July 26, 1941 and won their agreement.[74] In addition, the Russian general Aleksander Vassilevsky had signed an accord with Bohusz-Szysko regarding the "amnesty" of the prisoners the day before Retinger arrived.[75]

On the 13th, the Soviet Presidium issued an "amnesty decree" and Retinger was told that the Soviet government attached "great importance" to the agreement. It stipulated that Moscow

> would support on a large scale all welfare action undertaken by the Polish authorities for the Polish population. Moreover the Soviet authorities were anxious that the thousands of Poles residing in the USSR should work and live in adequate conditions and feel at home in the Union: that those fit to fight should fight, and those who wished to work should work.[76]

On the August 14, Retinger discussed with Molotov the issue of Poles being held in captivity.[77] The same day he met with Deputy Commissar Andrei Vyshinsky who praised ardently the recent Sikorski-Maisky Pact and promised support for "large-scale" welfare action for the Poles in camps. In addition to the "capital problems," the army and civilian welfare, Retinger had a list of items he regarded as of equal significance: a Polish newspaper and Polish radio broadcasts. Vyshinsky gave a positive response. Retinger pushed the issue of releasing the Poles but the Soviet representative Vyshinsky argued that they were moving slowly in fear of freeing a "spy."[78] They concluded by pledging "collaboration on the largest scale and in all fields."[79]

On the 16th, Retinger reported to Sikorski that the "amnesty" process seemed well underway. Retinger asked for formal confirmation of his status as chargé to facilitate his activities.[80] Through Cripps, Retinger was able to elevate the status of Anders to chief figure among the Poles in Soviet Russia: At this moment Anders began his career. He would become Poland's most famous World War II soldier, and later the president of the Polish government-in-exile. Retinger met with Anders and other officers who he, claimed, were very pleased with the pact signed with Maisky. According to Retinger, Anders criticized Sosnkowski harshly for his opposition; calling him "either stupid or ill-willed." Anders reported to Sikorski that he and Retinger saw eye-to-eye on fundamental problems, which must have pleased Sikorski.[81]

Retinger's first reports to Sikorski were extraordinarily positive even enthusiastic regarding Soviet cooperation.[82] Retinger saw Ambassador Bogomolov every day and praised him to Anders.[83] In addition, relations with the British could not have been better. Anders, Bohusz-Szysko, who came with the Polish delegation, as well as General Boruta (who had, like Anders, been a Russian captive) were most helpful.[84] He continued to assert this pro-Soviet and optimistic reporting when he returned to London and gave stories to the press.[85] He even spoke of a 200,000-man Polish army being formed in Russia.[86]

On August 22, Retinger presented the Commissariat for Foreign Affairs with a rather complex memorandum which concerned the implementation of Soviet efforts regarding interned Polish citizens spread throughout the USSR. Retinger asked that three Polish nationals assist the Russian authorities in all areas where there were large concentrations of Poles. The Polish Embassy would chose "un homme de confiance" who would approach local Soviet authorities concerning the conditions of the Polish population in the area, especially those in need of urgent care. This was to be broadcast as soon as possible.

Second, Retinger asked for the release of all Poles being held so that they could make it to the local "assembly stations" from where they would be processed according to their usefulness including possible military roles. The Soviets would supply "appropriate living accommodations, adequate food supplies and other indispensable needs." Moscow was also asked to provide each with some un-named "grant of money." The Polish government would do what it could to supplement these efforts. It would take eight weeks, because of the war's exigencies, to arrange for supplies the Poles had obtained from Washington and London to reach those in need.

For Poles currently "employed" by the Soviets, Retinger had a number of requests: that those unfit for heavy labor be transferred to less demanding tasks; that they be treated with the protections granted regular Soviet workers; that their food rations be the maximum; that those capable of military service were to be transferred "without delay to Polish military camps"; that women and children be allowed to relocate to places of their own choosing. The whole of this complex effort was to be directed by "mixed commissions" of Poles appointed by the embassy and a cooperating Soviet official. "Without delay" and before the onset of fall, local conditions should be investigated and the "sorting out" of the Polish population be effected at once. This was to apply especially to "the Moscow region, Kazakhstan, Novosibirsk and Arkhangelsk" the latter three well known for their brutal conditions. The mixed commissions were to depart immediately, and the matter was to be discussed directly with Molotov on the 25th. In a cheerful conclusion, Retinger noted that "the harmonious relations at present prevailing between the Polish and Soviet Governments" will make it "easy to work out the details."[87] The Soviet response six days later agreed on all main points, and promised to address subordinate issues soon.[88] However, several of the major issues affecting Poles scattered about under dreadful conditions had still not been addressed by late October, despite the efforts of Kot to remind Vyshinsky what Retinger had been promised.[89]

Retinger arranged for telegraphic communication to wherever large numbers of Poles were concentrated. They in turn would report to the Embassy in Moscow and to the Soviet authorities. This was what Keith Sword deems a "clever" solution to the problems of masses of Poles scattered about in isolation.[90] On August 30, 1941 the first Polish representatives, Retinger and Anders, had made a radio broadcast to the Poles living in Russia.[91] After his month-long sojourn in Soviet Russia, Retinger gave a report of the dreadful conditions under which the Poles were living in the Soviet Union. Any progress in this deplorable situation would be welcome.[92]

What Retinger apparently did not tell Sikorski was a conversation he had with Foreign Commissar Vyacheslav Molotov and Andrei Vyshynski. Vyshinsky praised Sikorski in his efforts to normalize relations between the countries. However, in an uncharacteristic show of honesty, he added that a Russian ambassador did really not need to leave – when we win the war we shall just take Warsaw.[93] Retinger's reaction to this was not recorded. On the 30th, Vyshinsky and Retinger had a conversation about an earlier memorandum Retinger had presented. It was quite obvious that Retinger was making policy without consulting Zaleski, and perhaps, on a very light rein from Sikorski.[94] Retinger had been the effective Polish ambassador to Moscow if not more.

When Retinger returned to Britain he was debriefed by the British as well as the American Ambassador Biddle. He told him that the Poles in Russia liked Sikorski's new policy towards the Russians, and were resentful of Sosnkowski for not grasping the larger issues at play. This was a "realist" policy which Retinger would demonstrate frequently during the war and afterwards. He admitted that the Russians had treated the Poles abominably, but insisted things had improved dramatically.[95] Ambassador Raczyński disagreed strongly with Retinger's optimism.[96] Retinger at once met with the representatives of the British Left: Hugh Dalton, who earlier called him a sewer-rat, and Ben Smith a Cabinet Minister. Among his new friends were the Americans Harriman and later Berle, whom he referred to as Roosevelt's "right hand," and also Biddle, who became the American representative to the exile governments in London. He also met John Foster Dulles, and later his brother Allen. He discovered that Berle and Dulles were "most ardent supporters" of the idea of European federation.[97] Dulles was also religious which appealed to Retinger.[98] On the other hand, Sumner Welles and William Bullitt disliked him.[99] There were a few others. Retinger, after long distrusting Americans, was now taking them into his circle of acquaintances.[100]

Retinger gave a dreadful interview to *The Times* upon his return to London. It was enthusiastic about the Soviets: they were entirely loyal to the stipulations of the Sikorski-Maisky agreement. Poles were being released and placed in good housing. Russia was doing all it could to ensure that a Polish army was assembled with all possible speed.[101] This enthusiastic portrayal of the Polish soldiers' attitude towards the Russians was nonsense, and British intelligence was well aware of it. At a meeting in early October, Retinger gave a very positive portrayal of Russian treatment of the Poles, though he was critical of the Soviet government saying that Hitler's regime was "child's play" compared to Stalin's empire.[102] Why Retinger spread this rubbish is difficult to grasp.[103] Probably because it is what London wanted him to say.[104] For their part, the British were aware that Retinger's effectively pro-Russian comments were resented by the London Poles who thought had "strong Communist sympathies." The British preferred to regard this as "Realpolitik."[105] They dismissed Retinger's insistence that Polish soldiers in the USSR were "full of sympathy" for the Russians, but, on the contrary, without exception they are very hostile to the Russians."[106]

The Soviets had dunned Retinger to "make open rebellion in Poland *now*." Retinger agreed with the British that it should be postponed. Moscow had earlier suggested that the Poles be urged to commit sabotage. The Russians then asked him to work on convincing the British of their view. Retinger informed the SOE. He declined, but urged the Russians that General Zhukov be sent to London and Retinger "would be able to arrange for him to meet some important British people." He suggested Jebb and Gubbins. Retinger also asked Sikorski to support this idea and urge a "making a formal agreement" between the Poles and the Russians in London. Eden apparently supported the idea and Moscow was ready to send Zhukov.[107] One of the intriguing aspects of this episode, which seemed to have no aftermath, is that Retinger reported it to the SOE, apparently after speaking with Sikorski. He obviously had active channels with the highly secret British organization.[108]

The SOE concluded that Retinger could persuade Sikorski of almost anything, but that the Polish military would not work with Zhukov. In a revealing SOE memorandum, it was noted that they"thought that it would be quite in order, in view of Retinger's position, to say that it was O.K. for Zhukov to come."[109] The British Military Mission in Moscow telegraphed the War Department that Poles there supported sending Zhukov.[110] Since he was a "prominent figure in Russian secret organisations," the Mission wanted the SOE to be involved and announced that Retinger, soon to return to London, had "more detail." He should be contacted upon his arrival.[111] Sikorski and Retinger told Eden that they wanted "far closer collaboration" with the Russians. They emphasized the importance of the Zhukov mission because, as Sikorski stressed, the principal goal of the Polish government was to raise an army in Russia.[112]

Shortly before, Mason MacFarlane of Military Intelligence, then in Moscow, had informed headquarters that the Poles wanted Zhukov in London to meet with *them*. The Poles were told not to make such invitations without first asking London's permission. The British responded to this initiative by stressing that Retinger's support of the idea was all that it took to convince Sikorski of its rectitude. The SOE noted that Russian intelligence was trying to infiltrate Polish secret organizations and were concerned, something enhanced by a possible visit from a high-ranking Soviet intelligence operative. Nonetheless the SOE seemed well-inclined towards the notion citing Retinger's support as a key ingredient.[113] It was Retinger, in the company of Anders who negotiated the preliminaries of an agreement for the Polish and Russian forces to share intelligence and liaise with underground forces in German occupied territory. Not long after, Sikorski signed on December 14, 1941.[114]

## Sikorski's visit to the Soviet Union[115]

Sikorski went to Moscow in early December, 1941, a dangerous time to travel. Retinger did not accompany him as he rarely did on matters that were essentially military.[116] Besides, Retinger the former chargé, and the newly installed ambassador Kot, who arrived on September 4, loathed one another. Neither was a happy choice. Kot was a "difficult character with a tendency to intrigue" besides knowing nothing about Russia. Retinger, he concluded, was "almost certainly a British political agent" whose interest may not have been exclusively Polish, a rather damning judgment.[117]

When Sikorski left England, Eden ordered Roberts to meet Retinger to "get quite clear" what Sikorski's actions in Moscow would be. Retinger said that, shortly before, the Poles had provided the Foreign Office with this information, but he was evasive. For London, Retinger, not Raczyński, was the link to the Poles.[118]

The meeting between Sikorski and Stalin was pleasant and they agreed to releasing 25,000 Poles from Russia to the Middle East and England. The soldiers plus civilian prisoners would gather around Tashkent. According to Cazalet, the two discussed the Polish-Russian border and signed an accord.[119] Over the army issue, Retinger was very positive: "The Russian government demonstrated concrete proof of the desire that the Polish army arose quickly as possible and a suitable area for exercises has been designated east of the Volga."[120] This is an indication of what was called the "eastern direction" of Sikorski's foreign policy, a direction Retinger had long agreed with and promoted diligently.[121]

Discussion of postwar territorial divisions were threatening. Stalin obviously had large ambitions. Cripps warned Sikorski that Stalin wanted the Curzon line (essentially the border wrought by the second partition of Poland in 1793) but was in favor of compensating Poland in the West which would in effect deprive Poland of all its eastern territories.

Sikorski's main goal was to gain Stalin's cooperation in improving the lot of the thousands of Polish prisoners still suffering under Soviet domination, and to convince Moscow that they should be released. Sikorski wanted the Polish prisoners, most of whom had no shoes, to be evacuated to Iran where they could be adequately provisioned and trained. Boorishly Stalin asked if the Poles really wanted to fight and Sikorski was outraged. The general realized the benefit of leaving Polish soldiers in Russia as a point, or points, of coalescence round which other scattered troops might rally and, idealistically dreamed of Polish-Russian reconciliation.[122] He even forced through a resolution by the Polish government endorsing the Poles helping form an eastern front.[123] Anders, on the other hand, wanted the Poles out. Retinger, astonishingly, supported Anders, not Sikorski.[124] Knowing what he had been through he can hardly be blamed. Sikorski, naively, but perhaps resignedly, accepted the withdrawal of 35,000 Polish soldiers.[125] This hardly generous settlement with the Poles has been deemed the pinnacle of Polish-Soviet cooperation during the war, the best indication of how dreadful they were. Retinger tried to get American help in supplying the Polish refugees and told them, as encouragement, that his negotiations with Moscow had gone well.[126]

The Poles were badly divided. Sikorski and Anders did not like each other and Kot did not trust him either. Kot and Sikorski were old friends and their view dominated. Anders acted as a rogue and demanded all Poles be evacuated. Anders was told supplies were inadequate to furnish the Soviet troops. Things were at an impasse: The Soviets would supply only 44,000. Anders already had 78,000 and the number was growing. He estimated 500,000 would soon face the possibility of leaving, or extinction. Sikorski wanted them to stay, and the Western Powers supported him in fear of offending Stalin.[127] Finally they were allowed to leave, with Soviet ill-grace and far too little provisioning.

The whole matter had an ugly denouement, Anders despised Sikorski for being gullible and another officer challenged Sikorski to a duel. The prisoners suffered endlessly. Britain and the Americans largely abandoned Poland to its fate. However, Garliński regards the outcome of the Sikorski-Stalin negotiations as "positive." When Sikorski left the Soviet Union on December 15, 1941 he had gained the Russians permission to withdraw Polish soldiers from the Soviet Union. Money was to be allocated to provide for civilian Poles in the Soviet Union, and efforts would be made to release them from work battalions. This seems rather mean, but compared to the situation obtaining before, it was a major step forward. Later in the year, the Soviets had either violated or misapplied all the agreements Sikorski had signed with Stalin. Nonetheless, by August, 1942 a substantial number of

Polish troops, two divisions plus ancillary troops, were sent to the Middle East where they joined units which had managed to leave in March.[128]

## Notes

1. Mackiewicz, *Zielone oczy*, 178–179. "From the time Sikorski arrived in London in 1939 he was the connection between British intelligence and the Poles"; ibid., 241.
2. Prażmowska, *Britain and Poland*, 61.
3. "Note made by General Sikorski on his conversation with Sir Stafford Cripps," June 18, 1941, *Documents on Polish-Soviet Relations, 1939–1945, Volume 1, 1939–1943* (London: Heinemann, 1961), 103–108 (hereafter DPSR and volume number); cf. Eugeniusz Duraczyński, ed., *Układ Sikorski-Majski: Wybór dokumentów* (Warsaw: Państwowy Instytut Wydawniczy, 1990), 87.
4. Retinger, "Agreement with Russia," Retinger Papers, drawer 1, BPL. Sikorski and Kot once raised the issue. Duraczyński, " Układ."
5. Stroński, *Polityka*, 1: 517ffcf. DPSR, I; 108–112 the contents of the meeting were long kept secret; Witold Babiński, *Przyczynki historyczne od okresu 1939–1945* (London: B. Świderski, 1967), 27.
6. Duraczyński, *Układ*, 6.
7. Cripps had alerted Sikorski to the attack a few days earlier and suggested the Poles make overtures to the Russians; see Retinger Papers, shelf 1, "Agreement with Russia," BPL. The original version differs slightly from Pomian's published version so I have relied on the former.
8. Terlecki, *Wielka awantura*, 74–76.
9. Retinger, "Agreement with Russia," Retinger Papers, shelf 1, BPL; "Polish Relations with the USSR," Shelf. 2, BPL.
10. "Polish Relations."
11. Pomian, *Retinger*, 217.
12. Babiński, *Przyczynki*, 55.
13. Garliński, *Poland in the Second World War*, 105.
14. An internal FO memorandum, probably by B. H. Summer, admitted that the British were "pressing them [the Poles] hard to conclude an agreement," "Polish-Soviet Relations," July 17, 1941, FO 371/26756, NA. Eden had many meetings with Sikorski in this period and found the general "intrepid." See Anthony Eden, *Memoires of Anthony Eden: The Reckoning* (Boston, MA: Houghton Mifflin), 314–315.
15. Retinger Papers, drawer 1, "Agreement with Russia," BPL; Sikorski's estimate of prisoners was 200,000; see Duraczyński, *Układ*, 10.
16. Zygmunt Nagórski, *Wojna w Londynie* (Księgarnia Polska w Paryżu, 1966), 128–129; for a very hostile evaluation of Polish participation, see Gabriel Gorodetsky, *Stafford Cripps' Mission to Moscow, 1940–42*. (Cambridge: Cambridge University Press, 1984), 190–193. The treaty was first brought before the Cabinet by the Foreign Office in April. It contained specific language that London would not agree to the Soviet demands for a border change with Poland. Sikorski had been assured that "the proposed treaty will be of benefit to Polish interests since it will establish the right of His Majesty's Government to concern themselves with the future frontier settlement in Eastern Europe, including the Polish-Russian frontier." The Poles were to be informed. This promise proved insubstantial; see "Proposed Anglo-Soviet Treaty," April 5, 1942, CAB66/23/24, NA, 1–2. In Annex II to the draft agreement however, the Polish border is not mentioned and vague words about: "the reconstruction of Europe after the war with full regard to the interests of both parties in their security as

well as to the desire of the U. S. S. R. for the restoration of its frontiers violated by the Hitlerite aggression, and in accordance with the two principles not to seek territorial aggrandizement for themselves and not to interfere in the affairs of European peoples." This left Polish claims to the 1939 frontiers hanging by a thread. See ibid., 7.
17 Tadeusz Wyrwa, "Układ Sikorski-Maisky," Zezyty Historyczne, 102 (1992), 200.
18 C. Dormer to FO, July 21, 1941, FO 371/26756, NA.
19 Pestkowska, Za kulisami, 87. Retinger seems never to have been present at the meetings of the Polish Council of Ministers; see Duraczyński, Układ, passim.
20 Zaleski brought the issue to the government, arguing that the Prime Minister should not be negotiating with a mere ambassador. Retinger defended Sikorski; see Marian Czesław Sokołowski, Dzieje prezydentury Rzeczypospolitej Polskiej na uchodźstwie (Warsaw: Peta, 2007), 54–55.
21 Pomian, Retinger, 139.
22 "Zeznanie własne," IPN BU 01136/69/D.
23 "Note on S.O.E.'s Work with the Poles," nd, HS4/136, NA.
24 Ibid.
25 Świderska, "Drobiazgi." 70.
26 Barbara Berska, Kłopotliwy sojusznik: Wpływ dyplomacji brytyjskiej na stosunkie polsko-sowieckie w latach 1939–1943 (Kraków: Księgarnia akademicka, 2005), 51 n. 19.
27 Nagórski, Wojna w Londynie, 246.
28 Untitled British minutes of the Sikorski-Maisky Pact, August, 1941, FO 371/26759/NA. The minutes also indicate that Retinger played an active role in exchanging documents between the Russians and the Poles.
29 The private conferences during the negotiations included only Retinger, Litauer, and Cazalet; see Mitkiewicz, Z Gen. Sikorskim, 157.
30 Retinger Papers, drawer 1, "Agreement with Russia," BPL. Curiously, Retinger's quotations in Pomian's recollections speak of Eden as impartial and helpful; see Pomian, Retinger, 142.
31 "Russo-Polish Agreement and Polish Cabinet Crisis," by MPX to M, nd, HS4/243, NA; the British press was also opposed to the Poles.
32 Anna M. Cienciala, "General Sikorski and the Conclusion of the Polish-Soviet Agreement of July 30, 1941: A Reassessment," Polish Review, Vol. 41 (1996), 407, December 6, 1944.
33 Retinger, "Agreement with Russia," drawer 1, Retinger Papers, PBL; The Foreign Office claimed that Eden worked "hard" for three weeks on the issue; Strand to Leeper, August 1, 1941, FO 371/26759, NA.
34 Eden, Memoires, 316.
35 Cabinet meeting of July 21, 1941, CAB65/19/8/ NA, 154.
36 Terlecki, Wielka awantura, 79.
37 Retinger, "Agreement with Russia," Retinger Papers, drawer 1, BPL.
38 "Zeznanie własne," IPN BU 01136/69/D.
39 Władysław Bułhak, "The Foreign Office and the Special Operations Executive and the expedition of Józef Hieronim Retinger to Poland, April–July. 1944," unpaginated MS. Courtesy of Władysław Bułhak.
40 July 29, 1941, Retinger, Notes from Conversation with Strang; in Duraczyński, Układ, 166; R. M. Makins to NN, July 20, 1941, FO 371/26757, NA.
41 Berska, Kłopotliwa, 103–104.
42 Strang to FO, August 7, 1941, FO 371/26757, NA; in turn, the Foreign Office called upon Retinger to get the Polish press to "drop these polemics" against the Polish-Soviet accord; see Cripps to FO, August 5, 1941, FO 371/26757, NA.

43 "Polish-Soviet negotiations," regarding conversation with Retinger, July 28, 1941; Strang to NN, July 28, 1941, both in FO 371/26756, NA.
44 See RG 59: Decimal File: Name Index, 1940–1944, Box No. P1-157-E-200, Box 345, USNA.
45 For the text of the agreement see DPSR, I:141–142.
46 Terlecki, *Wielka awantura*, 77–78.
47 Duraczyński, *Układ*, 139; the pact was signed on July 30, 1941.
48 Kacewicz, Great Britain, 109.
49 Strang to FO, July 29, 1941, FO 371/26756, NA; Prażmowska, *Britain and Poland*, 90. Retinger, in turn, was advised by the British as to how to approach Sikorski; see Strang memorandum, July 29, 1941, FO 371/26756, NA.
50 A British Intelligence memorandum argues this; see "Russo-Polish Agreement and Polish Cabinet Crisis," nd, from MPX to M; HS4/243, NA.
51 The possible American pressure on Sikorski awaits elaboration; for an argument along these lines see "Russo-Polish Agreement and Polish Cabinet Crisis," August 15, 1941 from "MPX" to "M" and "MX"; NA, HS4/137.
52 Ibid.
53 Strang memorandum, August 7, 1941, FO 371/26758, NA.
54 Richard C. Lukas, *The Strange Allies: The United States and Poland, 1941–1945* (Knoxville, TN: The University of Tennessee Press, 1978), 11.
55 Retinger quoting Sikorski in Retinger to Sikorski January 31, 1944, file 233, FO371/39421, NA. Of course this attributed quotation was very self-serving. It also disclosed the very high opinion Retinger had of his role in the Polish government.
56 Given his closeness to Polish and British leaders since early in the war: "Who was better to send than Retinger?" See Taverne, *Wat niemand*, 15.
57 Kot, *Listy*, 535.
58 Ibid., 536
59 NN minute to Cripps to FO, August 7, 1941, FO371/26757, NA. It should be noted, however, that the Foreign Office were dinning the Poles to send a representative, not championing Retinger.
60 Józef Garliński, *Poland in the Second World War*. New York: Hippocrene Books, 1985, 113.
61 Kot held a very powerful position in the Polish government; see Sokołowski, *Dzieje prezydentury*, 64. Retinger, "Agreement with Russia," Retinger Papers, drawer 1, BPL, cf. "Wyciąg z notatki informacyjnej z Dep. I z dn. 2.IV.1955r." May 3, 1955, IPN BU 0 1178/694. Foreign Office sources contradict any role for Eden in prompting Retinger's journey despite these later intelligence papers in Warsaw
62 Pestkowska, *Za kulisami*, 100; cf. Sokolowski, *Dzieje prezydentury*, 64.
63 DPSR, 1:582, See the clipping dated August 17, 1941 in AKC, 4386, Woźnicki Papers, BPP. The British were disgusted with Kot's dilatoriness, and were pleased when Retinger, "who enjoys General Sikorski's close confidence," left for Moscow; see Cripps to FO, August 10, 1941, FO371/26757, NA. As an interesting aside the FO noted that Kot had matters to "clear up" with Dalton before he left. Dalton was the head of the SOE. See Strang memorandum of August 7, 1941, FO371/26757, NA.
64 Kot, *Listy*, 19.
65 Pomian, Retinger, 115.
66 Retinger. "Agreement with Russia," drawer 1, BPL. Elsewhere Retinger names the second goal, the freeing of the incarcerated Poles, his chief goal.
67 Podgórski, *Retinger*, 111.

68 Anders, like Sikorski and Retinger, was an ardent anti-Piłsudskiite; see Zbigniew Wawer, *Armia generała Władysława Andersa w ZSRR, 1941–1942*. Warsaw: Bellona, 2012, 28.
69 A. Tarnowski to Molotov, 1941, *Dokumenty i materialy po istorii sovetsko-polsk'skikh otnoshenii. Tom VII, 1939–1943gg* (Moscow: Nauka, 1973), 211; Retinger asked Sikorski for the title almost at once; see "Appointment of M. Retinger as Polish Charge d'Affaires in Moscow," August 13, 1941, FO 371/26758, NA; Cripps to FO, August 13, 1941, FO 371/26758, NA. Molotov was insistent that Retinger gain this appointment as soon as possible; see Cripps to FO, August 14, 1941, FO 371/26758; Cripps to FO, minute by Mackenzie, August 6, 1941, FO 371/26757, NA.
70 Cripps to FO, August 13, 1941, FO 371/26758, NA.
71 Pobog-Malinowski, *Historja Polski*, 3:194–195. Piotr Żaron contends that Retinger's promotion to *chargé* was on the motion of Bohusz-Szysko; see his *Kierunek wschodni w strategii wojskowo-politycznej gen. Władysław Sikorskiego, 1940–1943* (Warsaw: Państwowe Wydawnictwo Naukowe, 1988), 50. The Polish Foreign Ministry was horrified.
72 Cripps to FO, August 14, 1941, FO 371/26758, NA; Pestkowska, *Za kulisami*, 100.
73 Ibid., 537–538; Biddle to Secretary of State, September 17, 1941, Exile Government, reel 2; August 14, 1941, PRM, 215, 217 see Duraczyński, *Układ* 215, 217.
74 Cripps to FO, July 26, 1941, FO 371/26756, NA. Terlecki, *Wielka awantura*, 79; Sword agrees with Terlecki but offers no evidence; see Keith Sword, *Deportation and Exile: Poles in the Soviet Union, 1939–1948* (New York: St. Martin's Press, 1984), 34; Stroński, *Polityka*, 2:164.
75 Stroński, *Polityka* 2:238–244. Eugeniusz Duraczyński, *Rzad Polski na uchodzstwie, 1939–1945* (Warsaw: Książka i Wiedza, 1993), 132–133.
76 Keith Sword, *Deportation and Exile: Poles in the Soviet Union, 1939–1948* (London: St. Martin's Press, 1994), 34.
77 Vyshinsky memorandum, August 14, 1941; *Dokumenty i materialy*, 214.
78 Stroński, *Polityka*, 2:247.
79 DPSR, I:145–146.
80 There is an important typescript by Sikorski which mentions that the freeing of the prisoners was due to Retinger. It was later penciled out. See Sikorski Papers, PISM, Retinger Collection 1, f. 2; Wapiński, "Retinger," 151.
81 Ibid., 31. Retinger warned Sikorski that Anders was loyal but was dangerously ambitious; ibid., 33cf. Janta, "Refleksye (3)," 3.
82 Cripps to FO, August 14, 1941, FO 371/26758. Sikorski seemed pleased with Retinger's work; see Cripps to ?, August 18, 1941, includes Sikorski to Retinger. FO 371/26758, NA.
83 Retinger to Anders, October 10, 1941, Retinger Collection, 68/28, PISM.
84 Retinger to Sikorski, August 14 and 29, 1941, Retinger Collection, 68/28, PISM; Pomian, *Retinger*, 116–119; Kot, *Listy*, 537–538. There is a lengthy account of Retinger's first days in Moscow in Stroński, *Polityka* 2: 238–244.
85 Kot, *Listy*, 104 Pomian, *Retinger*, 155 where Retinger praises the Russian attitude towards him. The British seemed equally optimistic regarding Russian cooperation with the Poles; see Roberts minute to "Soviet-Polish Agreement." August 4, 1941, FO371/26757, NA.
86 "Memorandum of Conversation between Dr. Retinger, Confidential Political Adviser to Prime Minister General Sikorski, and Mr. Schoenfield, Counselor of Embassy, June 28, 1941, Exile Government, reel 2, HMA. Brandes, *Grossbritanien*, 248.

87 "Note from Chargé d'Affaires Retinger to the People's Commissariat for Foreign Affairs on the application of the Polish-Soviet Agreement of July 30, 1941," *DPSR*, I: 153–155.
88 "Pro-Memoria of the People's Commissariat for Foreign Affairs," August 22, 1941, DPSR, I: 157.
89 "Note from Ambassador Kot to Deputy Commissar Vyshinsky," October 13, 1941, DPSR, I:175–178.
90 Sword, *Deportation*, 92–93; *Documents on Polish-Soviet Relations, 1939–1945* (hereafter DPSR), (London: Heinemann, 1961), 1, 157; Brandes, *Grossbritanien*, 248, 251.
91 Stroński, 2:269.
92 Ibid., 2:389.
93 Berska, *Kłopotliwy*, 118; Vyshinsky was known for his belligerent outbursts against the West, showing Russian chauvinism as well as Soviet imperialism, especially when drunk; see Pietro Quaroni, *Diplomatic Bags: An Ambassador's Memoirs* (David White Company, 1966), 120–121.
94 DPSR, 1: 153–155.
95 Biddle to Secretary of State, September 18, 1941; Exile Government, reel 5; Biddle to Hull, September 17, 1941, FRUS, 1941, Vol. 1. Retinger was careful to acknowledge that the American ambassador to Moscow, Steinhardt had been helpful to him. Cazalet noted that the Retinger-Stalin talks were amiable and successful; see his *With Sikorski to Russia* (London: The Curwen Press, 1942), 47–48.
96 Cecil Dormer to Eden, September 17, 1941, FO371/26760, NA; Retinger was very positive about the Russian negotiations from the start; see R. H. Bruce Lockhart to Strang, August 26, 1941; he even claimed that Poles in Russia is "not anti-Soviet." See. FO 371/26759, NA.
97 "America and the Americans," Retinger Papers, drawer 4, BPL.
98 Pomian, *Retinger*, 169.
99 Ibid.
100 Pomian, *Retinger*, 128–131.
101 The Polish-language version of this *Times*' interview of September 17 1941 can be found in Kot, *Listy*, 452–453.
102 The British virtually ignored the speech. See "Report on Lecture by Mr. Retinger," October 3, 1941,"HS4/243, NA.
103 "London Report No. SO/576, December 14, 1942 from "MX" to "AD4 (for G.400) "MPX" to MX, December 26, 1942, NA, HS4, file 137. Retinger later gave a more balanced, but still very optimistic report; see "Report on Lecture by Mr. Retinger at the Rubens Hotel," probably written by Lewis Namier, October 3, 1941.HS 4/243.
104 General Klimecki to NN, October 1, 1941, HS4/243, NA.
105 "Comments of London Report," 11.1.1942, HS4/243, NA.
106 "London Report Number SO/578," December 14, 1942, HS4/243, NA.
107 "Note of a conversation," September 16, 1941, HS4/243, NA; Cripps to NN, August 30, 1941, FO 371/26759; Cripps to FO, August 30, 1941, FO 371/26759, NA. Retinger had conveyed this effort to the British, Cripps to FO, August 30, 1941, FO 371/26759, NA.
108 "Notes of a Conversation" marked "secret" by C.E.O., September 16, 1941, NA HS4, file 243; Foreign Office to Cripps, September 15, 1941, FO 371/26760, NA.
109 Unsigned memorandum, nd, HS4/243, NA.
110 The Foreign Office noted that the Poles had somehow "got into close touch" with Zhukov; the obvious link was Retinger; see Roberts' memorandum of September 15, 1941, FO371/26760, NA.

111 "Most Secret Cypher Telegram," Military Mission in Moscow to War Office (DDMI), 8/9/1941, HS4/243, NA.
112 "Polish-Soviet Relations," NN, September 15, 1941, FO371/26760, NA.
113 Mason MacFarlane to DMI, September 8, 1941, marked "most secret." September 8, 1941, NA HS4, file 243.
114 Żaron, *Kierunek*, 103n.
115 The next several pages, unless otherwise noted, draw from the Lukas work.
116 Sikorski kept his planned visit to Russia to himself – though he told the British. The only Pole who knew was, it seems, Retinger; see Eden to Secretary of State for Air, October 13, 1941, FO 371/26760, NA. Apparently, Sikorski had wanted Retinger to accompany him; see Strang to NN, October 21, 1941, FO 371/26760, NA.
117 Garliński, *Poland in the Second World War*, 113.
118 Roberts to NN, October 26, 1941, FO371/26761. NA.
119 Cazalet considered the Russians virtual barbarians but regarded Stalin as friendly to the Poles – "very pro-Polish," and asserted that the Sikorski-Stalin talks were amiable and successful; see his *With Sikorski to Russia* (London: The Curwen Press, 1942), 47–48. Cazalet's naïve assessment of Stalin and Russian attitudes towards Poles is stunning.
120 Quoted in Żaron, *Kierunek*, 66.
121 Ibid., where this theme is developed; Babiński, *Przyczynik*i, 135.
122 Lukas, *Strange Allies*, 18.
123 Terlecki *Wielka awantura*, 96.
124 Ibid., 97; Z. S. Siemaszko, "Niektóre wypowiedzi płk. Bakiewicza," *Zeszyty Historyczne*, 29 (1974), 145; Jan M. Ciechanowski, "Notatki z rozmów z gen. Marianem Kukielem," *Zeszyty Historyczne*, 29 (1974), 148–149. Kukiel dates Retinger's friendship with Anders to this episode; Kacewicz, *Great Britain*, 145.
125 Mitkiewicz credits Retinger with changing Sikorski's mind about leaving the Poles in Russia; see his *Z Gen. Sikorskim*, 282.
126 Biddle to Hull, September 17, 1941, FRUS, 1941, I, 252–253.
127 Józef Smoliński, "General Zygmunt Bohusz-Syszko dowódca samodzielnej brygady strzelców podhalańskich, zastępca dowódcy 2 korpusu," in Stefan Zwoliński, ed., *Naczelni wodzowie i wyżsi dowodcy Polskich sił zbrojnych na zachodzie* (Warsaw: Wojskowy Instytut Historyczny, Egros, 1995), 105. Siemaszko argues that whereas Sikorski wanted them to stay it was the British who wanted them out, hence another example of Retinger's doing London's bidding; see his "Szara eminencja," 174–175.
128 Terlecki, *Wielka awantura*, 97; Retinger cabled the American State Department for support with the Russians; see Winant to Hull, August 31, 1942, *Foreign Relations of the United States, 1942, Volume III* (Washington, DC, 1961), 177.

## 9 The collapse of Poland's international position

On the day of Sikorski departure to the United States (March 11, 1942), there was a high-level meeting in London to discuss the agenda in Washington. Raczyński, leaving earlier, was already in Washington. At the meeting were Sikorski and Retinger on the Polish side and Churchill, Bevin, and Sir Archibald Sinclair (Secretary of State for Air) for the British. Sikorski expressed his hope of gaining American support for the upcoming British-Soviet talks. He even spoke of a "military uprising in Poland" in 1943 with American help.[1] But far more important was the fact that the United States had just become a belligerent and its almost unlimited war-making capacities were something of which the Poles were well aware. The Soviets had diminished provisioning for the Poles still in Russia and had recently become more aggressive regarding territorial issues. The fact that Retinger would be the only other Pole (save the translator, Rotmistrz Zamoyski), demonstrates how vital Retinger had become to Sikorski and the formulation of his policies.[2] Raczyński already met with Secretary of State Sumner Welles before Sikorski's arrival. Retinger, before leaving for the United States vouchsafed the British his rather skeptical views of American participation in the war and even suggested Washington might seek a separate peace. He wanted to go to the United States to form his own judgments. Nonetheless, he retained his long-established mistrust of the Americans.[3]

Feliks Gross urged Retinger to have Sikorski meet the Planning Board which, he averred, represented a "new conception" of European order.[4] Later in the year, Sikorski wrote to Roosevelt in support of the Planning Board and asked that Roosevelt approach Herbert Lehman, Director of Foreign Relief and Rehabilitation, to help the Board establish a research Institute at New York University. The president answered positively and agreed to take the matter up with Lehman.[5] Whether Roosevelt actually did anything in this regard cannot be found.

In his short visit – which included Retinger "as usual,"[6] it was immediately apparent that some-sort of bi-lateral treaty was not possible, so Sikorski raised three issues: the future of the western territories: Danzig (Gdańsk), Silesia, and West Prussia, about which Roosevelt knew nothing, as compensatory additions, not outright seizures from Germany. This immediately raised the Riga frontier and Polish eastern territories, an odd and awkward issue for Sikorski to bruit. Second, Sikorski wished to thank Roosevelt for the pledge of $12.5 million the American had promised to the Home Army (Armia krajowa, AK, Poland's forces in the homeland), and his promise not to raise territorial issues during the war, respecting the Atlantic Charter. After Raczyński's successful negotiations, it was bizarre that Sikorski raised with Roosevelt something Raczyński had just taken off the table, namely territorial issues. The general had hoped to be regarded as the representative of the smaller allied governments gathered in London, but this issue seems not to have arisen.[7] Sikorski was giddy with success when he reported to the Cabinet in London claiming, "we could look into the future with complete confidence." The government was more skeptical than the general but thanked him for his efforts.[8]

Retinger furnished an embarrassing sidelight to the Sikorski mission. Before departing for London, Welles handed Raczyński a memorandum concerning Retinger's problematical past: "Sikorski and Count Raczyński expressed themselves as being upset to learn that a record of this nature existed in the archives of our [the American] government."[9] It included such awkward details as the St. Louis arrest in 1925, Retinger's expulsion from the United States, his "alleged activities directed against 'American imperialism'" and the charge that he was a "fellow traveler."[10] Both Raczyński and Sikorski defended Retinger as a loyal patriot with whom Sikorski had been close to for many years. Raczyński later furnished Drexel Biddle with a brief, and most positive biographical sketch of Retinger and offered additional oral endorsement of him.[11] Biddle met with Sikorski a number of times over the matter to dispel Welles's doubts.[12] Nonetheless, though he acknowledged the receipt of the Biddle-Raczyński efforts at exoneration, he concluded that "additional information ... relating to the extent to which Dr. Retinger may or may not be trusted ...would be helpful."[13]

Biddle informed Washington that ever since March, 1941, when he became ambassador, stationed in London, Retinger had conducted himself with great loyalty to Sikorski, and the general sent him to Moscow to reopen diplomatic channels, a testimony to his faith in him, and that his service there was admirable. By implication, Biddle was arguing to let bygones be bygones. He referred to Retinger, when writing to Raczyński, as "our friend" and emphasized their joint efforts to "putting this matter straight."[14]

The one issue Sikorski did not address while in the United States was the deteriorating relationship with American Polonia. The Piłsudskiite minority had consolidated into a well-functioning lobby and bombarded Sikorski with criticism and questions.[15] The failure to raise a Polonia army early in the war was still a humiliation for both sides and Sikorski, evidently, regarded Polonia with some contempt.[16] Whether this conclusion was of his own or provoked by Retinger who had long held Polonia with disdain, is problematical.

A few months later, Sikorski made his third and last trip to Washington. It was little more than a disaster. Col. Mitkiewicz labels it "unsuccessful," "a failure," "a farce," idiotic," and "fatal." According to Ciechanowski, Roosevelt "acted as if he were intimidated by the Soviet military efforts against the Nazis."[17] Sikorski signed a treaty which virtually foreswore the Polish eastern territories and gained nothing in return.[18] Sikorski had wanted certain positive statements from Roosevelt. Instead, he received no firm declaration in support of Poland as there had been in March, no endorsement of prewar boundaries. In fact State Department officials rejected the Riga line and there was no endorsement of Sikorski's dream of a federative reorganization of postwar Europe. Sikorski gave Welles a memorandum on Poland's position in a Central European federation, but it made no impression.[19] It included Polish support for a Polish-Czech federation and one between Greece and Yugoslavia as first steps in a larger plan. Despite Welles', and hence American lack of interest, a few days before he died, Sikorski claimed that both the British and the Americans supported his federative plans. There was no justification for such a conclusion.[20] Indeed, Churchill found the American "profoundly ignorant of the Polish problem," a few months after the Sikorski visit.[21] Sikorski was "far too prone to take Roosevelt's oracular expressions of goodwill as strong support for the Polish cause."[22]

Retinger attempted an indirect approach to supplement Sikorski's efforts. He met with Assisstant Secretary of State Berle and again raised the issue of federation, but now with more specific aspects. Retinger, who Berle referred to as "General Sikorski's brain trust," said that he had "organizing the governments-in-exile" about peace plans. Retinger presented Berle with a geopolitical outline. Poland had to live with Russia despite the latter's dreadful behavior. This meant that the Poles had "had to work out something." Thus there would be, "two federations: a Northeast European Federation and a Southeast European Federation, which would be large, strong and capable of making economic and military headway against all comers," essentially the Sikorski argument.[23] But, Retinger went on, Eden and others had been making efforts "to come up with a general outline of an economically cooperative union "of Europe." The "principal difficulty" was the Czechs. But here the Poles had been working diligently for a "confederation." Berle was most uncomfortable. The Americans were largely ignoring Sikorski; now this strange little man was speaking of great notions already underway which had the support of the British. Berle wrote in his diary, "this is getting a little farther out then I had expected."[24] Retinger was pursuing an independent, though parallel, Polish path towards federation.

Again the Americans were suspicious and rather unhappy with Retinger's coming. Secretary of State Hull issued Retinger a visa only because Biddle assured him that Sikorski would find it "urgently inconvenient" to be without Retinger. Biddle had also assured Hull that Sikorski reposed the utmost trust in Retinger.[25] Biddle even wrote to the president in this matter.[26] He informed Washington that Churchill was a great admirer of Retinger and regarded him as the key member of Sikorski's staff.[27]

Sikorski had kept a frantic schedule, usually consisting of meaningless appearances. His meetings with Polonia brought promises of greater relief activity and the recruiting issue was mercifully gone.[28] His meetings with American political figures, including Roosevelt, seemed to accomplish nothing.[29] Retinger, nonetheless was joyous, or at least feigned satisfaction. In a meeting with Nagórski of the Polish press and Skalicki the Czech envoy, Retinger was gushing, despite reality:

> The trip was the biggest success of the general's life. The most important thing ... is that he did not speak only of Poland, but of all questions. He met with Roosevelt four times, twice in private – the first time lasted two hours, the second an hour. ...There was particular interest and discussion prompted by his military memorandum ...in Mexico Czechs and Poles spontaneously worked together.[30]

Sikorski, almost certainly at Retinger's urging, made a trip to Mexico. He went there, having secured the help of Washington, to discuss Mexico receiving Polish refugees stranded in Russia.[31] At least Retinger got to visit his old haunts.[32]

When he returned to London, British intelligence was desperate to debrief Retinger regarding his Washington trip.[33] Retinger told them that it had not been the time to bring up Poland's eastern borders, but he favored a Polish-Lithuanian federation. He went on at some length about his observations derived from the American trip, though how much of this he shared with Washington is unclear. Retinger, the unknown British agent reported, "spoke at some length" regarding a "larger Eastern European federation": "from the Baltic to the Aegean." It would include Hungary, but not Austria. If one federation were impossible, the Poles would support two: one including the South Slavs and Greece; the other Poland-with Lithuania, plus Czechoslovakia and Hungary. These federations should be built on an "economic and not [a] political base." If so, he insisted, "The USSR will not object to it." The "silly talk" of a cordon sanitaire," popular during the interwar era, should be dropped. Retinger's views on the Soviets were most naïve, or perhaps desperate. If they could have "sound strategic frontiers" they would not be "too rigid." Retinger then added a number of *obiter dicta*: Beneš had "disgusted" him: he asked for British information about Polonia (!); he had advice for British Greek policy; and, perhaps awkwardly, he brought up the point that the Americans considered the British as "a poor relation" something that "shocked" him.[34] Retinger was convinced that the smaller states of Europe were of no concern to Washington. Dujardin and Dumoulin have argued that in November, just before leaving for the third Washington trip, Retinger concluded that:

> The government of the United States pays little or no attention to the national plans but it is inclined to listen with interest suggestions made

to it by a group of European states. In the hypothetical case where these states do not manage to present common solutions, it is to be feared that the United States either will impose no solution or will disinterest itself in the European problem.[35]

In the spring of 1943, Retinger took Counter Intelligence (Dwójka) chief Mitkiewicz aside and told him that Poland's military strength was weak but Sikorski' political position was "very strong."[36] This unconvincing argument was based on Retinger's long-held belief that soldiers do not win wars but politicians do. He wanted Mitkiewicz to become involved in politics and was somewhat despairing of the current political landscape: there was the unimpressive peasant leader Stanisław Mikołajczyk, who many regarded as heir-apparent to Sikorski; Kot deserved negative rankings, and heroic general Anders was a political naïf. Mitkiewicz, to his discredit, found Retinger's arguments intriguing. In reality the Polish position was feeble and deteriorating. Before leaving, Retinger made an important report to the government. He was optimistic. Russia would withstand the German advance towards Moscow. However, he had no illusions about Soviet society of which he was very critical.

## Katyń

In April, 1943 the German discovered the graves of several thousand Poles near Katyń in the Smolensk region. The Germans at once blamed the Russians. The news put the Polish government in London into "convulsions."[37] Within two days the Poles called for an investigation by the International Red Cross. Retinger recalls that at the time of the crisis both Sikorski and Raczkiewicz were ill. Averill Harriman, the American diplomat, called the Poles and urged them not to make an issue out of it, even though he knew the Russians were guilty. Retinger agreed. "We were not responsible," he argued cryptically, for the decision to request an inquiry by the International Red Cross. "When we heard," he continued, "we tried to stop its official publication but it was too late."[38]

Stalin denounced the Poles for being the lackeys of German propaganda and severed relations with the Sikorski government. Under intense British and American pressure, the Poles withdrew their Red Cross request, but the Soviets stood firm and did not rescind their severance of relations. Sikorski, according to Siemaszko, was convinced that the Poles could work with the Soviets, but weeks before his death, under the influence of Anders, changed his opinion.[39]

On July 4, Sikorski, caught in a devastating dilemma, set out for an inspection of Polish troops in the Middle East. His plane, taking off from Gibraltar, crashed instantly into the sea killing all the passengers save the pilot. But Retinger was not among them. He was in London.[40] This is often cited as a demonstration of two intertwined legends: that Retinger had been alerted to the intention to kill Sikorski by British intelligence and avoided the trip as a result. This would require him to be a British agent as well as accusing the British of assassination.[41] Neither of these accusations has been proven and no serious historian accepts either. Indeed, it was the tradition that Retinger did not accompany Sikorski on trips of a purely military nature, so his absence was not unexpected. Indeed, perhaps the best proof of the fact that Retinger was not a British agent was the fact that London's special services were curious why Retinger was *not* with Sikorski.[42]

Fortunately, we have Retinger's notes from the time immediately following the Gibraltar catastrophe. They deserve to be summarized. On the 5th Retinger was awaiting Sikorski's arrival in Swindon when he was informed of the tragedy. He, with British help, returned at once to London, so that he could fly to Gibraltar. In London he received a note to meet Churchill at midnight immediately after a Cabinet meeting. Churchill wept when he saw Retinger. He said he regarded Sikorski as a younger brother and had followed his career with interest and sensitivity (czułościa).

When asked who would succeed Sikorski, Retinger told Churchill that Sikorski had always spoken of Mikołajczyk. The significance of Mikołajczyk to the British was eloquently expressed when Churchill admitted that he had no idea who he was and that, perhaps, he was the one who looked like "a fat balding old fox." Retinger himself did not have a high opinion of Mikołajczyk[43]. As for the commander in chief, Retinger said he hoped it would be General Sosnkowski. Churchill said he would not interfere, but he did not like him. It was obvious to Retinger then and later, that Churchill would not regard Mikołajczyk with the respect he had for Sikorski.[44]

## Retinger post-Sikorski

Retinger was the first Pole to meet with the heads of the British government after the death of Sikorski. On July 11, Retinger called on Minister of Foreign Affairs Raczyński to tell him that he had enemies in the government, the socialists, who did not wish to see him re-appointed as Foreign Minister, and that there were other political issues at large. Retinger, who always turned to the British over internal Polish politics, promised to see Eden the next day and report.[45] Retinger and Raczyński supported Mikołaczyk for the post of Prime Minister. This was largely because Sikorski had made his choice of a successor plain and the two wanted to continue Sikorski's control beyond the grave. A perhaps cynical aside is that Mikołaczyk was out of his depth in international affairs and thus probably would be more beholden to Retinger than Sikorski had been.[46]

Mikołajczyk was not a sophisticated man and he was lost in the world of British high politics. Terlecki is probably right when he wrote that for Mikołajczyk, Retinger was a "sorcerer."[47] He continued to accompany the new premier, as had been the case with Sikorski, to all the major meetings with the British.[48] He, not surprisingly, acted as translator at the first

Churchill-Mikołajczyk meeting but, Retinger seemed to feel adrift without Sikorski.[49] He certainly lost his powerful role in the activities of the Polish government which was based entirely on the Sikorski connection. He did not have the decades-long bond he had with Sikorski and the shared feelings about such issues as postwar federation. The British obviously had no respect for Mikołajczyk. His selection by Sikorski still astounds. Retinger resigned his position in the government and became a private citizen.

Katyń, the severance of relations with Moscow, and Sikorski's death were great blows to Poland's international position. Indeed, by 1943, an independent Poland within its prewar frontiers was doomed. In fact we could say that this was true by 1941 or even, to be pessimistic, by 1939. The November 1943 Tehran Conference, the decisions of which were held in secret until 1945, had consigned to the Soviets all of Eastern Poland, a fact the British did not want the Poles to know. Of this, Bułhak argued that, nonetheless, Retinger "must have been fully aware."[50]

## Notes

1 Untitled memorandum by Sikorski (?), March 24, 1942, Welles Papers, container 83, FDR Library.
2 Berska, *Kłopotliwy*, 163. *Rotmistrz* is a cavalry rank equivalent to senior captain. Terlecki's comment that Retinger played "no role" in the mission is clearly wrong. He was Sikorski's confidant in the various meetings. See his *Wielka awantura*, 91.
3 Gladdwynn Jebb to R. Makins, February 24, 1942, NA, HS4, 325.
4 Gross to Strakacz with copy to Retinger, March 23, 1942, Gross Papers, PIASA, f. 4.41.
5 Sikorski to Roosevelt, December 16, 1942; Roosevelt to Sikorski, December 28, 1942; Gross Papers, PIASA, f. 4.43.
6 Karol Popiel, *General Sikorski w mojej pamięci* (London: Odnowa, 1978), 172.
7 Regarding Sikorski's hopes in this regard see Biddle, Memorandum, February 28, 1942, Exile Government, reel 4, HMA.
8 Dymarski, *Stosunki wewnętrzne*, 213–218.
9 [A. J. Drexel Biddle], "memorandum," n.d. "Poland: Government in Exile Records [hereafter Exile Records]," reel 4, HMA; Raczyński to Biddle, April 22, 1942, Exile Records, reel 4. Raczyński felt moved to write: "He is not of Jewish extraction."
10 Pomian, *Retinger*, 87.
11 Ibid.
12 Biddle to Welles, June 26, 1942, Exile Records, reel 4. Retinger was convinced that both Welles and Biddle disliked him; see Retinger, "America and the Americans," BPL. drawer 5.
13 Welles to Biddle, July 15, 1942, Exile Records, reel 4.
14 Biddle to Raczyński, June 26, 1942, Exile Records, reel 4; Janta, *Refleksye* (3), 3.
15 Lukas *Strange Allies*, 108ff.
16 "Poles' Rif Bared by Sikorski Visit," *New York Times*, December 24, 1942, 5.
17 Lukas, *Strange Allies*, 30–31.
18 Mitkiewicz *Z Gen. Sikorskim*, 306–307; cf. Dymarski, *Stosunki wewnętrzne* 257ff.

19 Witkowski, *Retinger*, 68; Wandycz, *Czechoslovakian-Polish*, 88; Welles expressed disapproval; see Terlecki, *Generał*, 242. Witkowski has found a draft of the memorandum, written by Retinger who was thus its author; see Witkowski, *Ojcowie*, 78–79 Podgórski, *Retinger*, 304.
20 "Konferencja Generała Sikorskiego," 147–148. Pestkowska, *Za kulisami*, 150–151; Terry, *Poland's Place*, 298–314. Pieczewski claims that Retinger played a role in drating the federative memorandum; see his *Działalność*, 113. The British, curiously, considered the trip as a success; see illegible note to Prime Minister, February 12, 1943, PREM 3/351/13.
21 Churchill quoted in Lord Moran, *Churchill at War, 1940–45* (New York: Carroll & Graf Publishers, 2002), 268.
22 Polonsky, "Polish Failure," 590.
23 "Memorandum," December 7, 1942, Berle Papers, container 214, FDR Library.
24 "Memorandum," December 4, 1942, Berle Papers, container 214, FDR Library.
25 Biddle to Hull, September 2, 1942; Exile Government, reel 3; Winant to Hull, November 6, 1942, Exile Government, reel 3; Hull to Biddle, November 14, 1942, Exile Government, reel 3, HMA.
26 Ibid.
27 [Biddle] to NN, nd, Exile Government, reel 3, ibid.
28 Bloch, "Starania," 260–264.
29 Roosevelt later told Beneš that Sikorski had made a positive impression on him; hardly a policy commitment; see Feierabend, *Beneš mezi Washingtonem a Moskvou*, 33
30 Nagórski, *Wojna w Londynie*, 146–147. Sikorski later reported his American meetings to the leaders of other exile states who, it seems, were not pleased that Sikorski deigned to speak for them. For Sikorski report see "Discours prononcé par le General Sikorski," January 28, 1943, in PREM, 3/351/13, NA. For the displeasure of the other leaders, see illegible note to F. D. W. Brown, February 11, 1943; PREM, 3/351/13, NA.
31 Ibid. The trip was arranged by the State Department; Sikorski to Welles, January 1, 1943, Welles Papers, container 83, FDR Library; "Memorandum of Conversation," December 10, 1942; "Memorandum" [by Berle], December 18–22, 1942; "Memorandum of Conversation," December 24, 1942; "Memorandum of Conversation," December 28, 1942 all in Berle Papers, container 214, FDR Library.
32 Pestkowska, *Za kulisami*, 150; Terlecki, *Generał*, 244.
33 McClaren to Retinger, January 19, January 19, 1943 Retinger to McClaren January 28, 1943 # 15., Retinger Collection, PISM.
34 "London. Report Nr. S.O. /591, December 16, 1942, NA, HS 4 file 137.
35 Dujardon and Dumoulin, *Van Zeeland*, 457n.
36 Mitkiewicz, *Z Generalem Sikorskim*, 334.
37 Pomian, *Retinger*, 133.
38 "America and the Americans" [written ca. 1955], sz. 5, Retinger Papers, BPL.
39 This is an interesting thesis by Siemaszko, "Retinger-wysłannik," 227.
40 Retinger had arranged the visit with the British; see Resident Minister Algiers to FO, June 26, 1943; FO 371/34614A, NA.
41 As a matter of fact, British Intelligence exonerated him according to recently released documents, see Tebinka, "Wielka Brytania," 152.
42 Tebinka, *Churchill a Polska*, 152.
43 Cf. Retinger, "Winston Churchill," Retinger Papers, drawer 1, BPL; Podgórski, *Retinger*, 122.
44 Pomian, *Retinger*, 135.
45 Raczyński, *In Allied London*, 152–153.
46 Kochanski, *The Eagle Unbowed*, 349.

47 Terlecki, *Wielka awantura*, 114.
48 Katelbach, *Rok*, 155.
49 Janta, "Refleksye" (3), 3.
50 Bułhak, "Foreign Office," unpaginated.

# 10 Retinger's most controversial episode
## The mission to Poland, 1944

By early 1944, Soviet troops entering eastern Poland were encountering Polish AK units. The relationship between the Poles and the Russians was at a crossroads. The November, 1943 Tehran Conference had consigned to the Soviets all of eastern Poland. Hence, London was most interested to find out what the state of opinion was in Poland and what reaction the underground authorities were likely to have to Soviet entry into Polish territories.[1] More, they wanted to convince the Poles that they must cooperate with the Soviets and could not expect any support from London in opposing the Russians. The imbroglio in Poland, and perhaps bad conscience, made the British more amenable to extending help to the Poles in using aircraft to smuggle agents behind enemy lines (Operation Wildhorn), in a series of "bridging operations" (or what the Poles called "mosty," or bridges) from the SOE base in recently conquered southern Italy.[2] These were a subsidiary of the general flights to the continent known as Operation Riposte.[3]

There had been a Wildhorn I flight in mid-April 1944 which carried two couriers and brought back a number of Poles including General Stanisław Tatar, deputy chief of the AK, among others. Wildhorn II left at the end of May and was a complete success in bringing back a number of high-ranking Polish officers. However, it failed to fulfill a major responsibility: to get Józef Retinger out of Poland.

### Organizing Retinger's mission

Retinger's goal in going to Poland in 1944 was to explain to his fellow Poles in the homeland "How are we going to lose this war?"[4] In short, he had to make it clear to the Poles that the Russians would be victorious, that neither the British nor Americans would protect them, and that the eastern territories were lost.[5] This "realist" perception of Poland's position was already accepted by premier Mikołajczyk and other members of both the Polish government in exile and the émigré community, as well as the British. Even some members of the home army had come to this tragic conclusion.[6] It was Retinger's idea to go to Poland to inform his countrymen of this bitter reality and gauge their reaction to report back to the British.[7]

Retinger broached, in his own name, the idea of a Polish mission to General Colin Gubbins of the SOE reporting its prior approval by Mikołajczyk, a claim which might or may not have been true.[8] Retinger had apparently asked Gubbins shortly before and noted that Mikołaczyk had approved of the notion:

> The concept of going to Poland was from Retinger alone. According to Mikołajczyk he presented this as a necessity, upon which the English depended. To the English he explained that it mattered to Mikołajczyk.[9]

He convinced Mikołajczyk and the British to help him go; it was not a difficult task. Indeed, there is even the speculation that the British proposed the idea to Retinger![10] By 1944, after his long dealings with the Anglo-Americans, Retinger knew neither Washington nor London were inclined to take serious efforts on behalf of Poland, and that it was essential to disabuse the Poles of any misconceptions in this regard. These doubts were dampened, if not dispelled, by Mikołajczyk's assurance to the British that Retinger would be traveling "as my personal emissary."[11]

On January 7, 1944 Retinger turned to the Foreign Office. They seemed to be a bit skeptical about Retinger's personal diplomacy, but Walter Roberts, of the Foreign Office, wrote that actually Retinger had raised the matter informally "several weeks ago" and that it was "a bright idea of his own."[12] However, given his precarious position in the Polish government, Retinger claimed authorship, and hence blame for the idea.[13] Retinger told Gubbins that the plan "is not known about, and should not be revealed to any other Pole." He had not yet even raised it with Mikołajczyk.[14] Mikołajczyk, however, as Retinger assured the British, would soon approach them. In other words, the British knew of Retinger's proposed mission to Poland perhaps even before Mikołaczyk had heard of it, at least that was the impression Retinger wanted the British to have. This may well have been to keep the matter from being exposed too quickly. Deciding not to inform the Polish government was a controversial decision on Retinger's part. It was a manipulative *tour de force*.

Roberts recommended that London help Retinger but await a formal request from Mikołaczyk: Retinger was "a bit of an intriguer." And, as Roberts wrote in an aside: a "wild reporter."[15] Significantly Eden minuted this memorandum with the words "I do not entirely trust M. Retinger."[16] Mikołajczyk duly made the request on January 12th.[17] It was accepted by Eden.[18] In writing to the British, Mikołajczyk was careful to grant himself credit for conceiving the mission: "I thought it would be useful," and that Retinger was his "personal emissary."[19]

However, the relationship between Retinger and the British is not completely clear. A very telling piece of evidence is the letter Tadeusz Chciuk-Celt, very close to Retinger late in the war, wrote to Retinger in 1955. Chciuk-Celt accompanied Retinger to Poland and later risked his life to help him. He asked:

Because it is no longer a secret to anyone any more, that the English patronized [patronowali] your trip to the homeland. That you where the agent of the English government. Should I give away which (Foreign Office, SOE, or etc.), or also not make the identification any clearer? [20]

As for the question of whether it was the Foreign Office or the SOE which was more responsible for Retinger's mission, it was certainly the latter.[21] Indeed, the SOE was almost certainly the only intelligence agency involved in the mission.[22] "We were," Retinger wrote, "partners."[23] There is no evidence that Churchill played any role in the mission: it certainly was not his idea. As Pomian argued, Churchill did not send Retinger, but the latter could not go without his permission.[24] Retinger seemed to trust the British more than his own countrymen and wanted to be able to present a picture in Poland which reflected the British "line." Retinger was motivated by the idea of serving Poland; he was also a British sympathizer.

Retinger told the Foreign Office his motives for the trip. The Polish government in London was "quite convinced" that it must make sacrifices to Russia, but opinion was more "intransigent" in Poland. Mikołajczyk wanted to situation explained to the Poles in the homeland and support for his policy was won. The great fear the Foreign Office noted regarding Retinger's explanation was that "Mikołajczyk agreeing to conclude an agreement with the Russians under our pressure and then being disavowed by the Poles at home."[25] It would be, Retinger argued, "fatal" were the homeland to reject any of Mikołajczyk's agreement with the Russians.[26] As he wrote sincerely to Mrs. Sikorski: "the object of my mission is not to create a very powerful or great Poland but a happy Poland."[27] Shortly before departing Retinger wrote a touching letter to Mikołajczyk that Polish unity was central to the country's welfare. Poland had lost the war with Moscow, and the allies had won it because of them. A woeful position indeed. A "compromise" that would last a "long term." He was pleading for Polish patriotism, "our most important weapon." In contrast, "the megalomania of national honour has done us much harm."[28] He bluntly stated that Poland had lost the war, and some way forward must be found: an honorable compromise. He assured the Prime Minister that "he had no personal ambition at all." He had never been an "intriguer," a dubious claim: "My one desire is the good of my country." He asked that Mikołajczyk not try to save him should something happen, but use him for the Polish cause.[29] He ended by asking Mikołajczyk to care for his children.[30]

Chciuk-Celt describes Mikołaczyk giving him the details of his undertaking, including taking Retinger. Mikołaczyk, curiously, told Chciuk-Celt that he was talked into agreeing by Retinger but the mission was conceived by Eden, or Retinger talked Eden into agreeing.[31] Mikołajczyk discounted the rumor of Retinger as a British agent, though he would not directly deny it to Chciuk-Celt.[32] In this context, it is worth remembering that Mikołajczyk, at British insistence, kept knowledge of Retinger's mission even from Raczkiewicz the

President of Poland, and General Kazimierz Sosnkowski, the commander-in-chief.³³ When informed, Raczkiewicz wanted to know what orders he had been given. Mikołajczyk responded evasively that Retinger had the trust of the English and was well informed as regards political conditions in the West which he could impart to the underground. This was hardly a satisfactory, if not an outrageously evasive answer.³⁴

The motives for Retinger's trip are referred to by Chciuk-Celt who describes an emotional scene in which he met with Mikołajczyk who asked him to undertake this most dangerous mission for patriotic reasons: to inform Poles what the allies had done to them at Tehran. Indeed, Polish reports from Washington revealed that Roosevelt and his administration had already adopted a very accommodating attitude towards the Russians.³⁵ Roberts noted that the Poles "should not expect the impossible either from us or from the Americans." To which Retinger ruefully added that American assurances were not to be given much credence especially in light of an approaching election. This probably reflects reports he received from his friend Zamoyski in Washington. According to Zamoyski, the Americans, from Roosevelt downwards, had already decided on the territorial reduction of Poland and what amounted to its reduced post-1945 frontiers.³⁶

How this mission would "save the nation" as Chciuk-Celt records Mikołajczyk as saying is a bit hard to understand, sauve *que peut*, perhaps. Mikołajczyk spoke of trying to convince the underground that, just because one could not save everything one did not have to lose all.³⁷ It would be better, perhaps, to see this as Mikołajczyk's efforts to preempt, in advance his rejection by the Poles. If he could have Retinger convince the Poles that the West would provide nothing, concessions to the Russians which Mikołajczyk already regarded as inevitable, would be tolerable at home.³⁸ Retinger's state of mind at this moment must be considered. In his notes we find this despairing reference from March 8, 1944; amidst the welter of pro-Soviet propaganda in the West, "at the moment the allies are winning, Poland is losing, and that it would lose without consideration of the outcome of the war."³⁹ This was a thesis debated in both the upper reaches of the AK and among high-ranking officers in exile.⁴⁰ In Retinger's memoirs he, rather vaguely, suggests that he was going to explain why Poland rejected British pressure during the war:

> I must go to Poland to inform our leaders there of the whole history of our dealings with London, which explains to them how we were right in avoiding the temptation to trim our sails to changing external conditions.⁴¹

Perhaps as important, Retinger wanted to gather information about the situation in the homeland so as to inform the exile government, and the British, of the true state of affairs both within the underground government and military as well as the disposition of society in general.⁴² He was suspicious that the émigré government was making decisions without a clear knowledge of the true situation in Poland.⁴³ In a letter written to Raczkiwicz, delivered, *nota bene*, after he departed, Retinger summarized his motives: It was necessary to send a senior figure *au courant* regarding the situation in England. Retinger felt this role could only be played by him because of his connections with Sikorski and Mikołajczyk. His experience in Russia and America were additional assets. Further, he had avoided internal Polish politicking and was truly "non-party." Since many influential people among the allies held him in high regard, his report would make a profound impression. The mission would have lifted the morale of the Polish underground. But, most of all the mission would unite Polish views at a very difficult time. He concluded by asking for God's help.⁴⁴

The British had their own questions regarding the situation in Poland. As Norman Davies succinctly summarizes, the exile government was reporting horrific stories about Soviet behavior in Poland, on the other hand, the British embassy in London was "passing on the Soviet line.". An independent source was necessary to "find out where the truth really lay": Retinger.

> was being sent behind the backs of the exiled Government to report on the veracity of their statements. In particular, he would have been asked to explore three aspects: the level of popular support for the Communist and pro-Communist organizations; the chances of cooperation between the Communist and the democratic parties; and the likely reaction of the population to the outbreak of a Rising. It is a credible scenario.⁴⁵

Not all Poles supported the realist position, especially as it concerned the eastern territories. Sosnkowski was adamant about not compromising with the Soviets in this regard and he was not alone. Many of this military group thought of Retinger as a British, sometimes a Russian, or even an international agent.⁴⁶ The realists were closer to the British than to their own government.⁴⁷ As Siemaszko has noted, the premier of the Polish government turned to the British command to carry out an action which was completely unknown by Polish authorities.⁴⁸

Sosnowski's frustration, as well as his adherence to the non-realist position is captured in a dispatch he sent to the commander of the AK, General Tadeusz Bór-Komorowski. Mikołajczyk was

> sending by the next flight two of his couriers to Poland. The Premier has prohibited the base commander from informing me in this matter, which was arranged as a complete secret from me or the President. The chief agent as far as I know has the pseudonym Brzoza and is concealed by the English and he shall enter the airplane in a mask. I cannot prevent his flight, because of the role of the English in the whole matter ... I have reason to believe, that [the mission] deals with personal instructions for the Delegate of the government and their Commander of the Home Army [AK].

The secrecy of the episode and the role of the English in its organization suggests that that the envoy of the Premier may be regarded as proposed or under the orders of the English, the more so because as you know English efforts are encouraging us to relinquish our Borderlands for an insecure recompensation in the West and to enter into military cooperation with the Soviets even without a prior political understanding.[49]

Bór-Komorowski assured Sosnkowski that "Józef Brzoza" (Retinger) was regarded as an English agent and an international crook (agent angielski i międzynarodowy aferzysta).[50] Polish intelligence may well have informed Sosnkowski that Retinger was a Soviet spy, which it already suspected.[51] The Foreign Office was convinced that Retinger had been regarded by the Poles as a "Soviet agent" in the period before the war.[52]

## Going to Poland

The Poles had been importuning the British since the beginning of the year to bring the Commanding Officer of the AK to Great Britain. By January of 1944 the British relented describing the mission as "urgent." Although the memorandum asked for the AK commander to be brought to Britain, it also intimated that someone should go to Poland "to instruct its representatives" there.[53] Thus the Retinger mission was not without preamble. Retinger later claimed that the British government sent him after allowing him access to "all British secret documents referring to the position of the Polish government in the international scene." The information was to be conveyed to the Poles in the occupied homeland so they would realize "what kind of position the Polish government was now faced with."[54]

Retinger wanted to leave in early February and return in a week or two. Roberts thought this too optimistic and calculated that to be in Poland at that time would mean a departure on January 16. Roberts argued that the SOE's Gubbins arrange the mission.[55] Gubbins had the SOE agent in Italy inform the Polish base there that someone would be coming through, with Churchill's full knowledge, code-named Józef Brzoza.[56]

Retinger, in turn, had two requests: the first was "what line" the British wanted him to take in Poland, and could Eden see him? This was an obvious attempt by Retinger to be able to tell the Poles that he had met with Eden.[57] It is important that we note that it was Retinger who asked to see Eden and not the other way round. The initiative was always on Retinger's side and the British merely acquiesced to his importuning. Mikołajczyk's role was window-dressing. Eden saw Retinger the next day for a few minutes. Unintentionally, when the Polish underground heard of this, they concluded that Retinger was definitely a British agent.[58]

Retinger than added a most unfortunate *obiter dictum*: he told Roberts that while in Poland he would remind the Poles that it was in part their failure to cooperate with Russia in 1938–1939 which was to blame for the failure of British peace efforts.[59] This was in so many ways a bad idea for Retinger to raise. First the whole premise of blaming the Poles for the failure of the anemic British efforts is dubious at best. Second, casting aspersions on the Piłsudskiite regime – especially Colonel Beck, was a tradition for both Sikorski and Retinger and showed the Poles in a bad light.[60] Besides the very idea of telling members of the Home Army in Poland, among whom Piłsudski held legendary status, that his regime was guilty would have disastrous consequences for Retinger's acceptance among Polish officers. The Poles in the homeland, already depressed and forced to accept the loss of 40 percent of their country, did not need to be told that the war was partly their fault. It is not surprising that the British, who monitored events in Poland as best they could, were aware that Retinger would get "a poor reception" in Poland: "he is now regarded as a British agent."[61] This sorry situation was made all the worse by a series of particularly belligerent and uncompromising statements issued by Moscow which Ambassador Raczyński referred to as "brutal."[62]

Retinger wrote a disingenous letter to Raczkiewicz and apologized for not meeting with him for his instructions, but "the English who are arranging his trip without exception demanded that no one other than the premier would know about his trip." He then explained why he was going. He believed: someone conversant with the political situation should go; someone who had been close to Sikorski and Mikołaczyk; someone with experience in Russia, the United States and the Middle East, and in addition, many people trusted him (though he did not say that many people did *not*); and he finally hoped he would raise Polish morale in the homeland. He confirmed to Raczkiewicz that he had spoken to Mikołaczyk about his mission and that he was sure they reflected what he and the president had spoken of after Sikorski's death, a record that does not survive. As he did with Mikołaczyk, he asked the president to take care of his daughters if he did not return.[63]

Later, Retinger wrote a letter to Ambassador Raczyński. He argued that he had not had the opportunity to meet with him about the mission, which was obviously untrue. This failure was because "the British made it an absolute condition that nobody besides the premier should know that I was leaving." This was simply a lie, because it had been Retinger who insisted to the British that the Poles be kept in the dark. Retinger explained his mission to Raczyński as aiming to inform the Poles of the international situation, a task he was particularly well-prepared to do because of his closeness to Sikorski and contacts with the allies and Russia. Besides, he argued he was really non-party and had not become enmeshed in internal politics and had no real political preferences. Certainly, this was a dubious remark. Besides, he was trusted by the allies, which is also dubious given the many comments made in internal Foreign Office memoranda about him being a suspicious character and an intriguer. Finally, the mission would have propaganda value sure to lift Polish spirits. He would return in six weeks, and as always Retinger's invoked "God's" help when facing dire circumstances.[64]

In concert with Gubbins, it was decided that Retinger would parachute into Poland and later be taken out by plane, another Wildhorn operation. This flight to Poland was supposed to take place on February 28, 1944. But it was delayed almost two months.[65] By this stage of the war, southern Italy was already in allied hands, and the journey was to be undertaken from there by a Halifax, four-engined bomber. The preparations were carried out in elaborate secrecy in fear of agents.[66] Gubbins was concerned from the outset that Retinger – neither young nor in good health – should not undertake the mission.[67] However, the SOE was convinced that the realist course was essential for Poland and supported Mikołajczyk in his efforts.[68] Retinger admitted that, "I often cooperated with that mysterious organization during the war."[69] Retinger's was to have one companion, Chciuk-Celt, and was to report to Mikołajczyk personally, though through "the Chief of the British Office with whom you are in contact."[70] In the words of Witold Babiński, who had a rather sour disposition concerning Retinger: "he returned to his double role: the emissary of English Intelligence and the confidante of the Premier."[71]

Shortly before leaving, Retinger wrote Mikołajczyk a letter that is as much wistful as it is political. He again called for a compromise and to avoid "the megalomania of national honor" which has cost Poland so much. After waiting in isolation since January, he read Plato. Retinger, then called on Captain George Paisley and wearing a mask, left Bari on the night of April 3, 1944 and parachuted into Poland: "perhaps the oldest jumper" of all times.[72] The jump was successful and Retinger sustained no injuries.[73] He had $144,000 in cash and a sum of gold. He was accompanied by Chciuk-Celt, who previously when dropped into Poland used the code name Sulima.

Sosnkowski and Raczkiewicz found out about Retinger's departure within one day.[74] As the British observed, since only Mikołajczyk knew of the mission, it could well cause him problems within his government where he was none too popular anyway.[75] Polish intelligence was not informed of the mission, though British intelligence, at least the SOE, knew, of course.[76] The Poles were not pleased by having to piece together the undertaking by bits and scraps.[77] But, according to Tucholski, they really knew Retinger was going before he left.[78] Sosnkowski sent a message to the underground army command describing Retinger's goals as including cooperation with the Soviet army even without a previous political accord.

Mikołajczyk immediately sent a dispatch to the underground authorities: Retinger and Chciuk-Celt had his complete confidence; in addition Retinger had the trust of the British. His safe return has "particular significance."[79] Once in Poland, Retinger, or Captain Paisley as he was referred to at Bari, was to be known by his Polish code name Brzoza and had false identification with that name.[80] However, the British used the alias "Salamader" for Retinger. It is hard to believe that Retinger could remember who he was in which context.

Curiously, Mikołaczyk insisted that all communication with Retinger while he was in Poland were to be "addressed for me personally" and "sent only through the Chief of the British Office." Thus the British would monitor Retinger's activities before they were known to Mikołaczyk.

## In Poland

Retinger conducted himself with courageous, or thoughtless, nonchalance in Warsaw, openly visiting his old haunts, drinking too much, doing nothing to disguise his movements or appearance. Perhaps this reflects his motto that he "despised spying."[81] The subterranean world of espionage was utterly foreign to him, and his casual approach amazed and disconcerted his interlocutors, especially because Retinger calculated that the Gestapo were searching for him by the third day of his arrival.[82]

Zygmunt Zaremba of the underground immediately grasped Retinger's main goal: to work for reconciliation with the Soviets. This was particularly difficulty for Zaremba who complained bitterly that the West was already too pro-Soviet in its reporting:

> I concluded that the thing that most interested him was the possibility of finding some kind of compromise between the Underground and the communists and Soviet. Russia. He always returned to these themes and discussed each argument in detail which I raised in support of the thesis, that it was impossible to settle this in the country, because the question lay exclusively in the sphere of international relations for the Soviets. For me, and for all of us, it seemed obvious, that the problem of our future was to be found now more than ever in the hands of the western allies, who alone possessed the means to limit Soviet appetites. Retinger suggested nothing, only obviously wanted to uncover what our understanding and evaluation of the situation.[83]

Retinger immediately made contact with a host of key underground leaders: the delegate of the exile government (the so-called Delagatura), Jan Jankowski (code name Soból); chief of the Directorship of Civil Resistance, Stefan Korboński, a member of the planning commission for the Delagatura, Henryk Kołodziejski, and Chairman of the Council of National Unity (Rada Jedności Narodowej, RJN), Kazimierz Pużak and many others.[84] Jankowski, for his part, did not understand Retinger's mission and mistrusted him from the start. He really did not know who Retinger truly was.[85] Soon he discovered that Retinger, contrary to his reputation as a sphinxlike agent, was a "blabbermouth." Retinger met with the AK's General Tadeusz Bór-Komorowski,[86] and many more of the chief figures in the underground movement. Retinger's main liaison was Korboński.[87] There are reports that Retinger also tried to meet with Communists, but this is unconfirmed.[88]

His days were crowded with meetings, and not always as a passive observer: he met with and appealed to the RJN for unified action.[89] Pużak was very disconcerted by Retinger's lack of caution ("fanforonada") in conducting meetings which made a bad impression among the underground. He received up-to-the minute sabotage reports from Korboński. Retinger outlined his main points succinctly: a compromise with Russia was necessary and would require relinquishing the eastern territories, and the participation of Communists in the Polish government. In Britain, pro-Soviet sentiment was profound and growing and support for Poland was very little. Sacrifices now would, perhaps, lessen future losses. There needed to be immediate talks between the RJN and the Polish Communist Party (technically the Polish Workers' Party, *Polska Partia Robotnicza*, PPR). A crucial unanswered question was how much the PPR would demand.[90]

These arguments met with a mixed, often hostile audience. They were, in effect, the Sikorski-Retinger-Mikołajczyk, "realist" program. Babiński concluded that one of Retinger's tasks was to convince the underground that it was the premier not the military commander (General Sosnkowski) who was to be obeyed.[91] An indication of Retinger's detachment from the sentiments of the underground was when he told Chciuk-Celt, just days before its outbreak, that a rising in Warsaw would be "nonsense."[92] In general however, especially given the considerable length of time he spent in Warsaw, we know relatively little about his meetings there. The conversations with the PPR, like all Retinger's negotiations, have never seen the light of day.[93]

Nonetheless, some idea of what message Retinger carried to the underground was conveyed in a secret Foreign Office document dated August 8, 1944. Retinger's purpose was:

> To explain to Poles in Poland the necessity for supporting Mr. Mikołajczyk's policy of conciliation with Soviet Russia ... He expresses the opinion that Poland would follow Mr. Mikołajczyk in reaching agreement with Stalin even if this involved the loss of Wilno but not if it involved the loss of Lwów. He stated that there is much more unanimity among Poles in Poland than among those abroad and that the Polish Committee of National Liberation at present represents only 2% of the population, though as a result of Soviet Liberation this proportion might increase 15% but not more.[94]

General Marian Kukiel, in a generous appraisal of the political naïf Bór-Komorowski, summarized one, perhaps the chief, motive of Retinger's mission. He also implied that Retinger's purposes was vouchsafed him by the British:

> Mikołajczyk agreed to Retinger's jump into Poland because, after the occupation of Poland by the Russians, he could be an intermediary in conversations with Stalin. Bór-Komorowski should have spoken with Retinger about this. He [Komorowski] was not privy to the nuances of many questions. He was too straightforward. He did not see the many aspects of a very complicated problem.[95]

Indeed, Bór-Komorowski had been informed about Retinger by his commander Sosnkowski. The role of the British in this episode was obvious by the fact that the agents sent by Mikołajczyk reflected British designs to force Poland to surrender her eastern territories and to cooperate with the Soviets without some *a priori* political agreement.[96]

The Sosnkowski entourage despised Retinger regarding him as an obvious British agent, and probably a Soviet one who represented a policy of limitless concessions to Moscow. It was known throughout the military that Sosnkowski could not countenance Soviet territorial demands.[97] Bór-Komorowski shared these sentiments as did his lieutenants.[98] Mikołajczyk was adamantly opposed to Sosnkowski's role as commander-in-chief and tried to have him removed. There were deep divisions in the exile government and Retinger was heir to them.[99] Retinger was devotedly anti-Sosnkowski,[100] and Sosnkowski warned Bór-Komorowski that the secrecy surrounding Retinger's mission indicated that he was sent with various British proposals and recommendations. These were, in effect, to accommodate the Soviets.[101]

There were very sensitive questions about Retinger's stay on Poland. The first, as noted, is that he was in contact with the Gestapo. There are a few wisps of evidence suggesting it, but it is not convincing.[102] Korboński even supplies the name of the Gestapo agent, one Bruno Schultz with whom Retinger "had certain contacts." The Gestapo apparently decided to kill him regarding him as someone attempting to improve Polish-Soviet relations. The Gestapo was repeatedly "on his trail," but never caught him. What Bułhak refers to as a "sensational" source argues that the Gestapo did catch him and released him in exchange for his becoming their informant. Retinger, the account concludes, actually was a double agent from which the underground profited more than the Gestapo.[103] This was not a convincing thesis.

There is much more evidence that Retinger tried to meet with Communists while in Poland. The sources, however, are scanty about this aspect of Retinger's attempts, if any, to meet with Soviet representatives or Polish Communists. Retinger told the underground that pro-Soviet opinion in England was strong and had to be considered when contemplating Poland's future.[104]

The result of this was the complex issue of whether Polish counter-intelligence had decided to kill Retinger when he was in Poland. After an exhaustive analysis of immense and contradictory literature, Bułhak seems to regard the idea of attempted murder by poisoning as certain,[105] but, at whose orders?

Links between Polish intelligence in London and its counterpart in Warsaw apparently placed in motion actions by Izabella Horodecka (code name "Teresa") who belonged to "993/W," the "liquidation" bureau of the counter-intelligence division of the high command of the home army, the so-called "Dwójka."[106] In April, 1944 she was visited by her superiors in the Dwójka including the chief of the bureau, Colonel Kazimierz Iranek-Osmecki. He handed Horodecka, who had participated in twenty-three assassinations, a poison which would kill Retinger in a couple of weeks after he left Poland. She later contended that Iranek-Osmecki was required to fulfill this mission on the specific orders of Commander-in-Chief General Sosnkowski. Another Polish officer, *au courant* regarding the plan, later denounced it as "tasteless and shameless."[107] The issue is still very controversial and sensitive.[108] Horodecka contended that Retinger was to be poisoned because he was "a very dangerous emissary of foreign intelligence whose task was to collect opinions from the population of Poland about eventual agreements with Soviet Russia on conditions strongly harmful to Poland, and suggest the necessity of their acceptance." The poison to be used was "Tri-o-cresyl phosphate, or TCP." [109] Retinger's later crippling illness was therefore attributable to poison, not to a fall as has been widely concluded.

Sosnkowski, however, probably did not order the assassination *in verbis strictis*, though it is not impossible. Bór-Komorowski certainly did not order it. iI was ordered either by the London headquarters of Polish intelligence or more likely its Warsaw branch.[110] Retinger was convinced that there was a subterranean conspiracy which was arranging his murder:

> Before the war there existed in Poland a sanacja committee a "brain trust" composed of 10 or twelve people which directed the policies of the state. This committee, disorganized by the September campaign and partially enlarged ... had its cells in England, Amereka [sic], and in the homeland and continued to direct sanacja actions. There [the United States] the decision was taken to murder him in Poland and with this goal a message was sent from London to Iranek.[111]

The chronology of the possible attempt on Retinger's life is fascinating. Several days after arriving in Poland and conducting his first meetings, Retinger told Chciuk-Celt that he had found from a reliable source, which he would not disclose, that Dwójka, including its units in the underground high command, intended to murder him. Chciuk-Celt quoted Retinger as saying: "various people in London – who steadfastly believe that I am an English agent – and perhaps a Soviet one as well, that I have come to Poland to dismantle [rozladować] the patriotic Underground and subordinate it to the Communists insist that I be liquidated in Poland."[112] Retinger was, it seems, convinced that the efforts to kill him were sent from London but never revealed the name of who ordered the execution.[113]

Retinger, again according to the only witness, Chciuk-Celt, went on to justify has actions:

> You know why I came. The [Underground] Delegate knows as well. And the commandant of the AK. They know that I only want to convince them that it will be necessary in the future to cooperate with the Communists, because no English are coming here, only Russians. If we do not get along with them somehow, it will be a terrible tragedy, because we well know what Stalin and the NKVD are. And it's about trying to make people here understand this fact. And they want to murder me![114]

Chciuk-Celt immediately informed the *Delegatura* who admitted he knew of the plot and had already undertaken efforts to counteract it. It would not take place he assured Chciuk-Celt. When pressed what steps he had taken, the Delegatura, probably Jan Jankowski, answered in a word that he had met with the Bór-Komorowski. It was not clear from Chciuk-Celt's report whether the general had previously known about the plot or not, but he assured the Delegatura that it would not transpire. Komorowski had threatened the perpetrators with a military tribunal. Thus, the notion of killing Retinger did not arise from Warsaw but was brought to the country from London through Dwójka channels. Retinger believed Komorowski's denial of any knowledge of the attempts.[115]

A reliable report noted that

> [Retinger] told me that during his stay in Warsaw the Polish II Bureau [i.e. Dwójka] made two attempts on his life. In the first case he was to be shot with a gun, but he was shielded from the bullet by the accompanying woman at a critical moment ... The second attempt at murdering Retinger was made using poison, with which his food was laced. Since the dose was insufficient to cause death, he recovered and returned to health.[116]

Retinger's report to Polish intelligence that there was a *previous* attempt on his life in Poland arranged by Dwójka, from which he was saved by an unknown woman, is a mystery in itself.[117] Retinger, bizarrely, only learned of it in the final stages of the war and was unaware of it during his stay in Poland. Retinger did not disclose the man who had ordered the assassination, but later said he was still alive and living in the West.[118] We must conclude that, obviously, there was indeed a plan to kill him.[119]

In 1958, not long before his death, Retinger told a Polish intelligence agent what was more or less a summary of his stay in Warsaw in 1944: two attempts on his life, one by gunshot, one by poisoning. Retinger was later told by his friend Colonel Stanisław Gano that the Warsaw Dwójka had arranged the attempts on orders from Dwójka in London. The attempts were arranged hastily and incompetently. "Oskar" an operative of Communist Poland who met with Retinger several times after the war, suggested that it was the underground's General Tadeusz Pełczyński, at which Retinger visibly "came to life a little [ożywił się nieco]"[120] but said he did not wish to disclose the name.[121] He also did not wish to discuss the motive for the attempts. Speculating on them, Retinger suggested that it was "revenge" for his "sharp critique of generals and colonels of the sanacja in the presence of Sikorski." But it was more than this. Retinger was supposedly responsible for the "Rothesay Camp" where Polish officers hostile to Sikorski were shamelessly confined since the beginning of the war.[122] The sanacja officers hated Sikorski for years. They informed on Retinger to Sikorski as early as 1940 in Scotland.[123] But the two ridiculed the officers. Hence, the Piłsudskiite officers wanted to "remove" (usunąć) Retinger in order to have direct and greater influence on Sikorski. Retinger concluded by saying that he did not want to disclose any information regarding Gano.[124]

In conclusion, the evidence is insufficient to discern the ultimate source of the decision to kill Retinger. It was, as Bułhak argues, probably a remark by Sosnkowski to Demel of the London Dwójka which was vague. Demel then ordered the Warsaw branch of Polish counter-intelligence to kill Retinger. Iranek-Osmecki (in Warsaw), probably at Pełczyński's instruction, tried to carry out the order via Horodecka. It is an explanation which is supported by the available evidence, but not dispositive.[125]

The radical political right in Poland, the National Armed Forces (Narodowe Siły Zbrojne, NSZ) also, apparently, wanted to kill Retinger because of his reluctant acceptance of the future Soviet role in Poland.[126] Perhaps, argue others, the reason for the NSZ determination was Retinger's putative contacts with the Gestapo, a dubious thesis.[127] His leftist politics and rumors of being a British agent, let alone a Soviet one, were causes enough.

## The return

Retinger was to be evacuated on May 29–30, 1944. But the first, positive, reports of Retinger's return to Britain, Operation Wildhorn II, were in error. He was not on the plane. There was much confusion. Someone else was taken for Retinger. The plane did not wait for him and the second "Most" was a failure.[128] The fault lay with British incompetence.[129] Mikołajczyk was furious. The Ministry of the Interior was desperate to arrange Retinger's return, though why that ministry would be especially concerned is a curiosity.[130] Retinger wrote a frantic letter demanding another flight and insisted upon Gubbins's personal intervention.[131]

Retinger had run after the departing plane in the dark. In the chaos of retrieving him, he fell in the water and awoke the next day paralyzed. In Retinger's words:

> I fell ill from inflammation of the nervous system [zapalenie korzonków] losing control of my legs and hands. It happened suddenly, one day when I was on a tram returning to my conspiratorial apartment. I had the terrible feeling that I could not walk. For three or four days I could not even move my hands.[132]

A specialist told him movement would gradually return, but it would take months for a full recovery. He could not walk. The situation would, indeed, worsen and he would be in considerable pain.[133] He went to a clinic to recover, but the Gestapo was looking for him. He was taken to a hospital for venereal disease, which he found amusing. He and Chciuk-Celt took a train, sometime later, for Kraków. There were some colorful adventures there. In the meantime, the underground felt burdened by him.¹³⁴ However, Retinger's gravely compromised health really had nothing to do with the reported fall. It was really due to the partially administered poison by an agent of the Dwójka. The supposedly grievous injury was a "cover story."¹³⁵

In the meanwhile, as this Hollywood-like tale unfolds, the Polish underground had extraordinarily obtained portions of the V-2 rocket and it was vital to get them, and at least one specialist, to London. This information, and parts of it, were given priority over any person.¹³⁶ Also waiting in the passenger line was Tomasz Arciszewski, the elderly socialist, whom the underground wanted to replace the ailing Raczkiewicz as president.¹³⁷ Finally, the Poles were importuning the British to get Retinger out.¹³⁸ Notably, Retinger was given pride of place over Arciszewski.

According to Chciuk-Celt, they waited for days near a little village not far from Kraków. With the Russians approaching, the Germans threw together an air base in the vicinity. German cavalry were stationed close by, and the Gestapo were moving everywhere. On July 25th, Chciuk-Celt was informed the evacuation would be that night, Wildhorn III.¹³⁹ Retinger appeared with two AK officers. He sat in silence while the soldiers conferred over their hopeless situation surrounded by Germans. They finally boarded with Chciuk-Celt carrying Retinger in his arms. He wept as he left Polish soil.¹⁴⁰ He was reported to be "partly paralyzed and travelling under care."¹⁴¹ Similarly, when he eventually landed in England, he was treated with special attention due to his condition.¹⁴²

Lt. Jan Nowak was briefed on the evacuation of Retinger, though his name was not used. The "order of loading for the return trip" was:

> The special supplies this was particularly stressed – then the accompanying expert, 'Rafal;' 'Brzoza' goes next, then 'Tomasz', and last the two couriers. The order is important in case the total weight is too heavy for the aircraft. In that case you will not take aboard everyone scheduled but will leave some behind, starting from the bottom of their list. However the material and the expert must be taken aboard no matter what.¹⁴³

The return was a harrowing adventure. There was a last-minute change in landing destination because of the sudden appearance of German troops. This delayed the rendezvous. The landing was without incident, but the return was a near disaster. The plane took over an hour to take off and made three attempts. The problem was the muddy field from which it had to be dug-out. There was even the thought of setting the plane afire and abandoning the mission. The fourth effort was finally a success.¹⁴⁴

On his return Retinger, a "helpless cripple," met with Gubbins in Brindisi.¹⁴⁵ Roberts of the Foreign Office was anxious to meet with Retinger as well, and this is quite understandable: Retinger bore fresh news from an important theater and the British were naturally interested. The SOE also met with him in nearby Bari. Later, he met with Mikołajczyk, en route to

Moscow for a meeting with Stalin in Cairo on July 28, 1944.[146] The British had sent him to Egypt "with highest priority."[147] The British were "specially interested [in the] welfare of this body."[148] To his outrage, Arciszewski was kept waiting for the entire time. He exploded, quite insightfully to Zygmunt Nagórski:

> More than one hour I waited to speak with Mikołajczk, but before me he took Retinger and spoke with him for a very long time. Ordering me to wait – and I was very tired after this rather difficult trip from the homeland and I thought that my reports should interest the Premier of Poland most of all. I could not understand it, though I saw that Retinger, as an agent of the English could be for him such an important source of information. But he returned from the homeland and therefore could not have more fresh information than the English. And concerning the country, I knew a bit more and was better oriented than he. Who is this Retinger? I told him to his face in Cairo, that it seems he served three intelligence services simultaneously. He answered with complete casualness: only two –Polish and English – not a third.[149]

Retinger and Mikołajczyk had a four-hour conversation.[150] "Talks at the crossing of the London and Polish roads," said a Polish observer, and, perhaps also, "at the crossroads of our history." A subsequent conversation included an SOE agent, Lt. Col. Harold Perkins.[151] Mikołajczyk later flew on to Moscow without Retinger – who, incidentally, had asked to accompany him. Retinger instead returned to London along with Arciszewski, Chciuk-Celt, and one other whose name cannot be deciphered.[152] The details of Retinger's talks with Mikołajczyk have never been revealed.[153]

British intelligence wanted to meet with him at once after his return to London. They wanted to confer before he spoke with the Foreign Office: it was "urgent." Retinger was the "one and only person who can help us concerning it." It was not detailed what it was, but it revealed both the rivalry in British agencies and the high regard the SOE had for Retinger.[154]

In Britain, Retinger was not kept secret. He appeared at press conferences and gave interviews, informing the population of the situation in Poland and the desperate fate of the Jews. He also discussed his supposed polyneuritis. At one meeting he said underground Poland supported Mikołajczyk and would accept "any agreement" that he could reach with Stalin.[155] He dismissed the Polish Committee of National Liberation, a Russian created front organization, as "wholly unrepresentative." He emphasized the hatred of the Germans, national unity, and that people in the homeland "think differently from the Poles abroad on many questions social and political."[156] He noted, significantly, that Poland supported Mikołajczyk and was willing to make substantial territorial concessions, but would oppose "by force" any dictated agreement.[157] Nothing Retinger did or said would suggest pro-Communist sympathies

Indeed, Bułhak seems to have put to rest the notion that Retinger was a Soviet agent or even a crypto- Communist. The gossip that Retinger was pro-Soviet, or even a Russian agent, was obliterated by a public remark he made:

> There are only a few [Poles] in favor of Communism. In fact the Communists' influence has declined since the war. The Communist Party in Poland, which had 5000 members before the war, now has only 2000 in its ranks.[158]

Lavrenty Beria, the head of the NKVD, concluded that he was a British agent.[159]

Retinger also met with Foreign Minister Tadeusz Romer and Stanisław Grabski.[160] Retinger asked, again, to go to accompany Mikołajczyk to meet with Stalin in Moscow, but his health prevented it.[161] However Chciuk-Celt has written that Retinger had asked Mikołajczyk if he might go to Moscow in advance of the premier, as he had done in 1941 before Kot. Mikołajczk approved, but Retinger had apparently told Mikołajczyk that Eden had promised him a plane; which he had not. Retinger did not go.[162]

The 1944 mission has remained controversial ever since, and its secrecy and British involvement have done much to create the legend of Retinger as an agent of London.[163] The refusal of the British to release pertinent documents, and the failure of Retinger to discuss the operation in detail have not helped.[164] Even many years after the event, Retinger refused to speak to a young historian seeking information.[165] Retinger wrote to former paramour, Mary Louis Doherty, that his four months in Poland "was one of the most inspiring and thrilling adventures I have ever had."[166]

## Retinger adrift

Mikołajczyk's government was thrown into disarray by the failure of the Warsaw Rising of August–October, 1944 and the chaos it produced. He was completely discredited by his meeting in Moscow with the Russians and the browbeating and humiliation he suffered at Churchill's hands over Polish-Russian border issues.[167]

Retinger continued to advocate cooperation with the Soviets to the fall of 1944 if not later. He told *The Times* that despite all, he still favored collaboration with the Soviets-which he deemed the Mikołajczyk policy. He recalled Churchill's overly-dramatic words at the signing of the Sikorski-Maisky treaty that it represented "a new chapter in history." Both sides, Retinger argued, had made mistakes: the Poles' deep-seated mistrust of the Russians, while Soviet intentions were demonstrated by their treatment of the home army and the occupied territory. The real cause of the problem was not strategic, economic nor social, but psychological. The old traditions were obsolete in Poland. The Warsaw Rising was misunderstood in the West, whatever that meant. Peace in the east of Europe would be based on Soviet policy towards the smaller countries of which Polish-Soviet relations were the key: peace in Europe depended upon peace in its eastern part.[168]

Here we see, as was the case in 1916–1917, Retinger then trying to create a policy of reconciliation between Austria and Poland and by solving this problem, the continent itself would be at peace. Now, the reconciliation must be with Russia. However, Moscow had no need of cooperation with the Poles. Retinger was no friend of Russia, but was desperately trying to save Poland by elevating it to the means of continental harmony.

Churchill's abusiveness to Mikołajczyk was due to the fact that he had to admit betraying Polish trust. It was the passion of guilt. Mikołajczyk returned to London a broken man. He resigned on November 24th.[169] In mid-June 1945, he returned to Poland, no longer in political office, for reasons still unclear.[170] He briefly played a role in the transitory coalition government soon replaced by the Communists. Poland had failed to defend its borders, its sovereignty, and the West had betrayed it. Mikołajczyk returned to see if he could ameliorate the situation in the face of horrendous odds. He was as Paczkowski argues "a realist."[171] Perhaps "delusionary" would have been a better description.

Retinger wanted to go on yet another secret mission before the war in Europe concluded. He dunned the British over his "urgent desire" to visit France and Belgium in September 1944. Apparently the latter welcomed the idea, but the former's attitude is unknown. The Air Ministry was willing to provide transportation but wanted Foreign Office approval. Ostensibly he wanted to "see the Poles in the Lille area." The ultimate decision was to tell Retinger to wait.[172] The motivation for the mission is unknown.

In March, 1945 Retinger decided that he wanted to go to Moscow to "pave the way" for Mikołajczyk's return to Warsaw. Eden asked him why he wished this and Retinger replied that he wished to "aid" the British ambassador. When the British asked Mikołajczyk about this plan, which he had apparently not discussed with Retinger, he dismissed it, not seeing what or whom Retinger would represent: "It seems to me that he is simply put a busybody [wścibski] and his activities are more likely to do bad than good."

Retinger tried a last time to convince Cripps, in a "strictly secret and confidential" letter to send him to Russia as "some kind of advisor to the British embassy." Retinger had, apparently discussed this idea first with the Briton and then with General Anders, who replaced Sosnkowski as commander-in-chief of the Polish army in 1944. Retinger told Cripps that he had convinced Anders to negotiate with the Russians and approved Retinger's going to Russia. Moreover, as he told Cripps, Anders promised that, after his return "he would let himself be guided by my relations to the main problems." Retinger was, in effect, asking for the British to send him, ostensibly as a British official, to really work from Poland. He approached the British and suggested that he could unite British Polonia, dubious on the face, or be asked to be sent to Moscow to facilitate Mikołajczyk's activities. The request was refused. The latter dismissed this idea as essentially pointless.

Retinger's offer to aid the British embassy was rejected with derision.[173] The ambiguity of the arrangement is reminiscent of the 1944 mission to Warsaw. Retinger saw himself being the key player in the formation of an appropriate Provisional Government of Poland.

His fitness for this assignment was, as he argued to Cripps, that he was unaffiliated with any Polish political party and completely independent. Second, he was "the closest collaborator of General Sikorski in his Russian policy and settlement of 1941" and was later "the first Polish diplomatic representative in Moscow during the war." Therefore he was "an appropriate link between the past and future Polish-Russian collaboration." It was the same case he made in 1944 to go to Warsaw. He admitted the frequent criticism he endured from Polish quarters, but "I think I am trusted by them as far as the main Polish problem is concerned." This was especially true since, as Retinger claimed, he had spent the last months trying to arrange a "truce" among Polish factions. In addition to exile Poles, his 1944 visit to Warsaw allowed him to meet "most of those of my countrymen who can be considered as leaders of political activities in Poland." Someone had to go soon to Moscow because of the "growing moral terror against those who are for a settlement with the Soviet government may influence the decisions of those who are still willing to make a try." In a few weeks, no Pole would be "courageous enough" to go.[174] He suggested to the British that he be sent to Italy to meet with General Anders to do what the British called "Mikołajczyk propaganda."[175]

Near the war's end, with Poland's dismal fate plain to see, one of Retinger's close friends, perhaps a lover, from the Mexican years wrote to him, "One cannot believe that the present situation is the final solution. Your whole life's work too. No, it just can't be."[176]

## An end to Retinger's connections to the exile government

Retinger had been a sick man when he returned to England, suffering from bouts of paralysis, and was obviously most despairing. He was bedridden, and drinking heavily.[177] Mikołajczyk was replaced as premier of the exile government by the obscure socialist Tomasz Arciszewski. He, in turn, named, almost as an afterthought, Kot his replacement as head of the Peasant Party.[178] For all practical purposes the British ignored the London Polish government. It had been a sad and dramatic decline from the commanding Sikorski, the unimpressive Mikołajczyk, and now the invisible Arciszewski. Retinger openly distanced himself from the exile government and noted that "We want friendship and cooperation with Soviet Russia."[179] This was not a statement designed to ingratiate him to the ardently anti-Communist exile community. It was now, shortly after the war, that the Retinger legend, or legends, began to circulate: British spy, Soviet agent, Mason, Jewish conspirator. Retinger never answered, for the rest of his life, any of the aspersions beyond a blanket denial. He established close connections with the Sikorski Institute in London, but otherwise absented himself from émigré affairs; in many ways he was an outcast, long mistrusted.[180] Similarly, he severed contacts with his friends in Poland: their connection put them under the suspicion or worse of the Communist authorities. Ironically, he met with Warsaw's intelligence operatives. His motives here are incomprehensible.

Retinger's most fierce critics in postwar Britain were those ruined and bereft by the Russian occupation of Poland. If, indeed, as Prażmowska has argued, London "betrayed" the Poles in the war, Retinger's close association with them makes him doubly damned. There could be nothing worse than a pro-Russian British spy. This visceral reaction to Retinger's political machinations is not just bitterness and paranoia but understandable revulsion at someone who often appears in this most unsavory light.[181]

In Poland the Provisional Government of National Unity (Rząd Tymczasowy Jedności Narodowej) was in power, a Communist front with Mikołajczyk a suspended oddity. What the Poles stranded abroad should do was a problem. They could either return or remain in exile. Some, like Mikołajczyk, thought they could have an ameliorative effect on the Communist system by returning. Retinger admits he hesitated. Then, with no other political cards to play, "for the one and only time in my political career I worked exclusively on social issues and not politics."[182]

Retinger went to his two old friends Cripps and Dalton and asked them to help Poland in its misery. He records in his memoirs how he was haunted by the devastation he had seen during his 1944 mission there. In addition he used other channels. From the Trades Union Congress he asked for "international" workers' support for Poland where the workers' movement was under "government pressure." But it was the government which played the decisive role. Cripps told him, to Retinger's astonishment, that "of course we shall do everything, which is within our power, and we shall expect nothing in return."[183] It would all be for free, because Warsaw had no means to pay. However, there was a strange stipulation: the aid could not be officially from the British government; it had to come, ostensibly, from Retinger personally and he would be responsible for its dissemination. After further negotiations it was agreed that the Poles would pay for their shipment to the country, and the British would cover all loading and transfer costs. As it turned out the British paid for the transport too. Victor Cavendish Bentinck, the British ambassador in Warsaw, also lent his efforts.[184]

In a fascinating side note, the experts and others who organized the effort either donated their efforts, were paid by the British, or even by Retinger himself. The total value of the materials sent exceeded 4 million pounds. The aid included "blankets, field kitchens, tents, and even a few Bailey bridges" among many other things in large amounts, especially clothing and tools.[185] The Communist government never publicly thanked London nor Retinger.[186] Even those Poles who were ardently opposed to the new regime in Warsaw did not criticize Retinger's actions.[187] In addition, Retinger spent the immediate postwar years helping Polish refugees in many ways.[188]

Retinger's effort to aid his homeland in need was constant: A decade later, he raised money to aid those injured as a result of the anti-regime riots in Poznań in 1956. As would be expected, he turned to his old acquaintances on the British Left.[189] For this service to the Polish cause, Retinger worked closely with an antagonist from the war years, Raczyński. Retinger's friends noted that he followed developments in Poland very closely. Poland was always on Retinger's mind even when he was deeply involved in international affairs.[190] According to Warsaw, Retinger monitored Polish émigré affairs for the British government.[191] Another source claims that Retinger worked with the UNRRA regarding displaced Poles in the West.[192] He was also associated with a number of prominent exile Poles in creating some sort of political center.[193] There are a few reports that Retinger considered creating a "Polish Communist Party in emigration." This fantastic idea was explained by Warsaw intelligence as an attempted "diversion."[194]

In conjunction with his efforts, Retinger went to Poland three times between December 1945 and March 1946, his last visit to Poland.[195] He was able to meet with Premier Edward Osóbka-Morawski.[196] Departing, his assistant, Chciuk-Celt, was arrested. The Warsaw government claimed that he was traveling about the country taking pictures of "bridges, ports, railroad connections, and other industrial sites."[197] Retinger intervened personally with both Polish Prime Minister Jakub Berman, and even Molotov to get Chciuk-Celt and his wife released from imprisonment.[198] In what was a final bitter blow, the British would not grant him a visa to enter the United Kingdom. The reasons are not clear. For the rest of his life Retinger remained, to his satisfaction, stateless which gave him greater freedom in his international missionary work."[199]

Podgórski argues that these visits were really "to find a place for political activity in Poland." Retinger hoped he could play some role in relations between the newly installed communist government in Warsaw and the authorities in England. He was in regular contact with people in Poland especially PPS veterans.[200] Even the post of Warsaw's ambassador to London crossed his mind. But, suspicion that Retinger was a British intelligence agent convinced Moscow, and Warsaw, that he was not acceptable for the position.[201] This version of events is not entirely plausible and seems to be based only on Ministry of Security documents of the Communist regime in Warsaw.[202]

Retinger passed through an odd but retrospectively logical change after 1946. He was really rejected by both the exile community and the homeland. There was nothing more he could do for Poland after his touching relief efforts. He seemed to turn his enormous energies to larger, continental, problems. In concerning himself with Europe, Retinger always had Poland in his view. Helping the future of Europe was the way a patriot could best help his country. "Poland could only be helped indirectly."[203] Evidence suggests that the Communist authorities in Warsaw mused over the idea of establishing contact with Retinger in 1951,[204] despite their suspicion of him being a British agent.[205] Eventually they sent an agent, code-named "Oskar" to meet with Retinger in London in 1957. He was introduced to Retinger via the latter's friend, the poet J. Minkiewicz. The results of this group of meetings were most illuminating. Retinger was very talkative and had much to say on contemporary affairs, however, he also drank a great deal. Retinger followed Polish developments very closely and was actively involved in gaining loans for Poland from London, and especially the United States.[206]

Retinger was quick to point out that he never applied for British citizenship and always considered himself a Pole of which he was proud. He was, he assured Oskar "a Krakovian." His English, reported Oskar was poor, and spoken with a heavy accent. He "avoided English habits" and, in general "did not like the English as a people." Minkiewicz supported this conclusion. Despite this he was attached to his English friends among whom he named Churchill and his son-in-law Duncan Sandys. Retinger was bitter that his relief efforts for postwar Poland especially that: "Now of course nobody remembers this or me." He spoke of the probable Soviet spy Litauer as his postwar "friend"[207] Among Americans he mentioned Biddle, and was very proud that he still had friends and influence in the State Department.[208]

He insisted that he had a close friendship with Molotov and Vyshinsky from his time in Moscow. His mistrust of the Russians, however, was colossal and he suspected them of plotting a war against the West. The Americans, he told Oskar, neither trusted nor believed the Russians. This was his conclusion from meeting with high-ranking Americans. This reflects Retinger's life-long view of the Russians which he seemed to ameliorate from time to time, as in his conversations with Sikorski which we know about only by inference. But now, near the end of his life, his dislike of the Russians resurfaced. `He concluded pessimistically that Poland's return to freedom was not likely because the Russian were pursuing their traditional policy towards Poland.[209] We should keep this in mind when we discuss the last years of Retinger's life: the Pole as internationalist.

## Notes

1. Zbigniew S. Siemaszko, "Retinger-wysłannik Foreign Office i Mikołajczyka," *Zeszyty Historyczne*, 170 (2009), 213–214.
2. The Poles called these flights "mosty" (bridges). See Jonathan Walker, *Poland Alone: Britain, SOE and the Collapse of Polish Resistance, 1944* (Stroud: The History Press, 2008), 88ff. Kajetan Bieniecki, "Wildhorn," *Zeszyty Historyczne*, No. 88 (1989), 81–100.
3. "Operation Wildhorn (Operation Mosty or Bridges)," Online at http://www.polandin exile.com/exile13.htm. Accessed on October 31, 2013.
4. Bułhak, "Wokół misji," 5.
5. Bułhak, "Wokół misji," 15. This was a conclusion which Retinger had accepted as early as 1943; see Brandes, *Grossbritanien*, 480.
6. Bułhak, "The Foreign Office," unpaginated.
7. Pomian, among others, also argues that it was Retinger's notion at the outset; see Bułhak, "Wokół, "9–10.

8 Ibid., 10–11. Bułhak contends that it was the SOE with which Retinger had a special relationship, and not with any other British Intelligence body; ibid., 17. Retinger may, however, have raised the possibility of his mission to the Foreign Office before speaking to Gubbins: the chronology is not exact; Mikołajczyk originally opposed the mission vigorously and only consented after much protest; see Podgórski, *Retinger*, 124; Roberts to NN, nd, file 233, FO 371/39421, NA.
9 Janta quoted in Witkowski, *Retinger*, 40. Mikołajczyk consented to Retinger's proposal rather than having a hand in crafting it.
10 Bułhak, "Wokół misji," 9–10; Gubbins insists that Retinger had to make a "reiterated request" of Mikołajczyk to be allowed to go; see "Mr. Joseph Retinger," *The Times*, June 20, 1960, 16. This obituary was not published.
11 This is Bułhak's insight; see his "The Foreign Office,"unpaginated.
12 Roberts's memorandum, January 7, 1944, file 233, FO371/39421, NA, January 12, 1944.
13 Bułhak to author, January 5, 2015.
14 Roberts's memorandum, January 7, 1944, file 233, FO 371/39421, NA.
15 Roberts to NN, April 5, 1944, file 233, FO371/39421, NA
16 Ibid.
17 Mikołajczyk to Foreign Office, January 12, 1944, file 233, FO 371/39421, NA.
18 Eden to Mikołajczyk, January 14, 1944, file 135, FO371/39421, NA.
19 Quoted in Bułhak, "Wokół," 13; Chciuk-Celt place the *spiritus movens* behind the mission as Mikołajczyk; which I do not find persuasive; vide his letter MM, April 24, 1967, Retinger col., 75, PISM.
20 Tadeusz [Chciuk] to Retinger, March 15, 1955, Retinger Papers, box 18, folder G, BPL.
21 "Materiały dotyczące biografii Józefa Retingera," PISM, kol. 68, 13; 34. The latter reference suggests it was Mikołajczyk rather than the British who can be credited with the initiative.
22 Bułhak, "The Foreign Office," 44.
23 See Retinger's quotation in "Materiały dotyczące biografii Józefa Retingera," kol. 68, teczka 79, PISM, 20.
24 Pomian to Chciuk-Celt, February 1, 1997; Retinger collection, 75, PISM. The notion that Churchill technically did not send Retinger but witnessed approvingly the discussion of the issue was raised in Collection 68, teczka 79, "Materiały dotyczące biografii Józefa Retingera," PISM; cf. Garliński, *Poland in the Second World War*, 275.
25 Roberts' memorandum of January 12, 1944, file 233, FO 371/39421, NA.
26 Roberts's memorandum of January 17, file 233, FO 371/39421, NA.
27 Retinger to Mrs. Sikorski, January 31, 1944 [not delivered unit March 29], file 233, FO 371/39421, NA.
28 Retinger to Mikołajczyk, February 1, 1944, file 233, FO 371/39421, NA.
29 Retinger to Mikołajczyk, February 1, 1944, quoted in Pomian, *Retinger*, 188–190.
30 Retinger to Mikołajczyk, January 12 [?], 1944, Retinger Collection, #63, PISM.
31 Marek Celt, *Z Retingerem do Warszawy a z powrotem: Raport z podziemia* (Łomnianki: LT, 2006), 27–28. Retinger actually wrote about half this book, so it must be used with some caution; see "The Reminiscences of Tadeusz Celt"; #1077, Oral History Collection, Butler Library, Columbia University (hereafter Butler).
32 Ibid., 29–30.
33 Polish Intelligence discovered the details within twenty-four hours; see Bułhak, "The Foreign Office," unpaginated.
34 Pobóg-Malinowski, *Historja Polski*, 3:604. Keeping the mission secret from the Poles served no useful purpose and only heightened Polish Intelligence's suspicions.

35 Bułhak, "Foreign Office," unpaginated.
36 Bułhak, "Wokół," 15–16.
37 Celt, Z Retingerem, 90.
38 Retinger shared Mikołajczyk's views regarding concessions to the Russians; Podgórski, Retinger, 147.
39 See the "top secret" notes, dated March 8, 1944 in Retinger col., PISM, 68/47.
40 Bułhak, "Wokół," 9.
41 Retinger, drawer 3, "Secret Mission to Poland," BPL.
42 Pomian, Retinger, 143.
43 Terlecki, Wielka awantura, 120–121.
44 This letter, from mid-January, is reproduced in Pomian, Retinger, 187–188.
45 Norman Davies, Rising '44: The Battle for Warsaw. New York: Viking, 2004, 214–215.
46 Bułhak, "Wokół," 23–26.
47 Witold Babiński, "Wymiana depesz między Naczelnym Wodzem i dowódcą Armii Krajowej 1943–1944," Zeszyty Historyczne, 26 (1973), 160.
48 Siemaszko, "Retinger-wysłannik," 216. Years after the event, however, Foreign Minister Tadeusz Romer claimed to have been informed of the mission. This claim cannot be verified. Why this would be true is difficult to understand. Sosnkowski and Raczkiewicz were both Piłsudskiites; Romer however had been closely associated with the endecja movement. Perhaps some people in the government were privileged with the information. Here Retinger's anti-Piłsudski animus may be of issue. See Romer's remarks in box 25A "Kondolencje i Wspomnienia pośmiertnie" see letter from Adam Romer, Retinger Papers, BPL.
49 Sosnkowski to Bór-Komorowski, February 2, 1944, in Babiński, "Wymiana depesz," 160.
50 Bór-Komorowski to Sosnkowski, April 29, 1944, in ibid., 161. Retinger, when entering Poland was listed as ten years younger than he was. See "Operation Wildhorn," online at http://www.polandinexile.com/exile13.htm; accessed on October 13, 2013.
51 Bułhak, "Wokół misji," 24ff.
52 Roberts to NN, April 16, 1944, file 233, FO 371/39421, NA.
53 Memorandum "Operation WILDHORN," January 19, 1944; HS4, 4/180, NA.
54 Retinger is quoted in Walker, Poland Alone, 94.
55 Baliszewski,"Salamandra," 1; regarding Retinger's approaches to the SOE, see the FO memorandum, FO 371/39421, NA.
56 "U. M." [Probably according to Bułhak, Col. Marian Utnik; Bułhak to author, January 5, 2015] untitled memorandum dated September 3, 1958, IPN BU 01136/69/D. Churchill was ill at the time and Eden temporarily replaced him as Prime Minister. Thus it is probable that Churchill was not au courant regarding the early stage of the mission.
57 Ibid., cf. Roberts memorandum of January 13, 1944, Roberts memorandum of January 17, 1944, file 233, FO 371/39421, NA.
58 Bułhak, "Wokół," 24.
59 Ibid.
60 Sikorski even ridiculed Beck to Eden; see Avon Papers, diary entry for January 24, 1941, Cadbury Research Library, University of Birmingham.
61 Roberts to NN, April 16, 1944, file 233, FO371/39421, NA.
62 Bułhak, "Wokół," 17.
63 Retinger to Raczkiewicz, January 21, 1944, #64, Retinger Collection, PISM.
64 Retinger to Raczyński, March 29, 1944, file 233, FO 371/39421, NA.
65 Siemaszko, "Retinger-Wysłannik," 214.
66 There were "two aborted sorties," Gubbins to Editor, June 17, 1960, Gubbins Papers, 5/1–31, Imperial War Museum.

67 Terlecki, *Wielka awantura*, 118.
68 Bułhak, "Wokół misji," 19.
69 Retinger, "Introduction," Retinger Papers, BPL, 82/3.
70 Bułhak, "Wokół misji," 21.
71 Bibiński, *Przczyniki*, 245.
72 Wapiński, "Retinger," 151; "Secret Mission to Poland," drawer 2, BPL.
73 For Retinger's account of his flight and jump see the long quotation in Pomian, *Retinger*, 190–204.
74 Bułhak, "Wokół," 20.
75 Roberts to NN, April 16, 1944, file 233, FO 371/39421, NA; According to Jędrzej Tucholski, in addition to Mikołajczyk, the Minister of Internal Affairs (Minister Spraw Wewnętrznych), Władysław Banaczyk, was also aware of the Retinger mission previously; see Tucholski's *Spadochroniarze* (Warsaw: PAX, 1991), 126.
76 For this complex subject see Tucholski, S*padochroniarze*, 126–129. In 1960, Gubbins wrote that he had "discussed the possibilities" with Retinger sometime before the flight. See "Mr. Joseph Retinger." In Gubbins to "The Editor" [The Times], June 17, 1960, Gubbins Papers, 5/1–31.
77 This is carefully reconstructed by Tucholski, ibid., 125ff.
78 Ibid., 131.
79 Quoted in Terlecki, *Wielka awantura*, 123–124.
80 Podgórski, *Retinger*, 136.
81 Zygmunt Zaremba, *Wojna i konspiracja* (London: B. Świderski, 1957), 211–213. Pomian, *Retinger*, 164 Retinger, "Back into Exile," drawer 1, BPL.
82 Retinger, "Thrillers and Socrates," BPL, drawer. 3; he changes this to 200 looking for him the next morning; see Retinger, Secret Mission to Poland," drawer 3, Retinger col., BPL; Stefan Korboński, *W imieniu Polski walczącej* (London: B. Świderski, 1963), 84.
83 Zaremba, *Wojna*, 212; cf. Bułhak, "Wokół," 44. Retinger emphasized the pro-Soviet disposition prevalent in Great Britain.
84 Wapiński, 151. Regarding his relationship see the Pużak's "Wspomnienia 1939–1945," *Zeszyty Historyczne*, No. 279), 1977, 75.
85 Siemaszko, "Retinger-wysłannik," 224–225.
86 Ibid., 216–216; cf. Retinger, "Conspiracy in Poland," Retinger Papers, drawer 1, BPL.
87 There are brief recollections of Retinger, and his drinking in Korboński's *W imięniu Polski walczącej*, 83–86. Podgórski, *Retinger*, 137; Siemaszko, "Szara eminencja,"175; cf. Siemaszko, "Retinger-wysłannik," 216; also see Retinger," Conspiracy in Poland," drawer 1. BPL; Cf. Terlecki, *Wielka awantura*, 124–126.
88 Siemaszko, "Szara eminencja."
89 A good indication of his interminable meetings can be found in Celt's report, in his *Z Retingerem*, 181–206. Only fragmentary portions of his meeting survive.
90 Bułhak, "Wokół misji," 43–46.
91 Babiński, *Przyczyniki*, 258.
92 Celt, *Z Retingerem*, 139.
93 Baliszewski, "Salamander," 3; see Podgórski quoting Jan Nowak-Jeziorański in his *Retinger*, 148.
94 Document labeled "of particular secrecy," FO to Resident Minister, August 8, 1944, HS4 4/139, NA; Foreign Office to O. O'Malley, August 5, 1944, CAB 121/454. There is a summary in Bułhak, "Wokół misji," 72.
95 Jan M. Ciechanowski, "Notatki z rozmów z Gen. Marianem Kukielem," *Zeszyty Historyczne*, 29 (1974), 143.
96 Bułhak, "Wokół," 23–24.
97 Ibid., 23.

98 Ibid., 24.
99 See the document by the Ministerstwo Spraw Wewnętrznych dated July 5, 1943, entitled "Trójkąt" in the "Rząd Polski na emigracji" collection, file 701/9/5 at the Józef Piłsudski Institute of America [hereafter JPIA].
100 Pobóg-Malinowski, *Z mego okienka*, 715.
101 These are Sosnkowski's words quoted by Bułhak, "Wokół," 23.
102 Siemaszko, "Retinger-wysłannik," 217–221; cf. the more convincing Bułhak, "Wokół misji," 46–48. The issue is not definitely settled. Bułhak suggests that the radical right in the underground might have consipired to kill Retinger for his supposed contacts with the Germans; the whole issue is a maze; see Bułhak "Wokół," 48. Bułhak contends that contacts between the NSZ and the Gestapo, strange bedfellows indeed, may have been the source of German knowledge of Retinger's presence in Poland; Bułhak to author, January 5, 2015. For a mention of Retinger's contacts with the Gestapo see "Notatka," June 15, 1966, IPN BU 0 1178/694.
103 Bułhak, "Wokół," 47.
104 Ibid., 44.
105 See the discussion in Witkowski, *Ojcowie* which references a considerable literature; 49; cf. Podgórski, *Retinger*, 174–176.
106 Bułhak, "Wokół misji," 31.
107 Baliszewski, "Salamander," 3.
108 In the autumn of 1999, Telewizja Polska aired a program which claimed Colonel Kazimierz Iranek-Osmecki ordered Horodecka to kill Retinger, though others disagreed with the decision. She failed to carry out her orders. The program also claims that Retinger was a British agent since World War I, but that his file was burned in 1924, and that his incarceration in St. Louis during his Mexican sojourn had something to do with unexplained sabotage. See Jerzy Iranek-Osmecki's memorandum, "Retinger," dated January 24, 2000 in teczka 69, col. 68, Retinger Papers, PISM.
109 Ibid., 35; for details concerning the attempted poisoning, see ibid., 77–80.
110 For this discussion see Bułhak, "Wokół misji," 26–42, 79.
111 Retinger quoted in Bułhak, ibid., 39.
112 Celt, *Z Retingerem*, 111; Bułhak, "Wokół," 38ff.
113 Bułhak, "Wokół," 39.
114 Celt, *Z Retingerem*, 111.
115 Pomian, *Retinger*, 217; Tucholski argues that Bór-Komorowski was probably the one who over-ruled carrying out the assassination; see his *Spadochroniarze*, 134–135.
116 Quoted from Bułhak, "The Foreign Office," unpaginated. Elsewhere, Bułhak speculates that the woman in question was Jadwiga Gebethner of the famous publishing family; see his "The Foreign Office," 49.
117 The issue is murky.
118 Ibid., 39.
119 See for example the very careful evaluations in Bułhak, "Wokół misji," 26–42; cf. Jan Chciuk-Celt, "Who was Józef Hieronim Retinger," online at http://home.teleport.com/~flyheart/retinger.htm. Accessed on January 26, 2012.
120 IPN BU 0 1178/694IPN, 4.
121 General Tadeusz Pełczyński (code name "Grzegorz") was one of the most decorated and distinguished officers in the Polish army. A member of Piłsudski's Legions in 1914, he was long associated with Section II. During the war he was Deputy Commander of the Home Army and fought with great distinction during the Warsaw Rising of 1944. He died in 1986 in London.
122 "Stanislaw Kot," British Intelligence Files, NA, KV2/3429 (Stanislaw Kot).

123 There is a long list of sanacja officers who despised Retinger in the memorandum "Zeznanie własne," dated July 17, 1954 in Polish postwar intelligence files; see IPN BU 01136/69/D. It is noteworthy that one of the few officers Retinger was on good terms with was General Izydor Modelski, a vicious and vengeful man noted for his hatred of the sanacja and desire to purge them from the Polish army; see ibid. After the war, Modelski worked for the Communist authorities in Warsaw to "encourage Polish soldiers to seek repatriation." He later escaped to the West. See Kochański, *The Eagle Unbowed,* 557.
124 Oskar, Notatka, June 4, 1958, IPN BU 01136/69/D.
125 This very persuasive version is the work of Władysław Bułhak; Bułhak to author, July 5, 2016; author's files.
126 This evidence is the work of Siemaszko; see Podgórski, *Retinger,* 166; cf. "Retinger," IPN BU 01222/593/D.
127 The issue was not definitely settled. Bułhak suggests that the radical right in the underground may have planned to kill Retinger for his supposed contacts with the Germans; the whole issue is a maze; see Bułhak "Wokół," 48; for a mention of Retinger's contacts with the Gestapo see "Notatka," June 15, 1966, IPN BU 0 1178/694. No details or explanation are provided.
128 Celt, *Z Retingerem.* 113ff; Bułhak, "Wokół," 63ff.
129 Bułhak, "The Foreign Office," unpaginated.
130 Major Pickles to Lt. Col. Protasewicz, July 5, 1944, HS4/181, NA.
131 Bułhak, "Wokół," 66. Bułhak has subsequently argued that the II Bureau, Polish Military Intelligence, had some role to play in Retinger's missing this flight; see his "The Foreign Office," unpaginated.
132 Pomian, *Retinger,* 166. Gubbins refers to Retinger's malady as "polio"; see Gubbins, "Retinger," 16; his *New York Times* obituary refers to "poliomyelitis"; "Joseph Retinger, Polish Democrat," June 24, 1960, 27; cf. Gubbins to Editor, June 17, 1960, Gubbins Papers.
133 Pomian, *Retinger,* 167.
134 Terlecki, *Wielka awantura,* 126ff.
135 Bułhak, "Wokół," 32–38; Baliszewski, "Salamander," 3; Bułhak to author, October 28, 2014.
136 NN to Maryland, July 17, 1944, HS4 4/182, NA.
137 Pomian, *Retinger,* 170.
138 Major Pickles to Lt. Col. Protasewicz, July 5, 1944; HS 4/180, NA.
139 "Punch" to "Maryland," July 7, 1944, HS4/183, NA.
140 Terlecki, *Wielka awantura,* 136.
141 Punch to NN, July 26, 1944, HS4/182, NA.
142 IMU to MP, July 31, 1944, Air 23/7946, NA.
143 Jan Nowak, *Courier from Warsaw* (Detroit, MI: Wayne State University Press, 1982), 311–312; cf. Jan Nowak, "Operacja 'Whitehorn'," *Kultura,* 11 (July–August, 1949), 216–217. A different list of pseudonyms can be found in the memorandum of July 26, 1944 in HS4/181, NA.
144 Celt, *Z Retingerem,* 150–163; for Retinger's account see Pomian, *Retinger,* 223ff.; cf. Nowak, "Operacja," 222–223. Tucholski, *Spadochroniarze,* 137–138.
145 This is Gubbins's description, see Gubbins to Editor, Jun 17, 1960, Gubbins Papers, 5/1–31.
146 Apparently Retinger discovered that he was going to Cairo only when he landed in Bari; he was then an invalid; see Gubbins, "Retinger," 16; cf. "Back into Exile," drawer 1, BPL.
147 NN to Punch, July 26, 1944, HS4 4/182, NA.
148 Ibid.
149 Quoted in Nagórski, *Wojna w Londynie,* 268.
150 Nowak, *Courier,* 338.

151 Bułhak, "The Foreign Office," 52.
152 Cairo to FO, July 28, 1944, Air 23/7946, NA.
153 Babiński, *Przyczyniki*, 334. The British wanted to see Retinger as soon as possible. Eden minuted an internal FO memorandum that Retinger had performed "a gallant exploit and wanted to see him." This seems to be more a desire to extend congratulations than a desire for a debriefing.
154 Marsy McClaren to Retinger, January 3, April 7, August 5, August 8, 1944 Retinger Collection, f. 38, PISM.
155 "Poles back 1939 Frontier," *New York Times*, August 4, 1944, 5.
156 Bułhak, "Wokół misji," 74.
157 Ibid.
158 Quoted in ibid., 74.
159 Ibid., 75.
160 Arciszewski was furious that Retinger met with Mikołajczyk before he did. He referred to Retinger as an "English confidant" (powiernik); see Terlecki, *Wielka awantura*, 132.
161 Bułhak, "Wokół misji," 71.
162 Celt, *Z Retingerem*, 27–28n.
163 Podgórski even suggests Masonic dimensions to the mission; see his *Retinger*, 154ff.
164 Podgórski, *Retinger*, 140–141; Anna Cienciała to author, March 23, 2014.
165 Anna Cienciała to author, March 23, 2014.
166 Retinger to Doherty, August 28, 1944, Doherty Papers.
167 Richard C. Lukas, *The Strange Allies: The United States, and Poland, 1941–1945* (Knoxville, TN: University of Tennessee Press, 1978, 129–130).
168 Babiński, *Przyczyniki*, 442.
169 For a sympathetic reconstruction of Mikołajczyk's last days as head of government, see Andrzej Paczkowski, *Stanislaw Mikołajczyk: czyli klęska realisty* (Warsaw: Omnipress, 1991), 112–116.
170 Ibid., 130–131.
171 Ibid., 268.
172 Frank Roberts, Foreign Office to NN with Minutes, September 28, 1944, NA, FO 371/39541.
173 Hanna Świderska, "O Retingerze w Archiwum Foreign Office," *Zeszyty Historyczne*, 106 (1993), 226–227. These documents damage the notion that Retinger functioned as a British spy, or at least they suggest that the British had no further use for him after 1945.
174 Retinger to [Cripps], March 14, 1945, f. 50, Retinger Collection, PISM. Hanna Świderska, "O Retingerze", 227.
175 Roberts [Foreign Office], memorandum of December 5, 1944; NA, FO 371/39541.
176 Mary Louis Doherty to Retinger, February 9, 1945, Retinger Papers, Box 17, BPL.
177 Terlecki, *Wielka awantura*, 137.
178 Mikołajczyk to Kot, PISM, collection 25, Stanislaw Kot, file 25/2.
179 Retinger to Walter Citrine, [1945], drawer 5, Retinger Papers, BPL.
180 Regarding Retinger and the origins of the Sikorski Institute see "Sprawa Instytutu Generała Sikorskiego w USA," nd; "Report of the Committee of the General Sikorski Historical Institute for the Period 11th April 1946–1st October, 1946" both in Gross Papers, PIASA, f. 4, 122.
181 The very subtitle of Prażmowska's work on 1939–1943 is "the betrayed ally"; see also pp. 82–83 of her, *Britain and Poland*.
182 Pomian, *Retinger*, 183.

183 Quoted in ibid., 183 for Retinger's activities to convince the British authorities to aid the Poles see Pomian, *Retinger,* 239–244.
184 There is a valuable correspondence regarding this between Retinger and "Dzidek" (i.e. Chciuk-Celt), in folder D, Box 18, Retinger Papers, BPL; cf. Shackleford to Retinger, May 14, 1946, ME 328, HAEU.
185 "Who was," 6; Pomian, *Retinger,* 184.
186 Grosbois, "L'action," 79.
187 Retinger's official title was Chief Agent for Rehabilitation Supplies to Poland."
188 There is substantial correspondence to this effect in ME 328, HAEU.
189 See the packet of documents in folder P, Box 19, Retinger Papers, BPL.
190 There is considerable correspondence over Retinger's actions regarding relief for 1956 strikers in drawer 5, Retinger papers, BPL. Perhaps the most important letter is Pomian to Retinger, July 2, 1956. For the context of Retinger's concern for Poland in the mid-1950s see his "Analysis of Events in Poland," shelf, 2, BPL.
191 "Notatka informacyjna,"nd, IPN BU) 1178/694.
192 "Notatka," June 15, 1966, IPN BU 0 1178/694. Though this is from a Warsaw communist file it would not seem that this would be a misrepresentation.
193 Ibid.
194 Ibid.
195 Ibid.
196 Oskar, Notatka słuzbowa, July 2, 1957, IPN BU 01136/69/D.
197 H. Pietek, Director Department III, "Notatka," June 15, 1966, IPN BU 0 1178/694.
198 Cf. Retinger to NN, September 5, 1947; Box 17, files "Korespondencja," Retinger Papers, BPL; "Note Concerning T. Chciuk," Box 18, folder c, Retinger Papers, BPL; Retinger to Jakub Berman, April 14, 1956, ME 328, HAEU.
199 Geoffrey de Freitas, "Retinger," *The Times,* June 18, 1960, 12.
200 "Wyciąg z doniesienia ag. 64," November 11, 1947, IPN BU 0 1178/694.
201 Podgórski, *Retinger,* 198–199. In 1952 Polish Communist authorities suspected Retinger of being a British, and American, agent at the end of the war; see "Retinger," IPN BU 01222/593/D, 8–9; "Karta personalno-operacyjna," describes him as a close agent of British intelligence, IPN BU 01136/69/D; cf. Witkowski, "Kartka do pamiętnika," November 30, 1957, IPN BU 01222/593/D.
202 Pomian rejects this out of hand; Pomian to author, July 29, 2014.
203 Pomian, *Retinger,* 190.
204 NN to NN, "Plan nawiązania kontaktów z JHR," IPN BU 01222/593/D. Zubrzycka.
205 "Ankieta Personalna, Retinger," nd, IPN BU 1178/694; cf. "Ankieta Personalna, Żuławski," IPN, BU 1178/694. "Akta Personalna, Świerzewski," IPN BU 1178/694; "Notatka informacyjna," July 27, 1968, IPN BU 1178/694. "Były agent wywiadu angielskiego," in Nr. 1524/b, in IPN BU) 1178/694 "Notatka," June 15, 1966, IPN BU 0 1178/694. According to Warsaw Communist Intelligence, Retinger was also a "Jew," "Nr. 5," September 5, 1962, IPN BU 0 1178/694.IPN. The biography of Retinger also refers to him as a Jew; see "Notatka informacyjna," nd, IPN BU 0 1178/694cf. "Notatka," June 15, 1966, IPN BU 0 1178/694. See also "Plan," October 6, 1958, IPN BU 01136/69/D. They assembled quite a dossier on him; see "Przegląd akt," May 22, 1951, IPN BU 0 1178/694. They also kept careful track of his post-war travels, which were frequent. He was obviously very interesting to Warsaw; see "Notatka informacyjna," IPN BU 0 1178/694. However, by late 1958 he was regarded as not of practical importance. "Plan," IPN BU 01136/69/D.
206 W. Sienkiewicz, Dyrektor Departamentu I MSW, November 6, 1957, IPN BU 01136/69/D; Oskar, June 4, 1958, IPN BU 01136/69/D.

207 Oskar, "Notatka służbowa," July 2, 1957, IPN BU 01136/69/D; for more about Retinger's dislike of the English in later years see Oskar, "Notatka," February 21, 1958, IPN BU 01136/69/D.
208 Ibid.
209 Oskar, "Notatka," June 4, 1958, IPN BU 01136//69/D.

# 11 "In twenty years Europe will be united, together with Poland"[1]
## Retinger and the federal movement in European history

The notion of European federation has a long pedigree. Mommsen sees it fully developed by the Enlightenment but interrupted and derailed by what he deemed "hegemonic power politics."[2] Here he cites fascism and its derivative Nazism. We may also add Soviet Communism. It was only after World War II that a survey of the European terrain made the salvation of Europe so obvious and pressing an item on the agenda. However, proposal for federation really appeared before the war, of which the League of Nations was the most obvious example.[3] However, the league, a creature of the Versailles Treaty, was crippled by American non-cooperation and never evolved beyond its modest beginnings. Later, during the war, in specific historic circumstances: the enormous power of Germany and Russia made the rest of Europe appear helpless by comparison. Only some sort of federative structure, a multinational empire was preposterous, could provide enough strength to guarantee a modicum of democratic life in the Europe wedged between these two goliaths. Hence it was the war which made federation appear needed, and the destruction wrought by it seemed so necessary for a diverse, democratic and safe Europe to survive. Though it might have led to concrete structures after 1945, it had a long speculative history and a number of functional examples.

### The origins of federalism

In exploring the first model of European federalism, Pieczewski begins his survey with the Roman Empire, St. Augustine and Charlemagne as well as Dubois, a student of St. Thomas Aquinas.[4] Pierre Dubois advocated a Christian Republic in which international struggles could be brought before supranational tribunal. Christianity was, after all, as Witkowski reminds us, not only the basis of Europe's culture, but the criterion for belonging to the whole.[5] It was the model for integration. Indeed, we may later discern elements of a Roman Catholic culture and model throughout Retinger's work. In 1954, a Polish journal insisted that the Council of Europe was essentially informed by 1891's *Rerum Novarum*, and 1931's *Quadragesimo*, a Catholic moral basis.[6]

Denis de Rougemont, like Witkowski, offered a rather grand sweep of federal history, beginning in the fourteenth century and changing somewhat little thereafter. He invoked a number of luminaries in support of his views.[7] The speculations, highly utopian, of Poland's eighteenth-century king, Stanisław Lesczyński, should also be noted.[8] Dubois, again, Goethe, and Victor Hugo, represented a nineteenth-century French flirtation with European unity,[9] Sully, Montesquieu, Rousseau, and Saint-Simon to Churchill and from Leibniz through Kant, according to de Rougemont,[10] were all, united by great themes such as peace which would suppress any attempt at hegemony by the creation of "an authority higher than nations and princes." This was also a dominant theme of the Middle Ages. Second, they advocated "the establishment of a spiritual community supported by a common legal framework." De Rougement saw this in Dante who wanted a universal monarch to arbitrate in quarrels between individual states, an understandable desire for someone to be above the fragmentary chaos of the Italian peninsula. Currently, there was "a many-headed monster dissipating itself in conflicting efforts."[11] But following this epoch, de Rougemont emphasized that this was of importance during the Reformation and traced it through to the Enlightenment "in which sovereign states were formed; in the sixteenth through eighteenth centuries."

Finally, there is "the prosperity of all," a trend he traces to Jeremy Bentham, around 1800 up to the European Economic Community.[12] De Rougemont then cited some rather esoteric characters: the Bohemian Jiři z Poděbrad, Émeric Crucé, the Huguenot Duke of Sully's grand and rather well developed "Great Plan" which would create a "United States of Europe". The Moravian, Ján Amos Komenský, had a similar large vision and William Penn suggested a mechanism for a unified body. The Abbé de Saint-Pierre, the Jacobin, Saint-Simon, Proudhon, Nietzsche and Pálacký also had similar thoughts.[13] Each had contributed an arcane and problematical part to the four-section plan with which de Rougemont began his essay.[14]

There were also models of ad hoc or partial federations: the anti-Turkish league of Poděbrad; the Czech-Polish union of 1462;[15] the League of Augsburg formed in 1686 to restrict seventeenth-century French expansionism.[16] The Slovak-Czech interrupted federation of the twentieth century should also be included as well as the older-and much longer loose connection of the Union of Kalmar between Denmark, Sweden, and Norway which consisted of a series of personal unions between 1397 and 1523. To these we may add late eighteenth-century Hungary's call for Europeanism.[17] Indeed, every treaty claimed to increase the welfare of mankind and the security of the signatories.

Other than German speculation, and partial actions regarding a *Mitteleuropa*, a rather specific form of European integration, German ideas of unity were not free of what Loth deemed "hegemonic ambitions."[18] To this we might add German *Lebensraum* of a later era, and Soviet colonization and forced federation. Valerio dates Italian "Europeanism" to the post-World War I age, despite the earlier exemplars.[19] We also contend with the lasting "ambivalence" of Great Britain, fearing "entanglements," especially promoted in the twentieth century by the Labour Party, and the later Brexit referendum.[20]

According to Chodorowski, a model for European integration required four particulars: first, an ideologically founded rationale for upon which the action could be founded; second, there must be a close link between ideology and practice, concrete and specifics for the construction of the project; third, the presence of "theorists-architects," and fourth, workers carry out the plans, government officials, social leaders, and people capable of rendering changes. Pieczewski named only a handful of capable of fulfilling all four categories. These were Richard Count Coudenhove-Kalergi, Churchill, Retinger, Spaak, Alicide de Gasperi, Jean Monnet, Robert Schuman, and Konrad Adenauer. In the modern era, the federal structure of the United States often was cited as a model. This was hardly appropriate for Europe because of the similar quality of American states.[21]

## The Briand-Kalergi vision

During the interwar era there were a number of organizations dedicated to European unity. Some like the 1889 Interparliamentary Union predated the League of Nations which itself spawned a number of supporting organizations. However, modern plans for a federation are probably best traced to the efforts of French notables, especially Eduard Herriot and Aristide Briand.[22] Under the influence of Kalergi, who will be discussed later, in a speech to the League of Nations in September 1929, Briand called for a federal bond between the twenty-seven members of the League.[23] This body would be a "permanent regime of conventional solidarity for the rational organization of Europe." This would allow European nations "to at last become conscious of European geographical unity." Briand did not see this body weakening or replacing the league but contributing a "federative organization of Europe" to its overall structure. Adjustments and "mediations" would still fall under the league's supervision. One of the first goals of this federation would be the removal of restrictive customs barriers about which Briand was especially unhappy[24]

The "sovereign rights" of no state would be infringed upon. A "European union" would be created. Details of the functioning of the league followed. European "cooperation" would include economic matters, financial, and labor issues, "hygiene," "intellectual cooperation," administrative issues, and the notion of an "Interparliamentary Union."[25]

Twenty-six European countries responded to his 1920 remarks,[26] and the Poles issued a short reply. Their complaint was as follows: "The Polish government accepts the idea of a European union, and declares itself ready to participate in any preparatory work which the first European Conference may consider necessary." It emphasized the principle of national sovereignty. The union was to be a "regional understanding," a somewhat opaque passage, within the framework of the league.[27]

In general the Briand plan failed to attract sufficient and enthusiastic support and failed to materialized. Andrea dall'Oglio characterized the reaction as "considerable [notevole]," but objections from several important countries "doomed it to failure [l'iniziativa fra destinata a cadere]."[28] Similar French efforts were made by André Tardieu, restricted to the Danubian area, and a rather grander scheme by André-François Ponçet. Neither was longed-lived.

Meetings were held in Geneva in 1930 to discuss the Briand proposal and the main topics of conversation were whether the union meant an inevitable diminution of member sovereignty and whether Great Britain, would be included or not.[29] The world was moving towards integration and a Europe of 400,000,000 would be a mighty competitor for either the United States or Russia.[30]

## Count Richard Coudenhove-Kalergi

The epitome of interwar federalist and unionist schemes was undoubtedly Coudenhove-Kalergi, a singular figure.[31] Of distinguished and multi-Central European heritage, he spent his youth in Japan where his father was a Habsburg diplomat. While he was there, the young Kalergi married an aristocratic Japanese woman which added an element of the exotic to this plan for Europe.

His first foray into pan-European visions were conveyed in two precocious publications: *Die europäische Frage*, (1922), and the following year's *Pan Europa*. In 1922 he also founded the Pan-European League with Otto von Habsburg.[32] This was a global vision based on large groupings of the world based on cultural substructures and civilizational levels. As Retinger would later argue, the European world was ultimately threatened, by two powerful blocs, the economic power of North America, and the ideological, if not to say military threat, of the Soviet east. In light of this, the economic and political unification of Europe was a necessity.[33]

Kalergi's scheme for the unification of Europe went through several stages, as outlined by Pieczewski. First, there would be European unions, second, a European customs union, and third a United States of Europe based on the American model.[34] It would include a two-house parliament: a lower chamber which would elect one delegate for 1 million people, and an upper body, to which each state would send a single delegate. English would be the common language. The new European aristocracy would be a "leader nation" a new aristocracy of the spirit, composed of Jews. They would represent the coming mixed-race common humanity, a somewhat complex hierarchy.[35]

By 1924 this Pan-European Union had over one-thousand members" with its headquarters in Austria and other branches being formed. The next year Kalergi cited the United States and his own Pan-European union as his antecedents. The three pillars of the Pan-American union were the British Commonwealth, the united European continent, and "Pan American unions".

The Soviet Union and the British Commonwealth would be recognized as "independent political entities." He was not opposed to the league, but its membership. He did not regard it as whole without the United States and the Soviet Union. He boasted that his "utopian scheme" had now become "a political program that is favored by nine-tenths of all the political leaders of Europe."[36]

From 1926 to 1935 Kalergi organized four congresses. For the elite of Europe it had become a moral force with prominent French and German members.[37] In 1926 Kalergi attempted a reorganization of the League of Nations. He created a Congress in Europe in that year with an impressive attendance.[38] He wanted nothing less than control by the league of all the countries of the world, the United States, and Soviet Russia, and perhaps the British Commonwealth would be excluded. There would be international disarmament. Eastern Europe would come under Soviet control. Latin America in turn would fall to American suzerainty. The first step of this redesigned league would be to settle minority problems in Europe. The restrictions of the Versailles Treaty on Germany would be ended. The obvious initial goal was to win over German cooperation. It was his effectively pro-German disposition, regarding the abolition of the "Polish Corridor," which made Polish support for him impossible.

As Marszałek has pointed out, he was only able to form a small committee, composed entirely of masons, perhaps because of Kalergi's own devotion to Freemasonry. The territorial issue was probably enough to alienate Kalergi from a Polish patriot like Retinger. Certainly the notion that Freemasonry was a link in Retinger's activities is badly damaged by this fact. Either, as he repeatedly said, he was not a Mason, or it did not matter. In either case it is something we can dismiss in explaining Retinger.

During the war Kalergi called for "American principles of federation," an old shibboleth. He substituted Hitler's quasi-union with a peaceful and fair one. He called for the leading role of the United States to build a security system in conjunction with the Soviets. Whereas his admiration for the Americans was nothing new, his call for close cooperation between the democracies and Russia to rebuild Europe and the world departed from his warning about the ideological threat from the east before the war. By Briand's death (1932), Kalergi's focus shifted to Germany and revision of the Versailles Treaty.[39] During the war, Kalergi relocated to the United States. In 1943 he warned against Russia and Germany and offered various confederations to ward them off.[40] His vision of a future Europe was mapped in great detail, something Retinger never attempted. Ultimately, as Sadowski pointed out, in contrast to Kalergi, Retinger "was never a European visionary, rather a man of practical politics, who functioned in meanderings and snares much better than Kalergi."[41] Retinger wanted to find a path towards European unity, but Kalergi was sketching a utopia. Moreover, Kalergi's insistence on an important role for Russia, and the idea of America as a model, would hardly interest Retinger who disliked both.

After the war was over, his movement reappeared, and he claimed that most European parliaments favored such an outcome. Kalergi concluded that history was shaping the future before his very eyes. A continent-wide European union embracing a Charlemagne Union, that formed part of an Atlantic Union would in turn, rest in "the mighty framework of the United Nations."[42] His movement was in pieces and new movements had left him behind. His elitist plans were out of step with the mass movement in favor of the union. Kalergi was the most important theorist and organizer of the Pan-European movement of the interwar era. Retinger, *mutatis mutandis*, was his successor.

## Retinger and historic Polish federalism

Retinger played a special role with clear and long-standing goals: work for Poland, European integration, and transatlantic understanding. Poland had an unusual, if not unique federalist motif for most of its history.[43] This began in 1385 with the Union of Krewo with Lithuania, the brief union with Hungary in 1390, the Union of Horodło of 1413 and other clarifying accords with Lithuania, reaching its apogee in the more tightly binding 1569 Union of Lublin, all of which brought Poland and Lithuania into closer federal linkage.[44] The Commonwealth of Two Nations (Rzeczpospolita Obojga Narodów) was formed. But whether this meant the conjoining of two states of a rather looser alliance is a historiographical dispute between Polish and Lithuanian scholars. The Polish-Lithuanian federation (or at least quasi-federation) was almost supplemented by the Union of Hadziacz of 1658 which would have extended the 1569 Union of Lublin to Ukraine, when some Ukrainians briefly saw Poland as a lesser threat to its sovereignty than union with Russia. Belarus, lacking political form, more or less followed the Lithuanian path. During the brief fifteenth-century supremacy of the House of Jagiełło, this Polish dynasty also ruled Hungary and Bohemia as well, though the ties were brief and loose.

As analyzed by Dziewanowski, the Union of Hadziacz:

> Remained a *matrimonium ratum sed non consummatum*, one of those historical turning points at which history refused to turn. The dualist Commonwealth failed to transform itself into the trialist federation that would have corresponded more to its true nature. The failure was one of the contributing causes to the downfall of the Polish-Lithuanian state.[45]

However, this defeat, in the tradition of Polish political development was, itself, a sort of quasi-victory: it enshrined federalism as a cause to be sought rather than a reality merely to be accepted.[46]

The 1596 union of Brześć, which attempted to ameliorate differences between Catholics and Orthodox within the commonwealth, can be regarded as a religiously caparisoned political cementing of the lands of

Poland. It gave birth to the Uniates, a compromise Church, recognizing Rome but retaining many Orthodox practices. We should remember that the former Orthodox, many then accepting union, retained their Slavonic rite and many traditional practices which differentiated them from the Poles. This demonstrated a federal division and a relatively weak and unobtrusive central political authority, and a visibly different culture on the periphery.

Still, the significance of Poland's long association with Lithuania-Belarus, and the more problematic relationship with Ukraine made Poland's linkages to the east an integral part of its history contributing much to its structure, whether the eastern linkages were viewed as a etiolating dissolution of national sovereignty like the nationalist Roman Dmowski, or a symbol and reality of Polish greatness like Józef Piłsudski. In any event, the Polish federation was a powerful feature in Polish history and the eastern borderlands, the *kresy*, were fundamental to the Polish self-image to modern times. Poland without its federated eastern territories was not really Poland and federation was thus fundamental to the very concept of the nation. This should be remembered when we consider the sanacja's almost fanatical determination to hold the *kresy*, the borderlands of eastern Poland against the millennial foe, Russia.

Lane and Wolański see in the eighteenth-century writings of Charles de Saint-Pierre a direct inspiration for the modern Polish ideas of federalism. The list of Polish speculators concerning European integration, federal solutions, and geopolitical structures for peace is long indeed and it includes Leszczyński, Stanisław Skrzetuski, Prince Adam Czartoryski, Wojciech Jarzembowski among others. Curiously, in an early version of Atlanticism we have the notions of Stefan Buczyński.[47] The list continues up to Retinger's era.

In the nineteenth and early twentieth centuries Polish political thinkers like Zygmunt Miłkowski, Kazimierz Kelles-Krauz, and Bolesław Limanowski, all representing different political camps,endorsed continental federalism.[48] De Rougemont argues that the great poet Mickiewicz was one who "fought for a United States of Europe based upon the will of the peoples."[49] In 1917, Paderewski presented President Wilson an outline for a "United States of Poland," which Wilson ignored.[50] The last federalist of the era was Józef Piłsudski who tried to resurrect the commonwealth but whose military weakness made him settle for the Treaty of Riga (1921) with the Soviet Union which effectively shattered irretrievably the former commonwealth. It was the lands Poland held under the Riga agreement which the Russians coveted and the West ignored, or even disdained. To the Poles they were indescribably cherished.

In the interwar period, Kalergi's Pan-European movement attracted some prominent Polish adherents including Aleksander Lednicki, Stanisław Estreicher, Konstanty Srokowski, and Stanisław Posner. There was also student support which overlapped with advocacy of the League of Nations, and admiration for Briand's efforts.[51]

During the World War II, federalism was a popular concept in occupied Poland, as well as within the Sikorski camp,[52] The sad fate of the smaller nations of Central Europe demonstrated, it seemed, that without larger congeries, the future of these nations was doubtful at the least. Central European blocs, the need for a Polish-Czech collaboration, Poland as leading a defensive array against an aggressive Russia, were all recurring themes. The notion that underground Poland was especially concerned with "all existing plans for federation" issues is emphasized by Lipgens.[53]

Federalists like Retinger always presumed the existence of some version of Poland plus some significant segment of the eastern territories as fundamental to Polish participation in a federated Europe. Retinger combined the heritage of a Polish commonwealth with a larger vision of a federal Europe. What, however, we should never lose track of is the Polish nucleus of this greater vision: a bloc of nations sufficiently powerful to assure Poland a secure place between Russia and Germany; a remodeled version of Poland at its federalist zenith and power in the sixteenth and seventeenth centuries.

Retinger was, for Kalicki, a nineteenth-century diplomat not subject to public scrutiny. According to Hatch, Retinger, "came straight out of the Renaissance" and was characterized by "a deeply religious, passionate, daring character with the Jesuitical conviction that the end justified the means and a Borgian aptitude for intrigue. But the ends he sought were never selfish. They were good."[54] His intriguing biography rendered him "Polish Baron Munchhausen."[55] Retinger, as both Kalicki and Hatch remind us, was essentially a man of the past, the Polish past.[56]

Moreover, we must note with care that Retinger's close associates in his postwar efforts to work for European unity all came from Catholic cultures – even though some of them were lapsed Catholics or were no longer members of that community – such as Retinger's early connections with the Jesuits, the influence of his profoundly religious guardian Zamoyski, the Catholicism of many of his French aficionados like Boni De Castellane. During World War II, he was especially close to Belgians, Dutch, and Slovaks rather than the limp Catholic Czechs. Even among his later relationships we find the profoundly religious Cripps, and the Catholic Dulles family.[57] Indeed, the influence of the Roman tradition, coupled with the reinforcing influence of hid Polish heritage were the two informing principles of Retinger's passion for European unity.

Not long before he died, Retinger enumerated the two goals of his life. The first was Polish freedom and the second was "better understanding among peoples."[58] Retinger was always a patriot first, and a unified Europe was a system to ensure the security of Poland and this is the only way we can discern the essential consistency of his actions. All the federal efforts were examples of tinkering with the architecture of Europe to arrange a secure place for Poland.

Here it is curious to locate Retinger in the pantheon of modern Polish geopolitics. He shared features with both the Polish nationalist right, Dmowski and the endecja, and the federalists associated with Piłsudski, but with a far broader participation. Retinger shared Dmowski's fear of expanding Poland too far to the east and thus gaining too many national minorities. Here he broke with Piłsudski who saw in the restoration of the pre-partition Polish east the greatness of Poland and security of Europe, both threatened by Russian imperialism. But Piłsudski also realized that a nationally homogenous Poland was too small to exist in the dangerous world of East Central Europe, something Dmowski never seemed to grasp. It was at this moment that federalism arose: a rearrangement of the states of Europe into defensible blocs, pre-empting Russian, or German, aggression. He was a European federalist in service to a Polish patriotism and was neither Piłsudski nor Dmowski. Hence, the notion that Poland will be great or it will not be-attributed to Piłsudski – would be replaced by a more modest Poland in a more secure system achieving the same ends. The simultaneously gained advantage was increasing international comity and protecting the Christian cultural heritage of the West.

Retinger was a religious man. He prayed, believed in God and His saints, and respected the Church. He regarded religion, as "the most important thing in the world." "Religions played the first place role in the development of civilization."[59] Retinger "spoke a great deal about building the future on the basis Christian principles."[60] He was, a close relation remarked, "a devout Catholic in secret."[61]

## Notes

1. Oskar, Notatka służbowa, July 2, 1957, IPN BU 01136/69/D.
2. Wolfgang J. Mommsen, "Introduction," in Wolfgang J. Mommsen, ed., *The Long Way to Europe: Historical Observations from a Contemporary View* (Chicago: edition q. incorporated, 1994), 4.
3. According to Communist era intelligence Retinger flitted about the League and especially the International Labor Bureau, led by Albert Thomas. See "Rettinger," October 29, 1952, IPN, BU 01222/593/D.
4. Andrzej Pieczewski, *Działalność Józefa Retingera na rzecz integracji europejskiej* (Toruń: Adam Marszałek, 2008), 16–18.
5. Grzegorz Witkowski, *Ojcowie Europy: udział polaków w procesie integracji kontynentu* (Warsaw: Kontrast, 2001), 11.
6. "Plany zjednoczenia Europy i stworzenia związku państw europejskich," *Narodowiec*, August 29/30, 1954.
7. Lane and Wolański, *Poland and European Integration*, 7.
8. Ibid., 7–8.
9. François Bédarida, "France and Europe- from Yesterday to Today," Mommsen, *The Long Way to Europe*, 14–15.
10. Denis de Rougemont. "Europe Unites," online at http://www.proeuropa.org/rougemont.html. Accessed March 19, 1998; cf. Denis de Rougemont, *The Meaning of Europe* (New York: Stein and Day, 1965), 63–85. There is an analysis of European precursors, including a number of Poles, in Marszałek, *Z historii*, 11–32. Marszałek discusses the German conception of Mitteleuropa, 32–69.
11. DeRougement, *Europe Unites*, 4ff.
12. Ibid. 1.
13. For the contributions of these Frenchmen, see Witkowski, *Ojcowie*, 16–20.
14. Pieczewski, *Działalność*, 16–23; Denis de Rougemont, *The Idea of Europe* (Cleveland, OH: The World Publishing Co., 1968).

15 Witkowski, *Ojcowie*, 13–14.
16 Ibid., 15
17 Ivan T. Berend, "Hungary's Place in Europe: Political Thought and Historiography in the Twentieth Century"; Mommsen *The Long Way to Europe*, 135–165, 167–193.
18 Wilfried Loth, "The Germans and European Unification"; Mommsen, *The Long way to Europe*, 44.
19 Valerio Castronovo, "Italian Europeanism in the Twentieth Century," Mommsen, *The Long Way to Europe*, 67ff.
20 William Wallace, ""The British Approach to Europe," Mommsen, *The Long Way to Europe*, 107–108.
21 Wieslaw Bokajlo, "What kind of Federation for Europe?," in Lane and Wolanski, *Poland and European Unity*, 241–243.
22 Pieczewski, *Działalność*, 32–38; Antoni Marszałek, *Z historii europejskiej idei integracji międzynarodowej* (Łódź: Wydawnictwo uniwersytetu łódzkiego, 1996), 7, 107–133.
23 Retinger did not like Kalergi whom he dismissed repeatedly as "utopian." He regarded Kalergi as the motivator for Briand's speech and attributed the latter's actions to garner domestic political support; see the untitled memorandum by Retinger in teczka 79, Retinger Collection, PISM. Kalergi had bold plans for the reorganization of the world, often employing American models; see "Kalergi Proposes Reshaping League," *New York Times*, February 27, 1932.
24 Kalergi, "The European Idea-Past and Future."
25 All quotations are drawn from Briand's remarks which are reprinted in full as "Memorandum on the Organization of a régime of European federal union addressed to twenty-six governments of Europe, by M. Briand, Foreign Minister of France, May 17, 1930," in *International Conciliation: Special Bulletin, June, 1930*, (New York: American Association for International Conciliation, 1931), 325–353.
26 "Replies of Twenty-Six Governments of Europe to M. Briand's Memorandum of May 17, 1930," in ibid., 655–748. All subsequent quotations are taken from this document; cf. Marszałek, *Z historii*, 114–119.
27 Ibid., 682–684.
28 Andrea dall'Oglio, *Europa, unità e divisione*, 2nd ed. (Milan: dall'Oglio, nd), 243.
29 "Briand's Union Topic for Geneva Groups," *New York Times*, June 3, 1930, 11.
30 Ibid.
31 A good introduction is Marszałek, *Z historii*, 70–90cf. Witkowski, *Ojcowie*, 19–21.
32 Russel and Cohen, *Coudenhove-Kalergi*, 7. He was fascinated by the universalist panoramas of Roman Catholicism, Judaism, and Freemasonry; Marszałek, *Z historii*, 71–73.
33 Marszałek, *Z historii*, 74–78; Pieczewski, *Działalność*, 28–29; Richard Coudenhove-Kalergi, "European Union is Favored," *The New York Times*, December 22, 1942, 24.
34 He was a great admirer of the United States, considering Hamiltonian federalism "one of the greatest achievements owed to America"; see his *Crusade*, 251.
35 Pieczewski, *Działalność*, 29.
36 "Pan Europe Idea Affects America," *New York Times*, November 15, 1945.
37 Aristide Briand, Leon Blum, Edmond Herriott, Gustav Stresemann, Paul Boncour, Hjalmar Schacht, among others.
38 Kalergi, *An Idea*, 125ff.
39 Pieczewski, *Działalność*, 31.
40 Kalergi, *Crusade*, 258ff.

41 Sadowski, "Amerykańska teczka," 4.
42 Kalergi, "The European Idea-Past and Future."
43 Lane and Wolański, *Poland and European Integration*, 6ff.
44 Halecki even places the federal tradition before the rise of the Jagiellonians; see Oscar Halecki, "The Problem of Federalism in the History of East Central Europe," *The Polish Review*, 5–19. Himself a federalist, Halecki seems to have cooperated with Kalergi and not Retinger; see "Report of the Pan-European Conference," June 4–5, 1943, Gross Papers, PIASA, f. 4.59. Bokajlo considers Paulus Vladimiri as an early proponent of Polish federalism; see his "What Kind of Federalism," 244
45 M. K. Dziewanowski, *Joseph Piłsudski: A European Federalist, 1918–1922* (Stanford, CA: Hoover Institution Press, 1969), 19.
46 This paradoxical feature is explored in Andrzej Walicki, *The Three Traditions in Polish Patriotism and their Contemporary Relevance* (Bloomington, IN: Indiana University Press, 1988), 20–21.
47 There is a good summary of this in Lane and Wolanski, *Poland and European Integration*, 7–11.
48 Podgórski provides a long list of Poles he regards as representing "continental integration." See his *Retinger*, 207n.
49 Denis de Rougemont, *Europe Unites* (New York: Stein and Day, 1965), 77.
50 See M. B. B. Biskupski, "Polish Conceptions of Unity and Division in Europe: Speculation and Policy". In Johann P. Arnason and Natalie J Doyle eds., *Domains and Divisions of European History* (Liverpool: Liverpool University Press, 2010), 107.
51 Feliks Gross and M. Kamil Dziewanowski, "Plans by Exiles from East European Countries," in Lipgens and Loth, *European Integration*, 2: 354.
52 See "The Polish Underground Institute of Central Europe," pamphlet in Karol Popiel Papers, PIASA, folder 9.37.
53 Walter Lipgens, "East European Plans for the Future of Europe: the Example of Poland," in Lipgens and Loth, *European Integration*, 2:621.
54 Hatch, *H.R.H. Prince Bernhard*, 214.
55 Dobrowolski, *Memuary*, 34.
56 Wlodzimierz Kalicki, "Gracz który budował Europę," *Gazeta Wyborcza*, September 18–19, 2010.
57 Regarding Cripps religiousness and the question of European unity, see Phillip M. Coupland, "Western Union, 'Spiritual Union,' and European Integration, 1948–1951," *Journal of British Studies*, Vol. 43, No. 3 (2004), 7–8.
58 Retinger, "Introduction," sz. 4, BPL.
59 Pomian, *Retinger*, 282.
60 Ibid., 283.
61 Quoted in Bułhak, "The Foreign Office," 45n.

# 12 Retinger and the building of a united Europe

A valuable insight into Retinger's federal idea is a memorandum he prepared in 1943 where he outlined a detailed plan about the Poles taking the lead in "regional federation." It foreshadowed this later presentations, but was a bit more modest.

> A bloc of Poles, Czechs, Slovaks, Lithuanians, Romanians, Hungarians – to which would later be added Ukrainians – would form a federation with a joint army and tariff system, but otherwise be independent.

Poland should work for Balkan and Scandinavian federations. They, together with France, Germany, and Italy could form "a future European federation" strong enough to defend European against any imperialism: Russian, American, British, or Japanese. The idea behind this federation requires that we must work to "win over public opinion"; not so much in Central Europe as in England, France, and America. "We must promote an organization like the Friends of the League of Nations."[1]

This was far more refined in Retinger's major address to the Royal Institute of Foreign Affairs at Chatham House on May 7, 1946. Many of his old acquaintances were there. He presented a bold plan.[2] Europe was in ruins and peace and security must be established. As he told Winston Churchill, it was "a catastrophic moment in history."[3] In "modern times" there have only been two ideas for "unification": Hitler's "New Order," and Communism the other. Either would prevent nations "preserving their national culture and spiritual independence." The Poles, he contended, put forward "another idea" to get all to cooperate, and to preserve Poland.[4] It was a sweeping analysis of the history of Europe from the time of the Roman Empire. Britain was singled out for particular praise for its historic role, a reflection of his life-long Anglophilia.[5]

Intellectual and spiritual problems must be fundamentally addressed in a shattered continent; this he emphasized. A sense of European uniqueness and unity already began to disappear in the eighteenth century. Europeans in the colonies began to treat their new residences as their countries and abandon Europe. Second, foreign powers (here the Russians and Americans were intended) have been allowed to play basic roles in continental affairs and their interests were different from European ones. Finally, the smaller powers had been ignored.

All of this was very dangerous because "barbarians of the East" with an ever increasing population, would pursue "Lebensraum" in Europe which reflected the fact that from times immemorial there has always existed a tremendous antagonism between the Orient and the Occident: which has occasionally burst into a "major conflagration." After noting the fundamental differences in Western and Eastern civilizations, Retinger made this fascinating observation:

> Unintentionally and almost without seeming to pay attention to it, we are sliding into a renewal of the conflict of the East and the West, in which Russia will be the champion of the East and the Anglo-Saxons the protagonists of the West. Both are extra-European Powers, with the difference that the Anglo-Saxons are slowly withdrawing from the Continent while Russia is getting closer and closer to it. The battlefield will be the Continent.[6]

General Sikorski, he noted, had already elaborated these ideas "with the help of a handful of his friends." During the war years we "were maturing our ideas." Though these notions were clear before the war, the first presentation was Sikorski's November, 1939 speech at the Foreign Press Association in London. Retinger was the original promoter of Sikorski's federalism and now tried to build upon it. Thereby Sikorski, Retinger claimed, became "the first active European statesman to indicate publicly and officially that the European states ought to relinquish part of their sovereignty for the common interest."[7] Retinger should be understood as describing himself. It was "a clear continuity between wartime planning meetings and the post-war movements for European unity."[8]

"Our idea," continued Retinger, was five or six regional blocs basically of an economic nature. The Polish bloc would include Czechoslovakia, Hungary, Romania and perhaps Austria. The others "more or less equal in economic and military potentialities, which, though strong enough to defend themselves against attack, would be economic organizations whose foremost need would be Peace." This economic common interest would, as for instance in the case of the "Balkan Union," preclude dissension among Bulgars, Serbs, or Greeks "since all would be participating in the blessings of an improved economic fabric." More economic cooperation, with its obvious benefits to all, would pre-empt the political Armageddon of an East-West conflict Retinger referred to at the beginning of his remarks. Failing this economic amalgamation, the continent would face a few solutions.[9] It would become a "free-market for Anglo-American expansion, "or a mere "appendage" of the Russian Empire and a laboratory for experiments in Communism. This would result in the continent becoming "permanently divided" into two zones-which would only "perpetuate the present conflict." The best solution was a free continent, economically cohesive and politically unified, and hence, anti-authoritarian.

A solution to this situation would *not* be "a Congress of all the Continental Powers." This was quite impossible because the winners of World War II would insist on the exclusion of the losers, and the neutral powers would be resented. Besides, Russia and its satellites would reject it. But so would the Western Powers who "would see that the Continent would cease to be a pawn in their own campaign. What then, was the solution? The smaller powers should "initiate consultations and upon this framework a unified continent might well be built.[10]

This was really quite a large conclusion to a presentation gigantic in its argument, suggesting a civilizational war, a third world war, the enslavement of vast reaches of Europe, the American hegemony over Europe, or alternatively, Russian domination. All of these horrors were to be averted by "consultations" among the small powers.

Thus Retinger conceived a world where people like himself, by energetic, ceaseless, and protracted negotiations would save civilization, and the great powers would look on with benevolent patience. By comparison Piłsudski's earlier dreams of restoring the Polish Commonwealth appeared to be modest and easily obtainable. Indeed, the conclusion Retinger produced made the whole document appear fantastical.

## The Polish aspect of the address

Sikorski began discussions with the British, Americans, and Stalin over this topic early during the war. The start was to be the (ill-fated) Polish-Czech collaboration. Sikorski's death and the end of the war, Retinger asserted, "caused all our schemes to come to nothing – for the time being only hope."[11] Now, we were moving to two separate blocs with Europe "the battlefield." Two non-European Powers, the United States and Russia dominated this struggle in Europe between the East and the West. Russia, the United States, and Great Britain would not belong to the continental federation. In keeping with his Polish traditions, Retinger reminded his audience that Poland had been a pioneer in the creation of federative structures going back more than 500 years. It was clear that "He believed that unity would restore Europe's power and provide a framework within which Poland could find a safe haven."[12]

Retinger's internationalism was a function of his Polish patriotism:

> Poland could only be helped by an indirect route, by building an international order, returning power to Europe and creating a structure in which Poland could find protection. Retinger never believed in the so-called inevitable process of history's development. He believed, that an entity forges according to its will, and in line with its vision. Each who manages to put in process the unity of Europe and helped in its progress

would have the right to believe that he really caused the change in the course of history. [13]

Retinger's specific ruminations on Polish history were noteworthy. In the interwar era, Poland "suffered from the mutual jealousies of the Big Powers, from the lack of co-operation among the smaller ones and from the spirit of mutual suspicion that everywhere prevailed." Poland was not included in European plans for integration by many.[14] Poland suffered from the imperialistic schemes of some of her neighbors, but she suffered too from the expansionist plans of Marshal Piłsudski and his followers, the sanacja, and "the isolation these brought upon her in international affairs." By denying any credit to Piłsudski as a federalist and characterizing his followers as responsible for Poland's international isolation, Retinger told the British what they wanted to hear.[15]

Sikorski and Retinger – "and a few others" – determined that Poland "could not remain a marginal country" nor join "schemes that might appear to threaten her neighbors." This latter reference doubtless referred to both Piłsudski's militant federalist efforts, the phantom war scare of 1923, as well as the foreign policy efforts of Colonel Józef Beck after 1935.[16] Poland must seek states in "analogous positions" and act in unison and not at the dictate of larger states. This would require "far-reaching political compromises." Retinger cited the federation which produced the Polish-Lithuanian Commonwealth in 1569 "which inspired my late chief and friend, General Sikorski, to find a way of getting the Continental states to co-operate for the benefit of them all." [17]

The interwar period taught, first of all, that sound "economic foundations" were necessary. Here he warned of the great powers' propensity to betray economic and commercial agreements with smaller states. This could only be avoided if "nations and their governments [were] linked with ties that could not be broken." This alone suggested the federal idea whereby "blocks of nations federated in such a way as to ensure their cohesion and the maximum amount of willing co-operation among them."[18]

In support of this vision Retinger noted his wartime collaboration with Belgians, Yugoslavs, Dutch, and Greeks; "approaches" to senior officials of the British government and, in a perhaps rhetorical flourish, claimed that "everybody knows that Beneš and Masaryk were for a long time in open agreement with us." This was hardly an accurate description of the federalist negotiations between the Poles and the Czechs. Sikorski, he noted spent much time talking about these ideas with Stalin and Roosevelt, neither of whom, however, cared about Sikorski's geopolitical musings. Despite this, Retinger claimed that Stalin and Sikorski had long and fruitful discussion which made real progress, an astonishing thing to claim in 1946.

Retinger, at the time of the speech, was musing over what he called a "Congress of Europeans," to be followed by efforts in Britain and the United States, the reverse of what would be Churchill's March 5, 1946 Fulton,

Missouri speech famous for its reference to an "Iron Curtain," but also containing the passage: "The safety of the world requires a new unity in Europe, from which no nation should be permanently outcast." Retinger wrote of the "penetration of the idea of the organization" even into the Communist bloc. This was not as impossible as it seemed because many who do "lip-service" to the regimes are really not devoted to them. "I know how to approach the Poles and Czechoslovaks and some ways may be found to get the Yugoslavs into line." He was confident about the Greeks. Although it was important to have movements in neutral countries like Switzerland and Sweden, the center "must remain in Belgium and Holland."[19]

Here we must interject an observation which underlay much of Retinger's postwar thought, His almost equal dislike of the United States and the Soviet Union. He had been a Russophobe since childhood and his wartime experiences in Moscow and other places in the Soviet Union, the sight of their gross mistreatment of Poles, his postwar trips to Poland, and witnessing the misery there could not help but convince him that Soviet Communism was the enemy of civilization. On the other hand he had at best a patronizing view of the United States and a conviction that Washington was essentially an "imperialist" power. It returns us to his Mexican years and a very telling comment he made at about this time, namely, "Americans are like the barbarians of the Middle Ages at the outset of their historical mission."[20] Europe was not only necessary, but a Europe without Germany and Russia taking the lead for the reasons he stated at the outset. They had both attempted continental unity and it had been terrible. Now Europe must emerge as an independent block to defy both super powers and, by implication, Germany as well.[21]

In an addendum a few weeks after his Chatham House address, Retinger called for a free market for Anglo-American expansion. Here he demonstrated a realization that it would require Washington and London to work together to resuscitate Europe. a sort of surrender to realism and also reflecting a major motif in Churchill's Fulton speech. Second, Retinger argued the acceptance of Russian expansion and the experiment of Communism, the limits of this were, perhaps understandably, not detailed. The result was a two part division of the continent reflecting the reality of the postwar world. Here Retinger departed from his musings about post eighteenth-century decaying unity and again responded as a realist to the fact of two blocs confronting each other in the heart of Europe: The Anglo-Americans were a separate but sympathetic outsider. The new Europe, the free bloc, must be political united, characterized by a free economic system, and political liberty as well.

Churchill had endorsed an "international armed force" for the United Nations a rather naively planned concept as he developed it,[22] the essence of "Atlanticism" He proposed that the threats facing the world be confronted by a "fraternal association of the English-speaking peoples which he saw as a compliment to and not a rival for the UN."[23] He did not refer to European unity except indirectly when he noted that "Central and Eastern Europe" had lost their sovereignty, hardly a "Liberated Europe."[24]

The two speeches, Churchill's by far the better known, drew starkly different geostrategic concepts: the first a European confederation to replace international rivalry and the second a powerful Anglo-American accord to defend against Soviet encroachments. This was enlarged by remarks more significant for the European unity movement in the speech Churchill gave in Zürich on September 19, 1946. Here he called for "the recreation of the European family by the building of a kind of United States of Europe." The first step would be a German-French partnership.[25]

Churchill proffered what he deemed a "sovereign remedy" to Europe's plight: and cited as precursors Briand's "pan-European union," of 1929–1930 and, dubiously, the earlier League of Nations. He did not see his putative organization in conflict with the United Nations, rather he saw the latter strengthened by a "European group" inculcating a "sense of enlarged patriotism and common citizenship." A "Council of Europe" would be a first step. It would include all those states "who can" join. The "friends and sponsors" of this new Europe would be the United States, the British Commonwealth, and "I trust" Soviet Russia, but the Franco-German effort must be the first step.[26]

The centrality of the great powers was obvious in Churchill's conception. The smaller states were virtually omitted; the reverse of Retinger's vision. It was to be a world based on Western Europe; the reference to the Soviet Union seemed a rhetorical device. This was a Europe built from the top down, rather than from the bottom up. It reflected the fundamental difference of viewpoint from a stateless Pole, and the representative of a world empire. In some ways both approaches are reminiscent of the 1930 notion launched by Briand of a federal organization of Europe created under the umbrella of the League of Nations. Now several ephemeral organizations were formed in response to Churchill's proposals. This included a significant British group which counted a number of prominent politicians among its founding members. Duncan Sandys, Churchill's son-in-law, was its leader and it took the name the United Europe Movement (UEM).[27]

## The complex path to unity

Building a federation was daunted by its disparate pieces. By 1945 the parts that had traditionally constituted Europe, or at least to some, were scattered. Western Europe grouped its way towards federative structures. The nations of the Communist bloc were imperial territory removed from European experiment and evolution. Britain was sympathetic but saw a "special relationship" only with the United States and retained the historic British ambivalence towards the continent. Russia, whose "Europeaness" has always been problematic, dominated much of the continent.

After the Chatham House speech, Retinger began to undertake the blueprint he had sketched. He went to Belgium immediately after his speech, and met with Roger Motz, a Belgian senator, and his countryman Spaak, but particularly with Van Zeeland to discuss the economic aspects of integration. Long before he had espied the fundamental economic problems as the main barrier.[28] Van Zeeland had been discussing these ideas for some time and the visit from Retinger led to greater coordination regarding inter-European rationalization of the various economies. It was these questions which had to be solved first if a federation were to arise from the current economic chaos.[29]

A month after their Brussels meeting, Van Zeeland and Retinger met again. This time also present were the Dutch senator Pieter Kierstens who had been involved in the wartime Benelux discussions among others. It was decided there that Van Zeeland would approach the Belgian, French and Luxembourgian governments, and cultivate prominent industrialists. Retinger was to obtain the "benediction" of the British and American governments. Both multiplied their contacts subsequently, Retinger working with the Americans to find a suitable liaison, and more important, money. Retinger also met with the British whose support proved more difficult, and Van Zeeland aided Retinger in efforts to cultivate London. This proved to be a disappointment,[30] though by late in the year he had gained the interest of Sandys.[31]

Retinger and Van Zeeland agreed to propose an international organization tasked with defending European economic interests which would "convoke an international congress composed of *leading men* [sic] of the West and of the East to prepare a future structure for Europe.[32] As we have seen, Van Zeeland had been inspired by the Sikorski plan after 1942.[33] Retinger later modestly commented "I had started a Movement for the Unity of Europe."[34] Frantic efforts at recruitment followed.[35]

They agreed that it was too early for a political movement and the outcome was the birth of the European League for Economic Cooperation (ELEC), (Ligue Européenne de Coopération Economique, LECE), or (Ligue Independante de Cooperation Européenne, LICE), more simply, "the League"[36] Van Zeeland and Retinger, joined soon by Kerstens of Holland, also a Catholic, conceived the League in Brussels in June, 1946. A study group was to work on assembling the international elite favorable to a European union.[37] Its economic focus reflects Retinger's fear "not to be carried away by unrealistic Utopianism."[38] As Lipgens summarizes:

> Action must be taken to prevent the unthinking restoration of European national economies and that the European idea should be developed first and foremost in the economic sphere through an international 'independent league of experts.[39]

It was Retinger who seemed to be the imitator of the creation, with Van Zeeland his close collaborator, though it may have been the reverse. In any event both were the "spiritual fathers" of the organization.[40] Its organizing committee included Daniel Serruys (France), Randolph Churchill (the

United Kingdom), Retinger (Poland), Kerstens (the Netherlands), Guillaume Konsbruck (Luxemburg), Pipinelis (Greece), and an unnamed Belgian. The date of Retinger's memorandum, September 17, 1946, is regarded as the date of the formal founding of the League.[41] Retinger was secretary-general.[42]

Kerstens, Van Zeeland, and Retinger went to London to establish a British branch. They met with Prime Minister Clement Attlee and Retinger's old friend Cripps. Retinger, and Van Zeeland subsequently made visits to Paris, Luxembourg, and The Hague.[43] Retinger's devoted wartime friend Gubbins arranged funds from the wealthy Briton Edward Beddington-Behrens.[44] But Retinger lamented that, at this point, "we had nothing."[45]

In 1946, Van Zeeland travelled to the United States preaching that economic unity in Europe was the alternative to "disaster." Retinger accompanied him and they elicited interest in a planned "congress" with Retinger, as usual, in the background.[46] However, his elusive presence was much more important than it seemed. Finances for the conference were substantially provided "at Retinger's request" from the "Economic Cooperation Agency counterpart funds which subsidized the Office of Policy Coordination." The latter was a covert CIA agency.[47]

Retinger's main goal was to form an American branch of the League and based his hopes on Adolf Berle and the help of Averill Harriman, who, Retinger was convinced, was avidly in favor of European unity.[48] He was financially very helpful to Retinger. It had been with the ambassador's assistance, that Retinger went to the United States and there found a number of interested political and financial leaders as well as Sir William Wiseman, the British diplomat who had much involvement with Polish politics in the World War I era and was later a partner in Kuhn Loeb as well as a MI6 member;[49] Berle proved to be a major link for Retinger. He had been the only State Department official who "knew something about Eastern Europe," and had struck up a close friendship with Retinger which would prove very useful later.[50] Retinger re-established his link with Berle.[51] Berle agreed to head the American section, though it was inactive.[52] John Foster Dulles was of help, but whether he was a formal member is unclear.

Berle was to be the man to provide the nucleus of American support, though Retinger met with a number of prominent members of the State Department as well.[53] Berle arranged the American financing of the effort. This was an irony given Retinger's long-time distrust of the United States and his tendency to counterpoise Europe and the United States. His overtures to the Council on Foreign Relations were abortive because William Bullitt and Senator William Fulbright of the CFR were proponents of Kalergi and would not help. He tried to spread his efforts to academic circles and labor leaders, but these efforts failed. Washington's initial response was lukewarm: Retinger explained that the Americans did not wish to give the impression that they were interfering in European plans for recovery.[54] Retinger tried to convince John Foster Dulles to "sound" Moscow regarding the goals of the League, but Dulles demurred.[55] Moscow's response, in Retinger's words was that "they very much supported the idea of a united Europe under the condition that it would emerge under their control."[56] "An economic unity which might invigorate the Western democracies and their societies of freedom does not seem to appeal much to the Soviet leaders.[57] Closely associated with this is Retinger's endorsement of a sort of appeasement towards the Soviet Union, reconciliation between the American and Soviets, a notion he shared with Van Zeeland.

Purposely, no country's name was attached to the League for fear that it be thought of as a national body. Retinger prepared what amounted to an introduction for the League: autonomy but close cooperation; neutrality of ideology with no religious uniformity required; the eventual amalgamation of Eastern Europe; the inclusion of the United States, Canada, and even Soviet Russia.[58] Economic issues were at the heart of the creation.

As Retinger argued, the organization was designed to defend the basic values of Western civilization. He was "afraid of continental Europe becoming a playing field for the Anglo-Americans or the Russian Empire." That is why the smaller powers should "initiate consultation and upon this framework a unified Continent might be built." National committees in agreement quickly appeared in a number of European countries. Retinger was a member of the coordinating committee of this assemblage. Both Van Zeeland and Retinger could act rapidly because neither was attached to a specific government.[59]

Retinger tried to reconstitute the wartime group formed under Sikorski's inspiration.[60] It comprised Belgians, Van Zeeland, Spaak, and Senator Roger Motz and Dutch, Kerstens. Soon a British network evolved consisting of Cripps, Sir Harold Butler, diplomat and businessman, Beddington-Behrens, and Harold Macmillan among others.[61] In general, however, the British were not well-disposed.[62] Labour suspected that their arch-enemy, Churchill would play a leading role, and wished to distance themselves from the project.

Also in 1946 additional organizations were inaugurated for ostensibly more or less the same goals.[63] Already the curse of too many organizations is evident. It was, however, the central goal of the League to combine the various "similar movements," and Retinger became a sort of salesman for the League, a major and exhausting effort which had as its centerpiece the establishment of harmonious relations between Retinger and Churchill's UEM led by Sandys.[64] De Rougemont referred to all these meetings as "stepping stone conferences."[65]

The goal was to establish a branch of the League in every possible European country.[66] The first of these was probably that formed in Holland by Retinger's wartime associates, especially Kersten's.[67] The pro-Polish Gubbins, retired from the SOE and now in industry, founded the British branch, though he was not actively involved. Dorril argued that, though Gubbins had retired from the SOE. He still had ties to MI6 and it was this network that Retinger used to create his new team.[68] Gubbins had long shared Retinger's vision of European unity.[69] France proved a rather more difficult field of activity. Here they approached Serruys, who had been part of the French delegation at the Paris Peace Conference of 1919. He had become a major business figure after years of government service and was also close to Van Zeeland.

Through Serruys the French branch gained François-Poncet, Valéry Giscard d'Estaing and a number of others. Van Zeeland established, under Guillaume Konsbruck, a filium in Luxembourg. However Retinger failed in Italy where no branch was established, despite a preliminary creation under Senator Enrico Falck. There were similar failures in Portugal and Switzerland and hesitation in Austria and Sweden. It was decided to delay forming a German branch for political reasons; it only later appeared in 1948 in the person of industrialist Hermann Abs.

The Soviets would not let the satellite states cooperate. The ill-fated Jan Masaryk was interested, but was murdered, or committed suicide, before the meeting commenced. Van Zeeland wrote to Retinger that if the Soviets were favorably inclined, he wanted him to fly to Moscow to "explain our goal and our methods."[70] Retinger would thus repeat his mission of a few years earlier now representing a larger creation than Poland. It never happened.

Finally, representatives of the émigré political communities were invited including Mikołaczyk and Raczyński representing Poland.[71] Efforts to somehow include Eastern Europe failed despite earnest efforts by Retinger. The prominent Labour Foreign Secretary Ernest Bevin had addressed parliament just a few months earlier about the "Bevin Plan" which called for a "Union of Western Europe." This effectively ignored the east of Europe. Moreover, British participation also not mentioned in his remarks.[72] Efforts for the unofficial sponsorship of several governments met with mixed success: Belgium, Holland, and Greece agreed, the key, Great Britain, refused, citing the alleged unsavory pasts of Van Zeeland and Kerstens.[73]

Retinger was, as usual penniless. Two friends came to his aid in the initial steps in creating the European union movement, not so much because they were won over to the idea, but because they wished to support him financially. The two were David Astor, and Beddington-Behrens. Beddington-Behrens sent Retinger the money ostensibly to help Poland "the bravest of the brave." In addition to Beddington-Behrens and Astor, separate "covenants" came from other sources which the two managed to persuade.[74] This was yet another indication that those who worked with Retinger on international and federal schemes always realized he was a devoted Polish patriot, but a poor one.[75]

Lesser monies came from other sources, but his past came back to haunt him. The Communist government in Poland of course wanted nothing to do with movements to free Europe. Poles living abroad, contrariwise, frequently regarded him as pro-Soviet and a long-time foreign agent. In France and many other places he was looked upon as a British spy. He represented no one and had no country behind him. Two years before he died he dictated his memories of the first years on the international stage. "By 1946 I concluded that that once again the time had come to renew efforts towards European unity." [76] Over the next two years he was to have 200 meetings.[77]

In March 1947 the League met in New York which both Retinger and Van Zeeland attended. But when the Marshall Plan (or ERP, European Recovery Program) was agreed on June 4, 1947 "our American friends decided that it would be better if they concentrated their efforts in America." The plan would extend 13 billion dollars of US funds and technical assistance to members of the Organization for European Economic Co-operation, a body created to administer the American funds. Originally the nations of the Communist bloc were to be included, but under the pressure of Moscow, they refused to cooperate. As a result of this initiative, the Americans abandoned the League, and, after several months of activities, decided to restrict themselves to Western Europe only. Naturally, the League hailed the Marshall Plan and the League's Central Committee drafted a document supporting the plan. This was actually a great help: "Retinger had secretly persuaded Shepard Stone of the US High Commission in Germany to finance his [Retinger's] European Movement from so-called "counterpart funds," Marshal Aid repayments which the Americans banked in Europe."[78] Retinger claimed the plan was concurrent with his own visions.[79]

Retinger and van Zeeland and seven of the "most active" League members met to organize cooperation with the Marshall Plan. They replied with "a coordinated European plan and setting up a 'European Planning Board' for the purpose of combing the most urgent national needs into a single list and anticipating the removal of the trade and customs barriers that were partly responsible for Europe's troubles."[80] "Van Zeeland and Retinger and key members of the British group met in London on June 20, 1947 and drafted a memorandum "which [welcomed] the Marshall offer."[81] However, the Europeans "emphasized the need for a European partner with its own views and policy. This was intended to counteract the tendency for the United States to interfere in European economic affairs."[82] Simultaneously the League decided to restrict its own activities to Western Europe, though eventual expansion to Eastern Europe was contemplated.[83]

The League met in Paris on June 30, 1947 and expressed its support for Marshall's plan deeming it a "natural continuation" of the earlier pronouncements of the League," a claim not entirely convincing.[84] It was now in a position to make concrete economic proposals.[85] Retinger and Van Zeeland were its two principals, according to Dumoulin "the determinant influence."[86] Cooperation with the Americans to revive the European economy was emphasized, though as a marriage of free trade and central planning, a strange combination.[87]

Retinger decided that the League should turn to other organizations to seek cooperation. He met with Sandys of the UEM, and urged a coordinated effort to which Sandys agreed. A multi-part conference was held in Paris. This body was dominated by Retinger who repeatedly referred to it as "my committee."[88] It included, principally the League (Retinger), Sandys' UEM, and the Union of European Federalists (UEF), led by Henri Brugmans of the Netherlands. Kalergi's followers did not join. Retinger described the goal as "a common basis for the unity of Europe."[89] On July 20, 1947, the Liaison Committee of the Movements for European Unity was constituted: the United Europe Movement and the League were the nucleus of the later European Movement.[90] Witkowski considers this fragile agglutination an "enormous" success with Retinger's role considerable.

The initial focus of attention was on "practical" economic questions, given the sorry state of Europe. Reflecting this was the League's own desperate financial straits. In June, 1946 Retinger wrote to Van Zeeland that he had spent $10,000 "out of my own pocket." Not only did he need reimbursements, but the financial management of the organization was out of control. If something was not done hurriedly, "the League "must end in a fiasco,"[91]

We must depend on Retinger's recollections to reconstruct his relationship with these emergent bodies. The principal one was Sandys' UEM, maintained with the cooperation of a number of conservatives plus a few Liberals and Labour members.[92] The UEM worked closely with several other committees in Europe. It was the UEM which gave Churchill such a celebrated role in the origins of the later European Movement.[93] Indeed, Churchill wanted Europe to unite but without the British Isles. Federation, for Churchill was particular: "the British were keen to advance the cause of European integration but only on British terms."[94] This set him at odds with Sandys, who argued that Great Britain was an integral part of the European world.[95] Ironically, Churchill's vision specifically excluded his own country.[96] This was perhaps an omen: once he was re-elected Prime Minister, his support for European unity waned.

Retinger soon concluded that the organization was harmed by inexperience, impatience, and the desire to become rapidly a mass movement.[97] The elitist Retinger wrote a note to himself at the time: "start with an intellectual organization around the idea of the continent as a unit." It should have scholars, businessmen, "and lastly, politicians."[98]

Dissension soon broke out in the Liaison Committee. Sandys and Retinger argued for the primacy of economic and then military union; political coordination would come later while the UEF's De Rougemont demanded a "political federation" in contrast. Hence they were referred to as the "federalists." De Rougemont was characterized as demanding "revolutionary drive" versus "realistic tactics." The so-called realists regarded their opponents as acting prematurely.[99] The federalists were also reluctant to adopt an anti-Soviet stance. This reflects their leftist orientation; in contradiction with their more rightist, realist, opponents. Ironically, now Retinger had functionally migrated to the political right, at least as far as visions of Europe were concerned.

The Liaison Committee had a short life, July to November 1947 when it was transformed into a larger body: the International Committee of the Movements for European Unity, or ICMEU (sometimes referred to as JICMEU). Sandys presided, and Retinger was secretary-general. In planning the European unity movement's next steps, JICMEU envisioned a large world meeting at The Hague, in 1948 "whose goal was the creation of a western European parliament."[100] But there was more. It would be a meeting of "representative leaders of thought and action from as many countries of Europe as possible. The purpose of the conference would be to affirm the urgent need for greater unity among the nations of Europe and to recommend to governments practical measures to achieve it."[101] As Retinger told Walter Lippmann, "private and independent activities" were best able to work for European unity; governments are "overcautious and rather timid." He continued that "we …want to go further than the governments can." They would be informed of "our aims and tactics" and asked for suggestions.[102]

Thus it was not solely to be an intellectual conclave but the inception of a political action organization. In Hick's words "this Sandys-Retinger axis would effectively shape The Hague Congress campaign." [103] Hederman goes further and credits The Hague notion solely to Retinger.[104] Already in this early period frictions between Retinger and the somewhat erratic Sandys became manifest.[105] Kalergi was asked to take steps to form a suitable group to prepare the necessary reports on the moral and cultural aspects of the European problem. But his ego prevented him from cooperation. As Retinger's secretary wrote: "several times he agreed to take part in the work of the coordinating committee, but each time he withdrew after a few weeks, or even days."[106]

But, before The Hague Congress could convene, Kalergi created a rival body at his home in Gstaad in September, 1947 with well over 100 participants to convoke a "preliminary European parliament," the "European Parliamentary Union or EPU." Retinger, along with a few others generously urged all federalist parliamentary groups to cooperate with the EPU. Soon other federalist bodies appeared in other European countries. Retinger was aloof from this movement and he was not alone. It had plans which Retinger had regarded as "Utopianism," federal union and the summoning of a constituent assembly."[107]

Kalergi enlisted Senaor William Fulbright and OSS chief William Donovan in his efforts. Fulbright introduced a Senate resolution endorsing the notion of a "United States of Europe." [108] Within a few months, Kalergi was speaking of "American" and "European" branches of the Committee for a United States of Europe."[109] In April, 1948 they created the "American Committee on a Free and United Europe" under the chairmanship of Fulbright[110] Kalergi was the only "honorary member." There were a number of important collaborators, including Allen Dulles. However, it never met. Indeed, only in 1949, did a group gather to create some sort of organization. By this time the European unity movement was moving in a different direction.

## Notes

1 Untitled 15 page memorandum, in Retinger Papers, PISM, folder 18; cf. Sadowski, ""Retinger i jego amerykańska teczka," 2.
2 This speech is discussed in Andrzej Pieczewski, "Retinger's Vision," 5ff.

3 Retinger to Churchill, June 8, 1948, Centre Virtuel de la Conaissance sur l'Europe (CVCE at www.cvce.eu), herein cited as Archives historiques.
4 Joseph H. Retinger, "The European Continent: An Address given on 7 May, 1946, with a postscript dated 30 August, 1946, shelf 6, Retinger Papers, BPL, 3.
5 Grosbois, "L'action," 79.
6 "The European Continent."
7 "The European Continent," 5; Sikorski noted this fact days before he died, emphasizing its importance to small and medium-sized powers; see Terlecki, *Generał*, 293.
8 Cristina Blanco Sío-López, "Memories and Horizons: The Legacy of the Central and Eastern European Intellectuals in Exile and the 'Reunification' of Europe," *Pliegos de Yuste: Revista de Cultura, Ciencia y Pensamiento Europeo*, Número 11 (2012), 32. She refers to Retinger as someone whose role "should not be underestimated"; "he could be considered as an East European equivalent of Jean Monnet."
9 "The European Continent."
10 See the "Postscript" of August 30, 1946.
11 Ibid., 6–7.
12 Sío-López, "Memories," 32–33.
13 Pomian, *Retinger*, 250.
14 Andrzej Pieczewski, "Retinger's Version," 3; idem, "Joseph Retinger's Vision of a United Europe after World War II: Central and Eastern European Question," *The Polish Review*, Vol. 60, No. 4 (2015), 52ff.
15 Pieczewski, "Retinger's Version," 6–7.
16 Marek Kornat, "The Polish Idea of 'The Third Europe' (1937–1939: A Realistic Concept or an ex-post Vision?" *Acta Poloniae Historica*, Vol. 103 (2011), 101–126.
17 Pieczewski, "Retinger's Version," 6–8.
18 Ibid., 7.
19 Retinger notes, Box 17, folder "korespondencja," Retinger Papers, BPL; Dumoulin and Dutrieue, *La Ligue*, 23.
20 Retinger to Citrine [1945], drawer 5 Retinger Papers, BPL.
21 A convenient copy of the text is "Sinews of Peace," online at http://www.historyguide.org/europe/churchill.html.
22 Ibid., 2–3.
23 Ibid., 4–5
24 Ibid., 5–6.
25 "Recreating the European Family," *The Times*, September 20, 1946, 4. Dumoulin and Dutrieue, *La Ligue*, 20–21.
26 "Recreating the European Family," *The Times*, September 20, 1946, 6.
27 Pomian, *Retinger*. 258. In an undated memorandum the United Europe Committee [sic] stated that "The final elimination of war can be assured only by the eventual creation of a system of World Government," of which Great Britain must be a member and both Moscow and Washington must cooperate. See un-titled sheet issued by the United Europe Committee, signed by Churchill as Chairman, and Sandys as Secretary, not dated, in F. D. Sandys Papers, folder 54.5, CCA.
28 Witkowski, *Ojcowie*, 125. De Rougemont came to the same conclusion; see his *The Idea of Europe* (Cleveland, OH: The World Publishing Co., 1968), 424.
29 Retinger, memorandum, folder 79, PISM; Michel Dumoulin, "Les débuts de la Ligue européenne de Cooperation économique (1946–1949)," *Res Publica*, Vol. 29, 1 (1987), 100.
30 Dumoulin and Dutrieue, *La Ligue*, 24–25.
31 Retinger, "Winston Churchill," Retinger Papers, drawer 1. BPL. Sir Nigel Fisher once referred to Sandys as "the most ardent European in the Cabinet." Pomian to author, July 29, 2014.

32 Vincent Dujardin and Michel Dumoulin, *Paul Van Zeeland, 1893–1973*, Brussels: Editions Racine, 1997, 154. Retinger was quick to emphasize that nine months before Churchill's speech "I has started a movement for the unity of Europe," Retinger, "Winston S. Churchill, drawer 1, BPL; Dumoulin, "Les débuts," 102–103.
33 Ibid., 100 "The European Movement and its Affiliated Organizations."
34 Retinger, "Winston Churchill," Retinger Papers, drawer 1, BPL.
35 Retinger, "Unity of Europe," Retinger Papersn, drawer 5, BPL.
36 Retinger "Notes," Retinger Papers, BPL, drawer 3. It was otherwise known as the "Independent League for Economic Cooperation." In 1948 it changed its name to the European League for Economic Cooperation ELEC. An important study based largely on Belgian documents concerning the League is Dumoulin and Dutrieue, *La Ligue*. The organization changed its name to LECE (Ligue Européenne de Cooperation Economique in June 1948; it was also known by its English acronym, ELEC.
37 "The Origins of the ELEC in 1946," 5, in *Archives historiques de l'union européenne*, fonds code LECE, dossier no. 000272, "Dossier sur Joseph Retinger" (hereafter *Archives historiques*: Retinger dossier). His biographer notes that Van Zeeland accelerated his activities in 1946; cf. Drion du Chapois, *Paul van Zeeland, au service de la Belgique* (Brussels: Editions Labor, 1971), 73; Dumoulin, "Les débuts." 100ff. Regarding Kerstens, see M. van der Velden, *European League for Economic Co-operation* (Brussels: ELEC, 1995), 5. Other sources mention Serruys, Gubbins, and Sainte-Lorette as part of these negotiations; see Gisch, "ELEC," in Lipgens and Loth, *European Integration*, 3: 189, 197. Retinger, in 1955, took credit for founding the League; see Retinger to Joseph E. Johnson, May 28, 1955; box 26b, Retinger Papers, BPL; Retinger, "Unity of Europe."
38 Lipgens, *European Integration*, 341.
39 Ibid., 335–336.
40 Michel Dumoulin and Anne-Myriam Dutrieue, *La Ligue Européenne de Cooperation Économique (1946–1981)* (Berne: Peter Lang, 1993), 12, 17ff.
41 See M. van der Velden to Conrad Reuss; "Conference Retinger et note d'organisation," in Retinger dossier. There is some debate about the founding meeting: van der Velden argues for October 17, 1946; see his *European League*, 6; there is also an argument for a May inauguration; see Dumoulin, "Les débuts," 111; May 8 is occasional given as the inaugural date; see Van der Velden, *The Origins*, 10.
42 See European League for Economic Cooperation, 50th Anniversary of ELEC, 1946–1996: In remembrance of Joseph Retinger, Initiator of Elec (Brussels, 1996), and Andrzej Pieczewski to author January 13, 2015, author's files. I am grateful to Pieczewski for sharing this source for me.
43 Van der Velden, *The Origins*, 9–10.
44 Wilkinson and Astley, *Gubbins*, 240.
45 This quotation appears in the first draft of Retinger's "Report by the Secretary General," January 25, 1952, ME 297, HAEU.
46 Brigitte Henau, *Paul van Zeeland en het monotaire, sociaal-economische en Europee beleid van België, 1920–1960* (Brussels: Paleis der Academiën, 1995), 209; "League for Europe seeks Cooperation," *New York Times*, April 4, 1947, 12.
47 Wilford, *The CIA*, 228.
48 Ibid., 257. Retinger was very interested in gaining Harriman's active support of his EM efforts, see NN to Retinger, June 10, 1948, ME 268, HAEU.
49 According to Dorril, *MI6*, 461.
50 Berle, "Memorandum," February 24, 1942, Berle Papers, container 165, FDR Library.
51 Retinger to Berle, March 24, 1946, Berle Papers, container 84, FDR Library.

52  Retinger "Notes", drawer 3–4, Retinger Papers, BPL; Taverne, *Wat niemand*, regarding the fruits of the Retinger-Harriman cooperation, 19; cf. Gerald Sharp to Retinger, October 10, 1948, ME 177, HAUE. Berle's role, however, is a bit hazy.
53  Dumoulin and Dutrieue, *La Ligue*, 24n. The authors consider Retinger's American mission a major success; cf. Gijswijt, "Uniting the West," 9. Berle was, according to a Polish friend of Retinger, "very close to you," Ronikier to Retinger, September 19, 1950, ME 890, HAEU.
54  Notes from the ELEC Paris meeting, June 30, 1947; box 4, BPL, 5; cf. Aldrich, "OSS, CIA," 220, n. 20.
55  Dumoulin and Dutrieue, *La Ligue*, 28.
56  Retinger, "Notes," Retinger Papers, 4, BPL Pomian, *Retinger*, 195–196; Moulin and Dutrieue, *La Ligue*, 28.
57  John Foster Dulles quoted in Dumoulin. "Les debuts," 110.
58  See the discussion of Retinger's program for the League, "Jedność kontynentu, "in Witkowski, *Ojcowie*, 93.
59  Witlowski, *Retinger*, 83.
60  Pomian, *Retinger*, 194ff.
61  Ibid.
62  Dumoulin, "Les Debuts," 107; Beddington-Behrins had known Gubbins since World War I; a nice triangle with Retinger; see Wilkinsom and Astley, *Gubbins*, 18.
63  Van der Velden, *ELEC*, 8.
64  Retinger, memorandum, teczka 79, sik; cd. Retinger to Joseph E. Johnson, May 28, 1955, box 26B, Retinger Collection, PISM.
65  "Souvenirs de Denis de Rougemont sur le congress de La Haye," May, 1968. Archives historiques: Retinger dossier.
66  Henau, *Van Zeeland*, 209.
67  "Notes," Retinger Papers, BPL, drawer 3.
68  Wilford, *The CIA*, 250.
69  See Bułhak, "Wokół," 17n.
70  Dujardin and Dumoulin, *Van Zeeland*, 219.
71  Ibid., 228.
72  See "'Free Europe' Suggested," a letter by Kalergi in *The Times*, February 16, 1948.
73  For initial approaches to the British see van der Velden, *ELEC*, 6, 9. Surreptitious American money was also spent to combat British opposition to federalism; Aldrich, "OSS, CIA," 185.
74  David Astor to Retinger March 3, March 15, and 17, 1960 in Box 18, Folder A, Retinger Papers, BPL.
75  Behrens to Retinger, June 1, 1947, Retinger Papers, BPL, box 17, folder "korespondencja."
76  Pomian, *Retinger*, 250–254.
77  Pomian, "Slowo o autorze," np.
78  Fred Hirsch and Richard Fletcher, *The CIA and the Labour Movement* (Nottingham: Spokesman Books, 1977), 58.
79  Podgórski, *Retinger*, 305.
80  Lipgens, *European Integration*, 337; Dumoulin and Dutrieue, *La Ligue*, 30.
81  Gisch, "ELEC," Lipgens and Loth, *European Integration*, 4:188; Dumoulin and Dutrieue, *La Ligue*, 30.
82  Ibid., 4:202. There was no doubt that the ERP was a blow to the League and small continental organizations; see Sadowski, "Amerykańska teczka," 2.
83  Pomian, *Retinger*, 196; See the report of the Central Council of the League of July 23, 1957 in Edward Mayou Hastings Lloyd Papers, London School of Economics (hereafter LSE), folder 8/11.

84 Witkowski, *Ojcowie*, 100–101.
85 Pieczewski, Działalność, 138.
86 Dumoulin, "Les débuts," 118.
87 Ibid., 101; Dumoulin and Dutrieue, La Ligue, 30.
88 "Letter from Joseph Retinger to Morgan Phillips (London, 10 March 1948,"Centre Virtuel de la Connaisance sur l'Europe; Archives historiques.
89 Retinger, Memorandum, teczka 79, PISM.
90 Regarding the Liaison Committee, see Sandys to Retinger, July 22, 1947, ME 177, HAEU. Retinger to Shinwell, February 13, 1948, Archives historiques.
91 "European Movement Finances," box 17, Retinger Papers, BPL. See also the folder "Independent League for European Cooperation," in ibid. The bills were paid, up to the amount of 50,000 francs by Guillaume Konsbruck; see ibid.
92 Coudenhove-Kalergi, *An Idea*, 267–269.
93 Van der Velden, *The Origins*, 8.
94 McKay, *Federalism*, 38.
95 Spaak, *Continuing Battle*, 199–202.
96 See de Rougemont, *Meaning of Europe*, 82, 89. Churchill by 1951 was more "reserved" about European federation: he wanted the "first step" to be US-UK Commonwealth "solidarity" and only then a "second stage" of the "unification of Europe", see "Abroad" by Anne O'Hare McCormick, *New York Times*, July 7, 1951.
97 Pomian, *Retinger*, 197–198.
98 Retinger, folder "korespondencja," box 17, Retinger Papers, box 18, BPL.
99 Lipgens, *European Integration*, 665–666.
100 Wapiński, Retinger," 151. An idea of the list of prominent Europeans Retinger was canvassing is in "Aide Memoire for Dr. Retinger," December 30, 1947, Retinger Papers, BPL.
101 Retinger, "Congress of Europe," nd, Archives historiques.
102 Retinger to Lippmann, April 1, 1948, ME 177, HAEU.
103 Hick, "European Movement," in Lipgens and Loth, *European Integration*, 4: 326. The committee was also called "the Joint International Committee of the Movements for European Unity;" see "Congress of Europe," signed by Retinger in Archives historiques.
104 Miriam Hederman, "the beginning of the discussion on European Union in Ireland," in Lipgens and Loth, *European Integration*, 3:783.
105 Retinger [draft letter] to Morgan Phillips, nd., Archives historiques. Sandys was arrogant and overbearing though he usually worked well with Retinger; Pomian to author; Wilford, The CIA, 232–233.
106 Pomian, Retinger, 260.
107 Lipgens, *European Integration*, 609.
108 In twenty words the United States Congress was asked to endorse a "United States of Europe" early the next year, Senator William J. Fulbright introduced the motion into the Senate and Hale Boggs into the House: both passed. Kalergi seems to have initiated the Fulbright-Boggs action.
109 Kalergi to Dulles, February 5, 1948, box 3, folder 6, Dulles Papers.
110 "Minutes of Preliminary Meeting on the Organization of an American Committee," Dulles Papers, box 6, f. 3. For the membership, quite impressive, see "American Committee for a Free and United Europe," nd, Dulles Papers, Box 6, f. 3.

# 13 The Congress of Europe, 1948

Retinger confided to de Rougemont during "these sad days of Easter" that he considered a "manifesto" with a great many signatures to be gathered as an essential goal of the congress. This manifesto, addressed to "all men of goodwill" would form the basis for post-congress "conjoint behaviors." He wanted "millions" of signatures thus creating a "very strong popular movement." Governments "timid or recalcitrant" could even be subjected to some unspoken "supplementary pressure" (une pression supplementaire).[1] The manifesto was to be a "principal and immediate" accomplishment of the congress to make its ideas known to the general population-a mass movement.[2] Elitist Retinger's sudden interest in mass mobilization was noteworthy.

The manifesto would begin with "a definition of our moral conception of life," a "Charter" of human liberty. It should explain how only economic and political cooperation on the European continent could realize the security and prosperity for Europe, personal and national. It should condemn the perennial division of Europe. As regards political matters specifically, the manifesto should address the issue of national sovereignty. Then, it should be explained that the "organs of decision" are exercising rights bequeathed to it as the citizens of Europe. Nationalism, and here it cites pejoratively Mussolini's "egoismo sacrato," is really a means of enslaving people, and also reminds readers of the "perils of isolationism."[3]

In a rather disturbing aside, Retinger adds that contrary to the past, no "moral force" should dominate this assembly of Europe, and that "the interior and national policy" should not be "jealously guarded" (protégée jalousement) by the individual national governments but a "common norm of political morality" should be obeyed. Pursuant to that, the congress should "prevent (empêcher) the creation and propagation of immoral ideologies, such as totalitarian systems, hostile to the spiritualist conception of the world." Should this not be successful, Retinger concluded in a vague and disturbing passage, an "international tribunal" should be vested with executive powers to "to survey the path taken by national politics which risk adverse repercussions for the neighboring countries."[4]

The risks to national sovereignty long attributed to the European movement in general and Retinger in particular are exposed here in stark light. Of course, just having completed a massive war dominated by ideological conflict, his sensitivity to "immoral ideologies" is understandable. But this monitoring of the internal politics of member nations is disturbing as is the assumption of a prevalent and enforceable "common norm of political morality." What exactly is meant by the "spiritualist conception of the world" is also vague. Retinger, in his own ruminations, provided ammunition for his later critics who would cite schemes of international domination as the biggest danger in his propositions.

The largest obstacle to the organization, and success, of the congress was the fervid opposition of the British Left, especially the Labour Party.[5] They encouraged their members not to attend, denounced the congress for being dominated by "reactionary forces," criticized the exclusion of socialists, objected to the prominent role given to the conservative Churchill, and resented what they thought was a rigged selection process by Retinger's committee. Retinger wrote a series of ameliorative letters to explain that socialists were invited, that Churchill would speak only once, but so would French socialist Léon Blum, that selection had been equitable, and that deeming the participants "reactionary" misrepresented them. He noted, interestingly, that Labour objections might give the appearance of a Right vs. Left divide in Western Europe which, in turn: "Such a misunderstanding, I am sure you will appreciate, might even imperil the material and moral help which we expect to receive from our American friends." [6] In a curious side note, Retinger noted patronizingly that when he wanted Kalergi to speak at the plenary session it "came up against opposition on personal grounds." It was a pity, he observed, because Kalergi had devoted a "long year of pioneer work in the wilderness."[7]

Funds were short, and organizing efforts proved difficult: The meeting was designed for 750 people. Retinger, and Sandys, traveled about seeking support everywhere, and the Low Countries were the most generous.[8] Travel had to be subsidized for some, and organizational matters were very difficult.[9] Retinger's role is eloquently captured by Spaak, who was to play a major role in The Hague: "[Retinger] knew everybody and no door was closed to him. ... he was one of the best informed politicians. ... he was one of the most ardent partisans of European unity and deserves to be remembered as a pioneer of that cause."[10] Retinger drew up long lists of those he sought for the meeting, notably including those from the socialist Left.[11] No Americans were invited, though they might come as "observers" and only a "few" from Eastern Europe.[12]

Retinger was, unquestionably, the major figure in pre-conference efforts.[13] He sent the congress rules and guidelines to those who were to attend, and maintained a furious correspondence.[14] He gathered reports from the conference's committees in advance; they were all confidential.[15] The League, of which Retinger was secretary, dominated.[16] At the congress he was the League's representative regarding matters "cultural."[17] Technically, it was JICMEU, the umbrella organization for several movements that had organized the congress.[18] Days before the congress, Retinger outlined his plans to Allen Dulles. He shared with him the economic arguments already issued, and the inevitable perils of disunity. He referred to himself as the "founder" of ELEC and argued that this organization, plus a number of others, created JICMEU which had subsequently added participants. It was "private and independent organizations," not governments, which were necessary to pave the way for the effective unity of Europe.[19] The first important step in this was the upcoming Hague congress. Retinger invited Dulles to participate in the name of JICMEU as an "observer," and solicited his "advice."[20] Although Dulles could not attend, he said he had heard "a great deal" about the congress, and stressed the "urgency" of European unity.[21]

## The congress meets

On May 7–10. 1948 eighteen former prime ministers and twenty-nine former foreign ministers came to The Hague. There was even a German representative.[22] In all, there were 740 attending, a little fewer than anticipated, including both delegates and "observers."[23] Van Zeeland presided and Retinger was secretary. The conference underlined the essential role of solving basic economic difficulties first, barriers to commerce including customs, currency convertibility, coordination of economic development, and so on. De Rougement pointedly noted that for all its difficulties the conference was "accomplished...in a few months by an extraordinary moving spirit, the Polish citizen Joseph Retinger."[24] The only depressing note was the late decision of the British Labour Party to oppose the congress; nonetheless more than two dozen members attended despite their party's opposition.[25] Clement Attlee, the British Prime Minister, was convinced that European economic integration was not in Britain's interest.[26] Retinger tried desperately to convince Bevin to attend, but the latter feared Churchill's domination of the meeting.[27]

Despite this absence, Churchill gave a powerful speech, very reminiscent of his 1946 Zürich remarks which, unlike his earlier references, did not seem to exclude Great Britain from eventual participation.[28] Retinger later recalled that he wanted to counterbalance Churchill, so he invited Cripps and Bevin from Labour.[29] Regardless of behind the scenes politicking, de Rougemont insisted, "Everything began at The Hague."[30] There was even a dreadful "poème symphonique" written by Ernest B. Steffen to express favor for "European Unity."[31]

According to de Rougement the four basic themes undergirding the congress were "peace through federation," "suppressing the anarchy of sovereign states," a free European economy and the creation of a "spiritual community" based on Western civilization. The issue, he noted, of "common defense" was not discussed on purpose and was indeed rejected. Although he referred to the issue only in passing, it was apparent that he did not wish the congress to be dominated by the issue of unity in the face of the Soviet threat.³² The centrality of economics was ironic: Retinger neither liked nor understood economics.³³

In the weeks following the congress, Retinger and Sandys traveled about drumming up support. Subsequent international conferences, in Brussels, Lausanne, Rome, and Westminster, were indirect products of The Hague. After assembling a host of worthies from several countries to meet in December, Retinger decided on a preliminary unofficial meeting, very much his style and, as Pomian tells us, traveled all night standing and awake to reach Paris. This alone conveys Retinger's passion for the project, especially if we remember that he was old, tired, and not in good health.³⁴

There is a telling anecdote in Pomian's memoirs about Retinger's behavior at informal moments during these many preparatory meetings:

> He sat alone at a table, ordered a cognac with soda water and there occurred to him the notion of gathering a few people. To each of them he explained that his idea was so important that it would be better to keep it secret. Afterwards all of these would gather together in pleasant company, and he would go back to his chair alone, order another cognac with soda water and await the development of events.³⁵

He was, Pomian recorded: a superb inspirer.³⁶

## The American Committee on United Europe (ACUE) and the European movement

It was during the summer of 1948, shortly after the major success at The Hague, that Retinger, along with Sandys and Beddington-Behrens, came to the United States. The three Europeans acted in the name of the International Committee of the Movements for European Unity (JICMEU), and referred to themselves as the "International Coordinating Committee." They had meetings and the European Movement was aggressively marketed.³⁷ They discussed collaboration between the European Movement and a forthcoming American committee.³⁸ The three asked the Americans for $250, 000.³⁹

Retinger particularly impressed his European colleagues. His "friendships in high places were extraordinary." He was able to telephone President Truman and General Donovan directly and arrange immediate appointments, noted Beddington-Behrens.⁴⁰ Retinger met with Dulles on "several occasions," and also had a meeting with Fulbright. " ⁴¹ At a dinner on June 28, 1948 it was decided to organize the American Committee on United Europe (ACUE). Dulles would be "temporary" chairman to be succeeded by Donovan. Dulles told Fulbright that American actions regarding the European unity movement required a "review." He copied in Sandys and Kalergi. Kalergi's position had begun to "slip away."⁴²

Dulles also asked Fulbright to meet with him, stressing that there could be only one committee in the United States.⁴³ Fulbright agreed. This would eliminate Kalergi's nascent group which had been headed by Fulbright. Dulles argued that European union required "discreet pushing" from the Americans.[44] It was to clarify this issue that Dulles called this first, provisional meeting of the ACUE. He insisted that only American could join the new committee, which effectively ruled out Kalergi.[45] Dulles' intentions were clear.[46] He urged that Fulbright chair the new committee, but Donovan eventually emerged into this position.[47]

The result was the lucrative relationship with the emerging ACUE which had been in the planning stages since the previous April.[48] Former OSS stalwarts, CIA and NSC members were the founding fathers. Surreptitious CIA funding almost certainly began at once.[49] Members of the Committee were Dulles, George Franklin of the Council on Foreign Relations, and Thomas Braden also of the CIA as well as a number of other high-ranking members of the administration as well as union chieftains.[50] The ACUE was immediately sought by European federative agencies, including Kalergi's. Sandys wrote to Dulles and others and again asked for American money.[51] The Americans did not make the first step in funding the European unity effort.[52]

The ACUE did not convene its "preliminary meeting" until January 5, 1949, despite its origins a year earlier.[53] Dulles presided. He began by noting Kalergi's efforts of 1948 and the committee he formed under Fulbright's chairmanship. But, he announced, "certain things have happened" since then. "Re-examination" of the original plans was required. Dulles noted that JICMEU had "joined together" the major European unity movements at the Hague.

Kalergi had decided not to cooperate with what Dulles called the "Churchill-Sandys" movement. He had written Dulles repeatedly a few months before and argued that his organization had played "a very active part" at The Hague. He warned that The Hague movement was "at war" with the British Labour Party, while his movement had their cooperation.[54] He denounced Sandys and the European Movement as threatening to pre-empt the unity efforts and act, in reality, as a tool of London.[55] Dulles did not send a positive response. Donovan later sent Kalergi a rather blunt letter telling him that the ACUE had chosen the European Movement.[56] This disposition was doubtless aided when Churchill wrote to Donovan arguing the Marshall Plan was really an "unofficial counterpart" of the European Movement.[57]

## The Hague's accomplishments

De Rougement discerned several creations of the congress. First, the European Movement was born superseding JICMEU, on October 25, 1948. In April, Sandys, Retinger, and several others issued a memorandum, in the name of the European Movement, endorsing the idea of a European Council of Ministers and a European Consultative Assembly on the basis of the conclusions of The Hague meeting.[58] A "political commission" entitled the Council of Europe was founded by ten states on May 5, 1949 by the Treaty of London.[59] An associated court of human rights, and a consultative European Assembly at Strasbourg followed.[60] Churchill personally intervened to ask Donovan for American funds.[61] From this welter, the movement for European unity commenced. The original membership included Belgium, Denmark, France, Holland, Ireland, Norway, Sweden, Luxemburg, and Great Britain. As Pieczewski concludes: the European Council, the object of The Hague, was achieved: the "first institutional step" to the creation of supranational institutions in Europe. It was clear from the start that the council foresaw that the member states in the future must surrender a portion of their sovereignty. Since The Hague was the origins of the council we should attribute this insistence on the limitation on sovereignty to that meeting and thus to Retinger among others.[62] De Rougemont argued that the council led to a psychological stimulation and focus of the movement which "inspired" the proponents of "Europeanism."[63]

The council was thus a delayed child of the congress. Spaak, who became the first president of the council, credits Sandys and Retinger with the "most spectacular" preparatory task, the establishment of The Hague congress, an "astonishing success."[64] The accomplishments of The Hague caused Allen Dulles of the CIA to dump Kalergi in favor of the European Movement as a recipient of American money. The council openly described itself as the "heirs and Executors" of The Hague congress.[65]

The council reflected American European policy. Covert operations would further interdependent goals of European unification, a barrier against Soviet Communism, and a concomitant way to "solve the German problem." American money increased after 1949 and was probably two-thirds of the European Movement budget by 1952. This reflected Donovan's words to Walter Bedell Smith of 1949 that American financial support was crucial.[66] Donovan asked Retinger to provide him a report of European Movement activities along with similar reports from the other European Movement leaders.[67] Donovan referred to Retinger as someone who had "done so much to advance the cause of European union."[68] Retinger, according to Wilford, must have had a "pretty good idea" that these were covert CIA funds.[69] Indeed, he later admitted it.[70] Donovan would turn to Retinger to provide information about the European Movement's situation.[71]

Sandys stunningly attempted to "disband" the European Movement during the winter of 1949–1950. He misdirected American funds intended for the European Movement to a British organization to which the European Movement had become indebted.[72] Members of the European Movement were not immediately informed. However, Sandys was criticized for incompetence, and further American subvention was put at risk.[73] Sandys virtually begged the Americans for money immediately.[74] Donovan found the European Movement's situation "confusing."[75] The Sandys scandal, according to Braden of the ACUE, was "handled" by Spaak and Retinger:

They have succeeded in getting the promise of his resignation in July, found a minor honorary office in the Movement for him, and kept the whole fracas from reaching the public. They also prompted the decision of the European Movement Executive Committee, announced in the minutes of April 10, that 'all funds which may be forthcoming from the American Committee on United Europe will be used for the European Movement.'[76]

The Retinger-Sandys relationship was a curious one. However their relations at The Hague were probably not good and they were in a deplorable state soon thereafter. In the end, Retinger accused Sandys, the president, of corruption, incompetence, inaction, presumptuously acting without authorization, discourtesy, squandering, and, in general, having ruined the European Movement through neglect. His actions were "wholly unacceptable." He threatened to denounce him for his transgressions. Sandys in general accused Retinger of traveling too much and spending too much money.[77] By his own admission Retinger maintained an extraordinary travel schedule almost until the end of his life.[78] He admitted, in 1951, that he had "spent most of my time travelling around."[79]

Sandys insisted that Retinger resign, and Retinger swore he would because of the problems Sandys was causing. By 1950 Sandys was, according to Retinger, doing nothing. Moreover the Americans were suspicious of Sandys and the Labour Party would not cooperate because of him, Retinger insisted.[80] In 1951 Sandys let it be known that his Conservative Party would, like Labour, not support British cooperation in a European federation. Sandys had, in effect, severed his connections to the European Movement.[81] The matter became personal and Retinger called his adversary "unfair, immoral, and [a user of] bad tactics." They each asked the other to resign.[82] Sandys also, most importantly, seemed to have a change of heart regarding the effects of European unity on Great Britain.

Efforts by Retinger to convince the British to play a part failed. The "United Europe Movement [the British branch of the European Movement] has been paddled into a quiet back-water where it makes no effort and is completely ineffectual." It was also broke.[83] British refusal to be an active participant had devastating consequences for the Council for Europe.[84] American funding declined.[85] Retinger was very critical of the council's inaction, the executive committee as it were of the movement, which seemed to be unable to achieve any practical results.[86] It was a crisis for the movement.[87]

Retinger toured Europe in 1950, visited twelve countries and met with forty leaders asking each what could be done next. He combined their answers as a compendium of letters sent to the American committee.[88] Most of the responses were lofty and avoided clear answers or a definite program. Spaak laid out a five part program for immediate action, Van Zeeland urged haste, Bevin, contrariwise, preached caution, as did the Italian Prime Minister de Gasperi, and Foreign Minister Count Carlo Sforza, and Finn

Moe the Norwegian parliamentarian.[89] The others indulged themselves in lofty rhetoric or vague formulations.[90] The collection of statements endorsing the idea of European unity, which Retinger gathered, had a practical motive: to convince the Americans that Europe has a "sincere determination to achieve unity," or Marshall aid would be cut,[91] hence the propagandistic collection. Retinger was, though doubtless not acting on his own initiative, trying to link the United States and Europe more closely, something that characterized his thought and action after the war and with increasing passion as time passed. He even appeared at a press-conference with Donovan and Braden.[92]

A "political reorganization" of the European Movement was decided. Retinger was given $6000 to make the necessary changes including moving the center of activities to Brussels from London and Paris. [93] In justification of this expenditure The Hague conference and the creation of the Council of Europe were cited.[94] Sandys was ousted. In the interim the ACUE paid the European Movement's expenses. A separate sum of $3000.00 was granted to the European Cultural Center, the creation of the European Movement [95] Donovan referred to the European Movement in 1951 as "the overall organization representative of almost every private group in Europe working for unity."[96] Thanks to Spaak's leadership, and American money, the European Movement had recovered by 1951.[97]

American interest in the ACUE was a mixture of both selfishness and hope for the future. As Hugh Wilford explains, the ACUE's federalism heralded a continent "made over in the image of the United States." Federation, moreover, would mean a "more rational and efficient Europe which would reduce the need for American assistance, as well as "containing German militarism and Soviet expansionism."[98] These goals had been adumbrated by both Retinger and Sikorski during the war. Indeed, as Aldrich has noted, the ACUE, and American policy in general were less the product of CIA strategy than the activation of a network of contacts created during the war. In such networks, Retinger was experienced and impressive.[99]

Thus American intelligence agencies, functioning under the umbrella of the ACUE, funded the European Movement to the tune of 3 million dollars between 1949 and 1960.[100] It was Kalergi, according to Aldrich, who was the first to interest the American in the federalist vision of Europe and first, notably, to arrange secret American financing for the idea.[101] Kalergi's success proved ephemeral. The Americans found him difficult to work with, a common complaint, and re-directed their support to the European Movement, with its titular leader, Churchill, with Retinger as secretary-general.[102] The money had originally been given to Sandys to dispose of. This was probably the source of the later bitter relations between Retinger and Sandys.[103]

The second Hague creation was an economic commission to discern common interests. De Rougemont claims that the European Coal and Steel Community of Robert Schumann and Jean Monnet was "accepted" as was the later Common Market.[104] The implied relationship to the Hague meeting is problematical. "Acceptance" certainly does not convey creation.

Finally, based on Retinger's proposal, a rather amorphous cultural commission was announced to be based in Strasbourg.[105] Salvador de Madariaga led this body. A "study office" was created in Geneva to plan for the center in February 15, 1949. After some delay, the European Conference of Culture was opened in Lausanne. It was particularly important to Retinger.[106] Its membership was limited to corporations of public law, international organizations, cultural institutions whether national or otherwise, people representing European bodies and (here we see Retinger's fingerprints) people from the world of culture who had contributed signal service to the European cause. The announcement went on to discuss organizational matters: how the conference would fulfill its mission, and how it would organize its activities. Retinger had attached high hopes for American funding for this effort, but was repeatedly rebuffed.[107]

This rather elaborate plan-housed in a humble office met in Geneva in June 1950. The meeting was organized by de Rougemont and Raymond Silva and was presided over by de Madariaga and a number of members of the cultural department of the European Movement. This included Retinger, listed as representing Poland, and described as "secretary-general" of the European Movement. There were six others who took part in the meeting.[108] Retinger became the Honorary Secretary of the Executive Committee.[109] The European College at Bruges was its crowning achievement.

## The Hague and the European movement in retrospect

The Hague, according to Spaak, was the turning point in the history of the postwar pan-European movement, "an Historic landmark in the annals of Europe." The Hague produced the European Movement, the basis for all subsequent efforts at European federation.[110] De Rougemont concluded:

> The European Movement was to become, during the next three or four years, not so much the vanguard of federalism, but rather the indispensable link between this vanguard and the authorities, i.e., the governments, parliaments, politicians and financial circles.[111]

The Hague was the culmination of Retinger's views going back to World War I.[112] Even Kalergi proffered a tentative merger with many conditions.[113] Probably its central creation was

> A historic-political movement which had been at the nadir of its hopes two years earlier was close to achieving political success in Western Europe...Its development was similar to that of all great historical movements. Individuals in pre-war days had first evolved the idea; later private groups and associations had championed it despite all set-backs;

now at last the movement had gained the support of all or most of the parties; the appointed channels of political opinion, and through them the realization of the European idea was in sight.

The European Movement was designed to pursue, according to a report by André Philip just a handful of goals:

> Our aim is to form a European Community: an economic community through the establishment of a single market comprising a number of unified institutions ... a military community through the creation of a unified army; a political community to control the other two.[114]

These were, of course, gigantic plans, obscured by succinct language. Loth summarized the significance of The Hague meeting.

> A representative body of European statesman and persons of influence was mobilized in favour of unity. ... The Hague Congress pointed the way towards the first great objective of the integrationist cause: an international assembly of parliamentarians to discuss the structure of a European community and prepare the way for its creation. ... After this success the Co-Ordinating Committee enlarged its scope to become the European Movement, to which all Europeanists associations were affiliated.[115]

It was, as Retinger modestly noted, "one of the great events of history."[116] It deserved "a decisive place in the evolution of a united Europe, and Retinger was at the heart of this process."[117] Perhaps most appreciation was voiced by Retinger's secretary, Pomian:

> A radical new order was defined and launched at a three day, non-governmental Congress organized at the Hague...while Joseph Retinger did much of the spade work, it was Winston Churchill who provided the inspiration, the political caution and the attraction. This ...Congress proved to be the 'Big Bang' which led to the creation of the E.U. and changed forever the course of European history.

Nonetheless, he concluded, Retinger has been forgotten, and Churchill's role all but ignored in Great Britain for political reasons.[118]

After The Hague, the European Movement organized the "Westminster Economic Conference" in London in April, 1949. The conference, expectedly, called for "European Economic Union" as its first resolution.[119] The first honorary presidents of the movement were, Spaak, Churchill, Léon Blum, and Alcide de Gasperi, and the vice-president was a British Liberal nominated by Churchill. The prestigious officers gave the European Movement access to powerful European leaders. Retinger played no visible role.

As far as the movement's American supporters were concerned Retinger was more than just the secretary-general. It was, in words addressed to him in a public document by Donovan,[120] "your guidance ... [that] has done so much to advance the cause of European unity."[121] Retinger responded with a brief outline of the movement since The Hague meeting to the creation of the Council of Europe. For his part, Donovan raised private money for what he deemed the "coming United Europe" inviting, for example, wealthy New Yorkers to a dinner at which: "There will be an opportunity for all of us to pledge our financial aid to the work of the American Committee on United Europe."[122]

## The Schumann Plan and the origins of the European Union

Economic issues resulted (1951) in the European Coal and Steel Community (ECSC) created by French Foreign Minister Robert Schumann and Jean Monnet by the Treaty of Paris,[123] and the Common Market began to appear. Originally intended to embrace "all free Europe," the Coal and Steel Community added Great Britain as an "associate member" in 1954. Others also joined. A series of subordinate organizations were formed. The ECSC had lofty goals including bringing Germany back into the European community of nations, creating supranational blocs, preventing war between member states; and laying the groundwork for a European Union. The role of the European Movement in the Schumann Plan is not clear, but it certainly reflected its overall aims. This is embodied in the Schumann declaration which "implied a partial transfer of sovereignty from the participating countries."[124]

The European Movement was very concerned about the Schumann Plan which one of its members described as a "slender structure" preserving the "façade of unity" and totally incapable of inspiring "loyalty and confidence in the event of Russian aggression."[125] In fact the Schumann Plan was the direct precursor of the European Union which largely eclipsed the European Movement and rendered it incidental. It was practicality's victory over lofty ideas.

Leaving the ECSC, in 1955, Monnet founded the Action Committee for the United States of Europe in order to revive European construction following the failure of the European Defense Community (EDC). It held its first meeting the next year and was dominated by labor leaders and members of the political Left. Along with the Bilderberg group, of which much more later, and the European Movement, these three were the "most important transnational elite groups emerging in the 1950s."[126]

## The European movement and commission for Central and Eastern Europe

Retinger was mindful of the absence of the East Central European Communist bloc countries from the council. Hence he created a "commission for Central and Eastern Questions" functioning inside the European Movement with the goal of eventually including Eastern Europe in its ranks.[127] In April, 1949, Retinger met with Harold Macmillan, Behrens, and several leading émigrés from the Eastern Europe. It was at this meeting that the commission was formed as a special committee for eastern affairs under the umbrella of the council.[128] Macmillan was its head.[129] Retinger, in addition to being credited as founder, served as honorary treasurer. The Central and East European Commission was, "particularly close to his heart." [130] Pomian was the secretary based in Paris and perhaps its most active member. Lord St. Oswald, an obscure member of the House of Lords, was the leader in London. Retinger seemed to be less involved as the years wore on, due perhaps to his declining health.

The organization was financed by private contributions from Great Britain, France and Belgium including personal contributions from Behrens. It had no office, and all members were unpaid volunteers.[131] The goals were cooperation among émigrés with the European Movement, and to popularize the idea of continental unity among these peoples. From this initial stage, it became a spokesman for the countries behind the Iron Curtain so that they did not disappear from the European agenda. In the words of the commission, it was to "propagate the idea of European unity" in Eastern Europe and to help "exiles" to "participate in the movement for European integration." The secondary goal was to "provide a suitable political platform for the exiles in Western Europe, and to help them to maintain contact with the Western political leaders."[132] Its "Political Declaration" stressed that when the countries of Eastern Europe regained their independence they would be "unconditionally" be accepted.[133] Each member nation had seven representatives. Despite its small budget, the commission was active in organizing meetings and conferences and acting as an advisory body, a kind of organizational Retinger.

He was able to convince a number of West Europeans to serve as well as representatives from ten countries of the region including the Baltic States. A number of members were well known in émigré circles and included, the Poles, Raczyński, and the Czech Ripka. A series of presidents followed, with Retinger acting as "honorary treasurer," a typically modest position. The secretary, Pomian, did not act without Retinger's consultation, which Pomian himself acknowledged.[134] It was Retinger's energy and contacts that propelled the commission. Up until 1952 none of the European Movement sessions was devoted to Eastern Europe. That year, in London, Retinger gave his last speech before 7,000 deeming the Commission as devoted to "peaceful and constructive" activities. A "Political Declaration was issued endorsing the inclusion of the Eastern European nations in a future united Europe.[135] The enthusiasm was short-lived, always poor, and the commission broke apart. Retinger and Pomian resigned and only sporadic and unofficial gatherings continued.[136] Retinger regretted the lack of British participation, and the long periods of inactivity of the commission.[137] The Czech, Jan Stránský, described, in May 1953, the commission as being in "sad shape" and "unable to survive without Retinger."[138] Pomian confirmed this dismal observation, noting that the commission was moribund, and adrift from the European Movement, and from Retinger. Pomian predicted its death in a matter of months.[139]

Not to be vanquished, Retinger by force of will re-constituted the commission. After the 1953 disaster the commission went on to accomplish what Pieczewski deems "much useful work," especially in the cultural field, but by issuing economic and other studies. In Westminster, a fairly large meeting was held with forty Western European participants lasting three days. It was trying to re-assess the commissions' goals after the death of Stalin.[140]

The commission, never a major focus of the European Movement, nonetheless played a role in reminding Europe that its east was part of the continent. Some members tried to expand the commission, including Germans and other non-Easterners, even an American and Retinger was opposed. Fears of American money capturing the commission were voiced by some members and the example of the "captive nations" organization was cited as a precedent.[141]

At the beginning of 1952, Retinger circulated a very lengthy "Report" analyzing the past and future of the European Movement. He was very critical of the progress of the movement after the success of The Hague. Although there were many causes, economic difficulties were the most significant, though these, he noted, seemed to be on the mend. Retinger suggested a reorganization of the European Movement because it was "in danger." The whole movement must be restructured. Contact with the "masses" must be undertaken as part of a "propaganda" campaign. Nonetheless, he was optimistic. It was time for "political plans." But first a "not very pleasant" analysis of the present state was required.[142] Although war was unlikely in 1952, "exhaustion and helplessness" would characterize Europe, harming the process of unification.[143]

Retinger's analysis was lengthy. The Council of Europe, envisioned as the "keystone" was not effective. This was due to the lack of support from many governments. Indeed, some were opposed to the very idea of European unity. Even more important was the lassitude of Western European governments. Their "bureaucracy" opposed any basic changes."[144] The Council thus could not play its intended role. Thus the very idea, which Retinger credited to Churchill, Van Zeeland, Spaak, de Gasperi, Brugmans, de Madariaga, and himself was in "difficulties." The founders were "responsible."[145]

This was more the pity because unity was "part of the logic of history" and "the only way of saving Europe economically." It also enjoyed general support from the European population. It was time for "energetic activity" in light of the gloomy forecast. To this end, he made a number of "proposals." There must be a "complete change of structure" of a more aggressive kind, "a surrogate for what a supranational European Government will ultimately contain." A kind of "shadow government" must be created of several departments to prepare "procedures" for the future. [146] This would require study and reorganization. Currently, most of the "national councils" were moribund.[147]

To make all these changes, more money was needed. Private backers, as had been the case of The Hague conference, would not suffice. In addition to aid from "great capitalists," "Governmental financial support" was necessary.[148] "Finally, there are the Americans." Heretofore they had only contributed 15 percent of the European Movement's costs, a problematical figure. The problem was getting more without "placing ourselves in their power." We must be "an equal partner." Eisenhower, Retinger added, agreed. In conclusion, Retinger rendered "today" his "irrevocable resignation as Secretary General."[149] As a result, he was appointed by Spaak to the less arduous position of "General Delegate for External Relations."[150] His position as secretary-general was assumed by Georges Rebattet who had been his deputy.

Many reasons have been suggested for his decision including the long-standing feud with Sandys. Despite his resignation, Retinger continued to play an occasional role in the organization. Witkowski is probably correct that by this time the European Movement had reached the level of intra-government relations, private actors, like Retinger, had lost their usefulness.[151] Lane and Wolański offered another argument:

> Retinger resigned...because the Movement had begun to break away from the general principles of the Hague Congress. He criticized it for supporting the ECSC [European Coal and Steel Community] and the proposed European Defense Community (EDC) to the almost complete exclusion of all other activities. There was no propaganda or information put out 'which had any bearing on Europe as a whole.' 'We must return he said 'to the general programme and tactics of 1948.'[152]

We can sense a feeling that the Pole saw his the homeland being left out in these comments. It was perhaps time for something different.

## Retinger and the Youth Commission

Once the infrastructure was laid, the European Movement dreamed of mass European support. The United States had collected substantial European funds due to the Marshall Plan and Retinger thought a "good cause" could tap into these funds. John McCloy was the American High Commissioner for Germany and working with him was Sheppard Stone. Robert Murphy was the American ambassador to Belgium and an old friend of Retinger's and a supporter of the European unity movement. All were well-disposed towards Retinger's notions.[153] In 1958, the Movement created the "Youth Commission" (Commission de la Jeunesse) with about eight members in leadership positions, including Retinger.[154] The president of the commission was Robert Schuman. In 1958 the commission made a huge effort to recruit youth including the issue of a massive amount of literature.[155]

Spaak joined the talks. McCloy, was "heavily involved in American psychological and covert warfare, immediately recognized the importance" of "mass propaganda campaigns among the European youth." He turned to Retinger. Retinger, Spaak and André Phillip decided to "map out the profile of the European youth campaign."[156] The European Movement was given substantial funds which allowed for a continent-wide youth movement in favor of European unity.[157] ACUE monies were directed towards this effort.[158] American funds were only slowly replaced by European monies. The ACUE was, according to a sharp critic, the founder of "instruments imperialists."[159] Retinger later admitted that the Americans provided "big subsidies" for the youth movement.[160] The efforts were, initially, successful:

By the end of 1951 almost every organized youth group in Western Europe had formed

> national councils of youth groups and elected representatives to a European Parliament of Youth. From the Parliament a six man committee was designed to work with the European Movement in a unity campaign to inform the masses of European youth of their obligations to themselves and the Free World.[161]

The "European Youth Campaign" was a failure. It tried to be all inclusive and became a "one-party" rather than a "democratic institution." Retinger made the disturbing observation that "We only want that section of European Youth capable of militant action, which can understand the importance of building European unity." They did not want "millions of morons," but "hundreds of thousands ...of combatants."[162] They wanted to "penetrate the minds" of the vast majority. This shows Retinger's elitism very starkly.

This ultimately raises the question about secret American financing of the European Movement in general. Ambrose Evans-Pritchard argues that "in the Fifties and Sixties" the "US intelligence community funded and directed" the movement via the ACUE. He observed Donovan of the American Committee and the OSS as the principal agent here.[163] The CIA's Allen Dulles and Walter Bedell Smith late of the OSS were also key actors. Other sources mention Frank Wisner and Tom Braden. The ACUE, according to Pritchard, provided, for example, 53.5 percent of the movement's funds in 1958. The ACUE not only provided funds, it also pressured the British to be more cooperative with the European Movement's agenda. American surreptitious funding caused Retinger considerable concern and led to controversy. This did not mean that Retinger was personally profiting from his relations with the Americans. He lived in poverty and depended on the generosity of friends. His travels were fantastic. Pomian, his secretary, regarded it as "unthinkable" that Retinger received American or other governmental funds. However, whereas he did not profit personally from these sources they certainly financed his activities.[164]

Whereas these specific charges cannot be verified, we know that Retinger worked closely with American intelligence directors for a number of years.[165]

Because ACUE support could not be openly admitted as it would provoke anti-American sentiment, a lot of the money came via the Ford or Fulbright Foundation, as well as covert sources. British opposition to the European Movement ultimately caused American funding to stop. But, after a couple of years, Retinger moved on to a new adventure, the Bilderbergs.[166]

## From political to religious Union[167]

From its inception, the European Movement was fascinated by the notion of religious union, something in which Retinger put much faith. He had long-standing but never explained, connections with the Vatican. Indeed, Sandys asked Retinger to arrange a "private audience" for him with the Pope.[168] Retinger was able to arrange the support of the Vatican and interest a number of Catholic dignitaries in The Hague meeting. The Vatican sent a nuncio, later Cardinal – Fernando Cento.[169] There were also leading Protestants involved. Congregational minister and Labour politician Gordon Lang was honorary secretary of the European Movement. The idea of building the movement according to Christian principles was an issue of much discussion. Retinger tried to create a Christian basis that would have the support of the various churches. Despite his best efforts, and the help of Van Zeeland, Retinger, for all his intelligence, could not find a means of injecting principles which would satisfy the membership.[170]

He sought support of prominent Catholics and Protestants. "It is very important," he wrote "to have the religious forces on our side in the long run."[171] He first turned to Cripps and Lord Halifax who were prominent figures in the Anglican Church and member of Christian Action.[172] Cripps told him to meet with Canon John Collins of St. Paul's Cathedral who had a reputation for bold action. But finding a corresponding voice in the Vatican was more difficult. The contact was Dr. Luigi Gedda, Pius XII's personal physician and good friend as well as a power in the Christian Democratic Party, and the Catholic Movement in Italy.[173] Gedda was, incidently, the recipient of CIA funds.[174] The two arranged for Collins to go to the Vatican for an initial meeting in May, 1950. There was even an ad hoc committee for the Catholic Secretariat to work in conjunction with the Council of Europe, but it seems to have played a very minor role.[175] The Vatican had made only a few positive remarks about the value of European federation.[176]

They met with the future Pope Paul VI, Giovanni Montini. The meeting concluded that, should a working agreement be reached, the next step would be a meeting with Geoffrey Fisher the Archbishop of Canterbury in hope that his support would encourage other Protestants to join the movement. Retinger had already established good relations with the Irish Church hierarchy.[177] The Montini meeting was highly secret and even Pomian knew virtually nothing of its contents other than the fact that Retinger returned "delighted" (uradowany). The Pope expressed his support for the unity movement. Retinger boasted of support from Catholic circles in several countries, notably France.[178] He later claimed to have met the Pope, but it is not clear whether he was referring to this occasion or not.[179] It was, as Pomian notes, too early for ecumenism.

By late June, 1950, there was to be another meeting including a private audience with the Pope. Unfortunately, after the required lapse of time, the atmosphere had changed and the Vatican was disinclined if not hostile to further meetings. Retinger "never discovered what had happened."[180] Whereas Van Zeeland continued his efforts, Retinger gave up and the effort collapsed. Pieczewski blames opposition from the Archbishop of Canterbury.[181] Mierzwa claims it changed Retinger's attitude towards the Church for the worse.[182] In any event, a meeting was held in which, *sauve que peut*, Retinger and Jean Drapait along with three Italians representing the European Movement planned to organize "une soirée d'information sur l'Europe." It was to discuss European unification "from the Catholic point of view." The Vatican decided to keep distant from the various European unity movements and not adopt a position regarding the proper "form" of the movement.[183]

## Notes

1 Retinger to de Rougemont, March 29, 1948, Archives historiques.
2 Ibid. Retinger started soliciting broad support almost immediately after the Congress closed; see the untitled letter (in French) nd, signed by Retinger on the stationary of "Comité international de coordination des mouvements pour l'Unité Européenne," Archives historiques.
3 Ibid.
4 Ibid.
5 Mackay to Dalton, July 14, 1948; Mackay to Sandys, April 13, 1948; Mackay to Retinger, April 13, 1948. Mackay Papers, LSE, folder 6/1; Retinger to E. Shinwell, February 13, 1948, ME 694, HAEU; Morgan Phillips to Retinger, March 24, 1948, ME 694, HAEU.
6 See the following letters by Retinger, all in Archives historiques: to Emmanuel Shinwell, February 13, 1948; undated letter on The Hague Congress; to Guy Mollet, April 15, 1948; to Morgan Phillips, March 10, 1948; as well undated and un-addressed letters.
7 Retinger to NN, April 15, 1948, Archives historiques.
8 "I'm travelling throughout Europe in my international work he wrote to an old friend; see Retinger to Natalja Drohojowska, March 2, 1948; Retinger Papers. Box 19, folder D, BPL. For Retinger's recruitment efforts see "Aide Memoire for Dr. Retinger," Retinger Papers, December 30, 1947, Box 17, BPL. A close observer of Retinger's activities is Denis de Rougemont. See his "A Biographical Sketch,"44–45. Other sources give the attendees as numbering only 600; see "Churchill Bids Europe Unite to Avoid Impending Perils," *New York Times*, May 8, 1948, 1.Pieczewski says both 750 and 800; see his *Działalność*, 84, 149. Witkowski suggests 800; *Ojcowie*, 115. For the financial backers of the Congress, see Pomian, *Retinger*, 262.
9 Pomian, 198–199. Apparently Retinger was dunning Van Zeeland for expense money and the latter had to plead poverty; see Box 17, "European Movement: Finances," Retinger Papers, BPL.
10 Spaak, *Continuing Battle*, 202.

11 See "European Movement: National Council," a correspondence file in Retinger Papers, Box 17, Retinger Papers, BPL. Retinger to Morgan Phillips, nd. March [?], 1948, Archives historiques.
12 Retinger to Lippmann, April 1, 1948, ME 177, HAEU.
13 Andrzej Pieczewski, "Komisja do Spraw Środkowej i Wschodniej Ruch Europejskiego (1949–1973) – głos emigracji w sprawie europejskiego zjednoczenia." Available at the Akademia Ekonomiczna in Kraków (hereafter AE). Sandys was also most active; see Sandys to Nelson Rockefeller, August 11, 1948, Dulles Papers, Box 51, f. 1
14 All last-minute telegrams from delegates were to be sent to him; see Retinger, "Congress of Europe," April 23, 1948, ME694, HAEU.
15 Retinger to Lippmann, April 1, 1948, ME 177, HAEU.
16 Edward Beddington Behrens emphasized Retinger's work regarding the European economy his principal accomplishment. However useful, the "European Movement" was "propagandist and political." See "Mr. Joseph Retinger," *The Times*, June 13, 1960, 12. A Polish scholar refers to Retinger as "the Polish Richard Coudenhove –Kalergi"; see the essay of that title by Marcin Święcicki, on-line at http://www.pro-europa.eu/index.php?view=article&catid=26%3Anotable&id=411%3As. Accessed on November 7, 2013.
17 "Répresentants de la L.E.C.E. aux commissions, July, 1948," ME 694, HAEU.
18 See the document "Congress of Europe," signed by Retinger, nd. Dulles Papers, box 3, f. 6.
19 Retinger to Dulles, April 15, 1948, Dulles Papers, box 3, f. 6.
20 Ibid.
21 Ibid.
22 Retinger, "Notes," 6.
23 The delegations were bizarrely concocted: 68 from Belgium, but only seven from much larger Spain; France 155, but Italy only 57; Poland 5, but smaller Czechoslovakia 10; the Saarland(!) 5; and other such oddities. See an analysis of the delegates in "Les délegations nationales. nd, Archives historiques.
24 Denis de Rougemont, "Europe Unites," on line at http://www.proeuropa.org/rougement.htm accessed June 16, 1999. Spaak was quoted as crediting Retinger and Sandys; for which see Terlecki, *Wielka awantura*, 144; cf. Lord Boothby, *My Yesterday, Your Tomorrow* (London: Hutchinson, 1962), 75. A good behind-the-scenes description of the Congress is de Rougemont, "Souvenirs de Denis de Rougemont," May 7.
25 Witkowski, *Ojcowie*, 113–114. See Retinger's efforts to induce the Labour members to attend: Retinger to M. Phillips, March 10, 1948 in Clemens A. Wurm, "Great Britain: Political Parties and Pressure Groups in the Discussion on European Union," in Lipgens and Loth, *European Integration*, 3:696–698. For a letter of militant opposition to the Hague Congress see Secretary Morgan Phillips to Leslie Hale, April 21, 1948, Archives historiques.
26 Podgórski, *Retinger*, 245. The British Labour Party even tried to persuade members of the continental left not to attend; Pomian, *Retinger*, 265.
27 Retinger quoted in Ibid., 266.
28 "Churchill Bids Europe," 1.
29 Retinger, "Winston Churchill," drawer 1, BPL.
30 De Rougemont, *Meaning of Europe*, 83.
31 Ernest B. Steffan to Retinger, April 3, 1948, Archives historiques.
32 "Europe Unites," 9–10.
33 See his "Domestic and External Politics," drawer 1, BPL.
34 Pomian, *Retinger*, 269–270.
35 Ibid., 276.
36 Ibid., 278.

37  Sandys to George Franklin, August 11, 1948, Dulles Papers, box 3, f. 6.
38  Sandys to Dulles, November 26, 1948, Dulles Papers, box3, f. 6.
39  Charles R. Hook to "My dear Mr. So and So," nd, Dulles Papers, box 4, f. 1.
40  Dorril, *MI6*, 466 where he quotes Beddington-Behrens.
41  Dulles to Fulbright July 7, 1948, Dulles Papers, Box 26, f. 24. Fulbright to Dulles, July 2, 1948, Dulles Papers, box 26, f. 24.
42  Dulles to Donovan, August 1, 1949, Dulles Papers, Box 17, f. 18.
43  Dulles to Fulbright, July 7, 1948; Dulles Papers, Box 26, f. 24.
44  Dulles to Kalergi, December 21, 1948, Dulles Papers, box 3, f. 6.
45  Kalergi phoned one of the committee's members to express his concern the morning of ther meeting; "Minutes of Preliminary Meeting.". Cf. Dulles to Arnold Zurcher, January 25, 1949; Fulbright to Dulles, February 12, 1949; Fulbright to Kalergi, February 12, 1949, Dulles Papers, box 3, f. 6. Fulbright was, effectively. "pushed out." See unsigned memorandum of February 17, 1949, Dulles Papers, box 3, f. 6; cf. Dulless to Fulbright, November 17, 1948, Dulles Papers, Box 26. f. 24.
46  "Minutes of Preliminary Meeting," Dulles Papers.
47  Dulles to Donovan, February 4, 1949, Dulles Papers, box. 3, f. 6.
48  Gijswijt, "Uniting the West. The Bilderberg Group, the Cold War and European Integration, 1952–1966," Ph.D. diss. Ruprecht-Karls-Universitat Heidelberg, 2007, 10. As late as 1951 Donovan was directing funds to the European Movement; the source is unclear; see de Rougemont to Retinger, February 21, 1951, ME 905–2, HAUE.
49  This is discussed in Hugh Wilford, *The CIA, the British Left, and the Cold War* (London: Frank Cass, 2003), passim. This information is repeated in Wilford to author, September 8, 2014.
50  Aldrich, "OSS, CIA," 185. See the "Note" in folder 79, of Retinger Papers, PISM, unpaginated.
51  Sandys to George S. Franklin, November 25, 1948, Dulles Papers, box 6, f. 3; Sandys to [Franklin], June 24, 1949, Dulles Papers, box 3, f. 7. Sandys also asked that American subvention be kept secret; see "Minutes of the Second Meeting of the Executive Committee," July 1, 1949, Dulles Papers, box 3, f. 7.
52  Aldrich, "OSS, CIA," 186.
53  "Minutes of Preliminary Meeting on the Organization on an AMERICAN COMMITTEE ON UNITED EUROPE," January 5, 1949, Dulles Papers. Box 3, folder 6.
54  Kalergi to Dulles, April 19, 1949; Dulles Papers, box 17, f. 18. Kalergi to Dulles, August 25, 1948, Dulles Papers, box 3, f. 6.
55  Kalergi to Dulles, November 30, 1948, Dulles Papers, box 3, f. 6. Kalergi denounced the European Movement as "violently opposed to him; Kalergi to Donovan, November 24, 1949, Dulles Papers, box 18, f. 17.
56  See the draft of Donovan to Kalergi, March 27, 1950, Dulles Papers, Box3, f. 8; Donovan and Dulles decided to give Kalergi a small amount of money to assuage him. See Dulles to Donovan, November 1, 1949, Dulles Papers, box 17, f. 18; cf. NN to Donovan, March 15, 1950, Dulles Papers, box 17, f. 19.
57  Churchill to Donovan, June 4, 1949, Dulles Papers, Box 12, f. 20.
58  Lipgens and Loth, "European Movement Deputation: European Consultative Assembly, 6 April 1949," *European Integration*, 4:399; "Creation de l'autorité politique européenne et des institutions spécialisées"; ADG 115, HAEU. Retinger signed for Poland.
59  Witkowski, *Ojcowie Europy*, 109.
60  De Rougemont, with his usual sarcasm, deems Retinger "the spiritual father but also the obstetrician of the Council of Europe"; see his "A Biographical

The Congress of Europe, 1948    267

Sketch," 45. For Strasbourg see "The Background," in *News from the American Committee on United Europe,* January 15, 1950. Dulles Papers, box 3, f. 8.
61  Churchill to Donovan, June 4, 1949, Dulles Papers, Box 17, f. 18.
62  "Plany zjednoczenia Europy I stworzenia związku państw europejskich," *Narodowiec,"* August 29/30, 1954 in Karol Popiel Papers, PIASA, folder 9.37.
63  Quoted in Pomian, *Retinger,* 281.
64  Spaak, *Continuing Battle,* 201. Retinger apparently invited Spaak, Churchill, Blum and Gaspari to become "Presidents of Honour of the European Movement; see Sandys to Spaak, September 12, 1948, Duncan Sandys Papers, Churchill College Archives, Cambridge University, Box 1 (hereafter CCA). It is unclear who chose these names or upon whose initiative they were invited, Retinger or Sandys; the implication is that it was Retinger. Their letters of acceptance are filed with the Sandys Papers in Box 1, CCA. See also the undated memorandum by Karol Popiel, "Rodzaje międzynarodowej współpracy," Popiel Papers, folder 9.37, PIASA.
65  "The Role of the European Movement in relation to the Council of Europe," Sandys Papers, Box 3, pt. 1, CCA.
66  Donovan to Smith, November 29, 1949, Smith Papers, Box 4, Dwight David Eisenhower Library [hereafter DDE].
67  Donovan to Retinger, December 20, 1949, Smith Papers, Box 4, DDE.
68  Donovan to Blum, Churchill, de Gasperi, and Spaak, December 20, 1949, Smith Papers, box 4, DDE.
69  Wilford. *The CIA,* 230.
70  Aldrich, "OSS, CIA," 211.
71  Donovan to Retinger, December 20, 1949, Dulles Papers, box 3, f. 7.
72  For details see Thomas W. Braden, "Confidential Memorandum," to Dulles, June 27, 1950, Dulles Papers, Box 3, f. 8. Braden though that Churchill supported Sandys which was "politically understandable" given British politics.
73  "Memorandum to General Smith," December 30, 1950, Smith Papers, Box 4, DDE.
74  Braden to Dulles, December 28, 1949, Dulles Papers, box 3, f. 7.
75  Donovan to Blum, Churchill, Alcide de Gasperi, and Spaak, December 20, 1949, Dulles Papers, box 3, f. 7.
76  Braden to Dulles, June 27, 1950, Dulles Papers, box 3, f. 8; Braden to Smith, July 6, 1950, Smith Papers, Box 4, DDE.
77  This brouhaha produced a considerable correspondence; see Retinger to Sandys, July 17, 1948; July 23, 1949; October 11, 1949; December 20, 1949 and March 12, 1950; Sandys to Retinger December 21, 1949 all in Retinger Papers, Box 4, f. 2. BPL; Aldrich, "OSS, CIA," 197.
78  [Oskar], "Notatka dot. Rozmowy z Retingerem," (September, 1957), IPN BU01136/69/D.
79  Retinger to Mrs. Imboden, May 18, 1951, ME 890, HAEU.
80  Melandri, *Les Etats-Unis,* 287.
81  William J. Donavan to Odlum, July 27, 1951.Odlum Papers, DDE.
82  Sandys to Retinger, nd; Retinger to Sandys, July 23, 1948; Sandys to Retinger October 11, 1949; Retinger to Sandys, March 12, 1950; Sandys to Retinger July 20, 1950; Retinger to Sandys, July 20, 1950; Retinger to Sandys, November 18, 1949; all in box 12, Retinger Papers, BPL.
83  Brian Goddard to Retinger, box 3, Retinger Papers.BPL; Aldrich, "OSS, CIA," 195ff.
84  This is discussed in Boothby, *My Yesterday,* esp. 70–92.
85  Aldrich, "OSS, CIA," 196ff.
86  The Council had two parts: a Consultative Assembly, rather large, and a smaller Committee of Ministers. It was this latter body which attracted Retinger's ire.

For the original organizational structure of the European Movement see Sandys Papers, nd, Box 1, CCA "The Grand Council" took precedence.
87  Aldrich, "OSS, CIA," 196.
88  Ibid., 9–10; cf. Retinger, "Introduction to the Work by Secretary General of the European Movement," February 10, 1950, Dulles Papers, box 4, f. 1.
89  Van Zeeland was an ardent proponent of European unity and his ardor occasionally led to "accents pathétiques," Chabois, *Paul van Zeeland*, 80.
90  See ibid., passim (9–75).
91  Ibid., 7.
92  Pierre Melandri, *Les États-Unis face a l'unifacation de l'Europe, 1945–1954*. Paris: Editions A. Pedone, 1980, 248–249.
93  "Annual Report" May 1952, ACUE, Smith Papers, Box 4, DDE.
94  Ibid.
95  Ibid., regarding the center see de Rougemont to Hoffman, June 25, 1951 in ME 205-2, HAEU.
96  Donovan to Owen J. Roberts, July 12, 1951; Smith Papers, Box 4, DDE.
97  Gijswijt, "Uniting the West," 10. By 1954 the CIA had provided the European Movement with $5.4 million, some of which may have come from the State Department.
98  Hugh Wilford, "Calling the Tune? *The CIA, the British Left, and the Cold War*. London: Frank Cass, 2003, 227.
99  See Sławomir Łukasiewicz, "Polish Federalist in the United States after 1940 and their Efforts to Influence American Policy towards Central Europe," where Richard J. Aldrich is quoted in Lane and Wolański, *Poland and European Unity*, 158.
100 Richard J. Aldrich, "OSS, CIA and European Unity: The American Committee on United Europe," *Diplomacy and Statecraft*, Vol. 8, No. 1 (March, 1997), 184–185.
101 Aldrich, "OSS, CIA," 190.
102 Ibid.
103 Ibid., 194.
104 De Rougemont, *Meaning of Europe*, 83–84. De Rougemont was somewhat unhappy that the Common Market was attributed to Monnet and not as a derivative of The Hague; see his *Meaning of Europe*, 119.
105 "Europe Unites," 9–10; Mierzwa, "Polish Link," 253.
106 Witkowski, *Ojcowie*, 128. For the European Movement's Conference of Culture" see "Conférence Européenne de la Culture,"ADG 115, HAEU.
107 Dana S. Creel to Rougemont, nd; David Rockefeller to Retinger, September 13, 1954; Retinger to Berle, Gross, and Dulles, October 3, 1953; box 4, file 3, BPL.
108 "Création d'un Centre européen de la Culture a Genève," issued in Berne, June 28, 1950, in Documents Diplomatiques Suisses, o.B.64.101-TZ, Schweizerisches Bundesarchiv (hereafter SB).
109 See Hick, "European Movement," in Lipgens and Loth, *European Integration*, 4:420, 426. Great Britain insisted that the Council be virtually powerless and similarly they refused to take part in the European Coal and Steel Community (ECSC) negotiations preferring a close working relationship with the United States; see Wurm, "Great Britain," 628.
110 See the memorandum "The European Union" which includes the organization's constitution; see Sandys Papers, Box 1. Interestingly enough, there was apparently a brief moment when the European Movement was to be referred to as the European Union. That is the title used and later crossed out on the constitution; see Sandys Papers, Box 1, CCA. There are a number of printed versions of the constitution in this box.
111 De Rougemont, "A Biographical Sketch," 45.

112 On the first European Movement papers, Retinger is listed as the Polish representative on the "Reconuversance (?) des Conciles Nationaux," Sandys Papers, Box 2, part 1, CCA.
113 Kalergi to European Movement, February 6, 1949, Sandys Papers, Box 3, pt. 1, CCA. The European Movement immediately quizzed him on matters financial, how many votes he wanted and they needed the answers in five days; see Sandys to Kalergi, February 19, 1949, Sandys Papers, Box 3, pt. 2, CCA.
114 André Philip, "Europe and the United States [1951]," Smith Papers, Box 4, DDE.
115 Loth, "General Introduction," in Lipgens and Loth, *European Integration*, 3:4.
116 Retinger to Paul Ramadier, Archives historiques.
117 Sío-López, "Memories and Horizons," 33.
118 Pomian, letter to the author, September 14, 2014.
119 "European Economic Conference of Westminster, April 20– 25, 1949," in Dulles Papers, box 3, f. 7.
120 Donovan was, in 1950, the Chairman of the American Committee on United Europe. Its members included such worthies as Allen Dulles, and Francis Adams Truslow.
121 See Donovan's letter of December 20, 1949 in *American Committee of United Europe, The Union of Europe: Declarations of European Statesmen* (New York: American Committee of United Europe in Cooperation with the European Movement, nd), 5–6. This document was addressed, *nota bene*, to Retinger personally.
122 William J. Donovan to Floyd Odlum, May 3, 1952, Floyd Odlum Papers, ACUE, Box 1, General Correspondence Series, 1951–52. DDE; cf. Donovan to Odlum, July 27, 1951, in ibid.
123 The ECSC disappeared when the Treaty of Paris lapsed in 2002. Its institutions had been absorbed by the European Union.
124 Piotr S. Wandycz, "Regionalism," 247.
125 Brian Goddagar, United Europe Movement, to Retinger, February 16, 1953, Box 3, Retinger Papers, BPL.
126 Aldrich, "OSS, CIA." 186.
127 Retinger to Joseph E. Johnson, nd, box 26B. Retinger Papers, BPL; cf. NN to Pomian, July 21, 1949, ME 268, HAEU.
128 Macmillan was later replaced by Sir Beddington Behrens. For the members of the Commission, see Pieczewski, *Dzialałność*, 171–192; Pieczewski, "Retinger's Vision," 11ff.
129 The Commission included what were deemed "all nine captive countries": Albania, Bulgaria, Czechoslovakia, Estonia, Hungary, Latvia, Lithuania, Poland, and Romania. The omission of Yugoslavia and the DDR, and the presence of the Baltic states is notable, as is the alphabetical order: see "Note on the History and activities of the Central and East European Commission of the European Movement," Archiwum Komisji do Spraw Europy Środkowej I Wschodniej Ruchu Europejskiego (hereafter Archiwum Komisji), folder 2, UEK.
130 Pomian made this observation after Retinger's death; see Pomian to Bernhard, September 9, 1963, folder 10, Archiwum Komisji, UEK.
131 Archiwum Komisji, folder 1, UEK.
132 Ibid. Retinger to Grigoire Gaffencu, March 8, 1951, ME 890, HAEU.
133 Pieczewski, "Retinger's Vision," 15.
134 Pieczewski, "Komisja," 7.
135 Pieczewski, "Komisja," ibid.
136 Ibid., 10. See also the effort to hold a series of lectures at New York University at the latter's expense, NN [probably Feliks Gross] to Retinger, February 17, 1952, Archiwum Komisji, folder 1, UEK
137 Retinger to Jan Stránský, May 27, 1953, Archiwum Komisji, UEK folder 8.

138 Stránský to Pomian, May 18, 1953, Archiwum Komisji, folder 1, UEK.
139 Pomian to Stránsky, May 27, 1953. Archiwum Komisji, folder 1, UEK.
140 See "Note on the history and activities of the Central and Eastern European Commission of the European Movement in Archiwum Komisji," folder 2, UEK.
141 Étienne de la Valée Poussin to NN [probably Pomian], June 10, 1958; Archiwum Komisji, teczka 3. Anna Mazurkiewicz to author, July 12, 2014.
142 Retinger, "Report by the Secretary General," January 25, 1952, ME 297, HAEU, 1–3.
143 Ibid., 5.
144 Ibid.
145 Ibid., 3.
146 Ibid., 7–8.
147 Ibid., 8–10.
148 Ibid., 13–15.
149 Ibid., 17. His written resignation was shortly thereafter.
150 Retinger to Spaak, March 26, 1952 with other drafts.ME 261, HAEU.
151 Witkowski, *Retinger*, 120–121; idem., *Ojcowie*, 131.
152 Lane and Wolanski, *Poland and European Integration*, 114.
153 Pomian, *Retinger*, 217.
154 There was a European Movement youth congress held in Paris in 1953 arranged by Retinger and aided by a number of Polish exiles; the relationship of this meeting to the 1958 movement cannot be reconstructed save by saying it indicates Retinger's long standing interest in youth activities by the European Movement; see NN "Wyciąg z notatki informacyjnej z dn 23.IV. 1953r," May 8, 1953; IPN BU 01222/593/D.
155 See the box, number 11, entitled "European Youth Movement," folder "1958–1959" in Retinger Papers, BPL, Box 11.
156 Aldrich, "OSS-CIA", 207.
157 See Retinger's "Campagne de la jeunesse," "fin septembre 1956," Retinger Papers, Box 3, BPL; Retinger was at the center of fund-raising for the movement. Funds he solicited from, for example, the CFR, were sent directly to him; see, for example, Retinger to George S. Franklin, March 20, 1958; Reinger to Franklin, April 2, 1958, ME 485, HAEU.
158 See "Campagne europeenne de la jeunesse," [December 13, 1951], ME 1477, HAEU.
159 Luis M. González-Mata, *Les vrais maîtres du monde* (Paris: Bernard Grosset), 1979.
160 Retinger, "Confidential," September 18, 1957, Retinger Papers, box 25a, 8, BPL; cf. there is an unfortunately unreliable account which discusses Braden and the youth movement; see "The Atlanticist Tendency of the Labour Party: How the European Movement was launched: The CIA and the Labour Party-part 5," *Working Class Movement Library*, online at http://www.wcml.org.uk/contents/international/cold-war/the atlanticist-tendency-of-the-lab. Accessed on February 28, 2013.
161 Wilford, *The CIA*, 239.
162 Ibid., 10.
163 See Retinger to Harry B. Friedgood, October 10, 1951, ME890, HAEU.
164 Pomian to author, [August 3, 2014].
165 Ibid.
166 Sadowski, "Teczka amerykańska," 4–5.
167 Unless otherwise noted, this very mysterious episode in Retinger's life is reconstructed on the basis of the unpublished memoirs and recollections of his then secretary Pomian.
168 Sandys to Retinger, January 9, 1948, ME 177, HAEU.

169 Podgórski, *Retinger*, 297.
170 Pomian, *Retinger*, 215.
171 Quoted in Mierzwa, "Polish Link," 254.
172 Pomian, *Retinger*, 283–284.
173 Regarding Gedda see Marco Invernizzi, *Luigi Gedda e il movimento cattolico in Italia*. Milan: Sugarco Edizioni, 2012.
174 Aldrich, "OSS, CIA," 212.
175 Dujardin and Dumoulin, *Van Zeeland*, 156–159.
176 Aldrich, "OSS, CIA," 212.
177 Hederman, "Beginning of the Discussion," in Lipgens and Loth, *European Integration*, 3:783–785.
178 Witkowski, *Ojcowie*, 113.
179 Oskar, "Notatka," October 31, 1957, IPN BU 01136/69/D.
180 Pomian, *Retinger*, 216–217.
181 Pieczewski, *Działalność*, 87.
182 Mierzwa, "Polish Link," 254.
183 See Phillipe Chenaux, *Une Europe Vaticane? Entre le Plan Marshall et les Traités de Rome*, Brussels: Éditions Ciaco, 1990, 108–109.

# 14  The Bilderbergs

Although Retinger resigned as the European Movement secretary in 1952, he began a yet more grand enterprise, the bringing together on a regular basis of prominent people from *both* the United States and Europe. This informal arrangement appealed to Retinger's history and personality more than a large, public body which the European Movement had become. He was returning to the *eminence grise* status so often attributed to him, the "Talleyrand without portfolio."[1] Perhaps he was even the "sphinx" which Janta called him.[2] As Valerie Aubourg noted, Retinger's informal discussions with exile politicians during the war encouraged him to attempt a similar means to a greater end.[3]

The original motive that caused Retinger to undertake another movement for unity was the fear that an intellectual and perhaps political rift was beginning to emerge between the United States and Europe. What was needed was a means to establish closer relations between the two. He was deeply troubled.[4] The principal problem, he believed, was European distrust of the United States, and reciprocal distrust by the Americans.[5] "Off-the-record discussions" were his means of addressing the problem.[6] This represented a shift from his traditional concentration on European problems to a transatlantic orientation.[7]

In Retinger's words:

> A few years ago a large number of people began to feel anxious about a growing distrust of America which was making itself manifest in Western Europe and which was paralleled by a similar distrust of Western Europe in America. This feeling caused considerable apprehension on both sides of the Atlantic and in 1952 I felt that it was of the first importance to try to remove this suspicion, distrust, and lack of confidence which threatened to jeopardize the post-war work of the Western Allies.[8]

Retinger believed that "public opinion followed the example of influential people." Here we note echoes of Morel and his "Mafia" of the 1920s. With this in mind, he decided to assemble a group of the most significant actors he could find to "revivify the situation in Europe and America," a vague goal.

The first step was to "invite a team of leading Europeans to prepare a report on the causes of European anti-Americanism." It would then be sent to an American group for "critique." The third, joint report, would become the founding document for a "group" (which would come to be known as the Bilderbergs), "elite," and "anonymous."[9]

A number of preparatory meetings were held so that "concerns" could be "accommodated" "in privacy," by holding "off-the-record" discussions.[10] At the beginning of 1952 Van Zeeland and Paul Rykens, old friends, met with Retinger.[11] They were to be the "three European Fathers" of the Bilderbergs.[12] The problem was finding a group of suitably influential colleagues. Retinger choose as a titular leader Prince Bernhard of the Netherlands, a wartime acquaintance of his who had prestigious contacts throughout Europe and America and thus was a fine choice to be the public face of the organization.[13] Rykens arranged a meeting with the Prince who was enthusiastic.[14]

The four drew up a list if those to be invited to a secret international conclave. Retinger later asserted: "I am myself responsible for all the spadework of the group as a whole."[15] Retinger "revealed almost mystical faith in Atlanticism" and "the extreme importance he still attached to the mobilization of elite, as opposed to mass opinion."[16] This was a late conversion for Retinger whose mistrust of American hegemony in Europe was evident during the war.[17] The Bilderbergs grew out of the same overlapping networks drawn from the European Community and the Western intelligence establishment: sincere support and surreptitious funding. They were trying to recruit an American contingent for the group through American intelligence.

Grosbois has argued, too bluntly, that "the Bilderberg Group...was set up with CIA money."[18] American clandestine funding, Aldrich concludes, was behind the group.[19] By contrast, Gijswijt has concluded:

> The Bilderberg Group was essentially a European creation. The claim that the group was co-founded or financed by the CIA does not stand up to scrutiny. It is true that Retinger and Prince Bernhard both relied on their high-level government contacts in the United States – including subsequent CIA directors Walter Bedell Smith and Allen Dulles – but the Eisenhower Administration was at first uninterested in assuming an active role in the Bilderberg.[20]

The real answer is a combination of both arguments. The Bilderbergs were a European, essentially a Retinger, idea, but CIA money was present from the very beginning.[21] Major financial backers of the organization were the Ford, Rockefeller, and Carnegie Foundations; whether under CIA pressure or not.[22] British support via MI6 seemed more likely with former SOE director Gubbins as the link. Philipsen concludes that there were "close ties" with the SOE veterans.[23]

Both Retinger and Bernhard wanted to recruit Harold Macmillan, but he refused. Eden was considered, but his Cabinet position made him impossible to maintain the proper secrecy [24] He intended to speak to Churchill, but no record of a meeting exists.[25] Nonetheless, Prince Bernhard wanted him involved "off the record." Hugh Gaitskell would, however, join[26] as well as Gubbins from England. Retinger also rounded up his wartime colleagues and members of the European Movement, Van Zeeland, and Rijkens. There were also Italian, French, German, and Danish members.[27] At this point, the differences between this new un-named group and the early stages of the European Movement are almost impossible to distinguish. Retinger wrote endless letters and traveled constantly to organize the group. Each participant was asked to prepare quickly a brief report in anticipation of the first meeting.

The preliminary gathering was in Paris on September 25, 1952. Van Zeeland was in the chair, but Retinger spoke first and explained the reasons for the meeting. He had warned that the organizational efforts must be completed as soon as possible, because of the approaching American election.[28] He outlined the earlier preparatory "conversations." Then the group would meet again to consider it. The existence of the group would not be disclosed.[29]

The birth of the movement which this conclave would create was captured by Quaroni who deserves to be quoted at length. He notes that finally Retinger had within his grasp the agency he had long dreamed of:

> We were seated along a large table in a small room. We agreed regarding basic questions, but how to reach them, how to organize, to whom to turn, where to find sources of funds. All these matters were obvious. Ideas poured forth from Retinger like a burst from a machine gun. Not all were excellent ideas, to be sure, but when one idea was rejected, he had up his sleeve ten others. He was the only one of us who had studied the problems on both sides of the Atlantic and had definite answers in this regard. The old intriguer had such an appealing manner, that we agreed with everything that he wanted.[30]

Retinger had just founded, by force of planning, will, and persuasiveness a new worldwide body. What would soon become the Bilderbergs were born, though still without a name.

There was a second meeting, held in strict secrecy, equally preliminary, at Zbigniew Morawski's home in Paris; Morawski was the stepfather of Retinger's secretary, Pomian. The principal agenda item was again to improve European-American relations by bringing together elites.[31] Retinger again dominated the meeting. This is the more curious because Retinger was very averse to speaking publicly.[32] He made a lengthy presentation based upon the several reports he had earlier solicited from the participants.[33] It was subsequently circulated to those in attendance to emend.

The Retinger report stated that close European-American relations were "the only basis for the recovery of Europe and for its defense."[34] "Bitterness" by Europeans towards America were "a general and spontaneous reaction which is throughout Europe and growing 'rapidly'." The major powers resented playing "second fiddle" to the Americans. This resentment was not without reasons "which cannot be overcome." This was due in large part to the "progress" in the United States being paralleled by the "retrogression" of Europe. Moreover, Americans serving in Europe were paid more than Europeans, and, whereas a "Welfare State" was being built in Europe, "private enterprise" ruled in America.[35] Although these factors could not be "altered" they could be "mitigated." This included the "energy" reflecting American youth which the Europeans found aggressive and offensive. This led to "psychological misunderstanding,"[36] evidenced by the lack of intercourse between Americans in Europe and the local population. Many Americans stationed in Europe were "deplorable." European behavior was also often blameworthy. American interference in Europe had "disastrous effects." This reflected the fact that many Americans had anti-European attitudes that had reached "dangerous proportions."[37] Those Europeans genuinely pro-American are "distrusted by the general public."[38] American interference in European colonial territories was also often objectionable. America was not "accepting a responsibility proportionate to her power": Europe was unable to do its share because the power relationship was probably "7 to 1."[39] European-American trade also did not favor the former. While American commerce suffered no ill-effects from the war "the trade of the free countries of Europe has suffered beyond bearing."[40] There were thus many problems and their solution could only be found only in "mutual understanding."[41] The necessity of American leadership was acknowledged.[42] The result, he concluded, with great optimism, will be that problems, "without too much difficulty" will be "removed and forgotten."[43]

Closer relations with the United States was the central concern. They decided to create a "corresponding group" in the United States."[44] This would complement the "Committee of Vigilance, which the group designated itself. This new committee would be "permanent" and work year-long. It will be "indispensable." It was decided that Retinger should go to the United States.[45]

Retinger expanded his whirlwind activities working especially on the Americans, awkward during a presidential election year. Retinger came to the United States in November 1952 and met with members of the Truman administration, especially Averill Harriman as well as members of the incoming Eisenhower government. Prince Bernhard had met with Harriman after the Paris conclave, and Retinger soon after told him that members would "exercise our influence" to have the draft report implemented.[46] He requested Harriman to provide an American "counterpart" to the report, and asked to meet with him to discuss the nascent group in "complete secrecy." Prince Bernhard had already appointed the diplomat Walter Donnelly to act as liaison, and Retinger mentioned Drexel Biddle as well.[47] When Harriman procrastinated, Retinger told him that discord between Europe and America was "fast increasing" but that the Paris meeting had "well laid" plans.[48]

The incoming Eisenhower administration seemed more inclined towards energetic cooperation than had been its predecessor.[49] Retinger met with Bedell Smith, John McCloy, and the CIA's George Franklin, as well as the agency's incoming chief Allen Dulles, and provided him with certain papers and the names of his group's major actors which Dulles sent to his colleague, Thomas Braden, a major OSS-CIA operative close to Dulles. Retinger had already provided other materials for Braden.[50] In addition, Adolf Berle had several meetings with Retinger[51] As a result, Retinger considered his December, 1952 American trip "completely successful." Dulles and Bedell Smith promised to form a small committee. Soon however, Retinger's optimism faded.

It is here we come upon one of the most fascinating episodes of Retinger's life. On December 1, 1952 Retinger came to see Berle and the two had a long conversation.[52] Retinger was "pessimistic" about Europe, and broached the subject of the European Movement's "Central and East European Commission" working with the CIA's American National Committee for a Free Europe [NCFE]," of which Berle was a prominent member as well as being the director of Radio Free Europe (RFE). Retinger explained that his "commission" was not a product of British intelligence, but was privately funded, Behrens committing £2,000 and Sir Henry Price £1,000. The Foreign Office, indeed, had not been particularly cooperative. Churchill and Sandys were supportive, but contributed only "good will" as did Harold Macmillan and a former Churchill Cabinet member Richard Law. Retinger would even move the commission's headquarters from London to Paris to allay American suspicions.[53]

Retinger was concerned about "tension" between his commission and the American NCFE. Berle promised to work on the idea of a "joint working arrangement," and discuss it with his colleagues.[54] Berle considered the differences minor as "both the United States and Britain" wanted the Russians out of Central and Eastern Europe." The meeting, therefore, ended on a promising note. However, afterwards, Berle appended a fascinating note to his "Memorandum." He found that Retinger's commission had been independent of the Foreign Office and Intelligence up to three months before. That had all changed. Eden then "took responsibility for its operation." He was "taking control." He even informed Washington that he had done so. Berle did not know Eden's plans, but had suspicions that Retinger and Behrens "prefer to tie up their project with NCFE rather than fall under the control of the British Foreign Office."[55] This would explain Retinger's approach to Berle, and his rather abrupt announcement that his commission was not a creature of British intelligence. Berle suggested the need for a "high-level meeting" between the British and Americans to avoid "working at cross-purposes."[56]

The same day, Berle wrote to Admiral H. B. Miller reflecting on the situation. Retinger was, he concluded, telling the truth when he said his group was "not controlled by the British Government." But London somehow was guiding Retinger's commission "by remote methods." He told Miller that he wanted to discuss the issue.⁵⁷ That night, Berle made a reflective diary entry. Retinger was "my good friend." But it was unclear what he was seeking. He had not mentioned Eden's reported take-over. Hence, perhaps Retinger did not know of it Berle conjectured.⁵⁸

Was Retinger somehow working very closely with the British-surreptitiously? This was a fact he would not even disclose to Berle. Or, was it Eden who was acting in the darkness, manipulating a take-over of Retinger's commission without telling him? There is no answer. It does, however, underline the large, perhaps secret, role played by the British in Retinger's postwar plans for European unity.

But Retinger was not through with Berle. A few days later he called on him again with far larger plans, some of which crossed the line into secret activities. Retinger was carrying a letter from CIA Director Dulles. Berle, because of his relationship with RFE which was CIA funded, understood the meaning of this clearly. Besides, Berle and Dulles were close friends.⁵⁹ Retinger explained "a majestic scheme rigged up to deal with anti-American sentiment in Europe." He had gathered a group, the Paris Vigilance Committee no doubt, which had produced a document which Retinger gave to Berle. It had about ten names affixed to it including Prince Bernhard, Van Zeeland, and both Gaitskell and Lord Portal, "Winston Churchill's man," from Britain. A certain "Roykins" from British intelligence was also a signatory.⁶⁰

Retinger had already met with Harriman and told him that he wanted Berle and John McCloy of OSS-CIA fame to "report for America and then join him for a "secret meeting" in Paris. Harriman had directed him to the CIA's Dulles, who suggested he speak with Berle. This was probably the impetus of the Retinger-Berle meetings and explained the letter Retinger was carrying. Dulles said that was "alright with him" if Berle "wanted to get mixed up in it." Berle decided to speak with Dulles and had Retinger talk to the former Assistant Secretary of War, McCloy. Berle would act the next day.⁶¹

Berle was enticed but a bit suspicious: he wondered whether Retinger was acting for "personal promotion." This was not an unreasonable thought. Berle concluded that, ultimately, the British were behind it. London "would like to take over direction of all American activities in Europe." Here, Berle concluded that Retinger's "connections with British intelligence gave him easy access to that sort of operation." Despite this, Berle concluded that Retinger's plan was not "an invention of the devil."⁶² However, Berle decided not to work with Retinger: as "Director of RFE" he would be "an interested party" and hence must stay away.⁶³

This is a most intriguing episode in Retinger's mysterious links to intelligence. In 1952, he was obviously seeking to work with the CIA at the highest levels and was having some success. At the same time, it seems at least possible that the British, possibly intelligence, or even Eden directly, were also involved. Indeed, they might have been the *spiritus movens*.

Eden also had prior experience working with American intelligence.[64] But whether he told this to Retinger is a different matter, though it would seem most probable. Retinger might well have been working as a link between the governments, at least their intelligence operations.

Retinger's efforts to create an American branch of his new creation still did not proceed. The American group formed very slowly.[65] The Council on Foreign Relations refused to join, but urged him to send his report to the new Under-Secretary of State, Bedell Smith.[66] Harriman had provided no report by mid-January, and the CFR refused put in jeopardy the goal of creating an American counterpart.[67] Retinger wrote a pleading letter to Dulles saying that the situation was "alarming" and sent a similar text to Bedell Smith. Prince Bernhard and Van Zeeland met with Dulles and Bedell Smith, but nothing was happening and the Paris meeting of what would evolve into the Bilderbergs was almost one year old and no American counterpart existed.[68] There was a lack of urgency in the United States.[69] An "anti-American" attitude was rapidly building in Europe and it had reached the level of "psychological crisis." [70] In a note to himself, Retinger foresaw "profound political divergences" and the very security of Europe was at threat.[71]

Retinger's report was regarded as "controversial" by the Americans. Bedell Smith did not regard it as particularly important and passed the matter off to subordinates. Prince Bernhard approached Smith, though results were poor.[72] Smith was not particularly interested in the idea. Finally, the "American wing" of the Bilderbergers was created and led by C. D. Jackson, Eisenhower's "psychological warfare coordinator,"[73] who quickly passed the job on to John Coleman president of the Burroughs Corporation, and Joseph Johnson director of the Carnegie Foundation.[74] Gubbins, in the meantime, prepared a memorandum urging "immediate action."[75] Gradually, American participation increased. Those chosen constituted a "typical East coast elite organization."[76] However, many Americans refused and Prince Berhhard found the list unimpressive.[77]

Jackson mistrusted Retinger and regarded him as a British agent with ties to close with Gubbins.[78] Retinger was "desperate" because the Eisenhower administration seemed disinclined. In large part this was due to doubts about Retinger, Prince Bernhard's "Richelieu."[79] American suspicions about Retinger's British intelligence connections "severely complicated the initial American response. Without Prince Bernhard's frequent and insistent interventions in Washington, Retinger's initiative "would in all likelihood have died a premature death."[80] After months of waiting, nothing was done and Retinger said that the Paris Vigilance Committee was "very worried."[81] It was only later that Prince Bernhard thought that the Americans were "seriously getting to work."[82]

Eventually, twenty Americans attended the first official Euro-American meeting at the de Bilderberg Hotel (hence the name) at Oosterbeek, near Arnhem, the Netherlands in May, 1954.[83] Retinger had been the key to selecting the participants. His World War II efforts were the basis of his choices.[84] They were selected on the basis of "their experience, their knowledge, and their standing."[85] Invitation was to be considered as "private."[86] The CIA was particularly interested in the gathering "in view of Retinger's background and interest in this meeting." They concluded that the meeting's "outcome would bear watching."[87] Despite American interest, and CIA funding, the Americans were still suspicious of Retinger's relationship with the British.[88] American discontent over this issue was crucial because Retinger dreamed of "transatlantic" gatherings and the Americans were thus indispensable.[89]

It was "the most unusual international conference ever held."[90] Eighty attended, a wide variety of businessmen, intellectuals, union leaders, bankers and politicians, among others. Officially Prince Bernhard, but more significantly, Van Zeeland and Coleman ran the meeting. The scene was captured by Hatch, Prince Bernhard's official biographer:

> There was absolutely no publicity. The hotel was ringed by security guards, so that not a singular journalist got within a mile of the place. The participants were pledged not to repeat publicly what was said in the discussions. Every person present ... was magically stripped of his office as he entered the door, and became a simple citizen of his country for the duration of the conference.[91]

Retinger was designated secretary-general: "he was the motor of all activities."[92] He chose the agenda. The elite meeting was designed to consider how public opinion might be "favorably influenced," Retinger said, because "the proper task of private individuals is to try to move public opinion in their own countries as close as possible to that of the other countries of the Western Alliance."[93]

The Oosterbeek meeting had several main themes: "Communism and the Soviet Union," "dependent areas and peoples overseas," economic "policies and problems," and, finally, European integration.[94] All subsequent meetings had similarly broad issues to discuss.[95] The official "Final Report" of the first meeting was prepared by Retinger in conjunction with Gubbins.[96]

Retinger decided that there would be only "one or two short communiqués" avoiding details and keep the press out of the meetings, and that no speaker would be mentioned "by name," and the "substance" of the discussions would not be discussed. This was done to ensure "frank" conversations. From the outset, the Bilderbergs were "not to concern" themselves with "policy making." But rather to seek a "common approach to the major problems of the Western Alliance." Those invited would be more or less, "one-third politicians and one-fifth business men and trade unionists, the remainder being intellectuals, professional men, and other leaders of public opinion." "Younger people" were constantly being sought. There was no office except Retinger's "flat" and no permanent organization.[97]

The conference ended by partially ameliorating European-American antagonisms. The Americans were impressed by the first Bilderberg meeting and "urged Retinger and Prince Bernhard to continue their good work."[98] Nonetheless, Jackson still did not trust Retinger whom he regarded as "a lone-man brain trust, whipper-in, and *rapporteur* for Bernhard. Who would crawl out "at the most awkward moment" with "invisible sources of income." Jackson was convinced that Retinger was both untrustworthy and a British agent" probably also with attachment to the CIA.[99] At the first meeting the American delegation expressed rather harsh criticism of Retinger's prominent role, referring to him as a "professional promoter." This suspicion in dealing with Retinger also dates, no doubt, from his long history of serious differences with the Americans.[100] In any event, he did not resign and the issue seemingly was suppressed.[101]

Almost at once after the first meeting Retinger and Bernhard pressed for a second meeting in 1955, perhaps two. The Americans acquiesced after some reluctance about coming together again so soon.[102] The two decided to send reports to NATO and Supreme Headquarters Allied Powers Europe (SHAPE) to "create greater interest in their organization." The second meeting, in France in 1955, was devoted to Communist infiltration in the West and policies towards neutral countries. The third, near Munich, was the largest yet and designed to "put the group definitely on the map."[103]

The agendas changed but always focused on whatever problems were most at issue at the time of the meeting. Only the body responsible for setting the agenda remained unchanged. Pomian concluded that what became the Bilderberg Group was: "The best possible forum to consider the most important problems of a given moment and certainly one of the best informed gatherings."[104] New participants were invited every year.[105] Internationalism was regarded as a requisite quality of the invited. Only they received the agenda and no views were attributed. Speakers were allowed only five minutes once the themes had been described. Good food was served, important particularly for Retinger who was a gourmand. The elegant quarters where the meetings were held were, and still are, reserved exclusively for the participants. No outsiders were registered at the hotel which was in a secluded place. The meetings moved about with no consecutive gatherings in the same place. Expenses were paid by the Bilderbergs in the country in which the meeting took place. "Private subscription" maintained the organization.[106] Retinger was here, again, the key: "most of the contributions were obtained as a result of personal interventions by Dr. Retinger. Nearly all of these interventions took place on the occasion of his foreign visits."[107]

Very quickly the elite status of the members attracted much attention.[108] It was, as Dujardin and Dumoulin noted, born in a halo of intrigue which encouraged all sorts of speculation as to its goals and its real membership."[109] Retinger was intimately involved, either alongside Prince Bernhard or as his own voice, until his health failed in 1959. The Prince himself admitted that Retinger was the "prime mover" of the Bilderbergs.[110] No participant, who spoke only for himself, brought advisors or consultants. Views were expressed, it seems, with complete frankness. There were few rules. Pomian recalls a 1956 meeting in Turkey at which matters became completely confused and Prince Bernhard and Retinger failed to coordinate their actions. Everybody went to a nearby bar and drank.[111]

The 1956 meeting in Denmark was focused on Asia. The fifth, in 1957, in America, discussed the Atlantic Bloc and problems of cooperation and defense. There was another meeting in Italy in 1957 devoted to armaments and the superpowers.[112] Retinger tried to arrange the participation of Field-Marshal Montgomery or Lord Mountbatten and, from the American side, General Alfred M. Gruenther, retiring Supreme Allied Commander of SHAPE, and General Walter Bedell Smith of the CIA, already a "member of our group" among others.[113] Through his contacts at SHAPE, Retinger was able to interest the French "our idea to get greater international cooperation in education."[114] Retinger also tried to involve himself in selecting the American leaders of NATO (the Assistant Secretary General of NATO). The Americans alerted their senior military officials of this strange effort by Retinger and Prince Bernhard.[115] Retinger was invited to visit SHAPE headquarters in Paris, but the details of this are unknown. Despite these contacts, SHAPE was unaware of the source of Bilderberg funds which they knew to be "considerable."[116] It was also aware of the attendees, and maintained a very large file, so big that a subordinate officer urged the Supreme Commander of SHAPE not to read it![117]

The 1958 meeting was in Great Britain and concerned NATO and free trade issues. Retinger was very active in preparing the conference and attached great importance to it.[118] Retinger's last conference was 1959 in Turkey, which had earlier witnessed the abortive meeting, and was three years in preparation. It was devoted to the Middle East. Retinger resigned as conference organizer almost immediately thereafter because of rapidly declining health. He was designated "Patron" of the group. Despite his enormous behind-the-scenes efforts, he had almost never spoken.

The key actor in organizing the conferences was by the "Steering Committee" which was responsible for "diplomatic work": choosing participants and setting the agenda. The secretariat's "diplomatic work" was "by far" its most important responsibility. This effort "has been assumed almost entirely by Dr. Retinger.[119]

Retinger did not like the random representation on the "Steering Committee" with some countries contributing no one, and others four. He wanted this changed to a one or two per Western country but "for obvious reasons" *ten* from the United States. But the Steering Committee was too large (twenty-eight) so Retinger noted that a "Management Committee" (ten) had been created with fewer members.[120] This committee would further appoint a financial sub-committee. This, again, was the curse of bureaucracy which bedeviled all these unity organizations. The creator of the body was Prince Bernhard who was listed first and immediately thereafter, Retinger. He also placed himself on the small Management Committee, again in second position. Surprisingly, Retinger's almost certainly last memorandum on the Bilderberg group was short, and largely concerned with details of management. We can conclude that he was pleased with what he had wrought.[121]

## Retinger's creation

Witkowski has concluded that:

> The Bilderberg group, created by Retinger, is one of the most important means by which decisions shaping the structure of the contemporary world are decided. In harmony with the wishes of its founder, it became a forum for working-out a common policy of the Western world; as a place in which the harmonization of goals and coordination of actions of the greatest political and military powers are wrought. From its very origin of its existence, until today, it gathers people able to undertake that level of decision.[122]

The European Centre of Culture pronounced this accolade:

> He was the motive force behind most of the important congresses, associations, and private institutions which have worked, since the end of the last war, to promote European unity. The European League for Economic Cooperation, the European Movement and our own European Cultural Central in particular would not have come into being without him. The Congress of Europe ... the Hague Conference was his work, and from it resulted in the Council of Europe. More recently, he again it was who conceived and encouraged the Bilderberg Group, dedicated to the cause of Atlantic unity.[123]

Gijswijt's conclusion was that the many Bilderberg meetings purposely "reached no binding conclusions." It was neither a "lobby nor an interest group." It's "influence" is not measureable, but it has led to a greater mutual understanding in the West, and encouraged cooperation among European powers, building a "transatlantic political culture," the essence of Atlanticism.[124] A group of others have concluded that the Bilderbergs are a "significant event" in the "Atlantic political calendar," which has had a major role in the development of this phenomenon.[125] In this effort Retinger played "the" decisive role as inspirer and organizer. His name, often used pejoratively, will always remain inextricably linked to the Bilderbergs

By the late 1950s, Retinger's increasing interest in Euro-American cooperation reached its apogee. He was a member of the international organizing committee which resulted in the Atlantic Conference in London in 1959. Weeks before he died he attended a meeting of the "Provisional Committee for the creation of an Atlantic Institute." As Geoffrey de Freitas observed:

In recent years he had come to believe that Europe and North America needed each other and he had worked as hard and as conscientiously for the Atlantic community as he had previously worked for the European Movement.[126]

## The final efforts

In his last months, Retinger became personal and vindictive. He claimed "nasty behavior" by the Americans. They were only devoted to Prince Bernhard because of their "snobbishness." Retinger was replaced as European Movement Secretary-General by E. H. Van der Beugel, a disappointment who would not even take calls from Retinger. This left Retinger burdened with the materials in his dingy flat.[127] Retinger also had views on where the headquarters should be: London rather than the Netherlands he thought. In general, parenthetically, Retinger had soured considerably on everything Dutch. He regarded the Netherlands as too insignificant to house the headquarters there.[128] Prince Bernhard wrote Retinger a scathing letter in late January, 1960 reprimanding him for a variety of indiscretions and insisting that he be consulted before actions were taken: "You've made my life difficult and complicated." Retinger's behavior was threatening to "undermine the future of our work."[129] Retinger puckishly observed that he did not wish to speak to Prince Bernhard: he was not "childish," but he was "senile." He was designated a "life patron" of the Bilderbergs. He had only weeks to live.

## The Bilderbergs as conspiracy

From its inception, the Bilderbergs have been highly controversial and have given rise to fantastic speculation. Doubtless one of the causes of this is the considerable secrecy surrounding the meetings. Secrecy, speculates Lawrence Black, was inherited from the influence of the SOE on key founders, including Retinger.[130] Funds were privately donated. Other than the three-day meeting, they did nothing. There were no resolutions or votes. Invitations to participate are decided by the "chairman" following consultation with the Steering Committee. Of the approximately 120, two-thirds were Europeans, the rest from North America.

The Bilderberg group gave Retinger much influence. He was able to interfere in important issues almost at random. The European Cultural Foundation, which he founded, and the Atlantic Congress eventually occupied most of his time.[131] He, late in life, tried to begin a Western-Asian dialogue, but virtually nothing resulted.[132] Retinger always wanted Eastern Europe to be a participant. Retinger concluded that winning the Noble Peace Prize for himself would be a means to involving the Soviet Bloc.[133] Despite efforts on his behalf, it was not to be. Retinger never emerged into the spotlight of European history. He remained to the end the man behind the scenes.

Both published works, and especially the internet, frequently discuss the Bilderbergs, often in lurid terms.[134] An almost random sampling makes clear what images the Bilderbergs have created among conspiracy theorists. However, some of the charges against Retinger and the Bilderbergs are based on fact. All of this, mostly nonsensical, conjecture, however, begins with two quite simple truths. Retinger did have a long and mysterious career which cannot be fully explained. His life was full of adventure and he moved in influential circles. He might not have been a spy, but was close to them. The second is that the Bilderbergs, which Retinger created were secretive, powerful, and international.

Certain themes are repeated endlessly about Retinger. He was, since his youth, part of a Vatican, or Jesuit, conspiracy. He was a proponent of Catholic hegemony. He was linked to incomprehensible and ancient religious conspiracies guided by "Babylonian Mysteries and the Occult; a member of the Illuminati."[135] He had dangerous Masonic, or similar, linkages and was anti-American. He had some sort of powerful "oil connections." He was in the pay of American intelligence among others. He was pro-Communist and a secret proponent of Soviet Russia. He was a Jew who hid his origins. He was, simply put, a man of mystery. People feared and hated him so much that they tried to kill him.

The problem with all of these notions is that all of them are at least partially true. He was, briefly, in Jesuit training and had close ties to the order and its leadership as well as probably to the Vatican. He tried to preserve Catholic Europe during World War I, although this was really more for Polish loyalties. He did regard religion as very important, and many of his closest collaborators during and after World War II were Roman Catholics. He was, we may venture, a "political Catholic." He did have close connections to British intelligence and, if the Caillaux issue is true, he was also an international agent during the First World War. He did work for the Mexican government in ways that cannot be reconstructed. And he was involved in international oil politics at the highest level. He certainly regarded the Americans of being a malign influence in the 1920s, and probably after. They jailed him once and mistrusted him for decades. Later, however, he was in the pay of American intelligence. In the 1920s he was very far to the Left and an apologist for the Soviets. Claims that he was pro-Moscow during World War II are exaggerated; though he certainly defended them occasionally.

He did work for international consolidation, and was behind a bewildering concatenation of European unity agencies. His methods were always secretive and involved undefined webs of power. He was convinced that it would be necessary to create a supranational authority upon which European federation would depend.[136] In 1948, in reference to The Hague Congress, he remarked: "maintaining national sovereignty is an obsolete thing."[137] After all, the "only logical thing is world government."[138] He was almost certainly of partial Jewish heritage. Masonic connections, which he repeatedly denied, were attributed to him by many people throughout his life. He was almost constantly being paid by someone or something, but it is frequently unclear who and why. Indeed, he was a mysterious figure.

It is similar with the Bilderbergs. They are secretive, powerful, support an international world order and economic union. We know little of what goes on at their meetings. Again, a great deal of this is true. The Bilderbergs do represent an "internationalist" outlook and favor world economic interrelationships. One critic's conclusions that the Bilderbergs favor "Global government and a centralized world economy" are not completely false.[139] The Bilderbergs are a collection of the most powerful people in the world. Their influence cannot be discerned, which makes them appear yet more sinister. One source makes the reasonable conclusion that "if the Bilderberg's purposes are truly benevolent, the Group could stand to be a little more open about its activities."[140] In so far as he built the Bilderbergs he incorporated his very personality and modus operandi into the organization. Nobody knows quite what he was about. There is virtually no evidence, and motives must be reconstructed *post factum*. As David Astor, an old friend of Retinger wrote that he "started up this old-boy network."[141] Charges that they are also proponents of moral corruption, and hence "intrinsically evil" are nonsense.

Jan Chciuk-Celt, son of Retinger's companion in 1944 Poland, has made a fascinating effort to combine an exoneration of Retinger with a possible indictment of the Bilderbergs. He writes that another author

> Very correctly raises some pretty hairy suspicions about the Bilderbergers ... [but] they meant well and were motivated by high ideals at the start [*sic*] ... and that the whole thing got a lot weirder a few years into it. In other words, Retinger was motivated by lofty ideals, not wicked schemes, when he first called the conference together at the Bilderberg Hotel in Holland.[142]

# Notes

1 Wilford quoting C. D. Jackson in *The CIA*, 242.
2 Janta, "Refleksye (3)", 3.
3 Valerie Aubourg, "Organizing Atlanticism: the Bilderberg Group and the Atlantic Institute, 1952–1963," in Giles Scott-Smith and Hans Krabbendam, The *Cultural Cold War in Western Europe, 1945–1960* (London: Frank Cass, 2003, , 92–93.
4 Hatch, *H.R.H. Prince Bernhard*, 214. Retinger traveled frequently to the United States after 1945; his sponsor was Averell Harriman; see Retinger to U.S. Embassy, London, Box 20, Retinger Papers, BPL; cf. Gijswijt, "Uniting the West," 10.
5 Retinger, "The Bilderberg Group," pamphlet dated, February, 1959 in 60.1, BPL.
6 "Bilderberg Meetings" [1993], 60.2, 1, BPL.
7 Wilford, *The CIA*, 242.

8   J. H. Retinger, "The Bilderberg group," 60.1, BPL.
9   Philipsen, "Diplomacy with Ambiguity," 44ff.; Wilford, CIA, 242.
10  "Bilerberg Meetings," 1, BPL, 199 60.2. Philipsen, "Diplomacy with Ambiguity," 44ff.
11  Van Zeeland's biographer describes Retinger as the moving force behind the Bilderbergers. Hena, *Van Zeeland*, 265; cf. Retinger, "The Bilderberg Group," BPL; Rykens to Retinger, June 2, 1948, ME 328, HAEU.
12  Philipsen, "Diplomacy with Ambiguity," 55ff.
13  It is also reported that Retinger only met the Prince at the Hague in 1948; Witkowski, *Retinger*, 122. This is false: in 1960 Retinger refers to knowing Bernhard for twenty years; see Retinger to Bernhard January 21, 1960, Box 20, Retinger Papers, BPL; Aubourg, "Organizing Atlanticism," 93–94, 95.
14  Gijswijt, "Uniting the West," 10.
15  Retinger, "The Bilderberg Group."
16  Wilford, *The CIA*, 242.
17  Groisbois, "Activities," 35.
18  Grosbois, "Activities," 17; cf. Aldrich, OSS, CIA, 216.
19  Aldrich, "OSS, CIA," 216.
20  Gijswijt, "Uniting the West," 59. After the initial meeting, subsequent Bilderberg meetings were ostensibly financed by the Ford Foundation. Philipsen essentially agrees with Gijswijt's conclusion; "Diplomacy with Ambiguity," 82–83; cf. Wilford, "Calling the Tune," 47.
21  Aubourg, "Organizing Atlanticism," 96.
22  Philipsen, "Diplomacy with Ambiguity," 82–83.
23  Ibid., 90. The SOE had been disbanded but Gubbins and other British Intelligence figures were among the organizers of Retinger's group. Gijswijt, however, dismisses MI6 involvement; see his "Uniting the West," 88.
24  Retinger to Van Zeeland, July 25, 1952, 219045-2, Archieve Nationaal.
25  Retinger to Van Zeeland, August 26, 1952, 219045-2, Archieve Nationaal.
26  Retinger to Prince Bernhard, July 25. 1952, 219045-2, Archieve Nationaal; Bernhard to Retinger, August 6, 1952, 219045-2, Archieve Nationaal.
27  Cf. Dujardin and Dumoulin, *Van Zeeland*, 224. Gubbins, a "founder member" considered his role in the Bilderbergs "the greatest honour of his life"; Wilkinson and Astley, *Gubbins*, 240; Retinger, "The Bilderberg Group," 3. According to Healey, a Bilderberg, Gaitskell and Gubbins were among the first to be aoppproached by Retinger; see Denis Healey, *The Time of My Life* (New York: W. W. Norton & Co., 1990), 195.
28  Retinger to Brauer, July 27, 1952, 219045-2, Archieve Nationaal.
29  "Meeting held in Paris on September 25th, 1952: Minutes," 219045-2, Bilderberg Archief, Nationaal Archief, der Hague (hereafter NA).
30  Quoted in Pomian, *Retinger*, 234.
31  Taverne, *Wat niemand*, 43.
32  Untitled document, dated III/30 [1955], 219045-4, AN.
33  Retinger to Van Zeeland, September 22, 1952, 219045-2, NA.
34  "Draft,", 25, 1952.
35  Ibid., 4.
36  Ibid., 6.
37  Ibid., 13.
38  Ibid., 13.
39  Ibid., 6–10.
40  Ibid., 12.
41  Ibid., 16.
42  Ibid., 17.
43  Ibid., 18.

44 Retinger, "The Bilderberg Group," 8.
45 Retinger to Øle Bjorn Kraft, December 16, 1952. 219045-2, NA.
46 Retinger to Harriman, October 10, 1952, 219045-2, NA.
47 Ibid., 3; Harriman responded positively; see Harriman to Retinger, October 18, 1952, 219045-2, AN; cf. Retinger to Pipinelis, October 29, 1952, 219045, NA.
48 Retinger to Harriman, October 31, 1952, 219045-2, AN; Retinger to Van Zeeland, November 12, 1952, 219045-2, NA.
49 Andrzej Pieczewski, "Józef H. Retinger – pomysłodawca i współtwórca grupy Bilderbergu," *Studia Polityczne*, Vol. 10 (2000), 204.
50 REL, Memorandum for Dulles, December 4, 1952; untitled penciled notes, nd; Retinger to Dulles, December 16, 1952; in Dulles Papers, box 47, f. 16.
51 Retinger to Prince Bernhard, December 16, 1952, 219045-2; Retinger to Van Zeeland, December 16, 1952, 219045-2; Retinger to Kraft, December 16, 1952, 219045-2, NA. Retinger had approached Berle for funding for his federalist schemes as early as November, 1946. Apparently there were no results; see Aldrich, "OSS, CIA," 220, n.20.
52 "Memorandum of a Conversation," December 1, 1952, Berle Papers, container 218, FDR Library.
53 Ibid.
54 Ibid.
55 Eden, we should remember, was much interested in European federalism for much of World War II. His interest in Retinger's schemes might well have played a role in his putative activities.
56 "Memorandum of a Conversation," December 1, 1952, Berle Papers, container 218, FDR Library.
57 Berle to Miller, December 1, 1952, Berle Papers, container 218, FDR Library.
58 See Berle's diary entry for December 2, 1952 in Berle Papers, container 218, FDR Library.
59 Dulles Papers, Box 8, folder 3. This folder contains a number of letters between the two witnessing their close friendship.
60 Berle diary, December 8, 1952, Berle Papers, container 218, FDR Library; for the activities of the Vigilence Committee see "Memorandum concerning the International Campaign for the Creation of a European Council of Vigilence," nd, and Braden to Walter Washington, January 4, 1950, Dulles Papers, box 4, f. 1.
61 Ibid.
62 Ibid.
63 Ibid.
64 James Srodes, *Allen Dulles: Master of Spies* (Washington, DC: Regnery Publishing), 1999, 388.
65 Retinger, "The Bilderberg Group," 8.
66 George S. Franklin to Retinger, December 31, 1952, 219045-2, NA.
67 Retinger to Franklin, January 19, 1953, 219045-2, NA.
68 Retinger to Allen Dulles, September 17, 1953, 219045-2; Retinger to Bedell Smith, September 17, 1953, 219045-2, NA.
69 Retinger to Prince Bernhard, nd, 219045-2, NA.
70 Retinger to NN, nd, 219045-2, AN.
71 "Notes for a Letter to: General Bedell Smith," nd, 219045-2, AN.
72 Aubourg, "Organizing Atlanticism," 94; Philipsen, "Diplomacy with Ambiguity," 55ff.
73 Aldrich, "OSS, CIA," 216. Jackson later served as president of the Free Europe Committee; see Anna D. Mazurkiewicz, "The Relationship Between the Assembly of Captive European Nations and the Free Europe Committee in the Context of U.S. Foreign Policy, 1950–1960," 92, *Polish American Studies*, Vol. 62–63.

74  For health reasons, Coleman surrendered his leadership of the American group to Dean Rus, and Bedell Smith; Retinger, "The Bilderberg Group," 8.
75  RUSK, *CIA*, 243–244.
76  Aubourg, "Organizing Atlanticism," 95.
77  Philipsen, "Diplomacy with Ambiguity," 66–67.
78  Gijswijt, "Uniting the West," 26. The fact that the CIA only financed the initial Bilderberg meeting reflects, in some degree, Jackson's conviction that the organization was run by a "British secret agent" – Retinger. See Wilford, *Calling the Tune*, 48.
79  Gijswijt, "Uniting the West," 26.
80  Gijswijt quoted in Philipsen, "Diplomacy with Ambiguity," 74.
81  Retinger to Prince Bernhard, August 31, 1953, 219405-2, NA.
82  Prince Bernhard to Retinger, July 22, 1953, 219045-2; Retinger to van Zeeland, July 28, 1953, 219045-2, NA.
83  Retinger solicited $15,000 from the Americans shortly afterwards; see Retinger to R. M. Bissel, October 4, 1954, Box 20, Retinger Papers, BPL.
84  Ibid., 236. For the criteria, see Gijswijt, "Uniting the West," 35–36.
85  "Bilderberg Meetings," 60.2, BPL.
86  Pieczewski, "Retinger," 6.
87  Deputies' Meeting, DM-297.May 21, 1954, doc.c no. CIA-RDP80BO1676R002300150013-9, CREST: 25 Year Program Archival Collection, CIA Archives.
88  Ibid., 88; Philipsen, "Diplomacy with Ambiguity," 82–87.
89  Ibid., 81.
90  Alden Hatch, *H.R.H. Prince Bernhard of the Netherlands*. London: George G. Harrap & Co., 1962, 212.
91  Ibid.
92  Witkowski, *Ojcowie*, 263.
93  Retinger quoted in Philipsen, "Diplomacy with Ambiguity," 71.
94  Philipsen, "Diplomacy with Ambiguity," 71.
95  For an outline of meeting agendas from 1954–1992 see "Bilderberg Meetings," 60.2, BPL.
96  Gijswijt, "Uniting the West," 12ff., 33.
97  "Bilderberg Meetings," 5–6.
98  Ibid., 39, 60.
99  Ibid., 245. Gijswijt, "Uniting the West," 25–26; Wiford,*The CIA*, 242ff.
100 The Americans accused Retinger of being a "professional promoter" and making considerable money from his operations. As a matter of fact Retinger was almost always penniless; see Retinger to Joseph E. Johnson, box 26B, Retinger Papers, BPL.
101 Witkowski, *Ojcowie*, 143.
102 Gijswijt, "Uniting the West," 65ff.; Philipsen, "Diplomacy with Ambiguity," 76, this was the beginning.
103 Ibid., 81.
104 Pomian, *Retinger*, 235.
105 Hatch argues that it was Retinger, utilizing his long-established contacts, who was able to attract "many men of the non-Communist but radical left," see his *H.R.H. Prince Bernhard*, 220.
106 "Bilderberg Conferences," 60.2, BPL.
107 "Note on the organization," 60.3, 3, BPL.
108 "Bilderberg Conferences," 60.2, BPL.
109 Dujardin and Dumoulin, *Van Zeeland*, 224.
110 Prince Bernhard, "In Memoriam," 3.
111 For the early stages of the Turkey conference see "Memorandum from Joseph E. Johnson," February 25, 1959, C. D. Jackson Papers, Box No. 36, DDE.

112 The agenda and list of participants can be found in Papers of Lauris Norstad, Box 77, Personal Name Series. Bilderberg Conference at Fiuggi, DDE. Norstad commander of SHAPE was to prepare a report on disarmament; cf. HGW memorandum, September 12, 1957, Norstad Papers, Box 77 (DDE). Retinger arranged for Norstad to be met and lunch with the American ambassador to Italy.
113 Retinger to General Alfred M. Gruenther, November 13, 1956, Alfred M. Gruenther Papers. Box 39: General Correspondence Series, DDE.
114 H. Glen Wood to Retinger, January 28, 1956, in ibid.
115 HGW to General Schuyler, January 7, 1956, in ibid. cf. HGW to Schuyler, January 5, 1956, in ibid. Schuyler and Retinger met and communicated with each other a number of times; see Retinger to Gruenther, September 28, 1955 in ibid.
116 Gruenther to Retinger, November 29, 1955, in ibid.
117 HGW to General Schuyler, January 5, 1956, Box 4, NATO Series, Alfred M. Gruenther Papers, DDE.
118 [Oskar], "Notatka," October 31, 1957, IPN BU 01136/69/D.
119 "Note on the organization and activities of the Bilderberg Group Secretariat," nd, 60.3, BPL. This document was probably prepared by Pomian.
120 The Steering Committee later worked with the other committees to decide who would be invited; "Bilderberg Meetings,"1, 60.2, BPL.The Committee's work began at least four months before the conference and lasted about a month after; see "Note on the organization and activities of the Bilderberg Group Secretariat," nd, 60.3, BPL.
121 "Notes on the future organization of the Bilderberg Group," September, 1959. Retinger Papers, box 27B, BPL.
122 Witkowski, *Retinger*, 136.
123 Introduction to *Tribute to a Great European: J. H. Retinger*, published by the Centre Européen de la Culture, nd. Retinger himself claimed that concrete action regarding Western investment in the Middle East was the result of a Bilderberg meeting; Retinger, "The Bilderberg Group," 12.
124 Gijswijt, "Uniting the West," 293–294.
125 See the forceful argument in Ian N. Richardson, Andrew Kakabadse, and Nada Kakabadse, *Bilderberg People: Elite Power and Consensus in World Affairs* (London: Routledge, 2014), 30–31 et passim.
126 Geoffrey de Freitas, "Dr. Joseph Retinger," *The Times*, June 18, 1960; cf. Prince Bernhard, "In Memoriam," *Tribute*, 3.
127 V. J. Konigsberg to Retinger, January 5, 1960; Retinger to Rykens, January 19, 1960; Rykens to Retinger, February 8, 1960; BPL, box 26b.
128 Retinger to Rykens, January 5, 1960, Box 26B, Retinger Papers, BPL.
129 Prince Bernhard to Retinger, January 30, 1960; box 26b, Retinger Papers, BPL.
130 Cited in Philipsen, "Diplomacy with Ambiguity," 9.
131 Retinger to Joseph R. Johnson, box 26B, Retinger Papers, BPL.
132 David Astor to Viscount Monckton of Brenchley, August 21, 1959; Dean Rusk to Retinger, April 30, 1959, no document numbers, BPL.
133 In parallelism Kalergi had been nominated for the Prize in 1945; see "Count Urged for Noble Prize," *New York Times*," October 15, 1945.
134 Philipsen, "Diplomacy with Ambiguity," 4ff.
135 Mizzie Jones, "The Mysteries, Freemasonry, Jesuits, and the EU – A History," online at http://troyspace2.wordpress.com/2008/02/12/themysteries-fr. Accessed on July 8, 2014.
136 Quoted in Pomian, *Retinger*, 172.
137 Ibid., 268.
138 Retinger, "My Part in the Movement for the Unity of Europe," drawer. 2, BPL.

139 "Origins of the Bilderberg meetings," www.bilderberg.org/bildhist.htm. Accessed September, 18, 2012
140 "Origins of the Bilderberg," Bilderberg Index, nd, on-line at http://site 034145.primehost.com/mx/articles/bilderberg01.htm; accessed on June 23, 1999.
141 Astor to Monckton, August 21, 1959, BPL.
142 See the updated version of Jan Chciuk-Celt, "Who was Józef Hieronim Retinger?" online at http://teleport.com/-flyheart/retinger.htm. Accessed on October 25, 2013.

# 15 Conclusions

According to Alden Hatch's adulatory account of Retinger, he was "brilliant," which was certainly true; he was an intriguer, an SOE operative; a champion of uniting the West in opposition to the threat from the East, and a Polish patriot. His adventures rivaled James Bond.[1] In conclusion he was "the key figure in most of the great European union. The League of European Economic Cooperation (from which evolved the Common Market), the European Movement, the European Centre of Culture would not have seen the light without him. The Congress of The Hague was his doing, and the Council of Europe grew out of that." Sío-López credits Retinger with a major contribution to its creation, Retinger was "its very energetic and accomplished organizer."[2]

These claims are substantially persuasive. As for the central creation, the rudiments of the European Union, Pomian for one has concluded that the center of Retinger's life work was "his outstanding contribution to the creation of the EU which was to change European history and constitute a milestone in the history of mankind." It "dwarfs in importance all his other achievements and acts of courage both moral and physical."[3]

Beddington-Behrens singles out the 1948 Hague Conference as a major step "accomplished by an extraordinary moving spirit," the Polish citizen Joseph Retinger: "everything else flowed from the Congress."[4] It was "a major turning point in the movement for European unity, and among its leadership and ardent supporters were prominent East Central Europeans."[5]

> It was the living synthesis of the four traditional themes of union, concretely expressed in its three commissions – political, economic and cultural, representing *peace* through federation, suppressing the anarchy of sovereign states; *prosperity* by means of an economy at once free and organized; and the *spiritual community*; gathering together the living forces of culture, beyond frontiers and nationalisms. What is striking is the fourth theme, that of *common defense*, which had nearly as always figured in the argument up to that time, was quite absent from the discussions and from the final Manifesto.[6]

His services to the European Movement were stressed by all of those associated with the cause.

Through either self-delusion or dissimulation, Retinger seemingly convinced himself that it was only after World War II, that he was able to look beyond the problems of Poland and consider the larger design of a united Europe, and that this structure would be a creation of multiple federations. Retinger earlier argued that it was only with his departure from Mexico that he embraced the notion of international federation for Europe. Actually, none of this was true. Retinger was noteworthy for his consistency, not his tergiversations. Indeed, Retinger in 1947 was essentially the same man he was during World War I. What did he work for during World War I? Was it the preservation of the Habsburg federation, the isolation of Russia, and the prevention of a German dominated Europe.

During World War II, a generation later, Retinger made overt declarations adumbrating a European federation, convincing, or sharing, this vision with Sikorski. The Polish-Czech federation, soon to be followed by a series of other formulations, was designed to protect Europe from Russian domination – the same goal as it has been during World War I, and to prevent Germany from having the hegemonic power to control the continent. The "imperialist" Americans were to be kept at arm's length.

Despite all the talk of "world government," Retinger continued to espouse the same vision: a community of nations, built on federation, including Eastern Europe, with dubious attitudes towards the United States. Again the relationship towards Russia oscillated between trepidation and rejection. Note it was the United States that at first resented Retinger, the same power that he had feuded with in the 1920s, and had gained an unfavorable image of in 1914. Retinger's inclusion of Americans among the Bilderberg Group and the courting of their elites was motivated substantially by fear of Russia, and later advocating Atlanticism, joining North America with Europe. He also wanted money.

Britian represents a special case. Retinger was devoted to the British. Though he, oddly, did not like them. He might, as we have seen, even have been in their employee, or worked in very close cooperation. There is a thin and faint line between cooperation and collaboration and it was all that separated Retinger from British Intelligence, notably the SOE. What role did he envision for the British in a federated and united Europe? Here the answer is not clear and Retinger did nothing to elucidate the situation. By the late 1940s Churchill's seeming endorsement of union, plus the energetic activities of Sandys seemed to suggest that Great Britain was now to be considered a part of a European union. Most people in Britain, did not want to belong, and Labour was ardently opposed to it. This still persists today, to some extent. Did Retinger want Great Britain in his European union, perhaps not. Britain was a necessary part of a European world required to restrain Germany and block Russian imperialism. Beyond that it was not part of what Retinger considered the essential Europe: Western and Eastern Europe linked by a series of federations.

Hence, it was simple: solve the Russian and German problems; build a federation on tradition and Christian principles, and avoid self-destruction. But these were the goals of World War I. The factor which proved consistent, that knitted these various permutations together was the freedom of Poland. Despite claims that he was an architect of the modern continent and a great European, Retinger was both more and less than that. He was born 100 years after Poland had lost its independence into a patriotic, and Catholic family. He pursued, for the rest of his life, the goals of such a heritage: the re-creation of a free and secure Poland, Catholic and traditional. This would require a series of federations to nullify the threat of Germany and Russia. Absent those threats, Poland could live in freedom. Retinger never did anything to harm the interests of Poland. Even when he supported the Sikorski-Maisky Pact, or went to Poland in 1944 to convince the Poles to accept a Soviet future, he did so in order to *sauve que peut*.

He never worked to the detriment of Poland. Britain was always the possible savior of Poland, as it briefly seemed to be after 1939; but the British ultimately betrayed the Poles, even though by force of circumstance. Germany and Russia were dangerous. The French were a remnant of the past: they had for a long-time past relinquished the role of restraining Germany. They were, in many ways, just another small European power. Their historic mission had concluded. Sikorski was deluded. The small, persecuted, and forgotten nations of Europe would combine to save themselves and for one they were not conscious of. They would save Poland. This was the life-long goal of Józef Retinger.

Near the end, Retinger wanted desperately to go to Poland and even wrote to Premier Józef Cyrankiewicz in this regard. He apparently wanted his promise that he would be allowed to return to the West. Cyrankiewicz never answered.[7] Retinger lamented that in Poland he was regarded as a certain British agent: "therefore I cannot even briefly go to Poland." Ironically, Retinger noted that he could go to Moscow without problems, but not to Warsaw. Still he wanted to go in 1959, if only to visit "my Kraków."[8]

When he died in 1960 he was in dire poverty. He had paid no taxes "for 3–4 years." He lived in a small apartment over Harrods department store. He bequeathed all of his books to the Jagiellonian University library in his birthplace, Kraków. A great amount of money passed through his hands, but he managed none of it. He frittered away a considerable inheritance. He had the "nature of a gypsy." He neglected his family and had uncountable romances throughout the Western world. When asked, late in life, what he would have been if he had had any choice, he answered instantly, "a Pole."

He died after receiving the Last Sacraments of the Church. He was the godfather of the European Union. And, one of the great modern Poles.

## Notes

1 Hirsch and Fletcher, *The CIA*, 58.
2 Sío-López, "Memories and Horizons," 33.
3 Pomian to author, September 14, 2014.
4 Ibid., 9.
5 Sío-López, "Memories and Horizons," 33. The latter goal was largely a failure; ibid., 33–34.
6 Pomian, *Retinger*, 9.
7 Oskar, "Notatka," August 13, 1958, IPN BU 01136/69/D.
8 Ibid.

# Bibliography

## Unpublished materials

### Abilene, KS

*Dwight D. Eisenhower Presidential Library and Museum*

Alfred M. Gruenther Papers, "Retinger, Dr. J. H." Box 4, NATO Series.
Alfred M. Gruenther Papers, "Retinger, Dr. J. H." Box 39: General Correspondence Series.
C. D. Jackson Papers.
Floyd Odlum Papers, American Committee on United Europe; American Institute for Foreign Trade. Box 1, General Correspondence Series, 1951–52 files.
Lauris Norstad Papers, "Raymond thru Retinger (2)" [Bilderberg Conference at Fiuggi], Box 77, Personal Name Series.
Walter Bedell Smith Papers, "American Committee on United Europe (1) (2)," Box 4.

### Amherst, MA

*Amherst College*

Dwight W. Morrow Papers.

### Bern, Switzerland

*Eidgenössisches Departement des Innern, Schweizerisches Bundesarchiv*

Diplomatische Dokumente der Schweiz, Online Datenbank Dodis: 8649.

### Birmingham

*Birmingham University, Cadbury Research Library*

Avon Papers.

## College Park, MD

### United States National Archives

Record Group 59, Records of the Department of State Relating to the Internal Affairs of Mexico, 1910–1929, microfilm roll 138.
Record Group 59, Records of the Department of State Relating to World War I and its Termination, microfilm roll 374.
Record Group 65, Records of the Federal Bureau of Investigation, f. 202600, microfilm roll 935.
Record Group 165, War Department General & Specific Staffs: Military Intelligence Division.

### Special Collections, University of Maryland Libraries, Hornbake Library

Mary Louis Doherty Papers.

## Florence, Italy

Historical Archives of the European Union.

### European University Institute

Archives historiques de l'union europeenne. Online.

## The Hague, Netherlands

### Nationaal Archief

Archief van de Bilderberg Conferenties.

## Hyde Park, New York

### Franklin D. Roosevelt Presidential Library and Museum

Adolf A. Berle Papers.
Roosevelt Papers as President.
Sumner Welles Papers.

## Kew Gardens, Great Britain

### National Archives (formerly Public Record Office)

AIR 23, Air Ministry and Ministry of Defence.
CAB 24, Cabinet memoranda.
CAB 65, Second World War conclusions.
CAB 66, Second World War memoranda.
CAB 67, Second World War memoranda.
CAB 121, Special Secret Information Centre: Files.

CAB 129, Cabinet memoranda.
FO 371, Foreign Office.
FO 688.
FO 371, Sir Robert Bruce-Lockhart Papers.
FO 954/19B.
HS4 Special Operations Executive, Eastern Europe: Registered Files.
KV 2/3429 (Stanislaw Kot).
PREM 3/351/13.

*Kraków, Poland*

*Archiwum Narodowe w Krakowie*

Archiwum J. Retingera.
Korespondencja Józefa Hieronima Retingera, f. 8060–8068.
Z Papierów Jana Hulewicza.

*Biblioteka Uniwersytetu Jagiellońskiego*

Zamorski, Pamiętniki, f. 9075III.

*Uniwersytet Ekonomiczny Krakowski*

Archiwum Komisji do Spraw Europy Środkowej i Wschodniej Ruchu Europejskiego.

**London**

*Biblioteka Polska w Londynie*

Joseph Retinger Papers.

*Imperial War Museum*

Sir Colin Gubbins Papers.

*Polish Institute and Sikorski Museum*

Retinger Collection.

*General Władysław Sikorski Papers.*

General Marian Kukiel Papers.

*British Library*

Lord Bertie Papers.
Arthur James Balfour Papers.

### London School of Economics Library

Edward Mayou Hastings Lloyd Papers.
Ronald William Gordon Mackay Papers.
Edward Hugh John Neale Papers.

### New Haven, CT

*Yale University: Sterling Library*

James Rockwell Sheffield Papers.
Henry Lewis Stimson Papers.

### New York

*Columbia University. Oral History Collection*

#1077 "The Reminiscences of Tadeusz Celt."

*Józef Piłsudski Institute of America*

Rząd Polski na emigracji.

*Polish Institute of Arts and Sciences in America*

Feliks Gross Papers.
Karol Popiel Papers.
F. D. Sands Papers.

### North West Digital Archives

Guide to the Zygmunt William Birnbaum Papers. 1920–2000 [with appended documents] online at http://nwda.orbiscascade.org/ark:/80444/xv09585. Accessed January 7, 2017.

### Ottawa

*Public Archives of Canada*

Mackenzie King Diaries on line at http://www.collectionscanada.gc.ca/obj/001059/f4/50003V60.gif. Accessed January 7, 2017.

### Oxford

*Bodleian Library, Oxford University*

Sir Horace Rumbold Papers.

## Paris

### Archives Nationales

605AP, Fonds Théodore Lescové.
324 AP, André Tardieu: Guerre 1914–1918: Documents et Raports.

### Biblioteka Polska w Paryżu

Archiwum Kazimierza Woźnickiego.
Stanisław Lam, Materiały do słownika biograficznego polaków w świece litera "R"; Sygn 1263.

## Poznań, Poland

### Wojewódzkie Archiwum Państwowe w Poznaniu

Polizeipräsident in Posen, f. 2721; f. 2723.

## Princeton University, Princeton, NJ

Seeley G. Mudd Library.
Allen Dulles Papers.

## Warsaw, Poland

### Archiwum Akt Nowych

Stanisław Kauzik Papers.

### Instytut Pamięci Narodowej

File BU 01136/69/D.
File BU 01178/694.
File 01222/593/D.

## Washington, DC

### US Holocaust Memorial Museum Archives

Record Group 1998A.0371. Poland, Government in Exile Records, 1940–1945.

### Federal Bureau of Investigation Archives

Jane Anderson Papers.
CIA Archives (online).

## Wrocław

### Ossolineum

Papiery Wacław Gąsiorowskiego, f. 15226/II.
Papiery Rozwadowskich, Jana Rozwadowskiego działalność publiczna, f. 8005/II.

## Works by Retinger (Published)

Retinger, J. H. "The Bilderberg Group," n.d. online at https://publicintelligence.net/bilderberg-group-retinger/. Accessed January 7, 2017.

Retinger, J. H., *Tierra Mexicana: The History of Land and Agriculture in Ancient and Modern Mexico*. London: Noel Douglas, 1926.

Retinger, J. H., *Morones of Mexico: A History of the Labour Movement in that Country*. London: The Labour Publishing Company Limited, 1926.

Retinger, Józef H., "Historja i polityka: O obiektywny komentarz," *Wiadomości Literackie*, November 13, 1938.

Retinger, J. H., "The European Continent: An Address given on the 7th May 1946, with a postscript dated 30th August, 1946." London: Chatham House, n.d.

Retinger, J. H., *Conrad and his Contemporaries*. Miami, FL: The American Institute of Polish Culture, 1981.

Retinger, Józef H., *Polacy w cywilizacjach świata: Do konca wieku XIX*. Gdańsk: Krajowa Agencja Wydawnicza, 1991 [1937].

Retinger, J. H., *The Poles and Prussia*. No Publisher or place of publication indicated: n.d.

Retinger. J. H., *La Pologne at l'équilibre Européen*. Charleston, SC: Bibliolife, 2001 [1923].

## Published documents

Babiński, Witold. "Wymiana depesz między Naczelnym Wodzem i dowódcą Armii Krajowej 1943–1944," *Zeszyty Historyczne*, 26 (1973), 116–165.

Bán, András D., *Pax Britannica: Wartime Foreign Office Documents Regarding Plans for a Postbellum East Central Europe*. Boulder, CO: East European Monographs, 1997.

Ciechanowski Jan M., "Notatki z rozmów z Gen. Marianem Kukielem," *Zeszyty Historyczne*, 29 (1974), 130–143.

Ciechanowski, Jan M., "Józef Retinger (1888–1957) w świetle raportów brytyjskiego wywiadu z lat 1913 do 1941," *Zeszyty Historyczne*, Vol. 59 (1982), 196–205.

*Documents on Polish-Soviet Relations 1939–1945*, two vols. London: Heinemann, 1961–1967.

Duraczyński, Eugeniusz, ed. *Układ Sikorski-Majski: Wybór dokumentów*. Warsaw: Państwowy Instytut Wydawniczy, 1990.

"European Federal Union. Replies of twenty-six governments of Europe to M. Briand's Memorandum of May 17, 1930," *International Conciliation: Documents for the Year 1930*. (New York: Carnegie Endowment for International Peace, nd), 651–769.

*Foreign Relations of the United States, 1941. Volume I*. Washington, DC: Government Printing Office, 1958.

*Foreign Relations of the United States, 1942. Volume III*. Washington, DC: Government Printing Office, 1961.

Katelbach, Tadeusz, "Akt pierwszy dramatu," *Zeszyty Historyczne*, Vol. 5 (1965), 29–107.

Kirkor, Stanislaw, "Rola Benesz w sprawie polskie w 1944 roku," *Zeszyty Historyczne*, Vol. 26 (1973), 39–56.

Kisielewski, Tadeusz, "Z archiwum Józefa Retingera. Listy do przywódców ruchu ludowego z lat 1938–1939," *Dzieje Najnowsze*, Vol. 24 (1992), 91–104.
"Konferencja Generala Sikorskiego w Bejrucie, 23 kwietnia 1943," *Zeszyty Historyczne*, Vol. 74 (1985), 139–148.
Krzyżanowski, Ludwik, "Joseph Conrad: Some Polish Documents," in Ludwik Krzyżanowski, ed., *Joseph Conrad: Centennial Issues*. New York: Polish Institute of Arts and Sciences, 1960.
Lipgens, Walter and Wilfried Loth, eds. *Documents on the History of European Integration*, 4 vols. Berlin: Walter de Gruyter, 1985–1991.
"Memorandum on the Organization of a Régime of European Federal Union Addressed to Twenty-Six Governments of Europe, by M. Briand, Foreign Minister of France, May 17, 1930," *International Conciliation: Documents for the Year 1930*. New York: Carnegie Endowment for International Peace, n.d. 325–353.
*Parliamentary Debates: House of Commons Official Report*, Vol. 333, No. 152, Wednesday, July 20, 1938. London: HMSO, 1938.
Sikorski, General Władysław, *Modern Warfare*. New York: Roy Publishers, 1943.
Sikorski, General Władysław, "Poland Wants Peace [as told to Alfred Toombs]," *Colliers*, April 3, 1943, 11, 61–62.
"Sienkiewicz o legionach, NKN i akcie 5 listopada 1916," *Komunikaty towarzystwa im. Romana Dmowskiego*, Vol. 1 (1970–1971), 289ff.
Sokolowski, Marian Czeslaw, *Dzieje prezydentury Rzeczypospolitej Polskiej na uchodźstwie*. Warsaw: Peta, 2007.
Suchcitz, Andrzej, "Listy Wojciecha Korfantego do Józefa Retingera," *Zeszyty Historyczne*, Vol. 73 (1985), 222–230.
Świderska, Hanna, "O Retingerze w Archiwum Foreign Office," *Zeszyty Historyczne*, Vol. 106 (1993), 226–227.
*The Union of Europe: Declarations of European Statesmen*. New York: American Committee on United Europe, n.d.
Van der Velden, M., *European League for Economic Co-operation: The Origins of the European League for Economic Co-operation*. Brussels: ELEC, 1995.

## Memoirs, diaries and letters

Anders, Władysław, *Mémoires, 1939–1946*. Trad. J. Rzewuska. Paris: La jeune parque, 1948.
Babinski, Witold, Przyczynki historyczne od okresu 1939–1945. London: B. Swiderski, 1967.
Beneš, Eduard, *Memoirs of Dr. Eduard Beneš: From Munich to New War and New Victory*. Boston, MA: Houghton Mifflin Company, 1954.
"Benesz a Polska," *Zeszyty Historyczne*, Vol. 76 (1986), 79–88.
Borkowski, Zygmunt, "Wspomnienia z Drugiej Wojny Światowej-1939–1943," *Zeszyty Historyczne*, Vol. 29 (1974), 186–201.
Brandes, Detlef. *Grossbritannien und seine osteuropaischen Allierten, 1939–1943: Die Regierung Polens, der Tschechoslowakei und Jugoslawiens im Londoner Exil vom Kriegsausbruch bis zur Konferenz von Teheran*. Munich: R. Oldenbourg Verlag, 1968.
Caillaux, Joseph, *Devant l'histoire: Mes prisons*. Paris: Éditions de la Sienne, 3rd ed., 1920.

Calles, Plutarco Elías, *Correspondencia personal, 1919–1945* (ed. Carlos Macías). México, DF: Fideicomiso archivos Plutarco Elías y Fernando Torreblanca, 1993.

Celt, Marek, *Z Retingerem do Warszawy i z powrotem: Raport z podziemia, 1944*. Lomianki: LTW, 2006.

Coudenhove-Kalergi, Count Richard, *Crusade for Pan-Europe: Autobiography of a Man and a Movement*. New York: G. P. Putnam's Sons, 1944.

Coudenhove-Kalergi, Count [Richard], *Paneuropa*. Vienna: Paneuropea-verlag, 1926.

Coudenhove-Kalergi, Count [Richard], *An Idea Conquers the World*. London: Hutchinson, 1953.

Davies, Norman, *Rising,44: The Battle for Warsaw*. New York: Viking, 2003.

Dobrowolski, Stanisław W., *Memuary pacyfisty*. Kraków: Wydawnictwo Literackie, 1989.

Feierabend, Ladislav Karel, *Beneš mezi Washingtonem a Moskvou: vzpomínky z Londýnske vlády. Od jara 1943 do jara 1944*. Washington, DC: PRO, 1966.

Gil, Emilio Portes, *Autobiografía de la revolución Mexicana: un tratado de interpretación historica*. Mexico, DF: Instituto mexicano de cultura, 1964.

González-Mata, Luis M., *Les vrais maîtres du monde*. Paris: Bernard Grasset, 1979.

Hull, Cordell, *The Memoirs of Cordell Hull, Volume II*, New York: Macmillan, 1948.

James, Robert Rhodes, *Victor Cazalet: A Portrait*. London: Hamish Hamilton, 1976.

Janta, Aleksander, "Refleksye Retingerowskie: czy był i czyim był agentem?," *Wiadomości*, August 22 (1971), No. 1325, 2.

Janta, Aleksander, "Refleksye Retingerowskie (2)," *Wiadomości*, September 12, (1971), No. 1328 3.

Janta, Aleksander, "Refleksye Retingerowskie (3)," *Wiadomości*, October 3, 1971, No. 1331, 3.

Janta, Aleksander, Refleksye Retingerowski (4)," *Wiadomości*," December 12, (1971), No. 1341, 3.

Jaspar, Marcel-Henri, *Souvenirs sans retouche*. Paris: Librairie Arthème Fayard, 1968.

Jean-Aubry, G., *Conrad: Life and Letters*. Vol. 2. New York: Doubleday, Page & Co., 1927.

Karl, Frederick R. and Laurence Davies, eds., *The Collected Letters of Joseph Conrad: 1912–1916*, Vol. 5, Cambridge: Cambridge University Press, 1996.

Katelbach, Tadeusz, *Rok złych wróżb*. Paris: Instytut Literacki, 1959.

Kirkor, Stanisław, "Rola Benesza w sprawie polskiej w 1944 roku," *Zeszyty Historyczne*, Vol. 26 (1973), 39–56.

Korboński, Stefan, *W imięniu Polski walczącej*. London: B. Świderski, 1963.

Kot, Stanisław. *Listy z Rosji do Gen. Sikorskiego*. London: Jutro Polski, 1955.

Kwiatkowski, Eugeniusz, *Sylwetki. W takim żyliśmy świecie polityków*. Kraków: Znak, 1990.

Langenhove, Fernand Van, *La sécurité de la Belgique: contribution à l'histoire de la période 1940–1950*. Brussels: Éditions de l'université de Bruxelles, 1971.

Lednicki, Wacław, *Pamiętniki. Tom II*. London: B. Świderski, 1967.

Lerski, Jerzy, *Poland's Secret Envoy, 1939–1945*. New York: Bicentennial Publishing Compamy, 1988.

Martin Jim, *Bilderberg Diary*. Washington, DC: American Free Press, 2005.

Mitkiewicz, Leon, *Z Gen. Sikorskim na obczyznie (Fragmenty wspomnien)*. Paris: Instytut Literacki, 1968.
Moran, Lord, *Churchill at War, 1940–45*, New York: Carroll & Graf Publishers, 2002.
Nagórski, Zygmunt, *Wojna w Londynie*. Paris: Księgarnia Polska w Paryżu, 1966.
Nowak, Jan, "Operacja "Whitehorn: Kartki z pamiętnika kuriera," *Kultura*, Vol. 11 (1949), 207–225.
Nowak, Jan, *Courier from Warsaw*. Detroit, MI: Wayne State University Press, 1982.
Onacewicz Włodzimierz, "Komentarze do książki Leona Mitkiewicz 'Z Generałem Sikorskim na obczyźnie.'" *Zeszyty Historyczne*, Vol. 18 (1970), 154–184.
Pobóg-Malinowski, Władysław, *Z mojego okienka: Fakty i wrażenia z lat 1939–1945. Tom I 1939–1940*. Łomianki: LTW, 2013.
Pużak, Kazimierz, "Wspomnienia 1939–1945," *Zeszyty Historyczne*, No. 41 (1977), 3–196.
Popiel, Karol. *Generał Sikorski w mojej pamięci*. London: Odnowa, 1978.
Popiel, Karol. *Wspomnienia polityczne*. Warsaw: Ośrodek dokumentacji i studiów spolecznych, 1983.
Quaroni, Pietro, *Diplomatic Bags: An Ambassador's Memoirs*. London: David White Company, 1966.
Raczyński, Count Edward, *In Allied London*. London: Weidenfeld and Nicolson, 1962.
Radolin, Hugo Prince, ed., *Mémoires de Boni de Castellane, 1867–1932*. Paris: Libraries Academique Perrin, 1986.
Seyda, Marjan, *Polska na przelomie dziejów*. Poznań: Księgarnia św. Wojciecha, 1927.
Siemaszko, Z. S., "Niektóre wypowiedzi płk. Bakiewicza," *Zeszyty Historyczne*, Vol. 29 (1974), 144–156.
Sosnkowski, Kazimierz, *Materiały Historyczne*. London: Gryf Publications, Ltd., 1966.
Spaak, Paul-Henri, *The Continuing Battle: Memoirs of a European, 1936–1966*. Boston, MA: Little, Brown and Company, 1971.
Stroński, Stanisław, *Polityka rządu polskiego ma uchodźstwie w latach 1939–1942*. 3 vols. Nowy Sącz: Goldruk, 2007.
Suarez, Georges, *Briand: sa vie-son oeuvre-avec son journal et de nombreux documents inédits. IV: La Pilote dans la Tourments, 1916–1918*. Paris: Librarie Plon, 1940.
Suchcitz, Andrzej, "Listy Wojciecha Korfantego do Józefa Retingers," *Zeszyty Historyczne*, Vol. 73 (1985), 225–228.
Šťovíček, Ivan and Jaroslav Valenta, eds., *Československo-polska jednani o konferaci a spojenectví, 1939–1944*. Prague: Karolinum vydavatelstvi univerzity karlovy a historický ustav akademie ved České Republiky, 1995.
Świderska, Hanna, "O Retingerze w archiwum Foreign Office," *Zeszyty Historyczne*, Vol. 106 (1993), 226–227.
Tyszkiewicz-Łącki, Janusz, "Byłem adiutantem Generala Sikorskiego," *Zeszyty Historyczne*, Vol. 89 (1989), 68–90.
Wilkinson, Sir Peter, "Sikorski's journey to England, June 1940," in Keith Sword, ed., *Sikorski: Soldier and Statesman: A Collection of Essays*. London: Orbis Books, 1990, 158–167.

Witos, Wincenty, *Moja tułaczka*. Warsaw: Ludowa Spółdzielnia wydawnicza, 1959.
Zaremba, Zygmunt, *Wojna i konspiracja*. London: B. Świderski, 1957.
Zochowska, Maria and Stanislaw Zochowski, *Nasz Pamiętnik, 1914–1984*. Brisbane: Poets and Painters' Press, 1984.

## Secondary sources

Aben, Henk, "Sprong naar gouden ELES," http://www.dds/nl/ecbn/europavan morgen/archief.evm/nr12/12eles.htm. Accessed August 24, 2016.
Aldrich, Richard J., "OSS, CIA and European Unity: The American Committee on United Europe, 1948–1960," *Diplomacy & Statecraft*, Vol. 8 (1997), 184–227.
Aldrich, Richard J., *The Hidden Hand: Britain, America, and Cold War Secret Intelligence*. Woodstock: The Overlook Press, 2002.
Alvarez, David, "A German Agent at the Vatican: The Gerlach Affair," *Intelligence and National Security*, Vol. 2 (1996),
"American Interference via European Movement," *Democrat*, May–June 2011, Online at http://www.caef.org.uk/d123cia.html. Accessed February 28, 2013.
Arnason, Johann P. and Natalie J. Doyle, eds., *Domains and Divisions in European History*. Liverpool: Liverpool University Press, 2010.
"The Atlanticist Influences in the British Labour Movement: Some Roots of New Labour," *Working Class Movement Library*, March 21, 2009. http://wcml.org.uk/Main/en/contents/international/cold-war/the-atlanticist-tendency-, accessed February 28, 2013.
Babiński, Kazimierz, *Kazimerz Sosnowski: Myśl, praca, walka*. London: Veritas, 1988.
Balcerak, Wiesław, *Polityka zagraniczna Polski w dobie Locarna*. Wrocław: Ossolineum, 1967.
Baliszewski. Dariusz, "Misja, Salamandra." *Wprost*, Vol. 28 (2004). Online at http://niniwa2.cba.pl/retinger_misja_salamandra.htm. Accessed September 5, 2012.
Baumgart, Marek, *Wielka Brytania a odrodzona Polska 1923–1933*. Szczecin: Uniwersyten szczeciński, 1990.
Bereš, Witold and Wojciech Pięciak, "Europa, tuż za szyba," *Tygodnik Powszechny*, January 5, 1992, 4–6.
Barrès, Maurice. *En regardant au fond des crevasses*. Paris: Émile-Paul Frères, 1917.
Berska, Barbara. *Kłopotliwy sojusznik: Wpływ dyplomacji brytyjskiego ma stosunki polsko-sowieckie w latach 1939–1943*. Kraków: Księgarnia akademicka, 2005.
Bevay, P., P. Hazebroucq, and B. Henau, *Paul van Zeeland, 1893–1973. Un Sonegien Premier Ministre*. Soignies: Cercle archeologique du Canto de Soignies, 1993.
Bienicki, Kajetan, "Wildhorn," *Zeszyty Historyczne*, Vol. 88 (1989), 81–100.
Biskupski, M. B. B., "Pierwszy wstęp ‚szarej eminencji?: Józef Retinger, Polonia amerykańska i sprawa wojska polskiego na obczyźnie," *Niepodległość*, Vol. 20 (1987), 181–187.
Biskupski, M. B. B., "Spy, Patriot, or Internationalist? The Early Career of Józef Retinger, Polish Patriatrch of European Union," *Polish Review*, Vol. 43 (1998), 23–67.
Biskupski, M. B. B., "Canada and the Creation of a Polish Army, 1914–1918," The Polish Review, Vol. XLIV, No. 3 (1999), 337–378.
Biskupski, M. B. B., "Polish Conceptions of Unity and Division in Europe: Speculation and Policy." In Johann P. Arnason and Natalie J. Doyle, eds.,

*Domains and Divisions of European History*. Liverpool: Liverpool University Press, 2010, 93–111.
Biskupski, M. B. B., *The United States and the Rebirth of Poland, 1914–1918*. Dordrecht: Republic of Letters, 2012.
Biskupski, M. B. B., "Polonia's Ambassador to the United States: The Mystery of Jerzy Jan Sosnowski, 1917–1918," *Polish American Studies*, Vol. 73, No. 1 (Spring, 2016), 83–95.
Bloch, Czesław, ed., *Władysław Sikorski-Ignacy Paderewski*. Lublin: Katolicki Uniwesytet Lubelski, 1988.
Broż, Adam, "Retinger-błyskotliwie inteligentny i bezinteresowny," *Kurier Polski* (New York), February 22, 2014, 5.
Brożek, Andrzej, "Polonia w Stanach Zjednoczonych wobec inicjatyw Ignacego Jana Paderewskiego oraz Władysław Sikorskiego w I i II wojny światowej." In Czeslaw Bloch, *Władysław Sikorski-Ignacy Paderewski*. Lublin: Katolicki Uniwesytet Lubelski, 1988, 269–303.
Bułhak, Henryk, "Działalność Władysława Sikorskiego w dziedzinie polityka zagranicznej w latach 1922–1925." In Henryk Bułhak, ed., *Z Dziejów polityka i dyplomacji polskiej*. Warsaw: Wydawnictwo Sejmowe, 1994, 255–268.
Bujak, Waldemar, "Stronnictwo Pracy – partia generała Władysława Sikorskiego," *Przegląd Polonijny*, Vol. 7, No. 2 (1981), 89–106
Bułhak, Władysław, "Wokół misji Józefa H. Retingera do kraju, kwiecień-lipiec 1944r," *Zeszyty Historyczne*, Vol. 168 (2009), 3–80.
Bułhak, Władysław, "The Foreign Office and the Special Operations Executive and the Expedition of Józef Hieronim Retinger to Poland, April–July, 1944," *Polish Review*, Vol. 61, No. 3 (2016), 33–57.
Calder, Kenneth J., *Britain and the Origins of the New Europe, 1914–1918*. London: Cambridge University Press, 1976.
Cano, Fabio Barbosa, *La CROM de Luis N. Morones a Antonio J. Hernández*. Puebla: ICUAP, 1980.
Centre européen de la culture, *Tribute to a Great European, J. H. Retinger*. n.p., n.d.
Chapois, Drion du. *Paul van Zeeland, au service de la Belgique*. Brussels: Editions Labor, 1971.
Chciuk-Celt, Jan, "Who was Jozef Hieronim Retinger?," n.d. online at http://home.teleport.com/~flyheart/retinger.htm. Accessed January 26, 2010.
Chenaux, Philippe, *Une Europe vaticane? Entre le Plan Marshall et les traités de Rome*. Brussels: Éditions Ciaco, 1990.
Ciechanowski, Jan M., *The Warsaw Rising of 1944*. Cambridge: Cambridge University Press, 1974.
Ciechanowski, Jan M., "Brytyjskie służby wywiadowcze i specjalne, " *Zeszyty Historuczne*," Vol. 143 (2003), 3–40.
Cienciala, Anna M., "The Question of the Polish-Soviet Frontier in British, Soviet, and Polish Policy in 1939–1940: The Litauer Memorandum and Sikorski's Proposal, *The Polish Review*, Vol. 33 (1988), 295–324.
Cienciala, Anna M., "General Sikorski and the Conclusion of the Polish-Soviet Agreement of July 30, 1941: A Reassessment," *Polish Review*, Vol. 41 (1996), 401–434.
Cookridge, E. H., *Set Europe Ablaze*. New York: Crowell, 1967.
Coppens, Filip, "The Priory of Sion. Part 4: My Way," n.d. online at http;//www.perillos.com/pos1_4.html. Accessed February 28, 2013.

Coutouvidis, John, "Sikorski's Thirty-day Crisis, 19 June–19 July, 1940," Keith Sword, ed. *Sikorski: Soldier and Statesman*. London: Orbis, 1990, 114–138.

"Cultural Cold War: Origins of the Congress for Cultural Freedom, 1949–50," *Culture, Communication and Control: CIA Covert Operations in the 1950's/60's, European Arts Scene*," n.d. Online at http://www.bilderberg.org/ccf.htm. Accessed February 28, 2013.

Czubiński, Antoni, *Centrolew: Kształtowanie się i rozwój demokratycznej opozycji antysanacyjnej w Polsce w latach 1926–1930*. Poznań: Wydawnictwo Poznańskie, 1963.

Dall'Oglio, Andrea, *Europa, unità e divisione*. Milan: Dall'Oglio, n.d.

Drozdowski, Marian Marek, "Paderewski-Sikorski. Współpraca i przyjaźń w świetle korespondencji z lat 1928–1941." In Czesław Bloch, ed., *Sikorski-Paderewski*, Lublin: Katolicki Uniwesytet Lubelski, 1988, 185–219.

Dufoix, Stéphane, *Politiques d'exil: hongrois, polonais, et tchécoslovaques en France après 1945*. Paris: Presses universitaires de France.

Dujardin, Vincent and Michel Dumoulin, *Paul Van Zeeland, 1893–1973*. Brussels: Éditions Racine, 1997.

Dumoulin, Michel, "Le début de la Ligue européenne de Coopération économique," *Res Publica*, Vol. 29, No. 1 (1987), 99–118.

Dumoulin, Michel and Anne-Myriam Dutrieue, *La Ligue Européenne de Cooperation Économique (1946–1981): un groupe d'étude et de pression dans la construction européenne*. Berne: Peter Lang, 1993.

Duraczyński, Eugeniusz, *Rząd Polski na uchodźstwie, 1939–1945*. Warsaw: Książka i Wiedza, 1993.

Duraczyński, Eugeniusz and Romuald Turkowski, *O Polsce na uchodźstwie, 1939–1945: Rada Narodowa Rzeczypospolitej Polskiej*. Warsaw: Wydawnictwo Sejmowe, 1997.

Dymarski, Mirosław, *Stosunki wewnętrzne wśród wychodzstwa politycznego i wojskowego we Francji i w Wielkiej Brytanii, 1939–1945*. Wrocław: Wydawnictwo Uniwersytetu Wrocławskiego, 1999.

Dziewanowski, M. K., *Joseph Piłsudski: A European Federalist, 1918–1922*. Stanford, CA: Hoover Institution Press, 1969.

Edwards, John Carver, *Berlin Calling: American Broadcasters in Service to the Third Reich*. Westport, CT: Praeger, 1991.

Engel, David, *In the Shadow of Aushwitz: The Polish Government-in-Exile and the Jews, 1939–1942*. Chapel Hill, NC: University of North Carolina Press, 1987.

Eringer, Robert, *The Global Manipulators: The Bilderberg Group, the Trilateral Commission: Covert Power Groups of the West*. Bristol: Pentacle Books, 1980.

Estulin, Daniel, *The True Story of the Bilderberg Group*. Walterville, OR: TrineDay LLC, 2007.

Evans-Pritchard, Ambrose, "Euro-federalists financed by US spy chiefs," *The Telegraph*, September 19, 2000.

Frančič, Mirosław, "Ignacy Jan Paderewski widziany oczyma historyków," *Przegląd Poloninjy*, Vol. 9, No. 1 (1983), 91–102.

Garliński, Józef, *Poland in the Second World War*. New York: Hippocrene Books, 1985.

Garliński, Józef, *Poland, SOE and the Allies*. London: Allen and Unwin, 1969.

Gąsiorowski, Wacław, *1919–1925: Historja armji polskiej we Francji*. Warsaw: Dom Książki Polskiej, 1931.

Giertych, Jędrzej. *Rola dziejowa Dmowskiego: Tom I: Rok 1914*. Chicago, IL: Towarzystwo imienia Romana Dmowskiego, 1968.

Giertych, Jędrzej, "Õ Józefie Retingerze," *Komunikaty towarzystwa im. Romana Dmowskiego*, Vol. 1 (1970–1971), 316–381.

Gniazdowski, Mateusz, "Kontakty Piłsudczyków ze Słowakami w latach 1939–1945," *Niepodległość*, Vol. 55 (2005), 107–150.

Gonzales, Michael J., *The Mexican Revolution, 1910–1940*. Albuquerque, NM: University of New Mexico Press, 2002.

Gorodetsky, Gabriel, *Stafford Cripps' Mission to Moscow, 1940–42*. Cambridge: Cambridge University Press, 1984.

Grin, Gilles, *The Battle of the Single European Market: Achievements and Economic Thought*. London: Kegan Paul, 2003.

Grosbois, Thierry, *L'idée européenne en temps de guerre dans le Benelux (1940–1944)*. Louvain-la-Neuve: Academia, 1994.

Grosbois, Thierry, "L'action de Józef Retinger en faveur de i'idée européenne 1940–46," *European Review of History*, Vol. 6, No 1 (1999), 59–82.

Gross, Feliks, "The Future of the Mid-European Union," *Journal of Central European Affairs*, Vol. 16, No. 4 (January, 1957), 353–370

Hall, Linda B., *Oil, Banks, and Politics: The United States and Postrevolutionary Mexico, 1917–1914*. Austin, TX: University of Texas Press: 1995.

Halverson, John and Ian Watt, "Notes on Jane Anderson, 1955–1990," *Conradiana*, Vol. 23 (1991), 59–87.

Hamerow, Theodore S., *Why We Watched: Europe, America, and the Holocaust*. New York: W. W. Norton & Co., 2008.

Hatch, Alden, *H. R. H. Prince Bernhard of the Netherlands: An Authorized biography*. London: George G. Harrap & Co., Ltd., 1962.

Hay, Eloise Knaap, "Reconstructing 'East' and 'West' in Conrad's Eyes." In Keith Carabine, Owen Knowles, and Wiesław Krajka, eds., *Contexts for Conrad*. New York: Columbia University Press, 1993.

Henau, Brigitte, *Paul van Zeeland en het monetaire, social-economische en Europese beleid van België, 1920–1960*. Brussels: Koninklijke Academie voor Wetenschappen, Letteren en Schone Kunsten van België, 1995.

Herzog, Jesús Silva, *Historia de la expropiación de las empresas petroleras*. México, DF: Instituto Mexicano de las Investigaciones Económicas, 1964.

Hirsch, Fred and Richard Fletcher, *The CIA and the Labour Movement*. Nottingham: Spokesman Books, 1977.

Hodges, Donald C. and Ross Gandy, *Mexico. The End of the Revolution*. Westport, CT: Praeger, 2002.

Hodža, Milan, *Federácia v strednej Európe a iné štúdie*. Bratislava: Kalligram, 1997.

Holzer, Jerzy, *Mozaika polityczna Drugiej Rzeczypospolitej*. Warsaw: Książka i Wiedza, 1974.

Holzer, Jerzy and Jan Molenda, *Polska w pierwszej wojnie światowej*. Warsaw: Wiedza Powszechna, 1973.

"How the European Movement was Launched: The CIA and the Labour Party," *Working Class Movement Library*, January 17, 2009. Online at http://www.wcml.org.uk/contents/international/cold-war/the-atlanticist-tendancy-of-the-lab. Accessed February 28, 2013.

Jeleński, K. A., "Prekursor anachroniczny," *Kultura*, No. 7/165–8/166 (1961), 190–195.

"Józef Retinger: Happy Birthday, Józef!" 2013 http://bilderberg2013.co.uk/jozefretinger/. Accessed May 9, 2013.

Kacewicz, George, *Great Britain, the Soviet Union and the Polish Government in Exile, 1939–1945.* The Hague: Martinus Nijhoff, 1979.

Kalicki, Włodzimierz, "Retinger, gracz, ktory budował Europę," *Gazeta Wyborcza*, September 18–19, 2010, 26–27.

Kane, N. Stephen, "American Businessmen and Foreign Policy: The Recognition of Mexico, 1920–1923," *Political Science Quarterly*, Vol. 90 (Summer, 1975), 293–313.

Kaplan, Lawrence S., "Coudenhove-Kalergi, Richard." In Warren F. Kuehl, ed., *Biographical Dictionary of Internationalists* (Westport, CT: Greenwood, 1983), 172–174.

Katelbach, Tadeusz, "Loże," *Zeszyty Historyczne*, 3 (1963), 199–208.

Kisielewski, Tadeusz, *Federacja środkowo-europejska: Pertraktacje polsko-czechosłowackie 1939–1943.* Warsaw: Ludowa Spółdzielnia Wydawnicza, 1991.

Kochanski, Halik, *The Eagle Unbowed: Poland and the Poles in the Second World War.* Cambridge, MA: Harvard University Press, 2012.

Kohout, Luboš, *Edvard Beneš-demokrat, vlastenec, politický realista, proti legendam c vzniku průběhu, důsledcích Druhé Světově Války.* Prague: 1984.

Korbonski, Stefan, *The Polish Underground State: A Guide to the Undergroumd, 1939–1945.* New York: Hippocrene, 1978.

Korpalska, Walentyna, *Władysław Eugeniusz Sikorski: Biografia polityczna.* Wrocław: Ossolineum, 1981.

Krzyobłocka, Bożena, *Chadecja, 1918–1937.* Warsaw: Książka i Wiedza, 1974.

Lacroix-Riz, Anne, "Le Vatican et le buts de guerre germaniques de 1914 a 1918: Reve d'une europe allemande," *Revue d'histoire moderne et contemporaine*, Vol. 42 (October–December, 1995), 517–555.

Landau, Zbigniew and Jerzy Tomaszewski, *Kapitały obce w Polsce, 1918–1939.* Warsaw: Książka i Wiedza, 1964.

Lane, Thomas and Marian Wolański, *Poland and European Integration: The Ideas and Movements of Polish Exiles in the West, 1939–1991.* London: Palgrave Macmillan, 2009.

Larsh, William, "W. Averell Harriman and the Polish Question, December 1943–August 1944," *East European Politics and Societies*, Vol. 7 (1993), 513–554.

Lato, Stanisław. *Ruch Ludowy a Centrolew.* Warsaw: Ludowa spółdzielnia wydawnicza, 1965.

Latour, Francis, "De la spécifité de la diplomatie vaticane durant la grande guerre," *Revue d'histoire moderne et contemporaine*, Vol. 43 (April–June, 1996), 349–365.

*Die LECE im europäischen integrationsprozess zwischen 1947–1957*," n.d. online at http://www.ess.ch/housi/lece.htm. Accessed February 24, 2000.

Łepkowski, Tadeusz, *Polska – Meksyk, 1918–1939.* Wrocław: Ossolineum, 1980.

Lerski, Jerzy J., "Socjaliści polscy do brytyjskich," *Zeszyty Historyczne*, Vol. 75 (1986), 122–139.

Leslie, R. F. ed., *The History of Poland since 1863*, Cambridge: Cambridge University Press, 1980.

Lewis, John S., "Conrad in 1914," *Polish Review*, Vol. 20 (1975), 217–222.

Lipgens, Walter, *A History of European Integration. Volume 1, 1945–1947.* Oxford: Clarendon Press, 1982.

Łossowski, Piotr, ed., *Historia dyplomacji polskiej. Tom IV. 1918–1939*. Warsaw: Wydawnictwo Naukowe PAN, 1995.
Lukáč, Pavol, "Stredoeurópanstvo Milana Hodžu." In *Milan Hodža, Federácia v strednej Európe a iné štúdie*. Bratislava: Kalligram, 1997, 11–37.
Lukas, Richard C., *The Strange Allies: The United States and Poland, 1941–1945*. Knoxville, TN: The University of Tennessee Press, 1978.
Łukasiewicz, Sławomir, "Dzieje Związku polskich federalistów w Stanach Zjednoczonych," *Zeszyty Historyczne*, 143 (2003), 57–84.
Łukasiewicz, Sławomir, *Polacy w europejskim ruchu federalnym po II Wojnie Światowej*. Warsaw: Centrum Europejskie Natolin, 2005.
Łukaszewski, Jerzy, *Cel: Europa. Dziewięć esejów o budowniczych jedności europejskiej*. Warsaw: Noir sur Blamc, 2001.
Mackiewicz, Stanislaw, *Zielone oczy*. Warsaw: Instytut Wydawniczy PAX, 1958.
Marszalek, Antoni, *Z historii europejskiej idei integracji międzynarodowej*. Łódź: Wydawnictwo uniwersytetu łódzkiego, 1996.
Mazur, Grzegorz and Kazimierz Ostrowski, "Przyczynek do pobytu Józefa Retingera w Polsce," *Studia Historyczne*, Vol. 32 (1989), 621–628.
Mazurkiewicz, Anna, "The Relationship between the Assembly of Captive European Nations and the Free Europe Committee in the Context of U.S. Foreign Policy," 1950–1960, *Polish American Studies*, Vol. 62-63 (2008).
Melandri, Pierre, *Les États-Unis face a l'unification de l'Europe, 1945–1954*. Paris: Éditions A. Pedone, 1980.
Meyer, Lorenzo, *México y los Estados Unidos en el conflicto petrolero (1917–1942)*. México, DF: El Colegio de México, 1968.
Mierzwa, Edward A., "Józef Retinger – A Political Link in the European Unification," *Politics and Society*, Vol. 8 (2011, 247–265).
Najder, Zdzisław. *Joseph Conrad: A Chronicle*. New Brunswick, NJ: Rutgers University Press, 1983.
Nowak-Kiełbikowa, Maria, *Polska-Wielka Brytania w dobie zabiegów o zbiorowe bepieczeństwo w Europie 1923–1937*. Warsaw: Państwowe Wydawnictwo Naukowe, 1989.
Onacewicz, Włodzimierz, "Komentarze do książki Leona Mitkiewicza Z Generałem Sikorskim na obczyźnie," *Zeszyty Historyczne*, Vol. 18 (1970), 154–185.
"Operation Wildhorn (Operation Mosty or Bridges)," online at http://www.polandin exile.com/exile13.htm. Accessed October 31, 2013.
Paczkowski, Andrzej, *Stanisław Mikołajczyk: czyli kleska realisty (zarys biografii politycznej)*. Warsaw: Agencja Omnipress, 1991.
Pająk, Henryk, *Retinger, mason i agent syjonizmu*. Lublin: Retro, 1996.
Pease, Neal, *Rome's Most Faithful Daughter: The Catholic Church and Independent Poland, 1914–1939*. Athens, OH: Ohio University Press, 2009.
Pestkowska, Maria. *Za kulisami rządu polskiego na emigracji*. Warsaw: Rytm, 2000.
Peszke, Michael Alfred. *The Polish Underground Army, the Western Allies, and the Failure of Strategic Unity in World War II*. Jefferson, NC: McFarland & Co., Inc., 2005.
Pieczewski, Andrzej. "Józef H. Retinger-pomysłodawca i wspołtwórca Grupy Bilderbergu," *Studia Poliyuczne*, No. 10 (2000), 203–208.
Pieczewski, Andrzej. *Działalność Józefa Hieronima Retigera na rzecz integracji europejskiej*. Toruń: Adam Marszalek, 2008.

Pieczewski, Andrzej. "Komisja do Spraw Środkowej i Wschodniej Ruchu Europejskiego (1949–1973) –wołanie o jedność całego kontynentu," *Studia Polityczne*, Vol. 21 (2008), 197–224.

Piszczkowski, Tadeusz, *Anglia a Polska, 1914–1939: w świetle dokumentów brytyjskich*. London: Ofycyna poetów i malarzy, 1975.

Pobóg-Malinowski, Władysław, *Najnowsza historia polityczna Polski, 1864–1945. Tom trzeci: Okres 1939–1945*, 2nd ed. London: Gryf, 1981.

Podgórski, Bogdan, "Józef Hieronim Retinger, 1888–1960," online at www.kangur.uek.krakow.pl. Accessed January 7, 2017.

Podgórski, Bogdan, *Józef Retinger: Prywatny politik*. Kraków: Universitas, 2013.

Polonsky, Antony, "Sikorski as Opposition Politician, 1928–1939," In Keith Sword, ed., *Sikorski: Soldier and Statesman: A Collection of Essays*. London: Orbis Books, 1990, 43–74.

Pomian, Jan, *Józef Retinger: Życie i pamiętniki pioniera Jedności Europejskiej*. Warsaw: Pavo, 1994.

Prażmowska, Anita J., *Britain and Poland, 1939–1943: The Betrayed Ally*. Cambridge: Cambridge University Press, 1995.

Przybyłski, Henryk, *Front Morges w okresie II Rzeczypospolitej*. Warsaw: Państwowe Wydawnictwo Naukowe, 1972.

Przybylski, Henryk, "Współpraca Ignacego Paderewskiego z gen. Władsławem Sikorskim w latach 1926–1941," *Przegląd polonijny*, Vol. IX, 1 (1983), 5–16.

Przybyłski, Henryk, "Dzieje współpracy politycznej Ignacego Paderewskiego i Władysława Sikorskiego (1926–1941)." In Czesław Bloch, ed., *Sikorski-Paderewski*, Lublin: Katolicki Uniwesytet Lubelski, 1988, 167–182.

Przybyłski, Henryk, *Paderewski. Między muzyką a polityką*. Katowice: Wydawnictwo UNIA, 1992.

Przybyłski, Henryk, *Front Morges*. Toruń: Marszałek, 2007.

"Quest for a United States of Europe: Role of the USA, CIA and Winston Churchill," *Democrat* (July–August), 2010, online at http://www.caef.org.uk/d119route3.html. Accessed February 28, 2013.

Raczyński, Edward and Tadeusz Żenczykowski, *Od Genewy do Jałty*. Lublin: Katolicki Uniwesytet Lubelski, 1991.

Richardson, Ian N., Andrew Kakabadse, and Nada K. Kakabadse, *Bilderberg People: Elite Power and Consensus in World Affairs*. London: Routledge, 1914.

Riede, David C., "Retinger, Joseph Hieronim." In Warren F. Kuehl, ed., *Biographical Dictionary of Internationalists*. Westport, CT: Greenwood, 1983, 606.

Ross, Stanley Robert, "Dwight Morrow and the Mexican Revolution," *The Hispanic American Historical Review*, Vol. 38, No. 4 (November 1958), 506–528.

Rougement, Denis de. *The Meaning of Europe*. New York: Stein and Day, 1965.

Rougemont, Denis de, *The Idea of Europe*. Cleveland, OH: The World Publishing Co., 1968.

Rougement, Denis de, "A Biographical Sketch," in *Tribute to a Great European: J. H. Retinger.*, n.d. 20–50.

Rougemont, Denis de, "Europe Unites," online at http://proeuropa.org/rougemont.html. Accessed January 7, 2017.

Russell, Jessie and Ronald Cohn, *Richard Nikolaus von Coudenhove-Kalergi*. Edinburgh: Bookvika Publishing, 2012.

Rutkowski, Tadeusz Paweł, *Stanisław Kot 1885–1975: Biografia polityczna*, Warsaw: DiG, 2000.

Sadowski, Jeremi, "Józef Retinger i jego amerykańska teczka, Wolna Europa," n.d. online at http://wolmnaeuropa.org/index2.php?option=com_content&task=view&id=89&pop=1&page, 1–5. Accessed February 8, 2013.
Seeholzer, Heinrich, *Die Politik des Grafen Boni de Castellane*. Zürich: Leeman & Co., 1913.
Siemaszko, Z. S., "Szara eminencja w miniaturze," *Zeszyty Historyczne*, Vol. 23 (1973), 172–185.
Siemaszko, Z. S., "Cazalet, Sikorski, 'Anna'," *Zeszyty Historyczne*, 61 (1982), 218–222.
Siemaszko, Z. S., "Retinger w Polsce w 1944r.," *Zeszyty Historyczne*, Vol. 59 (1982), 56–115.
Siemaszko, Z. S., "Wojskowi o Retingerze," *Wojskowy Przegląd Historyczne*," Vol. 37 (1992), 90–91.
Siemaszko, Z. S., "Brytyjczycy zaangażowani w sprawy polskie," *Zeszyty Historyczne*, Vol. 112 (1995), 77–94.
Siemaszko, Z. S., *Sprawy i troski, 1956–2005*. Lublin: Norbertinum, 2006.
Siemaszko, Z. S., "Retinger-wysłannik Foreign Office i Mikołaczyka," *Zeszyty Historyczne*, Vol. 170 (2009), 205–229.
Sierpowski, Stanisław, "Benedetto XV e la questione polacca negli anni della Grande Guerra." In Giorgio Rumi, ed., *Benedetto XV et la pace – 1918*. Brescia: Editrice Morcelliana, 1990.
Síu-López, Cristina Blanco, "Memories and Horizons: The Legacy of the Central and Eastern European Intellectuals in Exile and the 'Reunificaction' of Europe," *Pliegos de Yuste: Revista de Cultura, Ciencia y Pensamiento Europeo*, No. 11 (2012), 31–40.
Śladkowski, Wiesław, *Opinia publiczna we Francji wobec sprawy polskiej w latach 1914–1918*. Wrocław: Ossolineum, 1976.
Smoliński, Józef, "Generał Zygmunt Bohusz-Syszko dowódca samodzielnej brygady strzelców podhalańskich, zastępca dowódcy 2 korpusu." In Stefan Zwoliński, ed., *Naczelni wodzowie i wyżsi dowódcy Polskich sił zbrojnych na zachodzie*, Warsaw: Wojskowy Instytut Historyczny, Egros, 1995.
Spenser, Daniela, *The Impossible Triangle: Mexico, Soviet Russia, and the United States in the 1920s*. Durham, NC: Duke University Press, 1999.
Stape, J. H., "The Chronolgy of Conrad's 1914 Visit to Poland," *Polish Review*, Vol. 20 (1975), 65–71.
Stęborowski, Stanisław Piotr, *Geneza Centrolewu, 1928–1929*. Warsaw: Książka i Wiedza, 1963.
Stout, Janis P., *Katherine Anne Porter: A Sense of the Times*. Charlottesville, VA: University Press of Virginia, 1995.
Suleja, Włodzimierz, "Szara eminencja." In Zbigniew Fras and Włodzimierz Suleja, eds. *Poczet agentów polskich*. Wrocław: Ossolineum, 1995 155–164.
Sukiennicki, Wiktor, *East Central Europe During World War I: From Foreign Domination to National Independence*, 2 vols. Boulder, CO: East European Monographs, 1984.
Świderska, Hanna, "Drobiazgi jałtańskie," *Zeszyty Historyczne*, 106 (1993), 63–83.
Sword, Keith, ed., *Sikorski: Soldier and Statesman: A Collection of Essays*. London: Orbis Books, 1990.

Sword, Keith. *Deportation and Exile: Poles in the Soviet Union*. New York: St. Martin's Press, 1994.
Szerer, Mieczysław, *Federacje a przyszłość Polski*. London: P. S. King & Staples, 1942.
Szumowski, Tadeusz, "Wokół przesilenia lipcowego 1940 roku." *Kwartalnik Historyczny*, Vol. 87, No. 1 (1980), 85–95.
Taverne, W. C., *Wat niemand schunt te weten: J. H. Retinger en het streven naar een verenigd Europa*. Hoogeveen: Horizont, 1987.
Tebinka, Jacek, *"Wielka Brytania dotrzyma lojalnie swojego słowa": Winston S. Churchill a Polska*. Warsaw: Neriton, 2013.
Tendyra, Bernadeta, "Władysław Sikorski w oczach brytyjczyków," *Zeszyty Historyczne*, Vol. 97 (1991), 24–53.
Terlecki, Olgierd, *Generał ostatniej legendy: Rzecz o Gen. Władysławie Sikorskim*. Chicago, IL: Polonia, 1976.
Terlecki, Olgierd, *Wielka awantura*. London: Polska Fundacj Kulturalna, 1978.
Terlecki, Olgierd, *Kuzynek diabła*. Kraków: Krajowa Agencja Wydawnicza: 1988.
Terry, Sarah Meiklejohn, *Poland's Place in Europe: General Sikorski and the Origin of the Oder-Neisse Line, 1939–1943*. Princeton, NJ: Princeton University Press, 1983.
Tosstorff, Reiner, *Profintern: Die rote Gewerkschaftsinternationale 1920–1937*. Paderborn: Schöningh, 2004.
Unrue, Darlene Harbour, *Katherine Anne Porter: The Life of an Artist*. Jackson, MS: University Press of Mississippi, 2005.
Van der Velden, M., *The European League for Economic Co-operation: The Origins of the European League for Economic Co-operation (ELEC)*. Brussels: E.L.E.C., 1995.
Victorian, Armen, "The Bilderberg Group: The Invisible Power House," *Nexus Magazine*, Vol. 3, No. 1 (December, 1995–January 1996), online www.nexusmagazine.com. Accessed January 7, 2017.
Walicki, Andrzej, *The Three Traditions of Polish Patriotism and their Contemporary Relevance*. Bloomington, IN: Indiana University, 1988.
Walsh, Thomas F., *Katherine Anne Porter and Mexico: The Illusion of Eden*. Austin, TX: University of Texas Press.
Wandycz, Piotr S., "Regionalism and European Integration," *World Affairs Quarterly*, Vol. 28, No. 3 (October, 1957), 229–259.
Wandycz, Piotr S., "Poland in International Politics," *Canadian Slavonic Papers*, Vol. 14, 3 (1972), 401–420.
Wandycz, Piotr S., "Pierwsza Republika a Druga Rzeczpospolita," *Zeszyty Historyczne*, Vol. 28 (1974), 3–20.
Wandycz, Piotr S., "Dwie próby stworzenia związków regionalnych w Europie Wschodniej." In Piotr Wandycz, *Polska a zagranica*. Paris: Instytut Literacki, 1986, 109–126.
Wandycz, Piotr S., "Tentatives et projets d'union regionale en Europe central (XVIIIe et XX$^e$ siècles)," *Les cahiers de Varsovie*, Vol. 22 (1991).
Wandycz, Piotr S., "O stosunkach polsko-czechsłowackich: garść refleksji," *Zeszyty Historyczne*, 108, (1994) 112–120.
Wandycz, Piotr S., "Benešův rozhovor se Sikorským 3. Února 1942," *Acta Universitatis Carolinae-Philosophica et Historica*, Vols 3–4 (1995), 345–353.
Wandycz, Piotr S., "Western Images and Stereotypes of Central and Eastern Europe." In André Gerritis and Nanci Adler, eds., *Vampires Unstaked: National*

*Images, Stereotypes ND Myths in East Central Europe*. Amsterdam: Nord Holland, 1995, 5–23.
Wandycz, Piotr S., "Konfederacja polsko-czechosłowacka: Dokumenty," *Zeszyty Historyczne*, Vol. 116 (1996), 186–190.
Wandycz, Piotr S., *Aleksander Skrzyński: Minister Spraw Zagranicznych II Rzeczypospolitej*. Warsaw: Polski Instytut Spraw Międzynarodowych, 2006.
Wandycz, Piotr S., "Rozmowa Beneša z Sikorskim 3 lutego 1942 roku," in Piotr Wandycz, ed., *O czasach dawniejszych i bliższych: Studia z dziejowa Polski i Europy Środkowo-Wschodniej*. Poznań: Wydawnictwo poznańskie, 2009, 357–365.
Wandycz, Piotr S., "Recent Traditions of the Quest for Unity: Attempted Polish-Czechoslovak and Yugoslav-Bulgarian Confederations 1940–1948," *Cahiers de Bruges*, N.S. 25, nd, 37–93.
Wapiński, Roman, *Władysław Sikorski*. Warsaw: Wiedza Powszechna, 1978.
Wapiński, Roman, "Retinger, Józef," *Polski Słownik Biograficzny*, 1988, Vol. 128, 148–152.
Wawer, Zbigniew, *Armia generala Władysław Andersa w ZSRR, 1941–1942*. Warsaw: Bellona, 2012.
Wilford, Hugh. *The CIA, the British Left, and the Cold War*. London: Frank Cass, 2003.
Wilkinson, Peter and Joan Bright Astley, *Gubbins and SOE*. South Yorkshire: Pen & Sword Books, 1993.
Witkowski, Grzegorz, *Józef Retinger: Polski inicjator integracji europejskiej*. Warsaw: Zbliżenie, 2000.
Witkowski, Grzegorz, *Ojcowie Europy: Udział polaków w procesie integracji kontynentu*. Warsaw: Kontrast, 2001.
Wolański, Marian S., "Federalism as a Doctrine and a Method in the Activity of the Union of Polish Federalists." In Thomas Lane and Marian S. Wolański, eds., *Poland and European Unity: Ideas and Reality*. Wrocław: Wydawnictwo Uniwersytetu Wrocławskiego, 2007, 53–80.
Wyrwa, Tadeusz, "Układ Sikorski-Majski," *Zeszyty Historyczne*, Vol. 102 (1992), 198–203.
Żaron, Piotr. *Kierunek wschodni w strategii wojskowo-politycznej gen. Władysław Sikorskiego, 1940–1943*. Warsaw: Państwowe Wydawnictwo Naukowe, 1988.

# The press

*Monitor*
*The Times* (London)
*The New York Times*
*The Telegraph*
*Wiadamości*

# Unpublished materials

Andrews, Gregg, "'Shoulder to Shoulder': Samuel Gompers, Imperialism, and the Mexican Revolution, 1910–1924."

## 314  Bibliography

Buford, Nick, "A Biography of Luis N. Morones, Mexican Labor and Political Leader," Ph.D. diss., Louisiana State University and Agricultural and Mechanical College, 1971.

Bułhak, Władysław, "The Foreign Office and the Special Operations Executive and the expedition of Józef Hieronim Retinger to Poland, April–July, 1944."

Cazalet, Major V. A., *With Sikorski to Russia*. London: Printed at the Curwen Press for Private Circulation, 1942.

Cienciala, Anna M., "Retinger." January 30, 1997.

Grosbois, Thierry, "Joseph Retinger's Vision of United Europe after World War II: Central and Eastern European Questions," 2014.

Horn, James John, "Diplomacy by Ultimatum: Ambassador Sheffield and Mexican-American Relations, 1924–1927," Ph.D. diss., State University of New York, Buffalo, 1969.

Latawski, Paul C., "Great Britain and the Rebirth of Poland, 1914–1918: Official and Unofficial Influences on British Policy," Ph.D. diss., Indiana University, 1985.

Marcoux, Carl Henry, "Plutarco Elías Calles and the Partido Nacional Revolucionario: Mexican National and Regional Politics in 1928 and 1929," Ph.D. diss., University of California, Riverside, 1994.

Martula, Anka, "The Double Life of Józef Retinger during World War II," M.A. thesis, Central Connecticut State University, 2010.

Melzer, Richard, "Dwight Morrow's Role in the Mexican Revolution: Good Neighbor of Meddling Yankee?" 2 vols. Ph.D. diss., University of New Mexico, 1979.

Rice, Sister M. Elizabeth Ann, "The Diplomatic Relations between the United States and Mexico, as affected by the Struggle for Religious Liberty in Mexico, 1925–1929." Ph.D diss., Catholic University of America, 1959.

Soustos, Constantine Peter, "Vatican Peace Diplomacy during World War I," M.A. thesis, University of Virginia, 1992.

Watkins, Holland Dempsey, "Plutarco Elias Calles: el jefe máximo de México." Ph.D. diss., Texas Technological College, 1968.

## Letters

Richard J. Aldrich to author, March 4, 2013.
Władysław Bułhak to author, October 28, 2014.
Władysław Bułhak to author, January 5, 2015.
Wladyslaw Bulhak to author, July 5, 2016.
Anna Cienciala to author, March 23, 2014.
Marya Fforde to author October 8, 2014.
Anna Mazurkiewicz to the author, July 12, 2014.
Neal Pease to author, July 3, 2012.
Jim Pegolotti to Nancy Howe Webster, April 17, 2000.
Jan Pomian to author, nd [ca. February, 2000].
Jan Pomian to author, July 26, 2014.
Jan Pomian to author, July 29, 2014.
Jan Pomian to author [August 3, 2014].
Jan Pomian to Author, August 28, 2014.

Jan Pomian to author, September 14, 2014.
Piotr S. Wandycz to author, July 31, 2002.
Hugh Wilford to author, September 8, 2014.

## Interviews

Jan Karski, Rochester, NY, 1983.
Jan Pomian, London, July 12, 2000.
Piotr S. Wandycz, June 10, 2013.
Zbigniew Siemaszko, July 23, 2013.

# Index

Abd el-Krim 82
Adenauer, K. 222
AFL-CIO 62
Aga Khan 29
Albania 152
Aldrich, R. x
Algeria 116
American Committee on United Europe (ACUE) 251–3, 255, 258, 262
American Polonia 18–22, 31, 34, 44, 45, 119, 136–7, 158, 182, 184
Anders, W. 168–71, 173, 174, 185, 207–8
Anderson, J. 30, 43–4, 60–1, 65, 68, 77, 80
Anschluss 104
Anti-Semitism 6, 10
Archbishop Bourne 11
Archduke Charles Stephen 33, 37
Arciszewski, T. 204–5, 208
Armstrong, A. xi
Askenazy, S. 27
Asquith, H. 17, 18, 26–7, 35, 43, 128
Atlantic Charter 182
Atlanticism 4, 226, 235, 273
Attlee, C. 80, 238
Austria 3, 6, 17–18, 20, 24, 28, 31–3, 37, 38, 93, 104, 143, 152, 207, 232, 240
Austrophilism 3, 21, 23, 25, 29, 31, 33, 38, 39, 43, 93

B'nai B'rith 2, 12
Balfour, A. 17
Beck, J. 102–4, 107, 125, 138, 151, 196, 234
Beddington-Behrens, E. 1, 238–40, 251, 259, 291

Belgium 121, 127, 151–5, 236, 240, 253
Benelux treaty 153, 237
Beneš, E. 95, 102, 138–45, 234
Bennett, A. 8, 10, 24
Bentinck, V. 209
Berle, A. 137, 143, 171, 183, 238, 276–7
Berlin 9, 27, 31, 37
Berman, J. 210
Berthelot, F. 11–12, 26, 156
Bevin, E. 80–1, 140, 151, 181, 240, 250, 254
Bilczewski, J. 11
Bilderbergs x, 2, 4, 80, 258, 263, 272–85, 292
Bogomolov, Ambassador A. 126, 165, 170
Bohusz-Szysko, General Z. 167, 170
Bolshevik 40, 42, 67, 70, 118
Bór-Komorowski, T. 194–5, 198–202
Boyer, F. 76–7
Braden, T. 252–3, 262
Briand, A. 35, 40, 222–3, 226, 236
British Communist Party 2
Brodetsky, S. 157–8
Brygiewicz, J. 77
Brześć 100, 115
Bucareli Accords 64
Bulgaria 152
Bułhak, W. x, 187, 200, 206
Bullitt, W. 172, 238
Burián, S. 30

Cadogan, A. 165
Caillaux, J. 25–8, 32, 35–9, 42, 128
Calles, P. 62, 63, 68–9, 72–4, 78–9, 80
Canada 31, 136–7, 239
Capel, A. 40

Index 317

Cardinal Alfred-Henri-Marie Baudrillart 7
Cardinal Montini (Paul VI) 2, 263
Cardinal Rampolla 6
Carr, M. x
Catholic 4, 6, 9, 24–6, 38, 40, 66, 72, 72, 78–9, 119, 142, 152, 156–7, 220, 225, 227–8, 263–4, 284
Cazalet, V. 124–5, 136, 152–3
Central and East European Commission 258, 260
Central and East European Planning Board 155–6, 181
Central National Committee (Centralny Komitet Narodowy) 11, 18, 22, 23
Central Powers 18, 22, 27, 34, 36
Centrolew 100
Chciuk-Celt, T. 191–3, 197, 199, 201–6, 285
Chicago 19, 60, 62
Christian Democratic Party 101
Church of England 2
Churchill, W. 17, 117–18, 122–5, 127, 142, 151, 153, 181, 183, 186–7, 192, 206–7, 222, 231, 234–6, 239, 242, 249–50, 253, 255, 257, 260, 274, 276–7, 292
CIA 4, 238, 252–3, 255, 262, 273, 276–7, 279–81
Ciechanowski, J. 120, 136, 156, 183
Cienciala, A. x, 166
Cieński, T. 11
Clemenceau, G. 25–7, 40, 42
Clerk, G. 18
Cleveland, G. 72
Colby, B. 68
Cold War x
Comintern 2, 71
*Comité Général* 21
Common Market 256, 291
Confederación Regional de Obreros Mexicanos (Regional Confederation of Mexican Workers, CROM) 61, 75, 121
Conrad, J. 10–11, 19, 22–7, 30, 36, 44, 60
Consul Robertson 68–9
Coolidge, C. 70, 136
Coudenhove-Kalergi, R. 222–6, 238, 241, 243, 249, 251–3, 256
Council of Europe 253, 260, 263
Council on Foreign Relations (CFR) 238, 278
Count Mensdorff-Pouilly 27, 32–3, 36

Cripps, S. 10, 80–1, 106–7, 127, 141, 143, 152, 155, 163, 166, 169, 173, 207–9, 238, 250, 263
Curzon Line 174
Czechoslovakia 95, 100, 102, 104, 119, 137–44, 150, 152–4, 157, 167, 183, 225, 227, 231–2, 292
Czernin, O. 32–3
Czyrnianski, I. 7
Czyrnianski, M. 7

Dąbski, J. 11
Dalton, H. 118, 120, 151, 167, 171, 209
de Castellane, B. 7, 8, 24–7, 37, 39, 40, 43, 227
de Rougemont, D. ix, 239, 242, 248, 250, 252, 255–6
Dęblin 115
Denmark 152, 253, 281
Dmowski, R. 8, 11–12, 27, 29, 31, 32, 33, 34, 37, 42, 43, 101, 226–8
Doherty, M. 65, 206
Donovan, W. 243, 251–3, 258, 262
Drexel-Biddel, A. 116, 137, 154, 171, 182–3, 275
Drummond, E. 35
Duchess of Uzès 39
Duff, G. 11
Dulles, A. 172, 243, 250–3, 262, 273, 276–7
Dulles, J. 171–2, 238
Duncan, I. 43
Dunkirk 121

Eden, A. 106, 120, 142, 153–5, 164–8, 172, 183, 186, 191–2, 195, 206–7, 273–4, 276–8
Eisenhower, D. 261, 273, 275–6, 278
England 7, 10, 11, 17, 21, 29–30, 36, 39, 45, 62, 80, 104–6, 123, 137, 144, 151, 154, 167, 171, 173
European Coal and Steel Community 255, 258
European Conference of Culture 256, 291
European League for Economic Cooperation 2, 152, 237, 241, 291
European Movement 2, 251, 252–62, 264, 272, 274, 283, 291–2
European Union 291

Fall, A. 67, 74
Faury, L. 116

FBI 65
Federalism 4
Fiala, V. 3
Fimmen, E. 93-4
France 7, 11-12, 17, 21, 24, 30-2, 34, 37, 39, 40-3, 45, 77, 80, 93-4, 115-17, 122, 127, 139, 150, 152, 221, 239-40, 253, 264, 280
Frankfurter, F. 12, 65
Fritsch, C. x
Front Morges 101-3, 106, 115, 117, 120-1, 125
Fulbright, W. 238, 243, 251, 263

Gaitskell, H. 274, 277
Galicia 6, 8, 12, 18, 21, 23, 31
Galician rising (1846) 6
Gamelin, M. 102
Gano, S. 202-3
Gdański (see Danzig) 105, 181
Gdynia 77
Germans 9, 10, 292
Germany 3, 7, 8, 20, 28, 30, 38, 80, 94, 105-6, 114, 121, 123, 150-1, 156, 181, 227, 231, 235
Gide, A. 8
Godębski 7, 40
Gompers, S. 62, 68
González, P. 67
Gould, A. 8
Gould, J. 8
Grabski, S. 103, 206
Grabski, W. 98-9
Grand Duke Nikolai 18
Greece 152-4, 183-4, 240
Grey, E. 18, 20
Grosbois, T. ix-x, 79, 139, 151-3, 273
Gross, F. x, 155-7, 181
Grünwald (1410) 9
Gubbins, C. 2, 120, 129, 172, 191, 195, 197, 203, 239, 273-4, 278-9

Habsburgs 3, 7, 8, 11, 21, 24, 26-8, 32-4, 36, 39, 81
Hague Congress 242-3, 248-52, 257-8, 261, 282, 284, 291
Hall, L. x
Haller, J. 101-2, 115-16, 158, 168
Haller, S. 168
Hanna, P. 68, 69
Harding, W. 72, 74
Harriman, A. 144, 154, 171, 185, 238, 275, 277

Hemmerling, L. 97-8
Hitler, A. 104, 121, 172, 231
Hitler-Stalin Pact (1939) 114
Hlond, A. 116
Hodža, M. 140-1
Holland 1, 152-4, 239-40, 253, 273, 278, 283, 285
Home Army (Armia Krajowa, AK) 182, 190, 194-8, 201
Hoover, H. 68, 74, 136
Horodecka, I. 200-1, 203
Horodyski, J. 34-5
House, E. 35, 42
Hudak, A. x
Hull, C. 137, 183
Hungary 32, 119, 137, 143, 151-2, 184, 225, 231-2

International Committee of the Movements for European Unity (JIC-MEU) 242, 249-52
Iranek-Osmecki, K. 200-1, 203
Ireland 253
"Iron Curtain" 235
Italy 7, 8, 35, 114, 150, 152, 190, 197, 240, 281

Jackson, C. 278, 280
Jacques, M. xi
Jagiellonian University 7
Janas, L. x
Jankowski, J. 198, 202
January Insurrection (1863-1864) 7
Januszajtis, M. 102
Japan 35, 37, 151, 231
Jaskulski, K. 77
Jasper, M. 152-3
Jebb, G. 155, 172
Jesuit Order 1, 4, 26, 39, 73, 79-80
Jews (Jewish) 2, 6, 9, 12, 41, 101, 119, 137-8, 157-8, 205, 208, 223, 284
Jodko-Narkiewicz, W. 23
Joffre, J. 35

Katyń 163, 185, 187
Kellogg, F. 71, 72
Kerstens, P. 152, 237-40
Kiernik, E. 100
King Edward VII 7
King, M. 137
Koc, A. 158
Koller, G. x
Korboński, S. 198-200

Korfanty, W. 100–1, 104–7
Kot, S. 96, 100–1, 104, 115–16, 123, 140, 157–8, 165, 168, 171, 173–4, 185, 206, 208
Kraków 6, 7, 8, 11, 28, 95, 203–4, 293
Kucharski, W. 97–8
Kukiel, M. 115–16, 199
Kulturkampf 9

*La Pologne* 40–1
Labor Party (Stronnictwo Pracy, SP) 103
Labour Party, British 10, 66, 80, 97–8, 104, 120, 137, 140, 151, 239, 240, 249–50, 254, 292
Latvia 155
League of Nations 151, 156, 220, 222, 224, 226, 236
Ledóchowski, W. 26–7, 36
Leeper, R. 119
Leo XII 7
Liaison Committee 242
Lieberman, H. 100–1
Lipski, J. 153
Litauer, S. 118–19, 125–6, 129, 164–5, 168, 211
Lithuania 104, 119, 151–2, 184, 225–6, 231
Lloyd George, D. 32, 35, 36
Łódź 77
London 1, 8, 10, 17, 21–3, 27, 29, 30, 32, 34–5, 42, 44, 69, 93, 101, 105–7, 116, 118, 126, 139, 150, 153, 164, 170, 181, 190, 259, 276
Lord Addison 104
Lord Kitchener 17
Lord Northcliffe 8, 26, 43
Luxembourg 152, 155
Lwów 11, 18, 77, 115, 199
Lyautey, H. 7

MacDonald, R. 99
Macmillan, H. 239, 259, 273
Maisky, I. 163–4, 167, 170
Mandel, G. 42–3
Marquis Pierre de Dampière 43, 76–7
Marshall, L. 12
Marshall Plan 241, 252, 261
Masaryk, J. 140–4, 155–7, 240
Masaryk, T. 234
Masonry 2, 79, 95–6, 208, 224, 284
Mastin, H. x
McCarthy, M. xi
McCloy, J. 261–2, 276–7

Mexico 1, 3, 40, 44, 60, 61–6, 68–70, 72, 74, 93, 99, 121, 184, 284, 292; Oil politics 76, 78, 82
MI5 29
MI6 36
Mikołajczyk, S. 129, 136, 185–7, 190–200, 203, 205, 207, 240
Mitkiewicz, L. 123, 125, 136, 182–3, 185
Modelski, I. 116
Molotov, V. 164, 169, 171, 210–11
Molotov-Ribbentrop Pact 164, 168
Monnet, J. 222, 255, 258
Morel, E. 80, 272
Morocco 82
Morones, L. 60–5, 68–9, 71, 73–4, 80–1, 121
Morrow, D. 69–71, 75–6, 79
Morskie Oko 7
Mościcki, I. 102–3, 105, 116–17
Moscow 66, 70
Moss, W. x
Motz, R. 152
Msgr. Borgoncini di Duca 79
Muller, M. 99
Munich 8, 138

Napoleon III 7
Narutowicz, G. 95
National Armed Forces (Narodowe Siły Zbrojne, NSZ) 203
National Council (Rada Narodowa, RN) 8, 10, 11
National Democratic Party (Narodowa Demokracja, ND) 101, 227–8
NATO 280, 281
Netherlands 1
New York 19, 20
Nicolson, A. 18–19, 35, 36
Nicolson, H. 44
Niedziałkowski, M. 97–8, 100–1, 104–5
Niven, W. 67–8
NKVD 201, 206
Noël, L. 116
Norway 152–5, 253

Obregón, J. 61–2, 64, 66–8, 71, 79
Operation Riposte 190
Operation Wildhorn 190, 197, 203
Oskar 202, 211
OSS 243, 262, 276–7
Ovey, E. 62, 63, 69, 70, 74

Paderewski 1, 10, 21–3, 31, 34, 37, 42, 101–3, 115–17
Pająk, H. ix
Pams, Senator 42–3, 44
Paris 7, 10, 17, 22, 27, 29–30, 32, 34, 44, 101, 107, 121, 125
Paris Peace Conference 12, 240
Paris Vigilance Committee 275, 278
Patricians of Poland 9, 41
Peasant Party (Stronnictwo Ludowe-Piast, SL-P) 100
Pease, N. x
Pełczyński, T. 202–3
Penfield 11
Perlini, G. x
Peszke, M. x
Pétain, P. 121
Philips, S. 80
Pichon, S. 11, 43
Pieczewski, A. ix–x, 3, 141, 220, 222, 253, 264
Pierlot, H. 153
Piłsudski, J. 23, 39–40, 42, 64, 65, 93, 99, 101–3, 117, 138–9, 196, 226–8, 233–4
Pipinelis, P. 141, 238
Platt, D. x
Podgórski, B. ix, 6, 10, 210
Poland 4, 9, 18, 22, 25, 28, 31, 39–41, 43–4, 64–6, 72, 77, 81, 103, 105, 121, 126, 136–7, 140, 150, 152–3, 156–7, 181, 190, 194, 256, 293
*Poland and Peace* 98
Polish Bureau for the National Council 10
Polish Committee of National Liberation 205–6
Polish General Staff (Intelligence Division) (Dwójka) 2, 96, 185, 200, 202–4
Polish government-in-exile 2
Polish Information Bureau 21
Polish National Committee (Komitet Narodowy Polski, KNP) 31, 34, 43
Polish nationalism 8
Polish Press Agency (PAT) 118, 125
Polish Question 8, 10, 26, 28–9, 32, 34, 39
Polish Socialist Party (Polska Partia Socjalistyczna, PPS) 97, 101, 104, 167
Polish-Soviet War (1919–1920) 64, 95
Polish Workers' Party (Polska Partia Robotnicza, PPR) 199

Pomian, J. ix–x, 6, 17, 43, 61–2, 70, 71, 122, 251, 257, 259–60, 262, 263, 280, 291
Pope Paul VI 6
Popiel, K. 22, 100–1, 115–16
Porter, K. 63, 66–70, 73
Portugal 152, 240
Poulenc, F. 8
Prague 95, 101, 107, 142
Premier Edward Osóbka-Morawski 210
Prince Bernhard 1, 273–6, 278–80, 283
Prince Kazimierz Lubomirski, K. 65
Prince Sixte de Bourbon-Parma 8, 25–7, 32, 33, 39
Protestant 26
Protestantism 9
Provisional Government of National Unity (Rząd Tymczasowy Jedności Narodowej) 209
Prussia 8, 9, 25

Raczkiewicz, W. 117, 125, 163, 165–6, 185, 192–4, 196–7
Raczyński, E. 118, 125–6, 128, 137, 144, 155, 164, 171, 173, 181–2, 186, 196, 210, 240, 259
Raczyński, R. 116
Radio Free Europe (RFE) 276–7
Rataj, M. 105, 116, 121
*Rerum Novarum* 7, 220
Retinger, J. 20, 60
Retinger, J. H. ix x 1–6, 8–12, 17, 18, 20, 22, 28; 1944 assassination 200, 203, 284; 1944 mission 2, 190–211; 1916 mission to Poland 22–3; and American Polonia 18–22, 31, 34, 44, 45, 119, 136–7, 158, 182, 184; and Austria 10–11, 17, 21, 23–4, 28–30, 34, 81, 93; and Catholicism 4, 6–7, 9, 25–6, 37–9, 42, 44, 72–3, 78, 80, 228, 263–4, 284, 293; and Conrad 10–11, 19, 22–7, 30, 36, 44, 60; and espionage 2, 10, 18, 22, 27–8, 35–7, 39, 41, 96, 117, 127, 129, 168, 172, 185–6, 192 195, 197, 200–1, 203, 205–6, 208–11, 238, 240, 262–3, 273 276–8, 284, 292; and federalism 4, 38, 41, 93, 95, 119–20, 139–45, 150–7, 183–4 227–8, 231–6, 292; illness 203–4; and Jews 6, 12
Retinger, J. H. Sr. 6–7
Rif revolt 96
Ripka, H. 140–2, 259
Roberts, F. 195, 204

Romania 102, 114, 116, 119, 137, 143, 151–2, 231–2
Rome 116
Roosevelt, F. 136–8, 143–4, 171, 181–4, 193, 234
Rothstein, A. 125, 165, 168
Russia 3, 4, 17, 18, 28, 30–1, 33, 70, 72, 75, 105, 114, 117, 121, 123, 125–6, 138–9, 142, 144, 155–6, 163, 168, 173–4, 183, 224, 226–7, 232–3, 292
Rykens, P. 273

Sanacja 95, 100–3, 107, 116, 202, 226
Sandys, D. 211, 236–7, 239, 241–3, 249, 251–5, 261, 263, 276, 292
Scandinavia 143, 151
Schumann, R. 222, 255, 258, 261
Serruys, P. 239–40
Seyda, M. 98, 167
SHAPE 280–1
Sheffield, J. 63–4, 69, 70
Sienkiewicz, H. 21
Sikorski, W. 1, 2, 3, 4, 23, 93, 97, 99, 100–1, 103, 105–6, 114–29, 136–45, 150–8, 163–74, 181, 185–6, 194, 196, 199, 202–3, 208, 226, 232, 234, 255, 292–3
Sikorski-Maisky Treaty 163–7, 169, 172, 206, 293
Silesia 181
Skirmunt, K. C. 97, 126
Skrzyński, A. 94, 97–9, 120
Skrzyński, W. 32–3, 36–7, 43
Slavs 9
Slovakia 140, 151
Śmigly-Rydz, E. 102, 114–16
Smith, W. 253. 262, 273, 276, 278, 281
Smuts, J. 33
Sokołow, N. 12
Sosnkowski, General Kazimierz 115, 119, 124, 136, 166, 170–1, 193, 195, 197, 200
Spaak, P. 127, 152–4, 222, 237, 239, 249, 253, 255–7, 260, 262
Spain 43, 44, 60, 152
Spanish Civil War 96
Special Operations Executive (SOE) 2, 118, 120, 129, 155, 172–3, 192, 195, 204, 239, 273, 283, 291–2
Spies x
Stachiewicz, W. 116
Stalin, J. 127, 144, 169, 172–4, 185, 199, 205, 234

Stańczyk, J. 155, 167
Stefanicka, A. x
Stimson, H. L. 137
Strakacz, S. 156
Strang, W. 153, 165–7
Stroński, S. 103, 117–18, 121
Suleja, W. 11
Summerlin, G. 62–3
Sweden 152, 240, 253
Switzerland 11, 21–2, 27, 29, 31–3, 35, 37, 44, 102, 121, 240
Szczypien, J. x

Tarnów 7
Tarnowski, A. 32
Tatar, S. 190
Taverne ix
Teapot Dome 69
Tehran Conference 187, 190, 193
Teodorowicz, J. 11
Teutonic Knights 9
The Hague 243, 249–50, 252–7, 260–1, 282, 284, 291
*The Poles and Prussia* 8
*Tierra Mexicana* 70, 72
Treaty of London 253
Treaty of Riga 165, 167, 182–3, 226
Truman, H. 251, 275
Turkey 143

Ukrainians 77, 119, 138, 151, 225–6, 231
Union of Hadziacz 225
United Europe Movement (UEM) 236, 239, 241–2
United Nation 235–6
United States 1, 18–20, 25, 31, 34, 36–7, 39, 43–5, 63–4, 72, 75, 114, 117, 136, 151, 156–7, 181, 184, 211, 224, 235, 261, 272, 275
Upper Silesia 77

Van Kleffens, E. 153
Van Zeeland, P. 152, 154, 237–42, 250, 254, 260, 264, 273–4, 277–9
Vatican 1, 2, 4, 24–7, 36–9, 79–80
Versailles Treaty 220, 224
Vevey committee 21–3
Vickrey, R. xi
Vienna 11, 23–4, 27, 32–3, 40, 93
Villa, P. 61
Viscount Halifax 106, 126, 263
von Tschirsky, H. 11
Vyshinsky, A. 169, 171

Wandycz, P. x, 139, 142, 154
Wapiński, R. x
Warsaw 1, 23, 38, 77, 101, 105–6, 114, 116, 138, 142, 198, 208
Warsaw Rising (1944) 206
Washington 20, 32, 62, 65, 69, 71, 136–7, 191
Weizman, C. 12
Welles, S. 137, 143, 172, 182–3
Westminster Economic Conference 257, 260
Wieniawa-Długoszowski, B. 116–17
Wilford, H. ix, 2
Wilno 115, 199
Wilson, W. 32, 34–5, 37, 68, 72, 226
Wise, S. 12, 138
Witos, W. 1, 97–8, 100–7, 115, 121
Wojciechowski, S. 103
World War I 1, 3, 4, 7, 10, 12, 20, 31, 38–9, 41, 80, 81, 95, 127, 138, 256, 284, 292–3

World War II 1, 2, 4, 38, 81, 94–6, 100, 104, 114–15, 122, 128, 138–9, 227, 278, 284, 292
Wróbel, P. x

Youth Commission 261–2
Yugoslavia 152, 155, 183

Żabotyński, W. 12
Zaleski, A. 23, 118, 124–5, 128, 136, 158, 165, 171
Zamorski, J. 43
Zamoyski, S. 136, 181, 193
Zamoyski, W. 6–8, 11, 37, 39, 227
Zapata, E. 61
Zaremba, Z. 198
Żeligowski, L. 115
Zhukov 172–3
Zimmermann, A. 27
Zionism 12, 157
Zubrzycki, M. 10
Żuławski, Z. 80–1, 98, 101